A TEXT WITH ADAPTED READINGS

PART ONE / ELEMENTS OF SOCIOLOGICAL ANALYSIS   I INTRODUCTION   II SOCIAL ORGANIZATION   III CULTURE   IV SOCIALIZATION   V PRIMARY GROUPS   VI SOCIAL STRATIFICATION   VII ASSOCIATIONS   VIII COLLECTIVE BEHAVIOR   IX POPULATION AND ECOLOGY

PART TWO / ANALYSIS OF MAJOR INSTITUTIONS   X RELIGION   XI EDUCATION   XII LAW

PART THREE / MASTER TRENDS   XIII URBAN MAN   XIV INDUSTRIAL MAN   XV POLITICAL MAN

SOCIOLOGY A TEXT WITH ADAPTED READINGS

SOCIOLOGY

FOURTH EDITION

HARPER & ROW, PUBLISHERS
NEW YORK, EVANSTON, AND LONDON

A TEXT WITH ADAPTED READINGS

LEONARD BROOM
UNIVERSITY OF TEXAS, AUSTIN

PHILIP SELZNICK
UNIVERSITY OF CALIFORNIA, BERKELEY

ACKNOWLEDGMENTS

The chapter on SOCIALIZATION was written, with our collaboration, by Gertrude Jaeger Selznick, who also contributed extensively to RELIGION.

For generous collaboration on this or earlier editions we extend thanks to Robert Blauner, Burton R. Clark, Donald R. Cressey, Norval D. Glenn, Helen Beem Gouldner, William Kornhauser, Richard T. Morris, Philippe Nonet, Jerome H. Skolnick, and Ralph H. Turner.

We are greatly indebted to Gretchan N. Broom for her creative and unstinting collaboration in editing and writing, and for carrying the burden of administrative tasks.

To all editions of this book Phyllis M. Barnett, editor, contributed complete knowledge of publishing and the highest standards of performance.

Special thanks are due to Saul Geiser for able research assistance on this edition. In addition to others whose help we acknowledged in previous editions, we express our appreciation for the assistance and guidance of Mary Alden, Gerald Brandmeyer, Elliott Currie, Robert Cushing, Judy Dewing, F. Mark Ethridge, Caleb Foote, Jerrold Guben, Paul Jacobs, Sanford H. Kadish, John I. Kitsuse, Emily Knapp, Ruth Kornhauser, Leo Lowenthal, Herbert McClosky, Anthony E. Mellor, Sheldon L. Messinger, Arlene S. Skolnick, John H. Smith, John Warner, and Prudence J. Wood.

Other debts are recorded in footnotes and credit lines, but we wish especially to thank the authors of the original works from which our Adaptations are drawn.

L. B.

P. S.

CONTENTS

Part one   ELEMENTS OF SOCIOLOGICAL ANALYSIS

CHAPTER I   **INTRODUCTION**

1. The discipline of sociology   Sociology and the social sciences   3

Adaptation 1 / Trow   NOTES ON SOCIOLOGICAL RESEARCH   6

2. Plan and content of the book   Forms of presentation   8

Adaptation 2 / Wallis and *Roberts*   READING A TABLE   10

CHAPTER II   **SOCIAL ORGANIZATION**

1. Introduction   Social systems   Levels of social organization   14

2. The individual and social organization   Interaction and
relatedness   Roles and role strain   Social organization
and social control   17

Adaptation 3 / W. H. Whyte, Jr.   THE WEB OF FRIENDSHIP   20

Adaptation 4 / Durkheim   SUICIDE AND SOCIAL INTEGRATION   26

3. The group structure of society   Types of groups   Kinship and
social organization   Group relations   30

∗ KINSHIP TERMS   32

Adaptation 5 / Talmon-Garber   FAMILY AND SOCIETY IN ISRAEL   38

4. Basic patterns of social organization   Kinship   Fealty   Status
Contract   Bureaucracy   The master trend   42

CHAPTER III   **CULTURE**

1. The concept of culture   The symbolic order   Cultural values and
norms   Culture and social organization   50

∗ *Orwell:* NEWSPEAK AND EXPRESSIVE SYMBOLISM   53

2. The impact of culture   Pervasiveness of culture   Language and
culture   Culture shock   Conformity and deviation   57

∗ *Items marked with an asterisk are brief illustrative materials.*

Chapter III **Culture**—*Continued*

* *Thomsen:* THE CULTURE SHOCK OF QUIET DEATH   62

Adaptation 6 / Hall   THE SILENT LANGUAGE   64

3. **Cultural diversity**   The constant and the variable   Ethnocentrism and cultural relativism   Subcultures   68

Adaptation 7 / D. Lee   INDIVIDUAL AUTONOMY AND SOCIAL STRUCTURE   73

4. **Cultural adaptation and change**   Culture, civilization, and evolution   Technology and culture   Acculturation   75

* *MacNeish:* THE RISE OF CIVILIZATION IN TEHUACÁN   78

CHAPTER IV **SOCIALIZATION**

1. **Introduction**   Biological basis of socialization   Aims of socialization   Socialization and conformity   84

2. **Socializing the child**   Responses to the child   Responses of the child   The emergence of a self   88

Adaptation 8 / Mead   MIND, SELF AND SOCIETY   94

3. **Agencies of socialization**   Reaching the person   The family   Peer groups   98

4. **Adult socialization**   Parent-youth conflict   Social roles and personality   Resocialization   104

Adaptation 9 / Dornbusch   SOCIALIZING THE CADET   110

5. **Culture, personality, and human nature**   Basic personality   Sex and temperament   Human nature   113

Adaptation 10 / Malinowski   AUTHORITY AND SOCIALIZATION IN A PRIMITIVE SOCIETY   117

CHAPTER V **PRIMARY GROUPS**

1. **Introduction**   The primary relation   The primary group   120

2. **The primary group and the individual**   How the primary group helps   126

Adaptation 11 / W. F. Whyte   STRESS AND STATUS IN STREET CORNER SOCIETY   128

Adaptation 12 / Roethlisberger and *Dickson*   THE BANK WIRING ROOM   130

3. **Primary groups in large-scale organizations**   Sustaining the individual   The mediating primary group   Primary groups and society   133

Adaptation 13 / Shils and *Janowitz*   PRIMARY GROUPS IN THE GERMAN ARMY   135

Chapter V   **Primary Groups**—*Continued*

　　　4. *Internal structure and dynamics*   Task groups   Patterns of
　　　communication   Family systems   Negro families   140

　　　Adaptation 14 / Frazier   THE NEGRO FAMILY   145

　　　Adaptation 15 /   THE TECHNIQUE OF THE SOCIOGRAM   148

CHAPTER VI   **SOCIAL STRATIFICATION**

　　　1. *Introduction*   Strata and classes   Approaches   153

　　　Adaptation 16 / Morris   EXERCISES IN STRATIFICATION RESEARCH   157

　　　2. *Inequality*   Economic inequality   Prestige   Power   161

　　　3. *Status and life-styles*   Correlates of social stratification   Life
　　　at the top   Life at the bottom   Status consistency and
　　　inconsistency   170

　　　∗ INTERPRETING CORRELATIONS   173

　　　∗ *Lord:* SOCIAL RANK AND DISASTER AT SEA   175

　　　4. *Social mobility*   Kinds of social mobility   Intergenerational
　　　mobility   Individual mobility   Caste and open-class societies
　　　Changes in the opportunity structure   Trends in mobility   178

　　　5. *Class and society*   The Marxist model   Critique   The case of
　　　England   Class consciousness in the United States
　　　Is stratification inevitable?   187

CHAPTER VII   **ASSOCIATIONS**

　　　1. *Introduction*   194

　　　2. *Formal structure*   Elements of formal structure   Democratic and
　　　authoritarian forms   Bureaucracy   196

　　　Adaptation 17 / Bavelas   COMMUNICATION PATTERNS IN TASK GROUPS   199

　　　3. *Informal structure*   201

　　　4. *Cohesion and morale*   Socializing the organization member
　　　Organization units as social groups   Primary relations   203

　　　5. *Communication and social status*   206

　　　Adaptation 18 / Dalton   STAFF-LINE CONFLICT IN INDUSTRY   208

　　　Adaptation 19 / Gardner and *Moore*   THE LINE OF AUTHORITY AND
　　　COMMUNICATION   211

　　　∗ *Gardner* and *Moore:* A CASE OF JITTERS   212

Chapter VII   **Associations**—*Continued*

6. *Institutionalization*   215

Adaptation 20 / Michels THE "IRON LAW" OF OLIGARCHY   218

CHAPTER VIII   **COLLECTIVE BEHAVIOR**

1. *Introduction* Conditions of collective behavior   221

2. *Crowds and collective excitement* Emotional contagion Crowds
   Mobs Riots Rumor   223

* *Churchill:* THE HOUSE OF COMMONS AND PARLIAMENTARY PSYCHOLOGY   224

Adaptation 21 / RACE RIOT: LOS ANGELES, 1965   230

3. *Public opinion and propaganda* Publics Values, attitudes, and
   opinions Group basis of public opinion Ascertaining opinion
   Propaganda   235

* *Hyman:* EVALUATING PERCENTAGES   238

* *Lee* and *Lee:* THE TRICKS OF THE TRADE   244

Adaptation 22 / Odegard THE ANTI-SALOON LEAGUE   246

Adaptation 23 / Likert PUBLIC OPINION POLLS   251

4. *Social movements and social change* Perspectives and doctrines
   Social movements   254

CHAPTER IX   **POPULATION AND ECOLOGY**

1. *Introduction*   258

Adaptation 24 / THE UNITED STATES CENSUS   261

2. *Composition* The sex ratio Age composition   266

* THE POPULATION PYRAMID OF A MINORITY   270

3. *Fertility and mortality* The measures of fertility Mortality   274

* THE CASE OF THE G.E. BABIES   276

4. *Population change* World population growth International migration   281

Adaptation 25 / Ryan FERTILITY AND FAMILY ORGANIZATION IN CEYLON   289

5. *Ecology* Introduction Ecological succession Limited alternatives   292

* *Robinson:* ECOLOGICAL CORRELATIONS   296

Part two   ANALYSIS OF MAJOR INSTITUTIONS

CHAPTER X   **RELIGION**

    1. Introduction   Foundations of religion   The elements of religion   301

    2. Social organization   Fusion of religion and group life   Religion
        differentiated   Religion and social cohesion   306

    3. Culture   Religion and art   309

    4. Socialization   Religion and personal autonomy   Conversion and
        assimilation   313

    5. Primary relations   Religion and marriage   Sex, love, and
        birth control   316

    6. Stratification   Social composition of the churches   Social class
        and religious involvement   Religion and class interest   319

    7. Associations   The church and the sect   The Catholic *aggiornamento*   324

    Adaptation 26 / S. D. Clark   THE METHODIST CHURCH AND THE
        SALVATION ARMY   327

    8. Collective behavior   The origin of religion   Religion and
        expressive behavior   333

    9. Population and ecology   Religions of the United States   336

CHAPTER XI   **EDUCATION**

    1. Introduction   Functions of education   Basic dilemmas   339

    2. Social organization   Institutional autonomy   344

    3. Culture   345

    Adaptation 27 / B. R. Clark and *Trow*   COLLEGE SUBCULTURES   347

    4. Socialization   Education and basic attitudes   Education of the
        disadvantaged   350

    5. Primary relations   Teacher-student relations   Student peer groups   355

    6. Stratification   Differential access   Education, occupation,
        and income   359

    7. Associations   Bureaucracy and allocation   364

    8. Collective behavior   367

    * *Schachner:* ANTI-STUDENT PROTEST: OXFORD, 1354   368

    Adaptation 28 / Kornhauser   STUDENT PROTEST: BERKELEY, 1964   370

    9. Population and ecology   Trends in enrollment   Ecology of schools   375

CHAPTER XII   **LAW**

     1. Introduction   Foundations of law   Types of law   Sociology and law   379

     2. Social organization   Law and the division of labor   Self-help and the adversary principle   Law and order   385

     3. Culture   Conceptions of law   Law and morals   389

     Adaptation 29 / U.S. Supreme Court   POLYGAMY, MORALITY, AND THE MANN ACT   394

     4. Socialization   The sense of justice   Psychiatric justice   Criminality as a product of socialization   398

     Adaptation 30 / Piaget   THE CHILD'S CONCEPTION OF JUSTICE   402

     5. Primary relations   Marriage and divorce   Primary groups and social control   406

     6. Social stratification   The bias of the law   Differential administration   The right to counsel   411

     7. Associations   Administrative justice   The official perspective   415

     8. Collective behavior   Civil disorder and freedom of expression   418

     9. Population and ecology   The amount of crime   Age and sex ratios   421

     Part three   **MASTER TRENDS**

CHAPTER XIII   **URBAN MAN**

     1. Urbanization   Early cities   The Asian city   Urban and rural   427

     Adaptation 31 / Adams   THE ORIGIN OF CITIES: ARCHAEOLOGICAL EVIDENCE   434

     2. Urban society   Diffusion of urban life-styles   Urban culture and personality   437

     3. Urban ecology   Segregation   Ecological patterning   443

     * UNITS OF ECOLOGICAL ANALYSIS: CENSUS TRACTS   448

     Adaptation 32 / CHICAGO AS A SOCIAL LABORATORY   449

     4. Changing cities   Central city and suburb   Megalopolis   Urban neighborhoods   454

CHAPTER XIV   **INDUSTRIAL MAN**

     1. Early industrialization   Social relations and industrial capitalism   Religion and capitalism   Industrialization in non-Western societies   462

Chapter XIV   **Industrial Man**—*Continued*

        Adaptation 33 / Theodorson   INDUSTRIALISM AND SOCIAL RELATIONS
           IN NON-WESTERN SOCIETIES   469

        2. Management and labor in transition   Types of industrial management
           Unions and society   Prospects   473

        * *Jacobs:* DEAD HORSE AND THE FEATHERBIRD   478

        3. Technology and human relations   Alienation   Industrial
           variations   Automation   Group performance   480

        Adaptation 34 / Coch and *French*   AN EXPERIMENTAL STUDY OF
           RESISTANCE TO CHANGE   487

        4. The labor force   The world labor force   The United States
           labor force   491

CHAPTER XV   **POLITICAL MAN**

        1. Introduction   497

        2. The creation of nations   Colonialism as nation-building
           Nationhood and modernization   499

        * *Berger:* EGYPT'S POPULIST REGIME   506

        3. The age of social revolution   The meaning of social revolution
           The revolutionary situation   The natural history of
           revolutions   Nationalism and social revolution   509

        Adaptation 35 / Johnson   PEASANT NATIONALISM AND COMMUNIST POWER   516

        4. Totalitarian society   519

        5. Social foundations of freedom and democracy   Power and
           legitimacy   Pluralism   Participation   522

        Adaptation 36 / Tocqueville   THE DEMOCRATIC AGE   529

        Name index   537

        Subject index   543

PART ONE

ELEMENTS OF SOCIOLOGICAL ANALYSIS

CHAPTER I

INTRODUCTION

SECTION 1 THE DISCIPLINE OF SOCIOLOGY

Sociology is one of the social sciences. Its long-run aim is to discover the basic structure of human society, to identify the main forces that hold groups together or weaken them, and to learn the conditions that transform social life. In this, sociology, like any pure or basic science, is a disciplined, intellectual quest for fundamental knowledge of the nature of things. Most sociologists believe that they stand only at the outermost rim of this understanding.

Although some sociologists devote themselves to the development of first principles and fundamental concepts, others pursue relatively restricted inquiries, including careful reporting of significant events, the compilation and interpretation of sociological statistics, and the testing of hypotheses about limited topics. Some of this work has a practical orientation, such as the desire to control juvenile delinquency or to reduce absenteeism of factory workers; much of it is stimulated by intellectual curiosity, the desire to understand a puzzling fact or to comprehend an important event. This book draws on the sociological enterprise as a whole, both on attempts to formulate basic principles and on more modest efforts to contribute to the fund of verifiable knowledge.

When one seeks to draw general conclusions, he must be *selective*. The scientist is interested in *kinds* of things, in placing phenomena into categories, and this means looking at special aspects of the concrete world. Sciences are known by what they select for study and how they go about it. The same "thing" can be understood in a number of different ways. Consider your instructor's chair. If a specialist in the branch of physics called mechanics were to study it, he would see it as a combination of weights and balances; a biologist specializing in anatomy would see it as a receptacle for the human form and might assess its effect on the spinal column; an economist might see it as an item of mass production or a unit of cost and price; the psychologist might see it as part of the perceptual frame of the student; and the sociologist might see the chair as a symbol of status.

Thus like any other field of inquiry, sociology is selective. It highlights and illuminates aspects of social life that otherwise might be only obscurely recog-

August Comte (1798–1857), French social philosopher, gave sociology its name. As a "positivist" Comte stressed the need to base scientific theories on observation, but his own writings were highly speculative. He saw in human history three stages of "universal progress"—theological, metaphysical, scientific. He also offered elaborate proposals for a new Positivist State in which there would be a supreme priesthood of sociologists to direct society. Few of Comte's specific ideas are now accepted, but he gave impetus to the discussion out of which present-day sociology emerged. His major work was The Positive Philosophy, *first published in French in six volumes, 1830–1842.*

nized and understood. Its specialized knowledge about basic elements and processes in the social world can enrich understanding and may have practical uses as well. The sociologist may be called upon for help with a special problem, such as racial conflict, urban blight, or the war on poverty. However, sociology's present capacity to give "answers" to social problems should not be exaggerated. At this time the sociologist's practical contribution lies in the ability to clarify the underlying nature of social problems, to estimate more exactly their dimensions, and to identify aspects that seem most amenable to remedy with the knowledge and skills at hand.

Adaptation 1, pages 6–8, discusses some of the objectives, methods, and problems of sociological inquiry.

SOCIOLOGY AND THE SOCIAL SCIENCES

There has been diminishing controversy about whether sociology should be called a science or a more neutral name such as "discipline." Some believe that sociology is not a science and that because of the nature of its subject matter it cannot be one. They point to the difficulty of applying the experimental method to social phenomena as a major obstacle.

However, science is not a single method or routine, such as the classic before-after experiment or the use of special implements such as glass tubing or lenses or precise measuring instruments. Each of the old and established sciences has developed more or less distinctive techniques, instruments, and routines. But research procedures, which vary from discipline to discipline and from time to time, should not be confused with science itself. All science is characterized more nearly by an attitude, an approach, a point of view, than by any special technique. One is entitled to call sociology a science if its theories are progressively refined and tested by observation, and if the ideals of objectivity and exactness guide inquiry.

By a variety of research methods, the social scientist attempts to go as far as he can toward uncovering what is persistent and repeatable in the social world. He recognizes, however, that for him "nature" is more elusive and inconstant than it is for the physical scientist.

Sociology shares with other social sciences—notably anthropology, economics, political science, and social psychology—the task of scientific exploration of social behavior and its products. There is no hard and fast division between one social science and another, nor should there be. There are, however, important differences of emphasis that mark off one discipline from another.

Social psychology is largely concerned with connections between group experience and the psychology of the individual, an area of knowledge to which both sociologists and psychologists contribute. In their attempts to understand individual behavior and personality, social psychologists recognize the need to see the influence of interpersonal relations and group membership. This has led to studies of social roles, of the emergence of personality in social interaction, of the analysis of attitudes, and the investigation of small groups. In social psychology the emphasis is placed on the direct effect of groups on individuals. Aspects of social psychology are treated in the study of SOCIALIZATION,[1] PRIMARY GROUPS, and COLLECTIVE BEHAVIOR.

Anthropology is partly a biological and partly a social science. Physical anthropology deals especially with the biological origins of man and with variations in the human species, including the study of race. Because of the social importance of race differences, sociology texts have traditionally given much attention to this problem. We have not done this because the study of races (though *not* of race-conscious groups) is now recognized as a technical problem in genetics and human biology. We have also excluded discussion of such topics as fossil men and the characteristics of the lower animals.

Social and cultural anthropology have contributed greatly to the comparative analysis of societies by exploring the ways of life among preliterate communities throughout the world. We have drawn upon these materials and the ideas developed from them largely in CULTURE, SOCIALIZATION, and Part Three. In many ways, anthropology and sociology have drawn closer together in recent years, particularly as anthropologists have turned to the study of literate societies. A central emphasis on the analysis of culture, however, continues to characterize anthropological inquiry. In sociology this is a significant but not a predominant preoccupation.

Economics deals with the phenomena of cost and price, of savings and investment, of supply and demand. The economist necessarily makes assumptions about the goals men seek in economic life, and sometimes he questions those assumptions. When he does, psychological and sociological analyses are indicated. Furthermore, the economic order is related to and dependent upon many noneconomic forces, including government, public opinion, family life, and migration. Sociologists help to explore these relations and to see their significance for industrial stability and change. The chapter on INDUSTRIAL MAN is in part an introduction to the sociological analysis of economic institutions.

Political science is mostly concerned with the study of government, and traditionally it has had a strong legal and administrative orientation. In recent years, however, there has been a growing interest among political scientists in exploring all of the factors that influence political and administrative decisions, not merely the legal and official relationships. The political order does not stand alone but is rooted in culture and social organization. These considerations, added to the rapidly increasing importance of political decisions for many areas of social life, have stimulated a renewed interest in political sociology. This subject is treated in POLITICAL MAN.

History is classified by some as a social science, by others as one of the humanities. In either case historical documentation is invaluable for sociological research, and sociological analyses are of interest to historians of the contemporary scene.

Sociology is complementary to the other social sciences. It explores the varieties of group structure and the ways they affect political, psychological, and economic relationships. Sociologists are not interested in business decisions *as such,* but they are interested in the social conditions that make certain types of business relations possible. For example, they study the effect of kinship on economic participation in newly industrialized countries or the effect of group relations on factory output. Although not specialists in military science, sociologists study leadership and morale in military units.

---

[1] To facilitate cross-reference, the titles of chapters appear in small capital letters throughout the book.

Adaptation 1 / Trow **NOTES ON SOCIOLOGICAL RESEARCH**

Growing up in a society teaches its members much about how it works, but there are some kinds of knowledge that one is not likely to gain in the pursuits of everyday life. For example, adult Americans are aware of prejudice and discrimination against Negroes. But in the ordinary course of events the individual may not learn much about what lies behind these feelings and actions. Nor is he likely to know very accurately how widespread anti-Negro sentiments are, what forms they take, how they differ in different parts of the country and among different groups in the population, and whether such sentiments are on the rise or are declining in extent and intensity. Similarly, many people are aware that college enrollments are growing rapidly, but few people know how fast, what kinds of institutions are absorbing the bulk of the growth, and how this growth is affecting the character of higher education.

Sociological research is the purposeful effort to learn more about society than one can in the ordinary course of living. How the sociologist goes about his work depends on (1) his objectives, (2) the available materials or data, and (3) the knowledge and theory already established on the same or similar topics.

Sociological description For many purposes, what is needed is a factual account of an event, such as a political rally, or a summary of the characteristics of a population, such as the proportion of aged or the number of divorced persons. In this sense, sociology is a kind of reporting. However, sociological reporting has two special characteristics:

1. *Precision.* The sociologist tries to be as precise as possible in his descriptions. If he can do so, he finds ways of counting and measuring, but much valuable sociological research does not involve the use of statistics. It may consist of the careful study of historical records or the close observation of some single event, situation, or group. The evidence may be assembled and analyzed with care even though numbers are not used.

Accuracy in reporting and analysis has two basic requirements: *objectivity* in observation and *skepticism* toward other people's reports of what is going on. Objectivity does not require that the observer approach the world with a blank mind; rather, he should be equally prepared to find that the facts do or do not support his prior beliefs. Skepticism does not require that the scholar doubt everything he hears or reads, only that he try to distinguish reliable from un-

reliable reports, knowledge from opinion.

In numerical descriptions of populations a number of questions must be considered. For example, were the data collected or reported according to uniform criteria? The importance of uniform criteria is illustrated in the following hypothetical case. Suppose a sociologist compared juvenile delinquency rates for a number of small and large cities and found higher rates in the larger cities. He might then go on, very sensibly, to investigate what it is about large cities that makes for greater delinquency. His efforts might be pointless, however, if it happened that the smaller cities were in states that defined a juvenile as any person under eighteen, while the larger cities were in states that defined a juvenile as anyone under twenty-one. Thus the higher delinquency rates of the larger cities might reflect merely a more inclusive legal definition of who is a juvenile.

Many similar problems arise in the use of official statistics. Record-keeping is often more complete and detailed in cities than in rural areas, and this difference may distort comparisons between areas. There are similar problems in making comparisons over periods of time. At least part of the reported increase in juvenile delinquency in

SOURCE: Adapted from an unpublished paper by Martin A. Trow.

recent years is due to changes in official reporting rather than changes in juvenile behavior.

Besides using public records, sociologists gather data on their own, often by interviews and questionnaires. A sociologist interested in a community's attitudes toward an increase in school taxes would have to gather his own data. Since he could not interview everyone, he would select a sample. If his findings are to describe accurately the distribution of attitudes in the population, his sample must be "representative," that is, it must be a reflection in miniature of the whole community. There are scientific ways of constructing such samples and of estimating the probability that they are representative. When a sample is used to assess the characteristics of a whole group or population, the precision with which it is chosen is of fundamental importance.

On the other hand, much can be learned from studies that do not use representative samples. Detailed interviews with ten members of a college fraternity can tell many things about fraternity life. But unless the men interviewed (the "respondents") are selected according to principles of scientific sampling, the findings cannot be applied to the fraternity as a whole.

2. *Guidance by sociological ideas.* Precision alone does not make a description distinctively sociological. The sociologist has a fund of ideas that help him to form hypotheses about the particular situation or problem he is studying. These leading ideas or "concepts" comprise a large part of what the student of sociology learns. They are his armory of analysis, his guides to inquiry.

From description to explanation Sociologists are rarely content with simply counting things or with straight reporting. They want to understand and explain, to go beyond descriptive fact-gathering to comparison, interpretation, and the assessment of how different aspects of the social world are related.

The search for an explanation may in turn require new facts. For example, it has long been known that high school boys from working-class backgrounds are less likely than middle-class boys to go to college. Why? Some of the difference, but not all, can probably be accounted for by the expense of a college education. But this is not the whole story. In pressing for a fuller explanation, sociologists have applied another idea—the notion of a group atmosphere or "climate." Recently researchers have investigated the influence on college-going of different high school climates, especially attitudes in the student body toward academic achievement.

One study demonstrated the following: fewer middle-class boys from predominantly working-class high schools went to college than boys from the same backgrounds who had attended high schools with predominantly middle-class students. Conversely, more working-class boys in predominantly middle-class high schools aspired to college than boys from similar backgrounds in high schools whose students were mostly working-class in origin. By looking more closely at the students, studying their school environments as well as their origins, a more accurate and a more sophisticated understanding of the conditions affecting college-going can be achieved. Thus sociological description becomes a search for explanations.

Empirical indicators Many things sociologists want to study cannot be seen or measured directly. An example is the "morale" of a team of working men or a company of soldiers. Morale is said to be high when there is cheerful obedience to orders, confidence in supervisors or officers, and willing participation in the life of the organization. But to refine this idea, and to study the factors that affect morale, one needs some way of measuring the level of morale in one group as compared with others.

The strength of morale can be indicated by directly observable events that usually accompany high or low levels of morale. Thus morale can be measured by such *indicators* as rates of absenteeism, rates of infraction of rules, number of men who report themselves sick, willingness to put in extra work, and other acts or attitudes. An empirical indicator is an *observable* sign of some *un*observable or obscure characteristic of an individual or a group. To rely on empirical indicators in sociology is like relying on the observation of smoke as an indicator of fire.

One of the continuing tasks of social research is to test the *validity* of empirical indicators. For example, using the number of men who report themselves sick as an indicator of low morale may not always give valid results. Unhealthful living or working conditions might also produce higher sick-call rates in one group than in another with which it is compared. For this reason sociologists often try to find more than one indicator for the same phenomenon. In the case of army units, low morale would be expected to show up in high rates of absence without leave (AWOL), high rates of sick call, high rates of disobedience, and other signs of discontent.

The search for valid indicators also helps to clarify ideas. For example, the meaning of morale as used above includes *both* willing participation in group life *and* confidence in leaders. But when morale is measured, it may be found that participation and confidence do not necessarily go together. The members of a group may work well together with considerable satisfaction but in opposition to their leaders. Conversely, men may have confidence in their leaders but show little interest in active participation, as is often the case in trade unions and political organizations. Such findings invite a clarification of the working definition of morale.

Critical analysis of indicators may also lead to the discovery that the same behavior may have different meanings for different people. For example, is cutting classes a good indicator of "commitment to education"? Some students cut classes because they are indifferent to studies; for them high rates of cutting indicate low levels of commitment to education. For other students, however, cutting classes may point to a serious but independent pursuit of learning.

Sociological research is a union of observation and analysis, of gathering data and reflecting on it. Doing research on social life and theorizing about it can scarcely be distinguished. At every step the design of research is guided by and contributes to the body of sociological ideas.

SECTION 2 PLAN AND CONTENT OF THE BOOK

In order to present a systematic introduction to sociology, this book follows a carefully designed plan, the understanding of which is essential to the most efficient use of the book. Reference to the detailed Table of Contents (pp. vii–xiii) will be helpful in reading the following discussion.

Part One: Elements of sociological analysis Part One covers the main topics in the subject matter of sociology.

The distinction between Part One and Part Two reflects two kinds of specialization in sociology. First, a sociologist may be interested in certain phenomena found in all societies or in most areas of society. For example, he may be a specialist in the study of social stratification, in the analysis of population data, or in the study of how personality is influenced by group experience. These specialties are discussed in Part One, which sets out the main skills and interests comprising the sociologist's tools of analysis. Secondly, a sociologist may specialize in applying sociological analysis to a particular area, such as religion or education as in Part Two.

The division between Part One and Part Two is *not* a strict division of theory and application. Each Part One chapter includes factual material as well as concepts, application as well as theory. However, Part One draws on many different areas to illustrate points, while each Part Two chapter concentrates on a special area. For example, the chapter on ASSOCIATIONS in Part One includes material on political parties and factories illustrating general principles in the sociology of large-scale organizations.

Taken together, the Part One chapters present the main ideas with which the sociologist approaches any special area. The number of chapters, and the way they are divided, is largely a matter of convenience and emphasis. For instance, Chapter IX combines two closely related fields, POPULATION AND ECOLOGY, while separate chapters are given to ASSOCIATIONS and PRIMARY GROUPS. The chapters are not neat and watertight compartments. The broad subject of SOCIAL ORGANIZATION, for example, includes the study of primary groups, associations, and social stratification. But these important and specialized aspects of social organization are also given detailed treatment in separate chapters. There is no separate chapter on the study of the family, but that subject is treated in other chapters, especially SOCIAL ORGANIZATION, CULTURE, SOCIALIZATION, and PRIMARY GROUPS.

Part Two: Analysis of major institutions Part Two brings sociological analysis to bear on three selected institutions. Each Part Two chapter is divided into *sections* corresponding to the Part One chapters. In this way, the elements of sociology are reexamined in the course of studying several specialized areas. For example, the study of SOCIAL STRATIFICATION or COLLECTIVE BEHAVIOR is not limited to its treatment in Part One; it is pursued in Part Two in chapters on RELIGION, EDUCATION, and LAW.

The list of topics in Part Two could have been extended to include other areas such as the sociology of rural or military life or health and medicine. It would be a challenging project for a class to apply the pattern of Part Two chapters to a field not included in this book, that is, to develop its own Part Two chapter. One of the topics just mentioned might be used, or the approach might be applied to the study of a community, region, or nation. Experience has taught us that this is a good way to sharpen understanding of sociological concepts and at the same time to achieve a broad introduction to a special area. We do not imply that all elements of sociology are equally relevant to all areas of social life. For narrow subjects, only some of the sociological elements are relevant, and even broad areas do not call for equal emphasis of the several elements.

Part Three: Master trends Three major themes characterize modern society: (1) the development of the city as the predominant site of human residence, association, and work, (2) the ascendance of an industrial order with new problems of organization and control, and (3) the transformation of the political order. These trends are the subjects of three related chapters that form a distinct unit of the book. The chapters are presented within a framework emphasizing social change; at the same time they introduce the student to the main ideas and findings of

urban, industrial, and political sociology. Illustrations are drawn from emergent as well as advanced societies, from nations still at the threshold of modernity as well as from the more fully developed industrial societies. The chapters are entitled URBAN MAN, INDUSTRIAL MAN, and POLITICAL MAN.

FORMS OF PRESENTATION

The subject matter is handled in two main ways, in *Text* and in *Adaptations*. The text gives a coherent exposition and analysis. Separately identified adapted readings present aspects of important studies published in books, monographs, and learned journals. Because much of the material was prepared originally for a professional public, we have often simplified, condensed, and reorganized it to make it as useful as possible to beginning students of sociology. That is, we have "adapted" to the introductory level studies that illustrate or further develop discussions in the text. In a number of cases we have adapted only a portion of a major work or we have presented in Adaptation format our own summaries and interpretations of important books. In every case, Adaptations further develop points covered in the text discussion or are complementary to it.

Some Adaptations are primarily reports of research and are included for their factual and interpretive detail: for example, "Fertility and Family Organization in Ceylon," "Family and Society in Israel," "Race Riot: Los Angeles, 1965," and "Student Protest: Berkeley, 1964." Others are more theoretical: Mead on "Mind, Self and Society" and Michels on "The 'Iron Law' of Oligarchy." Still other Adaptations are simple research exercises or comments on research methods: "Exercises in Stratification Research" and "Public Opinion Polls."

Brief illustrative materials or, in the language of the printer, "text inserts," highlight particular topics and are set off from the rest of the text, for example, "Evaluating Percentages," "A Case of Jitters," and "The Case of the G.E. Babies."

Extensive use is made of charts and tables, which are essential parts of the text and should be studied with as much care as pages of exposition. See Adaptation 2 on "Reading a Table," pages 10–12.

Student research and privacy Outlines of research procedures ("Exercises in Stratification Research" and "The Technique of the Sociogram") are included to encourage the student to try his hand at original research. Such work should be undertaken only after careful review and planning with the instructor. Studies that depend on observation or interviewing are potentially invasions of privacy. It should be clearly understood that the privacy of informants and subjects will be protected. Real people and real social relations are the subject matter of the sociologist. He shares with other scientists the obligations of objectivity and rigor. To these, whether he is a mature scholar or a new student, he must add respect for the privacy and personal integrity of his subjects. For example, experiments that deceive subjects in order to gauge their responses, or that lead them to lie, raise serious ethical problems.

Adaptation 2 / *Wallis* and *Roberts* READING A TABLE

Once the reading of tables is mastered, the reader's time is economized by studying the tables carefully and then skimming the text for anything that is not evident in the table, or perhaps not in the table at all. This approach to study not only saves time but often results in a better understanding: verbal descriptions of any but the simplest statistical relationships are usually hard to follow, and besides, authors sometimes misinterpret, misrepresent, or ·overlook important facts in their own tables.

By following a systematic procedure it is possible to grasp quickly the information presented in a table. Here are the main steps (using Table I:1):

1. *Read the title carefully.* A good title tells precisely what the table contains. In this case, the title shows that the table tells about illiteracy in relation to the variables of age, color, and sex, that the data are for the year 1959, and that they are presented as rates—percent illiterate.

2. *Read the headnote or other explanation carefully.* The headnote of Table I:1 gives a more precise indication of the basis for classifying people as illiterate. It was taken for granted that any person who had completed six or more years of school was literate. The mentally deficient, criminals, and others in institutions have been excluded, as have the armed forces, so that the data relate to people in everyday civilian life. Finally, we note that the data are based on a large sample of the population 14 years old and over. Information of the kind given in this headnote is often not attached directly to a table but must be sought elsewhere in the accompanying text.

3. *Notice the source.* Is the original source likely to be reliable? In this case, the answer is definitely "yes," for the Bureau of the Census is one of the most competent statistical agencies in the world. The primary publication source is the Bureau's *Current Population Reports,* and the secondary source is the *Statistical Abstract,* which is a model of its kind. But, as presented here, the data are from a tertiary source—this book. At each step in the copying process errors can creep in. If there is ever a reason to question data in any table, the primary source should be checked.

4. *Look at the footnotes.* They affect the data you will study. Sometimes a footnote applies to every figure in a row, column, or section, but not every figure to which it applies has a footnote symbol. Although Table I:1 has no footnotes, many tables do. See Table V:1, page 137.

5. *Find out what units are used.* Reading thousands as millions or as hundreds is not uncommon. Long tons can be confused with

SOURCE: Abridged and adapted from W. Allen Wallis and Harry V. Roberts, *Statistics: A New Approach* (Glencoe: The Free Press, 1956), pp. 270–274. Published in this form by permission of The Macmillan Company. Copyright 1956 by The Free Press, a Corporation. The latest available data (for 1959) are substituted for the 1952 example used in the original, and this substitution has called for additional alterations in the text.

short tons or metric tons, meters with yards, nautical with statute miles, rates per 1,000 with rates per 100,000, and so on. In Table I:1 illiteracy is expressed in percent—incidence per 100—and age in years.

a. Know what column headings and stubs mean. Stubs are the age categories at the left in Table I:1.

The foregoing steps are, in a sense, all preliminary orientation. They do not take long and ought to become habitual, but if you omit them you may suffer a rude awakening later—or never awaken at all.

6. Look at the overall average. The illiteracy rate for all ages, both colors, and both sexes—the whole population, in other words—is shown in the lower right-hand corner as 2.2 percent, or one person in 45. This may surprise you,

for probably not one in 450 of your acquaintances 14 years of age or older is illiterate. On a matter like this, for a country that in 1959 had about 140 million people 14 or older, neither one's own impressions nor the consensus of friends' impressions are valid. You are a member of a college population which by the definition in the headnote has no illiterates, and you are likely to know people much like yourself.

7. See what variability there is. It is quickly evident that there are percentages less than 1 and more than 25 in the table. There is, therefore, large variation in illiteracy among the twenty-four basic groups into which the population has been divided (two sexes, two colors, six age classes).

8. See how the average compares with each variable.

a. Age. In the section for

"both colors," look down the column for both sexes. We see that the illiteracy rate is lower than the average of 2.2 percent from ages 14 to 44, but it is average or higher through the remainder of the age classes to a rate of 6.5 percent in the highest age class. This is 5.9 percentage points larger than, and nearly eleven times as large as, the rate of 0.6 in the lowest age class. (Avoid phrases such as "illiteracy increases with age" or "rises sharply," which suggest that individuals change as they age.) These data are taken from a cross section of the population at a given point in time, and there is no implication that individuals become illiterate with age. We know from other evidence that older people on the average have had less schooling, and the association between age and illiteracy is, therefore, about what we would expect.

TABLE I:1   ILLITERACY RATES BY AGE, COLOR, AND SEX, UNITED STATES 1959

[Excludes Alaska and Hawaii. Based on a sample of about 76,000. Persons unable to both read and write in any language were classified as illiterate, except that literacy was assumed for all who had completed six or more years of school. Only the civilian, noninstitutional population 14 years of age and over is included.]

AGE (Years)	WHITE			NONWHITE			BOTH COLORS		
	Male	*Female*	*Both*	*Male*	*Female*	*Both*	*Male*	*Female*	*Both*
14 to 24	0.7	0.3	**0.5**	1.7	0.7	**1.2**	0.8	0.3	**0.6**
25 to 34	0.9	0.6	**0.7**	5.1	3.4	**4.2**	1.3	0.9	**1.1**
35 to 44	1.1	0.6	**0.9**	9.1	3.5	**6.1**	1.9	0.9	**1.4**
45 to 54	1.6	1.1	**1.3**	15.0	5.8	**10.2**	2.9	1.5	**2.2**
55 to 64	2.5	2.2	**2.3**	16.5	9.6	**13.0**	3.7	2.8	**3.2**
65 and over	5.3	5.0	**5.1**	28.3	23.0	**25.5**	6.9	6.2	**6.5**
14 and over	1.7	1.4	**1.6**	9.8	5.4	**7.5**	2.5	1.8	**2.2**

SOURCE: *Statistical Abstract of the United States: 1966,* Table 159, p. 116. Original source: Bureau of the Census, *Current Population Reports,* Series P-20, Nos. 45 and 99.

b. Sex. In the both-colors section, comparison of the entries at the bottoms of the male and female columns—totals that apply to all ages—shows that the illiteracy rate for males (2.5 percent) is about 39 percent larger than that for females (1.8 percent).

c. Color. To see the association with color, we compare the entries at the bottoms of the both-sexes columns in the white and nonwhite sections and find that the nonwhite rate (7.5 percent) is 4.7 times the white rate (1.6 percent). At the youngest age the percent illiterate is low for both colors (compare the "both" columns under white and nonwhite), but more than twice as high for nonwhites as for whites. At the older ages nonwhite illiteracy is much greater.

This fact, too, is what we would expect from the trend in education. The older age groupings went to school when educational facilities for nonwhites were far from equal. The younger part of the nonwhite population had the advantage of improved, but not yet equal, educational facilities.

To this point we have used only summary data from the margins of the table. But this is not all that can be gleaned from reading a table. Turning to the cells in the body of the table we could compare the differences between males and females separately for whites and nonwhites. For every age bracket the illiteracy rate without exception is higher for males than for females. That is, white and nonwhite males show higher illiteracy

rates than white and nonwhite females respectively. We would also find that nonwhite females have a greater advantage over nonwhite males than white females have over white males.

However, without further attention to detail, some main conclusions that can be read from Table I:1 may be summarized. Illiteracy in 1959 among the civilian, noninstitutional population 14 years of age and older—

1. Averaged 2.2 percent.
2. Varied greatly with age, color, and sex.
3. Was higher for older people than for younger.
4. Was higher for males than for females.
5. Was higher for nonwhites than for whites.

SOURCES AND READINGS

R. E. L. Faris (ed.), *Handbook of Sociology* (Chicago: Rand McNally, 1964).

Julius Gould and William L. Kolb (eds.), *Dictionary of the Social Sciences* (New York: The Free Press of Glencoe, 1964).

Statistical Abstract of the United States, published annually since 1878 by the U.S. Bureau of the Census.

Encyclopedia of the Social Sciences (New York: Macmillan, 1938), 8 volumes.

International Encyclopedia of the Social Sciences (New York: Macmillan, 1968).

Periodicals

The following journals contain articles on topics pertinent to each of the chapters in this book and are not separately listed in succeeding chapters.

Acta Sociologica

American Journal of Sociology, until 1935 the official journal of the American Sociological Society, now Association. See the Index to Volumes 1–70, 1895–1965.

American Sociological Review, established in 1936 as the official journal of the American Sociological Association. See the Index to Volumes 1–25, 1936–1960 and the Index to Volumes 26–30, 1961–1965.

Annals of the American Academy of Political and Social Science

Australian and New Zealand Journal of Sociology

Behavioral Science

British Journal of Sociology

Canadian Review of Sociology and Anthropology

Current Sociology

European Journal of Sociology

Human Organization

International Journal of Comparative Sociology

International Social Science Journal

New Society

Pacific Sociological Review

Rural Sociology

Social Forces

Social Issues

Social Problems

Sociological Abstracts

Sociological Analysis (formerly *American Catholic Sociological Review*)

Sociological Inquiry

Sociological Quarterly (formerly *Midwest Sociologist*)

Sociology and Social Research

Sociometry

Southwestern Social Science Quarterly

Trans-action

Transactions of the World Congress of Sociology, published by the International Sociological Association.

CHAPTER II
SOCIAL ORGANIZATION

SECTION 1 INTRODUCTION

Whether his subject of study is student life, poverty, crime, the urban revolution, or the emerging nations, the student of society gives a large share of his attention to discovering *how persons and groups relate to each other*. In a specific inquiry, his task is to identify the kinds of relations and their effects on individual conduct and institutional history. Social organization is the pattern of individual and group relations. Every human setting has some degree of social organization.

Many writers refer to social organization as "the social fabric," a metaphor which suggests that human relations are closely interwoven and that strains on one part may weaken the whole fabric in unanticipated ways. This figure of speech emphasizes the harmonious, the interdependent, and the cohesive. Social organization consists also of relations that isolate people or groups and that foster disharmony and conflict. For example, the social organization of a business may segregate blue-collar from white-collar employees and create conflicts of interest among various groups within the enterprise.

In placing the adjective "social" before "organization," the sociologist emphasizes that individual and group relations are mostly unplanned, adaptive outcomes of social processes. *Social* organization emerges in day-to-day interaction—problem-solving, conflict, and cooperation. By itself the word organization connotes a technical arrangement of parts and does not suggest the complexity and texture of human association.

A good way to grasp the general idea of social organization is to consider a familiar case, for example, a modern American university. On the campus there is a wide variety of groups, some permanent and formally recognized, others formed *ad hoc* for special tasks and occasions. In addition, but less discernible, are the lines of communication and influence best known only to the most active participants in campus life. The student government may be a "sandbox" with little power and little communication with the student body, or it may be a source of effective leadership. None of this can be read from an organization chart or official description. The social organization of the campus can be discovered only in the course of experience or through systematic inquiry. And it is a dynamic, living thing, changing from year to year.

SOCIAL SYSTEMS

In pursuing the study of social organization, the sociologist often uses the term "social system." This idea emphasizes the interaction and interdependence of social phenomena. Separate social facts or units are studied as parts of interrelated wholes.

The concept of social system is useful for two reasons. First, it encourages a *contextual* view of individual and group behavior. By studying the social system of a prison, a neighborhood, or an occupation, it is possible to observe the limits that constrain participants as well as the opportunities opened up to them. Their decisions and activities are seen in context, that is, as conditioned by the social situation.

Second, the idea of social system invites attention to relationships that are not ordinarily visible and for which there are no commonsense names. For example, the interdependence of police and informers constitutes a social system; its reasons for being and its effects on law enforcement are not obvious. Social systems may cut across or extend beyond what are conventionally defined as social units. Thus the intersection of military, political, and industrial life may form a significant unity or complex, and may properly be thought of as a social system. Sometimes the analyst is interested in only selected aspects of a larger whole, for example, the communication system or the status system within a particular group or community.

Social systems may be small or large, stable or unstable. The idea of system encourages the analyst to look for contexts and connections; it does not tell him what he will find. It cannot be known in advance whether systematic connections will be found or, if they are discovered, how stable they may be. Indeed, the most important thing one may learn about a system is its internal stresses and tensions, that is, the sources of instability that are breaking it down or changing it into something else.

For example, in studying the social system of a family—how its members respond to one another, how their activities are organized, how they depend on one another—the sociologist is at least as interested in the tensions within the family, both actual and potential, as he is in the smooth accommodations that have taken place. Similarly, when Marx analyzed what he called the "capitalist system," he was interested both in the forces that held it together and its latent internal conflicts. He saw the system as producing a "class struggle" and thereby generating problems it could not solve.

Some sociologists avoid the term "social system" because it seems to them to connote too great an intellectual concern for integration or stability, or to be an undesirable prejudgment about the existence of stable systems. "Patterns of social organization" can serve much the same purpose, with perhaps fewer special connotations, and some prefer that usage.

LEVELS OF SOCIAL ORGANIZATION

It is helpful to think of social systems as located at three levels of social organization—the interpersonal level, the group level, and the social-order level.

1. *Interpersonal relations.* (See Sec. 2, pp. 17–20.) An interpersonal relation is the most elementary social bond, occurring when two persons stand in some relation to each other, such as leader to follower, neighbor to neighbor. The term *interpersonal* means between persons and does not imply that the relation must be a personal one; it may be either impersonal or intimate.

The study of interpersonal relations is fundamental to the science of sociology because they are the "building-blocks" of social structure. Although groups differ they are all made up of the same elementary units, especially roles and modes of interaction. In a criminal gang, or any group, some men are in authority over others, some are friends, some may be teachers. The more that is understood about authority and friendship as general phenomena, the more readily will *any* group be understood. Therefore the student of social organization may devote himself to a detailed investigation of the dynamics of leadership as such or to some other important interpersonal relation. He studies the conditions that sus-

the interpersonal level	ordered interactions role behavior
the group level	initiates, builds upon and sustains interpersonal relations distinctive characteristics of various types of groups relations among groups
the social order level	broad patterns of group life that characterize an entire community or society

FIG. II:1   Levels of social organization

tain the relation and the strains to which it is subject. In doing so, he contributes to knowledge of the basic elements of all groups.

Although the study of interpersonal relations may concentrate attention on limited elements of social life, the implications may be far-reaching. Particular interpersonal relations, such as those involved in kinship, slavery, or the relations to a feudal lord, may be so pervasive and important that they characterize an entire society. In that case, intensive analysis of the interpersonal bond is vital to understanding the whole community and broad social changes.

2. *Group relations.* Section 3 (pp. 30–38) treats the interaction of groups and the stable or uneasy arrangements that result as well as the group structure of society. There is a great deal of difference between intergroup relations and interpersonal relations. When groups oppose one another, the individual members are often hostile, but by no means always. And the group may not be able to do what an individual can do, such as withdraw from a trying situation.

Knowledge of the group structure of a community or society gives clues to potential conflict or solidarity, as well as to forces that may determine the future character of the society or subsociety. New occupations or new patterns of residence may sig-

nificantly alter the group structure of the society. Behind the headlines reporting dramatic events such as the eruption of conflict—in industry, or in a racial ghetto, or in the Middle East—there is a history of groups and their relationships.

3. A *social order* exists when an entire community or society for a significant portion of its history is characterized by distinctive and interwoven patterns of social organization. A social order is a *type of society,* a comprehensive social system. For example, European feudalism was a type of society. This system had a number of key characteristics: a personal tie of loyalty between lord and vassal, the binding of serfs and villeins to the soil, a manorial system of agriculture, and decentralized military control by barons who dominated the countryside from fortified castles. These and other features define the ingredients of a feudal order, its weakness and strength.

Sociologists are also interested in the distinctive features of other social orders: nomadic societies, the modern American society, totalitarian social organization, and other large social systems. Not all of these are readily reducible to a few simple elements, but the sociologist is primarily concerned with finding out how the social order functions as a system, what it depends upon, and the main points of inner strain and conflict.

These studies have largely been the province of historical sociologists interested in social orders that embrace and give form to large systems and long epochs. The study of social systems can also be applied to limited areas of life. The medical world, for example, is strongly controlled by professional organization, by a specialized technology requiring centralization of many activities in large hospitals, by the doctor-patient relationship, and by the way the private physician cooperates with hospital personnel. Anyone interested in medical care needs to understand this network of social relations that extends from the doctor at his patient's bed to the social ranking of hospital personnel.

No sharp separation can be made between studying large institutional settings and small-scale situations. The social organization of the medical world reaches into the hospital ward and affects the human relations within it, just as the social organization of feudalism left its mark on personal interaction in the baronial halls and in the fields.

SOURCES AND READINGS

Michael Banton, *Roles: An Introduction to the Study of Social Relations* (New York: Basic Books, 1965).

Bruce J. Biddle and Edwin J. Thomas (eds.), *Role Theory: Concepts and Research* (New York: Wiley, 1966).

Peter M. Blau, *Exchange and Power in Social Life* (New York: Wiley, 1964).

Lewis A. Coser, *The Functions of Social Conflict* (Glencoe: The Free Press, 1956).

H. H. Gerth and C. W. Mills, *Character and Social Structure* (New York: Harcourt, Brace & World, 1953), Part Three.

Scott A. Greer, *Social Organization* (New York: Doubleday, 1955).

George C. Homans, *The Human Group* (New York: Harcourt, Brace & World, 1950).

George C. Homans, *Social Behavior: Its Elementary Forms* (New York: Harcourt, Brace & World, 1961).

Robert K. Merton, *Social Theory and Social Structure* (revised and enlarged ed.; Glencoe: The Free Press, 1957).

Robert E. Park and Ernest W. Burgess, *Introduction to the Science of Sociology* (Chicago: University of Chicago Press, 1924).

Robin M. Williams, Jr., *American Society: A Sociological Interpretation* (2nd ed.; New York: Knopf, 1960), Chaps. 12–14.

SECTION 2 THE INDIVIDUAL AND SOCIAL ORGANIZATION

A major objective of this book is to explore the following general principle: *the way men behave is largely determined by their relations with each other and by their membership in groups.* Social relations are at the foundation of both motivation and control. The goals and aspirations that set people into motion are greatly influenced by their social relations. Social relations are also instruments of control, for they limit action and restrain impulses that might threaten the orderly arrangement of independent lives.

A corollary of the basic principle stated above is that individuals respond most to the immediate situations in which they find themselves. A member of a street gang or a sales force is also a member of groups that touch him less closely, but in his everyday life it is the proximate membership that has the greatest effect. It follows that behavior determined by social relations is not necessarily conformist from the standpoint of the larger society. The individual may be drawn into delinquency while conforming to immediate group influences.

INTERACTION AND RELATEDNESS

In his daily life an individual continually meets people, cooperates with them, obeys them, irritates them, ignores them. Even to begin a list of such actions shows how diverse are the ways human beings deal with each other. The process of acting in awareness of others, and adjusting responses to the way others respond, is called *social interaction.* Much interaction follows an established pattern; as soon as an individual identifies another person as his teacher or employer, for example, he knows how he is expected to respond.

Other interactions, however, are less closely governed by established patterns.[1] In Western society the individual is faced with many alternatives—whom to have as friends, whom to marry, where to work, what political party to join, and many others. In the course of making these choices, he establishes ties with other individuals, accepts membership in many groups (for instance, when he becomes a student or employee) and gradually comes to have a settled place in the world. The individual's interactions and his group memberships are determined more by how he solves the problems of everyday life than by a fixed set of rules. As an outgrowth of the individual's daily choices and decisions, enduring relations are established, and he thus makes a contribution to social organization. These topics are illustrated in Adaptation 3 which describes interaction and social organization in a suburban housing development.

The sociologist is mainly concerned with interactions that attain stability, that is, those that are recurrent and patterned. This central concern for stable, recurrent interactions does not mean that the less stable ones are uninteresting or unimportant. Sociologists also study spontaneous, relatively uncontrolled forms of human behavior, such as fads and fashions, panics and riots, but in doing so particular attention is given to the emergence of shared patterns of behavior, even though they are transitory. Sociologists also recognize that in the more stable relations, such as marriage, there is room for a variety of responses and adjustments. While searching for what is orderly, it must be remembered that change and instability are characteristic of social life. Much interaction is casual, tentative, or unstable, and does not lead to enduring social bonds.

The variety of social relations is enormous. Friendship, fatherhood, employment, leadership, neighborliness, partnership, citizenship, marriage, and a host of other terms signify important and differing relations. The sociologist tries to understand the nature of these relations by examining their elements, classify-

ing them, and studying what happens to them under changing conditions.

Some social bonds are strong and others weak. A shipboard romance is a notoriously weak social relation; marriage, even in present-day society, remains a relatively strong and stable relation. Some social relations, such as family relations, have lasting significance for the entire life of the individual while others, even if they endure, are far less meaningful. Some relations are of great importance to the community because they involve tasks that must be performed, such as the care of children. Other relations, for example a friendship, may be of little concern to anyone except those who are immediately involved.

The strength of a social relation depends in part upon its scope and whether it fits into a larger pattern. For example, if a marriage involves the husband in economic ties to his wife's family, this broadens and often strengthens the foundation upon which the marriage rests, despite the fact that it also introduces unusual strains. In addition, the strength of a relation depends on whether it serves or frustrates the needs of the individual. Both aspects of any social relation—its place in a larger social setting and its significance for personal satisfaction—affect whether the relation is strong and enduring or weak and transitory.[2]

ROLES AND ROLE STRAIN

A role (sometimes called "social role") is a basic unit of social structure. It may be defined as a pattern of behavior associated with a distinctive social position, e.g., that of father, teacher, employer, or patient. The *ideal* role prescribes the rights and duties belonging to a social position; it tells the individual what is expected of him in his role as father or teacher, to whom he has obligations, and upon whom he has a rightful claim. *Actual* role behavior is always subject to the influence of a specific social setting as well as the personality of the individual.

Some sociologists restrict roles to the ideal or pre-

---

[1] For studies of interaction with emphasis on situational rather than established patterns, see R. F. Bales, *Interaction Process Analysis: A Method for the Study of Small Groups* (Reading, Mass.: Addison-Wesley, 1950), and Erving Goffman, *The Presentation of Self in Everyday Life* (Garden City, N.Y.: [Anchor] Doubleday, 1959).

[2] For a treatment that relates interaction to larger social structure, see Peter M. Blau, *Exchange and Power in Social Life* (New York: Wiley, 1964).

scribed pattern, using role *performance* to designate the actual conduct.[3] However, the distinction between ideal and actual breaks down in the case of informal or emergent roles for which there are no clearly defined expectations. For example, in small-group interaction one person may be a sparkplug or idea man, another a joker who helps relieve tension. These roles are often independent of formally assigned positions or tasks and tend to be expressive of personality traits and group needs. From such role behavior stable expectations may in time develop, but at first there is no ideal or prescribed role.

Most roles are more complex than they appear to be at first glance. A mother is a mother in relation to a child; yet being a mother is more than just one social relation. It is a bundle of relations to other members of the family and to the community, as well as to the child. Part of the role of mother may involve membership in the PTA, just as part of the role of employer may involve membership in a Chamber of Commerce. Although many roles are rather definitely specified, in practice they are often too complex to be learned except through experience. The mother, the employer, the student, the foreman only gradually learn through their interactions with others what is expected of individuals in their social position.

To analyze a role completely it is necessary to specify in detail the social position with which it is associated. In some respects, all students occupy similar social positions. Insofar as this is true, it is possible to describe general features of the student's role. But there are many ways of being a student, even within a particular college. The married student, the disciple, the student leader are all significantly different in the positions they occupy within the social structure of the college. Close analysis usually reveals specific roles, reflecting the particular way a given family, school, or other group is organized.

Role conflict   In the course of his role behavior the individual is subject to conflicting pressures and strains.[4] Some of these strains arise because different and inconsistent kinds of behavior are required. For example, a role may call for friendship or intimacy but also may require impersonal judgment or command. To the extent that a professor's role leads him to attempt to influence some students deeply, he needs to be on friendly terms with them, to treat them as unique persons, and to develop a sense of mutual loyalty. But the professor must also be a judge who evaluates the work of the student, and makes decisions that may affect the latter's career. These conflicting demands require painful adjustments.

Some roles are designed to meet this type of problem. To preserve authority, close personal relations between those in command and their subordinates may be carefully avoided. For example, the impersonality and severity of military discipline are supported by creating a strong sense of social distance between officers and enlisted men. This is not always a satisfactory solution, however. A more personal leadership is necessary to win deep loyalty or to summon extraordinary energies in battle; and distance between ranks handicaps effective communication even in everyday activities. Hence, the wise leader seeks various ways of overcoming the distance between himself and his followers. For example, he may show by public acts that he is proud of his men and understands their problems.

Role conflicts in industry and military life arise when the attempt is made to create a bridge from the commanding group to those who must obey. Many noncommissioned officers in the army and foremen in industry play this bridging role. They are men "in the middle." They must communicate orders from above, but they must be close enough to the working group to understand how these orders will be received; they must have the confidence of the working group lest fear and hostility undermine effective communication and the will to cooperate. At the same time, these lower-level leaders must be able to take the point of view of their superiors whose orders are to be communicated and enforced. The result is a continuing necessity to take account of two approaches to daily experience and of two sets of interests that are often in conflict.

[3] See Erving Goffman, *Encounters: Studies in the Sociology of Interaction* (Indianapolis: Bobbs-Merrill, 1961), p. 85.
[4] William J. Goode, "A Theory of Role Strain," *American Sociological Review, 25* (August, 1960), 483–496.

Thus strains and inconsistencies are *built into the role*. When these built-in conflicts are known, the problems set for the individual by his role are also known. His role involves him in relations that make demands upon him, limit the alternatives he can choose, and create the problems he must try to solve. This point illustrates the dynamic, motivating, and problem-setting nature of social organization.

SOCIAL ORGANIZATION AND SOCIAL CONTROL

The individual gains much from his involvement in social organization, but he always pays a price. That price is the acceptance of restraints, of limitations on the freedom to do as he pleases.

Social organization produces social control mainly because people are *dependent* on each other. One way of mapping the social structure of a group or community is to explore the mutual dependencies that have been created.[5] The more people an individual is dependent upon for his satisfactions, the more claims will there be upon him to exercise self-restraint lest he offend those he needs and risk the loss of their cooperation.

Dependency is not necessarily an expression of narrow self-interest. Dependency may invoke ideals that might otherwise be inoperative. The social ideals of parenthood do not have much influence on a bachelor. His behavior cannot be restrained by responsibility to children he does not have. It is only through relations to others and by participating in social institutions that responsibilities arise; only in this way do ideals become effective instruments of social control.

Isolation and control Social isolation weakens social control. If a person is uninvolved with others, there are fewer occasions to assess the consequences of his actions either for himself or for others dependent upon him. Durkheim's explanation of the different rates of suicide (see Adaptation 4) is grounded in a theory of social organization. He pointed out, for example, that unmarried people are "freer" to choose suicide as a response to despair than are married people, because the unmarried are relatively isolated from controlling social bonds.

[5] Richard M. Emerson, "Power-Dependence Relations," *American Sociological Review, 27* (February, 1962), 31–41.

Adaptation 3 / *W. H. Whyte, Jr.* THE WEB OF FRIENDSHIP

Students of social organization are interested in both the *sources* and the *consequences* of patterned interaction. In the new suburb, one may observe the spontaneous growth of social organization among people previously unrelated to each other. The effects of this patterning on the personal lives of the residents can then be analyzed.

This procedure is followed in Whyte's description and interpretation of life in Park Forest, Illinois. He traces the emergence of different micro-communities that develop their own social characteristics. These characteristics are based on the physical placement of homes by the designers of the housing development and on the patterns of relations established by the first residents.

Also considered are the effects of the highly patterned and intense social life of these small subcommunities on (1) civic participation and (2) the individual's dilemma of personal autonomy and group loyalty.

SOURCE: Abridged and adapted from *The Organization Man* by William H. Whyte, Jr. (New York: Simon and Schuster, 1956), pp. 330–361. Published in this form by permission of William H. Whyte, Jr.

In suburbia, friendship has become almost predictable. Given a few physical clues about the area, you can come close to determining its flow of "social traffic," and to a diagnosis of who is in the gang and who is not.

Park Forest has the principal design features found in other suburbs: its 60 x 125 plots are laid out in the curved superblocks typical of most new developments, and the garden duplexes of its rental area are perhaps the most intense development of court living to be found anywhere. Park Forest is like other suburbs, only more so.

The architects wanted a good basic design that would please people and make money for the developers—but not since the medieval town have there been neighborhood units so well adapted to the predilections and social needs of its people. In many ways, the courts are remarkably similar to the workers' housing of the fifteenth century. Like the Fugger houses in Augsburg, the courts are essentially groups of houses two rooms deep, bound together by lines of communication, and the parking area unifies the whole very much as did the water fountain of the Fugger houses.

When the architects designed the 105 courts and the homes area, they tried hard to introduce some variety, and no two courts or superblocks are physically alike. But neither are they alike socially; some neighborhood units have been a conspicuous social success from the beginning, others have not. Each court produces a different pattern of behavior, and whether newcomers become civic leaders or bridge fans or churchgoers is determined to a large ex-

tent by the gang to which chance assigns them.

Court residents talk about these differences a great deal. In some areas, they will tell you, feuding and cussedness are chronic. "I can't put my finger on it," says one resident, "but as long as I've been here this court has had an inferiority complex. We never seem to get together and have the weenie roasts and parties they have in B 18 across the street." In other courts they will talk of their *esprit de corps*. "At the beginning we were maybe too neighborly," says one housewife. "Your friends knew

more about your private life than you did yourself! But it's still real friendly. The street behind us is nowhere near as friendly. They knock on doors over there."

A routine plotting of the rate of turnover in each area, the location of parties, and similar data revealed geographical concentrations that could not be attributed to chance. For example, when the location of leaders of church and other civic organizations was plotted, certain courts displayed a heavy concentration while others showed none at all. The pattern, furthermore, was a persistent one.

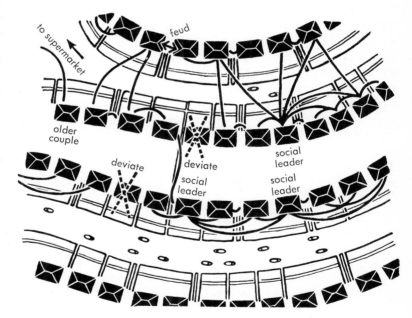

How Homeowners Get Together: (1) Individuals tend to become most friendly with neighbors whose driveways adjoin theirs. (2) Deviates or feuding neighbors tend to become boundaries of the gang. (3) People in the most central positions make the greatest number of social contacts. (4) Street width and traffic determine whether or not people make friends across the street. (5) People make friends with those in back of them only where some physical feature creates traffic—such as the short-cut pavement one woman on the lower street uses on her way to the supermarket.

When leaders for the same organizations as of two years earlier were studied, the same basic pattern emerged. Several leaders were still hanging on, but there had been enough turnover to show that the clustering was closely related to the influence of the court.

Other indexes show the same kind of contagion. The map of active members of the United Protestant Church indicates that some areas habitually send a good quota of people to church while other areas send few. Voting records show heavy voter turnouts in some areas, apathy in others, and this pattern tends to be constant—the area that had the poorest showing in the early days is still the poorest (six people voting out of thirty-eight eligibles). The same courts may also make more complaints to the police about parking-space encroachments, litter left on the lawns, and similar evidences of bad feeling. Courts that keep on producing an above-average number of complaints prove to be the ones with relatively poor records of churchgoing and voting. Another key index is the number of parties and such communal activities as joint playpens. Some courts have many parties, and though the moving van is constantly bringing in new people, the partying and the group activities keep up undiminished. On closer investigation, areas with high partying records usually prove to be the ones with the physical layout best adapted to providing the close-knit neighborly group that many planners and observers feel needs to be re-created.

Court traditions Of all the factors making for differences among the courts, the character of the original settlers seems the most important. In the early phase, the court's inhabitants must function as a unit to conquer such now-legendary problems as the mud of Park Forest, or the "rocks and rats" of Drexelbrook. During this period, though the level of communal sharing and brotherhood is high in all courts, the impact of the strong personality, good or otherwise, is magnified. Two or three natural leaders concentrated in one court may so stimulate the other people that civic work becomes something of a tradition in the court; or, if the dominant people are of a highly gregarious temper, the court may develop more inwardly, along the one-big-family line. Conversely, one or two troublemakers may fragment a court into a series of cliques, and the lines of dissension often live long after the troublemakers have gone.

In time, the intensity of activity weakens. As the volunteer policemen are replaced by a regular force, as the mud turns to grass, the old *esprit de corps* subsides into relative normalcy. First settlers will tell you that the place is in a dead calm. But what seems like dead calm to them will not seem so to anybody from the outside world, and for all the settling down the court continues to be a hothouse of participation. Occasionally, there are sharp breaks in the continuity of tradition; in one court, several forceful women ran for the same post in a community organization, and the effect of their rivalry on the court spirit was disastrous. Most courts, however, tend to keep their essential characters. Newcomers are assimilated, one by one, and by the time the old leaders are ready to depart, they have usually trained someone to whom they can pass on the baton.

Space and sociability The social patterns show rather clearly that a couple's behavior is influenced not only by which court they join but by the particular part of the court in which they are placed.

It begins with the children. There are so many of them and they are so dictatorial in effect that a term like *filiarchy* would not be entirely facetious. It is the children who set the basic design; their friendships are translated into the mothers' friendships, and these, in turn, into the family's. "The kids are the only ones who are really organized here," says the resident of a patio court at Park Merced in San Francisco. "We older people sort of tag along after them." Suburbanites elsewhere agree. "We are not really 'kid-centered' here like some people say," one Park Forester protests, "but when your kids are playing with the other kids, they force you to keep on good terms with everybody."

That they do. With their remarkable sensitivity to social nuance, the children are a highly effective communication net, and parents sometimes use them to transmit what custom dictates elders cannot say face to face. "One newcomer gave us quite a problem in our court," says a resident in an eastern development. "He was a Ph.D., and he started to pull rank on some of the rest of us. I told my kid he could tell his kid that the other fathers around here had plenty on the ball. I guess all we fathers did the same thing; pretty soon the news trickled upward to this guy. He isn't a bad sort; he got the hint—and there was no open break of any kind."

Placement of driveways and stoops: If you are passing by a row of houses equally spaced and want a clue as to how the different couples pair off, look at the driveways. At every second house there are usually two adjacent driveways; where they join makes a natural sitting, baby-watching, and gossip center, and friendship is more apt to flower there than across the un-broken stretch of lawn on the other sides of the houses. For the same basic reasons the couples who share adjoining back stoops in the courts are drawn together, even though equidistant neighbors on the other side may have much more in common with them.

Lawns: The front lawn is the thing on which homeowners expend most time, and the sharing of tools, energies, and advice tends to make family friendships go along and across the street rather than over the back yards. The persistence of this pattern furnishes another demonstration of the remarkable longevity of social patterns. At first, some people thought that lack of over-the-back-fence fraternization was strictly temporary. It has not proved to be so. As the areas have matured, some of the reasons for the concentration of activity in the front area have disappeared; but despite this fact and despite the turnover, over-the-back-fence socializing is still the exception.

Centrality: The location of your home in relation to the others not only determines your closest friends; it also virtually determines how popular you will be. The more central one's location, the more social contacts one has. In the streets containing rental apartments there is a constant turnover; yet no matter who moves in or out, the center of activity remains in mid-block, with the people at the ends generally included only in the larger gatherings.

Some Park Forest veterans joke that a guide should be furnished newcomers so that if they had a choice of sites they would be able to tell which would best suit their personality. Introverts who wished to come out of their shell could pick a house in the middle of a block; while introverts who wished to stay just as they are would be well advised to pick a unit more isolated.

Barriers: The rules of the game about who is to be included, who left out, are not simple. Suppose you want to give a party? Do you mix friends out of the area with the neighbors? How many neighbors should you invite? Where, as social leaders chronically complain, do you draw the line? Physical barriers can provide the limiting point. Streets, for example, are functional for more than traffic; if it is a large street with heavy traffic, mothers will forbid their children to cross it, and by common consent the street becomes a boundary for the adult group.

Because of the need for a social line, the effect of even the smallest barrier is multiplied. In courts where the parking areas have two exits, fences have been placed across the middle to block through traffic; only a few feet high, they are as socially impervious as a giant brick wall. Similarly, the grouping of apartment buildings into wings of a court provides a natural unit whose limits everyone understands.

Ambiguity is the one thing the group cannot abide. If there is no line, the group will invent one. They may settle on an imaginary line along the long axis of the court, or, in the homes area, one particular house as the watershed. There is common sense behind it. If it is about time you threw a party for your neighbors, the line solves many of your problems for you. Friends of yours who live on the other side understand why they were not invited, and there is no hard feeling.

In this need, incidentally, the deviant can be of great benefit. The family that doesn't mix with the others or is disliked by them frequently furnishes a line of social demarcation that the layout and geography do not supply. So functional is the barrier family in this respect that even if they move out, their successors are likely to inherit the function. The new people may be normal enough themselves, but unless they are unusually extroverted the line is apt to remain.

The outgoing life The effect this web of friendship has on the individual is a problem suburbanites think about a great deal. One of the first points they make is how it has altered their personality—or how they and the rest of the group altered someone else's. For the good. "I've changed tremendously," says one typical transient. "My husband was always the friend-maker in the family—everybody always loves Joe; he's so likable. But here I began to make some friends on my own; I was so tickled when I realized it. One night when the gang came to our house I suddenly realized I made these friends."

The cumulative effect can be summed up in a word. People are made *outgoing*. If the person is too shy to make the first move, others will take the initiative. In almost every court, patio, or super-block there is usually someone who enjoys doing the job, and the stiffer the challenge, the more the enjoyment. "When Mr. and Mrs. Berry came, they wouldn't give you the time of day," one leader recalls. "But I knew they were real shy and unhappy beneath it all. I said to myself, 'I'm going to conquer them if it kills me.' I have, too. She was one of the organizers for the Mothers' March and he's gotten tremendously interested in the school. They're part of the gang now—you wouldn't know they were the same people."

The sin of privacy On the matter of privacy, suburbanites have mixed feelings. Fact one, of course, is that there isn't much privacy; people don't bother to knock and they come and go furiously. The lack of privacy, furthermore, is retroactive. "They ask you all sorts of questions about what you *were* doing," one resident puts it. "Who was it that stopped in last night? Who were those people from Chicago last week? You're never alone, even when you think you are."

Few things are sacred. "It's wonderful," says one young wife. "You find yourself discussing all your personal problems with your neighbors—things that back in South Dakota we would have kept to ourselves." As time goes on, this capacity for self-revelation grows; and on the most intimate details of family life, court people become amazingly frank with one another.

No one, they point out, ever need face a problem alone.

In the battle against loneliness even the architecture becomes functional. Just as doors inside houses are disappearing, so are the barriers against neighbors. The picture in the picture window, for example, is what is going on *inside* —or, what is going on inside other people's picture windows. Walls in the new apartments are thin, but there is more good than bad, many transients say, to the thinness. "I never feel lonely, even when Jim's away," goes a typical comment. "You know friends are near by, because at night you hear the neighbors through the walls."

Even the most outgoing, of course, confess that the pace of court life occasionally wears them down, and once in a while they reach such a point of rebellion they don't answer the phone. One court resident moves his chair to the front rather than the court side of his apartment to show he doesn't want to be disturbed. Often a whole court or a wing of it will develop such a signal; a group in one Drexelbrook court has decided that whenever one of them feels he or she has finally had it, she should draw the venetian blinds all the way down to the bottom of the picture window. The rest spot it as a plea to be left alone—for a little while, anyway.

But there is an important corollary of such efforts at privacy— people feel a little guilty about making them. Except very occasionally, to shut oneself off from others like this is regarded as either a childish prank or, more likely, an indication of some inner neurosis. The individual, not the group, has erred. So, at any rate, many

errants seem to feel, and they are often penitent. "I've promised myself to make it up to them," one court resident recently told a confidant. "I was feeling bad that day and just plain didn't make the effort to ask them in for coffee. I don't blame them, really, for reacting the way they did."

The moral basis of conformity However one may view this responsiveness to the group, it is important to acknowledge its moral basis. That friendship in the new suburbia transcends personal characteristics so much is due in part to the increasing homogeneity of American middle-class values. But it is also due to a very active kind of tolerance, and unless this is recognized one cannot appreciate the true difficulty of the suburbanites' dilemmas.

Very consciously, they try to understand one another's backgrounds and prejudices, and make a great effort to meet one another half way. Farm-bred Republicans learn to appreciate that not all urban Democrats are Communists. "The people who lived in the other half of our duplex," recalls one Republican, "were as different as could be from us. They were the kind who worshipped F.D.R.'s name. But we got to like them just the same. We just didn't talk politics. We used to go bowling together and that sort of thing. I didn't make him a Republican, but I think he appreciates my views a lot more than he did before, and I understand him better."

This seeking of common values applies markedly to religion. The neighborhood friendship patterns would be impossible unless religious beliefs had lost much of their segregating effect. And it is more than a passive, live-and-let-live attitude.

Even where there is conflict, suburbanites lean over backward to see the other point of view. "When Will and Ada had to dash East last month—they're devout Catholics—I took care of little Johnny for them," recalls one non-Catholic. "It really tickled me. Here I was picking Johnny up at St. Irenaeus School every afternoon and seeing to it that he said his Rosary every night before he went to bed." Park Forest abounds with such stories, and the good will implicit in them is real.

The suburban group also has a strong effect on relations between husband and wife, in many ways a beneficent one. The group is a foster family. In the transient organization life the young family has to take a good part of its environment with it; no longer is there the close complex of aunts and uncles and grandparents to support the couple, and when they come to their first crisis this absence can have a devastating effect. All the other young couples are in the same boat, and in a sort of unspoken mutual assistance pact they provide for one another a substitute for the big family of former years.

What unites them most are the concerns of parenthood, and this preoccupation with children is a potent factor in keeping marriages on keel. "The kind of social situation you find here discourages divorce," says the United Protestant Church minister. "Few people, as a rule, get divorces until they break with their groups. I think the fact that it is so hard to break with a group here has had a lot to do with keeping some marriages from going on the rocks."

The group as friend and tyrant
But the group is a jealous master. It encourages participation, indeed it demands it, but it demands one kind of participation—its own kind—and the better integrated with it a member becomes the less free he is to express himself in other ways.

When we first went to Park Forest we thought that the courts and blocks most notable for their friendliness and social activity would contribute the greatest number of civic leaders. As a check we plotted the location of all the leaders in the principal community organizations. To our surprise, the two did not correlate; if anything, there was a reverse relationship. By and large, the people who were active in the overall community did not tend to come from the courts that were especially "happy."

The cause-and-effect relationship is not too difficult to determine. For some people, of course, it does not make much difference whether the neighborly gang is a happy one or not; they would be leaders in any event. But such people are a minority. The majority are more influenced by the good opinion of the group, and its cohesiveness has a considerable bearing on whether they will become active in community-wide problems. Where the group has never jelled enough to stimulate a sense of obligation, the person with any predilection for civic activity feels no constraints. The others would not be annoyed if he went in for outside activity; they don't care enough. If the group is strong, however, the same kind of person is less likely to express such yearnings. It would be divisive. There are only so many enthusiasms a person can sustain, only so many hours in the day, and the amount of leisure one expends outside the group must be deducted from that spent inside.

It is not merely that the group will resent the absenteeism. The individual himself feels a moral obligation to the group. A young housewife had been toying with the idea of getting involved in the little theater, for she felt she and her husband were culturally very lacking. But she decided against it. "If we do it'll mean we'll have to spend more of our free evenings away from the gang. I'd hate to be the first to break things up. The two play areas for the kids—my, how we all pitched in on that! I know we spend too much time just talking and playing bridge and all. Frankly Chuck and I are the only ones around here who read much more than the *Reader's Digest*. But have we the right to feel superior? I mean, should we break things up just because we're different that way?"

Is this simple conformity? Consider the man who is wondering about something he knows would upset the group—like not painting his garage white, like the rest. He may have been one of the first settlers of a block where the people have suppressed potential dislikes in a very successful effort to solve their common problems. Quite probably, a piece of bad luck for one of the group might have further unified them. If one of the wives had come down with polio, the rest might have chipped in not only with their money but with their time to help out the family through the crisis.

In other words, there had been a great deal of real brotherhood, and the man who is now figuring about his garage faces a decision that is not entirely ludicrous. He knows instinctively that his choice will be construed by the others as an outward manifestation of his regard for them, and he does feel a real obligation to help sustain the good feeling.

If he goes along with them he is conforming, yes, but he is conforming not simply out of cowardice but out of a sense of brotherhood too. You may think him mistaken, but grant at least his problem. The group is a tyrant; so also is it a friend, and *it is both at once*. The two qualities cannot easily be separated, for what gives the group its power over the man is the same cohesion that gives it warmth.

Adaptation 4 / Durkheim SUICIDE AND SOCIAL INTEGRATION

The French sociologist, Emile Durkheim, was interested in the various types of social integration and in social disorganization, the weakening of social bonds. He used rates of suicide as an index of social integration. The suicide rate was higher for Protestants than for Catholics, higher for the unmarried than for the married, higher for soldiers than for civilians, higher for noncommissioned officers than for enlisted men, higher in times of peace than in times of war and revolution, and higher in times of both prosperity and recession than in times of economic stability.

Durkheim reasoned that since different groups have different suicide rates, there must be something in their social organization that prevents or fails to deter people from suicide, or which may even prompt them to it. He acknowledged that individual reasons were many and varied: financial distress, disappointment in love, failing to pass an examination, ill health, and so on. But these reasons did not explain why some groups have higher suicide rates than others.

Durkheim suggested that the degree to which the individual was integrated into group life determined whether he could be motivated to suicide. However, he recognized that no single set of circumstances explains suicide. The individual can be motivated to suicide at either of two extremes: if he is highly integrated or if he is only superficially integrated into society.

Altruistic suicide When the individual is tightly bound into a highly integrated group with a strong sense of solidarity, he accepts the values and norms of the group as his own. He does not distinguish between his interests and those of the group, nor is he likely to think of himself as a unique individual with a life separate and apart from the group. Under these circumstances what would prompt him to commit suicide?

He will be willing to sacrifice his life for group goals. The Japanese *Kamikaze* of World War II is an example of military self-sacrifice. Japanese airmen crashed their planes onto enemy ships in order to disable them, despite the fact that it meant certain death. In

SOURCE: A summary and interpretation of Emile Durkheim, *Le Suicide* (Paris: Alcan, 1897). English translation and introduction by George Simpson (Glencoe: The Free Press, 1951).

highly integrated societies where there is a strong sense of social solidarity, self-destruction may be looked upon as self-affirmation and fulfillment; death, as well as life, has meaning and value. Closely related to this kind of suicide is ritualistic self-sacrifice. In India a practice called *suttee,* now outlawed, was sometimes performed, in which the Hindu widow threw herself on her husband's funeral pyre.

If the individual fails to meet group standards, death may appear preferable to life. Identification with the group can be so intense that group condemnation is tantamount to self-condemnation. Failure in such a case is total and absolute. The individual puts all his eggs in one basket. He stakes his entire self-respect on approval of one particular group; when that is withdrawn, he has no other basis for self-esteem.

Suicide that results from an excessive degree of group integration Durkheim called *altruistic,* and it is committed for the sake of the group or according to group norms of conduct. Altruistic suicide may be a manifestation of overinvolvement in one group and social isolation from other groups.

Durkheim used his theory of altruistic suicide to explain why the suicide rate was higher for soldiers than for civilians, higher for noncommissioned officers than for enlisted men, and higher for volunteers and those who reenlisted than for conscripts. He suggested that suicide increases as the soldier identifies himself more completely with the values and norms of military life. The officer is better integrated into the military organization than the ordinary soldier,

the volunteer more involved with military life than the conscript. The more fully the soldier is integrated into military life, the greater is his isolation from other groups in society; the more dedicated he is to military values, the more he stakes his self-respect on success in the army. No other paths are open to him.

Egoistic suicide What happens to the individual when he is only weakly attached to the social order?

1. He lacks the restraints that intense participation in group life imposes on him. If he has an inclination to commit suicide, he is not deterred because of deeply felt obligations to others. Nor does he consider the consequences of his suicide for the group. An individual not bound to others is free of any claims that they may have on his survival.

2. The individual lacks the emotional attachments to others that make life worth while and less self-centered.

3. The individual lacks the emotional supports that deep immersion in group life can provide. He is thrown back upon his own resources. He gains no satisfaction from the achievements of the group; success or failure are his alone. Wrongdoing is not defined solely by group standards, but is a matter of personal judgment and responsibility. Under the burden of individual responsibility, the individual is susceptible to the emotional disturbances which may lead to suicide, and he cannot fall back upon relations with others to help him over a personal crisis.

This kind of suicide Durkheim called *egoistic.* It is self-centered

Emile Durkheim (1858–1917), a profound student of social organization. His lifelong interest was in the forces that hold a society together or tend to disorganize it. In The Elementary Forms of the Religious Life, *he studied the contribution of religion to social cohesion; his* Division of Labor in Society *analyzed two basic types of social solidarity and introduced the concept of* anomie. *Another of his studies of social integration was* Suicide, *one of the first modern examples of the use of statistical method in social research.*

rather than group-centered. Altruistic suicide occurs because the individual is deeply involved in group life; egoistic suicide occurs because the individual is uninvolved and detached.

According to Durkheim, the relatively higher rate of Protestant suicide could be explained as egois-

Suicide as a demonstrative political act: the ultimate personal decision may reflect the strength or weakness of group ties.

unmarried are both socially and emotionally isolated from others. They have fewer responsibilities as well as fewer attachments. The married are restrained by both formal obligations and emotional ties. They are also apt to be less self-centered. Their lives are perforce taken up with the care of others, and they develop shared interests and values and find emotional support in their interpersonal relations.

During wars and revolutions people are led to forget themselves and their troubles in uniting for a common effort. At least temporarily, social crises result in a stronger integration of society. For this reason, Durkheim claimed, the suicide rate tends to fall during social disturbances and wars.

Anomic suicide A highly integrated and unified group develops norms to regulate behavior and interpersonal relations. The group provides the individual with a sense of security by establishing clear rules of right and wrong and by limiting his aspirations to what he can hope to achieve.

Durkheim believed that an ever-present source of acute anxiety is unrestrained aspiration. When people live without established, attainable goals and definite alternatives, when there is "only empty space above them," they are subject to emotional distress. When group norms are weakened, the individual feels less restraint on his aspirations and conduct. At the same time, he loses the security that group control and regulation provide. His ambitions soar beyond possible fulfillment and he is uncertain of what is right and wrong.

tic. Both Catholicism and Protestantism condemn suicide, but Catholicism makes its injunction effective by attaching the individual to the church as a social institution. Protestantism, on the other hand, makes salvation a matter of individual faith and religious belief, of personal responsibility. It tends to detach the individual from all religious constraint except his own conscience. In doing so, however, it removes the very social restraints that would be most effective in deterring him from suicide.

The relatively higher suicide rate among the unmarried is also an instance of egoistic suicide. The

According to Durkheim, a society that lacks clear-cut norms to govern men's aspirations and moral conduct is characterized by *anomie,* which means "lack of rules" or "normlessness." Suicide resulting from anomie Durkheim called *anomic.*

Anomic and egoistic suicide both spring from low social integration, but they are nevertheless independent. Although the egoistic suicide does not have the personal bonds that would deter him from the act, he has not necessarily rejected social norms. On the contrary, the egoistic suicide may be a highly moralistic person who feels a deep sense of personal responsibility for his behavior. His morality, however, stems from "principle" rather than from felt loyalties to other persons or institutions. Indeed one of the sources of his emotional disturbance may be that he is overdisciplined, that he conforms in an overly rigid way. According to Durkheim, egoistic suicide is apt to occur among intellectuals and professionals, people who are primarily concerned with ideas and are only loosely attached to specific persons or groups.

In anomic suicide, on the other hand, the individual may be deeply involved in society, but group life fails to provide him with controlling standards of behavior. Life may be unbearable to the egoistic suicide because of *excessive* self-discipline; life may be unbearable to the anomic suicide because of *inadequate* self-discipline.

Durkheim offered two kinds of evidence to support his theory that a lack of limiting norms would result in a high suicide rate.

1. He noted that the rate was higher in countries that permitted divorce than in countries that did not permit it, and the rate was still higher where divorce was frequent. Durkheim reasoned that by allowing divorce a society weakened an important regulatory principle.

When the relation of suicide to divorce is considered, a distinction must be made between the fact of divorce and the possibility of it. The fact of divorce tends to isolate the individual and thereby contributes to the rate of egoistic suicide. The possibility of divorce reflects permissive norms that open up alternatives and generate anxiety; therefore it is relevant to anomic suicide.

2. Durkheim also noted that suicide is associated with economic conditions. In periods of depression the suicide rate is high. However, the cause is not the hardship of poverty but rather the dislocation attendant upon economic crises. Spain was much poorer than France but had only a tenth as many suicides, and rates were generally low in areas of persistent poverty.

Durkheim felt that any abrupt economic changes, whether of boom or of depression, would unsettle established expectations. Sudden prosperity is unsettling, for it brings increased desire and excitability. "Poverty protects against suicide because it is a restraint in itself. . . . Wealth, on the other hand, by the power it bestows, deceives us into believing that we depend on ourselves only. Reducing the resistance we encounter from objects, it suggests the possibility of unlimited success against them. The less limited one feels the more intolerable all limitation appears." [6]

Durkheim's generalization about poverty was correct. The high suicide rates of depressions are due to the suffering that accompanies a *relative* loss of wealth or social standing. But his hypothesis about prosperity is rather weakly supported in *Suicide* and has not been confirmed.[7]

Conclusion   His study of suicide furthered Durkheim's broader interest in the nature of social order and social disorganization. The significance of *Suicide* is the light it casts on human relatedness, both to groups and to group norms. The types of suicide—altruistic, egoistic, anomic—point to the phenomena of integration and isolation.

The concept of anomie has a prominent place in contemporary sociological thought. It has helped focus attention on the personal disorientation that can occur when people lack a sense of belonging to a secure moral order.[8]

[6] Emile Durkheim, *Suicide* (Glencoe: The Free Press, 1951), p. 254.

[7] Andrew F. Henry and James F. Short, Jr., *Suicide and Homicide* (Glencoe: The Free Press, 1954), p. 23.

[8] See Marshall B. Clinard (ed.), *Anomie and Deviant Behavior* (New York: The Free Press of Glencoe, 1964).

Suicide was published in 1897 and was based on data that seem crude by modern standards. On the other hand, many of Durkheim's conclusions have been supported by later studies,[9] and the ingenuity of his analysis and interpretation is a continuing challenge to contemporary social scientists.

[9] A number of findings are reviewed in Henry and Short, *op. cit.,* Appendix I. See also Jack P. Gibbs and Walter T. Martin, *Status Integration and Suicide* (Eugene, Oregon: University of Oregon Books, 1964).

SECTION 3 THE GROUP STRUCTURE OF SOCIETY

Sociological analysis contributes to the understanding of the group structure of a community or nation, industry, or political order. In the study of political behavior sociology inquires into the group basis of politics:[10] instead of conceiving the political community as made up of individual citizens, account is taken of the social divisions within the public, based on their occupational, ethnic, family, or other affiliations. In industrial studies the sociological approach has helped counter the "rabble hypothesis," [11] which viewed employees as individual wage earners unaffected by the social life of the factory.

TYPES OF GROUPS

The word "group" is used in a very general sense. It refers to any collection of persons who are *bound together by a distinctive set of social relations.* This includes everything from members of a family, adherents to Catholicism, participants in a mob, to citizens of a national state. Two persons form a group if they are friends or partners or otherwise *held together and set apart from others* by their relationship. Groups can be highly organized and stable or very fluid and temporary.

Groups and social categories People who have similar incomes or who are alike in other ways, such as age, occupation, or reading habits, do not necessarily form social groups. Such classifications may be called statistical aggregates or social categories. A persistent interest of sociology is the study of the conditions under which various social categories become or produce social groups.

The aged are a significant social category, and there is considerable interest today in the kinds of groups older people are likely to form or accept. Is there an old-age style of life that can be the natural basis for separate housing? Or do older people feel little sense of identity with each other despite their similar age and dependency? There have been some old-age political pressure groups, such as the Townsend movement of the 1930s. Should more and increasingly powerful groups of this sort be expected as the proportion of older people in the population rises? What effect would this have on the political order? These questions indicate the problems raised when the group potential of a social category is explored.

Although *consciousness of kind*—the awareness of belonging to a certain category—is an important element in the formation of groups, it is not indispensable. Many workers belong to lodges, bowling clubs, and other groups that are distinctively working-class in character; yet if asked, they would not necessarily identify themselves as belonging to any particular social category. Nevertheless they unconsciously enter and create ways of group life based

[10] See David B. Truman, *The Governmental Process* (New York: Knopf, 1951), Chap. 2, "Groups and Society."

[11] Elton Mayo, *The Social Problems of an Industrial Civilization* (Boston: Harvard University Graduate School of Business Administration, 1945), Chap. 2.

on similarities of occupation and income. Similar life experiences lead to social interaction and the formation of groups, even though people are not aware of why and how this takes place.

Comprehensive and specialized groups A *community* is a comprehensive group with two chief characteristics: (1) within it the individual can have most of the experiences and conduct most of the activities that are important to him; (2) it is bound together by a shared sense of belonging and by the feeling among its members that the group defines for them their distinctive identity. Theoretically, the member of a community lives his whole life within it; he feels a sense of kinship with others who belong to it; and he accepts the community much as he accepts his own name and family membership.

Communities are usually based on locality—a village, city, or nation. The geographical area and a sense of place set the boundaries of common living and provide a basis for solidarity. However, without respect to geography, one may speak of the "Catholic community," in the sense that there is a unique set of Catholic activities and institutions which, taken together, permit many Catholics to live out much of their lives within boundaries set by religious affiliation. They can be educated as Catholics, live in a Catholic neighborhood, work for a Catholic organization, belong to a Catholic professional society, and read a Catholic newspaper. Similarly, one may speak of a Japanese-American community, a Jewish community, and even an academic community. However, most fully developed communities do share a common locality.

Special-purpose organizations, such as trade unions, corporations, and political parties, are called *associations*. In this category are factories, where the main incentive to participation is money income, as well as "voluntary associations," such as clubs or veterans' groups.

Associations are usually based on limited, utilitarian interests. However, there are variations in the range of interests served and in the resulting meaning of membership. The more specific and practical an association's objectives, the more impersonal and narrow will be the individual's relation to the group.

When an association serves broad rather than narrow interests, and does so in an accepted, orderly, and enduring way, it may be called an *institution*. The word institution also refers to practices, to *established ways of doing things*. Constitutional government, marriage, private enterprise, and Thanksgiving dinner are called institutions, although they are practices rather than groups. This book follows common usage and refers to both of these related phenomena as institutions. An institution, therefore, may be a type of group or it may be a formalized practice or procedure. In this sense, the Methodist church is an institution, and it conducts itself in institutionalized ways.

Considered as a type of group, an institution is less specialized than other associations and therefore has some of the attributes of a comprehensive group. One hears of a "university community," even though it may be difficult to achieve the ideal of community in the large "multiversity." Perhaps the most important difference between comprehensive and specialized groups is the capacity of the former to treat the individual as a unique and total person rather than as an instrument for the achievement of specialized goals. Discussions of the "organization man" have centered on this problem, emphasizing the dilemmas that arise when a large, impersonal business enterprise seeks broad loyalty from the employee as well as conformity to an approved pattern of life.[12]

KINSHIP AND SOCIAL ORGANIZATION [13]

For most people, group affiliation begins with membership in a family. The family mediates between the individual and society, helping him to take his place in the larger world and at the same time providing an island of protection and privacy. In every society kinship has at some time been the key unit of social organization, asserting its influence in the

---

[12] See William H. Whyte, Jr., *The Organization Man* (New York: Simon and Schuster, 1956).

[13] This discussion draws on material written in collaboration with Ralph H. Turner and included in earlier editions of this book.

KINSHIP TERMS

A technical vocabulary is necessary to describe precisely the intricate web of kinship. The following selection of important kinship terms suggests the variety of family types and relationships in preliterate and modern societies:

Choice of partners

Exogamy—partner must be chosen from outside a defined group, e.g., members of the same extended family lineage may not marry
Endogamy—partners must be members of the same group, e.g., a religious community

Number of partners

Monogamy—marriage of one man to one woman
Polygamy—marriage involving more than two partners:
Polygyny—one man to two or more women
Polyandry—one woman to two or more men (rare)

Descent

Patrilineal—the privileges and duties of descent follow the male line (e.g., child to father to father's father, etc.)
Matrilineal—follow the female line
Bilineal—follow both lines

Residence

Patrilocal—husband and wife take up residence with the husband's parents
Matrilocal—with the wife's parents
Neolocal—husband and wife reside by themselves

Authority and dominance

Patriarchal—father dominant
Matriarchal—mother dominant
Equalitarian—equal dominance of father and mother

economy, political life, religion, and even in warfare.
Sometimes kinship *is* social organization:

There are cultures with little or no economic organization beyond division of labor, by sex, within the family. This is true of the Polar Eskimo who live in the bleak environment of the shores of Smith Sound, N.W. Greenland, the furthermost northern settlement. Without agriculture and with few wild vegetable foods, they depend for meager subsistence upon hunting, fishing, and collecting. To survive, they must live in small groups, which (during the summer) usually consist of one or two primary families who hunt caribou and fish. Even in winter, when they live in villages, the community rarely exceeds seven or eight families. The village is transitory and has no head. Since hunting bands may include members who are not kin, there is some economic organization apart from the family, but not much.[14]

In anthropological studies of social organization, kinship is the major topic. For example, Murdock's *Social Structure*,[15] which includes a chapter on "Evolution of Social Organization," is entirely devoted to the family and kinship.

Meaning of kinship Broadly speaking, kinship is a relationship that is close and enduring enough to sustain a sense of common origin or commitment. Theoretically kinship can be founded in long association and shared tradition, with only a vague biological reference. But a more definite way of recog-

[14] M. F. Nimkoff (ed.), *Comparative Family Systems* (Boston: Houghton Mifflin, 1965), p. 33.

[15] George Peter Murdock, *Social Structure* (New York: Macmillan, 1949). However, Robert H. Lowie's *Social Organization* (New York: Holt, Rinehart, and Winston, 1948) includes discussion of property, law, and political organization.

nizing relatives is necessary to fix specific rights and responsibilities. Hence a reckonable common ancestry is the usual basis of kinship, supplemented by other recognized ties, such as affinity through marriage or adoption.

The essential point is that who is counted as kin is socially defined. The biological basis is a convenient starting point, but it is not the sole determinant. Kinship may be closely defined—for example, tracing ancestry only in the father's line—or every conceivable relative may be counted. The *consanguine* family is based on biological relatedness; it is the family of blood relatives and is the main basis of kinship. The *conjugal* family is the group formed by marriage. The children have blood (consanguineal) ties to their siblings, parents, and parents' relatives, but the married partners or conjugal pair may or may not be counted as kin. Although every marriage creates a network of in-laws, the latter may have few or many responsibilities to each other, and they may not be recognized as kin at all.

Kinship is a more inclusive idea than family, for kinship does not necessarily define a functioning group. Sometimes, however, family is used as a synonym for kin, for example, "family tree" in reckoning genealogy. It is important to distinguish between a network of relationships, i.e., *kin* and a kin-based cooperative unit or household, i.e., *family*.

Universality of the nuclear family Linton suggests that the conjugal family is a more basic social unit than the consanguine family, because the conjugal family reflects the biological facts of sexuality, especially the absence of a clearly defined human mating season, and the need for security and satisfaction in personal relationships. According to Linton the consanguine family ". . . is a social artifact

whereas the conjugal family is a biological unit differing little, in its essential qualities, from similar units to be observed in a great variety of mammalian species." [16] This point of view is supported by Murdock's finding, based on a study of 250 societies, that some form of *nuclear* family is found in every society. The nuclear family consists of a conjugal pair and their offspring, sometimes augmented by other individuals. From the standpoint of husband and wife, the nuclear family is the conjugal family; from the standpoint of the children, it is part of the consanguineal family.

Murdock's conclusion that the nuclear family is universal is widely accepted, but it has been questioned.[17] The sticking-point is his insistence that the nuclear family always has "the distinctive and vital functions" of the family—sexual, reproductive, economic, educational.[18] It is argued that not all of these functions are necessarily performed by the nuclear family, and in rare cases the nuclear family may be attenuated or disappear altogether. In Adaptation 5 one such setting is discussed—the Israeli Kibbutz at an early stage of its history.

Another apparent exception to the universality of the nuclear family was the social system of the Nayar caste in India during the nineteenth century, before British rule. The Nayar husband owed most of his responsibilities to his sister's children, but had minimal obligations to his conjugal family and was usually absent as a mercenary soldier. Although there was a concept of marriage and paternity, the nuclear family defined as including the husband hardly existed.[19]

The kin-based unit that most often supplements the nuclear family—and theoretically may displace it—is the *extended* family. In one form of extended family, three generations live together under the

[16] Ralph Linton, "The Natural History of the Family," in Ruth Nanda Anshen (ed.), *The Family: Its Function and Destiny* (rev. ed., New York: Harper & Row, 1959), p. 34.

[17] Marion J. Levy and Lloyd A. Fallers, "The Family: Some Comparative Considerations," *American Anthropologist, 61* (August, 1959), 647–651.

[18] Murdock, *op. cit.,* p. 3.

[19] See Joan P. Mencher, "The Nayars of South Malabar," in Nimkoff, *op. cit.,* p. 176; also E. Kathleen Gough, "Is the Family Universal?—The Nayar Case," *Journal of the Royal Anthropological Institute, 89* (1959), Part 1, reprinted in Norman W. Bell and Ezra F. Vogel (eds.), *A Modern Introduction to the Family* (New York: The Free Press of Glencoe, 1960), pp. 76–92.

same roof or in a family compound. Several married siblings, their spouses and offspring, and the grandparents together form a residential, economic, and educational unit. In such a setting, where perhaps twenty closely related people live together, the nuclear family, as such, is less important and less sharply defined. The economic unit is the extended family, and aunts, uncles, and cousins have a part in child rearing. Nevertheless, most nuclear families in nearly all societies retain their identity and some of their distinctive functions, despite being embedded in an extended family system.

Another kind of composite or extended family is the *polygamous* family. The most common form of polygamy (plural marriage) is *polygyny,* where one man has several wives. In this arrangement, two or more nuclear families share the same husband-father:

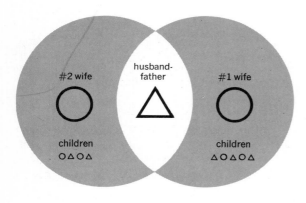

The extended family in its various forms is frequently found where agriculture is the main occupation. Smaller, independent families predominate in hunting-gathering economies and in modern industrial society. "The hunter is mobile because he pursues the game; the industrial worker, the job." [20]

Social change and the family A basic fact of modern history is the decline of extended kin groups and the emergence of the detached nuclear family as the representative form of family life. This trend is associated with (1) free choice of mates, in the sense that marriages are contracted without reference to the larger kin group; (2) more divorce as marriage has become increasingly a matter of choice rather than necessity (see Fig. II: 2); (3) greatly increased residential mobility, with accompanying weakening of kinship ties; (4) emancipation of women and their entry in large numbers into the labor force; and (5) diminished responsibility of children for their parents and grandparents.

The detached nuclear family maximizes freedom, but it also takes on a heavy burden of responsibility and is subject to severe internal strains. Although there is less responsibility for kin who are not members of the nuclear family, there is greater responsibility for children and for the psychic well-being of husband and wife. When divorce occurs in the American system, extensive readjustments in economic arrangements, care of children, social participation, and emotional involvements are necessary.

In sharp contrast, in the Hopi pattern the married couple lives with the wife's parents and her sisters and their husbands, sharing in many communal activities.[21] Loss of an adult from the Hopi extended family requires only minor readjustments. Children are already part of the larger kin group, and all the adults have served to some degree as parents. Because intimacy between husband and wife is only slightly greater than among all the adults in the extended unit, the suffering over loss of a spouse is minimized. There is little disruption in the life of a divorced wife who has a steady pattern of sociability and close cooperation with kin.

The detached nuclear family in contemporary America is also strained by the new and often uncertainly defined role of women, as well as by the dependence of all participants on the small family unit for psychic gratification. The small nuclear family has limited resources and offers few alternative

[20] M. F. Nimkoff and Russell Middleton, "Types of Family and Types of Economy," *American Journal of Sociology, 66* (November, 1960), 225.

[21] Stuart A. Queen and John B. Adams, *The Family in Various Cultures* (Philadelphia: Lippincott, 1952), pp. 23–43.

divorces per 100 marriages

FIG. II:2   Divorces per 100 marriages in the same year: United States, 1870–1965

For simplicity of presentation, decade figures are used, except for the 1945 peak and for 1965.

SOURCE: Ruth S. Cavan, *The American Family* (New York: Crowell, 1953), pp. 645–647, and the *Statistical Abstract of the United States, 1966,* Table 48.

year

opportunities compared to the extended family with many siblings and other relatives. Furthermore, the American nuclear family, which is seldom a unit of economic organization such as a family farm or small family business, lacks the sustaining continuities of shared work and responsibility.

Conditions of suburban life in the United States have given rise to a *matricentric* [22] family pattern within a formal patriarchalism. Because commuting keeps the husband out of touch with the family during daylight hours, because the wife controls day-to-day expenditures, and because she is the family "social secretary," she makes most decisions about the domestic and social life of the family, and the children look to her as the effective authority. The tension created by this imbalance between formal authority and working control is a recurring theme in popular comic strips. The husband may resort to arbitrary acts to validate his formal authority, and the wife may fret alternately over the authority the husband does exercise and over his failure to be a sufficiently strong and masculine figure.

While there is some decline in family stability,

as shown in Fig. II:2, there is no apparent decline in the acceptance of family living. (See Fig. II:3.) Much of the increase in percent of the population married during recent decades is due to earlier marriage, especially for men. But even allowing for this and other factors, marriage still shows no decline and a possible increase between 1890 and 1965.

Persistence of kinship   Although the detached nuclear family is the dominant form in modern life, it is not the exclusive form. Kinship ties remain important, especially in the working class, but among middle-class people too. A study of Bethnal Green, a community in East London, showed an extensive kinship network, with important effects in economic life (father-son succession in occupations, helping relatives to get jobs), as well as in personal relationships. However, the same study shows the importance of residence, of staying in the same immediate community, for the nurturing of kinship ties. Families who moved to a new housing "estate" less than twenty miles away from Bethnal Green tended to become more isolated. [23]

[22] Ernest W. Burgess and Harvey J. Locke, *The Family* (New York: American Book Co., 1953), pp. 111–113.

[23] Michael Young and Peter Willmott, *Family and Kinship in East London* (rev. ed.; Baltimore: Penguin Books, 1962). See also Herbert J. Gans, *The Urban Villagers: Group and Class in the Life of Italian-Americans* (New York: The Free Press of Glencoe, 1962), pp. 45 ff.

The relation of family and community under conditions of change and stress are explored in Adaptation 5, "Family and Society in Israel."

GROUP RELATIONS

At any given time, there are dominant groups and subordinate ones, allies and enemies. Some are dependent, others relatively independent. Some are strategically located and can communicate with or influence many parts of the community; others are on the fringes with limited access to other groups. Knowing the pattern of group relations is essential to understanding a community or society and the processes of social control.

Group structure is not static; it is the product of continuous interaction in which the relations among groups are tested and transformed. A few of the basic forms of group interaction, and the stable relations that they produce, are considered here.

Competition, rivalry, and conflict The interests of one group are often inconsistent with those of others. For example, several organizations may want to recruit the same people: colleges may compete for the better students or staff; several nations may want the same economic resources; many retail stores want to sell to the same customers. *Competition* is

this mutually opposed effort to secure the same scarce objectives.

Competition does not necessarily involve direct interaction; it may be impersonal and unconscious. Cotton farmers in Mississippi compete with cotton farmers in Egypt, but they may be unaware of each other. When groups become aware that they are in competition they are called rivals. *Rivalry* is a form of conscious competition between specific groups: for example, the Democrats and Republicans, the Ford Motor Co. and General Motors, the Army and the Air Force, the U.S.A. and the U.S.S.R. This kind of competition is more direct, with mutual awareness and often self-conscious strategy and tactics.

When the clash of interests is so keen that groups do not merely compete for the same scarce goals but seek to injure or even destroy each other, there is *conflict,* and the group itself is endangered in a direct way. Intense feelings may be aroused and, as a result, the rules governing competitive and rivalrous activity may be abandoned.

Rivalry and conflict are *dissociative* forms of interaction. They pull groups apart rather than bind them together. However, these processes are not *purely* dissociative. Rivalry is usually based upon commonly accepted rules, as in athletics. Conflict tends to increase the *internal* solidarity of opponents.

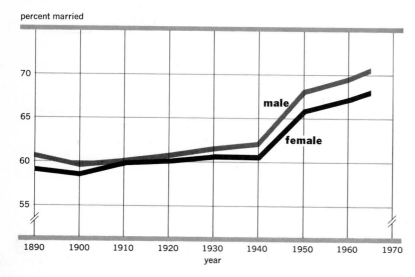

percent married

70

65

60

55

1890 1900 1910 1920 1930 1940 1950 1960 1970

year

male

female

FIG. II:3 Percent of the population married, fourteen years old and over, standardized for age, 1890–1965

Because the age distribution of the United States population has changed since 1890, figures reporting only percent married would be misleading. Above percentages are, therefore, standardized to the 1950 age distribution, i.e., each percent married has been recomputed as if the age distribution were the same as that in 1950.

SOURCE: Data in the *Statistical Abstract of the United States, 1966,* Table 31.

It is sometimes believed that conflict is a result of poor communication, that conflict arises because people do not understand each other. If communication means the ability to see another's point of view, then some conflicts truly rooted in false perceptions may be eased by increasing communication. However, many conflicts are grounded in mutually inconsistent needs and aspirations. Increased contact and improved communication may intensify conflict by making groups aware of their differences, increasing their fears, and revealing opposing interests of which they were unaware.

Accommodation and assimilation   After a long and bitter strike, union and management may come to agreement and the men go back to work, but hostility may persist. Each side may prepare to renew open conflict at another time. Under such circumstances, the agreement represents an unstable accommodation. *Accommodation* is the mutual adjustment of groups that retain their own identity and interests. In an unstable accommodation a temporary adjustment is made and the conflicting groups adapt themselves to immediate realities, despite the existence of unresolved issues.

In settling conflicts, accommodation must first be achieved. The problem is not to gain full communication or understanding but to discover what is essential to each group if it is to cease hostilities and offer the essential minimum cooperation. The American Constitution written *after* the Revolution was an accommodative document. It adjusted the interests of large and small states, of Southerners and Northerners, and thereby won support for the foundation of the United States. It was not essential that the states see all things alike or that the citizens cease to view themselves as Virginians and New Yorkers.

A stable accommodation resolves the major differences of interest, particularly those vital to continued group existence. If stable accommodation is reached, there is a basis for deeper harmony involving more extensive mutual understanding. Groups may then enlarge their contacts and even come to think of themselves as sharing a single identity.

The process by which the identity of groups is fused is called *assimilation*. In this process the breakdown of communication barriers is essential. In the assimilation of immigrants in the United States the schools have carried a heavy burden. Many classes were conducted in large cities to teach adult immigrants the English language and some essentials of American history and government. Despite these efforts, few first-generation immigrants are really assimilated. Differences in social background persist as barriers to effective communication.

Cooperation   Group cooperation is agreed-upon joint action. Agreement may be based on similar group aspirations, e.g., organizations interested in preventing delinquency; groups may have a common enemy and thus have temporarily convergent interests; or they may agree upon a set of common rules to regulate their competition. The amount of communication depends on the basis of cooperation; when people act together out of loyalty to family or community, there is much more communication than when there is a limited alliance in defense against a temporary threat.

In cooperation each group gains, either in an immediate advantage or indirectly in seeing its ultimate goals advanced. However, they need not gain *equally*. Weak groups usually gain more from cooperation than do strong groups, and the latter are therefore often reluctant to enter agreements with weaker groups. They may feel impelled to do so, however, when they share the social ideal that cooperation is a good thing.

Cooperation as well as conflict can threaten group independence. When two groups cooperate, communication between them is greatly increased. The boundaries of group membership may become obscure, and leaders may be called upon to justify the independent existence of their organizations. If pressure is generated for the amalgamation of groups, it may threaten the vested interests of the leaders as well as the long-run aims each group represents. This is a serious problem among churches, government agencies, and political groups. Leaders of government agencies—for example, of the different military services—carefully examine proposals for administrative cooperation with other agencies to see what the consequences will be for the sharing of public credit, for the justification of independent budgets, and for maintaining the distinctive loyalties and outlooks of their staffs. Cooperation among community welfare agencies raises similar problems. They need to be reassured that their independent existence is not threatened by a proposed joint venture, such as fund-raising through a community chest.

Because cooperation is highly valued, the word easily becomes a symbol to which people must pay their respects. In fact, however, responsible leaders who are alert to group interests always pose the question, "Cooperation for what and with whom and at what price?"

Adaptation 5 / *Talmon-Garber* FAMILY AND SOCIETY IN ISRAEL

This study analyzes the impact of radical and rapid social change on patterns of family organization and on the relation between the family and the community. Three types of family found in Israel are considered: (*a*) the family in collective settlements (Kibbutzim), (*b*) the family in cooperative settlements (Moshavim), and (*c*) the family among European refugees in the Israeli cities. Three distinct modes of interaction between family and community are portrayed. In the Kibbutzim the community is supreme and the family is subordinated to it. The traditional family in the Moshavim is kinship centered: the elementary family is subordinated to wider kin groupings that mediate between it and the community. The isolated refugee family in urban centers is cut off from kin and estranged from the community.

THE COLLECTIVIZED FAMILY

The *Kibbutz* (plural: *Kibbutzim*) is a form of collective settlement, first founded in 1910, long before the establishment of the State of Israel in 1948. The early settlers of the Kibbutzim were young and unattached migrants from Eastern and Central Europe, who were unaccompanied by parents or other relatives.

In the Kibbutz, which may range from less than 100 to 2,000 members, there is common ownership of property, except for a few personal belongings. The members agree to subordinate their personal interests to the attainment of communal goals and to seek self-expression only through service to the community. In theory, and to a large extent in practice, devotion to communal ideals takes precedence over kinship obligations. Feeling for fellow members and for the community is more significant than family loyalty. Relatives who are not members are by definition outsiders, almost strangers.

The revolutionary phase From its inception the Collective Movement realized the risk of conflicting loyalties and set out to redefine and curtail family obligations. The community took over most of the traditional functions of the family. Many ingenious devices were evolved to prevent the consolidation of the family as a distinct and independent unit. Members of the

SOURCE: Abridged and adapted from Y. Talmon-Garber, "Social Change and Family Structure," *International Social Science Journal, XIV,* No. 3 (1962), 468–487. Published in this form by permission of the Unesco publication, *International Social Science Journal.* At the time of her death in 1966, Dr. Talmon-Garber was Associate Professor of Sociology at the Hebrew University, Jerusalem.

same family were not assigned to the same place of work. All meals were taken in the common dining room. Families looked after their own rooms but had few other household responsibilities.

At this stage the family was not even relied on to maintain the community's population or to rear its children. The Kibbutzim ensured their continuity and growth by recruiting volunteers rather than by natural increase. The care and rearing of children were basically the responsibility of the Kibbutz, not of the parents. In most Kibbutzim children lived apart from their parents. They slept, ate, and studied in special children's houses.

Children met their parents and siblings in off-hours and spent the afternoons and early evenings with them. On Saturdays and holidays they stayed with their parents. There were thus frequent and intensive relations between parents and children; but mainly the child was in the hands of community agencies.

Persistence of the family   Even during the earliest phases, when antifamilism was strongest, the family remained a distinct unit. Although premarital sexual relations were permitted, there was a clearcut distinction between casual sexual experimentation, love affairs, and more durable and publicly sanctioned unions. By asking for a room of their own, a couple made public their wish to have permanent relations and eventually to have children. Residence in a common bedroom-living room allocated by the Kibbutz conferred legitimacy on the couple. While children did not share a common domicile with their parents, they visited the parents' room every day, and it was their home by reference. The parents could exert influence on the trained personnel in charge of their children. Interaction among family members, though less frequent than contacts with friends and work associates, was often more meaningful and intense. The emotional ties that bound husband and wife and parents and children were much more intimate and exclusive than their ties with other members of the community. The family's unconditional love and loyalty insulated its members from communal pressures and enhanced their security.

Changes in the Kibbutz   As the Kibbutz became better established and its work more routine, as it accepted new groups of settlers, and as a new generation grew up within it, the community became more heterogeneous and less cohesive. There were more different types of people with different interests and perspectives. New settlers, who joined the founders at different stages of the community's development, contributed to this process of differentiation. In time the collectives became more tolerant of the existence of subgroups, and hostility toward the family abated. It was assigned a place among other subgroups.

The coming of the second generation gradually transformed the relations between the generations. Whereas the first settlers broke away from their own parents, the children of the Kibbutz are expected to continue their life work in the Kibbutz. Parents and children are now members of the same community. They live in close proximity and share, at least to some extent, the same ideals; identification with one's family reinforces identification with the collective.

Restoration of family functions   The new emphasis on continuity between the generations is expressed in a partial "emancipation" of the family. As the family regains some of its lost housekeeping functions, more meals are eaten at home, "rooms" become "flats," and more of the couple's personal allowance is spent on the flat. The flat is an important symbol of family solidarity and a physical manifestation of its separateness.

At the same time, the family increases in importance as an agency of reproduction and child rearing. There is a considerable increase in the fertility of the women of the Kibbutz. The difficulties experienced by the Kibbutzim in recruiting and absorbing new immigrants have underscored the importance of natural increase. Emphasis has shifted from recruitment of volunteers to expansion from within. The family is now called upon to help the Kibbutz ensure its continuity and growth. As a corollary, the parents take a more active role in the care and education of the child. There is more parental supervision of behavior and parental involvement in choice of friends, reading habits, and future occupations. In some Kibbutzim, which have introduced a more radical reorganization, children no longer sleep in the separate children's houses. They stay with their peers during the day but return home every afternoon.

The tendency toward a more familistic pattern may be discerned in many ways. Marriage now normally precedes the establishment of a family. Husbands help in household duties, but in most families women are mainly responsible for domestic work. In spite of a blurring of the roles of father and mother, there are signs of differentiation.

There is also a subtle transformation of informal relations and leisure-time activities. Free time spent in public has diminished. Members of the Kibbutz are less eager to attend public meetings. Husband and wife spend most of their free time together, and it is now considered impolite to invite only one spouse.

The resurgence of familism has brought with it a gradual development and renewal of wider kinship ties. In the early days most members did not have any kin except their own elementary family living in the same community. However, when the Kibbutz embraces three generations, relatives who live in the same community establish close contacts through frequent visiting and mutual help. Wider kinship ties serve as connecting links with the outside world, and members tend to renew their contacts with relatives who live outside the Kibbutz. Kinship ties have thus broken through self-imposed isolation.

Persisting tension In spite of the changed position of the family, the Kibbutzim remain basically nonfamilistic. The Kibbutzim make far-reaching demands on their members. The proper functioning of the Kibbutz depends on wholehearted identification with its aims and ideals. The collectives cannot allow the family to become independent and self-sufficient. They still fear that the family may become the main focus of loyalty and satisfaction, with kinship ties more important than ties among members.

The militant antifamilism of the revolutionary phase has abated but not disappeared. It is superseded by a moderate collectivism which regards the family as a useful though uneasy ally. The Kibbutzim control and limit the family and employ it for the attainment of collective goals.

THE TRADITIONAL FAMILY

A second important pattern of immigration and settlement in Israel is illustrated by North African Jews who migrated to Israel later than the founders of the Kibbutzim and after the establishment of the State of Israel.

Historically Jews in North Africa lived in small communities composed of large patriarchal families of three or four generations. The father directed his married and unmarried sons in work and maintained discipline within a common residence. There were close kinship ties. Males customarily held dominant positions, and female roles were limited to home and family. The synagogue was an important place of male gathering. Allegiance to Jewish ritual and observance centered around the synagogue and religious schools.

This traditional pattern remained more or less intact in the villages and small towns, but it was undermined in the cities of North Africa. Rapid urbanization dispersed relatives and splintered the kinship group. Young men became independent, their ways secularized.

The traditionalist North African Jews went to Israel with a deep sense of Jewish solidarity and a vague Messianic striving. The more urbanized migrant from North Africa was mainly interested in security and economic advancement. But neither shared the basic values and dynamic aspirations of the new Israeli society. They took their old life with them and hoped to continue their former ways unmolested. Families, neighborhoods, and sometimes even whole communities migrated together.

The Moshav Some of the North Africans were settled in cooperative communities known as *Moshavim*. The Moshav presumes a semi-independent family working on a family farm. In the Moshav a familistic division of labor is combined with mechanized farming and centralized management of cooperative institutions. Land and machinery are publicly owned. There is rough equality in size of farm and basic investment, cooperative marketing and purchasing, and a ban on hired labor.

The Kibbutzim were formed by volunteer pioneering groups who sought to realize both personal and national ideals. The Moshavim are "administered communities," planned and managed by governmental and quasi-governmental agencies. State planners, guided by defense considerations and by a desire to disperse the Israeli population, ordered the construction of 274 cooperative settlements and directed new immigrants to these villages.

The settling agency regarded the traditional kin-centered social organization of the immigrants as inimical to the development of modern cooperative villages. The planners did not take into consideration the former group composition of the settlers and intentionally disregarded their former attachments and loyalties. In organizing the settlements, kinship groups were dispersed.

Reassertion of kinship The traditional kinship structure soon reasserted itself. Settlers sought out their relatives and encouraged them to settle in the same village. After a period of reshuffling, most villages have emerged with two or three major kinship groups. Although the Moshav economy is based on the nuclear family and each nuclear family has a separate household and a separate farm, there is much cooperation among members of the same extended family.

Reunion of kinsmen occurred more easily and rapidly in traditional families which had maintained wider kin ties and had arrived in the country in family or neighborhood groups. However, even relatives who were separated before they left North Africa and had not seen each other for years sought each other out. In the unfamiliar and unstructured social setting, kinship ties regained their lost significance and served as a major basis of spontaneous organization.

Kinship and social structure In this setting kinship has pervaded the social structure of the village. It is the keynote of the social system. Village politics center on control of community institutions, especially the central committee, which brings practical advantages as well as prestige to the family. The kin groups become rival factions, each struggling with the

other for power. The political history of each village involves a continuous struggle among the kinship groups, and politics reinforces the ties of kinship. Paradoxically, in this context, radical modernization has strengthened and revived the kin-dominated traditional order.

Kinship solidarity has been helpful to the immigrants as well as to the new community. The kinship group is itself a strong cooperative unit: authority, obedience, and the incentive to help others are supported by emotional ties and long-established expectations. The extended kin group mediates between the nuclear families and the community, and thereby links the traditional order to the new one.

Yet the growing dominance of the kinship group is troublesome to the village community. Village officers, elected on the basis of kinship ties, discriminate without compunction against nonrelatives. The nepotism of officeholders breeds inefficiency and suspicion, as well as bitter feuds. Deadlocked factions may immobilize the management of cooperative institutions for many months. It sometimes becomes necessary to transfer one of the warring factions to another village. The solidarity of the kinship group develops at the expense of the solidarity of the village community.

The planners have come to realize that the kinship groups are vitally important units in the absorption of traditional immigrants. On the other hand, they understand the risks. They therefore accept the kinship groups but try to limit their influence on central cooperative institutions. In some of the villages, there is a growing tendency to replace officeholders by hired

experts who have no kin in the village. They are not involved in the village feuds and are better trained. Consequently, they are more objective and more efficient. Management is thus partly disentangled from the kinship network, and cooperative institutions can continue to function even when there is conflict among the families.

THE ISOLATED FAMILY

European Jewish refugees who settled in Israel after World War II did so under conditions of great stress and suffering. In many centers of Jewish population only a few people managed to escape the Nazi annihilation, and few families remained intact. Uprooted and isolated, they arrived with few, if any, relatives. Their former lives were destroyed and most had spent long periods of compulsory collective living in concentration camps.

The refugees were unprepared for the difficult conditions of settlement in the new country. Many remembered their shattered prewar past with nostalgic yearning and tended to idealize it. They had diffuse positive attitudes toward Israel but no strong identification with its aims and values. The experience of concentration camp life had left them with a deep desire for privacy and undisturbed personal development. This preoccupation with personal aspirations ran counter to the ideological and collectivist orientations of the absorbing society.

The family turns inward The reaction to isolation and alienation is a wholehearted attachment to the nuclear family, which withdraws to its small and isolated private world. The immigrants seek solace and security in the intimacy of family life. They defend the independence of the family against the demands of the absorbing society. In the family they are their own masters and need not constantly accommodate to outside influences. They can continue to cultivate their former ways of life.

The immigrants work indefatigably to benefit the family, but are unconcerned with purely occupational problems and uninterested in the wider implications of their work. Isolated families develop only a few significant contacts outside the family circle. Informal relations and recreation are family-centered. The members refrain from joining organizations, distrust authorities at any level, and hold political parties in cynical contempt. They keep aloof from political or social activities and are apathetic to the goals of the society as a whole.

Costs of isolation The isolated family protects the uprooted individual and supports him, but eventually the self-imposed isolation adversely affects family unity. The outside world does have its effect as the children gradually adopt the values of the surrounding society. The parents cannot help their children find a place in the Israeli society. The children become ambivalent and frustrated. Isolation of the family thus weakens its own solidarity on which it has staked so much.

Local agencies have tried to cope with these problems by conducting periodic campaigns among members of isolated families, calling on them to participate in voluntary activities, recruiting them to various associations and nominating them to committees. These efforts meet with success only when they concentrate on activities that affect the family directly. Participation in local school committees is the best example. Taking an interest in the school is a way of relating to the problems of the children. The school may serve as a major link between the isolated family and the wider social setting.

Conclusion Immigration to Israel deepened the solidarity of the traditional and isolated families. Moshav and refugee families segregated their members from the larger society, which was perceived as threatening and hostile.

In the early Kibbutz, on the other hand, the youth of the settlers, their pioneering spirit, their socialist ideology, and an intense communal life made the family irrelevant—for a time.

Each situation had its distinctive problem: the Kibbutz faced the problem of allowing family units more privacy and independence without harming the cohesion of the community. The Moshav had to preserve the unity of the kinship group while limiting its influence on village management. The communities containing a considerable number of isolated families had to preserve the internal solidarity of the elementary families and, at the same time, find ways of extending their participation and identification.

SECTION 4 BASIC PATTERNS OF SOCIAL ORGANIZATION

Individual and group relations are best studied in the historical and sociological context within which they developed. Students of social organization attempt to describe the general features of whole societies or social orders. They try to identify the most important institutions, the most pervasive social relations, the basic social trends.

When the broad patterns of organization and change are known, individuals and groups are seen as part of larger settings. The roles of factory worker, professor, minister, and middle-class mother are all placed within the context, for example, of industrial society. The implications of industrial society for work, education, religion, and family life are thus brought into focus. No study of an important group or role is complete without some consideration of how it reflects a pattern of change, such as increasing specialization, or how it fits into the dominant features of the society or the epoch.

Because human societies are so complex, it is difficult and risky to formulate generalizations regarding broad patterns or trends in social organization. Nevertheless, much scholarship has been devoted to this task, and it is possible to state some conclusions with confidence.

This section discusses five *key forms* of social organization: (1) kinship, (2) fealty, (3) status, (4) contract, and (5) rational coordination. In various societies or historical periods one or another of these modes of organization has been salient. If it is considered the chief foundation of social order in a society or age, it gives the society its distinctive character. But no matter how dominant a principle of order may be, *all* of the key forms will be found *in some degree*.

KINSHIP

As discussed above, pages 31–32, in some societies kinship is the most important social bond and the family is the basis of social organization. The family firm and the family farm are reminders of economic activities based upon the family. Only a few centuries ago, in England, families vied for preeminence in politics, for the right to rule as the Royal House, or to be counted among the more favored nobility. Nor is this unknown in contemporary United States, as the political activities of the Kennedy family make plain.

Societies may be called *familistic* when the family is the dominant type of social group and carries the main burden of maintaining order, producing goods, and propitiating the gods. In such a society the individual is dependent on his relatives. They are his chief sources of practical aid, and they hold the keys to social esteem. The interests of the family—wealth, honor, continuity—are placed above the interests of the individual.

FEALTY

Another fundamental social bond is the *personal relation of follower and leader*. Fealty is the recognized obligation of one person to be faithful to another, to be "his" man. More than a contract of service is involved. Fealty presumes a personal commitment to do whatever may be needed to serve the interests of the leader, to take the bad with the good. In a limited sense, it is like a marriage. And indeed, oaths of fealty have sometimes matched the sacredness and binding character of marriage vows.

In Europe and England, for about four hundred years, fealty was a principal social bond. This was the epoch of *feudalism*, which may be roughly dated from about the tenth century, when its outlines were already clear, to the thirteenth century, when it began a gradual decline.

A chief characteristic of feudal life was lordship—a system of political obligation in which a group of followers, allies, and servile dependents owed personal loyalty and service to a powerful individual. An especially powerful lord might be called a duke or a king. In the heyday of feudalism, a great hierarchy of lords and their respective dependents, all knit together by bonds of loyalty and protection, gave the social order a remarkable symmetry and a precarious cohesion.

The development of lordship presumed that no effective central authority existed, and this was so in western Europe and England after the decline of Roman power. Moreover, lordship was an alternative to the bond of kinship. Some men sought the protection of lords, who were not their relatives, because there was no kin group capable of establishing order at the local level.[24]

Functions of fealty As feudalism developed, increasing emphasis was placed on the fidelity of a man to his lord, and the most important crime was treason against a lord. The bond of fealty had a dual importance. First, fealty helped create a small but devoted band of personal followers for the king or local

[24] Marion Gibbs, *Feudal Order* (New York: Henry Schuman, 1953), p. 21.

lord. In the formative period of feudalism, power was in the hands of small bodies of armed men. The lord was the leader of such a band and his influence depended on his capacity to maintain continuing loyalty. The development of a code of honor, with loyalty to the lord a supreme virtue, was helpful in sustaining this relationship.

Second, fealty was a way to maintain the cohesion of a society made up of local domains, each ruled by a supreme personal leader. As feudalism matured, the local barons became entrenched in their power. They were vassals of the king and took an oath of fealty to him, but they had independent power, with troops and resources of their own. Fealty and vassalage were in effect ways of recognizing an alliance or creating a federation. It was as if the governors of the fifty United States were considered personal rulers and recognized the central government by taking an oath of personal loyalty and submission to the President.

As a social bond, fealty belongs not only to a remote and exotic age, but also to contemporary society. Many executives of large enterprises rely on the personal loyalty of a few staff members. When an executive is promoted or moves to another organization, he often takes with him the key assistants on whose personal loyalty he can rely and who help him in establishing effective control over the organization he manages.

Ties of fealty are of continuing significance in modern political life. Because elections are often popularity contests and center on the man rather than on the party, politics tends to be based on personal leadership. In many areas, candidates create their own political organizations to supplement the work of the regular political party. To build campaign organizations often requires ties of personal loyalty, and in practical politics the capacity to win loyalty is of great value to the leader, the capacity to give it is highly prized in the follower.

Despite the continuing importance of fealty, it cannot be said to be a major principle of social organization in modern society. The trend is toward more impersonal modes of organization, and the areas within which ties of fealty count are few.

STATUS

The term "status" as used by students of society has two different but related meanings, distinguished by the context in which the word is used.

1. Status may refer simply to a person's social position. Each role in society is associated with a social position or status. (See above, p. 18.) In this meaning, status does not necessarily have any connotation of higher or lower.

2. Status is also used to designate an individual's place within a system of social ranking. Thus, sergeants rank higher than privates, and the whole set of ranks may be referred to as a "status system." This second meaning is narrower than the first, and is focused on the idea of rank.

Where status is a dominant principle of social organization, the society depends for its stability on the widespread belief in the rightness and permanence of one's "station" in life. Social discipline is maintained by inculcating and reinforcing the view that every man has a proper place within the social scheme of things. His place tells him how to conduct himself in relation to others, and it defines the limits of his aspirations.

A society based on fixed status emphasizes rank and uses many devices to maintain distinctions of place and privilege. In such a society a man's occupational status is stable and is usually transmitted from generation to generation. The cobbler sticks to his last and teaches his trade to his son.

Traditional Japan offers a striking example of a society based on fixed status, where personal qualities and expectations depend on social rank.

At all levels the lamentable principle prevailed that a man's status was irrevocably fixed at birth; and to the present day Japanese life is governed by the subtle ubiquity of the concept of *mibun* (personal position); a person's *mibun,* which depends on his sex, age, birth, education, rank, and occupation, governs his behavior at all stages. This means that the same conduct can be praiseworthy, indifferent, or actually reprehensible, depending on a person's *mibun.* The merchant's duty is to enrich himself, but a samurai who concerns himself with money is unworthy of the name; a second son is permitted amorous adventures; indeed they earn him applause and respect; his elder brother, however, is expected to behave irreproach-ably. . . .[25]

As European and English feudalism matured, status became more important as the foundation of social order. In the earlier period, kingship was highly personal, and the hereditary principle was not well established. A king was a king because he won and maintained the personal loyalty of a group of fol-lowers. Later a subtle and decisive transformation took place. The king received loyalty as a right *be-cause he was king*. At the same time, hereditary mon-archy, based on status fixed by birth, was strength-ened. Thus status joined fealty as a cardinal principle of feudal order.

In the contemporary world *fixed* statuses are less important to the social order, but the desire to achieve status and the effects of status are continuing features of everyday life. The assignment of status remains a powerful device for allocating respect and defining an individual's social worth. Man's desire for the respect of his fellows is a large part of the hu-man condition. The allocation of status in modern society is treated in SOCIAL STRATIFICATION.

CONTRACT

Under feudalism men could determine their obli-gations by entering into free agreements, mainly to exchange services for the lord's protection. The con-tract was especially important for the lower classes, to whom the idea of fealty, with its connotations of per-sonal honor, was not relevant. Later, rights originally established on the basis of contract and fealty became entrenched and hereditary, and were conceived of as attributes of status.

In the post-feudal era there was a basic trend toward contract as a principle of social organization. By the sixteenth century, society was beginning to be seen in a new light. The Renaissance, the Protestant Reformation, and the growth of business enterprise all helped give the individual a new hold on the po-litical, economic, and philosophical imagination. More and more, the basis of obligation was sought in

the agreements made by freely acting, personally re-sponsible individuals. This perspective advanced steadily and reached its greatest influence in the nine-teenth century.

In contract a bond is created based upon an ex-change of one promise for another; or a promise may be made in consideration of some act already done. The relation is a *specific* one and covers only those matters about which the promise is made. No commitment beyond the terms of the contract is in-tended or required. In contrast, marriage and fealty are more than contracts, since they entail a broad responsibility of one person for another. Marriage contracts are typically either promises to marry or agreements to define some special aspects of the re-lationship, such as the disposition of property. For the most part, marital responsibilities are *diffuse* rather than specifiable; they cannot be completely foretold nor restricted to a particular exchange of services.

When the principle of contract is a dominant fea-ture of social organization, private initiative and autonomy are encouraged. Especially during the nineteenth century, contract became almost a sacred principle to those who believed most strongly in indi-vidualism and in private rather than government ini-tiative.

In today's commercial civilization, contract is a significant part of social organization. It is the insti-tutional mainstay of the market economy. Neverthe-less, there are signs that unregulated, voluntary agreement is losing ground within the social order. Government is assuming an increasingly active role in limiting freedom of contract by setting standards, especially where the parties to the bargain are un-equal in power. The most striking examples are in labor relations, but the trend is growing in the fields of consumer economics, food and drug administra-tion, and the regulation of rates charged by tele-phone and power companies.[26]

Contract and social organization are discussed further in LAW, Section 2, pages 385–386.

[25] Fosco Maraini, *Meeting with Japan* (New York: Viking, 1959), p. 240.

[26] See W. Friedmann, *Law in a Changing Society* (Berkeley and Los Angeles: University of California Press, 1959), Chap. 4.

Herbert Spencer (1820–1903) was one of the most influental English writers of the late nineteenth century. He developed a theory of evolution which he summarized in the following famous "formula": "Evolution is an integration of matter and concomitant dissipation of motion; during which the matter passes from an indefinite, incoherent homogeneity to a definite, coherent heterogeneity; and during which the retained motion undergoes a parallel transformation."

On the basis of this resonant principle Spencer worked out a sociological system emphasizing an evolution toward greater social complexity and increased individualism. Society, he said, is like a complex organism in delicate balance, and only natural processes of evolution should be allowed to affect its development. This emphasis on individualism and on natural adaptation led him to oppose reform through governmental action.

BUREAUCRACY

The principle of social organization most characteristic of twentieth-century industrial society may be called *rational coordination*. In this pattern men are brought together in complex organizations run by professional managers. The managers are often called "bureaucrats" and the organizations they run are known as "bureaucracies." [27]

During the past two generations, many writers have called attention to the increasing bureaucratization of human activity. By this they mean that more and more spheres of life are dominated by large organizations and increasing numbers of people are becoming employees of the big corporation or government. The "organization society" produces the "organization man."

Few aspects of modern society can be studied without reference to the bureaucratic trend. Most obviously in the business world and in modern military establishments, the coordination of specialists in accordance with an impersonal logic of efficiency is highly developed. The same trend may be observed in educational institutions and even in church organization.

Where bureaucracy develops, there is increased specialization, impersonality, reliance on general rules, and distance between top management and the ordinary worker, citizen, or soldier. Up to a point, this is usually associated with increased efficiency, but there is growing evidence that new techniques are needed to offset some of the characteristics of bureaucracy that tend to limit initiative and personal satisfaction.

THE MASTER TREND

Over many centuries, Western society has shifted from an emphasis on kinship and status to a reliance upon more impersonal and instrumental modes of organization. This broad historical development is characterized by two attributes: (1) specialization, and (2) secularism and rationality.

Specialization   The historical trend toward *social*

[27] For the characteristics of bureaucracy, see ASSOCIATIONS, p. 199; INDUSTRIAL MAN, pp. 473 ff.; POLITICAL MAN, p. 508.

differentiation (specialization and heterogeneity) may be seen in the separation of major institutions from one another, in the development of the division of labor, and in the growth of many social groups with varying perspectives and interests.

1. *Differentiation of institutions.* The major economic, political, and religious institutions have become increasingly distinct and specialized. In earlier times, for example, church and state were fused or, at least, their responsibilities overlapped. Citizenship made one subject to the jurisdiction of the church, which could command obedience. The head of the state was also the "defender of the faith." Secular and religious education were not distinct. The separation of these institutions was marked by centuries of conflict, sometimes violent, sometimes carried on in the obscurity of legal argument over the jurisdiction of ecclesiastical and secular courts.

2. *Division of labor.* Even primitive society has a division of labor, based largely on age and sex. Modern industry and commerce have pushed specialization to an extreme. Consequently, new interests and groups are created, because those engaged in the same specialized activities tend to see the world alike and have a common stake in it. In addition, the individual's life is less unified and more compartmentalized.

Secularism and rationality Western society has moved away from reverence for and uncritical acceptance of established institutions. Few things are removed from worldly, secular judgment. Modern man feels freer to ask, "What good is it?" The world has become "disenchanted," more "sensate," more "materialistic," less "spiritual," to use terms that have been applied to this trend toward *secularism.*

Secularism encourages *rationality* in social organization. Group ways of acting are consciously designed and measured by effectiveness and efficiency. Weber studied the increasing emphasis on rationality in modern industry, military organization, and other spheres of life.[28] He saw that the business world, in

Georg Simmel (1858–1918) was a German philosopher who influenced the pioneers of sociology in the United States, particularly through the translations of Albion W. Small. A generation ago Simmel was best known for his effort to identify the distinctive subject matter of sociology, which he conceived as the study of "forms of social interaction," such as subordination, competition, and division of labor. Today there is more interest in his perceptive analyses of sociability, city life, the money economy, and the consequences of group size.

its drive for efficiency, was becoming increasingly impersonal and machinelike. Weber traced the emergence of what has already been mentioned as one of the characteristic social forms of our time, the bu-

---

[28] See the biographical note, p. 464. In his *The Protestant Ethic and the Spirit of Capitalism,* Weber studied the contribution of religious austerity and self-discipline to the development of rationality in early capitalism. (See INDUSTRIAL MAN, pp. 464–466.)

reaucratic administrative hierarchy, in which the principle of rationality in social organization is fully developed.

Secularism and rationality are associated with *impersonality* in human relations. With a weakened sense of kinship and with a utilitarian orientation, it is easy to treat people as means rather than as ends. Simmel showed how the growth of a money economy contributes to impersonality in social relations. When compensation is based strictly on money, people tend to restrict their relations with one another and to ignore personal considerations. A money economy brings into association people who have no other interactions. Their relations may be limited to the exchange of goods or services for money without further involvement.[29]

From Gemeinschaft to Gesellschaft Tönnies contrasted two types of society, *Gemeinschaft* (communal society) and *Gesellschaft* (associational society).[30] In a *Gemeinschaft* people feel they belong together because they are of the same kind. Broadly speaking, they are kin and cannot freely renounce their membership, which involves emotional meaning for the group as well as for the individual. People do not decide to join a *Gemeinschaft*. They are born into it or grow into it in the way the bonds of friendship grow. This model of a communal society closely fits the "folk" or primitive society and the ideal conception of the feudal social order. The decline of *Gemeinschaft* is a decline of the sense of kinship with other members of a community.

To this type of society Tönnies contrasted the *Gesellschaft,* in which the major social bonds are voluntary and based upon the rational pursuit of self-interest. People enter into relations with one another not because they must or because it is "natural," but as a practical way of achieving an objective. The typical relation is the contract, and the typical group is the voluntary special-purpose association. The long historical trend is toward the *Gesellschaft,* with more and more activities governed by the voluntary action of freely contracting individuals.

Gesellschaft weakens traditional bonds and encourages rationality and the division of labor.[31] The result is a mass society made up of individuals who are only loosely bound together. "Mass" suggests an aggregate rather than a tightly knit social group. Mass society is the "participant society." [32] In earlier periods, small well-insulated minorities controlled decision-making in the major institutions. The rest of the people lived out their lives within the confines of work, household, and parish. In mass society popular demand tends to govern policy in many areas, including government, education, and the production and distribution of consumer goods. Mass democracy is discussed in POLITICAL MAN.

Countertrends The trends culminating in mass society represent a movement away from a highly integrated social order to a more loosely knit one based on individualism and group autonomy. In the twentieth century these trends have come to their fullest development, but this century has also seen the rapid development of countertrends leading to closer social integration. Two of these countertrends are centralization and the "quest for community."

1. *Centralization* is a dominant theme in modern society, especially in political and economic life. The centers of decision have moved away from local areas and small units to the capital cities of government and industry.

[29] See *The Sociology of Georg Simmel,* translated and edited by Kurt H. Wolff (Glencoe: The Free Press, 1950); also N. J. Spykman, *The Social Theory of Georg Simmel* (Chicago: University of Chicago Press, 1925), pp. 219 ff.; and Lewis A. Coser (ed.), *Georg Simmel* (Englewood Cliffs, N.J.: Prentice-Hall, 1965).

[30] Ferdinand Tönnies, *Gemeinschaft und Gesellschaft* (1st ed., 1887), tr. and ed. by C. P. Loomis as *Fundamental Concepts of Sociology* (New York: American Book Co., 1940). (See PRIMARY GROUPS, p. 124.)

[31] See especially Karl Mannheim, *Man and Society in an Age of Reconstruction* (New York: Harcourt, Brace & World, 1949); also Jose Ortega y Gasset, *The Revolt of the Masses* (New York: Norton, 1932); and William Kornhauser, *The Politics of Mass Society* (Glencoe: The Free Press, 1959).

[32] See Daniel Lerner, *The Passing of Traditional Society* (Glencoe: The Free Press, 1958), p. 60 *et passim.*

2. The *quest for community* also runs counter to the emphasis on rationality and individualism. Millions feel the need to find or reaffirm a common identity, and this sometimes leads to a denial of individualism and a revived but distorted sense of kinship. The most extravagant example is Hitler's Germany, which purported to offer a rebirth of *Volksgemeinschaft,* a communality of "blood and soil."

In every age there are certain key words which by their repetitive use and re-definition mark the distinctive channels of faith and thought. . . . In the nineteenth century, the age of individualism and rationalism, such words as *individual, change, progress, reason,* and *freedom* were notable. . . .

Today a different set of words and symbols dominates the intellectual and moral scene. It is impossible to overlook, in modern lexicons, the importance of such words as *disorganization, disintegration, decline, insecurity, breakdown, instability,* and the like.[33]

The survival of rationality and of individual freedom depends upon man's ability to solve the problems which these ideals, together with industrialism and urbanization, have set for the modern world.

[33] Robert A. Nisbet, *The Quest for Community* (New York: Oxford University Press, 1953), pp. 3–4, 7. Reprinted by permission of Oxford University Press.

CHAPTER III
CULTURE

SECTION 1 THE CONCEPT OF CULTURE

As commonly used in the social sciences, the term culture refers to a *social heritage,* that is, all the knowledge, beliefs, customs, and skills that are available to the members of a society. The social heritage is the product of a specific and unique history; it is the "distinctive way of life of a group of people, their complete design for living." [1]

The idea of culture has a rich intellectual background.[2] In the philosophical, literary, and historical tradition, culture refers mainly to ideals of enlightenment and refinement, especially in the realms of intellect, morality, and art. This *humanist* view of culture emphasizes creativity and excellence. The cultured man in this tradition is sophisticated, sensitive, and educated. He can appreciate and perhaps teach the richness of his cultural tradition.

In the nineteenth century, especially in Germany, a connection was made between culture as a moral and intellectual ideal and culture as the distinctive "genius" of a people or an epoch.[3] Styles of art, conceptions of law, philosophical systems, religious orientations, and literary themes were studied for the way they reflected and shaped the *ethos,* or fundamental character, of a people. While the emphasis remained on intellectual, aesthetic, and moral attainment, a transition was made toward applying the idea of culture to certain aspects of a whole society at a stage of its history.

Nineteenth-century anthropologists often used "culture" and "civilization" interchangeably, and they were fascinated by the possibility of an evolution of society from lower to higher stages. (See Sec.

[1] Clyde Kluckhohn, "The Study of Culture," in Daniel Lerner and Harold D. Lasswell (eds.), *The Policy Sciences* (Stanford: Stanford University Press, 1951), p. 86.

[2] See A. L. Kroeber and Clyde Kluckhohn, *Culture: A Critical Review of Concepts and Definitions* (New York: Vintage Books, 1963); Raymond Williams, *Culture and Society, 1780–1950* (Garden City, N.Y.: [Anchor] Doubleday, 1960).

[3] See Kroeber and Kluckhohn, *op. cit.,* Part I; also George L. Mosse, *The Culture of Western Europe* (Chicago: Rand McNally, 1961); Bruce Mazlish, *The Riddle of History: The Great Speculators from Vico to Freud* (New York: Harper & Row, 1966).

4, p. 75.) Culture was something man attained as he developed his skills and rational capacities. Gradually, however, the ideas of culture and civilization were disentangled.[4] Civilization retained its evaluative connotation, but culture came to refer to the *way of life* of a people, whatever that might be.

At the same time that evolutionary theories of society were being proposed and debated, anthropologists were trying to delimit the races of man and assess the influence of race differences on human accomplishment. Some attempted to account for different ways of life by the influence of biological heredity, and the achievements of Western civilization were claimed to be due to the inherent superiority of the "white" race. For example, Gobineau's *Essay on the Inequality of Human Races* (1853–1855) argued that white "Aryans" or "Nordics" were responsible for the development of civilization.

Anthropologists like Franz Boas, however, read the lesson of cultural variation differently. They showed that biological heredity was of minor importance compared to social heredity. The difference between one people and another was a matter of historical opportunity, not of biological endowment.

Anthropologists wanted a concept of culture that would (1) be descriptive, free of value judgments, useful for analysis of any people's way of life, no matter how crude or primitive they might seem; and (2) direct attention to the social rather than biological influences on human nature and human achievement.

By the early decades of the twentieth century the anthropological concept of culture had come to center on the social heritage taken as a whole. The humanist concept, with its selective emphasis on ideas and the arts, was set aside as unsuitable for anthropological inquiry:

Culture is not restricted to certain special fields of knowledge; it includes ways of behaving derived from the whole range of human activity. The designs for living evident in the behavior of the Eskimos, the natives of Australia, or the Navahos are as much a part of culture as those of cultivated Europeans and Americans. Culture includes not only the techniques and methods of art, music, and literature, but also those used to make pottery, sew clothing, or build houses. Among the products of culture we find comic books and popular street songs along with the art of a Leonardo da Vinci and the music of a Johann Bach. The anthropologist does not employ the contrast "cultured versus uncultured," for this distinction of popular usage represents only a difference in culture, not its absence or presence.[5]

This viewpoint rejects provincialism and underscores the receptiveness of the social scientist in studying cultures other than his own. A comprehensive, inclusive idea of culture avoids invidious distinctions. It assumes that man's humanity may be achieved through any sustained social experience. A forest pygmy, an Eskimo, an ancient Roman, an advertising account executive, a member of a delinquent gang, or a "hippie" are all equally human and all participate in culture.

Thus the history of anthropology and its moral concerns have encouraged a comprehensive view of culture as equivalent to the entire social heritage. Within that broad definition, however, certain topics stand out as bridges between the interests of the social scientist and those of the humanist. These include: (1) culture as symbolism and (2) culture as the realm of values.

THE SYMBOLIC ORDER

Of all the animals man alone has culture, because only he is capable of creating symbols. Without symbols there could be social life, as there is among other animals, but it would be rudimentary.

A symbol [6] may be broadly defined as anything that

---

[4] See George W. Stocking, Jr., "Matthew Arnold, E. B. Tylor, and the Uses of Invention," *American Anthropologist, 65* (1963), 783–799, and "Franz Boas and the Culture Concept in Historical Perspective," *American Anthropologist, 68* (1966), 867–882.

[5] Ralph L. Beals and Harry Hoijer, *An Introduction to Anthropology* (New York: Macmillan, 1953), p. 207.

[6] Some writers use "sign" as the most general term to include "natural signs" (smoke is a sign of fire) and conventional signs, or symbols. See Ernest Nagel, "Symbolism and Science," in Lyman Bryson, *et al.* (eds.), *Symbols and Values: An Initial Study*, Thirteenth Symposium of the Conference on Science, Philosophy and Religion (New York: Harper & Row, 1954), pp. 39–71. This volume contains a number of articles pertinent to the present discussion.

stands for or represents something else. The word "pencil" is a symbol; it may stand for the idea of a pencil or for a specific object. The meaning of a symbol is social in origin: meaning is given to a symbol by those who use it. Thus symbols are always man-made. While words are the most common symbols, acts or objects are symbols too, for example, a threatening gesture or a river that marks a boundary.

For the purpose of understanding culture, two kinds of symbols should be distinguished, the *referential* and the *expressive*.[7] Referential symbols are *de*notative, they are words or objects that have a specific reference; they are instrumental. "Portable typewriter" is a referential symbol; it is a convenient way of referring to a specific class of objects.

Expressive symbols are *con*notative. They evoke associations that are diffuse and open-ended rather than specific and limited. The word professor *de*notes one who holds a position on a faculty, but the same word *con*notes a wide range of associations, not fully specified, suggesting authority, knowledge, and wisdom, or perhaps subversion and impracticality. "Cross" denotes a physical arrangement, but it connotes religious martyrdom and the perspectives of Christianity.

Expressive symbols have a special importance for culture. When symbols are narrowly denotative and technical—for example, a code for filing books in a library—they do not sustain personal and group identity. A symbol invested with connotation evokes responses that are personally meaningful, that is, the connotations are experienced by the person as comforting or threatening, uplifting or degrading. Thus "home" is a more expressive symbol than "house"; "boss" probably conveys more person-centered meanings than "employer"; "convocation" evokes associations of a ritual occasion while "meeting" is more narrowly referential. Expressive symbolism is capable of contributing to social solidarity by affirming shared ideals and perspectives.

Group-sustaining symbolism is not restricted to such clear-cut examples as flags and rituals. Etiquette, for example, has symbolic meaning:

On a relatively obvious plane of symbolism etiquette provides the members of society with a set of rules which . . . express society's concern for its members and their relation to one another. There is another level of etiquette symbolism, however, which takes little or no account of such specific meanings but interprets etiquette as a whole as a powerful symbolism of status. From this standpoint, to know the rules of etiquette is important, not because the feelings of friends and strangers are becomingly observed but because the manipulator of the rule proves he is a member of an exclusive group. [One who affirms his group membership in this way is not necessarily without malice or individuality.] By reason of the richly developed meanings which inhere in etiquette, both positive and negative, a sensitive person can actually express a more bitter hostility through the frigid observance of etiquette than by flouting it on an obvious wave of hostility.[8]

George Orwell's novel *1984* depicts the decay of social relations and culture in a totalitarian society dominated by "Big Brother." A phase of that decay is described in "Newspeak and Expressive Symbolism," page 53.

Symbolism and the arts   In all societies, though in varying degrees, expressive symbolism is sustained and enriched by aesthetic activity—dance, music, sculpture. The arts help celebrate occasions that are significant to the group. The artist is a specialist in creating symbolic representations that convey the spirit of a culture or an age, though he may be unaware that he is doing so. Artistic creations are therefore important to the student of culture. In the study of expressive symbolism the humanist and the social scientist find common ground.

However, expressive symbolism is not restricted to the arts. Any repetitive human act, any object, however simple or routine, can have expressive meaning. A meal, a form of dress, a greeting, a

[7] Edward Sapir distinguished referential and "condensation" symbolism, the latter "allowing for the ready release of emotional tension in conscious or unconscious form." "Symbolism," *Encyclopedia of the Social Sciences, 14* (1934), 493.

[8] Sapir, *ibid.,* p. 494.

NEWSPEAK AND EXPRESSIVE SYMBOLISM

The name of every organization, or body of people, or doctrine, or country, or institution, or public building, was invariably cut down into the familiar shape: that is, a single easily pronounced word with the smallest number of syllables that would preserve the original derivation. In the Ministry of Truth, for example, the Records Department was called *Recdep,* the Fiction Department was called *Ficdep,* the Tele-programs Department was called *Teledep,* and so on. Even in the early decades of the twentieth century, telescoped words and phrases had been one of the characteristic features of political language; and it had been noticed that the tendency to use abbreviations of this kind was most marked in totalitarian countries and totalitarian organizations.* It was perceived that in thus abbreviating a name one *narrowed and subtly altered its meaning,* by cutting out most of the associations that would otherwise cling to it. The words *Communist International,* for instance, call up a composite picture of universal human brotherhood, red flags, barricades, Karl Marx, and the Paris Commune. The word *Comintern,* on the other hand, suggests merely a tightly knit organization and a well-defined body of doctrine. *Comintern* is a word that can be uttered almost without taking thought, whereas *Communist International* is a phrase over which one is obliged to linger at least momentarily. In the same way, the associations called up by a word like *Minitrue* are fewer and more controllable than those called up by *Ministry of Truth.*

What was required, above all for political purposes, were short clipped words of unmistakable meaning which could be uttered rapidly and which roused the minimum of echoes in the speaker's mind. For the purposes of everyday life it was no doubt necessary, or sometimes necessary, to reflect before speaking, but a Party member called upon to make a political or ethical judgment should be able to spray forth the correct opinions as automatically as a machine gun spraying forth bullets. His training fitted him to do this, the language gave him an almost foolproof instrument, and the texture of the words, with their harsh sound and a certain willful ugliness, assisted the process still further.

The Newspeak vocabulary was tiny, and differed from almost all other languages in that its vocabulary grew smaller instead of larger each year. Each reduction was a gain, since the smaller the area of choice, the smaller the temptation to take thought. Ultimately it was hoped to make articulate speech issue from the larynx without involving the higher brain centers at all. This aim was frankly admitted in the Newspeak word *duckspeak,* meaning "to quack like a duck." Provided that the opinions which were quacked out were orthodox ones, it implied nothing but praise, and when the *Times* referred to one of the orators of the Party as a *doubleplusgood duckspeaker* it was paying a warm and valued compliment.

SOURCE: From "The Principles of Newspeak," Appendix to *Nineteen Eighty-Four* by George Orwell; copyright, 1949 (New York: Harcourt, Brace & World), pp. 309–311. Used with permission.

* For example, "Gestapo" from *Geheime Staatspolizei;* "Comintern" from *Communist International;* "Agitprop" from *Agitation* and *Propaganda* department.

dwelling, a public gathering-place—any of these may be rich with connotation. Thus culture includes everything that is produced by, and is capable of sustaining, shared symbolic experience.[9]

CULTURAL VALUES AND NORMS

A *value* is anything that is prized or of benefit. "Values do not consist in 'desires' but rather in the desirable, that is, what we not only want but feel that it is right and proper to want for ourselves and for others. [Values are] abstract standards that transcend the impulses of the moment and ephemeral situations." [10]

In the discussion of culture, value is usually considered from the standpoint of how the group acts, feels, or thinks. A *cultural value* may be defined as a widely held belief or sentiment that some activities, relationships, feelings, or goals are important to the community's identity or well-being. Because they are often held unconsciously, or are expressed as themes cutting across a variety of specific attitudes, the values of a people are not immediately apparent.

A suggestive effort to summarize the major value orientations in the United States has been made by Williams. One merit of this statement is its propositional form, which invites the reader to test the validity of each theme against his own knowledge. The list of themes follows a cautionary note:

(In the nature of the case, anyone—including the author—can think of numerous exceptions to each of these generalized formulations, as well as widespread alternative themes.)

1. American culture is organized around the attempt at *active mastery* rather than *passive acceptance*. Into this dimension falls the low tolerance of frustration; the refusal to accept ascetic renunciation; the positive encouragement of desire; the stress on power; the approval of ego-assertion, and so on.

2. It tends to be interested in the *external world* of things and events, of the palpable and immediate, rather than in the inner experience of meaning and affect. Its genius is manipulative rather than contemplative.

3. Its world-view tends to be *open* rather than closed: it emphasizes change, flux, movement; its central personality types are adaptive, accessible, outgoing and assimilative.

4. In wide historical and comparative perspective, the culture places its primary faith in *rationalism* as opposed to *traditionalism;* it deemphasizes the past, orients strongly to the future, does not accept things just because they have been done before.

5. Closely related to the above is the dimension of *orderliness* rather than unsystematic *ad hoc* acceptance of transitory experience. (This emphasis is most marked in the urban middle classes.)

6. With conspicuous deviations, a main theme is a *universalistic* rather than a *particularistic* ethic.[11]

7. In interpersonal relations, the weight of the value system is on the side of *"horizontal"* rather than *"vertical"* emphases: peer-relations, not superordinate-subordinate relations; equality rather than hierarchy.

8. Subject to increased strains and modifications, the received culture emphasizes *individual personality* rather than group identity and responsibility.

In broadest outline, then, American society is characterized by a basic moral orientation, involving emphases on active, instrumental mastery of the world in accordance with universalistic standards of performance. It is a pluralistic system in which it is not easy to secure unitary commitment to collective goals. It permits a wide range of goals for achievement.[12]

Thus whole cultures are sometimes characterized by values that reinforce each other and affect the most varied and important kinds of behavior.

Norms   Cultural norms are based on cultural values. They are guides to conduct, specifying what is

[9] See Gertrude Jaeger and Philip Selznick, "A Normative Theory of Culture," *American Sociological Review, 29* (October, 1964), 653–669.

[10] Clyde Kluckhohn, *Culture and Behavior* (New York: The Free Press of Glencoe, 1962), p. 289.

[11] A "universalistic" ethic emphasizes the application of uniform rules or principles, e.g., that all men are equal before the law or should have equal opportunities. A "particularistic" ethic emphasizes claims to special treatment on the basis of friendship, kinship, social status, or other specific criteria.

[12] Robin M. Williams, Jr., *American Society: A Sociological Interpretation* (2nd ed., rev.; New York: Knopf, 1960), pp. 469–470.

William Graham Sumner (1840–1910), influential sociologist and author of Folkways *and* The Science of Society *(with A. G. Keller). Sumner's work emphasized the conservative influence of custom. He was also a staunch conservative on both political and economic issues. Perhaps the best-known chapter title in social science is from* Folkways: *"The Mores Can Make Anything Right and Prevent Condemnation of Anything."*

appropriate or inappropriate, setting limits within which individuals may seek alternate ways to achieve their goals. Norms are usually framed as rules, prescriptions, or standards to be followed by people who occupy specified roles. Thus there are norms for the conduct of citizens, friends, parents, schoolteachers.

A value is more general than a norm. The society may value privacy, but the specific norms governing the handling of mail or the administration of public toilets necessarily depend on the situation and circumstances. While some norms apply to narrowly specified situations that may occur only rarely, others apply to the most common activities of everyday life.

When the occurrence is rare, as in the case of funerals and other ceremonies, specialists are needed to instruct the participants on proper conduct.

Norms vary in how closely they are connected with cultural values. Many norms are technical arrangements for organizing work or serving public convenience. They are important to the functioning of the society but they are not *experienced* as important, either symbolically or in their bearing upon cultural values. The _mores_ are culturally salient norms, such as prohibitions on murder and blasphemy or the prescriptions governing parental responsibility for children. Sumner observed that "the Romans used *mores* for customs in the broadest and richest sense of the word, including the notion that customs served welfare and had traditional and mystic sanction so that they were properly authoritative and sacred."[13]

Sumner distinguished mores from _folkways,_ which are less salient norms. The intensity of feeling associated with folkways is relatively low and conformity is more nearly optional. Norms specifying appropriate dress, for instance, evoke little emotion, except where the deviance is perceived as extreme.

CULTURE AND SOCIAL ORGANIZATION

Social organization is made up of interpersonal and group relations. The family is a unit of social organization, and the form of the family and much familial behavior are prescribed by the culture. One culture may value a kind of family in which the father is dominant; another may relegate him to a lesser role. Culture is the design and the prescription, the composite of guiding values and ideals. Hence, culture and social organization are interdependent. The separate treatment of the subjects is a matter of selective interest and emphasis.

On the other hand, much of social organization is not culturally prescribed but arises out of the give and take of personal and group interaction that is not entirely governed by definite rules. For example, a hierarchy of social classes may be culturally defined as it was in medieval Europe or classical China.

[13] William Graham Sumner, *Folkways* (New York: [Mentor] New American Library, 1960), p. 48. (First published in 1907.)

In American society stratification exists, but it has much less support in the design for living.

The interrelations between culture and social organization may be illustrated by the Tanala,[14] a hill tribe of Madagascar. Originally they subsisted by the cultivation of *dry rice*. They cut down and burned jungle growth, thus clearing the land for planting. After one or two crops the land had to be abandoned until the jungle overran it again. The jungle about a village was thus exploited until it was exhausted, and then the village was moved. There was no individual ownership of land; the village as a whole held the territory. Within the village *joint* families—groups of households connected through a common head— were the chief units of organization. Joint family members worked as a group and owned the crops from the land they cleared. The head of the joint family divided the crops among the households, and there was little variation in wealth between families. Forest products, such as game, belonged to whoever took them.

The adoption of *wet rice* cultivation from a neighboring people disrupted Tanala culture and social organization. Because at the outset wet rice planting was done on relatively small plots, it was cultivated by single households, and unlike the dry rice system, the land was in continuous cultivation. The idea of exclusive ownership of real estate developed, and because there was only a limited amount of suitable land, two classes—landholders and landless—became distinguished. Those who held wet rice land no longer

needed to be involved in the large joint-family effort in jungle clearing, and they did not want the villages to be moved. The landless, who continued dry rice cultivation, had to move into the jungle too far to return to the village at night. As a result they too began to develop separate household organization. There were numerous other effects: changes in the kinship and marriage system, in the practice of warfare, in the design of villages and village defense, in slavery, and in the growth of a centralized authority with autocratic control.

The Tanala case shows how changes in social relations are affected by changes in the key activities of a group and how the particular forms of adaptation and interaction are embedded in custom. When the food gathering technology was changed, the social system changed along with it. The sequence of changes was initiated by a modification in the technology—the shift from dry rice to wet rice cultivation. This was accompanied by changes in social organization: greater emphasis on the individual household, declining emphasis on the large joint family, and the stabilization of the site of the village. Accompanying these changes were shifts in cultural values: the joint family was displaced by the household as the chief object of loyalty, and land became valued not as something to be used temporarily but to be permanently possessed. Thus culture and social organization interact in the working out of man's relations to his physical environment and his fellow men.

[14] Ralph Linton, *The Study of Man* (New York: Appleton-Century, 1936), pp. 348–355; and Ralph Linton, *The Tanala: A Hill Tribe of Madagascar,* Anthropological Series Vol. XXII (Chicago: Field Museum of Natural History, 1933).

SOURCES AND READINGS

Ralph L. Beals and Harry Hoijer, *An Introduction to Anthropology* (3rd ed.; New York: [Free Press] Macmillan, 1965).

C. Daryll Forde, *Habitat, Economy and Society* (London: Methuen, 1934).

Edward Adamson Hoebel, *Anthropology* (3rd ed.; New York: McGraw-Hill, 1966).

Dell Hymes (ed.), *Language in Culture and Society* (New York: Harper & Row, 1964).

Clyde Kluckhohn, *Culture and Behavior* (New York: The Free Press of Glencoe, 1962).

Clyde Kluckhohn, *Mirror for Man* (New York: Fawcett World Library, 1964).

Dorothy Lee, *Freedom and Culture* (Englewood Cliffs, N.J.: Prentice-Hall, 1959).

Ralph Linton, *The Study of Man* (New York: Appleton-Century, 1936).

George P. Murdock, *Our Primitive Contemporaries* (New York: Macmillan, 1935).

Sol Tax (ed.), *Anthropology Today: Selections* (Chicago: University of Chicago Press, 1962).

Robin M. Williams, Jr., *American Society* (2nd ed.; New York: Knopf, 1960), Chapters 10, 11.

Periodicals

American Anthropologist

Comparative Studies in Society and History

Human Organization

Man (Journal of the Royal Anthropological Institute)

Southwestern Journal of Anthropology

SECTION 2 THE IMPACT OF CULTURE

The case of rice cultivation among the Tanala shows culture as a *dependent* variable, a product of other determining forces. Technological change affected social organization, which in turn influenced conceptions of property and the symbolic meaning of land. But culture is also an *independent* variable, a determinant of social patterns.

PERVASIVENESS OF CULTURE

Culture creates a world taken for granted; it forms the unconscious premises of thought and action. Culture tends to be pervasive, touching every aspect of life. The pervasiveness of culture is manifest in two ways. First, culture provides an unquestioned context within which individual action and response take place. Even rational action is subject to the cultural definition of what is a meaningful goal and what are available means. Emotional responses are governed by cultural norms that prescribe selective forms of emotion, such as appropriate feelings of grief, wounded pride, or romantic love. Culturally determined responses are built into the very physiology of the organism, for example, conditioning the individual to feel nauseated by sights, smells, or tastes, or to be sexually aroused by certain objects.

Second, culture pervades social activities and in-stitutions. There is a strain toward consistency in culture[15]—consistency of perception and style, as well as of values. This is the thesis of Benedict's discussion of integrating themes in three preliterate, relatively simple societies. Benedict based her analysis on the following postulate:

A culture, like an individual, is a more or less consistent pattern of thought and action. Within each culture there come into being characteristic purposes not necessarily shared by other types of society. In obedience to these purposes, each people further and further consolidates its experience, and in proportion to the urgency of these drives the heterogeneous items of behavior take more and more congruous shape.[16]

Although a strain to consistency is probably universal, the amount of consistency to be found in any particular culture is highly variable. As Benedict recognized, the more complex the society, and the more exposed it is to differing influences, the harder it is to identify and make generalizations about culture themes. The postulate of consistency calls attention to the pervasive effect of cultural symbolism and values; it is a way of saying that it is always pertinent to ask to what extent a given activity, such as warfare, economic organization, or politics, is taken for granted.

[15] Sumner, *op. cit.*, pp. 21, 49–50.

[16] Ruth Benedict, *Patterns of Culture* (Baltimore: Penguin Books, 1946), p. 42.

When radically different customs are compared, the impact of culture is obvious. But it is often necessary to examine the details of interaction, and the interdependence of language and thought, to grasp the full significance of cultural influence. See Adaptation 6, pages 64–68.

LANGUAGE AND CULTURE

Ordinarily language is taken for granted as a way of expressing ideas and feelings and of communicating messages. Because language appears to place no restraints on the flow of ideas, we assume that it is a medium equally fitted to convey any idea. According to this commonsense view, the various spoken languages of the world are merely different inventories for the same underlying reality; although different names and sounds are used in each language, the things named are actually the same. Though the "codes" may vary, the "messages" or thoughts expressed are fundamentally equivalent.

Such a conception of languages has been challenged by a number of linguists and anthropologists. Inspired especially by the work of Benjamin L. Whorf, social scientists have come to believe that language is more than an aid to thought: it pervades the content and style of thought itself. Language is not simply a set of labels for preexisting objects. Rather, language "constructs" reality by determining the kinds of objects we carve out of the flux of experience. Languages are more (and less) than different codes for the same messages; they restrict the kinds of messages that can be conveyed, and even the kinds of messages that can be conceived.

Language is a guide to "social reality." Though language is not ordinarily thought of as of essential interest to the students of social science, it powerfully conditions all our thinking about social problems and processes. Human beings do not live in the objective world alone, nor alone in the world of social activity as ordinarily understood, but are very much at the mercy of the particular language which has become

the medium of expression for their society. . . . No two languages are ever sufficiently similar to be considered as representing the same social reality. The worlds in which different societies live are distinct worlds, not merely the same world with different labels attached.[17]

While this statement may be somewhat overdrawn, it does point to one of the most important ways culture as a symbolic realm influences the human mind.

Selective attention By sensitizing the individual to certain aspects of the external world, language accentuates some features at the expense of others. An illustration is the use of verbs. In English, tense is an important aspect of conjugation. Since in English a verb must have tense, the speaker is cognizant of a time dimension whenever he uses the language. However, the Hopi Indian language conjugates its verbs for validity rather than time.[18] In naming an action the Hopi must indicate the nature of his evidence, that is, whether he is reporting (1) a direct experience, (2) a belief or expectation, or (3) a generalization about experience. For example, having watched a boy running down a footpath, the Hopi uses the verb-form *wari* (running, statement of direct observation); *wari* may be translated either as *he is running* or *he ran,* since the time of the action is unspecified. If the Hopi believes the boy is running down the footpath, but has no direct evidence for this, he uses the form *warikni* (running, statement of expectation); this form may refer to a past, present, or future action. Finally, if the speaker knows the boy runs as a matter of custom or habit, perhaps as a participant in racing games, he uses the form *warikngwe* (running, statement of a generalization or law). The Hopi language thus encourages the speaker to check his sources of information.

In Japanese, there are a number of sets of verbal triplets that denote the same action, one form indicating a humble attitude on the part of the speaker toward the listener, another an attitude of politeness,

---

[17] Edward Sapir, "The Status of Linguistics as a Science," in David G. Mandelbaum (ed.) *Selected Writings of Edward Sapir* (Berkeley and Los Angeles: University of California Press, 1958), p. 162.

[18] Benjamin Lee Whorf, *Language, Thought, and Reality* (New York: Wiley, 1956), p. 217. First published in 1940.

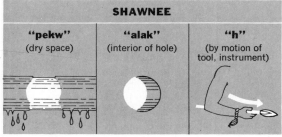

The three isolates from experience or nature used in English to say "I clean it (gun) with the ramrod."

The three isolates from experience or nature used in Shawnee to say "Nipekwalakha," meaning "I clean it (gun) with the ramrod."

FIG. III:1 Languages dissect nature differently

The different isolates of meaning (thoughts) used by English and Shawnee in reporting the same experience, that of cleaning a gun by running the ramrod through it. The pronouns "I" and "it" are not shown by symbols, as they have the same meaning in each language. In Shawnee ni- *equals "I";* -a *equals "it."*

(Redrawn after Whorf, *op. cit.*)

and the third a plain or abrupt attitude.[19] For example, *iku,* which is the plain form of *to go,* becomes *irrasharu* in the polite form, and *mairu* in the humble form; *taberu* (to eat, plain form) becomes *agaru* (polite form) and *itadaku* (humble form). Since the speaker is obligated to observe the status relationship between himself and his listener, the abrupt or plain form is used in the presence of inferiors, the polite form in the presence of peers, and the humble form

in the presence of superiors. In effect, the Japanese implicates himself within the social hierarchy simply by using a verb-form. European languages, too, have formal and informal modes of address, as in the French *vous, tu* and the German *Sie, du.*

Modes of discrimination Selective attention enforced by language reflects the distinctive problems and experiences of the society. In English, for example, the same word is used for falling snow, snow on the ground, snow packed hard like ice, slushy snow, wind-driven flying snow, and so on.[20] An Eskimo is acutely aware that these various types of "snow" are distinct phenomena, each presenting its own problems and opportunities. The more inclusive word is not useful in the Eskimo's environment, and the Eskimo language includes a large vocabulary of specific terms.

Languages differ not only in how precisely they differentiate experience, but also in the *way* they do so:

A Trobriand word refers to a self-contained concept. . . . For "A good gardener," or "The gardener is good," the Trobriand word would include both "gardener" and "goodness"; if the gardener loses the goodness, he has lost a defining ingredient, he is something else, and he is named by means of a completely different word. A *taytu* (a species of yam) contains a certain degree of ripeness, bigness, roundedness, etc.; without one of these defining ingredients, it is something else. . . .

There is no temporal connection between objects. The *taytu* always remains itself; it does not *become* overripe; overripeness is an ingredient of another, a different being. At some point, the *taytu* turns into a *yowana,* which contains overripeness. And the *yowana,* overripe as it is, does not put forth shoots, does not *become* a sprouting *yowana.* When sprouts appear, it ceases to be itself; in its place appears a *silasata.* Neither is there a temporal connection made . . . between events; in fact, temporality is meaningless. There are no tenses, no linguistic distinction between past and present.[21]

---

[19] Hide Shodara, "Honorific Expressions of Personal Attitudes in Spoken Japanese," Center for Japanese Studies, *Occasional Papers* (Ann Arbor: University of Michigan Press, 1962), No. 2, pp. 31–32.

[20] Whorf, *op. cit.,* p. 216.

[21] Dorothy Lee, *Freedom and Culture* (Englewood Cliffs, N.J.: Prentice-Hall, 1959), p. 109.

On first seeing a white man: A native of the Duna language area in the Southern Highlands District of New Guinea, photographed on his first encounter with a white man—June, 1955.

The Trobriand language orders the world in a way that may seem unnatural to one who is accustomed to thinking of the "same" entity as larger or smaller, earlier or later, ripe or unripe. This does not mean that Trobrianders are unable to conceive of entities that vary according to a temporal attribute. It would be more accurate to say that the language biases them against such categories.

Language and thought Because languages accentuate some features of experience and lend the world a special cast, they tend to produce different conceptions of reality and different thoughtways. The fact that some words are not translatable from one language to another "is merely the outward expression of inward differences between two peoples in premises, in basic categories, in the training of fundamental sensitivities, and in the general view of the world." [22] Consider the idea of time. There is much suggestive evidence that many peoples conceive of time differently. For example, the language of the Kachin people of North Burma seems to contain no single word that corresponds to the English *time*.[23] Instead, there are numerous partial equivalents. In the following expressions the Kachin equivalent of *time* differs in every case:

The *time* by the clock is	*ahkying*
A long *time*	*na*
A short *time*	*tawng*
The present *time*	*ten*
Spring *time*	*ta*
The *time* has come	*hkra*
In the *time* of Queen Victoria	*lakhtak, aprat*
At any *time* of life	*asak*

A Kachin is encouraged by his language to be aware of these distinctions.

Conceptions of time, space, and other aspects of the world are rooted in language. Concealed in the structure of each language is a set of implicit assumptions. By emphasizing features of experience, vocabulary and grammar carry an implicit message: This is important. That is not important. Always distinguish A from B.[24]

The extent to which language influences thought is not fully understood. It is clear, however, that the structure of language leaves its imprint on the consciousness and the thoughtways of a people.

[22] Clyde Kluckhohn, *Mirror for Man* (Greenwich, Conn.: Fawcett, 1964), p. 145. (First published in 1944).

[23] E. R. Leach, *Rethinking Anthropology* (University of London: The Athlone Press, 1966), p. 124.

[24] Kluckhohn, *ibid.,* p. 145.

CULTURE SHOCK

To the extent that a person is imbued with his culture's values, acts according to its assumptions, and lacks awareness of alternative ways, he may be said to be "culture bound." To some extent everyone is culture bound, at least about some premises and expectations.

When unquestioned expectations are shaken, "culture shock" may ensue. Culture shock is the experience of disorientation and frustration that occurs when an individual finds himself among people who do not share his fundamental premises. Usually, disagreement over abstract ideas or variation in modes of dress, eating habits, and other daily routines can be learned and adjusted to fairly readily. Acute culture shock is most likely to be experienced when expectations about personal feelings and interaction are violated. A case in point is the description by a Peace Corpsman of "The Culture Shock of Quiet Death," page 62.

CONFORMITY AND DEVIATION

Although culture is an important determinant of thought and feeling, it is not monolithic or irresistible. The impact of culture is *variable,* depending on the particular aspect of culture involved and the circumstances.

Cultural values specify ideals, not actual regularities of behavior. Ideals involve standards of perfection, whether in the skills of the fisherman, the behavior of parents, or the performance of the artist— in all societies, preliterate or modern. The medicine man, the expert storyteller, the skilled craftsman— each stands in a different position relative to his culture than does the average participant. Similarly, the knowledge of a passenger in a plane is not equal to that of the designer, even though both participate in what might be called the aeronautical culture complex.

Men participate in culture to different degrees and are more or less responsive to values and norms because most human action is *situational* and *problem-solving.* People live out their lives in specific circumstances. They spend most of their time dealing with

the problems, stresses, and opportunities of everyday life. Therefore, culture is always *mediated* by or filtered through the routine activities and interactions that preoccupy men. Men are not culturally determined automatons who merely act out values and follow rules. They do take rules into account and are often guided by them, but they also deviate from rules, both deliberately and unwittingly.

In many situations social organization, not cul-

Jeremy Bentham (1748–1832), no conformist, was a persistent critic of tradition and urged that all social practices be assessed according to their utility and the criterion of maximizing pleasure and minimizing pain. In his gift to the University of London, he required that his remains be preserved in University College, where his clothed skeleton is kept in a case with his skull between his feet.

THE CULTURE SHOCK OF QUIET DEATH

I had become friendly with a farm family who also ran a little cafe out on the road where the buses stopped. One morning I was sitting around waiting for a bus to take me down to the next village when one of the farmer's sons and his wife sat down by me. She was holding a baby in her arms who was dying of pneumonia, and I sat there listening to that unbearable gasping struggle for breath while the family calmly gathered around the child and watched. Only the mother seemed to be upset.

I was sure that they were waiting for the bus to rush the baby to a doctor, but as the bus came closer and finally into sight they made no move. And suddenly using the most beautiful Spanish of my life, completely out of control I was screaming at them, "Your baby's going to die; you've got to get him to a doctor. Now. Now."

The young mother began to pant; her husband looked to his father who simply nodded his head in a sort of permission without saying anything, and the young couple ran down to the road and stopped the bus.

When I got back that night they told me that the baby was dead.

The next afternoon I was about a mile from town buying some pineapples from a small farmer—just past the graveyard. As I was coming back I met the funeral procession, the toy-like coffin painted in white and sprinkled with a silver dust being negligently packed on a farmer's shoulder.

Behind him and strung out for a hundred yards the family and their friends followed. The men carried bottles of *traigo,* stumbling and reeling in the mud of the trail. But while they advanced with a sort of dignity, there was also something slapstick about it. Some of them stopped to offer me a drink.

The statistics, of course, I knew—that in the country areas [Ecuador] three out of five babies die before their third year. And I was also aware of the Catholic philosophy which makes these deaths bearable to the country people. They hold the profound belief that when a baby dies, it dies in a state of grace and flies directly to heaven.

Within this framework then, the death of a child is something to celebrate; he has been released without sin from a life of suffering and poverty to become one of God's angels.

But knowing all this, I still could not accept it. Two mornings later, drinking coffee in the same little open air cafe and once more waiting for a bus, I had to leave and stand in a drizzle of rain to keep from watching another baby dying. The calmness with which they accepted his death was obscene to me.

I began to develop a grudge against the town and would make wild generalizations in my mind about the town and the people in it. By the end of the second week I had pretty much decided that I really didn't much like the people and that it would be impossible to work with them.

What I was going to do in that unrewarding spot for 18 more months was something that when I seriously thought about it sent me reeling into a real depression. I locked myself in my room for about three days . . .

Well, I got straightened around, but it took a little time; it took at least a month. And I write about this experience now not because it is particularly interesting, but because it is so typical of a volunteer's first reactions to another, a different culture. It is a hard and unpleasant time, but I think almost all volunteers at one time or another go through it.

SOURCE: Moritz Thomsen, "The Culture Shock of Quiet Death," *This World,* San Francisco *Chronicle,* April 25, 1965, p. 26. Used by permission.

ture, is the chief determinant of behavior. Who depends on whom, who communicates with whom, who can reward and who can punish may be as important as what the pertinent rules or values may be. Because people are implicated in a web of social relations—a structure of opportunities and constraints—they are subject to many pressures that lead to deviant conduct. Thus deviance is socially determined just as is conformity.

Some norms are more specifically stated than others; some have wider ranges of application than others; some permit individual interpretation to a greater extent than others. Limits are indeed set by norms, but variation in conformity is often permitted, and exceptions are also provided for. For example, a person may have to choose between one norm and another. A driver who hits another automobile to avoid hitting a child violates one norm in order to conform to another. That he does so "automatically" shows how deeply ingrained the underlying values are. In this case the relative importance of the norms is clear and there is no conflict. On the other hand, a student who sees a friend cheating on an examination must choose between conflicting norms, especially if the school has an honor system. One norm instructs him to see that honesty is upheld, the other tells him to be loyal to his friend.

Norms in conflict Few acts are more repugnant to Western man than murder and cannibalism, few assertions more readily accepted than "Self-preservation is the first law of nature." What happens when these two norms directly conflict?

During the seventeenth century a small fishing party was driven far out to sea by a storm in the Caribbean.[25] Their few provisions were soon exhausted, and it became evident that it would take many days to reach land. One of the men proposed that lots be cast and that the loser sacrifice himself to be eaten, so that the others might live. Lots were cast,

and it so happened that the original proposer lost. However, no one would act as executioner and butcher, and it was necessary to cast lots again. A butcher was thus chosen, the man was killed and eaten. After 17 days the small boat reached port in a French island where the Magistrate did not hold the survivors. Because they were English, their case was again examined by an English judge on the island of St. Kitts. He released the prisoners outright saying ". . . the inevitable necessity had washed away the crime."

Can it be taken as a general principle that under the compulsion of *necessity* the strongest of laws and mores may be overridden? Examine this case from an incident in 1884.

At the trial of an indictment for murder it appeared, upon a special verdict, that the prisoners D. and S., seamen, and the deceased, a boy between seventeen and eighteen, were cast away in a storm on the high seas, and compelled to put into an open boat; that the boat was drifting on the ocean, and was probably more than 1000 miles from land; that on the eighteenth day, when they had been seven days without food and five without water, D. proposed to S. that lots should be cast who should be put to death to save the rest, and that they afterwards thought it would be better to kill the boy that their lives should be saved; that on the twentieth day D., with the assent of S., killed the boy, and both D. and S. fed on his flesh for four days; that at the time of the act there was no sail in sight nor any reasonable prospect of relief; that under these circumstances there appeared to the prisoners every probability that unless they then or very soon fed upon the boy, or one of themselves, they would die of starvation.[26]

The court held the prisoners guilty of murder and sentenced them to death. On the argument that the killing was an act of necessity, the court had this to say:

Who is to be the judge of this sort of necessity? By what measure is the comparative value of lives to be measured? Is it to be strength, or intellect, or what? It is plain that the principle leaves to him who is to

---

[25] See *Cox's Criminal Law Cases* (London, 1886), Vol. XV, p. 629.

[26] Regina *v.* Dudley and Stephens (1884), *Ibid.,* pp. 624–638. For another case bearing on the problem of necessity and a thoughtful assessment of norms and the law, see Edmond Cahn, *The Moral Decision* (Bloomington: Indiana University Press, 1955), pp. 61–71.

profit by it to determine the necessity which will justify him in deliberately taking another's life to save his own. In this case the weakest, the youngest, the most unresisting, was chosen. Was it more necessary to kill him than one of the grown men? The answer must be "No." [27]

It is probable that this court would have found that murder had been committed even if lots had been cast and one of the mature men had been the victim, for the verdict emphasized the importance of the normative principle:

We are often compelled to set up standards we can-

not reach ourselves, and to lay down rules which we could not ourselves satisfy. But a man has no right to declare temptation to be an excuse, though he might himself have yielded to it, nor allow compassion for the criminal to change or weaken in any manner the legal definition of the crime. [28]

Although sentence of death was passed, it was afterwards commuted by the Crown to six months' imprisonment. The original sentence defended a principle regarded as essential to the moral order; the commutation of the sentence acknowledged the exceptional circumstances of the crime.

[27] *Cox's Criminal Law Cases, op. cit.,* p. 637.
[28] *Ibid.*

Adaptation 6 / *Hall* THE SILENT LANGUAGE

Much cultural behavior is so deeply ingrained that the individual is unaware of it. Even such fundamental matters as dealing with space and time are approached with subtle and profound variations in different cultures. In "The Silent Language," anthropologist E. T. Hall treats the nonverbal aspects of communication.

1. Units of time gain their meaning in social situations that are culturally defined. Being an hour late in one culture is the equivalent of being five minutes late in another.

2. Comfortable interpersonal distance for a Latin American connotes undue intimacy or aggression to a North American.

3. Nonverbal communication may be as decisive as words in determining the effectiveness of the interactive process. Time and distance elements of a culture should, therefore, be studied as closely as the overt symbolic behavior of gesture, speech, and writing.

The voices of time Time talks. It speaks more plainly than words. The message it conveys comes through loud and clear. Not long ago I learned from the superintendent of the Sioux that he had been born on the reservation and was a product of both Indian and white cultures, having earned his A.B. at one of the Ivy League colleges.

During a long and fascinating account of the many problems his tribe was having in adjusting to our way of life, he asked: "What would you think of a people who had no word for time? My people have no word for 'late' or for 'waiting,' for that matter. They don't know what it is to wait or to be late." He then continued: "I decided that until they could tell time and knew what

time was they could never adjust themselves to white culture. So I set about to teach them time. There wasn't a clock that was running in any of the reservation classrooms. So I first bought some decent clocks. Then I made the school buses start on time, and if an Indian was two minutes late that was just too bad. The bus started at 8:42 and he had to be there."

SOURCE: Abridged and adapted from Edward T. Hall, *The Silent Language,* Chaps. 1, 9, and 10. Copyright © 1959 by Edward T. Hall. Used in this form by permission of the author and Doubleday & Company, Inc.

He was right, of course. The Sioux could not adjust to European ways until they had learned the meaning of time. The superintendent's methods may have sounded a bit extreme, but they were about the only ones that would work. The idea of starting the buses off and making the drivers hold to a rigid schedule was a stroke of genius; much kinder to the Indian, who could better afford to miss a bus on the reservation than lose a job in town because he was a day late. There is, in fact, no other way to teach time to people who handle it as differently from us as the Sioux. The quickest way is to get very technical about it and to make it mean something.

A well-known authority on children in the United States once stated that it took the average child a little more than twelve years to master time. This estimate is probably somewhat conservative. Why does it take a child so long to learn time? The answer is not simple. In fact when one begins to discover how many complications are involved he may wonder whether the full subtleties of time can be mastered at all.

In the social world a girl feels insulted when she is asked for a date at the last minute by someone whom she doesn't know very well, and the person who extends an invitation to a dinner party with only three or four days' notice has to apologize. How different from the people of the Middle East with whom it is pointless to make an appointment too far in advance, because their informal time system places everything beyond a week into a single category of "future," in which plans tend to "slip off their minds."

Even physiological urgency is handled quite differently by people around the world. In many countries people need less of what Americans would call urgency in order to discharge a tension. In the United States the need must be highly critical before people act. The distribution of public toilets in America reflects our tendency to deny the existence of urgency even with normal physiological needs. I know of no other place in the world where anyone leaving home or office is put to periodic torture because great pains have been taken to hide the location of rest rooms. Yet Americans are the people who judge the advancement of others by their plumbing.

Punctuality Informally, for important daytime business appointments in the eastern United States between equals, there are eight time sets in regard to punctuality: on time, five, ten, fifteen, twenty, thirty, forty-five minutes, and one hour early or late. In regard to being late there are "mumble something" periods, slight apology periods, mildly insulting periods requiring full apology, rude periods, and downright insulting periods. No right-minded American would think of keeping a business associate waiting for an hour; it would be too insulting. No matter what is said in apology, there is little that can remove the impact of an hour's heel-cooling in an outer office.

Even the five-minute period has its significant subdivisions. When equals meet, one will generally be aware of being two minutes early or late but will say nothing, since the time in this case is not significant. At three minutes a person will still not apologize or feel that it is necessary to say anything (three is the first significant number in the one-to-five series); at five minutes there is usually a short apology; and at four minutes before or after the hour the person will mutter something although he will seldom complete the muttered sentence. The importance of making detailed observations on these aspects of informal culture is driven home if one pictures an actual situation.

An American ambassador in an unnamed country interpreted incorrectly the significance of time as it was used in visits by local diplomats. An hour's tardiness in their system is equivalent to five minutes by ours, fifty or fifty-five minutes to four minutes, forty-five minutes to three minutes, and so on for daytime official visits. By their standards the local diplomats felt they couldn't arrive exactly on time; this punctuality might be interpreted locally as an act relinquishing their freedom of action to the United States. But they didn't want to be insulting—an hour late would be too late—so they arrived fifty minutes late. As a consequence the ambassador said, "How can you depend on these people when they arrive an hour late for an appointment and then just mutter something? They don't even give you a full sentence of apology!" He couldn't help feeling this way, because in American time fifty or fifty-five minutes late is the insult period, at the extreme end of the duration scale; yet in the country we are speaking of it's just right. If he had been taught the details of the local time system just as he should have been taught the spoken language, it would have been possible for him to adjust himself accordingly.

Coming to the point Our pattern allows very little switching of the position of "intervals" once they are set in a schedule, nor does it allow for much tampering with either the content or the position of the points on the time scale. How much this is a factor in other cultures has not been determined precisely. There are cases, however, where the content or "agenda" of a given period of time is handled quite differently. In the Middle East refusal to come to the point and discuss the topic of a meeting often means that the party cannot agree to your terms but doesn't want to turn you down, or simply that he cannot discuss the matters under consideration because the time is not yet ripe. He will not, moreover, feel it is improper to meet without ever touching on the topic of the meeting.

Our pattern calls for the fixing of the agenda informally beforehand. We do not, as a whole, feel too comfortable trying to operate in a semipublic situation, hammering out an agenda, the way the Russians do. We prefer to assume that both parties want to talk about the subject, otherwise they wouldn't be there; and that they are sufficiently involved in the topic to make it worth their while. With the Russians there is some indication that, while this is true, negotiation over the separate points of the agenda signals to the other side how the opponent is going to react during the actual conference. Softness on our part in early negotiation, because we do not technically fix the agenda but agree informally about what should be taken up, is often interpreted as weakness. Or it may give the impression that we are going to give in on certain points when we aren't at all.

By and large, the overriding pattern with us is that once you have scheduled the time, you have to use it as designated, even when it turns out that this is not necessary or advantageous. All of which seems very strange to the Arab. He starts at one point and goes until he is finished or until something intervenes.

Space speaks As one travels abroad and examines how space is handled, startling variations are discovered—differences we react to vigorously. Literally thousands of experiences teach us unconsciously that space communicates. Yet this fact would probably never have been brought to the level of consciousness if it had not been realized that space is organized differently in each culture. The associations and feelings that are released in a member of one culture almost invariably mean something else in the next. When we say that some foreigners are "pushy," all this means is that their handling of space releases this association in our minds.

"It's as much as your life is worth to ride the streetcars. They're worse than our subways. What's more, these people don't seem to mind it at all." As Americans, we have a pattern which discourages touching, except in moments of intimacy. When we ride on a streetcar or crowded elevator we "hold ourselves in," having been taught from early childhood to avoid bodily contact with strangers. Abroad, it's confusing when conflicting feelings are being released at the same time. Our senses are bombarded by a strange language, different smells, and gestures, as well as a host of signs and symbols.

The Latin house is often built around a patio that is next to the sidewalk but hidden from outsiders behind a wall. It is not easy to describe the degree to which small architectural differences such as this affect outsiders. American foreign aid technicians living in Latin America used to complain that they felt "left out" of things, that they were "shut off." Others kept wondering what was going on "behind those walls." In the United States, on the other hand, propinquity is the basis of a good many relationships. To us the neighbor is actually quite close. You can borrow things, including food and drink, but you also have to take your neighbor to the hospital in an emergency. In this regard he has almost as much claim on you as a cousin.

Another example has to do with the arrangement of offices. In this case one notices great contrast between ourselves and the French. Part of our overall pattern in the United States is to take a given amount of space and divide it up equally. When a new person is added in an office, almost everyone will move his desk so that the newcomer will have his share of the space. This may mean moving from positions that have been occupied for a long time and away from favorite views. The point is that the office force will make its own adjustments voluntarily. In fact, it is a signal that they have acknowledged the presence of the new person when they start rearranging the furniture. Until this happens, the boss can be sure that the new person has not been integrated into the group.

Given a large enough room, Americans will distribute themselves around the walls, leaving the center open for group activities such as conferences. That is, the center belongs to the group and is often marked off by a table or some object placed there both to use and save the space. Lacking a conference table, members will move their chairs away from their desks to form a "huddle" in the middle.

The French, by contrast, do not make way for each other in the unspoken, taken-for-granted way that we do. They do not divide up the space with a new colleague. Instead they may grudgingly give him a small desk in a dark corner looking toward the wall. This action speaks eloquently to Americans who have found themselves working for the French. We feel that not to "make a place" accents status differences. If the rearrangement which says, "Now we admit you to the group, and you are going to stay," fails to take place, Americans are likely to feel perilously insecure. In French offices the key figure is the man in the middle, who has his fingers on everything so that all runs smoothly. There is a centralized control. The French educational system runs from the middle, so that all students all over France take the same class at the same time.

Conversational distance Spatial changes give a tone to a communication, accent it, and at times even override the spoken word. The normal conversational distance between strangers illustrates how important are the dynamics of space interaction. If a person gets too close, the reaction is instantaneous and automatic—the other person backs up. And if he gets too close again, back we go again. I have observed an American backing up the entire length of a long corridor while a foreigner whom he considers pushy tries to catch up with him. This scene has been enacted thousands of times— one person trying to increase the distance in order to be at ease, while the other tries to decrease it for the same reason, neither one being aware of what was going on. We have here an example of the tremendous depth to which culture can condition behavior.

This was suddenly brought into focus one time when I had the good fortune to be visited by a very distinguished and learned man who had been for many years a top-ranking diplomat representing a foreign country. After meeting him a number of times, I had become impressed with his extraordinary sensitivity to the small details of behavior that are so significant in the interaction process. Dr. X was interested in some of the work several of us were doing at the time and asked permission to attend one of my lectures. He came to the front of the class at the end of the lecture to talk over a number of points made in the preceding hour. While talking he became quite involved in the implications of the lecture as well as what he was saying. We started out facing each other and as he talked I became dimly aware that he was standing a little too close and that I was beginning to back up. Fortunately I was able to suppress my first impulse and remain stationary because there was nothing to communicate aggression in his behavior except the conversational distance. His voice was eager, his manner intent, the set of his body communicated only interest and eagerness to talk. It also came to me in a flash that someone who had been so successful in the old school of diplomacy could not possibly let himself communicate something offensive to the other person except outside of his highly trained awareness.

By experimenting I was able to observe that as I moved away slightly, there was an associated shift in the pattern of interaction. He had more trouble expressing himself. If I shifted to where I felt comfortable (about twenty-one inches), he looked somewhat puzzled and hurt, almost as though he were saying, "Why is he acting that way? Here I am doing everything I can to talk to him in a friendly manner and he suddenly withdraws. Have I done anything wrong? Said something that I shouldn't?" Having ascertained that distance had a direct effect on his conversation, I stood my ground, letting him set the distance.

In Latin America the interaction distance is much less than it is in the United States. Indeed, people cannot talk comfortably with one another unless they are very close to the distance that evokes either sexual or hostile feelings in the North American. The result is that when they move close, we withdraw and back away. As a consequence, they think we are distant or cold, withdrawn and unfriendly. We, on the other hand, are constantly accusing them of breathing down our necks, crowding us, and spraying our faces.

Getting over a spatial accent is just as important, sometimes more so, than eliminating a spoken one. Advice to the foreign traveler might be: Watch where people stand, and don't back up. You will feel funny doing it, but it's amazing how much difference it makes in people's attitudes toward you.

SECTION 3 CULTURAL DIVERSITY

Studies of history and anthropology compel the conclusion that man is *one* and man is *many*. Everywhere the human being is the same in his biological and psychic nature. But upon that foundation he builds a remarkable diversity of motivation, custom, and belief. The interplay of man's oneness and his pluralism, his uniformity and diversity, is considered in this section.

THE CONSTANT AND THE VARIABLE

No feature of life in society is exempt from cultural variability—from language to physical posture, from concepts of property to ways of making love, from "great ideas" to the details of etiquette. To the reader of this book, many unfamiliar customs would be reasonable or even attractive alternatives to those of his own culture, for example, wearing an Indian sari or having more than one spouse. Other variations would be hard to accept, or even to think about without pain, such as circumcision rites for adolescent boys and girls or eating live witchetty grubs.

Not all variation is equally important. Variations in dress, for example, may or may not be *salient* to a culture. In some places costume has symbolic significance; elsewhere it is almost neutral, and changes in style may be easily accepted. What is salient can be known only if the culture as a whole is understood.

Cultural universals Despite manifest and even rampant diversity, there is striking uniformity. Murdock has listed the following common elements in all known cultures, arranged in alphabetical order:

Age-grading, athletic sports, bodily adornment, calendar, cleanliness training, community organization, cooking, cooperative labor, cosmology, courtship, dancing, decorative art, divination, division of labor, dream interpretation, education, eschatology, ethics, ethnobotany, etiquette, faith healing, family, feasting, fire making, folklore, food taboos, funeral rites, games, gestures, gift giving, government, greetings, hair styles, hospitality, housing, hygiene, incest taboos, inheritance rules, joking, kin-groups, kinship nomenclature, language, law, luck superstitions, magic, marriage, mealtimes, medicine, modesty concerning natural functions, mourning, music, mythology, numerals, obstetrics, penal sanctions, personal names, population policy, postnatal care, pregnancy usages, property rights, propitiation of supernatural beings, puberty customs, religious ritual, residence rules, sexual restrictions, soul concepts, status differentiation, surgery, tool making, trade, visiting, weaning, and weather control.[29]

This list could be extended if the items were analyzed further. For example, the word "authority" does not appear, as it would if the items "community organization" and "cooperative labor" were broken down into their elements.

When the constant and the variable are considered together, a more balanced response to strange customs is possible than when either aspect is considered alone. Among the polar Eskimo of Northwest Greenland, a man may lend his wife to a friend for the night, and the temporary exchange of wives is common.[30] The idea of sexual property is maintained (the

[29] George Peter Murdock, "The Common Denominator of Cultures," in Ralph Linton (ed.), *The Science of Man in the World Crisis* (New York: Columbia University Press, 1945), p. 124.

[30] George Peter Murdock, *Our Primitive Contemporaries* (New York: Macmillan, 1934), p. 213.

wife is not supposed to lie with another man without permission), but there is evidently no great value placed on exclusive physical intimacy. To someone reared in another tradition, wife-lending is a startling variation in what human beings can tolerate; on the other hand, he might find just as much cause for wonder in the fact that the ideal of hospitality is so widely subscribed to.

Cultural universals are general, not specific social forms. The content remains to be specified. Thus hospitality, the general phenomenon, may be offered in many different ways, of which wife-lending is one. What gives the Eskimo culture its distinctiveness is the particular way of extending hospitality and the special sensibilities associated with it. A culture is always made up of unique adaptations and elaborations. The universals, however, show that all peoples belong to the human species and the societies they create are *human* societies.

Cultural universals can be accounted for in three ways:

1. *The psychic unity of mankind*. Despite individual differences and cultural variation, all men are alike in being subject to conditioning, in having a similar range of emotions, in the need for security and response, in the capacity to symbolize, and in many other ways. This psychic unity does not determine specific adaptations; it does not make cultures *identical*, but it is a source of cultural *similarities*. When the same kind of organism responds to roughly similar circumstances, it is understandable that there should be similar outcomes.

2. *Requirements of group life*. Social life has functional necessities, that is, requirements that must be met if groups are to survive and flourish. Reciprocity, leadership, communication, specialization, and symbolic affirmations of group identity are not mere accidental developments. They are solutions to problems, rediscovered innumerable times as ways of dealing with the ever-present necessities of organization and solidarity. Here again, the common elements or universals are general, not specific. The particular form of leadership or feasting or exchange of goods reflects the experiences of the society.

3. *Limited possibilities*. Action and choice always take place within a framework of limited alternatives. Some limitations are set by the physical environment, especially when the society is isolated and has a low level of technology. In the polar north, shelters may be made of ice or skins, but few other alternatives are available. The principle of limited possibilities applies most clearly to the technical arts. There are many ways of making a boat or an oar, but certain conditions must be met if the boat is to float or the oar to pull; if, in addition, the quest is for a speedy boat or the most efficient oar, the technological limitations are even more severe. "The fewer the possibilities . . . the more likely are similar solutions." [31] The principle of limited possibilities also applies to language, which must have some sort of grammar; to social organization, for example, affecting modes of kinship or forms of leadership; and even to ritual, which relies for solemnity or exuberance on available modes of congregation, dance, and incantation.

Selective adjustment and elaboration Cultural diversity means cultural selection. From a broad range of possibilities each people selects ends and means that make up its way of life. "All cultures constitute so many somewhat distinct answers to essentially the same questions posed by human biology and by the generalities of the human situation." [32] Every culture faces similar problems, but each culture solves those problems in its own way. Some challenges must be met if the community is to survive; others may be neglected or not even perceived. What is conceived as a problem, for example, the attainment of a high standard of living or a low death rate, largely depends on cultural assessments. Nevertheless, all cultures go beyond bare survival: they provide opportunities for symbolic expression and the enrichment of experience.

[31] Alexander Goldenweiser, *Anthropology* (New York: Crofts, 1937), pp. 124 ff. Quotation at p. 125.

[32] Clyde Kluckhohn, "Universal Categories of Culture," in Sol Tax (ed.), *Anthropology Today: Selections* (Chicago: University of Chicago Press, 1962), p. 317.

In Adaptation 7 the value of personal autonomy is explored to show cross-cultural uniformity and diversity. The value appears in many cultures, but the ways of showing respect for the individual are diverse. However, comparison of cultures shows more than diversity: it helps identify the nature of personal autonomy and the conditions under which it flourishes. The author concludes (1) autonomy is found in freedom from subjection to the commands of other persons and (2) autonomy is compatible with, and indeed is supported by, the system of cultural norms. Conformity to an impersonal order or to objective rules is suggested as the key to freedom.

ETHNOCENTRISM AND CULTURAL RELATIVISM

Each group considers its way of life the natural and the best way. Strange groups, beliefs, or practices are treated with suspicion and hostility simply because they are strange. Identification with the familiar and the devaluation of the foreign is called *ethnocentrism*. It is the feeling that one's own culture is the best in all respects and that others are in varying degrees inferior—barbaric, heathen, or outlandish. Extreme ethnocentrism leads to a needless rejection of the richness and knowledge of other cultures. It impedes the sharing of ideas and skills that might bring a society closer to its own goals. Historically, man has improved his ability to cope with his environment through the exchange of techniques and knowledge among cultures. Ethnocentrism tends to inhibit this proved method of culture growth. Whether practiced by primitive or modern man, ethnocentrism denies the basic unity of mankind.

In less virulent form ethnocentrism appears as a cultural nearsightedness that takes one's own culture for granted and that passively rather than actively rejects others. Even a book like this, which tries to be sensitive to such problems, falls into ethnocentric terminology. The authors freely, if reluctantly, use "America" and "Americans" in the American (sic)

way. By "Americans," people in the U.S.A. mean nationals of the U.S.A. But it is a correct designation of all the people in North and South America. Latin Americans resent the proprietary way we use a word that belongs to them as much as to us. In polite parlance they use the term "Norte Americano," in colloquial speech the term Yankee, which can carry connotations ranging from friendly to bitter depending on intonation, and a repertoire of terms beginning with Gringo and ending with unprintable. From the standpoint of the "American" there is no convenient, neutral, all-purpose word that is the natural and readily-understood private property of citizens of the United States of America.

The critique of ethnocentrism is often associated with a moral and intellectual position called *cultural relativism*. This point of view was expressed by Sumner when he said, "Everything in the mores of a time and place must be regarded as justified with regard to that time and place. 'Good' mores are those which are well adapted to the situation. 'Bad' mores are those which are not so adapted." [33] In other words, there is no universal standard which an outside observer can use to evaluate cultures or cultural norms as good or bad. Each culture must be seen in its own terms. The worth of a custom can be judged only by the contribution it makes to the culture of which it is a part. In that sense, judgments and interpretations are relative; they must begin with an understanding of the social setting.

The social scientist looks to the cultural context to make moral sense of a particular practice, whether it be cannibalism or televised commercials. If he evaluates, he does so from the standpoint of the particular culture's own values and requirements. Cultural relativism encourages both a tolerant perspective on foreign ways and a closer inspection of what those ways really are and what their significance is.

Although cultural relativism is an important point of view for social science, certain limitations should be noted: [34]

---

[33] Sumner, *op. cit.*, p. 65.

[34] See David Bidney, "The Concept of Value in Modern Anthropology," in Tax, *op. cit.*, pp. 436–453; also Clyde Kluckhohn, *Culture and Behavior* (New York: The Free Press of Glencoe, 1962), especially Chaps. 16 and 17.

1. It is sometimes said that cultural relativism precludes the belief that some values are good for all mankind. In fact, however, cultural relativism itself posits a fundamental value: *respect for cultural differences.* Implicit in the doctrine is the view that all men need and deserve respect as a warrant of their common humanity.

2. Although it is proper to insist that cultural facts be interpreted according to their settings, it is nevertheless possible to discover aspects of morality that are cross-cultural:

Considering the exuberant variation of cultures in most respects, the circumstance that in some particulars almost identical values prevail throughout mankind is most arresting. No culture tolerates indiscriminate lying, stealing, or violence within the in-group. The essential universality of the incest taboo is well known. No culture places a value upon suffering as an end in itself. . . . In spite of loose talk (based upon an uncritical acceptance of cultural relativity) to the effect that the symptoms of mental disorder are completely relative to culture, the fact of the matter is that all cultures define as abnormal individuals who are permanently inaccessible to communication or who consistently fail to maintain some degree of control over their impulse life.[35]

These considerations should give pause to an extreme interpretation of relativism.

SUBCULTURES

Complex societies like the United States contain not one homogeneous culture but a multitude of ethnic, regional, and occupational subcultures with which people identify and from which they derive many distinctive values and norms, as well as social relationships and life chances. Some sociologists have suggested that there is no such thing as American culture, but instead that there is a conglomeration of subcultures. "American culture" can be thought of in several ways: as including all the subcultures, as consisting of only those elements that all subcultures share, or as restricted to the values and orientations that are subscribed to by a dominant element or the majority of the population.

A subculture is a pattern that is in significant respects distinctive but that has important continuities with a host or dominant culture. In other words, a subculture contains some of the dominant cultural values but also contains values, perspectives, or life-styles peculiar to itself. Every group has some patterns of its own, but the patterns of a specialized group do not necessarily affect the total life of its members and, therefore, do not comprise a subculture. A subculture, on the other hand, has a more general influence on the person and tends to give him a discernible identity.

A subculture may be based on an occupation, especially one that provides a total context for everyday life. Thus military subcultures are supported by the isolation of military garrisons, intensive training affecting deportment and outlook as well as skills, long-term career orientations, and the absorption of families into the military social system. Occupations that require special life-styles, setting the members off from the rest of the community, are especially likely to develop into subcultures.

More typical, however, is a subculture based on residential, ethnic, or social-class criteria. These subcultures tend to be coextensive with local communities and thus provide a setting for the entire round of life.

Continuities and discontinuities The concept of subculture has made a useful contribution to the study of juvenile delinquency. Some theories of delinquency stress the continuity of the delinquency-breeding subculture with its host society; other theories place greater emphasis on the uniqueness of the subculture.

A special sort of subcultural continuity is identified in Cohen's interpretation of the life-style of delinquent boys. The argument begins with a description of differences. The working-class boy grows up in a world that places no great store by self-discipline, high aspirations, deferred gratification, or community responsibility. "There is little interest in long-run goals, in planning activities and budgeting time, or in activities involving knowledge and skills to be ac-

[35] Kluckhohn, *ibid.,* pp. 294–295.

quired only through practice, deliberation, and study." [36] An immediate, close-knit world of family or gang dominates life and the rest of the world is seen as made up of victimizers and victims. These subcultural orientations are real, but the members of the subculture are not isolated from the larger society. When they come into contact with the middle-class school and other middle-class institutions, such as government agencies and large employers, they meet disapproval and rejection. The working-class boy becomes aware of his rejection and to some extent shares the low evaluation of himself. The delinquent behavior pattern is an aggressive reaction against this disapproval, both a hitting out against middle-class culture and an attempt to establish criteria of worth which the boy can meet, thus repairing his damaged self-respect.

The delinquent subculture functions simultaneously to combat the enemy without and the enemy within, both the hated agents of the middle class and the gnawing internal sense of inadequacy and low self-esteem. It does so by erecting a counterculture, an alternative set of status criteria.[37]

As a counterculture, a reaction-formation, the delinquent subculture shows its continuity with the host community. According to this theory, delinquent subcultures can be understood only by seeing their relation to the larger culture within which they develop.

A contrasting view emphasizes the autonomy and distinctiveness of lower-class culture. On this theory, the delinquent boy and his gang do not react against middle-class standards but act out values, such as masculinity, which are a positive aspect of lower-class traditions.[38]

Implications While the different interpretations of delinquency-related subcultures cannot be resolved at the present time, they point to a recurrent problem. Just as the sociologist attempts to eliminate ethnocentrism in his treatment of different cultures, so he must avoid the same bias in his analysis of subcultures. Because there are continuities with the host culture, the analyst may fail to recognize the existence and the viability of distinctive subcultural patterns. This failure may result in misleading assessments. For example, the phrase "culturally deprived" is often applied to lower socioeconomic strata in the United States and elsewhere. This signifies that in some way the cultural milieu does not prepare the members to compete in the larger social and economic world. Other writers have charged that the use of terms like "cultural deprivation" is but another instance of ethnocentrism, in this case "class ethnocentrism." They point out that while, indeed, lower- and working-class milieux may leave their members ill-prepared to compete in the middle-class world, these settings in fact constitute a distinctive subculture, adapted to lower-class conditions of deprivation and discrimination.

There can be no rule for deciding in advance when to treat a subculture as autonomous and when to see it as dependent upon or reacting against the larger cultural setting. Both perspectives can be valuable; each must be assessed for the light it sheds on a particular situation.

[36] Albert K. Cohen, *Delinquent Boys* (New York: The Free Press of Glencoe, 1955), p. 30. Another study emphasizing continuity is David Matza, *Delinquency and Drift* (New York: Wiley, 1964).

[37] David J. Bordua, "Delinquent Subcultures: Sociological Interpretations of Gang Delinquency," *Annals* of the American Academy of Political and Social Science, *338* (November, 1961), 125.

[38] See Walter B. Miller, "Lower-Class Culture as a Generating Milieu of Gang Delinquency," *Journal of Social Issues, 14* (1958), 5–19.

Adaptation 7 / D. Lee INDIVIDUAL AUTONOMY AND SOCIAL STRUCTURE

In every society we find some organized social unit; but not everywhere does the social unit provide freedom to the individual or the opportunity for spontaneous functioning. In some societies we find what amounts to dictatorship; in others the group may demand such sacrifice of individual uniqueness as to make for totalitarianism. On the other hand, in some societies we encounter conceptions of individual autonomy and democratic procedures which far outstrip anything we have practiced or even have conceived of as democracy.

It is often difficult for us to decide exactly how much our principle of personal autonomy involves. To what extent can we allow a child to make his own decisions, to speak and act for himself? At what point do we begin to allow him to do so? For example, when the mother first takes her infant to the pediatrician, she has to speak for him. Exactly when does she begin to remain silent, waiting for him to understand and answer the doctor's questions and to express his own likes and opinions and conclusions?

Permissiveness and respect Many of us feel that to allow a child to decide for himself and to act according to his own wish, that is, to be permissive, is to show respect for the unique being of the child. Yet for many of the societies we know, it would be presumption for any person to "allow" another to take what is essentially his prerogative—the right to decide for himself. These people do not "permit" others. When the children of the Wintu Indians ask "Can I" they are asking for information on the rules of the structure; for instance, they may be seeking clarification about a religious taboo or social custom. They are saying in effect, "Is it permissible for me to . . . ?" and not, "Do you allow me to . . . ?" These people do not "give" freedom to their children, because it is not theirs to give. If they do not impose an external time schedule on their infants, but feed them when they are hungry, and put them to bed when they are sleepy, they are not being "permissive"; they are showing their deep-seated respect for individual worth and their awareness of the unique tempo of the individual.

Ethnographers have presented us with many incidents, apparently commonplace and trivial, which point out for us an amazingly thoroughgoing implementation of respect for personal quality. For instance, one anthropologist visiting a Sikh household noticed that a small child, asked to entertain his baby brother, merely went up to the playpen and put in a toy truck. He did not show the baby how the truck worked; he gave the truck silently. This amazed the visitor, since she knew that the Sikhs were a people of great empathy and warmth, and with a great love for babies. She knew, also, that the child in question had approached the baby with friendliness and affection. Then she remembered the personal autonomy of the Sikh, and realized that the boy was acting consistently with the cultural values; he was furnishing the baby with the raw material for experience, and leaving him to explore without any attempt to influence him. He was expressing respect, not noninvolvement.

SOURCE: Abridged and adapted from Dorothy Lee, "Individual Autonomy and Social Structure," *Personnel and Guidance Journal*, 35 (September, 1956), 16–21. Published in this form by permission of Dorothy Lee and the *Personnel and Guidance Journal*. Copyright © 1956 by the American Personnel and Guidance Association.

Language and personal integrity Among the Wintu Indians of California, the principle of the inviolate integrity of the individual is basic to the very morphology of the language. Many of the verbs which express coercion in our language—such as to take a baby to (the shade), or to change the baby —are formed in such a way that they express a cooperative effort instead. For example, the Wintu would say, "I *went with* the baby," instead of, "I *took* the baby." And they say, "The chief *stood with* the people," which they have to translate into English as, "The chief ruled the people." To *live with* is the usual way they express what we call possession, and they use this term for everything that they respect, so that a man will be said to live with his bow and arrows. In Wintu, every interpersonal reference is couched in grammar which rests on the principle of individual integrity. Yet, for this people, the emphasis on personal inviolability did not mean that the individual was an isolate. There was such pervasive empathy among them that this, too, was expressed in the grammatical forms; if a boy was sick, the father used a special form of *to be sick* and said, "I-am-sick-in-respect-of-my-son."

Giving orders, following precepts A corollary of the principle of individual integrity is that no personal orders can be given or taken without a violation of personal autonomy. The individual takes his cues from the impersonal system of norms, not from the commands of another. In this sense, personal autonomy is compatible with, and supported by, an intricately developed social structure. In Burmese monasteries, for example, where novices performed menial tasks, the monks did not give orders. Instead, the work was structured throughout the day; and all the monk said to get the work done was, "Do what is lawful," reminding the novice to act according to the cultural tenet, not ordering him.

When the specific aspects of the structure are not clear, the people in such societies can turn to authority for clarification. And here we often find, as with the Burmese or the Navaho Indians, that the authority of the headman or the chief or the leader is in many ways like the authority of the dictionary, or of Einstein. There is no hint of coercion or command here; the people go to the leader with faith, as we go to a reference book, and the leader answers according to his greater knowledge, or clarifies an obscure point, or amplifies according to his greater experience and wisdom. He does not say: You must do this because I order you to. Yet he does use the *must* or its equivalent; he says, so to speak: As I see it, this is what must be done.

In Navaho autobiographies we often find the phrase, "I followed the advice of my parents," but rarely, "I obeyed my parents." The good Navaho does not command his child; and a mother who is aggressive toward her children, who "talks rough" to them, is strongly criticized. In teaching her children the tremendous number of taboos they have to learn for their well-being, the good Navaho mother does not say: I will punish you if you do thus-and-thus, but: Such-and-such an unpleasant thing will happen to you. If a child breaks a taboo, he is not "guilty." He has not committed a sin against the mother and is not in need of forgiveness. He has made a mistake which he must set right.

Guilt and self-respect This attitude is basic to all Navaho relatedness, so that here man is not burdened with guilt, and does not feel apologetic toward human or divine beings. He is neither grateful nor abject to his gods. As a matter of fact, he must never humble himself before them, since the process of healing, of the recovery of harmony with the universe, involves identification with the appropriate god, who would be slighted if the patient humiliated himself. The Navaho has, and indeed must have, as much respect and value for himself as for others. This is the Navaho version of the principle, discovered so recently in our society, that we cannot accept and respect others until we learn to accept and respect ourselves.

The competent child The Navaho do not differentiate between adults and children in the respect they show for personal autonomy. There is no minority status for children. For example, a good Navaho will not take it upon himself to speak for another, whether adult or child. A father, asked to sell his child's bow and arrow, will refer the request to a five-year-old boy, and abide by the child's decision not to sell, even though he knows the child is badly in need of the clothing that can be bought with the price of the toy. A woman, asked whether a certain baby could talk, said "Yes"; and when the ethnographer was puzzled by the "meaningless" sounds the baby was making, she explained that the baby could talk, but she could not understand what the baby said. Traditionally, parents do not force their children to do what they unequivocally do not want to do, such as going to school or to the hospital; children are not coerced even "for their own good."

For the Navaho mother, personal autonomy means that the child has the freedom to make his own mistakes. And the child has his freedom because the mother has faith in him. This does not mean that she has high expectations of him, but that she trusts

him. When the baby starts walking, the mother does not see to it that he is out of reach of the fire, and that all the sharp knives have been put away. The child gets burned a little and the mother helps him learn from this experience. By taking a chance on her child, the mother teaches him to be ready to meet and deal with danger, instead of warning him away from danger. This trust means that the child has freedom to move, to act, to undertake responsibility.

Coercion and leadership So the individual remains inviolate.

No one coerces another among the Navaho. There is no political coercion, and all leadership is traditionally incidental. Men do not seek leadership; and white employers have found that the Navaho are reluctant to become foremen, however able they may be, and in spite of the higher pay. It is "fundamentally indecent," according to Clyde Kluckhohn, a close student of the Navaho, "for a single individual to presume to make decisions for the group."

Conclusion If the societies mentioned here present an enviable consistency in the expression of the principle of individual integrity, it is well to keep in mind that there may be no special virtue in this; at the time these societies were studied, they enjoyed great social homogeneity, and were relatively unchanging over time. The children could learn the adult role at home by gradually sharing the life of the father or mother, as a matter of course, expecting and wanting to live the life of the parents, and to hold the same values and principles. However, the consistency was there; the principle was upheld by the various aspects of the culture, even by the very grammar of the language as among the Wintu.

The practices described here are not for others to copy. They are offered as evidence that law and limits and personal autonomy can coexist effectively, that spontaneity is not necessarily killed by group responsibility, that respect for individual integrity is not an end to be achieved by specific means, but that it can exist only if it is supported by deep conviction and by the entire way of life.

SECTION 4 CULTURAL ADAPTATION AND CHANGE

This section examines several aspects of culture dynamics: (1) evolution, (2) the impact of technology, and (3) acculturation.

CULTURE, CIVILIZATION, AND EVOLUTION

In the eighteenth and nineteenth centuries, the comparative study of societies was dominated by the idea of evolution. The rise of science, industrialism, and

democracy was accompanied by philosophies that celebrated the rationality of man, his freedom from traditional beliefs, and his moral progress from darkness to enlightenment. This point of view predated the theories of Charles Darwin, although nineteenth-century biological evolutionism and the discoveries of archaeology strengthened the conviction of men who believed in social evolution.

A leading evolutionist was Edward B. Tylor (1832–1917). Like others, he believed that culture evolves in successive stages: from savagery through barbarism to civilization. The idea of a *unilineal* (one-track) development through the three stages was well established by the late nineteenth century. It had been used earlier by the Scottish historian William Robertson (1721–1793) and the American ethnologist Lewis Henry Morgan (1818–1881).

Two strands were evident in the theory of evolution. One was *technical* progress, the advance of *homo faber* (man the maker) from primitive stone-chipper to master of complex machines. The other was *moral and symbolic* progress, the development of higher moral standards and of a more complex intellectual and aesthetic life. The separation of these two strands is a major theme in the critique of evolutionary doctrines.

Tylor thought of himself as a student of natural history, and he was well aware of the need to distinguish observed development from preferences and justifications:

The rites of sacrifice and purification may be studied in their stages of development without entering into questions of their authority and value, nor does an examination of the successive phases of the world's belief in future life demand a discussion of the arguments adduced for or against the doctrine itself.[39]

While Tylor believed that "civilization may be looked upon as the general improvement of mankind by higher organization of the individual and of society, to the end of promoting man's goodness, power, and happiness," [40] he recognized that there were difficulties in such a position. He noted exceptions to the general rule that technical progress leads to moral advancement:

Industrial and intellectual culture by no means advances uniformly in all its branches, and in fact excellence in various of its details is often obtained under conditions which keep back culture as a whole. . . . To have learnt to give poison secretly and effectually, to have raised a corrupt literature to pestilent perfection, to have organized a successful scheme to arrest free enquiry and proscribe free expression, are works of knowledge and skill whose progress toward their goal has hardly conduced to the general good. . . . If not only knowledge and arts [the technical arts], but at the same time moral and political excellence, be taken into consideration, it becomes yet harder to reckon on an ideal scale the advance or decline from stage to stage of culture. In fact, a combined intellectual and moral measure of human condition is an instrument which no student has as yet learnt properly to handle.[41]

Nevertheless, Tylor kept the faith as he saw it, concluding that there was a general tendency for "institutions which can best hold their own in the world gradually [to] supersede the less fit ones." [42]

Unilineal theories are usually criticized for arguing that all cultures follow a similar course of development. It is also important that Tylor's (and his predecessors') theories were comprehensive. A comprehensive theory of social evolution sees progress as an attribute of the whole cultural system. It assumes that, at least in the long run, there is a correlation between technical advance, moral enlightenment, and symbolic enrichment. The comprehensive theory uses "culture" and "civilization" as synonyms.

Contemporary thought More recent thought and research has preserved the idea of evolution but has done so *selectively*. Archaeological findings show the gradual development of technical skills and associated ways of life. For example, recently reported excavations in the Mexican valley of Tehuacán show an evolution over thousands of years, from primitive hunting and plant collecting, using simple stone implements, to a mainly agricultural society with extensive social organization and complex tools. (See "The Rise of Civilization in Tehuacán," p. 78.)

Savagery, barbarism, and civilization are terms still

---

[39] Edward B. Tylor, *Primitive Culture: Researches into the Development of Mythology, Philosophy, Religion, Language, Art, and Custom* (5th ed.; London: Murray, 1913), Vol. 1, p. 23. (First edition, 1871.)

[40] *Ibid.,* p. 27.

[41] *Ibid.,* pp. 27–28.

[42] *Ibid.,* p. 69.

used by British scholars, but with limited moral or aesthetic connotations. Some argue that "historical changes can be judged by the extent to which they have helped our species to survive and multiply." [43] Others would doubt that population growth in itself is a valid criterion of worth. However, the main stress is not on evaluation but on objective analysis of technological change and its contribution to social organization.

Savagery refers to a hunting and gathering economy beginning "perhaps 500,000, perhaps 250,000 years ago, with man emerging as a rare animal and a *food gatherer,* which lived like any other beast of prey, a parasite on other creatures by catching and collecting what food nature happened to provide." [44] This was the characteristic mode of life during the aeons of the Old Stone (Paleolithic) Age. *Barbarism* appears in the relatively recent past of the New Stone (Neolithic) Age, about 10,000–12,000 years ago, marked by animal husbandry, some agriculture, and permanent settlement. Civilization, the Age of Metals, is ushered in by the capacity of the economy to produce a surplus able to support urban centers and complex social organization; writing, metallurgy, commerce, and bureaucracy are hallmarks of the age.

In this scheme civilization and culture are not necessarily identical. A civilized society is one that has a highly developed technology, including a complex division of labor. It may or may not be a "good" society, and its culture may or may not be of higher quality than that of a society having a much simpler technology.

TECHNOLOGY AND CULTURE

Implicit in a number of the nineteenth-century theories of cultural evolution was a postulate of *technological determinism.* The growth of culture was seen as closely dependent on the capacity of man to control his environment. Specific ways of dealing with nature determined social organization, and the latter in turn decisively affected values, forms of government, even religion and the arts. (See the discussion of the Tanala, p. 56.)

The most influential evolutionary theory taking technological change as its starting point is found in the writings of Karl Marx (1818–1883). Marx, together with his collaborator Friedrich Engels (1820–1895), developed the doctrine of *historical materialism,* which holds that changes in technology invariably produce corresponding changes in the way work is organized. The latter includes, for example, the distribution of authority and power within the work unit. Taken together, the technology and the "relations of production" form the *material substructure* of the society. This substructure defines the nature of the society, for all the other institutions are "superstructure," ultimately serving and dependent upon the material base. For this reason Marxists think of "capitalist society" as defined by the economic substructure. Government, law, education, moral codes, family organization, and philosophy become "capitalist" institutions.

The following is a sample of Marx's argument:

These social relations between the producers, and the conditions under which they exchange their activities and share in the total act of production, will naturally vary according to the character of the means of production. With the discovery of a new instrument of warfare, the fire-arm, the whole internal organization of the army was necessarily altered, the relations within which individuals compose an army and can act as an army were transformed, and the relation of different armies to one another was likewise changed.

The social relations within which individuals produce, *the social relations of production, are altered, transformed, with the change and development of the material means of production, of the forces of production. The relations of production in their totality constitute what is called the social relations, society,* and, moreover, a society at a definite stage of development, a society with a unique and distinctive character. Ancient society, feudal society, bourgeois (or capitalist) society, are such totalities of re-

[43] V. Gordon Childe, *Man Makes Himself* (New York: [Mentor] New American Library, 1952), p. 17.

[44] V. Gordon Childe, *What Happened in History* (Baltimore: [Pelican] Penguin Books, 1964), p. 30.

THE RISE OF CIVILIZATION IN TEHUACÁN

The people of the valley of Tehuacán lived for thousands of years as collectors of wild vegetable and animal foods before they made their first timid efforts as agriculturists. Although the inhabitants of this arid highland pocket of Mexico were not the first or the only people in the Western Hemisphere to bring wild corn under cultivation, they were the first whose evolution from primitive food collectors to civilized agriculturists has been traced in detail.

From a hazy beginning some 12,000 years ago until about 7000 B.C., the people of Tehuacán were few in number. They wandered the valley from season to season in search of jackrabbits, rats, birds, turtles, and other small animals, as well as such plant foods as became available at different times of the year. Only occasionally did they manage to kill one of the now extinct species of horses and antelopes whose bones mark the lowest cave strata. These people used only a few simple implements of flaked stone: leaf-shaped projectile points, scrapers, and engraving tools.

Around 6700 B.C. this simple pattern changed, and from then until about 5000 B.C. the people shifted from being predominantly trappers and hunters to being predominantly collectors of plant foods. Most of the plants they collected were wild, but they had domesticated squashes and avocadoes, and they also ate wild varieties of beans, amaranth and chili peppers, but no corn. Among the flaked-stone implements, choppers appear. Entirely new kinds of stone tools—grinders, mortars, pestles, and pounders of polished stone—are found in large numbers. During the growing season some families evidently gathered in temporary settlements, but these groups broke up into one-family bands during the leaner periods of the year. A number of burials dating from this culture phase hint at the possibility of part-time priests or witch doctors who directed the ceremonies involving the dead.

By about 5000 B.C. a new phase had evolved. In this period only 10 percent of the valley's foodstuffs came from domestication rather than from collecting, hunting, or trapping, but the list of domesticated plants is long. It includes

SOURCE: From "The Origins of New World Civilization" by Richard S. MacNeish. Copyright © 1964 by Scientific American, Inc. All Rights Reserved.

lations of production, each of which denotes a particular stage of development in the history of mankind.[45]

In the Marxist scheme, technology generates economic institutions but then drops out as the immediately determining force. The economic system, not the technology as such, produces divisions within the society and vested interests that need to be defended. These aspects of the social system affect the rest of society and culture. As technology continues to develop, new forms of organization are called for, and these in turn tend to undermine established economic institutions. The technology of mass production, it is held, calls for very large organizations and state

[45] T. B. Bottomore and Maximilien Rubel (eds.), *Karl Marx: Selected Writings in Sociology and Social Philosophy* (New York: McGraw-Hill, 1956), pp. 146–147. Emphasis in original.

corn, the water-bottle gourd, two species of squash, the amaranth, black and white zapotes, the tepary bean, the jack bean, probably the common bean, and chili peppers.

Projectile points tend to be smaller than their predecessors; scrapers and choppers, however, remain much the same. The polished stone implements include forerunners of the classic New World roller-and-stone device for grinding grain: the mano and metate. There was evidently enough surplus energy among the people to allow the laborious hollowing out of stone water jugs and bowls.

In the next phase the people of Tehuacán made the fundamental shift. By about 3400 B.C. the food provided by agriculture rose to about 30 percent of the total, domesticated animals (starting with the dog) made their appearance, and the people formed their first fixed settlements—small pit-house villages. They lived at a subsistence level that can be regarded as a foundation for the beginning of civilization. In about 2300 B.C. this gave way to a culture marked by the cultivation of more hybridized, larger-yielding types of corn and the manufacture of pottery.

Thereafter the pace of civilization in the valley speeded up greatly. From about 1500 B.C. on, a more complex village life evolved with refinements of pottery and more elaborate cere-

monialism, including the development of a figurine cult, perhaps representing family gods. This culture led in turn to an even more sophisticated one that started about 850 B.C. Taking advantage of the valley's streams, the peoples of Tehuacán began to grow their hybrid corn in irrigated fields. Our surveys indicate a sharp rise in population. Temple mounds were built, and artifacts show signs of numerous contacts with cultures outside the valley.

By about 200 B.C. the outside influence on Tehuacán affairs shifted from that of the Olmec of the east coast to that of Monte Alban to the south and west. The valley now had large irrigation projects and substantial hilltop ceremonial centers surrounded by villages. In this phase some of the population proceeded to full-time specialization in various occupations, including the development of a salt industry. New domesticated food products appeared—the turkey, the tomato, the peanut, and the guava.

Starting about A.D. 700, Monte Alban influences gave way to the influence of the Mixtecs. This period saw the rise of true cities in the valley, of an agricultural system that provided some 85 percent of the total food supply, of trade and commerce, a standing army, large-scale irrigation projects and a complex religion. Finally, just before the Spanish Conquest, the Aztecs took over from the Mixtecs.

planning. At the same time, the great material surplus made possible by the new technology creates a potential for a new society and a new condition of man. Marx thought that capitalist society would inevitably be replaced by socialism. However, he did not anticipate the alternative forms that a post-capitalist world might take.

While evolutionary theory tended, on the whole,

to welcome technological advance and to look with optimism on its promise for mankind, the contemporary mood is more pessimistic, permeated by anxiety for the negative effect of technology on human values and the health and genetic constitution of all living things. It is urged that man's achievement should be judged by his symbolic life rather than by his conquest of nature.[46] Technology does not de-

[46] See Lewis Mumford, *The Myth of the Machine* (New York: Harcourt, Brace & World, 1967).

Woman with Loaves, *by Pablo Picasso (1905). Modern mass-produced bread—soft and frothy, thin of crust—is a distant relative of the loaves painted by Picasso. It has been argued that bread mechanized is bread degraded; that modern technology has made bread a less "organic" substance and thereby has reduced its capacity to serve as an expressive symbol of man's relation to nature. See Siegfried Giedion,* Mechanization Takes Command, *Oxford University Press, 1948, pages 169–208.*

velop evenly, and there is a continuing tension between technological achievements and the capacity of society to control their effects. The most obvious ex-

ample is the control of nuclear energy, but the same basic problem is created by the proliferation of automobiles and the widespread use of insecticides and antibiotics. A striking and unanticipated illustration was the disaster produced by the release of crude oil from a huge tanker disabled off the coast of England in 1967. The oil contaminated beaches of both England and France, destroyed birds, fish, and other marine life, and perhaps caused a profound dislocation of the natural environment.

Mass culture   When the technology of mass communication makes literature, music, drama and other activities available to very large numbers, as it does in contemporary America, intellectual and aesthetic standards are likely to be lowered and creative ideals may be jeopardized. This problem is not peculiar to the twentieth century. In eighteenth-century England, for instance, there was a mass market for literary goods, such as popular novels and magazines, and much discussion of the threat to standards of taste and morality.[47] Today there is similar concern among intellectuals that standards are being debased, that "mass culture" is pushing "high culture" into a precarious position.

Mass culture is oriented toward entertainment of large numbers of people and of course has become a major industry. It offers easy access to a part of the world of art and letters, and this is a key to its success. In order to win and hold their audiences, the producers of mass culture are ready to "give the people what they want" even if this means radically lowering standards.[48]

There is no doubt that some lowering of standards has occurred, but it is quite possible that improvement in popular taste has also taken place. This is not known to be so, nor is it known what effect mass culture has on the production of truly creative works of high standard. Perhaps the main question is

[47] Leo Lowenthal and Marjorie Fiske, "The Debate over Art and Popular Culture in Eighteenth-Century England," in Mirra Komarovsky (ed.), *Common Frontiers of the Social Sciences* (Glencoe: The Free Press, 1957).

[48] See Bernard Rosenberg and David M. White (eds.), *Mass Culture* (Glencoe: The Free Press, 1957); Max Lerner, *America as a Civilization: Life and Thought in the United States Today* (New York: Simon and Schuster, 1957). For an early but still valuable treatment of this subject, see Alexis de Tocqueville, *Democracy in America* (New York: Knopf, 1945), Vol. II, pp. 48, 51–52.

whether relatively low-grade forms of art necessarily drive out the good, or whether they can exist side by side in successful but uneasy accommodation. These matters have not been carefully studied.

ACCULTURATION

Acculturation refers to one people's taking on elements from the culture of another. The term has also been used as a synonym for *socialization,* the acquisition of ways of behaving and valuing by individuals. All cultural acquisitions are learned, and some writers use acculturation and socialization interchangeably. In doing so, they signify that they are chiefly interested in the molding of individual personality and behavior. (See SOCIALIZATION.) In this book we reserve the word *acculturation* for the process of cultural change induced by contact with foreign cultures. Usually both cultures in a contact situation are changed, although one may be more profoundly influenced than the other. In the modern world no culture is completely isolated and unaffected by others, but the intensity and duration of contact vary from place to place and from time to time. Many primitive peoples as well as modern men travel great distances, and in doing so, they carry with them cultural forms that are adopted by others and from whom in turn they acquire new practices. The Indians of North America traded their wares over a wide area. In the Southeast the population of whole villages visited neighboring tribes for a season of contests and recreation, and in the course of these social relations, acculturation took place.

Selectivity of acculturation   Except at the very end of the process, acculturation goes on selectively. This was the case, for example, at the time of the Norman Conquest (1066), which established a new upper class in English society as well as a new political control. The Norman French influence was reinforced by continuous contact with France. Changes induced in the English language testify both to the depth of French influence in English society and the

high status occupied by the French in other than political facets of English life.

It is a remark that was first made by John Wallis and that has been very often repeated, especially since Sir Walter Scott made it popular in *Ivanhoe,* that while the names of several animals in their lifetime are English (*ox, cow, calf, sheep, swine, boar, deer*), they appear on the table with French names (*beef, veal, mutton, pork, bacon, brawn, venison*). This is generally explained from the masters leaving the care of the living animals to the lower classes, while they did not leave much of the meat to be eaten by them. But it may with just as much right be contended that the use of the French words here is due to the superiority of the French *cuisine,* which is shown by a great many other words as well, such as *sauce, boil, fry, roast, toast, pasty, pastry, soup, sausage, jelly, dainty;* while the humbler *breakfast* is English, the more sumptuous meals, *dinner* and *supper,* as well as *feasts* generally, are French.[49]

Break with tradition: After World War II, young Japanese rapidly adopted "progressive" Western styles.

---

[49] Otto Jespersen, *Growth and Structure of the English Language* (New York: D. Appleton & Co., 1923), p. 89. Reprinted by permission of Appleton-Century-Crofts, Inc.

Foreign influences are received differently by different parts of a population. Some occupational or status groups, such as entrepreneurs or landholders or legal experts, may be in a strategic position to benefit from the introduced technology and knowledge. Others, such as technicians in aboriginal crafts or ceremonial experts, may perceive the foreign culture as threatening and destructive to vested interests and to be resisted at all costs.

Culture contacts of migrants Even the tourist in his native land encounters a sense of strangeness and unsureness in a different community. The customs of the new place must be learned if he is to be comfortable in it. But because the language difficulties are small, a minor matter of accent or dialect, and because customs are similar, he soon feels at home. The tourist in a foreign land has greater practical difficulties. Language and customs are strange, and he may be unsure of himself. Nevertheless, his tourist status lends him a degree of invulnerability, and he is not obliged to adjust fully to the land he is visiting. He is expected not to know; he can err without reprisal; he may even break some laws with impunity. His relations tend to be of a surface character, and if there is strain or conflict, it, too, is superficial. His ties to his homeland are unimpaired, and his native culture remains a steady reference for his judgments and actions.

The immigrant, however, by the very act of his movement alienates himself from his native culture. For an English immigrant to the United States or Australia or for a Portuguese immigrant to Brazil, the adjustment is relatively easy because cultural differences are not very great, but even in cases like these, there is strangeness, dislocation, and perhaps rejection of the new land and of its different ways.

For millions of immigrants, however, the cultural gaps are very great, and some people remain for the rest of their lives strangers in a strange land. The extent of dislocation of eighteenth- and nineteenth-century immigrants and their feelings of extreme insecurity are hard to appreciate in a time when cultural barriers have been reduced by easy travel and mass communication and when people of most nations are aware of other nations and, in a sense, prepared for differences. Although immigrants to the United States have come from diverse origins and statuses, many were peasants displaced from their land by economic and population pressures and the changing character of European society. Some had little conception of what awaited them in the New World, or indeed, of what their own land was like beyond their provincial confines. They knew intimately only their own locality, their neighbors, and the town to which they went to trade and for the Fairs. They were illiterate and uninformed or misinformed about the city and transportation, and the trip from farm to town to port city to the New World was a series of arduous experiences in which luck and native wit had to substitute for sure knowledge.

The qualities that were desirable in the good peasant were not those conducive to success in transition. Neighborliness, obedience, respect, and status were valueless among the masses that struggled for space on the way. They succeeded who put aside the old preconceptions, pushed in, and took care of themselves. This experience . . . [brought] into question the validity of the old standards of conduct. . . .[50]

The first culture conflict of the migrant was expressed as a conflict between the folk culture of the peasant and the cosmopolitan forms of an emerging commercial society. The conflict began in the migrant's homeland in his dealings with government officials and shipping agents who operated on the basis of rules strange to the migrant and mistrusted by him. It increased in the new land, where much more was strange and therefore suspect. In the New World the sense of rootlessness, of *anomie*, was compounded by more profound differences of language and custom. Only the expanding economy of America permitted so many with the skills of a folk culture to make their way in the culture of the New World. However well the immigrant learned the ways of his new country, there remained throughout his life important areas of knowledge and experience in which he was insecure and to which his adjustments

---

[50] Oscar Handlin, *The Uprooted* (Boston: Little, Brown, 1951), p. 61. Quoted by permission of Little, Brown & Co.

were faulty. He was, in a sense, "marginal" between the Old World and the New.

Stimulated invention Acculturative influences may stimulate inventions as well as modify or replace existing forms. One of the most remarkable cases of this kind was the invention early in the nineteenth century of a system of writing by Sequoyah, a Cherokee Indian. The stimulus for Sequoyah was an understanding of the function of writing as performed by the white man, and he wished to bring this art to his own people. Over a period of years he tried out a number of techniques, including picture writing, until he hit upon devising a separate symbol for each of the eighty-odd syllable sounds in Cherokee. The full execution of the idea required years of disciplined endeavor as well as the initial stroke of genius. The quality of Sequoyah's single-handed invention of writing and the extent of its immediate application are probably unique in recorded history.

The syllabary proved highly practical. Cherokee speakers needed only to memorize the symbols with their associated sounds in order to become literate in their language. In this respect the Cherokee system of writing is superior to English. A Cherokee can master reading and writing in a matter of a few months, compared with the three or four years of schooling required for basic knowledge of written English. On the other hand, compared with classical Chinese, for example, English has a writing system of only moderate difficulty. Chinese takes several times as much schooling as does English for comparable levels of literacy.

In a very short time after Sequoyah's invention was accepted, the Cherokee nation became literate, and this stimulated further developments. Type was cast in the syllabary, the Bible and other religious works were translated into Cherokee, and a newspaper was established. An unanticipated consequence of the invention was to give the medicine men a means for perpetuating their tribal learning. Traditions that had been handed down by word of mouth for many generations were preserved for posterity in the notebooks of the medicine men. A folklore became a literature.

CHAPTER IV
SOCIALIZATION

*by **Gertrude Jaeger Selznick** in collaboration*
with L.B. and P.S.

SECTION 1 INTRODUCTION

From the point of view of society, socialization is the way culture is transmitted and the individual is fitted into an organized way of life. Socialization is a life-long process. It begins very early, and in due course the child learns to take part in group life and to embody in some degree the values of his society and of groups within it. As the individual participates in new social forms and institutions, he learns new disciplines and develops new values. While parents are usually the chief agents for socializing the child, they are themselves socialized in taking on the parental role and the values of parenthood.

From the point of view of the individual, socialization is the fulfillment of his potentialities for personal growth and development. Socialization humanizes the biological organism and transforms it into a *self* having a sense of identity, capable of disciplined and ordered behavior, and endowed with ideals, values, and aspirations. Socialization regulates behavior, but it is also the indispensable condition for individuality and self-awareness. Thus socialization has two complementary meanings: the transmission of culture and the development of personality.

BIOLOGICAL BASIS OF SOCIALIZATION

The human infant comes into the world as a biological organism with animal needs and impulses and certain innate capacities. Man's biological nature makes socialization both possible and necessary. For example, socialization is possible because man has the inborn capacity to use language, but this capacity is realized only with socialization. The following are some of the biological characteristics of the human animal on which socialization is based:

Absence of instincts An instinct is a relatively complex behavior pattern biologically fixed for a species. Nest-building techniques among birds are a familiar example: they vary between species but not within species. If man possessed such biologically fixed behavior patterns, they would limit his learning and his socialization; variation and change would then be impossible.

Man has biological drives rather than instincts. A drive, such as hunger or sex, is an organic tension that is felt as discomfort or impulse but does not direct behavior to specific goals or in specific ways. A drive impels activity but does not determine it in detail. That man is activated by drives rather than by biologically fixed behavior patterns makes his needs amenable to social direction.

The absence of biological instincts makes socialization *possible*. Other aspects of man's biological nature make socialization *imperative*.

Interactional needs   Interaction with others during infancy is a biological need of many higher animals. If deprived of bodily contact and interaction in early life, rhesus monkeys develop behavioral aberrations and are unable to mate as adults.[1] A few females who were deprived in this way were impregnated but were incapable of maternal behavior and often beat, bit, and maltreated their young.

In an experiment, infant monkeys were taken from their biological mothers and each infant was placed in a cage with two mock "mothers," one constructed of wire, the other covered with soft cloth. Some monkeys were fed by bottles attached to the wire mother, others by bottles attached to the cloth mother. Even those infants that were fed by the wire mother spent most of their time clinging to the cloth mother. Primates appear to have a biological drive for bodily contact independent of the satisfactions of feeding.

When confronted with unfamiliar objects, the infant monkeys fled to the cloth mother. As their fears diminished, they explored the new objects, with occasional returns to the mother. If no mother or only a wire mother was present, the infants cowered in terror, screaming, sucking their fingers or toes, and otherwise manifesting fear and withdrawal. The cloth mother allayed fear, the wire mother did not.

Monkeys raised with cloth mothers did not show normal development, however, unless they had con-tact with other infant monkeys. Only then did they develop into socially and sexually competent adults. This shows the importance of interaction for biological development among primates.

These findings cannot be mechanically applied to human beings, but they are consistent with studies of children deprived of sustained human contact. One study used a Developmental Quotient to measure the progress of four groups of infants, one in a foundling home, the others in more normal environments.[2] The 61 foundling-home infants had an average Developmental Quotient of 124 for the first four months of their lives, the second highest of the four groups. Within the first year, their average DQ fell to 72 whereas the DQs of the other groups did not change. By the end of the second year the average DQs of the foundlings deteriorated to 45, which "would qualify these children as imbeciles."[3]

Two years after the end of the study the institution was revisited. Of 21 children between the ages of

Wire and cloth mother surrogates

[1] Harry F. Harlow, "Love in Infant Monkeys," *Scientific American, 200* (June, 1959), 68–74; Harry F. Harlow and Robert R. Zimmerman, "Affectional Responses in the Infant Monkey," *Science, 130* (August, 1959), 421–431; Harry F. Harlow and Margaret K. Harlow, "The Effect of Rearing Conditions on Behavior," *Bulletin of the Menninger Clinic, 26* (September, 1962), 213–224; Harry F. Harlow and Margaret Kuenne Harlow, "Social Deprivation in Monkeys," *Scientific American 207* (November, 1962), 137–146.

[2] René A. Spitz, "Hospitalism," in Rose L. Coser (ed.), *The Family: Its Structure and Functions* (New York: St. Martin's Press, 1964), pp. 399–425.

[3] *Ibid.*, p. 418.

two and four years who were observed, only five could walk unassisted, only one dressed alone, and only one spoke in sentences; most could not talk at all or knew only a few words.

Childhood dependence   Man has a longer period of physical dependence than other primates. This dependency is further prolonged by his need to learn the techniques of social living. Because the infant is helpless and the child socially inept, it is necessary to assign responsibility for child care and training. Social control transforms biological mating into the social institution of the family; the helplessness of the child thus contributes to socializing the adult.

The long period of physical dependence encourages long-term emotional dependence, and ties of feeling develop between the child and those who care for him, whether or not they are his biological parents.

Capacity to learn   The child is highly educable throughout the long period of childhood dependence. Although abilities vary from one individual to another, a high level of intelligence is an innate human biological potentiality. Man can learn more than other animals and can continue to learn more over a longer period of time. For a few years the young chimpanzee learns as well as, and in some respects better than, a human infant of the same age, but his relative rate of learning soon declines.

Language   Man's ability to learn is directly related to his capacity for language. Other animals have intelligence, but because he has language man alone has reason. When a chimpanzee fits some poles together to secure an otherwise unobtainable banana, he might be said to have insight into solving a problem. But without language he can neither reflect upon the principle nor elaborate it, nor can he convey it *as a principle* to another chimpanzee. Only through language can insight be formulated as knowledge and transmitted to and shared with others, thus becoming a social rather than merely an individual possession.

Language also expresses and arouses emotion, conveying values and attitudes as well as knowledge.

Whether as a vehicle for knowledge or for attitudes, language is the key factor in the creation of human society. By making possible the communication of ideas, it frees response and interaction from the limited confines of the purely biological. It makes possible *symbolic* interaction, upon which human society depends.

AIMS OF SOCIALIZATION

Through socialization society teaches the child what he needs to know to be integrated into the community, to develop his potentialities, and to find stable and meaningful satisfactions.

1. Socialization inculcates basic *disciplines,* ranging from toilet habits to the method of science. Undisciplined behavior is prompted by impulse. It ignores future consequences and stable satisfactions. Disciplined behavior restricts immediate gratifications by postponing, foregoing, or modifying them, sometimes for social approval, sometimes for the sake of a future goal.

Some disciplines reach so deep that they modify physiological responses; many people waken early whether they want to or not. Sometimes individuals become incapable of performing socially prohibited acts. A person may become physically ill after eating tabooed food. The sexual impulse may be so hemmed in by social prohibitions that impotence results.

2. Socialization instills *aspirations* as well as disciplines. Disciplines are often arduous and unrewarding in themselves, but aspirations help to sustain disciplines by making it easier and meaningful to give up immediate satisfactions.

Society transmits not only general cultural values that define its way of life but also specific aspirations. A religion organized around a priesthood must be able to motivate some of its adherents to become priests. An economy built upon an advanced technology must be able to motivate some of its members to become scientists and engineers. Such aspirations often entail self-denial, and socialization must inculcate these aspirations as ideals to be pursued for their own sake rather than merely for material reward.

3. Socialization teaches *social roles* and their supporting attitudes. Group membership calls for more

than a general ability to take account of others in a social relation; it requires the specific ability to play specialized roles.

4. Socialization teaches *skills*. Only by acquiring needed skills can individuals fit into a society. In simple societies, traditional practices are handed down from generation to generation and are usually learned by imitation and practice in the course of everyday life. In societies with advanced technology, inculcating the abstract skills of literacy through formal education is a central task of socialization. The individual who lacks intellectual skills is economically unproductive, relegated to the margins of society, and likely to feel alienated from both the society and himself. In other words, formal education is rapidly becoming a necessary condition for effective socialization.

Deliberate and unconscious socialization   Much of the socialization of the child, especially within the family, the school, and the church, is deliberate. Adults hold certain values explicitly, convey them verbally to the child, and support them with rewards and punishments. Cleanliness, promptness, obedience, and manliness are familiar examples of rewarded behavior.

Socialization is also a product of spontaneous human interaction and occurs without deliberate intent to train. Because the individual is part of the environment of others, people try to control and direct his behavior, not to educate him but to ensure their own comfort and well-being. The child who spoils a game of baseball because he has not learned the rules may be socialized by the scorn of his playmates, although their interest is in protecting their own enjoyment, not in socializing him. Parents are under many different kinds of pressure to socialize the child, and not the least is the fact that the undisciplined child is disruptive of the adult environment. The child responds at least as much to postural cues and expressions of feeling as to statements of approval and disapproval. Implicit values and unverbalized attitudes are important elements in socialization when they are embodied in behavior toward the child. Verbal injunctions that are not reinforced in

the lives and attitudes of parents are relatively ineffective.

SOCIALIZATION AND CONFORMITY

Socialization inevitably produces a degree of conformity. People brought up under similar circumstances tend to resemble each other in habits, values, and personality. However, socialization does not result in complete conformity. Many factors encourage individuality and uniqueness. Only three are mentioned here:

1. Socialization is not smooth and uniform. The individual is socialized by many agencies—the family, the school, his playmates, his occupation, and in a literate society by the written word. If they emphasize different values, the agencies may compete for the loyalty of the individual and, therefore, reduce his conformity to some group values. Bright children of lower-class families may be encouraged in school to pursue advanced study, but family values may discourage intellectual aspirations.

2. Nonconformity may be a value in itself and be transmitted, like any other value, through socialization. For instance, individuals may be taught to admire people who are independent or even rebellious.

3. The kind of socialization to which the individual is exposed is to some extent modified by his unique capacities. Little is known about the relation between the biological potentialities of the newborn infant and the abilities of the mature adult. Although all capacities depend on training for their full realization, some seem to be inborn—for example, intelligence and mathematical and musical talent. It may be that irritable or placid, responsive or passive temperaments are also biologically innate tendencies. To some extent, how a person is socialized depends upon these potentialities and tendencies. The child learns only what he is taught, but what he is taught depends to some degree upon what he can learn. This is evident in the case of extraordinary talent or lack of it, but the same principle is involved when parents adjust their discipline and aspirations to the responses of the average child.

Section 2 treats the socialization of the child and the emergence of the self with special attention to personal interaction and the interplay of response between parent and child. In Section 3 the agencies of socialization are considered, especially their unique functions and their capacities to influence the individual. Section 4 discusses adult socialization, including the importance of social roles in the development of individual personality. Section 5 deals with culture, personality, and human nature.

SOURCES AND READINGS

James H. S. Bossard and Eleanor S. Boll, *The Sociology of Child Development* (3rd ed.; New York: Harper & Row, 1960).

Orville G. Brim, Jr. and Stanton Wheeler, *Socialization After Childhood* (New York: Wiley, 1966).

Roger Brown, *Social Psychology* (New York: The Free Press of Glencoe, 1965).

Frederick Elkin, *The Child and Society* (New York: Random House, 1960).

S. L. Frost and G. R. Hawkes, *The Disadvantaged Child* (Boston: Houghton Mifflin, 1966).

Edwin M. Lemert, *Social Pathology* (New York: McGraw-Hill, 1951).

Alfred R. Lindesmith and Anselm L. Strauss, *Social Psychology* (Rev. ed.; New York: Holt, Rinehart and Winston, 1956).

Gardner Lindzey and Elliot Aronson (eds.), *Handbook of Social Psychology* (2nd ed. rev.; Cambridge: Addison-Wesley, 1968), 5 vols.

Eleanor E. Maccoby, Theodore M. Newcomb, and Eugene L. Hartley (eds.), *Readings in Social Psychology* (New York: Holt, Rinehart and Winston, 1958).

Daniel R. Miller and Guy E. Swanson, *The Changing American Parent* (New York: Wiley, 1958).

Jean Piaget, *Language and Thought of the Child* (New York: Harcourt, Brace & World, 1926).

Robert R. Sears, Eleanor E. Maccoby, and Harry Levin, *Patterns of Child Rearing* (New York: Harper & Row, 1957).

Tamotsu Shibutani, *Society and Personality* (Englewood Cliffs, N.J.: Prentice-Hall, 1961).

Neil J. Smelser and William T. Smelser (eds.), *Personality and Social Systems* (New York: Wiley, 1963).

Anselm L. Strauss (ed.), *The Social Psychology of George Herbert Mead* (Chicago: Phoenix Books, University of Chicago Press, 1956).

Periodicals

Journal of Personality and Social Psychology

Sociometry

SECTION 2 SOCIALIZING THE CHILD

The molding of the child, whether deliberate or unintentional, is accomplished through person-to-person interaction. The social response of the parent, though geared to an immediate life situation, is based upon needs and values already formed in a particular culture and society. The child responds in turn, and in this mutual interaction the drama of socialization is acted out. Thus socialization is a two-way process.

RESPONSES TO THE CHILD

The newborn infant is responded to as a biological organism; he is taken care of and given physical attention. His primary need is food, and his most important early experiences center around the act of feeding. Feeding habits differ from culture to culture and from family to family. In some groups the infant may be fed whenever he cries, in others, only at rigidly prescribed intervals. He may be breast-fed until well into childhood or weaned early. The way the infant's biological needs are met and the regularity with which he experiences satisfaction or deprivation convey an image of the world as either niggardly or indulgent, capricious or reliable. This image may remain as a permanent part of adult character, especially if it is reinforced by later experience.

The infant is also responded to in an emotional way. Attitudes of rejection or acceptance, approval or disapproval, tension or relaxation color the physical care he receives. The act of feeding, for example, is accompanied by the mother's attitudes and physical postures, which are prompted by cultural values or psychological traits. In the 1920s the middle-class culture of the United States dictated a degree of aloofness and rigidity toward the child, but in the 1940s permissiveness was encouraged in child rearing. The mother may regard the infant as a fulfillment or a nuisance, a natural product of marriage or a disruption of her life and interests.

Importance of emotional responses As the infant grows to childhood, emotional responses to his behavior take on increased importance. The adult's responses change from efforts to satisfy his bodily needs into attitudes of approval and disapproval designed to encourage him to exercise self-control. Thus the child is encouraged to feed himself and to renounce the satisfactions of being fed. He must learn to control his elimination and to stop depending upon his mother for cleanliness.

There are also emotion-laden responses to the child as a person, toward his appearance, his intelligence, and his temperament. The parents have cultural and personal images of what they are and what they expect the child to be. They respond to the child in terms of their own psychological needs, their position in the class, status, and role structure of society, and their ambitions for the child.

RESPONSES OF THE CHILD

The earliest reactions of the human infant are biological responses to his own inner states of comfort and discomfort. When he cries, he neither knows that he cries nor does he cry to gain attention. Gradually, however, he associates his crying with the attention and satisfaction he receives. He learns to cry purposively to bring a ministering response. By employing the cry to stimulate response in another, the infant enters into interpersonal communication. Later the child is able to forego crying and say instead, "I am hungry."

The physical dependence of the child upon the parents and in particular upon the mother soon develops into emotional involvement, largely because the parents are a source of *both* frustration and satisfaction.

1. *Rage and hostility*. The human organism does not suffer deprivation and frustration passively. It reacts by manifesting rage, anger, hostility, and aggression. As the child matures and is expected to control his impulses, part of his frustration and deprivation may be expressed as hostility and resentment against those adults who are the source of his frustration. One of the important problems the child faces in the course of socialization is the management of his aggressive impulses and his frustration.

2. *Anxiety*. Rage and hostility are immediate, sharply defined emotional responses, capable of being "discharged" by some act of aggression against the offending object. Anxiety, in contrast, is a diffuse emotional state that arises from threatening uncertainty, doubt, and inner conflict. Whereas fear is a response to a definite danger, anxiety is a vague, uneasy apprehensiveness. It is experienced when the outcome of a situation is in doubt or when one feels threatened by an unknown danger.

Man has been called the rational animal and the social animal. He has also been called the anxious animal. It may be that the prolonged dependence of the human child upon the care of others makes man peculiarly prone to anxiety. In Western society, where parents are usually the primary source of attention and care, the child's anxiety is probably greater than in societies where more people care for him.

As the child matures, other sources of anxiety are introduced. In Western society, a premium is placed upon independence and self-sufficiency. Before he enters school, the child is expected to be independent of his mother to the extent of feeding himself, managing his bodily functions, and controlling his aggressions and expressions of rage and hostility. He is then introduced to a formal and competitive system of education, where further demands are made upon his self-control. He is supposed to set goals for himself and to achieve them. Later, he is expected to choose a career, trade, or profession, to leave the parental home, and to make his own way. At every hand is the possibility of failure, and the fear of failure carries its burden of anxiety.

3. *Love and affection.* Little is known about the origins of human love. Love of the child for the mother was long thought to originate in the satisfaction of being fed. The experiments with rhesus monkeys (p. 85) separated feeding from bodily contact, which are almost invariably associated in real life. The findings suggest that the infant and young child need close bodily contact and without it normal responsiveness does not develop.

The studies of monkeys are important because they confirm what has long been suspected from the study of delinquent and maladjusted children: the child has an imperative need to evoke positive feelings from his parents or parent surrogates. Clinical studies have found that failure to evoke love in the parents may result in the atrophy of the ability to love and in what has been called a "fear" of loving.[4] In extreme cases, even when removed to environments of love and attention, some delinquent children were unable to return the positive feelings extended toward them with anything but further hatred and hostility. In less extreme cases, the failure to evoke love results in anxiety, in a sense of uncertainty, threat, and personal inadequacy.

THE EMERGENCE OF A SELF

The initial creation of the self takes place in the process of socialization. Whenever the individual takes on group values, some change in him and in his selfhood occurs.

Two important contributors to the understanding of the emergence of the self within the socialization process are the pragmatist philosopher, George Herbert Mead, and Sigmund Freud, the founder of psychoanalysis. Their views are not incompatible, but each stressed different aspects of the relation between the self and the social group. Mead, whose views are summarized in Adaptation 8, emphasized the emergence of human rationality and creativity. Freud, on the other hand, emphasized the repressive and frustrating aspects of group life.[5] Where Mead was interested in the potentialities of society for freeing the individual, Freud was interested in the ways group life constrains and distorts the self.

Both Mead and Freud divided the self into parts. Mead saw the self as partly conventional, that is, part of the self takes the attitudes and opinions of others into account; but he saw another part of the self as spontaneous and creative. Mead called this part the active "I," and the conventional and passive part of the self, the "me." If group life is rigid and restrictive, the "me" dominates the "I" and individuality is minimal. But, under appropriate social conditions, the "I" can actively and creatively influence and restructure the social process.

Freud divided the self into "id," "ego," and "superego." The superego is roughly equivalent to Mead's "me." The id is essentially the biological core of the self that society tries to but can never thoroughly domesticate. The ego is a kind of mediator trying to effect a compromise between the individual's biological needs and the demands of society. Where Mead saw the possibility of harmony between the "I" and the "me," Freud saw the potentialities for conflict among the various parts of the self.

From these views can be derived at least three important ways in which socialization creates a self.

1. *Socialization creates a self-image.* Through interaction with others and through language, the in-

---

[4] Fritz Redl and David Wineman, *Children Who Hate: The Disorganization and Breakdown of Behavior Controls* (Glencoe: The Free Press, 1951).

[5] Sigmund Freud, *An Outline of Psychoanalysis* (New York: Norton, 1949), pp. 19, 121.

GROWING SELF-AWARENESS

Margaret ignores the camera . . .

Karl and his playmate confront it tentatively . . .

. . . while Dotty's class poses proudly.

dividual comes to think of himself as an "I." As he perceives the attitudes of others toward this "I," he develops a self-image. He takes on a view of himself from observing the way others respond to him. For this reason Cooley spoke of a "looking-glass self." [6] The behavior of others toward him is the mirror in which the individual sees himself.

The attitudes that enter into the individual's self-image are, for the most part, emotive; they are attitudes of approval and disapproval, acceptance or rejection, interest or indifference. They are judgments upon the child, sometimes based on his genuine potentialities, sometimes reflecting the meaning of his potentialities for the life of the significant adults around him. In either case, the judgments that others direct toward the child, expressed in their attitudes toward him, are judgments the child is likely to make of himself.

The importance of self-images is most easily observed in pathological behavior, where socialization has created a self-image harmful to the person. In situations of neglect, deprivation, and rejection, the child may come to think of himself as inadequate; because he is unloved, he may think of himself as inherently unlovable.

2. *Socialization creates the ideal self.* From the attitudes of others toward himself, the individual also creates an image of what he ought to be in order to secure love and approval. The tendency of socialization to arouse in the child a need for love and approval and to construct an ideal version of himself is a double-edged sword. The identification of the self with ideal values, goals, and roles is an important aspect of socialization because it helps to sustain disciplines. On the other hand, if there is too great a discrepancy between the potentialities of the person and his ideal self, or if the ideal self makes extreme and unrealistic demands, the result will be a sense of inadequacy and failure.

3. *Socialization creates an ego.* Much of the behavior of parents toward their children after infancy is directed toward ensuring the child's self-control

and independence. As he matures, he is expected to develop *inner* controls, to establish his own relations to the world, and to set his own goals. Socialization is directed, therefore, toward creating a self capable of controlling and directing its own behavior.

The ego is what it does. It is a name for the integrative, controlling functions of the self, some of which are listed in Table IV: 1. In recent years the importance of these functions for the well-being of personality and its integration into society has been increasingly recognized.

Static and dynamic adaptation Part of socialization is more or less routine learning and adjustment, in which habits are formed and perceptions of the self and the world are acquired. Some adjustments, however, have deeper impact upon the personality and generate inner tensions, needs, and strivings. Fromm has distinguished static and dynamic adaptation:

By static adaptation we mean such an adaptation to patterns as leaves the whole character structure unchanged and implies only the adoption of a new habit. An example of this kind of adaptation is the change from the Chinese habit of eating to the Western habit of using fork and knife. A Chinese coming to America will adapt himself to this new pattern, but this adaptation in itself has little effect on his personality; it does not arouse new drives or character traits.
By dynamic adaptation we refer to the kind of adaptation that occurs, for example, when a boy submits to the commands of his strict and threatening father—being too much afraid of him to do otherwise—and becomes a "good" boy. While he adapts himself to the necessities of the situation, something happens in him. He may develop an intense hostility against his father, which he represses, since it would be too dangerous to express it or even to be aware of it. This repressed hostility, however, though not manifest, is a dynamic factor in his character structure. It may create new anxiety and thus lead to still deeper submission; it may set up a vague defiance, directed against no one in particular but rather toward life in general. . . . This kind of adaptation creates some-

[6] Charles Horton Cooley, *Human Nature and the Social Order* (rev. ed.; New York: Scribner's, 1922), p. 184.

TABLE IV:1 FUNCTIONS OF THE EGO

EGO FUNCTION	ADEQUATE EGO	INADEQUATE EGO
Tolerating frustration	Can substitute another goal for one that is blocked	Has a temper tantrum
Coping with insecurity, anxiety, and fear	Is able to develop psychological "defense mechanisms"	Can only flee or attack
Resisting temptation	Can resist immediate gratifications for long-range goals	Seeks promises of immediate gratification
Assessing reality	Adjusts behavior to particular circumstances and people	May see all authority figures as replicas of parents
Facing guilt	Has guilt feelings and can right a wrong	Has few guilt feelings and tries to evade them
Establishing inner controls	Can substitute inner control when external supervision is withdrawn	Quickly falls into disorganized behavior when outside controls are removed
Resisting group intoxication	Is slow to respond to group excitement	Easily loses control under impact of group excitement
Being realistic about rules and routines	Does not feel persecuted by rules and routines	Interprets rules and routines as directed against self
Dealing with failure, success, and mistakes	Can correct a mistake and is proud of success	A mistake signifies worthlessness; success, absolute worth
Maintaining ego integrity	Expresses, but does not lose, own values in group activity	Gives in easily to the authority of the group

SOURCE: Adapted from Fritz Redl and David Wineman, *Children Who Hate: The Disorganization and Breakdown of Behavior Controls* (Glencoe: The Free Press, 1951), Chapter III, "The Ego That Cannot Perform," pp. 74–140. This is a study of delinquent children with severe psychological and social difficulties.

thing new in him, arouses new drives and new anxieties.[7]

In part because of dynamic adaptation, there is often a considerable discrepancy between what parents want their children to be and the way they actually turn out.

Conclusions 1. *The child is active in socialization.* (*a*) Parents respond and adjust to the characteristics of the child. (*b*) The child does not absorb values as a sponge absorbs water; values may be smoothly accepted, or rejected, or modified in the course of dynamic adaptation.

2. *The self is social.* There is no self prior to interaction; the self develops only out of communication with others.

3. *The most significant interactions are emotional.* Not all communicative interaction has equal weight in the formation of personality. When interaction has emotional import, it reaches most deeply and has a more lasting effect on the core of personality.

4. *The management of impulse and tension is a strategic goal of socialization.* As a necessary condition for social participation and learning, this management is a critical point at which the normal and pathological begin to divide.

Caution To say that the self is social does not

[7] Erich Fromm, *Escape From Freedom* (New York: Holt, Rinehart and Winston, 1941), pp. 15–16. Reprinted by permission.

mean that it transcends its biological origins. The social self transforms but does not eradicate the biological. Nor is the self necessarily socialized in all its
aspects. Some biological impulses may not be adequately integrated with social goals. Furthermore,
the idea of a social self does not imply that the individual lacks a unique identity or is other than a
whole and independent person.

Adaptation 8 / *Mead* MIND, SELF AND SOCIETY

George Herbert Mead never presented his ideas in book-length form, and the four volumes
published under his name are for the most part stenographic reports of lectures. *Mind,
Self and Society* represents notes taken during 1927 and 1930 in Mead's social psychology,
a course he had given since 1900.

Both as philosopher and social psychologist Mead was concerned with socialization. As
a philosopher he was interested in the question: Which came first, the individual or society? Many philosophers, in trying to account for the existence of society, assumed that
individuals endowed with mind and self-consciousness could exist prior to or outside society. According to Thomas Hobbes's version of the contract theory of society, man first
lived in a state of nature in which each individual pursued his desires as best he could. This
wholly individual pursuit of satisfaction resulted, however, in "the war of all against all."
Therefore, in the interests of self-preservation and to render their satisfactions more secure,
men "contracted" with each other to accept authority and live according to rules, that is,
they agreed to create society.

Sophisticated contract theorists probably did not believe that a pure state of nature ever
actually existed, and in any case were more concerned to *justify* social norms than to trace
their historical origins. Nevertheless, their argument assumes a "natural man," who had
mind and selfhood prior to and outside society.

Mead considered the human individual endowed with mind and self as the *product*,
not the creator, of society. "The self . . . is essentially a social structure, and it arises in
social experience. After a self has arisen, it in a certain sense provides for itself its social
experiences, and so we can conceive of an absolutely solitary self. But it is impossible to
conceive of a self arising outside of social experience." (*Mind, Self and Society*, p. 140)

Mead thought the distinctive task of social psychology is to explain how society "gets
into" the individual, determines his behavior, and thus becomes part of his psychology,
or of his "selfhood." He also advanced specific hypotheses concerning stages in the development of the self from the narrow capacity to take on the attitudes of other individuals to
the more generalized capacity to relate to the community.

The essentials of Mead's point of view may be stated in a few key propositions. These are
briefly presented and explained in the following discussion.

SOURCE: A summary and interpretation of George H. Mead, *Mind, Self and Society* (Chicago: University of Chicago Press,
1934). Quotations by permission of The University of Chicago Press.

George Herbert Mead (1863–1931) was a member of the faculty of philosophy at the University of Chicago for many years. More than anyone else he clarified and illuminated the nature of social psychology. Mead disagreed sharply with the atomistic conception of man characteristic of seventeenth- and eighteenth-century "scientific" philosophy. This philosophy placed man firmly in the natural order of things; it was empirical in that it appealed to experience as the foundation of knowledge; yet it made the error of assuming that man was "naturally" endowed with both reason and self-consciousness. Mead contended that reason and self-awareness, though natural potentialities of man, could not be realized except in society. Early empiricism was atomistic because it conceived of individuals "forming" society the way atoms form matter. Mead recognized the atomistic analogy as a false one and showed that the individual is dependent upon society for his distinctive attributes as a human being, that is, for mind and self.

Preverbal interaction *S o c i a l interaction precedes language, mind, and self-consciousness.* Among many animal species sexual union and care of the young make necessary at least some continuing interaction with another individual; thus, rudimentary family life exists among species lower than man. In most cases common cooperation is made necessary by biological differences in capacity or function, of which sexual differentiation is the most striking example.

Among ants and bees, some individuals are biologically specialized to perform a single function, such as reproduction or food-getting. The survival of both individual and species depends upon the interaction of highly specific biological roles in a complex pattern of cooperative acts. In this way ant and bee "societies" arise. But their organization is, strictly speaking, a biological one, and interaction is based on physical and chemical cues.

Nonverbal communication must precede language. I n t e r a c t i o n, even on the biological level, is a kind of communication; otherwise, common acts could not occur. A dancing male bird does not deliberately intend to communicate a readiness to mate; yet communication occurs because it is more or less guaranteed by the nervous system of his species. As a rule, the dance does arouse an appropriate response in a female, much as if she "understood" the meaning of the male's behavior.

The dance communicates because it stands for something else. It is not an isolated, meaningless bit of behavior. It is a natural sign, a product and manifestation of a state of organic tension, of a physiological readiness to mate. The tensions behind the mating dance require for their relief appropriate behavior on the part of another. Thus, because the dance is a natural sign directed toward another, it can be viewed as a *gesture,* that is, as nonverbal communicative behavior.

If man could not first participate in a nonverbal "conversation" of gestures, he could never communicate by means of language. Before language can convey meaning *to* the child, the behavior of his mother must have meaning *for* him. He could never understand the meaning of "angry" or "hungry" unless he first understood an angry or a nurturing gesture. Nor would his mother's gesture have meaning for the child unless both were participants in a joint activity. The emergence of language depends upon the existence of already established, albeit primitive, social interaction.

The importance of language
Language creates minds and selves.
Despite interaction and communication, neither mind nor self-consciousness need be present in these primitive social acts; indeed without language they cannot be. Language alone makes possible ideas and communication by ideas.

The male bird's mating dance has meaning for the female when it prompts an answering response from her, but it cannot be said to have meaning for the dancing male. He is simply behaving. *He* is not telling the other he is ready to mate; if anything "tells" the other, it is the dance and not the dancing bird. The bird's behavior communicates, but not the bird.

Language makes it possible to replace behavior with ideas. Though the mother can teach her child the meaning of "I am angry" only by behaving in appropriate ways, once the child learns the words, the mother need not behave in an angry fashion in order to communicate displeasure. Having learned what the words mean, the child now has the idea of anger. Because mother and child now share an idea, the child can respond to what the mother says as well as to what she does. It is the mother (not merely her behavior) that now communicates.

Furthermore, having the idea of anger, the child can think about his mother's anger; it can have meaning for him even when she is absent or not angry. Thus as the child acquires language he acquires mind. He also becomes self-conscious as he reflects not only about his mother's anger but about himself and his own behavior. Thus he acquires a self. The attitudes of others, such as his mother's anger, lead him to modify his inner self as well as his external actions. As he matures, the child no longer adjusts merely to the immediate expression of approval and disapproval; he changes himself and his ways in order to achieve a stable adjustment to other people and his environment. He *takes the attitudes of others* into himself as enduring guides and standards, as part of his own personality.

The social self Mind and self are social. Much of language is factual, simply identifying objects about which people communicate. Though factual, these meanings are nevertheless social; they are shared and common meanings. In time "dog" and "cat" and "cow" come to have the same factual meaning for the child that they do for others.

Through language the child also learns the attitudes and emotions with which objects are viewed by his parents and others. The factual and emotive meanings of words are separable in analysis, but in practice they are learned together, and language transmits not only names of objects but appropriate or prescribed attitudes toward the objects named. Some of these are designed to enable the child better to deal with his physical environ-

ment; for example, attitudes of wariness and caution may go along with "dog" and "fire." Others are more distinctively social. Factually "cow" means the same to a Hindu as to an American, but to the Hindu child the meaning of "cow" also includes attitudes of religious reverence and respect. Thus as he learns language the child is initiated into a world of social meanings; he shares the meanings that objects have for his social group.

Just as the child learns to take the same attitudes toward objects in his environment that others take toward them, so he learns to take the same attitudes toward himself that others take toward him. When the mother tells the child that he has done something good or bad, right or wrong, she is not trying to teach him merely what the words mean. She treats the child as an object toward which she takes a certain attitude, and tries to induce the child to do the same. He is encouraged *to take himself as an object.* He evaluates and controls himself in the same way that he evaluates and controls other objects, and he does so from the standpoint of someone else. He is taught, in short, to make appropriate or prescribed responses to his own behavior just as he has been taught to make appropriate or prescribed responses to other objects in his environment.

Because this control occurs through taking the attitudes of others toward oneself, because it is control from the standpoint of someone else, it is distinctively social in nature. This is how society "gets into" the individual. Of all the animals, man alone is able to exercise self-criticism; but all self-criticism is social criticism insofar as the principles that guide it are the result of internalizing the attitudes of others toward oneself.

Prior to using the attitudes of others to think about himself, the young child is not *self*-conscious. As an animal, the human child is conscious. He has sensations, feelings, and perceptions of which he is aware. It is by thinking about himself in the light of the attitudes of others toward him that the individual becomes self-conscious and begins to acquire a social self.

Maturation and response to the other   As the individual matures he develops the capacity to respond to (1) *significant others* and (2) *a generalized other*. All higher forms of communication depend upon the capacity of each to put himself in the place of the other, that is, to control his own responses in terms of an understanding of what the other's responses are likely to be. As he learns to control his behavior in the light of another individual's attitudes either toward that behavior or toward the environment, the individual can be said to be learning *to take the role of the other*. He responds to himself and to the world as he anticipates the other would respond. The capacity to put oneself in the place of the other emerges only with maturity and in the process of social interaction and communication.

The child first internalizes the attitudes of particular individuals, primarily his parents, toward himself. At this stage he does not have the capacity to participate in organized group life or to engage in complex, cooperative games governed by impersonal rules. Social interaction is limited to interaction with specific individuals, and behavior is largely determined by the child's experience with those who are not merely others but *significant others* for him. At this stage of development, his play consists largely of simple role-taking. He plays at being a mother, father, doctor, or postman. He reenacts the behavior and attitudes of others as individuals.

The child gradually learns, however, a less personalized, more complex form of role-taking as expressed in his developing ability to participate in organized games. In baseball, for example, the acting out of a highly specific individual role is not required. The player adjusts his behavior from moment to moment, and does so in the light of what a number of others are doing and of the rules and purposes of the game. In performing his role, he responds to a *generalized other*.

Mead used this term to designate "The organized community or social group which gives to the individual his unity of self. . . ." (p. 154) One who takes the standpoint of the generalized other knows what is required to keep the group to its distinctive aims and rules. He sees not only his own role, not only the roles of particular others, but the ways roles are related in determining the outcome of group activity. Gradually the individual takes on the point of view of the community as a whole.

The "I" and the "me"   The *social self has a creative, spontaneous aspect*. To stress the essentially social nature of the self may seem to imply that the self is completely determined by the internalized attitudes of others. This is not so. To be sure, the internalized attitudes of others represent what the individual takes into account when he acts; they are the demands that group life actually or supposedly makes upon him. Nevertheless, his behavior has a large element of freedom and spontaneity. The demands of the social situation pose a problem to the acting individual, but there is considerable leeway in how he meets the problem. Furthermore, the individual can never predict precisely what his response in a given situation will be. The baseball player wants to play good ball; in this sense his behavior is determined by accepting the demands and standards of the group. But whether he will make a brilliant play or an error neither he nor anyone else knows beforehand.

Mead called the acting self the "I." The "me," on the other hand, is that part of the self that is an organization of the internalized attitudes of others. The "I" represents the self insofar as it is free, has initiative, novelty, and uniqueness. The "me" represents the conventional part of the self. The "I" responds to the "me" and takes it into account, but it is not identical with it.

There may be varying amounts of "I" and "me" in behavior. In impulsive behavior the "me" is absent; in Freudian language, the "I" is not being censored by the "me." Social control is present to the extent that the "I" is controlled by the "me." The oversocialized individual is overdetermined by his "me." In more normal circumstances the individual responds to a situation in its social aspects but does so with some regard for his own unique capacities and needs.

The most gratifying experiences are those in which the demands of the "me"—or of the social situation—permit the expression and realize the potentialities of the "I."

In primitive society the individual self is more completely determined than in civilized societies by the "me," that is, by the particular social group to which the individual belongs. Primitive society offers much less scope for the "I." Indeed, the development of civilization is largely dependent upon the progressive social liberation of the individual self. The "I" is the innovator, the source of new ideas and energy to initiate social change.

The enlargement of the self is dependent upon and in turn supports the breadth of community values. What the self is and how it develops depends upon the nature of the community whose attitudes the individual has internalized. Membership in a community is more than physical presence in it; the small boy belongs to his gang, not to the city in which he lives: ". . . until one can respond to himself as a community responds to him, he does not genuinely belong to the community." (p. 265)

The self will be isolated and alienated from other selves if it is a member of a socially isolated group or one with narrow or provincial values. The self becomes enlarged to the extent that it belongs to a group engaged in activities that bring it into contact with other groups. The rise of national states, which seems to be and often is a constraining and limiting influence, nevertheless encourages the development of internationalism and the extension of man's effective community. It does so because it fosters communication among nations rather than limiting it to communication among intranational groups. Similarly the self becomes enlarged to the extent that it belongs to a community that subscribes to universal values, such as the objective standards of science or a religious belief in human brotherhood.

Summary   1. Language is a biologically given potentiality of man. But man could not develop this potentiality without first being able to interact socially and communicate with others in a nonverbal, gestural way within shared, ongoing activities. Without social interaction language would not be possible. Out of social interaction accompanied by language human reason and self-consciousness emerge.

2. Social interaction, when accompanied and facilitated by language, leads "naturally" to social control and the development of human society.

3. Through language the individual takes on or internalizes the attitudes of others toward both the environment and himself. In this way the human being acquires a social self. The young child internalizes the attitudes of those who are significant others to him. With maturity the individual learns to relate to a generalized other, that is, to organized group activity and the community as a whole.

4. The individual need not and indeed cannot be totally controlled by the internalized attitudes of others, that is, by the "me" part of the self. The individual is also an "I," that is, someone who takes account of the "me" but is not necessarily dominated by it. The "I" may act upon, influence, and modify the social process.

SECTION 3 AGENCIES OF SOCIALIZATION

Many groups and institutions play a part in socializing the person. These agencies of socialization teach different things at different times. The delegation of specialized responsibilities to particular groups is partly a reflection of what the groups are competent to do. For example, although the family does much to educate the child, it cannot be relied upon to impart the degree of literacy that business and industry require of even "unskilled" employees. Consequently in Western society public education has become a basic social institution.

Socializing agencies may complement and support each other, but sometimes they inculcate independent or even conflicting values. This can lead to psychological conflict for the individual, but it is the necessary condition for freedom of choice among values and ways of life. During early childhood, his experience in the family is the only source of satisfactions and frustrations he knows, and the young child characteristically regards parental values as universal. As he grows older, particularly in a complex and varied society, he learns that there are alternative sources of satisfaction and approval and that a choice among values exists.

REACHING THE PERSON

In primitive and folk societies a great part of the culture has access to the child. The life of the society is lived out before his eyes; very little is not open to his direct observation; and most of the agencies support each other in socializing him. There is little competition for access to him. On the other hand, in a large and heterogeneous society, the agencies of socialization are faced with the problem of *gaining access* to the individual and of establishing the conditions which make for deep rather than superficial influence. A number of factors determine a group's ability to reach the individual and exert a significant socializing influence.

Conditions of effective access Communication is necessary in order to influence the person. In early life communication requires actual physical access to the child. Whoever wishes to influence the child from a distance can do so only through those who come into direct contact with him—his parents, his peers, or his school. In a literate society, the person is soon within reach from a distance through books, newspapers, movies, radio, and television. However, not all communication is equally effective in influencing the person.

Early access is likely to be most influential because the personality is still unformed. Groups that reach the individual in his formative years have an advantage, which largely explains the special importance of the family as an agency of socialization.

When *person-to-person interaction* permits the free play of emotion, it encourages intensive socialization. Such groups as the family, in which emotional relations are prominent, are called primary groups partly because they are primary agencies of socialization. The greater the need to influence the person deeply, the more important it is for socialization to take place in and through primary group experience.

The individual must be *psychologically accessible.* The person is ready for different influences at different times in his life. What appeals to him is related to his psychological needs and capacities. His present availability is also affected by the values he has acquired in the past. Some agencies of socialization, especially the early ones, tend to limit the areas in which the individual is open to influence by other agencies.

The more *exclusive* the access of a group to the individual, the more effective its influence is likely to be. For example, the initiation of the "swab" into the life of the Coast Guard Academy includes a two-month period of isolation from the outside world. Cut off from his former ties, he is more accessible to the Academy's influence. (See Adaptation 9, pages 110–113.)

THE FAMILY

Psychological theory has long stressed the link between early parent-child interaction and the emotional development of the individual. More recently, attention has centered on the relation between the intellectual or cognitive development of the child and patterns of interaction in the family. As discussed above, pages 94 ff., G. H. Mead theorized about a general relation between social interaction and the emergence of mind. More recent thought has traced specific connections between modes of interaction in the family and the ability of the child to learn.

Children from poorly educated, low-income families tend to score lower on intelligence tests and to do less well in school than children from middle-class families.[8] Differences are even greater for children from socially deprived minorities. These differences

---

[8] Virgil E. Herrick, "What Is Already Known about the Relation of the I.Q. to Cultural Background?" in Kenneth Eels *et al., Intelligence and Cultural Differences* (Chicago: University of Chicago Press, 1951), pp. 10–15.

tend to fix status differentials at birth and thus to violate the premises of an open society. If only for this reason, it is important to understand the relation between intelligence and modes of childhood socialization.

Intelligence tests were once believed to measure the innate capacity of the child to learn abstract materials. It is now recognized that intelligence and academic performance also depend on whether socialization arouses and develops a desire to learn. The child must "learn to learn" even when he possesses high innate capacity; whether he does learn to learn depends in part on his early experiences in the family.

Modes of socialization Methods of teaching, training, and otherwise socializing the child differ along a number of dimensions. These are presented in Table IV:2 as a set of contrasts. In practice, few parents are as consistent as the list implies. Nevertheless, research indicates that two broad patterns of socialization can be identified in American society.[9] One pattern, oriented toward obedience, may be called "repressive socialization," the other, oriented toward gaining the participation of the child, "participatory socialization."

Reward and punishment play a part in all learning, but one rather than the other may be stressed. Repressive socialization emphasizes punishing wrong behavior, participatory socialization rewards and thus reinforces good behavior. In toilet training, for example, parents may be on the lookout for mishaps to admonish; or they may ignore mishaps and concentrate on praising instances of self-control and compliance.

If the modes of socialization are compared with laboratory condition of animals, repressive socialization is similar to administering an electric shock to an experimental rat when he takes a wrong turn in a maze. Participatory socialization is like giving the rat a pellet of food when he selects the right path. Both forms of conditioning extinguish "wrong" behavior,

TABLE IV:2   TWO MODES OF SOCIALIZATION

REPRESSIVE SOCIALIZATION	PARTICIPATORY SOCIALIZATION
Punishing wrong behavior	Rewarding good behavior
Material rewards and punishments	Symbolic rewards and punishments
Obedience of child	Autonomy of child
Nonverbal communication	Verbal communication
Communication as command	Communication as interaction
Parent-centered socialization	Child-centered socialization
Child's discernment of parent's wishes	Parent's discernment of child's needs
Family as significant other	Family as generalized other

one by the negative act of punishment, the other by the positive act of reward.

In principle, participatory socialization gives the child freedom to try things out for himself and explore the world on his own terms. This does not entail leaving the child alone. On the contrary, a great deal of adult supervision is required, but the supervision is general rather than detailed and intrusive. Repressive socialization also requires supervision, indeed so much detailed supervision that it tends to be greatly modified in practice. As a result, punishment from the child's viewpoint is arbitrarily applied, depending on whether he is caught misbehaving and the parent is in a mood to administer punishment.

Repressive socialization emphasizes obedience, respect for authority, and external controls. Parents may indulge the child but also use corporal punishment, shame, and ridicule. Two-way conversation between parent and child is not encouraged. Communication tends to be downward from parent to child and to take the form of command. Gesture and

[9] Urie Bronfenbrenner, "Socialization and Social Class Through Time and Space," in E. E. Maccoby, T. M. Newcomb, and E. L. Hartley (eds.), *Readings in Social Psychology* (New York: Holt, Rinehart and Winston, 1958), pp. 400–425; Melvin L. Kohn, "Social Class and Parental Values," *American Journal of Sociology, 64* (January, 1959), 337–351.

nonverbal communication are conspicuous.[10] The child must learn to discern the seriousness of the parent's command to "shut up" by taking account of tone of voice, facial expression, and physical posture.

In participatory socialization communication takes the form of dialogue in which the child is expected to make his needs and desires known, as well as his responses to the adult world. Participatory socialization is child-centered rather than parent-centered: the adult assumes responsibility for discerning the child's needs rather than expecting the child to discern the parent's wishes.

Social class differences   The two types of socialization are not randomly distributed in society, but are correlated with social-economic level and education. For many years there was debate over whether blue-collar workers or the middle class were more repressive in socializing their children. Some of this disagreement seems to have reflected historical changes in middle-class socialization, and perhaps romantic images of working-class warmth and "freedom." However that may be, the evidence indicates that repressive socialization is now more characteristic of the working class. Participatory socialization is more likely to be found among middle-class families where in recent years the trend in parent-child relations has been toward greater permissiveness and warmth.

When asked what a good mother does, middle-class mothers emphasized understanding the child, relating lovingly to him, and making sure that he is happy and contented. Working-class mothers stressed keeping the child neat and clean, training him to regularity, and getting him to obey and respect adults.[11]

The apparent change in middle-class practices from more strict to more lenient has been related to changes in "expert" opinion as expressed in women's magazines and in *Infant Care,* the publication of the United States Children's Bureau.[12] Early editions of *Infant Care* stressed regularity, firmness, and determination in training the child. "Successful child training meant winning out against the child in the struggle for domination."[13]

In later years, the tone of *Infant Care* changed. The child was described in benign terms as mainly engaged in exploring the world, and in need of love and affection. "When not engaged in exploratory undertakings, the baby needs care and attention; and giving these when he demands them, far from making him a tyrant, will make him less demanding later on."[14] In the 1950s some doubts about permissiveness appear in the child-rearing literature and may represent yet another mode.

Practices of middle-class mothers seem to follow closely the changing trend of pediatric advice:

Both in the early and the later period, middle-class mothers were much more likely than working-class mothers to be exposed to current information on child care . . . to read Spock's best-seller, *Baby and Child Care,* and similar publications. Our analysis suggests that the mothers not only read these books but take them seriously, and that their treatment of the child is affected accordingly.[15]

Family organization   Repressive and participatory socialization are associated with different kinds of family organization. Lower-class families gain their cohesion and unity mainly through the complementarity of traditional roles. Father is breadwinner, mother is housekeeper; they often fulfill their roles with little reference to the other and little communication with one another.[16] In such families socializa-

---

[10] B. Bernstein, "Some Sociological Determinants of Perception," *The British Journal of Sociology, 9* (June, 1958), 159–174.

[11] Bronfenbrenner, *op. cit.*

[12] Martha Wolfenstein, "Trends in Infant Care," *American Journal of Orthopsychiatry, 23* (1953), 120–130; C. B. Stendler, "Sixty Years of Child Training Practices," *Journal of Pediatrics, 36* (1950), 122–134.

[13] Wolfenstein, *op. cit.,* p. 121.

[14] *Loc cit.*

[15] Bronfenbrenner, *op. cit.,* p. 411.

[16] Mirra Komarovsky, *Blue-Collar Marriage* (New York: Random House, 1962).

tion consists largely of teaching traditional roles and conveying traditional expectations to the child. Socialization thus tends to remain at the level of the "significant other" as Mead described it (see p. 97); the family represents a set of significant personal others who are role models for the child.

Middle-class families characteristically gain their cohesion by undertaking joint activities and developing common family goals. Traditional roles are modified, depending on the abilities and inclinations of the family members, and family goals are more varied. In such a setting, communication among family members is needed, because fewer goals and activities are determined by fixed notions of what is "right." Such families are better able to serve as a "generalized other" for the child. Socialization within a context of shared goals and activities is less direct and dependent on imitation and specific rules, than socialization in the traditional family. The understanding of means-end relations is stressed rather than the performance of prescribed roles.

School performance Repressive socialization and lack of verbal communication in the lower-class family contribute to the poor academic performance of socially disadvantaged children. The child's preschool experience does not motivate him to academic achievement because it does not teach him to govern his conduct in the light of symbolic rewards and future gratifications. Nor does it prepare him to interact with adults or to learn through the medium of language. Lower-class children "are much less likely than [middle-class] children to talk to themselves as an aid to 'thinking.' On ostensibly nonverbal tests and learning tasks which nevertheless require private verbal mediation, disadvantaged children perform especially poorly." [17] Not spoken to by others, these children do not speak to themselves and do not respond to the world with language. In the crowded home environment of the poor, a child's questioning curiosity may be rebuffed rather than welcomed. The

reaction of an unresponsive adult is at once a punishment and an impediment to exploratory behavior.

In theory, and to a considerable extent in fact, participatory socialization supports the motivation to achieve, and the middle-class family provides experiences in the home that are continuous with learning at school. However, middle-class permissiveness may lead to rejection of achievement.

Our data indicate that middle-class parents are becoming increasingly permissive in response to the child's expressed needs and desires. Yet, these same parents have not relaxed their high levels of expectations for ultimate performance. Do we have here a typical instance of Benedict's "discontinuity in cultural conditioning," with the child first being encouraged in one pattern of response and then expected to perform in a very different fashion? If so, there are days of disappointment ahead for middle-class fathers and mothers. [18]

It might be straining prophecy to relate the foregoing comment too closely to the emergence of the "hippie" in urban centers and around college campuses. Yet the hippies seem to come mostly from middle-income backgrounds and Bronfenbrenner's observation allows for something like a hippie-type dropout. Heretofore the dropout has been regarded as a characteristic product of disprivileged and impoverished environments, and such school failures are disproportionately from poor homes. The hippie as a self-selected dropout may be a transitory phenomenon, but it is a phenomenon that brings into question the inconsistency in child-rearing practices in many American homes.

PEER GROUPS

The individual is socialized by his equals as well as by his elders. In the peer group the individual associates with others who are approximately his own age and social status. The childhood peer group is typically a play group. In adolescence it takes on the character of a clique which introduces the child to status and class values. In adult life peer groups con-

[17] Alan B. Wilson, Arthur R. Jensen, and David L. Elliott, *Education of Disadvantaged Children in California,* Survey Research Center, University of California, Berkeley, Publication M-19, 1967, p. 26.

[18] Bronfenbrenner, *op. cit.,* p. 415.

tinue to provide a setting for social intercourse among equals.

Childhood peer groups and social control   1. The peer group introduces the child to *impersonal authority.* In the family, authority is vested in the parents as *persons,* and they determine what is right and wrong. In the play group, the child learns to obey the impersonal "rules of the game," to take an objective role such as pitcher in a game of baseball, and to develop a concept of justice which is applicable to all.[19] In time he himself becomes a representative of law and order; he conceives himself as a protector of the rules, and exercises social control over playmates who break them. (See LAW, pp. 402–406.)

2. Within the peer group the child *tests the limits of adult tolerance* with reduced fear of parental reprisal. Children in groups often behave more provocatively toward adults than the individual child feels free to do. At the same time, the child tests the extent to which his peers will go in defying the adult world and the degree to which he can rely on peer support.

3. The peer group may or may not support adult values. If it does, it is one of the most effective agencies for the *transmission of adult values.* The following example illustrates the power of the peer group and its role as the representative of adult class and status values:

Bill was a late adolescent who began to run around with a girl who not only lived on the other side of the railroad tracks, but who had most of the traits associated with that oft-used phrase. Bill's family was upper class, Bill was personally most attractive, and his mother knew the power of a peer group. Calling Bill to her, she explained with disarming friendliness that she had heard of his new girl and wanted to meet her. Wouldn't he bring her to the house, and to make it less formal, she would invite a few of his favorite friends. Upon securing Bill's wondering and semi-reluctant consent, the mother proceeded to promote, secretly, a gala event, to which she invited all of Bill's

extended clique. Bill's relations with the new girl just barely survived until the end of the party.[20]

Peer group values   The peer group exists for the sake of sociability. But behind this innocuous interest is a powerful force for conformity. Like any other socializing agency, the peer group represents a system of rewards and punishments, of approval and disapproval. It rewards the skills of sociability. It rejects the personality that disrupts the flow of good feeling and hinders smooth personal relations.

Riesman has suggested that the peer group is becoming the most important socializing agency. In present-day society people look primarily to their contemporaries for guidance and direction; modern man values most the judgment and approval of others in his environment. The most important values to modern man are the typical values of the peer group —for example, sociability, which minimizes differences and emphasizes similarities, cooperation, and getting along with others.

Other-directedness [21]   Riesman calls modern man "other-directed," and contrasts him with the "tradition-directed" and the "inner-directed" man. The tradition-directed type, e.g., in primitive and folk societies, looks to tradition and the past for guidance and models of behavior. The inner-directed type, exemplified by nineteenth-century man, guides his behavior by abstract ideals implanted in him as a child by family authority—ideals such as wealth, knowledge, and the moral life. The other-directed man, equipped with "radar," makes his way through the complexities and intricacies of modern life by picking up cues from his environment. Like the inner-directed man, modern man has a strong drive for success. But where the inner-directed man has internalized criteria of success, the other-directed man depends upon the approval of his peers to tell him what success is. (See Table IV:3.)

[19] See Jean Piaget, *The Moral Judgment of the Child* (London: Kegan Paul, 1932).
[20] James H. S. Bossard, *The Sociology of Child Development* (New York: Harper & Row, 1948), p. 507.
[21] David Riesman, in collaboration with Reuel Denney and Nathan Glazer, *The Lonely Crowd* (New Haven: Yale University Press, 1950).

TABLE IV:3 SOCIALIZATION AND CONFORMITY

SOCIAL CHARACTER	WHO SOCIALIZES?	WHAT GUIDES BEHAVIOR?	PSYCHOLOGICAL MECHA- NISM OF CONFORMITY	LIFE-STYLE
Tradition- directed	The clan, the tribe, the village	Detailed norms of village life learned by direct obser- vation	Shame: wrongdoing is a transgression against the group	Politically indif- ferent; subsistence oriented
Inner- directed	The parents	General principles laid down early in life; freedom for nonconformity within these limits; built-in gyro- scope steers individual	Guilt: wrongdoing is a violation of personal ideals	Politically moral- istic; production oriented
Other- directed	The peer group	Cue-taking in particular situations; being "hep"; built-in radar steers individual	Anxiety: the ultimate evil is being unloved and unapproved	Politically manip- ulative; consump- tion oriented

SOURCE: Adapted from David Riesman, in collaboration with Reuel Denney and Nathan Glazer, *The Lonely Crowd* (New Haven: Yale University Press, 1950).

SECTION 4 ADULT SOCIALIZATION

Adult experiences continue to shape and develop per- sonality. Adult socialization is most intensive during critical periods when adjustment to new situations must be made. If these adjustments are difficult to make and far-reaching in their effects, the individual may undergo great changes in his self-conception, habits, and values. Marriage, parenthood, divorce or death of a spouse, unemployment or financial success may serve to break up old behavior patterns and transform orientations. The person who moves from an urban center to the suburbs or from a Southern city to a Northern one has new experiences that may produce significant revisions of old attitudes and habits.

Specialized adult roles that depend on deeply in- ternalized social control require intensive socializa- tion. Adaptation 9 describes how a civilian youth is transformed into a military officer. (See pp. 110 ff.)

Three problems in continuing socialization are considered here: parent-youth conflict which may undermine earlier socializing influences, the interplay of roles and personality, and resocialization.

PARENT-YOUTH CONFLICT

In contemporary society adolescence is marked by conflict between the generations, and earlier close re- lations between parent and child may disappear. The adolescent looks to other authorities for guidance and support and often rejects parental values and ways. Some disparities between youth and age oc- cur in all societies, but there are special conditions that aggravate adolescent-parent antagonism in the United States.[22]

Differing Rates of Socialization. Socialization con- tinues throughout life, but it does so at a decreasing rate. The adolescent is at a stage of development

[22] This discussion is based on Kingsley Davis, "The Sociology of Parent-Youth Conflict," *American Sociological Review,* 5 (August, 1940), 523–535.

where learning is rapid and basic, but by the time the adult is a parent, he is no longer so able to acquire new ways or to undergo fundamental personality changes. If there is rapid social change, the habits and outlooks of the older generation will become "obsolete."

Differences in Opportunity and Participation. Youth is a period of opportunity and choice among alternatives. The adult has already made his choices. He has a settled way of life, an occupation, a defined position and role. He consolidates gains instead of exploiting opportunities. The choices open to youth may result in anxieties about the future.

Conflict between young and old may be less in societies that clearly specify appropriate behavior at all age levels. The young know that as they grow older they will automatically rise in the social hierarchy, and they do not experience anxieties about the future. The adult, backed by his superior ascribed status, is not so readily judged a failure by his children.

"The much publicized critical attitude of youth toward established ways is partly a matter of being on the outside looking in." [23] The young soldier who is "old enough to die for his country but not old enough to vote" may resent being excluded from political responsibility. The adolescent who knows how to drive an automobile may resent restrictions on his holding a license.

Adult Realism, Youthful Idealism. By its very nature, socialization encourages youthful idealism. As part of their education, children are taught the "official" ideals of the culture, and these are often at variance with its "operating" standards. Youth becomes exasperated with adult "hypocrisy," or may become cynical, dismissing all ideals as worthless and irrelevant.

SOCIAL ROLES AND PERSONALITY

Part of the socialization process is learning the specified and expected behaviors appropriate to social po-

sitions. A doctor's formal role specifies that he try to cure the ill, relieve suffering, help people, and be loyal to his profession. Additional behaviors are informally expected of a role, but these are not essential to it. A doctor is expected to be kind, well groomed, poised, and hard-working. These attributes are a kind of "halo effect" around the formal role, and a doctor can discharge his formal role without conforming to them.

Anticipatory socialization By specifying the terms of relationships, roles articulate the interactions of one person with another. The individual learns how to be a patient in relation to a doctor, a student in relation to a teacher, a husband in relation to a wife. Roles and their complementary roles, taken together, organize and integrate shared experience.

Insofar as roles consist of definite and known patterns of behavior, they provide blueprints for anticipatory socialization. The individual can prepare himself beforehand for an expected or hoped-for future role. Learning professional skills is one example of anticipatory socialization.

More significant than the learning of technical and social skills for the formation of personality is the acquisition of values, self-conceptions, and perspectives appropriate to an expected or admired role. The aspiring employee may view his fellow workers from the perspectives of the employer he would like to be. The prospective priest or nun may very early begin to acquire habits of self-discipline in preparation for the religious life. The medical student may take the role of doctor in his relations with nurses though he continues to see himself primarily as a student in his relations with faculty. [24]

Few roles are taught or learned in a wholly conscious and deliberate way. They emerge from personal interaction, and people learn what is expected of them by taking cues from others. The socialization of the person occurs in the role as he adapts himself

---

[23] *Ibid.,* p. 529.

[24] Mary Jean Huntington, "The Development of a Professional Self-Image," in Robert K. Merton, George G. Reader, M.D., and Patricia L. Kendall (eds.), *The Student-Physician* (Cambridge: Harvard University Press, 1957), pp. 179–187; and Howard S. Becker, Blanche Geer, Everett C. Hughes, and Anselm L. Strauss, *Boys in White* (Chicago: University of Chicago Press, 1961).

to its requirements and to the expectations that others have of him in that role. The medical student, for example, comes to realize that patients expect him to be wise and reassuring by observing their reactions to him when he is not.

To say that the patient "searches your face for clues" is no overstatement. . .when trying to palpate a baby once, I got a little confused and frowned in puzzlement. [I] sensed at once that the mother saw the frown and was alarmed. So I reassured her that everything was all right. I have always tried to remember not to do it again.[25]

Roles and personality integration All roles organize behavior, but some roles are so important that they serve to integrate the personality. They become part of the individual's self-conception, which is built around the behavior and the attitudes that go with a role. The individual sees the world from the point of view of a particular role and may find it difficult to take on other roles or to behave in ways alien to his critical role. Such roles are usually sex roles, family roles, and occupational roles, but an individual may also see himself as the "life of the party." He will be unhappy when this role is taken over by someone else, and he may try to act out this role even when it is inappropriate.

When identification is intense and a role is critical in personality integration, the individual may stake his self-respect on it. When deprived of his role, he loses self-esteem. People for whom a job has been the integrating element in life are disturbed by retirement and are often unable to find other sources of self-esteem and meaning.

Even where roles are satisfying to the individual and provide him with the opportunity to exercise his capacities, they may have a negative side. Attached to the role are characteristic risks, anxieties, and limitations. For example, successful business executives show common personality characteristics.[26] On the "positive" side are high achievement desires, strong

mobility drives, an attitude toward authority as helpful rather than inhibiting, high ability to organize unstructured situations, decisiveness, a strong sense of self-identity, and aggressiveness. These personality traits are "positive" in the sense that they support the social role and find expression within it. The "negative" traits are uncertainty, constant activity, continued fear of losing ground, inability to be leisurely, introspective, ever-present fear of failure, and limitations on the play of emotion in interpersonal relations.

Role distance Although people tend to identify with their roles, sometimes the individual may make clear to himself and others that his real self is not fully committed to a role. Such a person manifests "role distance." He shows that he does not take the role too seriously, that he has psychological distance from it, that he and the role are not identical.

Role distance signifies alienation from a role when the individual feels demeaned by what he is called upon to do:

. . . the subordinate is careful not to threaten those . . . in charge, he may be just as careful to inject some expression to show, for any who care to see, that he is not capitulating completely to the work arrangement in which he finds himself. Sullenness, muttering, irony, joking, sarcasm may all allow one to show that something of oneself lies outside . . . the role.[27]

Role distance of this kind may become part of a role style. The newly hired worker discovers that his training on the job includes learning role distance —how to goof off, joke about the work, and otherwise demonstrate to his fellow employees that he is not overly involved in his job.

Role distance may also occur when the individual feels so secure in his role that he can step out of it without fearing loss of identity, self-respect, or the respect of others. The "stuffed shirt" is one who can-

---

[25] Merton *et al., op. cit.,* p. 227.

[26] William E. Henry, "The Business Executive: The Psychodynamics of a Social Role," *American Journal of Sociology,* 54 (January, 1949), 286–291.

[27] Erving Goffman, *Encounters* (Indianapolis: Bobbs-Merrill, 1961), p. 114.

not step out of a formal role and is incapable of role distance. Overidentification with formal roles tends to be self-defeating, for then the individual cannot distinguish his personal needs from the requirements of the role. In this sense, a certain amount of role distance is needed for good role performance. Some sociologists see role distance as a way of maintaining personal integrity and freedom while conforming to role expectations.[28]

RESOCIALIZATION

Over the total life span, individuals change their attitudes, values, behavior, and self-conceptions as they assume new roles and undergo new experiences.

Adult change that is gradual and partial is called *continuing socialization. Resocialization* denotes change that is more basic and more rapid, especially the abandonment of one way of life for another that is not only different from the former but incompatible with it. Important examples of attempts at resocialization are "brainwashing," the rehabilitation of criminals, and the conversion of "sinners" to a religious way of life. In these cases, the aim is to make the person over in fundamental ways and to effect a break with the past.

Certain occupational and life roles demand extensive and intensive socialization, and training for them approaches resocialization. The role of priest or nun requires that the new religious life be all-encompassing and that a thorough break be made with the ways of the secular order. Adaptation 9 (pp. 110 ff.) describes some resocializing aspects of cadet life at the Coast Guard Academy.

Resocialization of the mature individual is difficult to accomplish. Generally speaking, it requires that the conditions of childhood socialization be reproduced in heightened, intense, and extreme form. Attempts at resocialization—whether forced upon the individual or assented to voluntarily—include some if not all of the following elements:

1. *Total control over the individual.*[29] The individual is isolated from society, from the countervailing influences of competing institutions and groups, and from his own past life. The resocializing institution has not only sole access but total access to the individual; every aspect of his life is under surveillance. The person is totally dependent upon the institution even for satisfaction of his physical needs. More significantly, he is dependent upon the institution for cues and "information" as to what is right and wrong, true and false, in his new environment.

2. *Suppression of past statuses.* Former statuses for which the person had approval or in which he took pride or pleasure are ignored. Within the resocializing institution the individual is initially devoid of status and is given approval only for the achievement of a new status defined by the resocializing agency.

3. *Denial of the moral worth of the old self.* Not only are past statuses ignored, the individual's past perspectives are seen as radically faulty, morally inferior, and blameworthy.

4. *Participation of the individual in his own resocialization.* The individual is encouraged to participate actively in the resocialization process by engaging in self-analysis, self-criticism, and "confession" of past and present failings.

5. *Extreme sanctions.* Resocialization agencies often employ extreme sanctions ranging from the negative sanctions of physical cruelty and social isolation to the positive sanction of the promise of eternal salvation.

6. *Intensification of peer group pressures and support.* Resocializing institutions rarely rely on "reforming" the individual by invoking a punishment and reward system administered from on high. Instead, efforts are made to increase the informal influence of the peer group, which is able to give and to withhold the often subtle but crucial satisfactions of group life and personal interaction.

[28] Peter L. Berger, *Invitation to Sociology: A Humanistic Perspective* (Garden City, N.Y.: [Anchor] Doubleday, 1963), pp. 135–136.

[29] See "On the Characteristics of Total Institutions" in Erving Goffman, *Asylums* (Garden City, N.Y.: [Anchor] Doubleday, 1961), pp. 1–124.

Brainwashing The term "brainwashing" is a translation from the Chinese and was first used in Communist China to refer to the reeducation of the Chinese people whereby all vestiges of the old, pre-Communist system would be "washed away." In the present context, the term refers to efforts at conversion of Westerners to the ideology of the Chinese Communist Party while they are being held prisoner.

Under the impact of brainwashing, many prisoners confessed to crimes of espionage that they could not possibly have committed and that they immediately repudiated upon liberation and arrival in Hong Kong. A few, however, appear upon release to have been "converted." Despite the brutality of their imprisonment, and their innocence of any crime, they made statements like the following:

In China today a person who is not guilty of a crime could never be arrested or convicted. Before I was arrested in my heart I knew that I was guilty of being a spy. The People's Government took care of us so well! We had no pressure put on us. In order to gain self-respect one has to confess. We are grateful for such light sentences.[30]

Such apparent conversions led to the widespread belief that the Communists had discovered "a new and powerful weapon to use against the mind of man."[31] However, reports by repatriated Westerners indicate that, although actual physical torture plays a part, brainwashing consists of an extreme, intensive, and in itself brutal application of the entire range of resocialization measures.

The process of "thought reform" or the "ideological remolding" of the individual begins with "total" imprisonment; the individual is entirely cut off from all contact with the outside world. Although he is charged with being a spy or an enemy of the Chinese people, no specific and refutable accusations are made. Instead he is made to review his past life in order to discover for himself what he did that was, from the point of view of his captors, morally wrong.

In order to be able to make a "sincere" confession that will satisfy his captors and secure his release, the prisoner must abandon his own concept of guilt and innocence learned in his past life, discover the concept of guilt and innocence held by his captors, and then use the latter to inspect and judge his past life. His confession must in effect consist of a moral condemnation of his entire previous self as the product of a capitalist, imperialist society. Although his confession must be buttressed by specific details—real or fabricated—the individual is required to repudiate, not only this or that specific act, but his entire past self as criminal.

Prisoners are commonly placed in a cell with other prisoners—usually all Chinese—who are well on the way to being reformed and who subject him to a process known as the "struggle" to help him recognize and admit his criminality. Hour after hour, from morning to night, they repeat the accusations against him and urge him to confess. They respond to him in no other way than as a criminal and as an object of a "struggle." The prisoner's past status as priest, doctor, or missionary is treated only as a "cover up" for his "spy personality."

. . . Each attempt on the part of the prisoner to reassert his adult human identity . . . ("I am not a spy. I am a doctor"; or "This must be a mistake. I am a priest; I am telling the truth.") was considered a show of resistance and of "insincerity" and called forth new assaults.[32]

The prisoner is never left alone, not even to perform the most intimate body functions. Until he is able to embark on the long road to a full and satisfactory confession, the prisoner is often put into chains. Besides being subjected to pain, he is rendered as helpless as an infant, and made totally dependent upon others for the satisfaction of every physical need.

When you get back [to your cell] you are obliged to stand with chains on your ankles and holding your

---

[30] Quoted by Edgar H. Schein with Inge Schneier and Curtis H. Barker, *Coercive Persuasion* (New York: Norton, 1961), p. 15.

[31] *Ibid.*

[32] Robert Jay Lifton, M.D., *Thought Reform and the Psychology of Totalism* (New York: Norton, 1961), p. 67.

hands behind your back. They don't assist you because you are too reactionary. . . . You eat as a dog
does, with your mouth and teeth. You arrange the
cup and bowl with your nose to try to absorb broth
twice a day. If you have to make water they open
your trousers. . . .[33] [Subjected to such treatment, the
person feels himself] deprived of the power, mastery,
and selfhood of adult existence . . . men began to
exist on a level which was neither sleep nor wakeful-
ness, but rather an in-between hypnogogic state. In
this state they were . . . more readily influenced.[34]

But the prisoner sometimes begins to internalize the
attitudes of others toward himself and to view himself
in the mirror of the degrading and humiliating treatment he is given. He begins to believe in his own guilt,
to acknowledge his utter dependence upon his captors, and to earnestly desire to be once again restored
to human society on any terms.

Sudden leniency on the part of prison officials is
often decisive at this point.

. . . An official came to see me and he spoke to me
in a very friendly voice. "The government doesn't
want to kill you. It wants to reform you. We don't
want to punish you at all, we just want to reeducate
you." . . . It was my first glimmer of hope. I felt
finally there might be a way out. I wasn't feeling so
hopelessly alone any more. The official had actually
shown some human quality.[35]

Once the prisoner begins to confess, he is subjected
to intensive "reeducation." Group study programs,
lasting as long as ten to sixteen hours, focus not
only on academic discussions of Marxist theory and
practice but on self-criticism and analysis to ensure
total intellectual and emotional agreement with official doctrine. Confession and self-condemnation are
continuously refined and elaborated during the period of imprisonment.

The evidence now available suggests that brainwashing is rarely successful in achieving a permanent transformation in the ideas and values of individuals subjected to it. This evidence is based almost
entirely on the experience of repatriated prisoners
who returned to a Western setting. It is not known
how successful brainwashing might be among prisoners who continue to live in China where their
"thought reform" would be supported and reinforced
daily or among Chinese themselves.

Several conclusions can be tentatively stated concerning both the success and the failure of resocialization by brainwashing techniques.

1. Resocialization is apt to be unsuccessful when,
as in brainwashing, it is submitted to under duress,
against the individual's will, and without "anticipatory socialization" on his part.

2. Attempts at "reform" can achieve some success
if they are related to values already held by the individual. Accounts of brainwashing often include
reports of efforts to arouse a sense of personal guilt
by invoking the failure of the individual to have lived
up to his own values in the past. This is illustrated
in the following exchange between a priest and his
prison "instructor":

Instructor: Do you believe man should serve others?
Priest: Yes, of course I do.
Instructor: Are you familiar with the Biblical say-
             ing, "I come on earth to serve, not to be served"?
Priest: Yes, as a priest it is my creed.
Instructor: Did you have a servant in your mission
             [in China]?
Priest: Yes, I did.
Instructor: Who made your bed in the morning and
             swept the floor?
Priest: My servant did this.
Instructor: You did not live up to your doctrine very
             well, did you, Father?[36]

3. Resocialization seems to succeed insofar as it
induces "spiritual humility" as in the above example.
But it is not likely to be successful if it degrades and
humiliates the person in his own eyes and those of
others.

[33] *Ibid.,* p. 22.
[34] *Ibid.,* p. 67.
[35] *Ibid.,* p. 73.
[36] *Ibid.,* p. 77.

4. Resocialization is unsuccessful in working a genuine transformation if it gains compliance merely by disorienting the person and then offering him a way out of his plight. When the individual is deprived of all social supports and psychological satisfactions, he is likely to suffer a mental breakdown or, at best, become confused, apathetic, and compliant in an external, mechanical way.

Adaptation 9 / Dornbusch **SOCIALIZING THE CADET**

The function of a military academy is to make officers out of civilians or enlisted men. The objective is accomplished by a twofold process of transmitting technical knowledge and of instilling in the candidates an outlook considered appropriate for members of the profession.[37]

The Coast Guard Academy, like West Point, Annapolis, and the Air Force Academy, provides four years of training for a career as a regular officer. Unlike the other service academies, however, the Coast Guard Academy's cadet corps is relatively small. This disparity in size probably produces differences in the methods of informal social control. Although all the findings reported here may not be applicable to the other academies, many of the mechanisms by which this academy socializes the cadet are probably used in a wide variety of social institutions.

The suppression of prior statuses The new cadet, or "swab," is the lowest of the low. The assignment of low status encourages the cadet to place a high value on successfully completing the steps in an Academy career, and requires that there be a loss of identity based on preexisting statuses. This clean break with the past must be achieved in a relatively short period. For two months, therefore, the swab is not allowed to leave the base or to engage in social intercourse with non-cadets. Complete isolation helps to produce a unified group of swabs, rather than a heterogeneous collection of persons of high and low status. Uniforms are issued on the first day, and discussions of wealth and family background are taboo. Although the pay of the cadet is very low, he is not permitted to receive money from home. The role of the cadet must supersede other roles the individual has been accustomed to play. There are few clues left which will reveal social status in the outside world.

Conflict between rules and tradition There are two sets of rules which regulate the cadet's behavior. The first is the body of regulations of the Academy, considered by the public to be the primary source of control. These regulations are similar to the code of ethics of any profession. They serve in part as propaganda to influence outsiders. In addition, official regulations help support the second set of expectations, the informal rules. Offenses against the informal rules are merely labeled as breaches of the formal code, and the appropriate punishment according to the regulations is then imposed. This punitive system conceals the existence of the informal set of controls.

In case of conflict between the regulations and tradition, the regu-

SOURCE: Abridged from Sanford M. Dornbusch, "The Military Academy as an Assimilating Institution," *Social Forces, 33,* No. 4 (May, 1955), 316–321. Published in this form by permission of the author and *Social Forces.*

[37] In the original paper the process of instilling an appropriate outlook is referred to as the "assimilating function" of the military academy. Cf. Robert E. Park and Ernest W. Burgess, *Introduction to the Science of Sociology* (Chicago: University of Chicago Press, 1921), pp. 735, 737.

lations are superseded. For example, it is against the regulations to have candy in one's room. A first classman orders a swab to bring him candy. Caught en route by an officer, the swab offers no excuse and is given fifteen demerits. First classmen are then informally told by the classmate involved that they are to withhold demerits for the swab until he has been excused for offenses totaling fifteen demerits. Experience at an Academy teaches future officers that regulations are not considered of paramount importance when they conflict with informal codes.

The development of solidarity

The control system operates through the class hierarchy. The first class, consisting of cadets in their third or fourth year at the Academy, are only nominally under the control of the officers of the Academy. Only one or two officers attempt to check on the activities of the first classmen, so that they are able to break most of the minor regulations with impunity. The first class is given almost complete control over the rest of the cadet corps. Informally, certain leading cadets are even called in to advise the officers on important disciplinary matters. There are one or two classes between the first classmen and the swabs, depending on the existence of a three- or four-year course. The middle classes haze the swabs. Hazing is forbidden by the regulations, but the practice is a hallowed tradition of the Academy. The first class demands that hazing take place, and, since they have the power to give demerits, all members of the middle classes are compelled to haze the new cadets.

As a consequence of undergoing unpleasant experiences together, the swab class develops remarkable unity. For example, if a cadet cannot answer an oral question addressed to him by his teacher, no other member of his class will answer. All reply, "I can't say, sir," leaving the teacher without a clue to the state of knowledge of this student compared to the rest of the class. Such group cohesion persists throughout the Academy period, with first classmen refusing to give demerits to their classmates unless an officer directly orders them to do so.

The basis for interclass solidarity, the development of group feeling on the part of the entire cadet corps, is not so obvious. It occurs through informal contacts between the upper classmen and swabs, a type of fraternization which occurs despite the fact it traditionally is discouraged. The men who haze the swab and order him hazed live in the same wing of the dormitory that he does. Coming from an outside world which disapproves of authoritarian punishment and aggressiveness, they are ashamed of their behavior. They are eager to convince the swab that they are good fellows. They visit his room to explain why they are being so harsh this week or to tell of a mistake he is making. Close friendships sometimes arise through such behavior, but the friendships must be concealed. One first classman often ordered his room cleaned by a swab as a "punishment," then settled down for an uninterrupted chat. Such informal contacts serve to unite the classes and spread a "we-feeling" through the Academy.

In addition, the knowledge of common interests and a common destiny serves to bind together all Academy graduates. This unifying force is expressed in the identification of the interest of the individual with the interest of the Coast Guard. A large appropriation or an increase in the size of the Coast Guard will speed the rate of promotion for all, whether ensign or captain. A winning football team at the Academy may familiarize more civilians with the name of their common alma mater. Good publicity for the Coast Guard raises the status of the Coast Guard officer.

Fostering self-esteem

The Coast Guard regulars are united in their disdain for the reserves. There are few reserve officers during peacetime, but in wartime reserve officers soon outnumber the regulars. The reserves do not achieve the higher ranks, but they are a threat to the cadets and recent graduates of the Academy. The reserves receive in a few months the rank that the regulars reach only after four grueling years. The Academy men therefore protectively stigmatize the reserves as incompetents. If a cadet falters on the parade ground, he is told, "You're marching like a reserve." Swabs are told to square their shoulders while on liberty, "or else how will people know you are not a reserve?" Myths spring up—stories of reserve commanders who must call on regular ensigns for advice. The net effect is reassurance that although the interlopers may have the same rank, they do not have equal status.

An increase in the cadet's self-esteem develops in conjunction with identification in his new role.

Military courtesy and discipline

Told that they are members of an elite group, respected by the community, most cadets begin to feel at ease in a superordinate role. One may be a low-ranking cadet, but cadets as a group have high status. When cadets visit home for the first time, there is a conflict between the lofty role that they wish to play and the role to which their parents are accustomed. Upon return to the Academy, much conversation is concerned with the way things at home have changed.

This feeling of superiority helps to develop self-confidence in those cadets who previously had a low evaluation of themselves. It directly enters into relationships with girls, with whom many boys lack self-confidence. It soon becomes apparent that any cadet can get a date whenever he wishes, and he even begins to feel that he is a good "catch." The cadet gains a new way of viewing the behavior of himself and others. As one cadet put it, "I used to be shy. Now I'm reserved."

Social mobility   The cadets are told that they will be members of the social elite during the later stages of their career. The obstacles that they meet at the Academy are then viewed as the usual barriers to social mobility in the United States, a challenge to be surmounted. And the Academy is perceived as a status machine, a vehicle through which to achieve higher social status.

Various practices at the Academy reinforce the cadets' feeling that they are learning how to enter the upper classes. There is a strong emphasis on etiquette, from calling cards to table manners. The Tactics Officer has been known to give long lectures on such topics as the manner of drinking soup from an almost empty bowl. The cadet must submit for approval the name of the girl he intends to take to the monthly formal dance. Girls attending an upper-class college in the vicinity are automatically acceptable, but some cadets claim that their dates with girls in low-status occupations, such as waitress, have been rejected.

Another Academy tradition actively, though informally, encourages contact with higher status girls. After the swabs have been completely isolated for two months, they are invited to a dance at which all the girls are relatives or friends of Coast Guard officers. A week later the girls at the nearby college have a dance for the swabs. The next weekend finds the swab compelled to invite an acceptable girl to a formal reception. He must necessarily choose from the only girls in the area whom he knows.

Justification of institutional practices   In addition to the social mobility theme which views the rigor of Academy life as training for higher status, there is a more open method of justifying traditional ways of doing things. The phrase "separating the men from the boys" is used to meet objections to practices which seem inefficient or foolish. Traditional standards are thus redefined as further tests of ability to take punishment. Harsh practices are defended as methods by which the insincere, incompetent, or undisciplined cadets are weeded out. Cadets who rebel and resign are merely showing lack of character.[38]

Almost all cadets accept, to some extent, the traditional view of resignations as admissions of defeat. Of the 162 entering cadets in 1944, only 52 graduated in 1948. The 110 resignations were largely voluntary, without pressure from the Academy authorities, and most of the resignations came at a time when the hazing was comparatively mild. Cadets who wish to resign do not leave when the hazing might be considered the cause of their departure. One cadet's history illustrates the desire to have the resignation appear completely voluntary. Asked to resign because of his lack of physical coordination, he spent an entire year building up his physique, returned to the Academy, finished his swab year, and then joyously quit. "It took me three years, but I showed them."

Every cadet who voluntarily resigns is a threat to the morale of the cadet corps, since he has rejected the values of the Academy. Although cadets enlist for seven years and could theoretically be forced to remain at the Academy, the usual procedure is to isolate them from the swabs and rush acceptance of their resignation. While they are waiting to be separated, cadets who have resigned are freed from the usual duties of their classmates. This action isolates them from cadets who might be affected by their disenchantment.

Conclusion Socializing the cadet goes beyond combat training or seamanship. Cadets are systematically isolated from the outside world, given a new personal and social identity, and instilled with a sense of solidarity. The new role is a new social world.

[38] "At each step of the ceremonies he feels that he is brought a little closer, until at last he can feel himself a man among men." A. R. Radcliffe-Brown, *The Andaman Islanders* (Glencoe: The Free Press, 1948), p. 279.

SECTION 5 CULTURE, PERSONALITY, AND HUMAN NATURE

Through socialization each culture places its distinctive mark on human personality. The more homogeneous the culture, the more likely it is to produce a characteristic type of person who reflects the dominant ethos or culture theme. In one society the representative personality may be relaxed and easygoing, careless of time, and tolerant of uncleanliness. In another society, quite opposite characteristics occur.

This sort of observation has been the commonplace of travelers for many centuries; but it is recognized that untrained observers leap easily to generalized images or stereotypes. Americans are apt to think of the English as "stuffy" and "unemotional," the English to think of Americans as "brash" and "crude," and both to think of Latins as "undependable" and "volatile."

BASIC PERSONALITY [39]

Anthropologists and sociologists approach the subject of representative personalities with caution because of the wide variation in personality observed within cultures and the difficulty of defining what is "representative." The concept of representative personality (sometimes called "basic personality," "modal personality," or "social character") points toward a *common core* of traits shared by members of a society, but there is some disagreement about the meaning of this.

1. "Representative" may mean simply the statistically frequent. Any item of behavior exhibited by a large number of people in a society would then be part of its "representative personality."

[39] For a discussion of "basic personality," see A. Kardiner, *The Psychological Frontiers of Society* (New York: Columbia University Press, 1945).

2. "Representative" may mean those common characteristics of personality which exist despite differences in overt behavior. Attention is then directed not toward the minutiae of observable behavior and response, but toward basic underlying orientations and outlooks, for example, Riesman's "tradition-directed," "inner-directed," and "other-directed" types. (See Table IV:3 p. 104.)

3. "Representative" personality sometimes means the personality which most fully expresses the spirit or ethos of a culture. In this sense the representative personality may be shared by only a minority. It is a kind of personality most easily integrated into dominant social institutions. The cultivated Englishman, product of a distinctive system of education, is representative in this sense.

Basic personality is culture as it is reflected in the individual's organized way of responding. If we assume that a culture tends to make the same kind of impress on the personalities it touches, the culture itself may be studied through the regularities in personality among the members of one society compared with another. This perspective reminds us that norms and patterns have reality only as they occur in someone's behavior or personality.

National character The emphasis on propaganda in contemporary international relations and the importance of national morale have led to efforts to assess national character, which is another term for basic personality when the subject of study is a whole nation. It is assumed that knowledge of basic personality will give evidence of the dispositions of a people to respond to certain types of propaganda, to go to war, to accept defeat, or to withstand great stress. Studies of national character have usually been carried on from a distance because they have been stimulated by interest in understanding an actual or potential enemy. Notable examples are the studies of Japanese character during World War II and more recent studies of Russian character.[40] These efforts involve considerable speculation, but they suggest the potential importance of studying basic personality.

Three limitations to this approach should be mentioned:

1. Modern societies are complex and heterogeneous. There are class differences, urban and rural differences, and ethnic differences, all of which may influence basic personality and lead to not one but a number of core types.

2. Even if there is a basic personality, it does not follow that decisions by political leaders are directly affected. Political decision is the outcome of many factors, and attitudes built up because of basic personality dispositions may be offset by other forces.

3. Even sound knowledge of basic personality is not necessarily specific enough to permit us to predict how people will behave in particular situations. If the representative personality of a culture is aggressive, for example, this does not tell what the object of aggression will be.

SEX AND TEMPERAMENT

All societies distinguish between the roles of men and women, assigning to each sex special tasks, duties, and prerogatives. In Western society, differences in the roles of men and women are associated with sharp and contrasting differences in temperament. The female is regarded as naturally nonaggressive and passive, the male as naturally aggressive and active. The contrasting temperaments of men and women have been associated with the dominance of one and the submission of the other. Thus, the more dominating a man, the more masculine he is thought to be; the more passive and pliant a woman, the more feminine.

Mead analyzed three primitive societies (Arapesh, Mundugumor, and Tchambuli), on the island of New Guinea, to determine whether temperamental differences between males and females are universal.[41]

[40] See Ruth Benedict, *The Chrysanthemum and the Sword* (Boston: Houghton Mifflin, 1946); Margaret Mead, *Soviet Attitudes Toward Authority* (New York: McGraw-Hill, 1951); and Alexander H. Leighton, *Human Relations in a Changing World* (New York: Dutton, 1949).

[41] This discussion is indebted to Margaret Mead, *Sex and Temperament in Three Primitive Societies* (New York: Morrow, 1935).

The ideal *Arapesh,* man *or* woman, is gentle, responsive, unaggressive, and "maternal." A child is not regarded as the result of a single act of impregnation, but must be fed and shaped in the mother's womb by repeated unions of mother and father. The verb "to bear a child" may refer either to a man or a woman. After an infant is born, the husband lies down at his wife's side and is said to be "in bed having a baby." Husband and wife together observe the taboos and perform the ceremonies that accompany the birth of a child. Later, the husband shares in child care.

The minute day-by-day care of little children, with its routine, its exasperations, its wails of misery that cannot be correctly interpreted, these are as congenial to the Arapesh men as they are to the Arapesh women. And in recognition of this care, as well as in recognition of the father's initial contribution, if one comments upon a middle-aged man as good-looking, the people answer: "Good-looking? Ye-e-s? But you should have seen him before he bore all those children." [42]

Sexual aggressiveness is attributed to neither sex. Rape is unknown among the Arapesh; their image of male sexuality makes it psychologically alien to them. The Arapesh permit polygyny (one husband, multiple wives), but it is not regarded as an ideal state.

Among the *Mundugumor,* both men and women are aggressive, harsh, and violent. In the structure of Mundugumor society the father and his daughters form one group, the mother and her sons another. Pregnancy is welcomed by neither parent, for the father fears a son and the mother a daughter. The crying infant is suckled only as a last resort, and then with the mother in a strained, standing position. The infant is removed as soon as he stops suckling. Weaning consists of slapping the child and thrusting him away.

Both sexes are regarded as sexually aggressive, and sex play, especially in premarital encounters in the bush, takes the form of mutual scratching and biting.

Polygyny is an ideal. Wives bring wealth and power by growing and curing tobacco, but new marriages are a further stimulus to hostility. Throughout life there is antagonism between the sexes. In this battle women ". . . are believed to be just as violent, just as aggressive, just as jealous [as men]. They simply are not quite as strong physically, although often a woman can put up a very good fight, and a husband who wishes to beat his wife takes care to arm himself with a crocodile-jaw and to be sure that she is not armed." [43]

Among the *Tchambuli,* sharply divergent roles are prescribed for the sexes and are accompanied by marked temperamental differences. The roles reverse Western notions about what is naturally male and female temperament. Tchambuli economic life is supervised by the women, and the men devote themselves in separate establishments to art and ceremony. The women work together in easy and bantering camaraderie, and the men are anxious, distrustful of each other, and given to "catty" remarks. The women are efficient and unadorned, the men self-conscious and arrayed in bird-of-paradise feathers. The women work and support the community; the men arrange ceremonies and dances to entertain and amuse the women.

Women are regarded as more actively and urgently sexed than men. The men's emotional life centers around the women. One source of this emotional dependence is the experience of the young male child. In infancy and early childhood he lives as an integral part of the women's community, where his experiences are pleasant and intimate. For a number of years, when he is considered too old to spend all his time with the women but is still too young to be accepted into the adult male community, he lives in a kind of emotional limbo. His earliest and deepest ties are to women, and these ties are never counterbalanced by his experiences in the male community.

Caution Although men and women do take on distinctive personality traits in different cultures, in

[42] *Ibid.,* p. 39. Reprinted by permission of William Morrow & Co., Inc.
[43] *Ibid.,* p. 210.

no society is there a dead level of temperament. Among the Arapesh, for example, there were noticeable differences in the degree to which individuals were unaggressive and nonviolent. Nevertheless, even the most active Arapesh child is less aggressive than a normally active American child.

HUMAN NATURE

Because the individual's own responses seem spontaneous and natural to him, he often regards them as part of his essential humanity rather than as the result of a particular training and experience. On the other hand, once the efficacy of socialization is understood, it is easy to fall into the opposite fallacy

Communication and basic humanity: A New Guinean, knowing no English, binds an Australian soldier's wounds and guides him for two days and nights through the jungle to his camp.

and to deny that there are limitations to human malleability.

When we speak of the "nature" of wood and water, we mean that it responds in ascertainable ways to known conditions. If too large a nail is driven into hard wood, it may crack; if water is heated to 212° F. at sea level, it will boil. To know the nature of anything is to know also its potentialities and limits. The problem of human nature should be understood in the same matter-of-fact way.

The idea of human nature is clear enough when it refers to the study of man as a physical organism. The more we learn about body chemistry and physiology, the more we can say about the organism's responses to the invasion of bacteria and to changes in temperature, pressure, and nutrition. Similarly, various psychological phenomena, such as learning and perceiving, seem to follow laws that are characteristic of the whole species. But man also has personality, characterized by dispositions to respond in emotional ways, by the development of a self, and by psychological defenses.

When we turn to the socially relevant aspects of man's psychic structure, such challenging questions as the following are raised: Are there universal psychological characteristics which affect the way men relate themselves to each other? Do these characteristics, if they exist, set limits on the kinds of social arrangements that are psychologically acceptable? Or are psychic tolerances so broad that *any* kind of social organization is possible? Are some aspirations, such as the quest for power, part of essential human nature, or are they products of socialization in a given culture?

Some of these questions have been explored in the comparative study of personality and society. Investigations such as Mead's study of sex and temperament and Malinowski's of the Oedipus complex test whether the asserted uniformities in human nature exist. (See Adaptation 10, pp. 117–119.)

A recent approach to the study of human nature is the attempt to identify emotional needs which demand satisfaction in social arrangements. Fromm asserts that man has a fundamental need for belonging, for being securely part of a community which can give him emotional support.[44] The growth of economic and political freedom in Western society has tended to isolate the individual and to bring about the withdrawal of older social supports. Fromm's analysis is based on neo-Freudian psychology. This point of view recognizes the importance of social influences but maintains that the human psychic structure is naturally fragile, because it grows out of and depends upon social interaction. The continued support of others through love, affection, and social approval is needed. The neo-Freudians hold that man is *anxiety-prone* and that social groups must provide conditions that alleviate anxiety. If these supports are lacking, the individual will seek a way out of anxiety, sometimes with severe consequences for political order. Anxiety may manifest itself in several ways; in overaggressiveness, submission to authority, or in apathetic withdrawal.

A common human nature does not necessarily lead directly to uniformities in behavior. What is observed depends on the conditions within which response takes place, and what is learned is *the disposition of the person to respond*. If the need for personal security is a fundamental part of human nature, the need will be revealed in a wide variety of ways. An understanding of the underlying psychic condition can reveal much about potential responses of children and adults to anxiety-provoking situations.

[44] Erich Fromm, *Escape from Freedom* (New York: Holt, Rinehart and Winston, 1941), and Erich Fromm, *Man for Himself* (New York: Holt, Rinehart and Winston, 1947).

Adaptation 10 / *Malinowski* AUTHORITY AND SOCIALIZATION IN A PRIMITIVE SOCIETY

Freud's theory According to Freudian psychoanalytic theory, the family universally gives rise to a typical constellation of feelings called the "Oedipus complex," in which the male child feels hostility toward his father because the child desires exclusive access to his mother. This hostility must be suppressed, but it manifests itself in later life as antagonism toward male authority figures. Freud held that the source of hostility to the father was sexual feeling on the part of the child for the mother. He believed that the Oedipus complex appears in disguised form in fairy tales, legends, and myths. For example, in the Greek mythical drama for which Freud named the complex, Oedipus unknowingly but inevitably killed his father and married his mother. Freud regarded the myth as evidence for the existence of the complex. The myth was a symbolic and socially acceptable form for expressing the repressed desire to return to a warm and intimate relation with the mother.

Malinowski's theory Malinowski approached the study of the Oedipus complex from the standpoint of anthropological studies, which show wide variation in family structure. He held that the pattern of "conflicts, passions, and attachments" within the family varied according to the structure. Malinowski's hypothesis was that the hostility of the male

SOURCE: A partial summary of Bronislaw Malinowski, *Sex and Repression in Savage Society* (New York: Harcourt, Brace & World, 1927).

child was directed against the father not in his role as husband of the mother, but in his role as authority over the child, and that the source of the Oedipus complex was not sexual jealousy but resentment of the father's power to dominate. He reasoned that if his hypothesis were correct, the Oedipus complex was not universal but a product of the middle-class family in Western society. This family is patriarchal, and the father has the dominant power within it. Other societies, however, distribute power differently, and the father has power in varying degrees. There are some societies in which he has very little power. Malinowski tested his hypothesis in the light of his extensive knowledge of the Trobriand Islanders (east of New Guinea), who vest authority over the child in the mother's brother rather than in the father.

The father The Trobriand Islanders are matrilineal, that is, kinship is reckoned through the mother only, succession and inheritance descend in the female line, and children belong to the mother's family, clan, and community. A boy inherits the social position and the possessions, not of his father but of his maternal uncle.

Matrimony is monogamous except for chiefs. The Trobrianders are ignorant of conception and do not regard the husband as the father of the children. He gives the children loving care and tender companionship in early childhood, but his authority over them is only by virtue of his personal relations with them. The mother's brother is the socially recognized source of authority.

Marriage in the Trobriand Islands is patrilocal: the wife goes to live with her husband in a house in his community. The children *live* with the father in childhood, but they *belong* to the mother's community. Their real home is where their maternal uncle lives.

The maternal uncle The child is integrated into the life of the community and learns his role and obligations in society from his mother's brother. This maternal uncle, not the father, directs the boy's occupations, teaches him tribal laws and prohibitions, and requires certain services of him. The work he does with his uncle contributes to his own community in which he will eventually take his place. Although he continues to work with his father, he does so out of good will and friendship, for this work contributes to his father's community of people who are legally strangers to him. The uncle holds the key to the boy's social status, wealth, power, and family pride. Therefore, to the Trobriand boy, the uncle is idealized as the model of right behavior and is the person to please and emulate.

During adolescence the young boy learns his duties, is instructed in traditions and magic, in arts and crafts. At this time relations between the boy and his uncle are most intimate and satisfactory, and the father suffers a temporary eclipse in the child's life.

The authority and discipline exercised by the uncle inevitably prove irksome to the child, and the ideal of behavior provided by him, a burden. Although the education received from his uncle is the road to mature status in the community, it requires from him the renunciation of childhood pleasures and the repression of childhood impulses. The child reveres his uncle, but he also resents him, and this hostility must be repressed and denied.

Unlike the father in our society, the Trobriand father escapes these feelings of hostility. Without authority and the power to discipline, he invokes no dislike on the part of the child. On the contrary, he provides a haven and a refuge when friction between the child and his uncle develops.

Myth and reality Following Freud's suggestion that repressed feelings find outlet in myth and legend, Malinowski examined Trobriand stories. He found that the father is not mentioned in their mythology. Myths are based upon the matrilineal family pattern, and the central male role is usually taken by the maternal uncle, who is typically the villain. He abandons the nephew or withholds the art of magic from him and is murdered by the nephew. These myths are double-edged. They may mean that the uncle finds his duties to his nephew irksome or that the nephew would be glad to be rid of his debt of gratitude to his uncle.

The mutual hostility and suspicion between uncle and nephew in myths have their parallel in reality. While it is the duty of the uncle to pass on to his nephew the family possessions, the nephew is in fact bound to make a substantial payment for inheritance. When a father gives gifts to his son, he always does so out of sheer affection, and magic is as often received from the father as a gift as it is inherited from the uncle. However, when magic is inherited from the uncle, there may be a suspicion in the nephew's mind that he has been cheated of his full share. Suspicion does not arise when the magic is a gift from the father.

Conclusion Malinowski disagreed with Freud on two counts. He concluded (1) that the Oedipus complex, as Freud described it, is not universal but a product of the patriarchal family in Western society, and (2) that the hostility found in the Oedipus complex is directed against the father, not because of his sexual relation to the mother, but because of his social relation to the child. This social relation is an *authority* relation, and hostility will center around whoever has dominant authority within the family.

The authority problem of the maternal uncle in Trobriand society lies in the divided loyalties of the uncle-father and the dilemma of authority and intimacy.

1. The family system of the Trobriand Islanders is subject to *divided loyalties.* The uncle is father to his own children and bound to them by ties of affection, and he may resent his obligations to his nephew—obligations which must have preference over his personal relations with his children and his wife. The nephew's fear of abandonment, hostility, and suspicion may, therefore, be not so much the result of rebellion against the uncle's authority as a recognition of the uncle's divided loyalties. By the standards of Trobriand culture, the uncle ought to be wholly committed to the nephew, but the nephew knows he is not.

2. The uncle is not only an authority figure for the nephew but his educator as well. Education must involve him in intimate relations with his nephew. When authority is combined with intimacy, it is likely to generate hostility. The intimacy leads to expectations that the person will be treated with affection and leniency, while the authority relation leads to a measure of impersonal judgment. In other words, it is not authority alone that engenders hostility, but authority combined with a personal or primary relationship.

Caution While Malinowski's study is an interesting attempt to test psychological hypotheses by anthropological investigation, it should not be concluded that the specific issue treated here is definitely settled.[45]

[45] For some of the debate on this topic, see Ernest Jones, "Mother-Right and the Sexual Ignorance of Savages," *International Journal of Psychoanalysis,* VI, Part 2 (April, 1925), pp. 109–130. See also Harold D. Lasswell, "A Hypothesis Rooted in the Preconceptions of a Single Civilization Tested by Bronislaw Malinowski," in Stuart A. Rice (ed.), *Methods in Social Science* (Chicago: University of Chicago Press, 1931), pp. 480–488.

CHAPTER V
PRIMARY GROUPS

SECTION 1 INTRODUCTION

Students of society have given much attention to the primary relation and the primary group—the characteristic setting within which intimate, person-centered interaction takes place. This chapter examines the nature of the primary group and shows its significance for the individual, for associations, and for society.

The term "primary group" was first used by Cooley to refer to groups

... characterized by intimate face-to-face association and cooperation. They are primary in several senses, but chiefly in that they are fundamental in forming the social nature and ideas of the individual. The result of intimate association, psychologically, is a certain fusion of individualities in a common whole, so that one's very self, for many purposes at least, is the common life and purpose of the group. Perhaps the simplest way of describing this wholeness is by saying that it is a "we"; it involves the sort of sympathy and mutual identification for which "we" is the natural expression. One lives in the feeling of the whole and finds the chief aims of his will in that feeling.[1]

For close analysis it is necessary to distinguish the primary relation and the primary group.

THE PRIMARY RELATION

A primary relation has the following chief characteristics:

1. *Response is to whole persons rather than to segments.* In the primary relation the participants interact as unique and total individuals. Uniqueness means that response is to a particular person and is not transferable to other persons. Wholeness means (*a*) that one responds to many aspects of another's character and background, and (*b*) that one responds spontaneously and freely, as a unified self, permitting feelings to enter the relationship. The less transferable the response and the more complete the interaction, the more primary is the relation.

[1] Charles Horton Cooley, *Social Organization* (New York: Scribner's, 1909), p. 23.

120

*Charles Horton Cooley (1864–1929) is rightly re-
garded as one of the founders of sociology. He is
best known for his writings on socialization and the
primary group. Like the American pragmatists
George H. Mead and John Dewey, Cooley emphasized the social nature of the self. It had been customary in Western thought to treat the relation between the individual and society as a philosophical
problem and to ask: Why should the individual take
on social values? Cooley and others held that the
relation between the individual and society is an
empirical one, and that the proper question is: How
does the individual take on social values? They
viewed socialization as a natural process.*

Many human relations are not primary because
they are highly transferable, readily directed and re-
directed to many persons, and because they are narrowly circumscribed. For example, the relation between clerk and customer is a transferable one; each
acts in standardized ways that are applicable to other
clerks and other customers. Furthermore, the relation
involves only those aspects of each person relevant
to conducting a business transaction. To take account
of another as a person instead of as a clerk or a customer is to become aware of and to adapt to many
facets of the other's personality.

Entering a primary relation presumes acceptance
of a whole person. For instance, the relation between
husband and wife is understood to be not a contract
but an unlimited commitment one to the other, where
each assumes full responsibility for the other's well-
being. In contrast nonprimary relations (often called
secondary) usually entail only limited, segmental
response of one individual to another, for example
the relation between many employers and employees.

2. *Communication is deep and extensive.* In the
primary relation few limits are placed on the range
and the mode of communication. In nonprimary relations communication is limited to specific topics. In
the primary relation, communication is often by
hints, clues, nonverbal and private behavior as well
as by words; feelings and needs are revealed that are
hidden in public situations. Nonprimary relations are
not meant to reveal the deeper layers of personality
and tend to be restricted to formal and public modes
of interaction.

The depth of communication in primary relations
is important because the expression of feelings and

Left, upper: The proprietor and friends are gathered around the stove in his Vermont general store.

Left, lower left: Rafer Johnson, Olympic decathlon champion, and C. K. Yang of Nationalist China. College friends, international competitors.

Left, lower right: A circus bicycle performer holds his sleeping baby just before his act goes on.

Below: A survey engineer talks with the captain of a labor gang in New Guinea.

PERSON TO PERSON

Each of these pictures is a study in personal relations, a blend of behavior defined by social roles and spontaneous person-to-person interaction. Spontaneity and intimacy afford opportunity for personal response and self-expression, but interaction is also governed and constrained by the situation, by the role, and by the past history of interpersonal experience.

beliefs tends to influence the feelings and beliefs of others. Although communication does not guarantee agreement, it does facilitate and encourage it, and where communication is intimate and extensive, similar attitudes and feelings naturally tend to develop. In nonprimary relations, though there may be agreement or understanding on some matters, it may not be carried over to other matters. In the primary relation, however, increased communication brings with it an increased opportunity for individuals to influence each other. Cooley emphasized the contribution of the primary group to the formation of character, for example, in the influence of parents upon children.

Primary relations do not presume unqualified affection and cordiality. All relationships involve tensions as well as positive responses, but they cannot long subsist on antagonism. The primary relation entails a positive valuing of the other, a sense of belonging together and sharing a common identity. When a personal relation is characterized by antagonism, communication is hampered and response is usually limited to a part of the other's personality.

3. *Personal satisfactions are paramount.* Individuals enter into primary relations because such relations contribute to personal development, security, and well-being. In the primary relation the individual is accepted for himself and not merely as a means to a practical objective. To the extent that a job gives psychological satisfaction, one may expect to find that primary relations have developed in the work situation.

Primary relations usually, but not necessarily, involve face-to-face interaction. Families, lovers, and friends may be separated physically yet maintain their primary relations. Obviously, many face-to-face settings are impersonal, for example a courtroom. Hence being face-to-face should not be considered part of the definition of a primary relation.[2] It is a congenial *condition* and a probable accompaniment rather than an essential feature.

The chief characteristics of the primary relation—

response to whole persons, deep and extensive communication, and personal satisfactions—are observable when the quality of "primaryness" is most fully developed. In experience, primary groups vary from the ideal type, and most primary relations are incomplete, even those between friends and lovers. Nevertheless, the primary relation model can help diagnose situations in which the incompleteness of the relation is a source of tension and frustration.

THE PRIMARY GROUP

A group is primary insofar as it is based upon and sustains primary relations. Where people live or work together closely for some time, groups based on primary relations usually emerge. Families, play groups, and neighborhood circles offer congenial conditions for primary group development.

However, not all small groups are primary. For example, a committee working together over a considerable time, but composed of men of varying backgrounds, ages, and ranks, may offer little opportunity for primary group formation. Small size facilitates primary group formation but in itself is not sufficient.

On the other hand, largeness, although not a congenial condition, does not necessarily prevent formation of primary groups. Sociologists sometimes speak of whole communities as based on primary relations. *Gemeinschaft* or "primary community" designates a type of society characterized by (1) an assignment of status to the whole person so that his job and the rest of his life form a unity; (2) a high degree of cohesion based on the widespread sharing of common attitudes and aims; and (3) a sense of unlimited commitment to the community, which is conceived as an enlarged kinship group, the source of one's personal identity. (See SOCIAL ORGANIZATION, p. 48.)

Such diverse groups as families, soldier groups, boys' gangs, and factory cliques can be classified together because they are based to a significant extent on primary relations and perform functions normally expected of primary groups, such as giving the indi-

[2] See Ellsworth Faris, "The Primary Group: Essence and Accident," *American Journal of Sociology, 38* (July, 1932), 41–50.

vidual emotional support. Clearly, however, all these groups do not protect or gratify the individual in the same way or to the same degree. A primary group within a factory can do some important things for the individual and can affect the factory organization; but it cannot do the family's job, just as the family cannot perform the factory group's functions. A primary group can be understood only in the social context within which it has developed.

Caution Because of this topic's connection with such experiences as love, friendship, and family life, the student may mistakenly conclude that primary relations are necessarily good and nonprimary relations are somehow inherently bad. It is true that primary relations bear closely on personal satisfaction. This does not mean, however, that just because a relation is primary, it is desirable, nor that direct personal satisfaction is the only criterion of social worth.

In many situations, it is advantageous to maintain relatively impersonal relations. Much business, military, educational, and legal experience suggests the wisdom of formalizing relations in order, for example, to establish equality of treatment. Formalization permits decisions to be made with reference to the task at hand. Professional standards can be upheld or individuals assigned to hazardous duties free from the pressures of personal claims on those in authority.

The relationship between faculty and students is an instance of the problem of formal *vs.* primary relations. Quite properly both professors and students value informal and easy contacts; yet such contacts are engaged in with real risks. The professor who is too easily accessible may find it more difficult to make objective judgments about grades, or he may be suspected of being influenced by his personal attachments. Because of this, many professors sacrifice part of their friendly relations with students rather than jeopardize impartiality and objectivity. The problem arises even more seriously for judges and other government officials. The long historic effort to achieve "a government of laws and not of men" reflects the social value of nonprimary relations in situations where objectivity is paramount.

SOURCES AND READINGS

Dorwin Cartwright and Alvin Zander (eds.), *Group Dynamics* (2nd ed.; New York: Harper & Row, 1960).

Charles Horton Cooley, *Social Organization* (New York: Scribner's, 1909).

Robert M. Golembiewski, *The Small Group* (Chicago: University of Chicago Press, 1962).

A. Paul Hare, *Handbook of Small Group Research* (New York: Macmillan, 1962).

A. Paul Hare, Robert F. Bales, Edgar F. Borgatta (eds.), *Small Groups* (rev. ed.; New York: Knopf, 1965).

George C. Homans, *The Human Group* (New York: Harcourt, Brace & World, 1950).

Josephine Klein, *The Study of Groups* (London: Routledge and Kegan Paul, 1956).

John W. Thibaut and Harold H. Kelley, *The Social Psychology of Groups* (New York: Wiley, 1959).

American Sociological Review, "Special Issue on Small Group Research," Vol. 19, No. 6, December, 1954.

Periodicals
Human Relations
Sociometry

SECTION **2** THE PRIMARY GROUP AND THE INDIVIDUAL

When Cooley first identified primary groups, he called them the "nurseries of human nature" [3] because of their importance in giving social direction to the individual's developing personality. The socializing function of primary groups has been considered in the preceding chapter. This section discusses the *individual-sustaining function* of the primary group, the kinds of support it can give to the person.

The primary group is the main link between the individual and society. It does the work society requires of getting the individual to want to work or fight or exercise self-restraint, because it serves his personal needs. Membership in a primary group gives him emotional support which binds him to the group and, through it, to the aims of the larger society.

The need of the individual for group support has long been recognized and is often used as a powerful instrument of social control. The extreme form of control based on this need is banishment, a technique regarded in some societies as equivalent to capital punishment. However, the severity of this punishment varies with the completeness of the personal isolation forced upon the individual. The more isolated an individual is from his immediate primary group and from the opportunity to create new primary relations, the greater is his distress. A political exile isolated from home ties may experience severe distress, but if he goes abroad with his family and a retinue of followers, he continues to be supported by primary group ties.

The problems of aging are undoubtedly aggravated by the weakening of primary group ties. The decay has two sources. First, the old person is deprived of companionship as his friends die; second, the limited number of home-centered activities in urban America provides slender basis for sustained mutual interests between the generations. Perhaps the rural home is a better environment for the old because there are more people and more activities—more opportunities for primary group interaction. It is not merely the fact of group membership that counts but the repeated opportunity to validate that membership by participation in activities meaningful to the group. Even activities of a routine and unemotional character perform this function as long as they draw the individual into the group.

The experience of the citizen soldier newly inducted into the army is another case in point. The organization, as he first encounters it, is impersonal, almost inhuman. All of the people are unknown quantities, and especially the recruit himself, for he discovers how dependent he is on the knowledge and judgment of people with whom he is intimate. Separated from them, he is unsure of himself. Early in his army career he depends on old ties to his family and friends. He tries to interpret new training activities in terms of the old relationships. Letters from home, visits from friends, and relatives, and daydreams about civilian life fill a large part of his unoccupied hours.

As new friendships are made with barracks mates, he comes to think of himself as a member of his army unit, and his dependence on civilian primary groups is lessened. In time of war the civilian primary group continues as a source of moral support. In the peacetime army a soldier's primary group may monopolize his relations. If he is married, his family becomes part of the army community. His wife is an army wife; his children are army "brats"; his army primary group and his family almost merge. In extreme instances, associations with civilian groups may vanish.

[3] *Op. cit.,* see especially Chap. 3.

HOW THE PRIMARY GROUP HELPS

What the individual gets out of the primary group and how it sustains him are not well understood, but the following elements are undoubtedly important:

1. In the primary relation uniqueness counts. The individual recognizes that he is accepted and wanted for himself. He does not need continuously to be on guard, to put forth his best effort, to *prove* himself. He can *be* himself.

2. From his primary group membership the individual derives an image of himself; continued membership in the group sustains his identity. When Joe's buddy moves to a new environment, he must reestablish his identity, or find a new one.

In Adaptation 11, pages 128–130, Long John was identified as "Doc's pal" until Doc left the Norton Street gang for Spongi's gang. No longer thought of as "Doc's pal" with the Nortons and unable to establish an identity with Spongi, Long John lost self-confidence and his bowling deteriorated. He was unprotected by his old identity and became an object of attack by his old gang. He could not establish a new image of himself either in his own or the group's eyes, and his psychological difficulties persisted until Doc once more identified Long John as his pal in both gangs.

3. The primary group protects the individual by reinterpreting and modifying goals and rules, and by adapting them to the capacities of the individual and to his special personal circumstances. In the case study reported in Adaptation 12, pages 130–133, the distant authority (management) of a large factory set standards that failed to take account of the working primary group. Although the primary group could not directly "get at" the distant authority, it effectively modified the expression of authority through the supervisor, whose difficult role was to compromise and interpret the formal standards of the factory in a way acceptable to both management and workers. If he had tried to make the formal system work in a literal way he would have been rejected by the primary group, and his usefulness to the company would have ended. On the other hand, he could protect the members of the group in minor violations of the rules only while the main objective of production was being satisfied. The workers were not interested in undermining production, but they wanted some control over the situation to reduce their dependence upon an impersonal industrial machine.

The large society must develop rules based on experience with average individuals. Groups that know the individual best, especially the family, intercede in his behalf and regulate his participation in the community. For example, parents may blunt the impact of the school by requiring a minimum of the child. Or they may support the standards of the school by helping the child to compensate for his learning difficulties or to exploit fully his special talents.

This soldier receives as he gives, acting out and reliving his own primary group experience.

Adaptation 11 / *W. F. Whyte* STRESS AND STATUS IN STREET CORNER SOCIETY

A stable and satisfying pattern of primary relations is of critical importance to self-security. In the following account of street corner groups, psychological difficulties and a breakdown in performance are traced to the disturbance of interpersonal relations.

The account is presented in the first person by the author. It concerns two street corner groups—the Norton Street gang and Spongi's gang—and the difficulties of two street corner members, Long John and Doc.

Long John's nightmares   Long John's position in the Norton gang was ambiguous. Although he was close friends with the Norton leaders, Doc, Danny, and Mike, and shared some of their prestige, he was not a leader himself and had little influence over the rank and file of the gang.

When Doc and Danny left the Norton Street gang to join Spongi's gang and Mike drifted away, the Nortons regrouped under the leadership of Angelo, a previous follower. Long John divided his time between Spongi's and the Norton Street corner, but the realignment of the two groups placed him in a new and vulnerable position.

Those who hung around Spongi's "joint" (a local gambling house) were divided into an inner circle and the hangers-on. Danny, Doc, and three others were in the inner circle. When Spongi went for "coffee-ands," for a drive, or to the movies, he would invite them, but

not Long John. Long John was excluded from the inner circle.

Without the support of Doc, Danny, and Mike, Long John lost his old standing among the boys who remained on Norton Street. Long John's bowling soon deteriorated, and he finished next to last in the individual competition that season. The first part of the next season brought no improvement. Doc and Danny, who still occasionally bowled, would say to him, "Well, it looks like you're not the man you used to be. This year maybe you won't be good enough to make the first team."

These remarks were made in a joking manner, but they were symptomatic of the changes in personal relations that had taken place. As if they sensed Long John's defenseless position, the Nortons redoubled their verbal attacks on him. The former followers had always attacked him more than they attacked Doc, Danny, or

Mike, but now they subjected him to an unrelenting barrage that was calculated to destroy his self-confidence. When he was bowling poorly, there was little Long John could say to defend himself.

One afternoon Doc came to consult me about Long John. He had confided to Doc that he had not slept well for several weeks. As Doc said, "I talked it over with him. . . . Whenever he gets half-asleep and the sheet comes up over his face, he wakes up thinking he's dead. . . ." I suggested to Doc that he might be able to dispel Long John's anxieties if he took him into Spongi's inner circle and if he and Danny began to defend Long John's bowling and encourage him when the others attacked him. Doc was doubtful but agreed to try. Within a short time he had fitted Long John into Spongi's inner circle. As he explained:

I didn't say anything to Spongi, but I already fitted with him. I just

SOURCE: Abridged and adapted from William Foote Whyte, *Street Corner Society* (Chicago: University of Chicago Press, 1943), especially pp. 3–25 and 255–268. Published in this form by permission of William Foote Whyte and The University of Chicago Press. The second edition issued in 1955 contains an extended appendix describing the field research methods used in the study.

made a lot of noise about Long John. If he wasn't around, I would ask the boys where he was. When he came in, I would say to him, "Here's Long John, the dirty bum," and I would ask him where he had been. I gave him so much attention that he moved in there right away. Spongi began asking him to go places with us. Now even when I'm not around John is right in there.

At the same time Doc and Danny began to support him at the bowling alleys. Long John's bowling began to improve. In a short time he was bowling as well as he had in the season of 1937/38. In the individual competition that climaxed the 1939/40 season, he won the first prize. He never again consulted Doc about his nightmares.

Doc's dizzy spells Doc's dizzy spells came upon him when he was unemployed and had no spending money. He considered this the cause of his difficulties, and, in a sense, it was. But many Cornerville men adjust themselves to being unemployed without serious difficulties. Why was Doc so different? To say that he was particularly sensitive is to name the phenomenon without explaining it. The observation of Doc's changing patterns of primary group relations provides the explanation.

Doc was accustomed to a high frequency of interaction with the members of his group and to frequent contacts with members of other groups. While he sometimes directly originated action for his group, usually someone would suggest a course of action, and then Doc would get the boys together and organize group activity. In 1938 Doc decided to run for the state legislature (he later withdrew from the campaign). The events of Doc's political campaign indicate that his usual pattern of interactions had broken down. Mike appointed himself Doc's campaign manager and was continually telling Doc what to do about the campaign. At the same time I was telling him what to do about getting a job. However, while we were suggesting action for him with increasing frequency, he himself was unable to originate action in group events. Lacking money, he could not participate in group activities without accepting the support of others and letting them determine his course of action. Since such a pattern conflicted with Doc's image of himself as a leader, he avoided associating with his friends on many occasions. When he was alone, he did not get dizzy, but, when he was with a group of people and unable to act in his customary manner, he fell prey to the dizzy spells.

When Doc finally got a job as the director of a recreation center, the spells disappeared. He was once again able to organize action, first for the boys in his center, but also for his own corner boys. Since he had money, he could again associate with his friends and could also broaden his contacts. When the job and money ran out, in the winter of 1939/40, the pattern of interaction on which Doc was dependent was once more upset. The dizzy spells came back, and shortly before Doc got a WPA job in the spring of 1941, he had what his friends called a nervous breakdown. When I visited Cornerville in May, 1941, he was once again beginning to overcome the dizzy spells. He discussed his difficulties with me:

When I'm batted out, I'm not on the corner so much. And when I am on the corner, I just stay there. I can't do what I want to do. If the boys want to go to a show or to Jennings or bowling, I have to count my pennies to see if I have enough. If I'm batted out, I have to make some excuse. . . . I don't want to ask anybody for anything. Sometimes I say to Danny or Spongi, "Do you want a cigarette?" They say, "No, we've got some," and then I say, "All right, I'll have one of yours." I make a joke out of it, but still it is humiliating. I never do that except when I'm desperate for a cigarette. Danny is the only one that ever gives me money.

I have thought it all over, and I know I only have these spells when I'm batted out. I'm sorry you didn't know me when I was really active around here. I was a different man then. I was always taking the girls out. I lent plenty of money. I spent my money. I was always thinking of things to do and places to go.

Conclusion Whyte's cases illuminate the importance of primary group support for individual security. They suggest that individual security is not merely a matter of belonging. Long John and Doc always belonged; neither was ever ostracized, but their old ways of belonging were upset.

The study indicates that even though primary relations approximate free, personal, and spontaneous conditions, they are nevertheless patterned and structured in definite social ways. Patterning was based on social rank. When Long John and Doc were deprived of their social rank, they were also deprived of those particular interpersonal relations that had been satisfying and supporting.

Whyte's study also suggests that personal maladjustment occurs within a social context and can be aggravated or ameliorated by changes within the individual's social situation. Doc helped to cure Long John's nightmares by changing his social situation. By bringing him into Spongi's inner circle, Doc reestablished the close relationship between Long John, Danny, and himself. In so doing, he protected Long John from the aggressions of the former followers. Then Long John's emotional troubles disappeared, and he again acted with the self-assurance that had previously characterized his behavior.

Doc showed that he was well aware of the nature of his own difficulties, but understanding was not enough to cure him. He needed to act in the manner to which he had grown accustomed. When that was impossible, he was socially maladjusted. A man with low standing in the group, one accustomed to rely on others to initiate group activities, would have experienced far less difficulty in coping with the problem of having no money. The dependence would have fitted in with the pattern of his behavior in the group. Because Doc had been a leader of the corner boys, there was conflict between the behavior appropriate to that position and the behavior necessitated by his penniless condition. Not until this conflict was resolved could Doc master his dizzy spells.

Adaptation 12 / *Roethlisberger* and *Dickson*

THE BANK WIRING ROOM

Between 1927 and 1932 an extensive program of studies on employee satisfaction was carried out at the Western Electric Company's Hawthorne plant in Chicago.[4] The data for these studies include management records of production, absenteeism and labor turnover, on-the-spot observation and record-taking, and an extensive and long-range interview program with management and workers.

The investigation reported here is one part of the famous Hawthorne studies, which had an important influence on industrial sociology. The interpersonal relations and social organization of a small group of factory workers are analyzed. These men wired telephone switchboards in what the company called the "bank wiring room."

The detailed study and observation of the bank wiring room was undertaken late in the research program. There was already evidence that social groups in shop departments were capable of exercising strong control over the work behavior of individuals. In some groups the wage incentive systems

SOURCE: Abridged and adapted from F. J. Roethlisberger and W. J. Dickson, *Management and the Worker* (Cambridge: Harvard University Press, 1939), Part IV. Published in this form by permission of the authors and Harvard University Press.

[4] The research was a joint activity of the company and the Harvard Graduate School of Business Administration. Henry A. Landsberger, *Hawthorne Revisited* (Ithaca, N.Y.: Cornell University, 1958) is an analysis of the research and a commentary on published critiques of *Management and the Worker*.

were rendered ineffectual by group pressure for controlled output. Informal practices which put certain workers under pressure and kept them in line were brought to light. There was evidence of informal leadership by persons who assumed the responsibility of seeing that the members of a group clung together and protected themselves from interference by company representatives. Such observations suggested the line of research.

These reports of social organization among employees, and its effects, were derived almost entirely from interviews. The investigators had little opportunity to observe the groups at work, they knew little about their output except what could be learned from departmental records, which were kept for practical rather than research purposes, and they knew almost nothing about the behavior of the employees toward one another and their supervisors. In order to get a more systematic and exact understanding of behavior in the shops, it was decided to study one group intensively.

The setting   For six months detailed observation was made of a group of fourteen men in the bank wiring room. The work group consisted of nine wiremen, three soldermen, and two inspectors. A completed job involved three main types of work: (1) a wireman connected the projecting points of "banks," (2) a solderman fixed the connections in place, and (3) an inspector tested the work of both men. The wired banks were assembled into a final product called an "equipment," which was ten or eleven banks long and two or three banks high.

Management's incentive system
The men worked under a system of group piecework. Part of their weekly earnings was based upon the number of equipments turned out by the group as a whole during the week. The wage incentive plan had the following three principal elements:

1. Every man was assigned an hourly wage rate based largely upon his own average individual output established by past performance. His basic hourly rate multiplied by the number of hours he worked constituted a worker's basic individual weekly wage. His basic wage was guaranteed by the company irrespective of group output.

2. The basic wage was supplemented by a "bonus" which depended upon the number of equipments the group as a whole had completed during the week. If group output went above a certain level, each man received his share of the increased earnings.

3. Since individual hourly wage rates were based upon a man's average output per hour, allowance was made for time lost by stoppages beyond his control. Otherwise the efficiency ratings of men who had been delayed would suffer when compared with ratings

The Bank Wiring Department, showing banks at different stages of completion.

of men who had lost little time.

This wage incentive plan assumed that the men wanted to maximize their earnings. Therefore it was expected:

1. Since each individual's total wage was determined to some degree by group output, each worker would try to increase output.

2. If the workers exerted pressure at all, it would be to increase the output of the slower workers.

3. To increase his hourly wage rate, each worker would strive to increase his individual average output.

The plan also assumed a high degree of cooperation between employees and management. Efficiency ratings, for example, were meant to assure a fair distribution of wages. In order to establish efficiency ratings, however, it was necessary to keep detailed records, both of individual output and of time lost. The plan could be fair, therefore, only if the employees did not thwart management's efforts at objective record-keeping.

Management's wage incentive plan was a workable one, promoting both efficiency and a fair distribution of earnings, only if the men acted in accordance with management's assumptions.

Restriction of output Actually, the men behaved quite differently. They had their own idea of a proper day's work—about two completed equipments per man—and they felt that no more should be turned out. So far as the company was concerned, total output was satisfactory, and the foreman felt that his "boys" worked hard. Nevertheless, the men had adopted an informal norm setting output below the level it might have

reached had each man worked as hard as he could.

If a man worked too fast or produced more than the group thought right, he would be ridiculed as a "rate-buster" or "speed king." On the other hand, if he produced too little, he would be called a "chiseler." Another penalty for nonconformity was a practice the men called "binging." This was a sort of game in which one man might walk up to another and hit him as hard as he could on the upper arm. His victim was then entitled to retaliate with a similar blow. One of the objects of the game was to see who could hit the hardest. But this practice was also used as a penalty and played a role in regulating the output of some of the faster workers. Thus:

First wireman: "Why don't you quit work? Let's see, this is your thirty-fifth row today. What are you going to do with them all?"

Second wireman: "What do you care? It's to your advantage if I work, isn't it?"

First wireman: "Yeah, but the way you're working you'll get stuck with them."

Second wireman: "Don't worry about that. I'll take care of it. You're getting paid by the sets I turn out. That's all you should worry about."

First wireman: "If you don't quit work I'll bing you." (He strikes him and finally chases him around the room.)

Observer, a few minutes later to the man who was "binged": "What's the matter, won't he let you work?"

Second wireman: "No, I'm all through though. I've got enough done." (He then went over and helped another wireman.)

The employees believed that their weekly average hourly output should show little change from week to week. They felt that if

their output showed much change either from day to day or from week to week "something might happen." An unusually high output might thereafter become the standard their supervisors would expect them to maintain. The men felt it would be a way of confessing that they were capable of doing better. On the other hand, they felt that a low output would afford their supervisors a chance to "bawl them out." If output were kept fairly constant, they thought, neither possibility could happen.

In attempting to keep his production record constant, the worker was repudiating management's assumption that he would try to increase his production and with it his hourly rate. Since average hourly output was calculated by dividing total output by hours of work, the men could keep their output records constant by claiming either more or less than their actual output or more or less than the time actually spent. In practice both methods were used. Most men reported more connections than they completed, but two men who worked quite fast usually reported a little less than their actual count. The men who reported less than their actual output also claimed the least time out.

Attitudes toward supervision The group felt that no worker should give the supervisor information which could be used to the detriment of his fellow workers. Anyone who did so was branded a "squealer" and made to feel unwelcome. One inspector was driven from the group with this treatment.

The group also felt that those in authority should not attempt to maintain social distance or act officious. The wage incentive plan provided one of the means by which the group was able in an informal way to decrease the social distance between themselves and their supervisor. To measure individual output the supervisor was supposed to make a daily count of the number of connections made by each wireman. But he did not have time for the job and left it to the wiremen to do themselves. Much the same thing occurred with regard to claims for time lost. The supervisor was responsible for deciding which stoppages were allowable and which were not, but because a clear distinction was often impossible, he approved most of the claims made. In effect, therefore, the workers supervised their own records, and by doing so were able to hold the supervisor to their own informal work norms.

Conclusion The work norms of the bank wiremen may be summarized as follows:

1. You should not turn out too much work. If you do, you are a rate-buster.

2. You should not turn out too little work. If you do, you are a chiseler.

3. You should not tell a supervisor anything that will be detrimental to an associate. If you do, you are a squealer.

4. You should not attempt to maintain social distance or act officious. For example, if you are an inspector, you should not act like one.

These norms, and the behavior supporting them, were spontaneously elaborated and enforced by the workers themselves, and were contrary to management's assumptions.

The function of the norms When the men were asked why they tried to limit output and to keep their output records steady, their replies were varied. "Someone might be laid off, hours might be reduced, the slower workers would be reprimanded, the rate would be cut." Although workers elsewhere have had experiences of this kind, the men at Hawthorne had not encountered any of the things they said they were guarding against.

Their behavior seemed to be guided by the desire to protect themselves from interference of any sort on the part of management. Fearing changes which might be detrimental to their interests, the workers guarded against all change. Despite the wage incentive system, the workers maintained by their own informal controls constant group and individual output.

The work norms controlled and regulated behavior within the group. The activities labeled "restriction of output" represented attempts at social control and discipline and were able to transform a collection of individual workers into a social group.

SECTION 3 PRIMARY GROUPS IN LARGE-SCALE ORGANIZATIONS

This section considers the function of the primary group in sustaining the cohesion of large organizations. The formal structure of an association is the official system of authority and communication. In this scheme officials are assigned powers and duties, the limits of their authority are set, and rules are prescribed for the conduct of the organization. Where such official patterns predominate, the organization is sometimes referred to as a formal organization.

In the study of associations, the phrase *informal structure* is used to denote those patterns that arise from the spontaneous interaction of personalities and groups within the organization. (See ASSOCIATIONS, pp. 201–203.) This discussion is restricted to one aspect of informal structure, the effect of primary relations upon the capacity of the organization to do its job effectively.

When individuals relate to each other as persons rather than according to their assigned roles, they tend to initiate primary relations. A characteristic outcome is the formation of friendships and cliques. The significance of this process is that *new lines of communication and influence* develop that are not accounted for in the officially approved patterns. For example, important information may be passed among friends even though they are not entitled to it according to the rules. Or a subordinate may have personal and informal access to a high official "over the head" of his immediate superior.

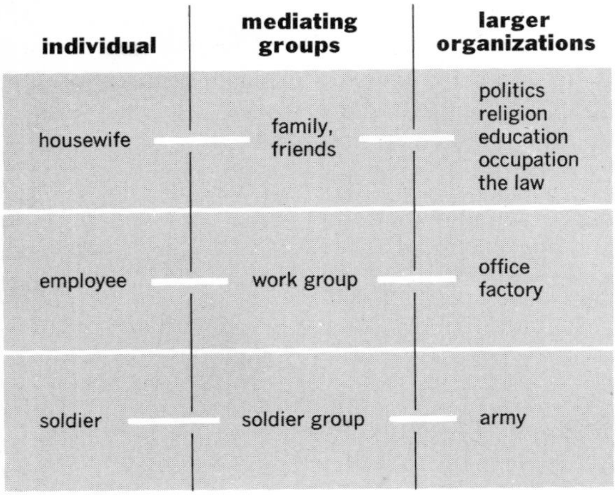

individual	mediating groups	larger organizations
housewife	family, friends	politics religion education occupation the law
employee	work group	office factory
soldier	soldier group	army

FIG. V:1 Mediating primary groups

Primary groups offer the individual personal affection and response as well as protection from arbitrary rules. If the primary group is effectively linked to a larger organization, it can heighten participation, but if the link is broken, morale and discipline may suffer.

SUSTAINING THE INDIVIDUAL

Since the goals of formal organizations are impersonal, individual needs tend to be subordinated. Because the members of formal organizations are not merely members but persons as well, they feel the need to be treated as unique individuals and not as impersonal instruments. They work to establish personal relations with other participants. If they fail they feel helpless and exposed to arbitrary treatment.

The most obvious way of escaping impersonality is to make friends with the boss, but cooperation with others of the same rank is also helpful. The Hawthorne wiremen banded together informally as a defense against possible arbitrary action by management. Groups of this kind act as havens where the individual's personal needs are taken into account. For example, if he is occasionally unable to do his work effectively, the group will protect him. On the other hand, he pays a price for his protection, for he must abide by the informal norms set by the group.

Double-edged significance of the primary group Primary groups may either support or undermine the officially approved pattern of communication and command. They may help to mobilize the participants for the achievement of prescribed goals or, on the other hand, they may have a subversive effect. An illustration of the subversive effect a primary group may have within a formal structure is the case of the Hawthorne wiremen who developed an organization of their own and whose activities resulted in a self-determined limitation of output. (See Adaptation 12.) All primary relations and groupings are potentially subversive of large-scale organizations because the special goals or interests of the self-protective group may be given priority over the official goals of the organization.

THE MEDIATING PRIMARY GROUP

The capacity of a large organization to mobilize and control members is increased if the members belong to it through a primary group. Such primary groups have a mediating function, binding the individual firmly into a larger social structure much as the family mediates between the individual and the larger society. The stronger the mediating primary group, the firmer the bond between the organization and the individual.

It should not be assumed that mediating primary groups are indispensable to the functioning of organizations. Many enterprises do not fully mobilize the energies and loyalties of their employees or members, and yet accomplish their purposes reasonably well. However, when ordinary incentives are inadequate, the individual's attachment to a mediating primary group may encourage greater participation and even personal sacrifice.

The role of mediating primary groups received special attention in the study of cohesion and disintegration in the Nazi army (Adaptation 13.) Although primary groups were important, they were not the only source of integration. The "hard core" of indoctrinated Nazis was a strong cohesive force which held the primary group to the organization's goals.[5]

PRIMARY GROUPS AND SOCIETY

If the primary group contributes to cohesion of large organizations, it may be expected to have an important role in knitting together whole societies. Many have speculated about the deterioration of primary relations and groups in modern industrial society, and the deterioration is sometimes suggested as the root of many symptoms of social and personal disorganization. Perhaps increasing mobility and urbanization have weakened individual ties to the extended family, the local community, and to small circles of lifelong friends. When such ties are weakened, social disciplines and aspirations are less effectively transmitted, and there may be new and sometimes pathological efforts to regain the benefits of primary group experience.

But it is not certain how much has been weakened, how far social disciplines and aspirations have deteriorated, nor the extent to which the new forms are pathological. The sociologist studies the weakening of primary relations and its consequences as one possible factor in any specific instance of social disorganization, just as he analyzes the influence of primary group ties on absenteeism in a factory. If there is evidence of high rates of mental illness, suicide, delinquency, or other manifestations of social disorganization, the sociologist will want to determine if the participants are deprived of normal primary group experience. The possible significance of the primary group in these cases offers a diagnostic hypothesis to be tested in the light of empirical research findings.

[5] On primary groups in the U.S. Army, see Roger W. Little, "Buddy Relations and Combat Performance," in Morris Janowitz (ed.), *The New Military* (New York: Russell Sage Foundation, 1964), pp. 195–223.

Adaptation 13 / *Shils* and *Janowitz* **PRIMARY GROUPS IN THE GERMAN ARMY**

This study was carried out by the intelligence unit of a Psychological Warfare Division. It analyzes the relative influence of primary and secondary group situations on the high degree of stability of the German Army in World War II. It also evaluates the impact of the Western Allies' propaganda on the German Army's fighting effectiveness.

Methods of collecting data included front-line interrogation of prisoners of war, intensive psychological interviews in rear areas, and a monthly opinion poll of random samples of prisoners of war. Captured enemy documents, statements of recaptured Allied personnel, and the reports of combat observers were also analyzed.

Although outnumbered and inferior in equipment, the German Army maintained its integrity and fighting effectiveness through a series of almost unbroken retreats over a period of several years. Disintegration through desertion was insignificant, and the active surrender of individuals or groups remained rare throughout the Western campaign.

The extraordinary tenacity of the German Army has frequently been attributed to the strong Nazi political convictions of German soldiers. It is the main hypothesis of this paper, however, that the unity of the German Army was sustained only slightly by the political convictions of its members, and that the determined resistance of the German soldier was due to the steady satisfaction of his *primary* personality needs.

The military primary group
Modern social research has shown that the primary group, the chief source of affection and accordingly the major factor in personality formation in infancy and childhood, continues to be a major social and psychological support through adulthood. In the army, when isolated from civilian primary groups, the soldier depends more and more on his military primary group. His spontaneous loyalties are to the members of his immediate unit whom he sees daily and with whom

he develops a high degree of intimacy.

A German sergeant, captured toward the end of World War II, was asked by his interrogators about the political opinions of his men. In reply, he laughed and said, "When you ask such a question, I realize well that you have no idea of what makes a soldier fight. The soldiers live in their holes and are happy if they live through the next day. If we think at all, it's about the end of the war and then home."

The combat effectiveness of the majority of soldiers depends only to a small extent on their preoccupation with the major political issues which might be affected by the outcome of the war and which are of concern to statesmen and publicists. There are, of course, soldiers to whom such motivations are important. Volunteer armies recruited on the basis of ethical or political loyalties, such as the International Brigade in the Spanish Civil War, are influenced by major political goals. In the German Army, a "hard core" of Nazis was similarly motivated.

In a conscript army, the criteria of recruitment are much less specialized, and the army is more nearly representative of the total population. Political or social values and ethical schemes do not have much impact on the determination of such soldiers to fight to the best of their ability and to hold

out as long as possible. For the ordinary German soldier the decisive fact was that he was a member of a squad or section that maintained its structural integrity and coincided roughly with the *social* unit which satisfied some of his major primary needs. If he had the necessary weapons, he was likely to go on fighting as long as the group had a leadership with which he could identify and as long as he gave affection to and received affection from the other members of his squad and platoon. In other words, as long as he felt himself to be a member of his primary group and therefore bound by the expectations and demands of its other members, he was likely to be a good soldier.

Weakness of secondary symbols
Problems and symbols remote from immediate personal experience had relatively little influence on the behavior and attention of the German soldier. Interrogation of prisoners showed that they had little interest in the strategic aspects of the war. There was widespread ignorance and apathy about the course of the fighting. Three weeks after the fall of the city of Aachen, many prisoners who were taken in the adjoining area did not know that the city had fallen. For at least a week after the beginning of the Battle of the Bulge—an important German counteroffensive toward

SOURCE: Abridged and adapted from Edward A. Shils and Morris Janowitz, "Cohesion and Disintegration in the Wehrmacht in World War II," *The Public Opinion Quarterly,* Summer, 1948; pp. 280–315. Published in this form by permission of the authors and *The Public Opinion Quarterly.*

TABLE V:1   ALLIED LEAFLET PROPAGANDA THEMES REMEMBERED BY GERMAN PRISONERS OF WAR

	DEC. 15–31 1944	JAN. 1–15 1945	JAN. 15–31 1945	FEB. 1–15 1945
Number of Ps/W	60	83	99	135
Themes and appeals remembered:				
a. *Promise of good treatment as Ps/W and self-preservation through surrender*	63%	65%	59%	76%
b. *Military news*	15	17	19	30
c. *Strategic hopelessness of Germany's position*	13	12	25	26
d. *Hopelessness of a local tactical position*	3	1	7	7
e. *Political attacks on German leaders*	7	5	4	8
f. *Bombing of German cities*	2	8	6	—
g. *Allied Military Government*	7	3	—	—
h. *Appeals to civilians*	5	4	2	—
	**	**	**	**

** The percentages add up to more than 100 percent since some Ps/W remembered more than one topic. Only Ps/W remembering at least one theme were included in this tabulation.

the end of the war—most of the troops on the northern hinge of the bulge did not know that the offensive was taking place and were not much interested when they were told of it after their capture.

Neither did expectations about the outcome of the war play a great role in the integration or disintegration of the German Army. The statistics of German soldier opinion show that pessimism about the outcome of the war was compatible with excellent combat performance. The relatively greater importance of considerations of self-preservation is shown by German prisoner recall of the contents of Allied propaganda leaflets (Table V:1). During December, 1944, and January, 1945, more than 60 percent of the sample of prisoners taken recalled references to the

preservation of the individual, and the figure rose to 76 percent in February of 1945. On the other hand, the proportion of prisoners recalling references to the total strategic situation of the war and the prospect of the outcome of the war seldom amounted to more than 20 percent, while references to political subjects never amounted to more than 10 percent. The general tendency was not to think about the outcome of the war unless forced to do so by direct interrogation. Pessimism was counterbalanced by reassuring identification with a strong and benevolent *Führer,* by identification with good officers, and by the psychological support of a closely integrated primary group.

Ethical aspects of the war did not trouble the German soldier

much. When pressed by Allied interrogators, the prisoners said that Germany was forced to fight for its life. There were very few German soldiers who said that Germany had been morally wrong to attack Poland or Russia. Most of them thought that if anything was wrong about the war, it was in the realm of technical decisions. The decision to exterminate the Jews was bad not because of its immorality, but because it united the world against Germany. The declaration of war against the Soviet Union was wrong only because it created a two-front war. But these were all arguments which had to be forced from the prisoners of war; left to themselves, they seldom mentioned them.

The "hard core" minority of fervent Nazis expressed strong political views. But National Socialism was of little interest to most of the German soldiers. "Nazism," said a soldier, "begins ten miles behind the front lines."

The soldiers did not react noticeably to attempts to Nazify the army. When the Nazi party salute was introduced in 1944, it was accepted as just one more army order, about equal in significance to an order requiring the carrying of gas masks. The *National Sozialistische Führungsoffiziere* (Nazi indoctrination officer), known as the NSFO, was regarded apathetically or as a joke. The NSFO was rejected not for his Nazi connection but because he was an "outsider" who was not a real soldier. The highly Nazified Waffen SS divisions were never the object of ordinary soldiers' hostility, even when they were charged with atrocities. On the contrary, the Waffen SS was esteemed, not as a Nazi formation, but for its excellent fighting capacity. Wehrmacht soldiers felt safer when there was a Waffen SS unit on their flank.

In contrast to the apolitical attitude of the German infantry soldier towards most secondary symbols, an intense and personal devotion to Adolph Hitler was maintained throughout the war. There is little doubt that identification with the *Führer* was an important factor in prolonging German resistance. Despite fluctuations in expectations regarding the outcome of the war, the trust in Hitler remained strong even after the beginning of the serious reverses in France and Germany. The attachment grew in large part from the feeling of strength and protection the soldier gained from his conception of the *Führer* personality.

However, as defeat became imminent, and the danger to physical survival increased, devotion to Hitler deteriorated. The tendency to attribute virtue to the strong and immorality to the weak boomeranged, and devotion to Hitler declined. Moreover, for most of the dishevelled, dirty, bewildered prisoners, Hitler was of slight importance compared with their own survival problems and the welfare of their families.

Impact of allied propaganda A monthly opinion poll of German prisoners found there was no significant decline in attachment to Nazi ideology until February and March, 1945, shortly before the German surrender in May, 1945. In other words, the propaganda attacks on Nazi ideology seem to have been of little avail until the smaller military units began to break up under heavy pressure. Much effort was devoted to ideological attacks on German leaders but only about five percent of the prisoners mentioned this topic, confirming the general failure of ideological appeals. Allied propaganda presentations of the justness of our war aims, postwar peace intentions, and United Nations unity were all ineffective.

Promises of good treatment as prisoners of war gained most attention and were best remembered. In other words, the best propaganda referred to immediate situations and concrete problems. The most effective single leaflet in communicating the promise of good treatment was the "safe conduct pass." It was usually printed on the back of leaflets which stressed self-preservation. The rank and file were attracted by its official lan-

guage and legal, document-like character. Where General Eisenhower's signature did not appear on the leaflet, doubt was cast on its authenticity.

As a result of psychological warfare research, a series of leaflets was prepared which aimed at primary group organization in the German Army and omitted reference to ideological symbols. Group organization depended on the acceptance of the immediate leadership and mutual trust. Therefore, this series of leaflets tried to stimulate group discussion and to bring attention to concerns which would loosen solidarity. One leaflet declared, "Do not take our [the Allies'] word for it; ask your comrade; find out how he feels." There followed a series of questions on personal concerns, family problems, the immediate tactical situation, and supply problems. Discussion of these problems was expected to increase anxiety.

Factors affecting primary group cohesion If the primary group was a crucial element in the German Army, it is important to know what factors strengthened or weakened primary group cohesion.

1. *The "hard core."* The stability and effectiveness of the military primary group depended in large measure on the Nazi "hard core," who approximated 10 to 15 percent of the total of enlisted men; the percentage was higher for noncommissioned officers and was very much higher among the junior officers. Most of these were young men between twenty-four and twenty-eight years of age who as adolescents were imbued with the Nazi ideology during its zenith. They were enthusiasts for the mili-

tary life. The presence in the group of a few such men, zealous, energetic, and unsparing of themselves, provided models for the weaker men, and their threats served to check divisive tendencies. Although, as we have seen, political ideology was not important to most soldiers, the "hard core" provided the link between the ordinary soldier in his primary group and the political leadership of the German Army and state.

2. *Community of experience.* German officers saw that solidarity is fostered by the recollection of jointly experienced gratifications and, therefore, the groups who had gone through a victory together when possible were maintained as units. This principle also guided replacement policy. The entire personnel of a division would be withdrawn from the front simultaneously and refitted as a unit with replacements. New members added to the division while it was in the rear had the opportunity to assimilate themselves into the group; then the group as a whole was sent forward. This system continued until close to the end of the war and helps to explain the durability of the German Army in the face of the overwhelming numerical and material superiority of the Allied forces.

Poor morale toward the end of the war was found most frequently in hastily assembled units. These were made up of new recruits, dragooned stragglers, air force men who had been forced into the infantry (and who felt a loss of status in the change), men transferred from the navy into the infantry, older factory workers, concentration camp inmates, and older married men who had been kept in re-

German prisoners: Note the varied ages of these prisoners from a mixed unit, captured near the end of World War II.

serve throughout the war and who had remained with their families until the last moment. These reluctant infantrymen, so diverse in age composition and background, could not quickly become effective fighting units. They had no time to become used to one another and to develop the type of friendliness which is possible only when loyalties to outside groups have been renounced—or at least put into the background.

3. *Family ties.* Correspondence

between soldiers and their families was generally encouraged, but the families of German soldiers were given strict instructions not to mention family hardships in their letters to the front. Even so, preoccupation with family affairs often conflicted with loyalty to the military primary group.

The pull of the civilian primary group became stronger as the coherence of the army group weakened under the pressure of Allied victories. Sometimes the strength of family ties was used to keep the men fighting in their units. For example, soldiers were warned that desertion would result in severe punishment of the deserter's family. Some men reasoned that the shortest way home was to keep the group intact and to avoid capture and a long period in an enemy prisoner of war camp. They thought those remaining in the defeated but intact army units would have only a short wait before they would be demobilized.

4. *Proximity.* Spatial proximity is important in maintaining the solidarity of military groups. In February and March of 1945, isolated remnants of platoons and companies surrendered in groups with increasing frequency. The tactical situation forced groups of three or four soldiers to take refuge in cellars, trenches, and other underground shelters. Isolation from the nucleus (officers and "hard core" elements) of the primary group reinforced fears of destruction and helped to break down primary group relations.

Conclusion At the beginning of World War II, many publicists and specialists in propaganda attributed much importance to psychological warfare operations. The legendary successes of Allied propaganda against the German Army at the end of World War I and the expansion of the advertising and mass communications industries in the ensuing two decades had convinced many people that human behavior could be extensively manipulated by mass communications. They emphasized that military morale was to a great extent a function of the belief in the rightness of the larger cause at issue in the war; good soldiers were, therefore, those who clearly understood the political and moral implications of what was at stake.

Studies of the German Army's morale and fighting effectiveness during the last three years of the war cast doubt on these hypotheses. Solidarity in the German Army was based only very indirectly and partially on political convictions or broad ethical beliefs. Where conditions allowed primary group life to function smoothly and where the primary group developed a high degree of cohesion, morale was maintained regardless of the political attitudes of the soldiers. When conditions fostered disintegration of the military primary group, effective propaganda ignored political issues and exploited the desire to survive.

SECTION 4 INTERNAL STRUCTURE AND DYNAMICS

Like all groups of significant duration, primary groups develop an internal structure, that is, relatively stable relations, mutual expectations, and patterned behavior. One way of describing group patterning is outlined in Adaptation 15, pages 148–152.

From the standpoint of internal structure and dynamics, the dilemma of the primary group is the tension between orientation to the person and social organization. To be free and spontaneous, to experience full communication and relatedness, to be taken account of as a unique person—these are values inherent in the primary relation. But the group has problems and obligations that require some degree of discipline, at least a modicum of leadership, and a sense of even-handed justice. The stronger these requirements, the more limits are put on freedom, spontaneity, and uniqueness.

It should not be concluded that primary relations are invariably impaired by social organization. On the contrary, primary relations may be sustained by formal arrangements that protect the relationship from being broken off too easily; and primary relations often gain in continuity and intensity from being embedded in a context of shared work and obligation.

TASK GROUPS

Many stable primary groups have goals to fulfill and tasks to perform. They are part of a work setting in which actions are initiated and directed, instructions are carried out, and some division of labor is instituted. Research on task groups emphasizes positive forms of social control, that is, the establishment of relations that satisfy the needs of the member for affection, respect, and a sense of meaningful participation. This research has been formulated as a "principle of supportive relationships":

The leadership and other processes of the organization must be such as to ensure a maximum probability that in all interactions and all relationships with the organization each member will, in the light of his background, values, and expectations, view the experience as supportive and one which builds and maintains his sense of personal worth and importance.[6]

A supportive approach to cooperation is important when people are asked to work hard and extend themselves.

However, when a group's members are mainly concerned with self-protection and defense against real or imagined threats, social control may be exercised in a negative way by aggressive or hostile behavior. Since such a group's aim is to secure passive conformity rather than to mobilize energies in a positive direction, it need not provide as many personal

satisfactions to its members. (For a case study of negative social control in a task group, see Adaptation 12, pp. 130–133.)

All cohesion and incentive do not stem from primary relations. Individuals may be united by fear of a common danger, and they may be coerced or persuaded to work or fight, quite apart from membership in primary groups. If, however, control is exercised through primary groups, then the conditions that make such groups effective must obtain. Among these conditions, in the case of task-oriented primary groups, is the creation of satisfying interpersonal relations.

PATTERNS OF COMMUNICATION

An experimental study[7] of supervised play groups investigated the effects of different kinds of supervision on two groups of children, ten to twelve years of age. One type of supervision was *authoritarian:* the children were allowed little voice in determining their own activities; direction was almost completely in the hands of the adult leader. The other type was *democratic:* the adult leader encouraged the children to make their own decisions and to plan group activities themselves.

Detailed observations were made of the children's conversation, behavior, and attitudes, both toward each other and toward the adult supervisor, in order to discover what differences existed under the two kinds of direction. The investigator found sharp differences in the patterns and quality of communication in the two groups. These differences were due to the kind of supervision over the children. The children with democratic supervision, where communication was relatively free, were able to form a more stable and complex group than the authoritarian supervised group. When communication is thwarted, as it was in the authoritarian group, individual needs are unexpressed and therefore may be unfulfilled.

If patterns limiting the free flow of communication develop within a primary group, the group is

---

[6] Rensis Likert, *New Patterns of Management* (New York: McGraw-Hill, 1961), p. 103.

[7] Ronald Lippitt, "An Experimental Study of the Effect of Democratic and Authoritarian Group Atmospheres," University of Iowa *Studies in Child Welfare, 16,* No. 3 (February, 1940), 43–195.

threatened by instability and divisiveness. A free flow of communication is necessary so that individual interests, especially of more passive members, can be known and taken into account. Another experimental study of communication within a small group (not, however, a primary group) showed that those who were not fully involved in the communication process set up by the experimenter were deficient in morale. (See Adaptation 17, pp. 199–201.)

Where self-protection and defense are the principal goal of a group, communication tends to be limited, designed not so much to evoke creative energies as to constrain and channel them.

FAMILY SYSTEMS

The nuclear family is properly considered the example par excellence of a primary group. More than most groups, the family is built upon and sustains primary relations. Affection, intimacy, openness, mutual commitment, and personal satisfaction are legitimate expectations. Relations between spouses, between parents and children, and among siblings tend to be governed by the primary relations model even if they fall short of fulfilling it.

But the family is more than a setting for primary relations. It is also a unit of social organization and as such has requirements that set limits on participation and interaction. For example, family membership is not necessarily voluntary, and members who feel "caught" may withdraw from free communication or otherwise undermine the primary group ideal. Furthermore, patterns of inequality and authority are inevitable if only because of the dependency of children.

As individuals, the members of the family have personality traits, goals, and outside involvements that affect how they act and respond. In American society adolescents often reject family intimacy; they may have much closer relations with their peers outside the family than with their parents; within the family a pseudo intimacy may be maintained out of a sense of duty and propriety. Thus the primary relations model cannot account for the complexity of interaction in the family setting. The family is a *kind* of primary group, not a "pure" example or prototype.

Although all primary groups tend to develop a system of relationships, wide variation is evident in the types of systems that emerge. Two groups are no more alike than any two individuals. In some primary groups there are permanent cliques and coalitions, rivalry and conflict; others are characterized by shifting coalitions, flexibility and harmony; still others have no cliques or coalitions, maintaining a very loose integration. Some groups are more or less isolated from the larger community, others are involved in it and susceptible to external influences.

The small social system can be described with reference to three features: (*a*) the *group boundary*, (*b*) the *role-system*, and (*c*) the *pattern of coalitions*. The interplay of these elements as applied to the family is traced in the following discussion.

The closed family system A closed family is turned inward. It tends to be isolated from the larger community: parents have relatively few contacts outside the family and children have few friends. The members tend to draw a sharp distinction between the family in-group and the outside world. (See the case of the Israeli urban refugee family discussed in Adaptation 5, pp. 41–42.) In an extreme case the outside world is viewed with apprehension while the internal life of the family is idealized.

High levels of commitment and cooperation are required by the closed family. The wife who does not look to outsiders for help and sociability expects more from her husband and children. The husband, having few outside involvements, is free to participate in household chores. One result may be a blurring of sex roles. A study in London found that relatively isolated families tended to turn inward, and in doing so broke down the sharp segregation between the duties of husband and wife:

Such continuity as they possess lies in their relationship with each other rather than in their external relationships. In facing the external world they draw on each other, for their strongest emotional investment is made where there is continuity. Hence their high standards of conjugal compatibility, their stress on shared interests, on joint organization, on equality between husband and wife. They must get along well together, they must help one another in carrying out familial tasks, for there is no sure external source of material and emotional help.[8]

The desegregation of sex roles in closed families is less likely to occur where the family is more than a consumption and child-rearing unit. If the family is a unit of the economy and runs a family farm or small business, there is a practical basis for close cooperation based on a clear division of labor.

There is some evidence, based on clinical studies of troubled families and families of schizophrenics, that the closed family is vulnerable to the formation of permanent coalitions.[9] A typical pattern is the coalition of a mother and one child. Mother and child form a deep, though frequently ambivalent, emotional attachment, creating a schism between themselves and the rest of the family, sometimes resulting in painful isolation of another member, or scapegoating, or pathological dependency.

The open family system The classic case of the open family system is the nuclear family embedded in a homogeneous, kin-based community. In such a setting the boundaries of the nuclear family are permeable and the members have sustained outside relations. Thus "nuclear families are open in closed societies."[10] The tightly organized community fully involves its members in participation, and obligations extend to the whole community.

The closely knit community fosters role segregation within the open family:

If both husband and wife come to marriage with such close-knit networks, and if conditions are such that the previous pattern of relationships is continued, the marriage will be superimposed on these preexisting relationships, and both spouses will continue to be drawn into activities with people outside their own elementary family (family of procreation). Each will get some emotional satisfaction from these external relationships and will be likely to demand correspondingly less of the spouse. Rigid segregation of conjugal roles will be possible because each spouse can get help from people outside.[11]

A fluid and amorphous environment, however, provides little support for open families. As a result the modern middle-class urban family has the task of balancing openness and withdrawal. To accomplish this it must create a semipermeable boundary, sufficiently closed to maintain the integrity of the family, yet open enough to draw upon the uncertain resources of the outside world and adapt to changing circumstances.

The adaptive family is characterized by *shifting* rather than permanent coalitions. In the American middle-class family the wife often accepts responsibility for managing internal relations within the family:

Insofar as this division of roles occurs, the wife is in the position of balancing the demands of the husband with those of the children. Successful mediation by the wife of the husband's and children's demands and needs is necessary for the smooth coordination of activities within the family.[12]

Effective mediation requires a sensitivity to the need for shifting coalitions. If the mother sides consistently with one family member to the exclusion of another, the family may become polarized and degenerate into conflict and permanent coalitions.

NEGRO FAMILIES

Some exceptions to the modal type of family unit, the complete nuclear family, are inevitable if only because of the exigencies of death. In the United States a high divorce rate is partially offset by a high remarriage rate. There are many incomplete families

[8] Elizabeth Bott, *Family and Social Network* (London: Tavistock, 1957), p. 95.

[9] Ezra F. Vogel and Norman W. Bell, "The Emotionally Disturbed Child as the Family Scapegoat," in Norman W. Bell and Ezra F. Vogel (eds.), *A Modern Introduction to the Family* (New York: The Free Press of Glencoe, 1960), pp. 382–397; also H. Lennard, M. R. Beaulieu, and N. G. Embrey, "Interaction in Families with a Schizophrenic Child," *Archives of General Psychiatry, 12* (February, 1965), 166–183.

[10] Bernard Farber (ed.), *Kinship and Family Organization* (New York: Wiley, 1966), p. 79.

[11] Bott, *op. cit.,* p. 60.

[12] Bernard Farber, *Family: Organization and Interaction* (San Francisco: Chandler Publishing, 1964), p. 321.

and families with a multiplicity of parents and foster parents. A heavy concentration of exceptional cases in some part of the population tends to become "visible" and to be defined as a social problem. The precarious status of many Negro families, especially in depressed urban areas, has recently become a subject of much popular awareness and concern. The Moynihan Report [13] and President Johnson's Howard University address in June, 1965,[14] brought to the attention of the public a complex set of problems that has been a topic of sociological inquiry for many years. Adaptation 14 (pp. 145–148) based on Frazier's classic monograph published a generation ago outlines the main types of Negro families as they existed before World War II. The chief family forms identified by Frazier persist, although in different frequencies, and many of the underlying forces that created the family types also persist.

Although the middle- and upper-income Negro families, which are increasing in number, closely resemble the conventional white American types, serious impediments remain to the development of effective and stable primary relations among many low-income families. The continued migration of poorly educated Negroes out of rural areas and into deteriorated urban centers both North and South is in itself a source of stress and at least temporary maladjustment.

Negro family formation and stability are complicated by some demographic and related factors.[15] In marital status more Negroes than whites are single, more Negroes are divorced, more Negroes are widowed, and many more Negroes are separated from their spouses. Whereas 87 percent of white families have both husband and wife living in the family group, only 72 percent of Negro families are complete units. Nine percent of white families have female heads but 25 percent of Negro families have female heads, and they tend to be concentrated in economically depressed areas. These statistics forecast the continued survival of the matriarchal-type family among Negroes. It is generally understood that Negro family income is lower than white and that families with female heads are characteristically poorer than husband-wife families. It can be seen in Table V:2 how this combination of facts affects Negro families with female heads. Because the birth rate for Negroes is higher than for whites, the Negro mother has a heavier responsibility for child care

TABLE V:2 MEDIAN FAMILY INCOME BY RACE AND FAMILY TYPE, UNITED STATES, 1965

FAMILY TYPE	WHITE	NEGRO
Husband-wife	$7,458	$4,581
Female head	$4,007	$2,473

SOURCE: *Current Population Reports,* Series P-20, No. 157, December 16, 1966.

with far less resources per child. She often tries to carry this responsibility while she is the chief or only wage earner. The nonwhite mother is four times as likely to die in childbirth, so that her child is exposed to a far greater risk of orphanhood.

From the beginning of World War II illegitimacy rates in the United States have increased. Perhaps one contributing factor is an excess of females of marriageable age. For every 100 white females over fourteen years of age there are about 92 white males; for every 100 Negro females there are about 88 Negro males. From a purely statistical point of view a Negro woman has less chance of finding a husband. But the number of eligible males is only one factor. Illegitimacy is correlated with poverty. The poor use contraception less effectively, and poor women are less likely to marry when they become pregnant or to hide an illegitimate birth.

---

[13] U.S. Department of Labor Office of Policy Planning and Research, *The Negro Family: The Case for National Action,* U.S. Government Printing Office, 1965; reprinted in Lee Rainwater and William L. Yancey, *The Moynihan Report and the Politics of Controversy* (Cambridge: The M.I.T. Press, 1967).

[14] "To Fulfill These Rights," reprinted in Rainwater and Yancey, *op. cit.,* pp. 125–132.

[15] The statistics in this discussion are derived or computed from the Bureau of the Census *Current Population Reports* and apply to the 1965–1966 period.

The facts listed here are significant because they are part of the structural conditions, largely rooted in poverty, that impair the building of strong and self-reliant families among the poor—and the poor include disproportionate numbers of Negroes.

It has been argued that an increase in the number of mother-father families would be the best way to strengthen poor (and poor Negro) family life. Al-though there is some validity in the supposition, there is no easy way to achieve it because the prospects for adoption of Negro children are not good. There will continue to be numerous families with female heads. Many of them are effective primary groups that rear well-adjusted and self-reliant children despite the handicaps of poverty, discrimination, and the absence of a parent.

Adaptation 14 / Frazier   THE NEGRO FAMILY

The several types of Negro families in the United States developed in the face of unique impediments to effective family organization. African family forms were largely destroyed by the transportation of captives into slavery and the forcible controls of the plantation. Slavery was not conducive to establishing new and stable types of family relations. The Civil War and Emancipation precipitated new disorganization and a high rate of geographic mobility. In this insecure environment Negro families attempted to adjust to new and uncertain trends.

Under slavery   There were few forces at work to contribute to the establishment of stable forms of familial association among slaves. Relations between slave men and women ranged from physical contacts, sometimes enforced by the master, to stable unions characterized by deep sentiment between spouses and parental affection toward children. However, the very nature of slavery in the United States, with its separations of family groups and its emphasis on absolute control of the slave, was not conducive to stable unions. Even where they did exist, the unions might be destroyed. For example, the death of the master might occasion the sale of his slaves.

Because of the conditions imposed by the slave system, the mother became the most dependable and important member of the Negro family. The father recognized the mother's more fundamental interest in the children and her authority in the household. A father might be sold and separated from his family, but when the mother was sold, the master had to take her children into account. Unions between white males and slave females lacked legal and moral support, and the Negro woman was head of the household of her mulatto children.

After emancipation   Immediately following emancipation there was widespread disruption in all phases of Negro life. Family disorganization was noticeable in the numbers of Negroes who became wanderers "to prove they were free," cutting themselves off from family ties and forming a promiscuous and demoralized population. The destruction of the master's authority brought about the uprooting of many stable families. On the other hand, the disintegration accompanying the Civil War and Emancipation often tested and proved the strength of marital and family relations that had developed during slavery.

The reorganization of the Negro family following the initial confusion of emancipation was assisted

SOURCE: Abridged and adapted from E. Franklin Frazier, *The Negro Family in the United States* (Chicago: University of Chicago Press, 1939). Published in this form by permission of E. Franklin Frazier and The University of Chicago Press.

E. Franklin Frazier (1894–1962)

His wide-ranging interests in community studies, ecology, stratification, socialization, and race and culture converged in the study of the Negro family and the influence of family life on behavior. Although best known for his work on the family, he wrote extensively on other topics. The acerbic quality of his Black Bourgeoisie, *first published in French in 1955, caused some consternation in the Negro middle class. In 1927 an article similar in tone analyzed race prejudice in terms of mental illness, and as a consequence he was forced to leave Atlanta by a white mob.*

toward stability by five forces: Northern missionaries, missionary schools, the Negro church, the pattern established by families free before the Civil War, and developments under slavery. Where slavery was experienced in its least malignant form, slave families frequently developed a degree of stability. A number of families persisted after emancipation and were able to acquire land and work it as family groups. Thus families had a new cohesive element—the economic tie of working on their own land, and they developed toward the patriarchal form, which was the American norm. But moral instruction and even force were un-

able to hold in check the widespread family disorganization which ensued when the Negro slave became a free agent able to form and break marital and other ties.

Recent status   Toward the end of the nineteenth century and the beginning of the twentieth century, two tendencies were apparent in the development of the Negro family:

1.   There was an extension, especially in the rural South, of the earlier mother-centered form of family.

2.   In both rural and urban communities there was an increasing

number of stable families modeled on the American pattern of family organization. They were not, however, characteristic of the Negro masses.

I. Rural South: *The Matriarchal Pattern*

The most striking feature of the Negro family of the rural South is the high proportion of families with female heads.

The grandmother is often the dominant figure in this type of family, and in many cases she is the *sociological mother* of the extended family group. That is, she may be the person who directly rears the grandchildren, and perhaps also nieces, nephews, and adopted children. She exercises authority, assumes responsibility, and is called upon during the major crises of life by her own family and those outside the family. She is a repository of folk wisdom, and her superior knowledge and authority are recognized in matters concerning childbirth and child care. Midwifery is still important in the Negro South. As late as 1940, four-fifths of live births of Negroes in Mississippi and South Carolina were attended by midwives, as compared with one-fourteenth of white live births.

In isolated rural areas courtship begins at an early age and often involves sexual relations. Where pregnancy results, the young people may or may not marry. Although the moral restraints of the larger community are absent and behavior is little influenced by white laws, the economic burden which pregnancy imposes operates as a restraint on sexual behavior. Both the girl's family and the father are obligated to help take care of the child. There is little, if any, guilt associated with illegitimacy, because the folk culture defines the bearing of children as the fulfillment of a woman's destiny. The birth of a child does, however, impose on the mother obligations which are increased if the others fail to discharge their obligations towards the child.

A large proportion of the marriages are common-law relationships; but from the standpoint of stability and community recognition, these relationships have the character of legal marriages. They conform to customs and mores which have grown up among the rural folk. As one moves from the rural South to the urban North and from lower to upper class, one finds a steady increase in the incidence of contractual marriage and observance of the formal codes governing family behavior.

II. Urban North: *The Class Pattern*

Lower class. The lower-class Negro families, which are composed in part of recent rural immigrants who have little experience with the conventional norms of marriage and divorce, most closely resemble the rural family forms. During the mass urban migration, which began at the time of World War I, many thousands of men and women cut themselves loose from their families to seek work and adventure. Family desertion remains one of the chief forms of family disorganization among urbanized Negroes.

Lower-class families are physically segregated to a large extent in the deteriorated areas where Negroes first secure a foothold in the community. They include a large proportion of families with female heads, as in the rural South. Between one-fourth and one-third of urban Negro families lack male heads. This is a result of the economic insecurity of the men and of illegitimacy. Although illegitimacy does not appear as a social problem in the rural South, sex relations and motherhood are redefined for the migrants in the city. Because of the precarious hold which women of this class have on men, their attitudes alternate between subordination to secure affection and domination because of their greater job stability and economic security.

Middle class. The effects of urban living have made possible the emergence of a substantial middle class in the Negro population. The middle class is differentiated by occupation and includes clerical and service workers and some business and professional people. Perhaps the most important accession to the middle class in the Northern cities has been the families of skilled workers. Among the middle class the male head of the family often has sufficient economic security to play the conventional role of provider for his family without the aid of the wife. The proportion of employed married women declines as the proportion of employed Negro males in industry increases.

The middle-class family is characterized by its emphasis on respectability in "getting up in the world," and it has a fairly democratic organization. The husband and father is recognized as the head of the family, but the wife and mother is not necessarily subordinated. She may work outside the home, temporarily or permanently, to help provide the extras for "getting up in the world." Her respected position derives from the tradition of independence among Negro women and is enhanced by her economic cooperation in buying a home or educating children.

Home ownership is an index of family stability among urban Negroes. The progressive stabilization of family life in the zones extending from the center of the community outward is indicated in some cities by a regular increase of the rate of home ownership in the successive zones. These increases are related to the tendency for the higher occupational classes to become concentrated on the edges of the Negro community.

Upper class. In upper-class urban Negro families, wives as well as husbands may be employed in professional occupations and other kinds of services. Among the upper class there are relatively few children per family and many childless couples.

Where the wife is employed, the upper-class family is usually equalitarian in its organization, and even where she is not employed, she enjoys considerable equality and freedom of activity. Respectability is taken for granted, but refinement and "culture" loom important. Individualism is a facet of upper-class behavior, and among the "emancipated" and "sophisticated" element a new type of intelligentsia has developed. The members of this group associate freely with white middle-class intellectuals and include interracial couples.

This adaptation has reviewed the evolution of Negro family types in the United States, the emergence of characteristic adjustments, and the forces making for stability and instability. The largely disorganizing heritage of slavery and the stresses of Emancipation have in part been overcome. In the rural South families based on common-law marriage and with a matriarchal organization persist, but trends toward conventional American forms are also apparent. In the urban North family types are correlated with socioeconomic status. Lower-income families show the highest incidence of disorganization and the highest rate of survival of rural, matriarchal norms. Middle-income families resemble the characteristics of white families of similar status and are organized for upward striving. Husbands in such families are able to assume full financial responsibility, although wives may continue to work. The husband and father is the nominal family head, but the relations among the family members are democratic. Upper-income families tend to be companionate units.

Adaptation 15 / **THE TECHNIQUE OF THE SOCIOGRAM**

Groups develop distinctive *patterns of interaction.* They contain subgroupings that differ from group to group and within a particular group over time. Some individuals are admired and sought out by many; others are isolated.

A casual participant or observer may notice some of the relationships and may sense the "tone" of relations within a small group. If, however, the group exceeds a few members, it is unlikely that even an astute and experienced observer will have a thorough grasp of the basic relationships without prolonged observation or the aid of objective measures. One technique for the objective presentation and interpretation of relations within groups is called the *sociogram.* It is a diagram of the *informal* relations within a group. (Charts of the *formal* relations are discussed in ASSOCIATIONS, pp. 196–197.) A sociogram shows the informal group structure, such as subgroup and friendship patterns, and the position of each individual among his fellows. A sociogram is a preliminary step in understanding group action or individual action in a group setting. It may be used to summarize verbal choices, written choices, or direct observations of a competent observer.

The student should gather data from a small group, preferably 12 or less in number, and follow through the basic steps outlined below. He may wish to ask questions regarding leadership or some other characteristic rather than friendship. The questions depend entirely upon the problem being investigated, but they must be phrased clearly and unambiguously. It is usually advisable to pretest the questions to ensure that they ask what is intended. Students may measure their degree of insight into group relations by predicting the choices that the members of the group will make and comparing them with the actual choices.

As an illustrative exercise a third-grade teacher asked her class of fifteen boys and fifteen girls to "Write the name of the child you like best in this class," and then "the name of the child you like second best." For simplicity we shall explain the processing of the boys' choices only. It is not necessary to show the whole sociogram because only three boys chose or were chosen by girls. The procedure is described below.

Interpretation 1. The outstanding finding of the first choices is William M's position as the *star.* He received 5 first choices from the other 14 boys and 2 second choices. Clinton received 2 first choices and 5 second choices, making him a strong runner-up to William M. Between them they received 14 choices, and their choices of Alfred create a *triangle,* which dominates the sociogram. The three boys combined received 19 choices.

2. In the first choice sociogram, there is one *mutual choice,* or *pair,* between boys—William M and Alfred—and one between a boy and a girl—Robert and Sally. Additional pairs show when the second choices are counted.

3. There is an *island* consisting of Melvin, Charles, Herbert, Robert (and Sally) on the first choices. In the second choices a bridge is thrown from the island to the main group of boys by Melvin's choice of Clinton, and there are additional ties between this group and the girls. The island has other girls who do not appear in the figure, and it is interesting that the girls in this group are only weakly inte-

grated with the main group of girls.

4. There are seven *isolates:* Skipper, Michael, Herbert, Donald, Morgan, Richard L, and William R. These boys received no choices.

5. One *error* appears in Richard L's failure to make a second choice.

Note that such errors reduce the *total* number of choices made by the group.

Variations in the use of sociograms This example of friendship choices is only one of many possible uses of the sociogram. By comparing the patterning of choices on different criteria (athletic partner, study companion, etc.), the consistency and diversity of ratings in a group can be observed. Sometimes investigators wish to study a particular factor or process in relation to group structure. Whyte (Adaptation 11, pp. 128–130) wanted to know how individual security was related to patterns of primary group relations. Although he did not ask the Nortons direct questions, such as "Who are your three best friends in this group?" his observations of group interaction provided him with data on their relations. He closely observed group activities until he was able to plot the informal relations of the group members. He was then able to relate behavior (for instance, Long John's nightmares) to breaks in the individual's usual pattern of primary group relations.

Roethlisberger and Dickson (Adaptation 12, pp. 130–133) studied group norms and informal controls in relation to group structure. Sociometric techniques were used to determine the informal

structure of a work group. The authors observed who talked most frequently to whom, which cliques played what sorts of games, between whom arguments took place, and so on. They were then able to plot the informal structure of the group. This led to a more detailed understanding of how group norms emerge and how they are enforced.

Applications and limitations Like any other research technique, the sociogram has its limitations.

1. *Validity.* Responses are influenced by the subjects' willingness to record their true feelings. If the respondents lack confidence in the investigator or if he is known to have strong preferences for certain individuals in the group, the results will probably be influenced. If there is resistance to making responses or to signing names to responses, it is unlikely that the results will be valid.

2. *Reliability.* A chart made at any given time is not necessarily a reliable indicator of relations at another time. Especially in groups of young children, there is evidence that relations are unstable. A series of sociograms would be needed to trace changes over a period of time.

3. *Cues.* We have already mentioned the possibility of cues from the investigator's preferences. Other cues should be avoided, too. For example, the students should not be given alphabetical lists of the group members. It is common knowledge that the order in which names appear on a ballot affects the number of votes candidates receive.

4. *Privacy.* The group should be confident that their choices will not be made known to others. If re-

procedure

1

We wrote each chooser's name on the left-hand side of a slip of paper with an arrow pointing to the name of his first choice, which was written on the right-hand side.

2

After a slip had been made for each choice, we sorted the slips of those who had named the same person as best friend. We found four subgroups, called *sets*, in which the same person had been named as best friend by several persons:

　　William M, chosen by Donald, Skipper, Michael, Clinton, and
　　　Alfred.
　　Alfred, chosen by William M and Morgan.
　　Clinton, chosen by William R and Curtis.
　　Robert, chosen by Charles and Herbert (and Sally).

3

The set with the most slips (William M's) was arranged to converge on his name.

4

William M chose Alfred, who was a member of another set. Because William M's and Alfred's choices were *mutual*, their slips were placed parallel to each other. The other choice in the 2nd set (in this case Morgan's choice of Alfred) was placed in position with the 1st set.

5

Another set which could be attached to the arrangement was Clinton's, and it was put in position.

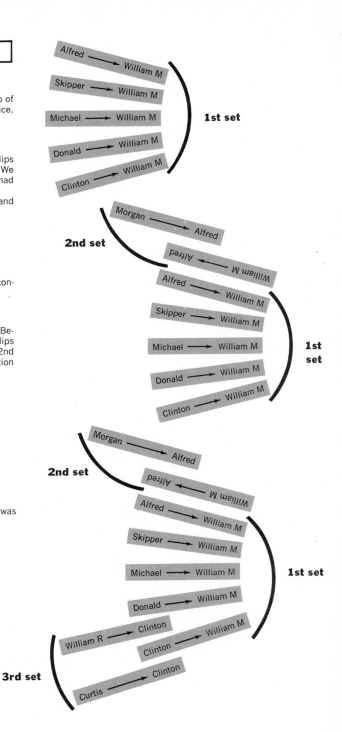

6

The 4th set (Robert's) did not attach to the other sets, and it was arranged by itself. Robert's choice was then placed in position.

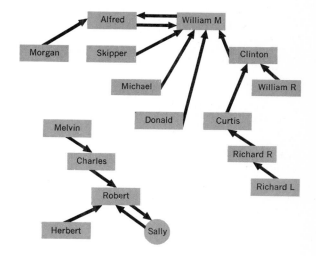

sociogram of first choices

7

The remaining individual slips were fitted into the arrangement, and the sociogram of 1st choices was completed by sketching the arrangement as a diagram.

sociogram of first and second choices

8

The second choices were processed in the same way, but a re-arrangement of the diagram was necessary to prevent an undue amount of crossing of choice lines. The completed sociogram of first and second choices is shown here.

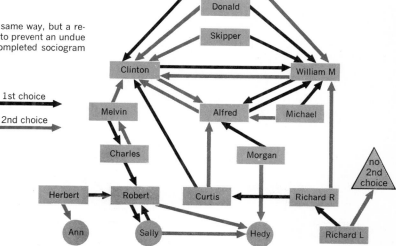

spondents are not assured of privacy, their choices may be clouded by anxiety or may reflect some factor other than the criterion asked for.

5. *Applicability*. The sociogram is especially useful in well-defined and limited groups. A small dormitory or fraternity house would provide a good experimental setting.

6. *The sociogram* is a beginning and not an end. It is usually a first step in the analysis of leadership, morale, popularity, or another aspect of informal structure.

CHAPTER VI
SOCIAL STRATIFICATION*

With the collaboration of
Norval D. Glenn

SECTION 1 INTRODUCTION

Social inequality and social ranking are so closely interwoven with the division of labor and with mechanisms of self-protection and self-aggrandizement that they are, inevitably, pervasive aspects of human society. Nothing is more likely to influence the individual or the social history of a nation than the system of stratification. For this reason stratification is the sociologist's favorite independent variable. He can usually trace a connection between stratification and almost any other social phenomenon, be it child training, voting, sexual behavior, or revolution.

The major *dimensions* of stratification are power, prestige, and wealth. However, any unequally distributed reward or resource that tends to order the relations among people is also a dimension of stratification. For example, in advanced societies, knowledge and skills are becoming increasingly important criteria for the allocation of positions in the occupational structure, which in turn largely determines the system of social ranking. In traditional societies,

privilege based on custom or law governed the importance and prerogatives of social positions. For instance, in feudal times, a villein could leave the estate only with the consent of his lord.

Vertical mobility Societies differ not only in how unequally their rewards and resources are distributed but also in the amount of upward and downward movement of individuals and families. Such movement is known as vertical mobility, a special kind of social mobility. There are no known societies, past or present, with a complete absence of vertical mobility, but in some the movement of families is so slow that it is hardly perceptible during a lifetime. In these same societies, however, there is usually a predictable and institutionalized change in the authority and privilege granted the individual as he progresses through the life cycle. The contemporary United States is an example at the other extreme—a society in which small to moderate movements are

---

* This chapter draws upon some material included in earlier editions written in collaboration with Richard T. Morris.

very common, and in which large and rapid movements are not infrequent.

STRATA AND CLASSES

Individuals or families in a group or society who have similar ranks on any one dimension of stratification constitute a social stratum, or a social level. Thus, there are prestige strata, power strata, economic strata, and so forth. For example, families who have incomes within a certain range constitute an income stratum, and people who have completed a given number of years of school are an educational stratum. The word stratum is meaningful only when the dimension of stratification is specified.

Usually, the number of strata identified in a society is arbitrary; there is no "natural" division of the individuals or families into discrete levels. We may arbitrarily decide that each one-thousand-dollar interval on the scale of annual income spans a stratum, or that the upper ten percent of the families constitute a stratum and that each lower tenth constitutes another. In some preindustrial societies, however, people are separated by a wide gulf. The nobility and serfs of medieval Europe are examples of such "natural" strata.

Some sociologists would restrict the term "social stratification" to these naturally divided social levels. Therefore, one may read of "stratified" and "unstratified" groups and societies. However, since the existence of discrete strata in modern societies and communities is in doubt, the term social stratification is increasingly used to refer to all forms of inequality, regardless of whether the distribution of the rewards and resources is discrete or continuous. In this sense, all societies and almost all groups are stratified.

Social classes The term "social class," which is widely used in popular as well as social stratification literature, has been defined in different ways. In the sense formulated by Marx, class refers to people who share a common situation in the organization of economic production. Classes were conceived as

structural units of society and not as arbitrarily delineated strata or statistical categories. (See p. 188.) In fact, the members of one class might fall into different economic strata, and the members of an economic stratum might be members of more than one class. For example, small-businessmen differ from industrial workers in their relation to economic organization, but they may have the same income and therefore "belong" to the same income stratum.

Max Weber distinguished three orders of stratification: (1) the *economic or class order,* based upon class situation defined in a way similar to Marx, (2) *the social order,* based upon the distribution of social honor, or status, (3) *the political order,* based upon the distribution of power. In distinction to class, a *status group* consists of people who share a common social estimation of honor. "With some oversimplification, one might thus say that 'classes' are stratified according to their relations to the production and acquisition of goods; whereas 'status groups' are stratified according to the principle of their *consumption* of goods as represented by special 'styles of life' . . . ."[1] The *party,* the third unit in Weber's analysis of stratification, is made up of people organized for the pursuit of power. The membership of a class, a status group, and a party may be almost identical, but this is not invariably the case, and according to Weber, the three kinds of units, and the dimensions that define them, should be kept analytically separate.

Furthermore, the idea of class has come into general use partly because of the public interest in popularized reports of social science research. However, class has entered common use not as a rigorous idea but in what may be called a "weak" sense as an omnibus term referring to all kinds of ranked, stratified, or authentically class behavior. This fact has presented the sociologist with a minor problem: whether to adhere to exact usage and employ specialized terminology or to use broad if somewhat imprecise terms, the sense of which will be readily recognized. In fact, he has done both: class is some-

---

[1] H. H. Gerth and C. Wright Mills (eds. and trans.), *From Max Weber: Essays in Sociology* (New York: Oxford University Press, 1946), pp. 180–184.

times used in the strong sense to connote groups who are conscious or at least potentially conscious of their common socioeconomic position, and in a weak, general sense to refer to all kinds of stratified phenomena.

APPROACHES

The principal ways of studying the complex reality of social ranking may be grouped under three headings: (1) reputational, (2) subjective, and (3) objective.

The reputational approach   Since prestige consists of the evaluations people make of one another, it is measured by observing actual social interactions or more usually by asking people to rank one another. For instance, the investigator may go into a small community, select a sample of long-term residents, and ask them to rate the other members of the community on a scale from highest to lowest with seven or some other number of points. In addition, he may ask the sample of judges whether they perceive distinct social levels. If they say they do, he will ask them to identify the levels and the names of people in each one. Then to find out what criteria the judges used in defining prestige, he may ask them why they rate specific people as they do.

This technique is adequate for measuring the prestige of *individuals* if the following conditions are met: (1) all raters know or know of most of the people to be rated, and (2) all raters use the same or very similar criteria of evaluation. In other words, the method is applicable only in small and culturally homogeneous groups and communities in which there is a commonly accepted and perceived prestige hierarchy.

The reputational technique can be used more generally, however, to determine the *relative* prestige of groups, categories, and roles. On college campuses, for example, there is usually a recognized prestige hierarchy among the clubs and social fraternities. Several studies have shown that there is approximate agreement among the different categories of people

in the United States on the prestige granted to occupations. (See pp. 166–168.)

Perhaps the most common deviation from consensus is in the assignment an individual gives his own occupation or organization. Almost invariably a person tends to rate his own organization higher than the ratings given it by other individuals. This tendency is known as the aggrandizement effect.[2] Such bias is best avoided by asking each judge not to rate anything with which he is affiliated.

The reputational technique is sometimes used in studies of the distribution of power in communities and groups by asking a panel of judges to identify those persons who can influence important decisions. However, the technique is less suited to the study of power than of prestige. Prestige consists essentially of reputation, whereas power does not. A person may be reputed to have power and not really have it, or he may have more power than he is reputed to have. Therefore, the reputational technique is of doubtful utility in the study of power unless it is combined with other methods. However, reputed power may be significant in itself, regardless of whether the reputation correctly reflects actual power.

The subjective approach   The self-rating or subjective approach investigates individuals' perceptions of their own positions in the pattern of inequality, and their self-perceptions may be quite important even though they do not correspond with their objective positions.

In this approach the investigator may ask people to indicate whether their economic standing in the society or the community is below average, about average, or above average. Or, he may be more specific and ask in what tenth or in what quarter of the population they would place themselves, in economic standing, in prestige, or in some other stratification variable.

Individuals whose objective ranks are the same may behave very differently in the system of social stratification, because they perceive their ranks dif-

[2] Theodore Caplow and Reece J. McGee, *The Academic Marketplace* (New York: Basic Books, 1958), pp. 45, 103–105.

ferently. People who see themselves standing at about the same ranks may evince similar feelings, even though their objective ranks are very different.

How people perceive their position in the system of economic inequality depends in large measure on their reference groups, that is, on the people with whom they compare themselves. For instance, a Negro who earns $10,000 a year, who lives in the ghetto and has few contacts with whites, may rate himself very high because his economic rank exceeds that of most people he knows. However, if he moves into a social circle that includes white professional people, his $10,000 income will seem relatively low. His objective economic position is unchanged, but his perception changes, and so may his reaction to it. Consequently, subjective stratification studies often try to determine the reference group or groups of the individuals studied.

In one commonly used subjective technique, persons are asked to name the "social class" to which they belong, or they are given a list of names of social classes and asked to indicate to which they belong.[3] For instance, the respondents may be asked to identify themselves as "upper class," "middle class," "working class," or "lower class." If there is a high degree of consensus about what class labels mean and if they are a common part of the social vocabulary of a large part of the population, a class-identification technique can be used to advantage. However, in some societies—and the United States is one of these—evidence of such agreed understandings is shaky. It cannot be assumed that the people who say they are middle class are thinking of the same things, are identifying with the same objective entity, or that their perceptions of their rankings on the major dimensions of stratification are similar. In fact, many respondents probably do not identify with any social class until they are asked the question.

The objective approach   The objective approach uses indicators that do not rely on the feelings, evaluations, or perceptions of the individuals studied or of a panel of judges. Delineation of strata in terms of income, years of school completed, occupation, or formal lines of authority exemplifies this approach.

These methods allow more precise measurement than the reputational and subjective approaches, and most of the measures can be used for studies of entire societies. Therefore, the objective approach is frequently employed on large populations and as an adjunct to community studies.

The objective method by itself leaves untapped significant aspects of the total reality. For instance, when one has identified all persons whose incomes fall within a certain range, he has not delimited a population for whom the social meaning and the social consequences of their income is the same. An income of $8,000 a year means one thing to a middle-aged skilled worker near the peak of his earning power, and it means something quite different to a young professional man just beginning his career. The significance of a given income also varies with factors such as past income, the level of income within one's reference groups, and the security of its source.

The foregoing discussion has referred to the self-rating approach as subjective and to indicators that do not necessarily involve awareness as objective. The distinction refers to types of information, not standards of evidence. Findings about socioeconomic status secured from an objective approach are not necessarily superior to subjective-type data based on attitudes and opinions. From the standpoint of scientific inquiry, the evaluation of reputational status can be as firmly founded on evidence as a measure of income, and the significance of one fact can make as dependable a contribution to the advancement of knowledge as the other.

Three exercises in the study of stratification are outlined in Adaptation 16. As presented, the methods are designed so that in the time required and the samples needed, they may be used as research projects by college classes. However, the interview schedules or questionnaires should be pretested under field conditions to make certain that they will be understood by the respondents.

---

[3] For instance, see Richard Centers, *The Psychology of Social Classes* (Princeton: Princeton University Press, 1949), p. 77.

SOURCES AND READINGS

Texts and collections

Bernard Barber, *Social Stratification* (New York: Harcourt, Brace & World, 1957).

R. Bendix and S. M. Lipset (eds.), *Class, Status and Power: A Reader in Social Stratification* (New York: The Free Press of Glencoe, 1953).

R. Bendix and S. M. Lipset (eds.), *Class, Status and Power: Social Stratification in Comparative Perspective* (2nd ed.; New York: The Free Press of Glencoe, 1966).

T. B. Bottomore, *Classes in Modern Society* (New York: Pantheon, 1966).

Norval D. Glenn, *Social Stratification* (New York: Wiley, in press).

Joseph A. Kahl, *The American Class Structure* (New York: Holt, Rinehart and Winston, 1957).

Thomas E. Lasswell, *Class and Stratum* (Boston: Houghton Mifflin, 1965).

Kurt B. Mayer, *Class and Society* (New York: Random House, 1955).

Leonard Reissman, *Class in American Society* (New York: The Free Press of Glencoe, 1959).

Other works

Peter M. Blau and Otis Dudley Duncan, *The American Occupational Structure* (New York: Wiley, 1967).

Ralf Dahrendorf, *Class and Class Conflict in Industrial Society* (Stanford: Stanford University Press, 1959).

Gerhard Lenski, *Power and Privilege: A Theory of Social Stratification* (New York: McGraw-Hill, 1966).

S. M. Lipset and R. Bendix, *Social Mobility in Industrial Society* (Berkeley and Los Angeles: University of California Press, 1958).

T. H. Marshall, *Citizenship and Social Class* (Cambridge: Cambridge University Press, 1950).

Herman P. Miller, *Income Distribution in the United States* (Washington, D.C.: U.S. Department of Commerce, 1966).

John Porter, *The Vertical Mosaic: An Analysis of Class and Power in Canada* (Toronto: University of Toronto Press, 1965).

Albert J. Reiss, Jr., *Occupations and Social Status* (New York: The Free Press of Glencoe, 1962).

Pitirim A. Sorokin, *Social and Cultural Mobility* (New York: The Free Press of Glencoe, 1959).

Kaare Svalastoga, *Social Differentiation* (New York: David McKay, 1965).

Southwestern Social Science Quarterly, 48 (December, 1967), special issue on community power, includes a comprehensive bibliography compiled by R. J. Pellegrin.

T. Veblen, *The Theory of the Leisure Class* (New York: Macmillan, 1912).

Bibliographies

Norval D. Glenn, Jon P. Alston, and David Weiner, *Social Stratification: A Research Bibliography* (Santa Barbara, Calif.: Glendessary Press, 1968).

S. M. Miller, "Comparative Social Mobility," *Current Sociology, 9* (1960), 81–89.

Adaptation 16 / Morris EXERCISES IN STRATIFICATION RESEARCH

Three research exercises have been designed to fit each of the methods discussed above (pp. 155 ff.). The samples and the research procedures called for can be readily dealt with in a classroom or some other small-scale study. Alternative phrasings of questions may be substituted but before being used in an actual study, they should be pretested to be sure they will be understood by the subject population.

SOURCE: Prepared especially for this book by Richard T. Morris.

THE SUBJECTIVE METHOD

The sample Use a large group in your school, or a combination of small groups, or an organization meeting. Try to get at least 100 people to participate. If you can get them all at once, so much the better.

The data The questions are meant to be read to the respondents. However, they can be given ruled and numbered forms with the lists on questions 5 and 6 already typed in.

Ask your subjects to write the answers to these questions:

1. To what class in the U.S.A. would you say you belong? (Write just the name of the class.)

2. To what class in the U.S.A. would you say your father belongs (or did belong, if he is deceased)?

3. To what class in your *own community or home town* would you say you belong?

4. To what class in his home community does (or did) your father belong?

5. Now please write the following words, one under the other: "Upper, Lower upper, Upper middle, Middle, Lower middle, White collar, Working, Upper lower, Lower." Please mark with an "O" your own class, the class in the U.S.A. to which you think you belong. Please mark with an "F" your father's class, the class to which you think your father belongs (or belonged).[4]

6. Now please write the following words, one under another: "Upper, Middle, Working, Lower." Mark one of these with an "O" to indicate your own class and an

"F" to indicate your father's class in America.

7. What is it about your father which made you place him in the class you did? What characteristic did you use to place him?

8. What made you place yourself where you did?

9. What is (or was) your father's main occupation? Be specific: do not just say "businessman"; say what kind of business and his position in that business. (Example: not accountant, but cost accountant in a newsprint papermill.)

10. What occupation do you plan to enter?

11. (Optional) If you were to vote in the next presidential election, would you be apt to vote Democratic, Republican, or other? (Specify.)

12. (Optional) How do you think your father will vote?

The findings To analyze the results, list separately all of the class names used in questions 1 through 4 and enter the number of people who used each of these names. Enter separately the number of people who placed themselves and their fathers in the various classes provided in questions 5 and 6. For each class in question 6 list separately the fathers' occupations from question 9 and the intended occupations from question 10. This might be compared with the occupational distribution in the classes derived from questions 1 through 5. For each class in question 6 list the criteria used for placement of father, question 7, and self, question 8. For each class enter the

number of political affiliations, questions 11 and 12.

The interpretation A study such as this will help you to answer the following kinds of questions as they apply to your particular sample:

1. Where do people place themselves when class names are not supplied in advance?

2. How does this differ from their self-placement when names are provided?

3. What does the "middle" or "working" class consist of?

4. How do occupations spread themselves over the classes?

5. Does voting intention differ by class?

THE REPUTATIONAL METHOD

The judges Use a small community (up to 5,000) for your study. Ask approximately five people who know a large number of individuals in the town to serve as judges. Bankers, clergymen, doctors, established businessmen, town officials, or a newspaper editor might be good possibilities. If you choose judges in the upper income and occupational brackets, however, bear in mind that you will get a picture of the class structure of the community as seen *from the top*. To compare this view with the perspectives from other levels, several investigators might choose judges from different strata in the same community. These judges should also know a large number of families. They might be milkmen, bill collectors, handymen, postmen, or policemen. (See the comment on privacy in INTRODUCTION, page 10.)

---

[4] Note the deliberate redundancy in the phrasing of these instructions. The purpose is to ensure clarity and therefore validity of response.

Judge A (5 classes)	Judge B (5 classes)	Judge C (3 classes)	Judge D (4 classes)	Judge E, F, G . . .
upper 6, 50	upper 6, 36	upper 6, 50	upper 6, 7, 36	
upper-middle 7, 12, 36, 41, etc.	upper-middle 50, 7, 12, 34, 22, etc.		upper-middle 12, 50, 34, etc.	
middle 22, 9, 34, 52, etc.	middle 9, 41, 52, 8, etc.	middle 7, 12, 36, 41, 22, etc.	middle 41, 22, 52, etc.	
lower-middle 8, 10, 26, 46, etc.	lower-middle 10, 26, 17, etc.			
lower 47, 17, 18 etc.	lower 46, 18, 47, etc.	lower 18, 47, etc.	lower 17, 47, 65, etc.	

FIG. VI:1   Example of plotting arrangement for reputational study

The numbers in the cells are the card numbers of the individuals ranked. Etc. indicates that additional rankings were made in the cell. Most judges will not rank all individuals in the sample.

The sample   Take a sample of the town's adults. If possible, get a city directory or other list that includes *all* of the people in the community. You might use a telephone directory, but if you do you will automatically bias your sample by excluding those who do not have telephones or who have unlisted telephones. A city directory is a less biased listing, but it omits people who recently moved to town.

Take each *n*th name. (For example, if there are 5,000, take each fiftieth name for an easily manageable sample of 100.) Write the name and address of each person selected on a separate card. If they are not included, add the judges' names to the set of cards. Number each card.

The data   Ask the judges to do the following operations:

1. Discard the cards listing people they do not know.

2. Sort the remaining cards into piles that represent groups of people who seem to belong together in terms of their general standing in the community. (They may make any number of groupings they wish.)

3. Arrange the piles in order of evaluation, with those who are most highly regarded in the community at the top, those least so at the bottom. (They may rate two or more groupings as having about equal value.)

After they have done this, ask the following information of the judges:

1. What do people generally call these groupings (if they have names for them)?

2. Do the groupings have any particular characteristics: in personality, character, or behavior?

3. What would you estimate is the percentage of the community in each grouping?

4. Are any important groupings omitted from this arrangement? (The judge may not personally know any people in them, or representatives of these groupings may not have been included in the original set of cards.)

5. Why did you group the individuals as you did? (What were the characteristics or criteria the judge used in his groupings?)

As the information is collected the investigator must:

1. Make a record of the cards discarded and of the groupings and ratings made by each judge. Save the discards for verification.

2. During each interview record the characteristics, estimated size, criteria, and names used for each of the groupings by each of the judges.

The findings After the data have been collected from all of the judges, make a summary of your findings. List the name or number of each judge, his position as estimated by the other judges and himself, the number of people he placed, the number of groupings he made, and their relative size.

Next, plot the rated individuals according to the positions assigned to them by the various judges. Use a large sheet of graph paper and enter the number of each individual's card in the class groupings made by each judge. This arrangement will provide a quick visual image of agreement between the judges in their perceptions of the social structure of the community. (See Fig. VI: 1.)

Make a summary statement of the characteristics, criteria, sizes, and names of the classes as perceived by the several judges.

The interpretation From such a study you may get a fairly clear picture of the class structure as seen by certain community members, the degree of agreement among them, and differences in the way the structure is seen from different vantage points.

THE OBJECTIVE METHOD

The sample Try to get about 100 people as subjects from a large college class or several small ones. Ask them the questions during a session.

The data Ask the students to write answers to the following questions, or give them mimeographed forms.

1. What is (or was) your father's main occupation? Be specific. Do not just say "businessman," but state the kind of business and your father's position in that business.

2. (Optional) What is your intended occupation? Be as specific as possible.

3. What was your father's approximate annual average income during his best five years?

4. (Optional) What income do you realistically expect to be making ten years after you graduate?

5. What educational level did your father attain? Use one of the following terms: grade school, some high school, high school graduate, some college, college graduate, some postgraduate, postgraduate degree.

6. What educational level did your mother attain? (Use the same terms as above.)

7. Now we would like to get some information about the personal tastes and preferences of your parents.[5] What sort of pictures are (or were) displayed in your living room at home? Use one of the following terms to indicate the kind of picture. If there is more than one kind displayed, indicate the most frequent kind by "1" for most frequent, "2" for second most frequent, etc.

   a. photographs of family members or friends
   b. photographs of scenery or animals
   c. reproductions of traditional or representational paintings
   d. reproductions of abstract or modern painting
   e. original traditional or representational paintings, including family portraits
   f. original abstract or modern paintings
   g. if others, describe
   h. no pictures

8. What kinds of entertainment do your parents prefer? If they had equal choice and opportunity to attend one of the following events, which would they choose? If more than one, number in order of preference. If mother and father differ, indicate separately by "F" and "M."

   a. ballet
   b. stage play
   c. night baseball, football, or basketball
   d. automobile races
   e. lecture or discussion
   f. symphony concert
   g. night club entertainment
   h. movie
   i. if others, describe

9. What magazines do your parents regularly read? Number in order of frequency if more than one. If mother and father differ, indicate separately.

10. (Optional) Ask questions 7, 8, and 9 of the students themselves.

The findings When the data have been collected, separate the occupations of the fathers as follows:[6]

1. Professionals, proprietors and high officials of large businesses, including gentlemen farmers

2. Semiprofessionals and lower officials of large businesses, clerical, sales, and kindred workers,

---

[5] Cf. Russell Lynes, *The Taste Makers* (New York: Harper & Row, 1954), pp. 310–333.

[6] For a finer breakdown, see W. L. Warner *et al., Social Class in America* (Chicago: Science Research Associates, 1949), pp. 140–141.

skilled workers, proprietors of small businesses including operators of modest-sized farms

3. Semiskilled workers and unskilled workers, including small-scale farmers

Separate the educational levels into:

1. College education
2. High school education
3. Grade school education only

Separate the income levels into:

1. Over $15,000
2. $5,000–$15,000
3. Under $5,000

Now distribute the answers to questions 7 through 9 according to the three kinds of strata. If you separate the strata differently, or make finer groupings, e.g., into seven categories instead of three, the differences in distribution may show up more clearly.

The interpretation The following are some of the questions that can be answered with your data. Does income, occupation, or education make the most difference in the preferences and tastes of your sample? Which area of preference is most clearly differentiated by which criterion, i.e., does artistic preference vary most by education while entertainment preference varies most by occupation? What is the relation between occupation, education, and income in your sample?

If the optional questions are asked about students' own positions and preferences, how do they differ from their parents? Which students differ most? Summarize your findings in tables like those on pages 171–172.

SECTION 2 INEQUALITY

ECONOMIC INEQUALITY

The distribution of family incomes in the United States in 1965 is shown in Figure VI:2. Median family income was $6,882, that is, half the families had incomes above that figure. Families with incomes of $25,000 and over were only 1.5 percent of the total, but 25 percent had incomes of $10,000 or more, and these included many families headed by manual workers. As recently as 1947, the proportion of families with incomes of $10,000 or more (in 1965 dollars) was only 8 percent; it was 10 percent in 1955 and 18 percent in 1960.[7] The society as a whole is now affluent, and yet in 1965 eight million families—17 percent of the total—had incomes below $3,000. Furthermore, the poor were disproportionately nonwhite as shown by the concentration of nonwhite families below $4,000 in Figure VI:3. The median income for white families was nearly double that of nonwhites.

The affluence, if uneven affluence, of the United States compared with other prosperous countries is illustrated in the following estimates of the time an industrial worker had to work in 1958 to earn enough to pay for a standard meal:[8]

United States	60 minutes
Canada	68 minutes
West Germany	131 minutes
United Kingdom	138 minutes
France	277 minutes
Italy	298 minutes

Comparison with underdeveloped nations would show even greater discrepancies.

There is a negative, but far from perfect, correlation between the level of prosperity of nations and the economic inequality within them. In other words, there is generally less inequality in the prosperous countries. This relationship is illustrated by the following estimates of the percentage of the total national income (before taxes) going to the most prosperous 5 percent of the families. The higher the

---

[7] U.S. Bureau of the Census, *Current Population Reports, Consumer Income* (Series P-60, No. 51, January 12, 1967), Table C.

[8] Zoe Campbell, "Food Costs in Work Time Here and Abroad," *Conference Board Business Record*, December, 1959.

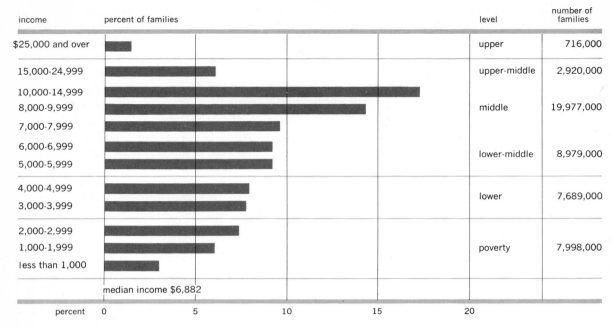

income	percent of families	level	number of families
$25,000 and over		upper	716,000
15,000-24,999		upper-middle	2,920,000
10,000-14,999			
8,000-9,999		middle	19,977,000
7,000-7,999			
6,000-6,999			
5,000-5,999		lower-middle	8,979,000
4,000-4,999			
3,000-3,999		lower	7,689,000
2,000-2,999			
1,000-1,999		poverty	7,998,000
less than 1,000			

median income $6,882

percent   0   5   10   15   20

FIG. VI:2   Stratification of U.S. families by income, 1965

SOURCE: U.S. Bureau of the Census, *Current Population Reports,* Series P-60, No. 49, August 10, 1966. Sample Survey.

percentage, the greater is the income inequality.[9]

United States	20%
Sweden	20
Great Britain	21
West Germany	24
Ceylon	31
Colombia	42
Kenya	51
Southern Rhodesia	65

Perhaps there is no society in which income is more evenly distributed than in the United States, although there may be slightly less inequality in such countries as Denmark, The Netherlands, and Israel.[10]

This discussion is not addressed to related but complicated questions of how earnings are spent and how subsidies for housing, health services, and the like should be evaluated. There is no study that takes all of these factors into consideration. However, it seems probable that the life of the lowest income persons in the Scandinavian states is healthier and more decent than of the poor in the U.S. This is the case even though the U.S. poor have larger cash incomes and more luxury products such as television sets and telephones.

The income distribution in the United States is to a large extent dependent on the educational and occupational distributions, which are shown in simplified form in Figures VI:4 and VI:5. However, as is pointed out in the discussion of status consistency,

[9] Simon Kuznets, "Quantitative Aspects of the Economic Growth of Nations," *Economic Development and Cultural Change, 11* (1963), Table 3.

[10] Herman P. Miller, *Rich Man, Poor Man* (New York: Crowell, 1964), p. 32.

there is not perfect correspondence between educational, occupational, and income levels (see page 177).

Poverty   The definition of poverty differs from society to society and from time to time in any one society.[11] In recent years, the poverty line in the United States has often been drawn, somewhat arbitrarily, at $3,000 for families and at $1,500 for single and unattached persons. As inflation reduces the value of the dollar and as socially defined consumer needs increase, the line should probably be drawn at a higher level; undoubtedly, there are now many poor families with incomes above $3,000.

By these standards, a majority of the people in the United States were poor only a few decades ago, and a great majority of the people in other countries are still poor. However, the social concern caused by poverty, and to a large extent the feelings of deprivation caused .by it, are relative to the contemporary standards in each society.

There is no simple answer nor a single cause to explain why so many people in the most affluent nation cannot afford amenities that most Americans take for granted. Ironically, however, the changes in technology and economic organization that have made the overall high level of income possible are to some extent responsible. The need for unskilled and semiskilled labor has diminished relative to the supply, so that many persons who can offer only muscle power on the labor market find it increasingly difficult to contribute to the economy. For example, modern earth-moving, ditch-digging, and tunnel-boring machines have replaced the pick-and-shovel crews that employed many immigrants and others in earlier years.

Many of the poorly educated and poorly trained are minority peoples. Past discrimination accounts for their relative lack of skills, and present discrimination makes it difficult for them to reap equitable rewards from the skills they have. Not surprisingly, Negroes are only about a tenth of the total popula-

[11] See Miller, *ibid.,* Chap. 5.

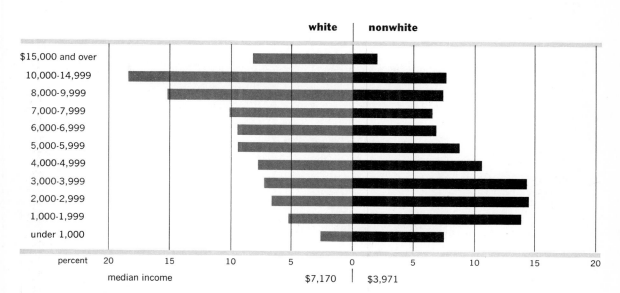

FIG. VI:3   Family income by color, United States, 1965

SOURCE: U.S. Bureau of the Census, *Current Population Reports,* Series P-60, No. 49, August 10, 1966. Sample Survey.

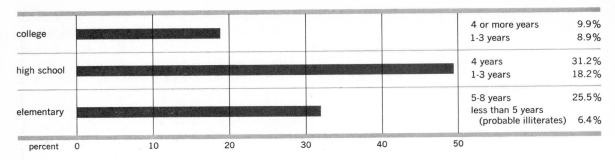

college	4 or more years	9.9%
	1-3 years	8.9%
high school	4 years	31.2%
	1-3 years	18.2%
elementary	5-8 years	25.5%
	less than 5 years (probable illiterates)	6.4%

percent 0   10   20   30   40   50

FIG. VI:4   Stratification of U.S. population twenty-five years old and over, by education, 1966

SOURCE: U.S. Bureau of the Census, *Current Population Reports,* Series P-20, No. 158, December 19, 1966, Table 3. Sample Survey.

tion but are more than a fifth of the poor. See Figure VI:3, which reports Negro and white family incomes.

Changes in technology and economic organization contribute to widespread poverty among farmers and farm laborers. In 1959, more than 15 percent of poor families lived on farms, but the proportion would be reduced somewhat if the value of food produced on the farm were included in the income data. Since 1959 many of these poor people have moved to cities, but often without the skills to compete adequately in the urban labor market. Large-scale commercial agriculture, using modern techniques and expensive farm equipment, has made the small fam-

ily farm obsolete and has eliminated the need for thousands of farm workers.

At least a fourth of all poor families have heads sixty-five years old and older, and more than half of all families with elderly heads are poor—another example of poverty exacerbated by changes in technology and economic organization. There is a secure economic niche for the elderly in agrarian societies, where age brings increased rights and privileges within the extended family, which is usually the producing unit. In contrast, the extended family in industrial societies is not an important economic unit, and the industrial society does not revere age nor

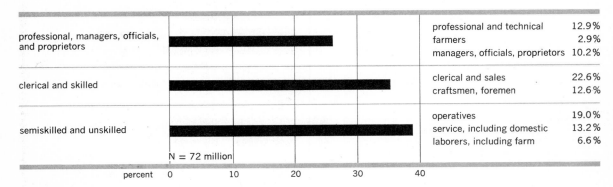

professional, managers, officials, and proprietors	professional and technical	12.9%
	farmers	2.9%
	managers, officials, proprietors	10.2%
clerical and skilled	clerical and sales	22.6%
	craftsmen, foremen	12.6%
semiskilled and unskilled	operatives	19.0%
	service, including domestic	13.2%
	laborers, including farm	6.6%

N = 72 million

percent 0   10   20   30   40

FIG. VI:5   Stratification of employed population of U.S. by occupational groupings, 1966

SOURCE: *Statistical Abstract of the United States: 1966.* Derived from data in Table 323.

provide so well for the aged. The plight of the elderly worsens as technology reduces the need for manual labor and tends to lower the retirement age. At the same time advances in medical technology and improvements in nutrition and living conditions increase longevity. Aside from these major categories of the poor, many people have low incomes because they are disabled or in poor health, because they are women with children but no husband, or because they suffer from other handicaps.

Since such a large proportion of the poor consist of the elderly, the middle-aged unskilled, husbandless women with children, and persons with severe mental and physical handicaps, poverty cannot be eliminated by increasing the productivity of the poor. Rather it can be significantly reduced only by modification of the traditional norm that the right to consume beyond a minimum provided by public "relief" is proportional to the value of the individual's contribution to the economy. Proposals for a negative income tax or a guaranteed annual income, recently made even by conservative economists, indicate that the norm is already weakening.

PRESTIGE

Prestige in small communities Early and influential studies using the reputational technique were conducted by W. Lloyd Warner and his associates in Newburyport, Massachusetts, a city of 17,000 north of the Boston suburbs, and in Morris, Illinois, a community of 6,000 a few miles south of the Chicago suburbs. In the research reports Newburyport is called "Yankee City" and Morris is "Jonesville," "Elmtown," "Hometown," or "Prairie City." A team of researchers supervised by Warner also studied a town of 10,000 population in the deep South, called "Old City," and other workers influenced by Warner investigated the distribution of prestige in communities from California to Connecticut.[12]

These studies found that people in a small, homogeneous community tend to use similar criteria in evaluating one another (that is, in granting prestige), but that there is not complete uniformity of criteria. At the lower economic levels money is a more important criterion whereas manners, taste, and family background count for more at the higher levels. Considering the community as a whole, Warner concluded that occupation was the most important basis for prestige in Morris. Among the variables measured and quantitatively analyzed, amount of income, source of income, house type, dwelling area, and amount of education followed occupation in that order.

The Warner researchers found that family background was salient in Newburyport and in "Old City" (in the deep South), but that it was less important in Morris. In the former two communities, an "upper-upper class" was differentiated from a "lower-upper class" on the basis of lineage. Although the lower-uppers had more money on the average than the upper-uppers, the latter were granted social superiority because they were from prominent old families.

Six prestige levels were distinguished in Newburyport and five in Morris. Although these levels are called "social classes" in the research reports, they are not classes in the strict sense but rather prestige strata. However, at least the higher levels appear to be cohesive social groupings, bound together by ties of intimate interaction. Therefore, they approximate

[12] The "Yankee City" Series (New Haven: Yale University Press): W. L. Warner and P. S. Lunt, *The Social Life of a Modern Community* (1941); W. L. Warner and P. S. Lunt, *The Status System of a Modern Community* (1942); W. L. Warner and Leo Srole, *The Social Systems of American Ethnic Groups* (1945); W. L. Warner and J. O. Low, *The Social System of the Modern Factory* (1947); W. Lloyd Warner, *The Living and the Dead* (1959).

The "Old City" study: Allison Davis, B. B. Gardner, and M. R. Gardner, *Deep South* (Chicago: University of Chicago Press, 1941).

The "Jonesville" studies: W. Lloyd Warner, Robert J. Havighurst, Martin B. Loeb, *Who Shall Be Educated?* (New York: Harper & Row, 1944); W. L. Warner and Associates, *Democracy in Jonesville* (New York: Harper & Row, 1949); W. L. Warner, Marchia Meeker, and Kenneth Eels, *Social Class in America* (Chicago: Science Research Associates, 1949); R. J. Havighurst and Hilda Taba, *Adolescent Character and Personality* (New York: Wiley, 1948); and A. B. Hollingshead, *Elmtown's Youth* (New York: Wiley, 1949).

For a summary statement see W. Lloyd Warner, *American Life, Dream and Reality* (Chicago: University of Chicago Press, 1962).

what Weber called "status groups" (see page 154).

Warner claims that the people not only arranged one another into a prestige hierarchy but that they also perceived discrete strata. Other studies have found that whereas people in small communities do perceive discrete levels, rather than a continuous array of individuals and families, there is little agreement on the number and relative size of the strata perceived.[13] The six- and five-layered prestige hierarchies Warner identified seem to reflect primarily the perceptions of some of his "upper-middle class" informants.[14]

The information about values, behavior, life-styles, and occupational characteristics of the "social classes" described by Warner and his associates has been widely disseminated among the American public, through social science courses in high schools and colleges and through popular books and periodicals. Such terms as "upper-middle class" and "lower-middle class" have become household terms, and the images they elicit probably approximate Warner's descriptions. For instance, the "lower-middle class," consisting of small-businessmen, clerks, salesmen, and a few skilled workers, is thought of as relatively conservative, work-oriented, thrifty, religious, temperate, chaste, and concerned with respectability.

However, Warner's picture of the different prestige levels is no longer accurate, if indeed it ever was pertinent beyond the communities where the research was done. The Newburyport study was conducted in the early 1930s and the Morris study in the early 1940s. Even then, small, static towns located just outside commuting range of large metropolises were not representative of the country as a whole, nor even of all small communities in the United States. It is hardly surprising, then, that recent national opinion poll data show clerical and sales workers to deviate markedly from Warner's "lower-middle

class."[15] Instead of being relatively temperate, they report the smallest proportion of teetotalers of any occupational category. Instead of being the most conservative, they are less conservative than people in the higher ranking occupations on most political and economic issues and are less conservative than farmers and all categories of manual workers on most issues relating to sex, religion, international relations, and civil liberties. Furthermore, they evince no unusual degree of thrift, commitment to work, or religious interest. There are similar disparities between recent national data and Warner's characterization of the other prestige levels.

In most large communities prestige criteria are less uniform than in small towns, and usually there is no commonly perceived prestige hierarchy. Prestige criteria differ between Negroes and whites and among the different ethnic communities. Such deviant subcultures as the underworld, the hippies, and the homosexuals have their own bases for prestige.

Occupational prestige Individuals who cannot be ranked accurately in overall prestige can be ranked in the prestige they derive from their occupations. Studies conducted in the United States since 1925 show a high degree of agreement in the prestige granted specific occupations. In the two best-known studies done by the National Opinion Research Center (NORC) in 1947 and 1963, 90 occupations were rated by a national sample. The ratings from the more recent study are shown in Table VI:1.

The prestige scores, which could vary from 20 through 100, correlate about equally well with median income and median educational attainments of workers in the occupations, but neither correlation is perfect. For instance, minister and schoolteacher rank higher in prestige than in income, but undertaker and singer in nightclub have less prestige than

[13] Harold F. Kaufman, "Members of a Rural Community as Judges of Prestige Rank," *Sociometry, 9* (1946), 71–85; and Gerhard E. Lenski, "American Social Classes: Statistical Strata or Social Groups," *American Journal of Sociology, 63* (1952), 139–144.

[14] Seymour Martin Lipset and Reinhard Bendix, "Social Status and Social Structure: A Re-examination of Data and Interpretations," I, *British Journal of Sociology, 2* (1951), 162.

[15] Norval D. Glenn and Jon P. Alston, "Rural-Urban Differences in Reported Attitudes and Behavior," *Southwestern Social Science Quarterly, 47* (1967), 381–400.

TABLE VI:1   THE RATINGS OF OCCUPATIONS

OCCUPATION	SCORE	OCCUPATION	SCORE
U.S. Supreme Court Justice	94	Newspaper columnist	73
Physician	93	Policeman	72
Nuclear physicist	92		
Scientist	92	AVERAGE	71
Government scientist	91	Reporter on a daily newspaper	71
State governor	91	Bookkeeper	70
Cabinet member in the federal government	90	Radio announcer	70
College professor	90	Insurance agent	69
U.S. Representative in Congress	90	Tenant farmer—one who owns livestock	
Chemist	89	and machinery and manages the farm	69
Diplomat in the U.S. Foreign Service	89	Local official of a labor union	67
Lawyer	89	Manager of a small store in a city	67
Architect	88	Mail carrier	66
County judge	88	Railroad conductor	66
Dentist	88	Traveling salesman for a wholesale concern	66
Mayor of a large city	87	Plumber	65
Member of the board of directors		Barber	63
of a large corporation	87	Machine operator in a factory	63
Minister	87	Owner-operator of a lunch stand	63
Psychologist	87	Playground director	63
Airline pilot	86	Corporal in the regular army	62
Civil engineer	86	Garage mechanic	62
Head of a department in a state government	86	Truck driver	59
Priest	86	Fisherman who owns his own boat	58
Banker	85	Clerk in a store	56
Biologist	85	Milk route man	56
Sociologist	83	Streetcar motorman	56
Captain in the regular army	82	Lumberjack	55
Accountant for a large business	81	Restaurant cook	55
Public schoolteacher	81	Singer in a nightclub	54
Building contractor	80	Filling station attendant	51
Owner of a factory that employs		Coal miner	50
about 100 people	80	Dock worker	50
Artist who paints pictures that are		Night watchman	50
exhibited in galleries	78	Railroad section hand	50
Author of novels	78	Restaurant waiter	49
Economist	78	Taxi driver	49
Musician in a symphony orchestra	78	Bartender	48
Official of an international labor union	77	Farmhand	48
County agricultural agent	76	Janitor	48
Electrician	76	Clothes presser in a laundry	45
Railroad engineer	76	Soda fountain clerk	44
Owner-operator of a printing shop	75	Sharecropper—one who owns no livestock or	
Trained machinist	75	equipment and does not manage farm	42
Farm owner and operator	74	Garbage collector	39
Undertaker	74	Street sweeper	36
Welfare worker for a city government	74	Shoe shiner	34

SOURCE: Robert W. Hodge, Paul M. Seigel, and Peter H. Rossi, "Occupational Prestige in the United States, 1925–1963," *American Journal of Sociology, 70* (November, 1964), 286–302. Used by permission of Professor Hodge and The University of Chicago Press.

predicted by income. One occupation, farm owner and operator, is granted more prestige than predicted by either income or education.

Obviously, the prestige of occupations is not a simple function of their economic rewards and educational requirements. Responsibility entailed, autonomy afforded, and similar characteristics may be important determinants.[16] Significantly, some manual occupations rank above several nonmanual ones, suggesting that the historic distinction between hand work and head work is not of overriding importance.

Many of the changes in the prestige scores between 1947 and 1963 are so small that they could result from chance differences in the samples of raters. (The correlation of the scores for the two dates is + .99.) However, consistency in the types of occupations for which ratings changed suggests that some of the changes are real. For instance, ratings of most scientific occupations increased while most artistic occupations declined, apparently reflecting a small, but perhaps meaningful, shift in American values.

International comparisons of occupational prestige reveal overall similarities but many moderate differences in the evaluations of specific occupations.[17] Correlations of foreign studies with the 1963 NORC study average higher for white-collar than for blue-collar occupations—an indication of greater variability of prestige of manual occupations. Some scholars conclude that an overall similarity of prestige rankings of occupations in countries with dissimilar cultures indicates that prestige reflects a "functional importance," not dependent on the peculiar values of the society.

POWER

Community power For practical reasons, the study of power in American sociology has been concentrated at the community level perhaps because it is so difficult to deal with national power systems.

Recent work on community power began with a study of Atlanta, the results of which were published in 1953.[18] Hunter reported a monolithic covert "power structure," that is, a small group of men, mostly wealthy businessmen, who did not occupy formal positions of political authority but had a determining voice in almost all important community decisions. Although the man in the street could not identify the members of the power structure, they were discovered through the reputational technique with a panel of strategically placed informants.

Other studies have found that the distribution of power in Atlanta described by Hunter is not typical of American communities and, in fact, may be rare.[19] Dozens of community studies since 1953 show a remarkable variety of power arrangements. For instance, the communities vary in the visibility of their leaders. Some have *visible* leaders, influentials who are almost universally recognized as such. Others have *concealed* leaders, known to strategically placed judges but not to the general public. Others have *symbolic* leaders with reputed but not real power. Some communities have leaders of each type. Communities also differ in the scope of influence of their leaders who may exert power on a wide range of community issues or only on a few. Finally, communities vary in the cohesiveness of their leadership; the different leaders may form a social group and

---

[16] A number of studies report some correlates of occupational prestige but there is no conclusive evidence of causation. For example, see Albeno P. Garbin and Frederick L. Bates, "Occupational Prestige: An Empirical Study of Its Correlates," *Social Forces, 40* (1961), 131–136.

[17] Robert W. Hodge, Donald J. Treiman, and Peter H. Rossi, "A Comparative Study of Occupational Prestige," in Reinhard Bendix and Seymour Martin Lipset (eds.), *Class, Status and Power: Social Stratification in Comparative Perspective* (2nd ed.; New York: The Free Press of Glencoe, 1966), pp. 309–321.

[18] Floyd Hunter, *Community Power Structure: A Study of Decision-Makers* (Chapel Hill: University of North Carolina Press, 1953).

[19] Charles M. Bonjean and David M. Olson, "Community Leadership: Directions of Research," *Administrative Science Quarterly, 9* (1964), 278–300.

exercise their influence in unison, or each may be more or less independent.

There is considerable but inconclusive evidence that the distribution of power in American communities is becoming more pluralistic and amorphous.[20] That is, power may be more widely distributed among competing individuals and groups, none of whom is able, nor perhaps motivated, to influence a wide range of decisions at the community level. Furthermore, interrelations of local organizations with national and regional ones may further diminish community power.[21]

National power If power is becoming more diffuse within American communities, it is not necessarily becoming more effectively shared by the population. The decline of discernible, well-defined monolithic power structures within communities may be a function of a nationwide centralization of decision-making. If few important decisions are made at the community level, local power elites have little reason for being, and there may be little motivation to monopolize local power. The apparent decline in the power of business in some communities is not proof of decline in the national power of business institutions.[22] If the most important decisions affecting business interests are now made at the state and national levels, business leaders may be quite willing to abdicate local power.

There is no conclusive estimate of the trend in the national distribution of power in the United States and in other industrial societies. Some evidence points to an increasing concentration of power in a fairly cohesive power elite; other evidence points to a wider distribution of power among a variety of interest groups that operate at the national level.

C. Wright Mills held that crucial decisions are made primarily by a rather cohesive power elite of not more than 200 to 300 individuals, consisting of (1) the *corporate elite,* major executives and board members of larger corporations; (2) the *military elite,* top-ranking admirals and generals; and (3) the *political elite,* made up of the President and the most influential members of the executive branch of the federal government.[23] Congress is relegated to what Mills calls the "middle levels of power," where relatively unimportant decisions are made. The power elite, he claims, decided to use the atomic bomb against Japan in 1945, to intervene militarily in Korea in 1950, and to set the course of United States policy in the "cold war." Furthermore, he claims that the members of the power elite are similar enough in background, outlook, and interests so that they tend to act in unison; the power of one segment does not offset the power of others.

Most sociologists and political scientists do not accept this thesis without qualifications. A contradictory "balance thesis" holds that major decisions tend to be compromises among the several interest groups, each of which has veto power that prevents decisions entirely contrary to its interests.[24] Those who hold this view believe that power in the United States has become more diffuse in recent decades, as a result of a proliferation of interest groups, modifications in the capitalist system, and a diversification of business interests.

Obviously, both views cannot be entirely correct, but each may emphasize important aspects of reality. In fact, Mills concedes that the balance thesis correctly describes the decision-making process at the "middle levels of power," and he is probably correct that the general public does not play an active role in major decisions of war and peace. Few would contend, for instance, that the decision to intervene

[20] John Walton, "The Vertical Axis of Community Organization and the Structure of Power," *Southwestern Social Science Quarterly, 48* (December, 1967); and Claire W. Gilbert, "Some Trends in Community Politics: A Secondary Analysis of Power Structure Data from 166 Communities," *ibid.*

[21] Roland Warren, "Toward a Reformulation of Community Theory," *Human Organization, 15* (1962), 8–11.

[22] A decline in El Paso, Texas, is reported in William D'Antonio and Eugene C. Erickson, "The Reputational Technique as a Measure of Community Power," *American Sociological Review, 27* (1962), 362–375.

[23] C. Wright Mills, *The Power Elite* (New York: Oxford University Press, 1956), Chap. 12.

[24] David Riesman, *The Lonely Crowd* (New Haven: Yale University Press, 1951), pp. 242–255.

militarily in Viet Nam was made by an informed and active general public; at the time, most of the public had no well-crystallized opinions and lacked adequate information to form them. However, it is doubtful that decisions of this nature affecting major aspects of international relations have ever been controlled by an active and informed general public.

SECTION 3 STATUS AND LIFE-STYLES

CORRELATES OF SOCIAL STRATIFICATION

Findings from hundreds of studies show that stratification is interwoven with the ways people live, act, and think. Examples of such data are summarized in the accompanying tables. Table VI:2 reports differences in life chances and privileges, Table VI:3 in attitudes and behavior. For illustrative purposes, cases were chosen that vary in an orderly manner from the higher to the lower strata.

The data show correlations, or statistical associations, between the stratification variables and the characteristics listed; they do not of themselves demonstrate causation. (See "Interpreting Correlations," page 173.) Many of the studies that treat stratification correlates are concerned with explaining the differences among the strata as well as describing them. The link between stratification and the correlated variable in some cases can be established as one of cause and effect, but in other cases remains a matter of statistical association. The several dimensions of stratification often show different relations to attitudes, behavior, and outlooks. For instance, Table VI:3 indicates that income is *directly* related to reported happiness, that is, the higher the income, the higher reported happiness. At most income levels, however, education is *inversely* related to reported happiness.

The differences among the social levels should not obscure the great variation in attitudes and behavior at each level. Except in cases where there is high consensus in the whole society, no social level in the United States shows a high uniformity of behavior or attitudes. Furthermore some data show an erratic profile with the middle strata deviating from the two extremes. However, the broad trend of findings points to the fact that position in the stratification system affects a multitude of details of life, behavior, and thought.

LIFE AT THE TOP

The consequences of variation in wealth, prestige, and power are most evident in the ways of life of the rich and the poor. At the top of society is a community of mutually aware families, most of whom inherit a substantial fortune, so they may, if they wish, live without working. But the rich do not always rank at the top in prestige; for instance, the names of many wealthy financiers and executives are not well known to the public. Some celebrities are not wealthy, and some very powerful men lack high prestige. Therefore, descriptions of elites depend on which dimension of stratification is used to define the elite.

Although wealth tends to be achieved before power and perhaps prestige, it may come as a consequence of recognition of accomplishments as it has for many generals and politicians. The attainments of individuals *qualify* them for membership in elites, but their full acceptance to newly won status in many cases depends on the acceptability of the whole family. There may be doubt about the existence of class consciousness at most levels of society, but there is little question about the self-awareness of the upper class.

One reason why so little well-documented infor-

TABLE VI:2 STRATIFICATION CORRELATES: LIFE CHANCES AND PRIVILEGES, UNITED STATES

RELATED FACTORS	(*)	STRATA		
		Lower	Middle	Upper
Standardized mortality ratios [a]	(O)	Unskilled workers: 120	Skilled workers: 96	Professionals: 82
Lifetime income [b]	(E)	Less than 8 years of school—$131,000	High school graduates—$246,000	College graduates—$386,000
Annual mean income [c]	(E)	Less than 8 years of school—$3,641	High school graduates—$6,693	College graduates—$10,062
Attend college [d]	(I)	Children from families with incomes under $5,000—9%	Children from families with incomes $5,000–$7,500—17%	Children from families with incomes of $10,000 or more—44%
Index of marital instability [e]	(I)	Low income—23	Middle income—10	High income—6
Dental visits per year per person [f]	(I)	Family income under $2,000—0.8	Family income $4,000–$7,000—1.4	Family income $7,000 or more—2.3
Obesity of women [g]	(I)	Low income—52%	Medium income—43%	High income—9%

* Parenthetical letters indicate the bases for stratification in the studies cited: (I) income, (O) occupation, (E) education.

[a] L. Guralnick, "The Study of Mortality by Occupation in the United States," (Washington, D.C.: National Office of Vital Statistics, September, 1959). (Ratio between the number of deaths and the number of deaths expected, adult white males, 1950).

[b] Statistical Abstract of the United States, 1966, Table 158. (Males only)

[c] Statistical Abstract of the United States, 1966, Table 158. (Males only)

[d] Herman P. Miller, Rich Man, Poor Man (New York: Crowell, 1964), p. 171.

[e] J. Richard Udry, "Marital Instability by Race and Income Based on 1960 Census Data," American Journal of Sociology, 72 (1967), 673. [The index is an estimate of the percentage of white males 25 through 34 years of age who have had one or more broken marriages. The index is higher for nonwhites at all income levels.]

[f] Statistical Abstract of the United States, 1966, Table 82.

[g] Robert G. Burnight and Parker G. Marden, "Social Correlates of Weight in an Aging Population," The Milbank Memorial Fund Quarterly, 45 (1967), 75–92.

mation is available about the life-styles of elites is that the rich and powerful can prevent the intrusions into their privacy that systematic and detailed study entails.[25] Nevertheless, the following characterization of the "old family" upper stratum in large American cities is probably both accurate and representative:

They live in one or more exclusive and expensive residential areas in fine old houses in which many of them were born, or in elaborately simple modern ones which they have constructed. In these houses, old or new, there are the correct furnishings and the cherished equipage. Their clothing, even when it is apparently casual and undoubtedly old, is somehow

[25] The "conspicuous consumption" and "ostentatious display of wealth" described by Veblen are more characteristic of the newly rich than of established upper-stratum people. See Thorstein Veblen, The Theory of the Leisure Class (New York: Macmillan, 1912).

TABLE VI:3   STRATIFICATION CORRELATES: ATTITUDES AND BEHAVIOR,
UNITED STATES

RELATED FACTORS	(*)	STRATA		
		Lower	*Middle*	*Upper*
Say they are "very happy" [a]	(I)	Income under $3,000 —14%	Income from $5,000–$6,000 —26%	Income $10,000 or more—38%
Think ideal number of children is three or less [b]	(O)	Laborers—27%	Clerical and sales workers —52%	Professionals and semiprofessionals—54%
Believe there is a Devil [c]	(O)	Laborers—72%	Clerical and sales workers —55%	Professionals and semiprofessionals—46%
Political conservatives [d]	(O)	Laborers—8%	Clerical and sales workers—39%	Professionals and semiprofessionals—41%
Church members [e]	(O)	Laborers—59%	Clerical and sales workers —80%	Professionals and semiprofessionals—87%
Report no close friends [f]	(O)	Unskilled workers —30%	Skilled, small business, and white-collar workers—13%	Professionals, top business, and officials —10%
Read a daily newspaper [g]	(O)	Laborers—59%	Clerical and sales workers—86%	Professionals and semiprofessionals—89%

* Parenthetical letters indicate the bases for stratification in the studies cited: (I) income, (O) occupation.

[a] Norman M. Bradburn and David Caplovitz, *Reports on Happiness* (Chicago: Aldine, 1965), p. 9.

[b] Gallup Survey *671* (1963).

[c] Gallup Survey *580* (1957).

[d] Gallup Survey *649* (1961).

[e] Gallup Survey *532* (1954).

[f] Joseph A. Kahl, *The American Class Structure* (New York: Holt, Rinehart and Winston, 1957), pp. 137–138.

[g] Gallup Survey *578* (1957).

different in cut and hang from the clothes of other men and women. The things they buy are quietly expensive and they use them in an inconspicuous way. They belong to clubs and organizations to which others like themselves are admitted, and they take quite seriously their appearances in these associations.

They have relatives and friends in common, but more than that, they have in common experiences of a carefully selected and family-controlled sort. They have attended the same or similar private and ex-clusive schools, preferably one of the Episcopal boarding schools of New England. Their men have been to Harvard, Yale, Princeton, or if local pride could not be overcome, to a locally esteemed college to which their families have contributed. And now they frequent the clubs of these schools, as well as leading clubs in their own city, and as often as not, also a club or two in other metropolitan centers.

Their names are not in the chattering, gossiping columns or even the society columns of their local newspapers. . . . For those established at the top are

INTERPRETING CORRELATIONS

Correlation is a measure of how accurately the magnitude of one variable can be estimated from another. For example, the correlation between years of school completed and personal income allows the investigator to estimate one variable from knowing another more accurately than he could by guessing. The highest possible correlation coefficient—1.00—indicates that two variables are so perfectly related that one can always be exactly stated on the basis of the other. A coefficient of 0.00 shows that no relationship exists between the two variables. A plus sign before the coefficient indicates that higher values of one variable are associated with higher values of the other, and a negative sign shows that higher values of one variable are associated with lower values of the other. The coefficient of correlation is symbolized by the letter "r."

Correlation in itself is never conclusive proof of cause and effect. A correlation between variables x and y may mean either that (1) x influences y, (2) y influences x, (3) x and y influence one another, (4) x and y are both influenced by another variable or a number of other variables, (5) the correlation is accidental, a result of chance, or (6) x and y contain a common component. Sometimes one or more of these possibilities can be ruled out by the sequence in which the variables occur. For instance, in any one generation, most formal education precedes occupational attainment, and therefore the latter usually cannot influence the former. However, the fact that education usually occurs first does not conclusively establish it as an influence on occupation (although for other reasons we know that it is). The correlation between education and occupation could partly reflect the common influence of family background, ambition, and similar variables on the two correlated variables.

Sometimes two variables are correlated because they contain a common component, in which case no causation of any kind should be inferred. For instance, two estimates, or indexes, of social standing may both be based partly on annual income, and for this reason alone they will be correlated. This is called *contamination* and means that something is being correlated with itself.

It is possible to estimate what proportion of the variation in one variable is explained by variation in another by squaring the coefficient of correlation. Suppose that income has a correlation of 0.50 with club membership. By squaring this correlation we find that income explains (accounts for) 25 percent of the variance in membership (or vice versa); 75 percent remains to be explained by factors other than income. A correlation of 0.50, although not statistically large, is fairly large in sociological research. Low correlations in social science may be due to imprecision in measurement, but more often they reflect the multiple causation of social phenomena; a social event or condition is rarely the outcome of only one or two other influences.

"proud"; those not yet established are merely conceited.

Almost everywhere in America, the metropolitan upper classes have in common, more or less, race, religion, and nativity. . . . In each city, they tend to be Protestant; moreover Protestants of class-church denominations, Episcopalian mainly, or Unitarian, or Presbyterian.[28]

[28] Mills, *op. cit.*, pp. 56–60.

In contrast to people at the middle levels, upper-stratum people are oriented to the past rather than the future, they emphasize "being" rather than "doing," and they are less individualistic and more concerned with lineage.[27]

According to one observer, there is a subtle upper-class accent in the United States that cuts across regional differences; it may be heard in Boston, New York, Chicago, San Francisco, or Philadelphia.[28] Furthermore, word usage differentiates the uppermost stratum from the middle levels. Euphemisms, circumlocutions, and pretentious speech are less common at the top; speech is simpler, more straightforward, terser, and by middle-class standards, often vulgar.

Fadiman gives the following impression of upper and non-upper usage: [29]

Upper	Non-upper
begin	commence
died	passed away
poor	underprivileged
kin	relative

Some observers believe that the social elites in the larger American cities are merging into a national upper class, largely as the result of the rise of national corporate enterprise and rapid communications and transportation.[30] Several institutions seem to have been instrumental in the growth of this class, the most important of which are the New England boarding schools and the fashionable eastern colleges. At these, the rich and well-born from all large cities intermingle, intermarry, and form ties that endure after they return to their respective communities. The development of the Episcopal Church into a national upper-class institution has both promoted

and been a result of the increased solidarity of the intercity moneyed elite in the United States.

LIFE AT THE BOTTOM

In contrast to the dearth of reliable information on upper-stratum life-styles, numerous studies deal with the culture and behavior of lower-class or working-class people.[31] However, the results of these studies are somewhat inconsistent, partly because the lower strata are not uniformly defined, and partly because lower-stratum values and behavior vary by race, ethnicity, religion, region, and community size. The description below is restricted to elements that several lower-class subcultures seem to have in common. Studies frequently include all manual workers in the lower stratum, but relatively few skilled workers evince the characteristics of the lowest strata.

Lower-stratum people tend to be politically liberal, but their liberalism is usually confined to welfare and labor issues that clearly involve their economic interests. In almost all other respects, lower-stratum people, considered as a whole, are more conservative than middle- and upper-stratum people. In religious beliefs, they are often fundamentalists. Even if they are not affiliated with a church or religious organization, they usually believe in a Devil, in the virgin birth of Christ, and in a literal interpretation of the scriptures. On the average, they are less favorable to civil liberties, more ethnocentric, more authoritarian, and more isolationist than people at higher levels.

In personal sex morality, a double standard prevails; males typically begin sex relations early and may consider frequent intercourse as necessary to health and to proof of masculinity, but many men expect their wives to be virginal at marriage.[32] Quite

---

[27] E. Digby Baltzell, *Philadelphia Gentlemen: The Making of a National Upper Class* (New York: The Free Press of Glencoe, 1958), p. 52.

[28] *Ibid.,* p. 50.

[29] Clifton Fadiman, "Is There an Upper-Class American Language?" *Holiday* (October, 1956), pp. 8–10.

[30] For instance, both Mills and Baltzell express this view in their publications cited in footnotes 23 and 27.

[31] Glenn and Alston, *ibid.*

[32] Alfred C. Kinsey, Wardell B. Pomeroy, and Clyde E. Martin, *Sexual Behavior in the Human Male* (Philadelphia: Saunders, 1948), pp. 374–384; and William F. Whyte, "A Slum Sex Code," *American Journal of Sociology,* 49 (1943), 24–31. More recent studies confirm these findings.

SOCIAL RANK AND DISASTER AT SEA

Britain of the Edwardian period was characterized by well-defined social strata and a strong sense of class identity. The great trans-Atlantic liners of the time with their sharp demarcations between classes of passengers were an expression of the status system in extreme form. The *Titanic,* a ship of the British White Star Line, was commissioned in 1912. The largest and most luxurious liner of her day, she was reputed to be the safest. She carried lifeboats for about 1,200 passengers, or only 30 percent of her total capacity, but safety regulations of the time required even fewer lifeboats. On her maiden voyage she collided with an iceberg in the North Atlantic and sank with the loss of more than 1,500 of her 2,200 passengers and crew.

A few years earlier when another White Star Liner, the *Republic,* sank, Captain Sealby told passengers entering the lifeboats, "Remember! Women and children go first, then the First Cabin, then the others." * There was no such rule aboard the *Titanic,* but the survivors were not a random sample of the passengers. Historical research and cold statistics suggest that a convergence of indifference, carelessness, luck, and location worked in favor of the first-class and against the third-class passengers. Of 143 women in first class only 4 were casualties (2.8 percent), and 3 of these were casualties "by choice." Of 93 women in second class there were 15 casualties (16.1 percent). Of 179 women in third class, 81 were casualties (45.3 percent). Only one of the 29 children in first and second class was lost, but only 23 out of 76 children in steerage were saved.

Investigations were held in both Britain and the United States, but in neither country was the moral drawn nor the statistical inference made. After the disaster new rules were passed governing lifeboats and safety measures. As Lord put it, "The night was a magnificent confirmation of 'women and children first,' yet somehow the loss rate was higher for Third Class children than First Class men. It was a contrast which would never get by the social consciousness (or news sense) of today's press." †

* Walter Lord, *A Night to Remember* (New York: Holt, Rinehart and Winston, 1955), pp. 107–109 *et passim.* Quotation at p. 109.

† *Ibid.,* p. 108.

often, neither the husband nor the wife expects the wife to enjoy intercourse; she yields only because it is her duty to do so, but this pattern is apparently changing.[33] Relations between husband and wife are frequently lacking in warmth and effective communication;[34] perhaps partly because of this, rates of marital dissolution are much greater than in higher strata.[35] The ideal of male dominance is strong but is probably less often realized than at higher levels; unemployment and low earnings tend to undermine the authority of the husband and father.

Working-class child-rearing practices have changed in recent years; once they were more permissive than middle-stratum practices, but now they are less so.[36] (See SOCIALIZATION, p. 101.) Physical punishment is more often used to discipline children, and threat of withdrawal of affection is less often used. Working-class parents discipline their children mainly to control their present behavior, whereas the higher strata are more concerned with inculcating standards and ideals that will guide future behavior.

Lower-stratum people participate much less in formal organizations than middle-stratum people, they report fewer friends, and much of their visiting and primary interaction is with kin. If relatives do not live nearby, vacations are likely to be spent with them.[37]

Lower-stratum people value education for its vocational and economic utility. They may sacrifice to send a son to college but think that sending a daughter is a waste of money.[38] If a daughter is sent to college, she is likely to be encouraged to go into elementary education or some other vocational curriculum. Neither a liberal arts education nor training in social skills is considered important.[39]

Many working-class people do not fit the above description, and with increasing education, they seem to be moving toward behavior characterized as middle class. However, the middle strata are also changing because the higher strata are often in the vanguard of cultural change.

The poorest families are often jobless and therefore detached from integrating ties with the world of work. Frequently the father has left the family group, and children are early thrown on their own resources. The very poor generally lack the confidence and social connections to make new friends once they have left school.[40] The resulting isolation and shortage of funds, often compounded by indebtedness, moves the women to seek jobs. Many husbands object, feeling their capacity to handle responsibility being challenged. A sense of isolation pervades interaction within the family so that on important issues, notably sexual matters, embarrassment or insecurity causes aloofness.[41]

Exposure to sexuality both at home, where overcrowding reduces privacy, and on the streets socializes the young to sexual roles by their early teens, and there is a high rate of adolescent illegitimacy.

Lower-class teen-agers find little reason for deferring gratification and applying themselves in school. Lack of opportunity perpetuates itself by inducing behavior which, by middle-class standards, appears aimless, defeatist, cynical, and irresponsible. An attitude that fate is fickle and that prior effort

---

[33] Lee Rainwater and Gerald Handel, "Changing Family Roles in the Working Class," in Arthur B. Shostak and William Gomberg (eds.), *Blue-Collar World: Studies of the American Worker* (Englewood Cliffs, N.J.: Prentice-Hall, 1964).

[34] Mirra Komarovsky, *Blue-Collar Marriage* (New York: Random House, 1964).

[35] William J. Goode, "Marital Satisfaction and Instability," *International Social Science Journal*, 5 (1962), 507–526.

[36] Urie Bronfenbrenner, "Socialization and Social Class through Time and Space," in E. E. Maccoby, T. M. Newcomb, and E. L. Hartley (eds.), *Readings in Social Psychology* (3rd ed.; New York: Holt, Rinehart and Winston, 1958), pp. 400–425.

[37] S. M. Miller and Frank Riessman, "The Working-Class Subculture: A New View," *Social Problems*, 9 (1961), 86–97.

[38] Lower-level Negroes are a significant exception to this generalization.

[39] Miller and Riessman, *op. cit.*

[40] Komarovsky, *op. cit.,* Chap. 14.

[41] Lee Rainwater, *And the Poor Get Children* (Chicago: Quadrangle Books, 1960), Chap. 5.

cannot prevent illness, injury, or misfortune increases an already high susceptibility to disruptive encounters.

Since lower-class people are going nowhere, their sense of time is vague and casual. Preoccupation with the immediate environment plus a cynical distrust of those in authority reduces interest in politics.

STATUS CONSISTENCY AND INCONSISTENCY

Ordinarily an individual ranks about the same on scales of prestige, power, income, and education because the dimensions are interrelated. For example, the highly educated are able to earn more, and wealthy families can afford better education for their children. Persons who are highly educated and wealthy have readily opened to them positions of responsibility and privilege. The same interrelations operate at any level of the scale. When an individual's scores are about the same on all the scales of social rank (income, education, prestige, etc.), he is said to be status consistent, regardless of whether his ranks are all high, all low, or all in the middle range.

Sometimes, however, the individual's ranks on the several scales are quite different, in which case he is status inconsistent. Inconsistency is often the result of different rates of upward or downward mobility on the dimensions of stratification. A newly rich person, for instance, is rarely able to gain the prestige or social standing commensurate with his wealth. In most societies money must go through an aging process before it has full buying power in social prestige. Knowledge of a person's less privileged background and outward signs of lower-level behavior may prevent the acceptance to which his wealth might otherwise entitle him. Or, ascribed characteristics such as race and ethnicity may keep him from attaining prestige consistent with his achievement. The Negro physician, for instance, is status inconsistent because he has low ethnic prestige and high occupational prestige.

It has been hypothesized that individuals with similar degrees of status inconsistency show common attitudes and behavior regardless of the particular combinations of ranks. If this is so, high prestige and low economic rank would have the same effects as low prestige and high economic rank. According to this line of reasoning, status inconsistent individuals tend to act toward others in terms of their own higher ranks, but others tend to treat them on the basis of their lower ranks. If one person has high educational and low-income status, he will tend to define his relations with others from the standpoint of his education, but others will tend to interact with him in terms of his income.

Early studies suggested that a discrepancy between expected and actual treatment leads to stress and is likely to be expressed in political liberalism and withdrawal from some kinds of social participation.[42] However, later research indicates that not all types of status inconsistency are conducive to stress. According to one study, most persons who rank high in income but low in education report themselves as relatively happy.[43] Furthermore, when status inconsistency does contribute to stress, the stress may be shown in ways other than political attitudes. For instance, high ascribed status combined with low achievement may lead to psychosomatic illness.[44]

[42] Gerhard Lenski, "Status Crystallization: A Non-Vertical Dimension of Social Status," *American Sociological Review, 19* (1954), 405–413; and Gerhard Lenski, "Social Participation and Status Crystallization," *American Sociological Review, 21* (1956), 458–464. "Status crystallization," as used by Lenski, is synonymous with status consistency.

[43] Norman M. Bradburn and David Caplovitz, *Reports on Happiness* (Chicago: Aldine, 1965), pp. 10–11.

[44] Elton F. Jackson, "Status Consistency and Symptoms of Stress," *American Sociological Review, 27* (1962), 469–480; and Elton F. Jackson and Peter J. Burke, "Status and Symptoms of Stress: Additive and Interactive Effects," *American Sociological Review, 30* (1965), 556–564. See also Hubert M. Blalock, "The Identification Problem and Theory Building: The Case of Status Inconsistency," *American Sociological Review, 31* (1966), 52–61; and Martin D. Hyman, "Determining the Effects of Status Inconsistency," *Public Opinion Quarterly, 30* (1966), 120–129.

SECTION 4 SOCIAL MOBILITY

KINDS OF SOCIAL MOBILITY

Vertical mobility is any upward or downward change in the absolute or relative rank of an individual or group. An alteration of position with no significant movement up or down in the system of social stratification is called *horizontal mobility*. For instance, the manager of a store in a supermarket chain who is transferred to another store with no change in salary, prestige, or authority is horizontally mobile. Change from one occupation to another at the same level of prestige and financial reward involves horizontal movement from one functional category or *situs* to another, but little or no vertical movement. Some changes entail both vertical and horizontal movement as, for instance, when a man moves to another company at a higher salary.

Examples of vertical and horizontal mobility are depicted in Figure VI:6. The strata and situses indicated are not single points but arbitrarily drawn bands. Mobility occurs within strata and within situses as well as between them. For instance, a change in occupation from accountant to bank manager in the figure would not count as mobility accord-

ing to the arbitrary delineation in the diagram. Yet according to the occupational prestige scores in Table VI:1 (p. 167), the accountant has moved from an occupation with a prestige score of 81 to a bank manager with a score of 85—small but measurable upward mobility.

Salience of occupation Vertical mobility is often inferred from occupational mobility, and the inference is generally justified because the position of the individual in the total pattern of inequality largely depends on his occupation. Change in status between father and son is called *intergenerational* mobility, whereas changes during the individual's work life are known as *intragenerational* or career mobility. Intergenerational studies of the mobility of females are usually made by comparing the occupations of father and husband. For instance, the daughter of a skilled worker who marries a professional man is considered upwardly mobile.

INTERGENERATIONAL MOBILITY

Apparently all societies have some intergenerational mobility as well as mobility associated with progres-

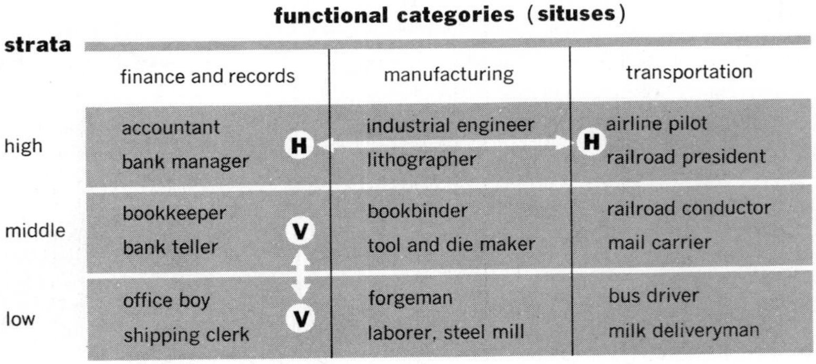

**FIG. VI:6
Types of mobility**

strata	functional categories (situses)		
	finance and records	manufacturing	transportation
high	accountant / bank manager **H**	industrial engineer / lithographer **H**	airline pilot / railroad president
middle	bookkeeper / bank teller **V**	bookbinder / tool and die maker	railroad conductor / mail carrier
low	office boy / shipping clerk **V**	forgeman / laborer, steel mill	bus driver / milk deliveryman

V = vertical mobility, from stratum to stratum
H = horizontal mobility, from situs to situs

TABLE VI:4 INTERGENERATIONAL MOBILITY (IN PERCENTAGES)

FATHER'S OCCUPATION	SON'S OCCUPATION,[a] 1950						
	Profes-sional	Busi-ness	Cler-ical and Sales	Skilled Labor	Semi-skilled	Service Workers	Laborers (includ-ing farm)
Professional	19	9	7	4	3	4	3
Business	25	34	22	10	10	15	8
Subtotal	**44**	**43**	**29**	**14**	**13**	**19**	**11**
Clerical and sales	12	7	15	4	4	5	3
Skilled labor	19	22	24	35	24	18	17
Farmers and farm mgrs.	5	13	8	15	20	26	39
Subtotal	**36**	**42**	**47**	**54**	**48**	**49**	**59**
Semiskilled	13	8	15	19	23	11	11
Service workers	5	4	5	4	5	12	3
Laborers (including farm)	3	3	5	8	12	8	15
Subtotal	**21**	**15**	**25**	**31**	**40**	**31**	**29**
TOTAL PERCENTAGE (deviations from 100% due to rounding)	**101%**	**100%**	**101%**	**99%**	**101%**	**99%**	**99%**
Number of sons (in thousands) projected from sample of 11,400 families	218	356	324	509	483	202	150

SOURCE: Herman P. Miller, *Income of the American People* (New York: Wiley, 1955), pp. 31–33. Based on unpublished data from the Occupational Mobility Survey conducted in 1951 in six cities: Philadelphia, New Haven, San Francisco, Chicago, Los Angeles, and St. Paul. For details of the survey see Gladys L. Palmer, *Labor Mobility in Six Cities* (New York: Social Science Research Council, 1954).

Note—Within each cell is entered the percentage of sons whose fathers were in each occupational category. Bold-faced type indicates the subtotal of each cell. Thus, in the upper left-hand cell 19% of the professional sons had fathers who were also professionals; 25% of the professional sons had fathers who were in business; 44% (the subtotal) of the professional sons had fathers who were either professionals or in business.

[a] The number of sons in farming was too small to be analyzed separately.

sion through the life cycle. There is fair consensus that intergenerational mobility, as measured between father's occupation and son's occupation, is limited, i.e., sons tend to follow their fathers' occupations or occupations of similar prestige and income.[45] However, Table VI:4 suggests that this generalization varies by occupation level. The middle of the occupational structure was most stable. More white-collar workers and skilled workers had fathers at their own level than did the higher occupations or the lower ones. Over half of the professionals and businessmen had fathers who were in lower occupational categories than themselves; about a fifth had fathers in the lowest occupational category of semiskilled, service workers, or laborers.

There was also a large amount of downward mo-

[45] Natalie Rogoff, "Recent Trends in Urban Occupational Mobility," in Bendix and Lipset, *Class, Status and Power* (1st ed., 1953), pp. 442–454. See also Reinhard Bendix and Frank W. Howton, "Social Mobility and the American Business Elite—II," *British Journal of Sociology*, 9 (1958), 1–14, for a comparative evaluation of research findings on the movement of individuals into the business elite.

bility: white-collar and skilled workers were almost as apt to be recruited from above as from below. Surprisingly, those in the lowest occupational level were *least* likely to be recruited from their own ranks. About two-thirds of the semiskilled, service workers, and laborers had fathers in higher occupational categories. Professionals were most frequently recruited from business, businessmen from their own ranks, white-collar workers from skilled labor, skilled laborers from their own ranks, semiskilled laborers about equally from skilled labor and their own ranks, and both service workers and laborers from farmers. Farmers' sons in urban occupations for the most part were in the lower occupations.

Conditions of intergenerational mobility The following conditions affect rates of mobility between the generations:[46]

1. *Differences between parents and offspring.* If a parent occupies an important position requiring high capacity, his children who are less capable are likely to be downwardly mobile. Even in rigidly stratified societies that have few institutionalized means for vertical mobility, extreme incompetents tend to be demoted. Conversely, children who are more capable than their parents are likely to be upwardly mobile, especially in open-class societies.

The reasons for disparities in capabilities between parents and children are both genetic and social. Children are genetically different from either parent, and they can be inferior to both. Or genetically superior offspring of capable and well-rewarded parents may lack the incentive to develop their capacities; they share the rewards that accrue to the parents and therefore do not need to earn high standing on their own. For instance, the college grades of highly born students average well below those of equal measured intelligence who come from lower social strata.[47]

Differences between parents and children in ambition, conscientiousness, ruthlessness, and similar qualities may promote vertical mobility. A son less capable than his father may nevertheless be upwardly mobile because he is more ambitious or because he is better able to perceive and take advantage of opportunities.

2. *Population change.* In industrial and industrializing societies, greater population expansion at the lower than at the higher levels contributes to upward mobility. Overall population growth creates new positions in the upper and middle levels, where growth is not great enough to fill the vacancies. Greater population increase at the lower levels may be due to an excess of births over deaths or to greater immigration at those levels. For instance, until World War I the steady stream of European immigrants into the lower strata created many new upper and middle positions into which native-born Americans and earlier immigrants moved. Throughout this century and probably earlier, families in the upper strata in this country have not produced enough children to replace themselves in upper-stratum positions. Therefore, there could be considerable upward mobility without downward movement.

In preindustrial societies, higher fertility or immigration at the lower levels does not necessarily generate upward mobility. Prior to the industrial revolution, downward movement seems to have exceeded upward movement in most societies.[48] More people were born in most of the strata than could find a secure niche in them, and the "surplus" population was relegated to a lower-lower stratum of "expendables," whose numbers were kept down by low fertility and very high mortality. For instance, beggars and highwaymen were among the "expendables" of medieval Europe.

3. *Changes in occupational structure.* Changes in the amount of inequality, in the proportion of people

---

[46] See Pitirim A. Sorokin, *Society, Culture and Personality* (New York: Harper & Row, 1947), pp. 435–437.

[47] Seymour Martin Lipset and Reinhard Bendix, *Social Mobility in Industrial Society* (Berkeley and Los Angeles: University of California Press, 1958), p. 246.

[48] Gerhard Lenski, *Power and Privilege* (New York: McGraw-Hill, 1966), pp. 289–291.

SECTION 4 SOCIAL MOBILITY
181

at each social level, and in the relative rewards and resources attaching to different social positions are not merely a matter of individuals changing their positions within a system of stratification. Vertical mobility due to changes in the system itself is called *structural* mobility.

A number of structural changes account for much recent vertical mobility in the United States. Many occupations have been upgraded or downgraded because their socially defined importance has changed. For instance, the relative financial rewards of physical scientists and technical workers increased during the late 1950s as a result of intensified technological competition with the Soviet Union. Other occupations have moved up or down because of changes in the scarcity of workers willing and able to perform their tasks.

The most important structural change contributing to mobility in advanced industrial nations is an expansion in the proportion of jobs in the higher levels of reward and a contraction in the lower levels. This change has led to a considerable balance of upward over downward mobility.

INDIVIDUAL MOBILITY

The following characteristics affect the individual's chances of moving up the social ladder:

1. *Community size.* In the United States, the probability that sons of manual workers will be upwardly mobile varies directly with the size of the place in which they spent their childhood and adolescence.[49] The same correlation does not hold for sons of nonmanual workers, presumably because aspirations of middle-class children are gained in the family. Larger cities generally offer better educational facilities and acquaint the manual worker's son with a wider range of occupations. The small-town boy who knows no architects or engineers and knows little of the nature of their work or the level of

their rewards is unlikely to aspire to such an occupation. Economic differences are usually greater and perhaps more apparent in larger cities and thus may be more likely to impart incentives to lower-level children.

2. *Number of siblings.* An only child and the child with only one sibling have the best chance of being upwardly mobile. Beyond one, the probabilities for upward mobility decline with each additional sibling.[50] Parents with many children must divide their resources and are less able to provide each child with a good education and financial assistance early in his career. In addition, and probably more important, the number of siblings affects aspirations and measured intelligence.

3. *Mother-dominance.* The strong-mother family seems to be more conducive to upward mobility than the egalitarian or father-dominant family.[51] The reasons for this are obscure. Possibly, dominant mothers are more ambitious, and mothers rather than fathers are primarily responsible for inculcating ambition and aspirations in their sons. In contrast, the family in which there is no father, or in which there is a succession of foster fathers, does not seem to be conducive to upward movement. (See page 144.)

4. *Late marriage.* European studies have shown marked differences in the mobility of persons who marry young and late.[52] According to a Danish study, males who married before age 25 tended to be downwardly mobile, those who married at ages 25 through 29 tended to be stable, and those who married at age 30 or later tended to be upwardly mobile.

There is some evidence that the same association exists in the United States. Ambitious, upwardly mobile males may postpone marriage so that they can more easily complete their education and become established in their careers. Or, postponement of marriage may be but one manifestation of a general ability and willingness to defer gratification in order

[49] Lipset and Bendix, *Social Mobility in Industrial Society, op. cit.,* Chap. 8.
[50] *Ibid.,* pp. 238–243.
[51] W. Lloyd Warner and James C. Abegglen, *Big Business Leaders in America* (New York: Harper & Row, 1955), pp. 64–107.
[52] Kaare Svalastoga, "An Empirical Analysis of Intrasociety Mobility Determinants." (Working Paper Nine Submitted to the Fourth Working Conference on Social Stratification and Mobility, International Sociological Association, December, 1957).

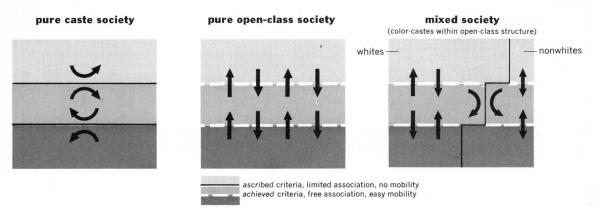

pure caste society   **pure open-class society**   **mixed society**
(color-castes within open-class structure)

whites —   — nonwhites

ascribed criteria, limited association, no mobility
achieved criteria, free association, easy mobility

FIG. VI:7   Caste, open-class, and mixed societies

to attain a future goal. For example, at the lower levels upwardly mobile males tend to begin sex relations at a later age and to be less active sexually before marriage than immobile males.[53] However, the upwardly mobile apparently do not differ much from immobile males at the upper and middle levels.

5. *Few children.* Upwardly mobile couples tend to have fewer children than immobile couples in the social levels into which they move.[54] Child rearing requires time, energy, and money, all of which are essential for mobility. It is not surprising that many ambitious couples allocate these resources to mobility rather than to children. However, the observed correlation is not universal. A study of the academic elite in Australia found fertility among upwardly mobile couples to be very similar to that among the immobile ones.[55]

CASTE AND OPEN-CLASS SOCIETIES

Ascribed status is based on characteristics with which the individual is born or into which he matures: race, sex, age, ethnic and family background. *Achieved* status depends upon characteristics over which the individual has more control: skills, knowledge, education, diligence, and the like. Both ascription and achievement occur in all societies, but one may predominate. Societies that are primarily ascriptive and have very little mobility are termed caste-like.

Until recently castes were conceived as closed social categories with no mobility, but probably no society has had true castes in that sense. However, it is useful to conceive of a hypothetical caste society as one ideal type and an open-class society as the opposite ideal type. (See Fig. VI:7.) All real societies are "mixed," but with varying emphasis on caste and open-class elements, that is, on ascription and achievement.

In open-class societies, the ascriptive barriers to mobility are absent. There is free movement up and down the strata, based on achievement.

An emphasis on achievement tends to be greater in industrial than in preindustrial societies. The complex division of labor and the greater number of social positions requiring scarce capabilities in industrial societies tend toward the demotion of highly-born incompetents and the promotion of capable and ambitious persons from the lower levels.

Nevertheless, even in the most technologically ad-

[53] Kinsey, Pomeroy, and Martin, *op. cit.,* p. 382.

[54] Charles F. Westoff, "The Changing Focus of Differential Fertility Research: The Social Mobility Hypothesis," *Milbank Memorial Fund Quarterly, 31* (1953), 24–38.

[55] H. Yuan Tien, "The Social Mobility/Fertility Hypothesis Reconsidered: An Empirical Study," *American Sociological Review, 26* (1961), 249–257.

vanced countries the allocation of rewards is based to a large extent on ascribed characteristics. Family background, race, and ethnicity still profoundly limit or enhance the chances for people to gain wealth, power, and prestige in the United States. The "mixed society" in Figure VI:7 is a simplified example of color being so defined that it imposes caste-like restrictions on mobility and limits the operation of achievement criteria.

Caste in India[56]   The caste order of India prior to modernization was a complex arrangement of thousands of groupings whose identity and relations were governed by rules of descent and marriage, ritual, ideas about purity and pollution, and occupation. Especially in Southern India there were restrictions on touching, approaching, or even seeing an individual of lowest caste. If a higher-caste individual did so, he would be polluted and would have to undergo purification. The lowest groupings (so-called untouchables) were excluded from temples and schools used by higher-caste groupings and were obliged to use separate paths and wells, and to live in isolated villages.

Public transportation, urbanization, and industrialization have broken down many caste rules and interfered with adherence to residential and food taboos. In 1949 the Indian government declared untouchability illegal, but the reforms engendered resistance and deep bitterness, which may have been involved in the assassination of Mahatma Gandhi. Although some caste practices are under strong pressure, the system persists in altered form throughout Indian society.

Contrary to popular impressions, the Indian castes are not strata. The castes, numbering in the thousands, vary widely on all dimensions of stratification, and several castes may be at the same level. Therefore, a given caste usually does not comprise a complete stratum on any stratification variable but rather shares its standing with other castes.

Despite the elaborate regulations of the system, castes move up and down in prestige, power, and privilege. Members of a caste may perceptibly improve their collective standing over a period of years by closely adhering to standards of behavior that apply to the high-ranking castes. Furthermore, there is variation in prestige and influence within castes, and individuals and families move within this hierarchy. There is even institutionalized intercaste mobility, although the movement is to a lower-ranking caste, a penalty for failure to adhere to the standards of the caste of origin.

Although many traditional occupations are linked to castes, the castes are not identical with occupational categories. Rather, certain castes have a right to engage in certain occupations if they wish to do so. Some occupations, such as agriculture, trade, and military service, are open to all castes.

On the one hand, older caste groups such as the barbers and washermen are breaking down into smaller units because so many of their members no longer follow the traditional occupation and tend to despise those who do. On the other hand, new caste groups are being formed around new occupational specialisms—skilled mechanical work, semiskilled dock and plantation work, and so on—because caste affiliations are used, all over India, to facilitate labour recruitment. Once a caste group has attached itself to a particular kind of work it soon increases its hold by bringing into it only fellow members of the same group.[57]

The survivals of the caste system of India are, therefore, of continuing interest to the student of stratification because of their impact on occupation and the tendency for mobility to be by groups rather than by individuals.

CHANGES IN THE OPPORTUNITY STRUCTURE

Changes in the pattern of inequality in the United States during recent years have on balance tended toward upward mobility. The more important trends are as follows:

---

[56] See M. N. Srinivas, *Caste in Modern India, and Other Essays* (Bombay: Asia Publishing House, 1962), and *Social Change in Modern India* (Berkeley and Los Angeles: University of California Press, 1966); E. R. Leach (ed.), *Aspects of Caste in South India, Ceylon and North-West Pakistan* (New York: Cambridge University Press, 1960); H. N. C. Stevenson, "Status Evaluation in the Hindu Caste System," *Journal of the Royal Anthropological Institute, 84* (1954).

[57] H. N. C. Stevenson, "Caste (Indian)," *Encyclopaedia Britannica 5* (1967), 24–33; quotation at p. 29a.

1. *Expansion in the upper and middle strata.* Technological changes and growing affluence have greatly increased opportunities for professional and technical workers, salaried managers and executives, clerical workers, and some kinds of service workers. At the same time, the demand for unskilled and semi-skilled labor has declined. The expanding lines of work are on the average more highly rewarded, both with money and prestige, than the contracting lines. The percentage of employed persons in nonmanual occupations increased from less than 20 percent in 1900 to 32.7 in 1940 to 45.7 in 1966. The proportion in professional and technical work increased from 7.5 in 1940 to 12.9 percent in 1966.

The proportions in the upper educational and income levels have increased even more. In 1940, only 24.1 percent of the persons twenty-five years old and older had completed four or more years of high school, but by 1965 the percentage was 49. In the same period, the percentage who completed four or more years of college also doubled from 4.6 to 9.4.

Reliable data on income are not available for dates earlier than 1947, but even since then there has been significant change. If dollars for earlier years are converted into the value of 1964 dollars, 31 percent of the families in 1947 had incomes under $3,000; by 1964, the percentage had dropped to 18. In 1947, only 7 percent of the families had incomes of $10,-000 or more; by 1964 the percentage had risen to 22, and 6 percent had incomes of $15,000 or more. It is estimated that in the prosperous predepression year of 1929, more than half the families had incomes of less than $3,000 in 1964 dollars and would, by present standards, be considered below the poverty line.[58]

Obviously an impressive upward movement has occurred in the economic and educational dimensions. Even most persons whose relative standing has declined have experienced an improvement in abso-lute standing. There is, therefore, a pervasive feeling of upward movement. However, those who have not shared in the upward movement, who have experienced sharp losses in relative standing, or who are more aware of their relatively low standings may feel increasing deprivation. The poignancy of their condition is heightened by contrast with the general affluence. This fact undoubtedly underlies much Negro discontent.[59]

2. *Changes in rewards of occupations.* As indicated on page 168, the prestige of the 90 occupations covered by the National Opinion Research Center studies was surprisingly stable from 1947 to 1963. In fact, few changes in occupational prestige have occurred since 1925, but pronounced changes in relative fianancial rewards are discernible. During World War II, the gap between the higher- and the lower-ranking occupations tended to close, only to widen during the 1950s.[60] Recent experience indicates that the range in inequality of rewards among occupations narrows during times of war-induced high employment and widens during recessions and periods of moderate unemployment.

The net change from 1947 through 1964 involved an appreciable increase in the relative economic rewards of craftsmen and salaried managers and a moderate increase in the relative incomes of clerical and sales workers and operatives. The relative standing of professional and technical workers remained about the same, and that of service workers and nonfarm laborers declined moderately. The relative status of farmers and farm laborers declined steeply.

3. *Changes in formal education.* At the end of the Civil War most of the population of the United States had no more than grammar schooling, and most of the small minority who went to secondary school were preparing to enter a college or university.[61] (See EDUCATION, pp. 375–376.) Therefore, economic and occupational differentiation was based

[58] Herman P. Miller, *op. cit.,* p. 27.

[59] Thomas F. Pettigrew, *A Profile of the Negro American* (Princeton, N.J.: Van Nostrand, 1964), Chap. 8.

[60] Herman P. Miller, *op. cit.,* pp. 61–65.

[61] See Martin Trow, "The Second Transformation of American Secondary Education," *International Journal of Comparative Sociology,* 2 (1961), 144–166.

less on education than on ambition, initiative, luck, and skills acquired out of school.

During the early decades of this century, and especially between the two World Wars, secondary schooling became redefined as terminal education for the many as well as college preparation for the few. As more and more people not bound for college started and finished high school, the educational differentiation of the population increased and became a more important basis for economic and occupational differentiation.

Now, an equally important change is occurring. Secondary education is once again becoming college preparation, but this time for the many instead of the few. Already a majority of each cohort (persons born within a given period) is completing high school; soon this will be a large majority, and ever greater numbers will complete at least a year or two of college. Thus the trend is toward a new stage of educational homogeneity at an even higher level.

The average difference in income and occupational status associated with a year's difference in education is increasing.[62] In 1946 high school graduates earned on the average 26 percent more than grammar school graduates; by 1958, the difference was 48 percent.[63]

Education is now almost essential for attaining highly rewarded positions, but completion of a degree or course of study is not enough. Such factors as reputation of one's college and college grades may become even more influential than they are in occupational recruitment and advancement.

4. *Economic inequality.* Although no completely reliable data are available, economic inequality in the United States probably declined from the turn of the century through World War II, and the war itself seems to have had an important leveling influence. After the mid-1940s, however, the trend toward equality was interrupted if not halted.[64] Since 1947, the proportion of the total income going to the upper fifth of the families, to the lower fifth, and to each fifth in between has remained virtually stable. The percentage of the total income going to the highest fifth was 43 in 1947 and 41 in 1964.[65] The percentage going to the lowest fifth was 5 at both dates. The stability is explained by two countervailing trends. The movement of people out of the lowest paid occupations—farming and unskilled labor—tends to lessen inequality, but the growing income disparity between these lower-level occupations and others tends to increase it. The net result is practically no change in the income shares of the higher and lower segments of the population.

TRENDS IN MOBILITY

Intergenerational mobility   Until a few years ago, most sociologists believed that intergenerational occupational mobility in the United States was diminishing, that the system of social stratification was becoming more rigid.[66] Such rigidity was believed to be the inevitable result of mature industrialization, the near cessation of immigration, the decline in fertility differentials among the social strata, the closing of the frontier, and the evolution of the "break in the skill hierarchy." This last phrase means that it is no longer possible to start at the bottom of the industrial hierarchy and work one's way to the top.[67] The worker may become a foreman or through an apprenticeship program, a craftsman, but it is now almost impossible to go from manual work to the higher managerial and executive levels. Rather, the higher levels recruit well-educated young men who have never worked at the lower levels, except perhaps temporarily.

[62] John K. Folger and Charles B. Nam, "Trends in Education in Relation to the Occupational Structure," *Sociology of Education, 38* (1964), 19–33.

[63] Lenski, *Power and Privilege, op. cit.,* p. 393.

[64] Herman P. Miller, *op. cit.,* pp. 49–53.

[65] *Statistical Abstract of the United States,* 1966.

[66] J. O. Hertzler, "Some Tendencies Toward a Closed Class System in the United States," *Social Forces, 30* (1952), 313–323.

[67] Warner and Low, *op. cit.* See footnote 12.

The community studies by Warner and his associates found that few people at the upper and intermediate prestige levels had come from the lower levels. In fact, they found no mobility from the lowest to the highest level, and upward movement of more than one level was very rare.

When reliable data on nationwide mobility trends became available, they showed the earlier impressions to be incorrect. In recent decades, intergenerational occupational mobility has not declined, and it may have increased moderately.[68] The small communities used in the Warner studies undoubtedly contained few upwardly mobile people, but those who generalized from these communities to the entire society overlooked the fact that upwardly mobile persons born in such communities as Newburyport and

Morris generally went to larger cities to escape the constraining local situation with its limited opportunities.

A schematic summary of the chief mobility channels in the United States is given in Figure VI:8. The young man born in a lower stratum is just as likely to move up now as he was thirty or sixty years ago, but different channels of mobility are open to him. He has little chance of becoming an independent farmer or businessman. Although thousands of manual workers each year quit their jobs to go into business for themselves, few succeed as entrepreneurs. Among those who remain small-businessmen for a number of years, many never attain income or economic security greater than they could have attained as wage workers. Any upward mobility they

[68] Otis Dudley Duncan, "The Trend of Occupational Mobility in the United States," *American Sociological Review, 30* (1965), 491–498; Elton F. Jackson and Harry J. Crockett, Jr., "Occupational Mobility in the United States: A Point Estimate and a Trend Comparison," *American Sociological Review, 29* (1964), 5–15; Natalie Rogoff, *Recent Trends in Occupational Mobility* (New York: The Free Press of Glencoe, 1953).

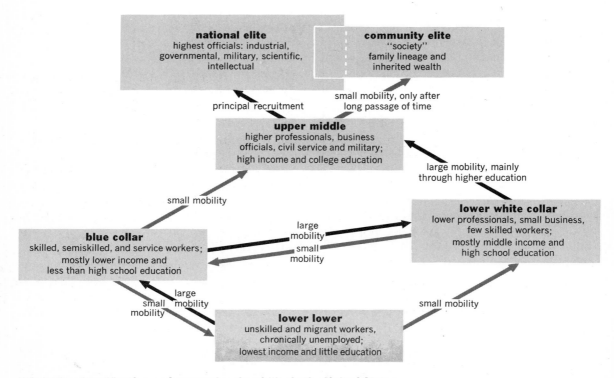

FIG. VI:8   Stratification and generational mobility in the United States

experience is on the power or prestige dimensions, and there is usually little of that. As mentioned earlier, upward mobility from the lowest strata increasingly requires formal education. Even mobility to the upper-lower or intermediate levels usually requires specialized vocational training or apprenticeship. Therefore, the foundations for upward mobility are laid during adolescence and young adulthood or not at all. Opportunities for the upward movement of poorly educated and unskilled older adults have declined, a clear product of the forces of technological change.

In spite of the fact that intergenerational mobility in the United States has not declined, its volume is only a fraction of what would occur if people born at all levels had an equal chance to attain any given level. For instance, the sons of physicians and janitors will not end up distributed in the same manner among the social levels. In fact, there will be little overlap in their distributions. Most people experience some mobility relative to their parents, but only a few move up or down very far. Therefore, whether the rate of vertical mobility in the United States is high or low depends on the perspective from which it is viewed. It is similar to the rates of the recent past, similar to the rates in other highly industrialized countries, and higher than the rates in preindustrial societies.[69] Viewed in this light, it might be termed at least moderately high. However, viewed in relation to the rate that would exist if there were complete equality of opportunity, the present rate of vertical mobility in the United States is low.

[69] S. M. Miller, "Comparative Social Mobility," *Current Sociology, 9* (1960); and Lipset and Bendix, *Social Mobility in Industrial Society, op. cit.*

SECTION 5 CLASS AND SOCIETY

Two perspectives in the study of stratification may be distinguished. The first looks at the system from the standpoint of how *individuals* are distributed, whether by income, prestige, influence, education, or some other dimension; and the consequences of stratification most closely studied are those affecting life-chances and life-styles of individuals. In the second perspective social classes are seen as group formations and as dynamic forces in history; group interest and power are the major themes. The latter perspective is used in this concluding section.

THE MARXIST MODEL

The discussion of class and society is to a large extent a dialogue between the Marxist view and its critics. Although Karl Marx (1818–1883) never set forth a systematic theory of social class, the idea of class was central to his thought, and a reasonably coherent argument can be gleaned from his voluminous writings.[70]

The elements of the Marxist theory may be summarized as follows:

1. *Origin of social classes.* Social classes arise out of the "relations of production," that is, the way work is organized. Some people own land, others are tenant farmers; some work for wages, others are employers; still others are self-employed. By examining the social structure of production, it can be determined who depends on whom, who dominates whom, who has what resources, what problems and interests arise, and what the potentialities are for action based on common concerns. Marx did

[70] T. B. Bottomore and Maximilien Rubel (eds.), *Karl Marx: Selected Writing in Sociology and Social Philosophy* (New York: McGraw-Hill, 1956); "Karl Marx's Theory of Social Classes," in Bendix and Lipset, *Class, Status and Power, op cit.*; Ralf Dahrendorf, *Class and Class Conflict in Industrial Society* (Stanford: Stanford University Press, 1959); and Lewis S. Feuer (ed.), *Marx and Engels: Basic Writings on Politics and Philosophy* (Garden City, N.Y.: [Anchor] Doubleday, 1959).

Karl Marx (1818–1883). His general system, dialectical materialism, includes a sociological system called historical materialism. In this theory Marx emphasized technology as a generator of social change and a direct influence on the nature of work and human relations. Technology and the forms of economic organization constituted the "material foundations" of the social order. All else was called "superstructure," a reflection of the problems set by technology and economic class relations.

not identify class with occupation. He saw social class as a more general phenomenon, rooted in the key roles such as employer and employee, that cut across most industries and occupations and that characterize a period of economic history.

2. *Major divisions.* In the Marxist model the major social classes of the modern era, following the breakup of feudalism, are the landowners, the owners of capital, and those who work for wages. Marx recognized that the system was more complex, but he foresaw an increasing polarization that would divide society into two great camps. On one side would be the capitalists, or *bourgeoisie,* including the commercial farmers; and on the other the *proletariat,*

composed of the large mass of men who owned nothing but their labor power. On this theory the small farmer, small-businessman, and independent professional would gradually be squeezed out, most of them forced into the proletariat as employees of large business organizations owned by a few wealthy capitalists.

3. *Objective class and subjective class.* Whether or not they are aware of it, people are thrown into common circumstances by the organization of production. *Objective conditions* define the individual's class position and his class interests. If he is an employer his interests are counterposed to those of his employee, whatever may be his subjective thoughts or desires. If a worker identifies himself as middle class, this does not change his objective class position. Marx distinguished between a class "in itself" (in German, *Klasse an sich*) and a class "for itself" (*Klasse für sich*). A class "for itself" is one that has transformed its latent, objective interests into awareness and cooperation.

Marx believed that the major classes of society would in time become such subjectively as well as objectively. He noted, however, that some social groups in the system of production, though they share common interests and life situations, do not have the objective potential for becoming a fully developed social class. Thus he wrote of the French peasantry, who were the mainstay of Louis Bonaparte (Napoleon III) in the 1850s:

The small-holding peasants form a vast mass, the members of which live in similar conditions, but . . . their mode of production isolates them from one another, instead of bringing them into mutual intercourse. The isolation is increased by France's bad means of communication and by the poverty of the peasants. . . . Each individual peasant family is almost self-sufficient; . . . A small holding, the peasant and his family; alongside them another small holding, another peasant and another family. A few score of these make up a village, and a few score of villages make up a Department. In this way, the great mass of the French nation is formed by simple addition of homologous magnitudes, much as potatoes in a sack form a sack of potatoes. In so far as millions of families live under economic conditions of existence that separate their mode of life, their interests, and their culture from those of the other classes and put them in hostile opposition to the latter, they form a class. In so far as there is merely a local interconnection among these small-holding peasants and the identity of interests begets no community, no national bond, and no political organization among them, they do not form a class. They are consequently incapable of enforcing their class interest in their own name, . . . They cannot represent themselves; they must be represented.[71]

Unlike the peasants, the workers would inevitably become an organized and self-conscious class. The conditions of life in the factory bring the workers together in ways that make them aware of their common interests as well as their common strength.

4. *Class rule and class struggle.* In all past societies, with the exception of "primitive communism," a few have ruled and the many have been ruled. But ruling is not best understood in purely political terms. Rather, a dominant economic class controls the mainsprings of society, including the government. Modern governments are *bourgeois* governments because in the last analysis they serve the interests of the capitalist class. Thus politics is subordinate to economics, and important social conflicts occur between an ascendant class and a defeated one, or between a ruling social class and an occasionally desperate subordinate one, as in the case of peasant revolts.

5. *Progressive and reactionary classes.* Through class struggle history renews itself continuously. With changes in technology and social organization, new classes arise to challenge the old and carry history forward to a higher stage. The ascendant capitalist class was "progressive," for it furthered the development of new forces of production and created the conditions that made a new class—the industrial proletariat—possible and inevitable. The capitalists were reactionary, as were the feudal magnates before them, when they acted to hinder rather than further social development.

6. *The end of the class system.* The proletariat incorporates most of society and has the widest as-

pirations. Therefore the victory of the proletariat is a final victory, ushering in a new form of social organization—the classless society. Marx argued that his concept of socialism was scientific, in that the conditions for its attainment were prepared for by previous history. He referred especially to the vast increase in productivity under capitalism and the creation of "socialized" property in the form of corporate enterprise.

CRITIQUE

Marx's theories reflected a distinctive intellectual perspective and political impulse. Therefore Marxism is not easily formulated as a set of hypothetical conclusions subject to the self-corrective method of science. Because it is both a philosophy of history and a political program, Marxism has generated loyalties and responses that go beyond the realm of scholarship. Nevertheless, the Marxist model is a continuing source of intellectual stimulation and a framework for thoughtful inquiry.

Criticism of Marx centers on the following points:

1. The model overemphasizes the significance of economic class for individual conduct as well as for the explanation of historical trends. Other sources of personal identification and group action are often more important. For example, nationalism remains an enduring social force, largely overshadowing class divisions; and other dimensions of stratification, especially prestige, often are more compelling in their influence on human thought and action. While the effect of class interest on politics is at times decisive, there is much evidence that politics goes its own way, independent of class influences.[72]

2. The concept of a "ruling class," though not without scientific merit, has limited relevance to a complex, industrialized nation. Even the idea of a "power elite" does not support Marx's contention of rule by the bourgeoisie through its governmental representatives. Although business interests often dominate government policy, the same interests are often defeated.

[71] Karl Marx, "The Eighteenth Brumaire of Louis Bonaparte," in Feuer, *op. cit.,* pp. 338 f.

[72] See Dahrendorf, *op. cit.,* Chaps. 7–8.

3. Marx did not give sufficient weight to the forces that mitigate the class cleavage he observed in the mid-nineteenth century. Although he hailed the advent of universal suffrage in England, he saw its inevitable result as the supremacy of the working class. Marx did not rightly gauge the significance for social integration of expanding civic participation and the enlargement of social rights.[73]

4. The thesis of a polarization of classes has not been upheld, although it is true that modern society has become an "employee society" and that there is great concentration of wealth and power in a relatively small number of corporate entities. But polarization has been offset by the proliferation of strata based on occupation, education, and prestige. The middle classes have changed their character since Marx's time, but they have not disappeared.

5. The prediction that workers under capitalism would develop class consciousness and revolutionary aspirations has been borne out only to a very limited extent.

6. Perhaps the most important failing of the Marxist model lies in its vision of the post-capitalist future. Marx thought that a proletarian victory would bring an end to exploitation of man by man and that government would be replaced by "the administration of things." He did not foresee the rise of totalitarianism as a more likely alternative to capitalist democracy than the benign and humanist socialism he expected.

These criticisms correct but do not discredit the contribution of Marxist thought to sociology, and especially to social history. Although modern scholars do not use the specific categories or adopt the detailed arguments of the Marxist model, they are made alert to the role of class in history and to some extent they follow lines of thought that Marx began.

THE CASE OF ENGLAND

The enduring contribution of Marx to social history is his insistence that the emergence of new classes, the reconstitution of old ones, and conflict among the classes, should be a leading preoccupation.of the historian. This idea is not unique, for Tocqueville, too, thought of social classes as the principal actors of history, but Marxism has been especially influential.

Analysis of social class is an essential part of modern historical inquiry. For example, a major problem is the relation between the transformation of classes and social stability. In England, during the sixteenth and seventeenth centuries, the social classes in the countryside were the *landed nobility,* the well-to-do *gentry,* the *yeomen,* and the *peasantry.*[74] In addition there were the business interests of the towns. The government of the period was a monarchy attempting to establish its dominance over the feudal nobility out of which it arose.

Although England experienced a civil war in the seventeenth century, there was no social upheaval comparable to what occurred in France 150 years later. The English social structure made a relatively smooth transition to modernity, and this continuity probably made possible the emergence in England of a stable constitutional democracy.

Social stability in England depended on the absence of a clear-cut class struggle. There were bloody conflicts, but they tended to cut across class lines and to involve issues, such as religion, that blurred class antagonisms. Among the conditions that created this situation were the following:

1. A clash between the rising bourgeoisie and the landed classes was avoided because a considerable *amalgamation* of these classes occurred. Thanks partly to the wool trade, agriculture was commercialized, and many landowners became, in effect, landed capitalists. "Adapting early to the world of commerce and even taking the lead in the march into the new era, the landed aristocracy of England was not swept away by the convulsions that accompanied the change." [75]

2. Unlike France, Germany, and Russia, England

---

[73] See T. H. Marshall, "Citizenship and Social Class," in *Class, Citizenship, and Social Development* (Garden City, N.Y.: Doubleday, 1964).

[74] See Barrington Moore, Jr., *Social Origins of Dictatorship and Democracy* (Boston: Beacon Press, 1966), Chap. I.

[75] *Ibid.,* pp. 22–23.

had no peasant problem. In the sixteenth and seventeenth centuries the small peasants were pushed off the land by "enclosures," which allowed the larger landowners, from yeomen to aristocrats, to take over what had once been open fields.

These factors, and others, allowed the landed establishment to dominate English government for 300 years. But if this was a ruling class, it was not isolated from the rest of the social system. It helped create conditions that made capitalism flourish, and it gave way relatively gracefully to the demand for social progress in the nineteenth and early twentieth centuries.

In this historical case study, the importance of class is underlined, but the Marxist model is modified by (1) taking account of a diversity of classes, and (2) allowing the historical record to say how much and what kind of class struggle occurred, with what effects on the political order.

CLASS CONSCIOUSNESS IN THE UNITED STATES

The term "class consciousness" is now widely used in sociology, but often with a connotation somewhat different from that given it by Marx. It may refer to one of a number of related phenomena such as awareness of the range of inequality, or of one's place in the pattern of inequality, or awareness of cultural differences among the social strata. Most often the term implies a feeling of identification with others in a "social class," however class is defined, and a feeling of difference from, and perhaps opposition to, persons in other classes.

Class consciousness in this latter sense and the unity of outlook within a class are not common in the United States. Public opinion poll data and voting studies show greater unity of opinion and of voting within occupational categories in Western European countries than in the United States. Broadly defined occupational categories in the United States contain a wide diversity of opinions and political inclinations. Furthermore, there is little feeling among most occupational groupings that their interests conflict sharply

with the interests of others. Some interest groups in the United States are highly effective, but only a minority of the people strongly identify with and actively participate in them.

A number of explanations have been offered for the relatively low level of class consciousness and class solidarity in the United States:

1. Because of widespread belief in opportunities for upward mobility, efforts to improve status typically are individual mobility striving rather than concerted collective effort. For some manual workers, opportunities for upward movement may be more illusory than real, but perception of reality rather than reality itself influences class consciousness. Many wage workers retain hope that they will go into business for themselves well beyond the ages at which radical, class-oriented political activity is likely.[76] Workers who know they will never move to a higher occupation often hope their children will be upwardly mobile, and many have relatives at higher levels.

2. A leveling of differences in the life-styles of manual and nonmanual workers lessens class consciousness. Many working-class people have houses and wear clothes similar to those of higher-level people. Important cultural differences still exist among the social levels, but there may be little awareness of these differences among upper manual workers.

3. A steady improvement in the living standard of blue-collar workers tends to lessen discontent and class solidarity, even though their relative economic position may be declining. Increasing numbers of wage workers are able to own houses and equipment that were once restricted to the higher levels. This trickling down of consumer goods gives manual workers the illusion of upward mobility.[77]

4. Racial, ethnic, religious, and regional differences in culture and perceived interests tend to crosscut and inhibit class consciousness and solidarity. For instance, conflict and acrimony between Negro and white workers have prevented working-class unity in the South. Although these non-class divisions appear

[76] Eli Chinoy, *Automobile Workers and the American Dream* (Garden City, N.Y.: Doubleday, 1955), Chap. 7.
[77] Lloyd A. Fallers, "A Note on the 'Trickle Effect,'" *Public Opinion Quarterly, 18* (1954), 314–321.

to be persistent, class consciousness might increase if they diminish.

Class consciousness is relatively low in the United States, but is not absent. A Detroit study, for instance, found a rather high level of certain measures of class consciousness among Negroes and recent migrants from rural areas.[78] Surveys find a fairly high degree of political unity of manual workers in the largest cities.[79] Nor is class conflict absent; strikes, labor disputes, and even the recent battle between the American Medical Association and the supporters of Medicare are examples of the American version of the class struggle. This conflict, however, is over issues and the division of spoils. It is a far cry from the proletarian revolution envisioned by Marx. In the words of one observer, the conflict has become "institutionalized";[80] it proceeds in accordance with established rules and rarely commands the attention or the efforts of more than a minority of the population. It leads to piecemeal changes in social institutions but to no radical changes in social structure.

In the institutionalization of class conflict, the democracies of Western Europe resemble the United States. In fact, in some of these countries, the expansion of welfare-state activities may have reduced the more disruptive types of class conflict to a point below that in the United States.

IS STRATIFICATION INEVITABLE?

One school of thought holds that social inequality is inevitable and functional (beneficial) to the society as a whole.[81] According to this view social inequality must exist in all societies with a complex division of labor in order to assure that important and necessary tasks are performed efficiently and conscientiously by well-qualified people. Some tasks are more im-

portant and some require scarce skills and abilities. If a position is relatively important and requires relatively scarce skills, it must be more highly rewarded than many other positions. Skills may be scarce either because they call for unusual talent or because their acquisition requires a long and arduous period of training.

The idea that people could not be socialized to prepare for and enter important positions requiring scarce skills if they were not relatively highly rewarded has been challenged.[82] The following questions have been raised: (1) Could people who have the potential to become doctors, engineers, scientists, and executives be so socialized that they would feel obliged to enter these occupations even if they anticipated no higher reward than unskilled workers? (2) Would the intrinsic enjoyment of highly skilled work be sufficient to motivate them to prepare for their jobs and perform them diligently? (3) Is the long training undertaken by people in highly rewarded occupations a sacrifice or is the training itself essentially rewarding?

There are no conclusive answers to these questions. However, widespread agreement is emerging on the following related points:

1. Even though some degree of inequality in rewards may be necessary, not all the existing inequality in any society is necessary. For instance, the salary spread between top-ranking executives and lowest-paid employees in private corporations in the United States seems to be far greater than necessary to fill the top positions with qualified and conscientious persons.[83] The fact that the spread is much smaller in many publicly controlled organizations that adequately perform similar functions suggests that such a wide spread is unnecessary.

---

[78] John C. Leggett, "Sources and Consequences of Working-Class Consciousness," in Shostak and Gomberg, *op. cit.,* pp. 235–247.

[79] Seymour Martin Lipset, *Political Man* (Garden City, N.Y.: Doubleday, 1963), pp. 265–266.

[80] Dahrendorf, *op. cit.,* part II.

[81] Kingsley Davis and Wilbert E. Moore, "Some Principles of Stratification," *American Sociological Review, 10* (1945), 242–249.

[82] Melvin M. Tumin, "Some Principles of Stratification: A Critical Analysis," *American Sociological Review, 18* (1953), 387–393.

[83] Lenski, *Power and Privilege, op. cit.,* pp. 352–356.

2. In almost all societies, many people are highly rewarded who neither occupy important positions nor possess scarce skills that are applied to socially useful tasks. Indeed, some people are highly though unintentionally rewarded for criminal activities, and others derive large "windfall" profits from legitimate but rather unproductive activities.

3. The importance of positions as measured by their rewards is not necessarily determined by their contribution to the survival or improvement of the society. High rewards for certain positions may merely mean that the function performed satisfies culturally defined and perhaps ephemeral needs and tastes, as in the case of the sale of cigarettes.

4. Some inequality in one generation may be necessary for the development and efficient utilization of talent, but no such claim can be made for inequality transmitted from generation to generation. The latter kind of inequality tends to inhibit rather than foster the discovery and utilization of talent. And since the extent of intergenerational transmission of inequality tends to vary directly with the degree of inequality in the parent generation, inequality above a certain amount tends to be detrimental. Inequality in all societies probably exceeds the level that would be determined by the criterion of efficiency.

5. An amount of inequality greater than is beneficial to the society as a whole is probably inevitable. Once established inequality gives some people the means for maintaining or improving their relative standing. For instance, a differential distribution of authority is an essential aspect of social organization. Although authority is granted as a resource to be used for assigned tasks, some who possess authority are very likely to use it for their own aggrandizement.

6. High prestige may substitute for high financial rewards in motivating people to occupy responsible positions and conscientiously to perform their duties. The importance of prestige as a reward is evidenced by the fact that high-income and even moderate-income people will often make financial sacrifices to gain the prestige of an appointment with civic importance or to participate in more interesting or challenging work.

Niccolò Machiavelli (1469–1527) served the city-state of Florence for fourteen years as administrator, politician, and diplomat. Forced out of office, he retired to his study and wrote down his reflections on power and society. His most famous works are The Prince *and* Discourses on the First Ten Books of Titus Livius. *Machiavelli is one of the fathers of the theory of elites—the view that political life depends on the energy and character of active minorities who have the strength and the will to rule. The rise and fall of elites, and with them the flowering and degeneration of political communities, is in the nature of things; the cycle will be repeated without end. "For, virtue begets peace; peace begets idleness; idleness, mutiny; and mutiny, destruction: and then* vice versa: *that ruin begets laws; those laws, virtue; and virtue begets honor and good success."*

CHAPTER VII
ASSOCIATIONS

SECTION 1 INTRODUCTION

The word *association* as used in this book is a synonym for formal organization or, simply, organization. This chapter is called ASSOCIATIONS in order to minimize confusion with the broader idea of social organization. The association is a *special-purpose* group. The term *formal organization* is often used to emphasize that most such groups have explicit goals and official ways of doing things. An association or formal organization should be distinguished, for example, from a "web of friendship," as discussed in Adaptation 3, pages 20–26, or from a system of social stratification. The latter are examples of social organization, but they are not associations.

Schools, prisons, factories, and clubs all have distinctive characteristics, as do organizations of rural dwellers or of minorities. Different environments and different functions produce widely varying patterns of participation. In the sections on associations of the chapters in Part Two, the special characteristics of religious, educational, and legal organizations are discussed.

The sociologist views an organization figuratively

as a little society. In specialized associations are many of the features of societies, including the processes that bind them together or disrupt them. For example, stratification, socialization, and primary-group formation are important phases of organizational experience, affecting the capacity of the organization to achieve its objectives.

Whatever its special purpose, every organization attempts to coordinate the activities of human beings. Therefore, organizations have a number of common characteristics, which will claim most of the attention of this chapter. Every association must:

1. Provide *incentives* to its members so as to win and sustain their participation;

2. Set up an effective system of internal *communication;*

3. Exercise *control* so that activities will be directed toward achieving the aims of the organization;

4. Adapt itself to external conditions that may threaten the existence of the organization or its policies, that is, maintain *security*.

If these requirements of effective organization are

to be fulfilled, the social relations among the persons involved must be consistent with them. A major task of the sociologist is to explore the ways in which incentive, communication, control, and security depend on the underlying relations among persons and groups. Figure VII:1 outlines how the essential elements of organization are influenced by social processes.

INCENTIVE is increased when	COMMUNICATION is facilitated when	CONTROL is strengthened when	SECURITY is fostered when
socialization builds organization's goals into personality by identification.	**socialization** transmits the organization's point of view —"decisional premises."	**socialization** creates homogeneous organization—permits authority to be delegated without loss of control.	**socialization** strengthens group loyalty —members protect the organization, e.g., its reputation.
primary relations provide personal satisfactions which reinforce monetary or other rewards.	**primary relations** break down formal barriers to communication.	**primary relations** provide a source of informal discipline.	**primary relations** create personal attachments that bind the individual to the organization.
stratification affords added rewards of prestige and privilege.	**stratification** tells if the message comes from an authoritative source.	**stratification** locates and stabilizes authority.	**institutionalization** adapts the organization to its social environment.

FIG. VII:1 Social relations and effective organization

SOURCES AND READINGS

Peter M. Blau and W. Richard Scott, *Formal Organizations: A Comparative Approach* (San Francisco: Chandler Publishing, 1962).

Theodore Caplow, *Principles of Organization* (New York: Harcourt, Brace & World, 1964).

Amitai Etzioni, *A Comparative Analysis of Complex Organizations* (New York: The Free Press of Glencoe, 1961).

Erving Goffman, *Asylums* (Garden City, N.Y.: [Anchor] Doubleday, 1961).

Daniel Katz and Robert L. Kahn (eds.), *The Social Psychology of Organizations* (New York: Wiley, 1966).

Rensis Likert, *New Patterns of Management* (New York: McGraw-Hill, 1961).

James G. March and Herbert A. Simon, *Organizations* (New York: Wiley, 1958).

James G. March (ed.), *Handbook of Organizations* (Chicago: Rand McNally, 1965).

Robert Presthus, *The Organizational Society* (New York: Knopf, 1962).

Harold L. Wilensky, *Organization Intelligence: Knowledge and Policy in Government and Industry* (New York: Basic Books, 1967).

Periodical

Administrative Science Quarterly

SECTION 2 FORMAL STRUCTURE

The distinction between formal and informal relations is important in understanding the sociological aspects of organizations. (See PRIMARY GROUPS, pp. 133 ff.) Sociologists have given most attention to informal patterns, but the working organization is a product of the interaction of both formal and informal patterns of behavior. Informal relations develop in the environment of the formal system.

ELEMENTS OF FORMAL STRUCTURE

Figure VII:2 is a somewhat simplified organization chart of the formal structure of a large oil company. It should be referred to throughout this discussion of company organization:

1. *Division of labor.* The company's operations have four main divisions: one produces the oil, another refines it, still another handles transportation, and a fourth is responsible for marketing. Problems of personnel are also divided. In the division of labor according to a definite plan, *specialization* is the guiding principle. Responsibilities are delegated to particular individuals and groups. This delegation of responsibilities creates new groups, and the larger association becomes an organization of organizations.

2. *Delegation of authority.* The boxes and lines of the organization chart show the chain of command. Typically, there is a *hierarchy,* in which some individuals and groups are given the right to issue orders to others. The four main operating divisions are on the same level in the hierarchy. Although apparently one step higher, the personnel department does not have the formal right to give orders directly to the operating divisions. Ordinarily, a personnel department is a staff or auxiliary group. It receives instructions from the higher administrative and policy levels and makes recommendations to those levels without directly supervising the lower operating divisions. However, actual practice may differ considerably from the official or formal pattern.

3. *Channeled communication.* Some complex organizations, notably the military services, go to some pains to ensure that individuals transmit information or requests through channels. For example, according to the organization chart, which shows the officially approved paths for information, requests, and commands, a vice-president who wants to communicate with a member of the board of directors will not bypass the president of the company. Similarly, if the manager of an oil field, who is subordinate to the chief of the production division, wishes to communicate with the manager of an oil refinery on a matter of policy, he is expected to do so through his chief. The latter in turn communicates with subordinates in the refinery division through the chief of that division. Rules of this sort are not rigidly held to because they may interfere with the ability of subordinates to solve their problems. But even in the most relaxed organization, the wise subordinate remembers channels when dealing with important matters. Otherwise, his chief will not have the information he needs to make decisions or to defend the actions of his division when questioned by higher authority.

4. *Coordination.* In order to attain the advantages of specialization, labor is divided, but it is necessary to maintain a united and consistent effort by the organization as a whole. This is the job of the administrative and policy levels, which review the activities and recommendations of the various divisions, consider conflicts that must be resolved, and develop new policies that may be needed. Such coordinating officials often act as judges, weighing the arguments presented by divisions that differ on company policy or that have complaints against each other. Organiza-

tions differ in the extent to which top management initiates activity or simply reviews actions initiated at the working level.

Rationality and discipline   There are many procedural rules and sanctions, such as the rules governing hours of work, that do not appear on the chart. In addition, the official goals of the organization may be considered part of the formal system. These elements of formal structure are governed by two related ideals: rationality and discipline.

Under a system of *rationality,* the goals of the organization are to be attained as completely as possible and at the lowest cost. This assumes that attainable goals can be formulated in a clear-cut way. However, in many multipurpose associations such as churches, universities, political groups, and even some businesses, the formulation of attainable aims is difficult and consequently administrative rationality is only partly achieved.

Discipline is necessary because the organization is basically a system of roles. When a man is given a job, he is expected to act out the role assigned to him. Since activities, not persons, are coordinated, a single individual may be assigned more than one

role. He "wears two hats," but he is expected to keep his two roles separate, and this calls for a special kind of self-discipline. Disciplined role behavior is necessary to a rational formal system. But, like rationality, it is an ideal that is never completely fulfilled.

Formal structure defined   The formal structure of an organization is a system of rules and objectives defining the tasks, powers, and procedures of participants according to an officially approved pattern. The pattern specifies how the work of the organization is to be carried on, whether it is producing steel, winning votes, teaching children, or saving souls.

The officially approved pattern is not necessarily codified or written down, nor is it always fully understood by the participants. There may not be an organization chart. Sometimes the official, formal relations are so simple and well understood that there is no need to write them down. On the other hand, the relations may be so complex that a chart of the whole system would be too complicated to be helpful. To find out what patterns of a complex organization will be recognized and enforced as part of official policy is no simple task. Many patterns

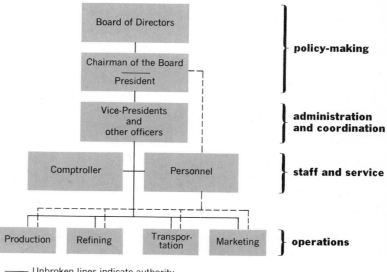

FIG. VII: 2   Abbreviated organization chart of an oil company

ADAPTED from *Planning and Developing the Company Organization* by Ernest Dale (New York: American Management Association, 1952), p. 28.

receive (or are denied) official approval only when they are challenged and must be submitted to the controlling officials for review.

DEMOCRATIC AND AUTHORITARIAN FORMS

Some organizations encourage their members to participate in decision-making, while others restrict this privilege. For example, the Parent-Teacher Association, the League of Women Voters, the Republican party, and the United Automobile Workers Union are so organized as to permit, at least formally, a wide degree of membership control. On the other hand, bank tellers, soldiers, pupils, and boy scouts are not expected to participate significantly in the control of their organizations.

Differences in organizational form may reflect the values people hold, but they also arise out of practical necessity. Authoritarian controls are associated with sustained and coordinated activity. If a group does no more than meet occasionally for discussions, democratic forms may be adequate, but groups that carry on more extensive and continuous activities usually add authoritarian forms. It is convenient and effective to assign to a single individual or small group of executives the responsibility for a job. They select others who accept direction, and thus a unified effort is carried out according to a definite plan. All large organizations follow this procedure, though they vary in the rigidity of discipline, extent of supervision, and the autonomy of component units.

Democracy may be useful to an organization as well as be prized for its own sake. When other incentives are not available or are insufficient, the chance to participate in decisions adds an incentive. Usually where participation is involuntary or where it is fully compensated in money or services, democratic forms are only weakly developed. They are not needed to induce or sustain participation. But if high levels of loyalty and zeal are required or if the individual is expected to take risks, democratic forms are appropriate. Even in a factory, where authoritarian controls predominate, the company may introduce democratic participation in decision-making in order to maintain high morale.

The universe of formal organizations is not neatly divisible into democratic and authoritarian types. In fact, both forms are found in many large organizations. The United Steelworkers of America, the American Farm Bureau Federation, the National Association of Manufacturers, and the Standard Oil Company are alike in their formal provisions for meetings and elections to be held by members or stockholders. They all have large staffs of employees whose activities are controlled in accordance with ideals of rationality and discipline. Democratic forms may control the relations between the members and the top officials. But the officials have an authoritarian relation to the employees of the organization. From a sociological point of view, the employees are also members, but they may not be recognized as such within the organization. A sense of membership is most often found among professional participants, such as members of a college faculty in which case the employee is a staff member. The professional "joins" an organization, and the minister is "called," but the blue-collar worker is "hired."

Not all organizations controlled from the top are equally authoritarian. Some corporations and agencies permit considerable decision-making by committees, wide autonomy for subordinate officials, and action initiated from below. Organizations that encourage these patterns may be thought of as democratic in spirit and to some extent in form, even though final responsibility and authority remain at the top.[1]

Sometimes an executive is criticized as authoritarian because he shows a lack of regard for the opinions or feelings of his subordinates. Authoritarian *behavior* of this kind may be found in authoritarian *organizations,* but the two should not be confused. Some army commanders or corporation officials are authoritarian in their dealings with subordinates; others show tolerance and respect. Some pride themselves on lone-wolf decisions; others consult with subordinates. But in all armies and in most businesses, authoritarian *procedures* predominate.

The word authoritarian has a sinister ring. Indeed, if the kind of discipline and decision-making

[1] On the balance between compliance and initiative in bureaucratic structures, see Reinhard Bendix, "Bureaucracy: The Problem and Its Setting," *American Sociological Review, 12* (October, 1947), 493–507.

that prevails in an army or even a corporation or government agency were extended to the whole society, self-government could not survive. But authoritarian forms, when limited to specific activities and controlled by law and custom, do not necessarily challenge the cultural ideals of a democratic society. So long as the men at the top, who stand in an authoritarian relation to their subordinates, are themselves responsible to some membership or electorate, and are controlled by legal or other norms that restrain arbitrary action, authoritarian forms can readily be accepted or even required. For example, there is authoritarian administration within most government agencies, but the head of the agency is responsible to a governor or a president who must stand for election.

BUREAUCRACY

Formal structure is often referred to as bureaucratic structure. That term is widely used, but occasions some misunderstandings. The following points should be kept in mind:

1. Bureaucracy as used in social science refers to the formal organization of *administrative officials*. It does not include the nonsupervisory work force in a factory or the members of a trade union. Nor does it usually include the top policy-making leaders or directors. Formal structure is a more general term, designating the prescribed roles and procedures of *all* participants.

2. Webster's *New International Dictionary* (Second Edition) gives the following definition of *bureaucracy*: "A system of carrying on the business of government by means of departments or bureaus, each controlled by a chief, who is apt to place special emphasis upon routine and conservative action. . . . Hence, in general, such a system which has become narrow, rigid, and formal, depends on precedent, and lacks initiative and resourcefulness." This definition, reflecting ordinary usage, associates bureaucracy with something undesirable, even pathological. It is important to be clear that social scientists do not define the term in this way, though they may agree that under certain conditions officials are indeed apt to overemphasize routine and otherwise take on the traits suggested in the dictionary definition. A bureaucrat is simply an official within a formal system. The social scientist may study the likelihood that bureaucrats will exhibit certain tendencies, such as narrowed perception and lack of initiative, but he does not limit the idea of bureaucracy to these tendencies.

Adaptation 17 / Bavelas COMMUNICATION PATTERNS IN TASK GROUPS

In addition to determining the division of responsibility and lines of authority, formal structure establishes communication patterns. How do these fixed patterns affect the work and life of a group? Bavelas and his associates undertook some experiments to find out whether different *imposed* patterns of communication make for differences in group performance, leadership, and morale. This work (1) provides a fresh way of looking at formal structure and (2) shows how certain features of formal organization may be studied experimentally.

SOURCE: Abridged and adapted from "Communication Patterns in Task-Oriented Groups" by Alex Bavelas, *Journal of the Acoustical Society of America*, 22 (1950), 725–730. Published in this form by permission of Alex Bavelas and the Acoustical Society of America. The experiment was conducted by Sidney Smith. The full article may also be found in Dorwin Cartwright and Alvin Zander (eds.), *Group Dynamics: Research and Theory* (2nd ed.; New York: Harper & Row, 1960), pp. 669–682.

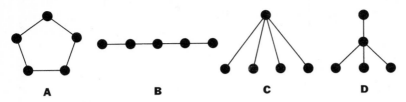

FIG. VII:3 **Some different communication patterns**

Each line represents a communication linkage.

Communication links Let us vary the ways in which five individuals are linked to one another, it being understood that every individual in the group will be linked to at least one other individual in the same group. To be "linked" means that individual p can communicate to q and q to p. What different kinds of communication patterns may we produce that might affect human beings in some way? First impressions of the patterns may prove misleading. (See Fig. VII:3.) Students commonly remark, upon seeing patterns C and D for the first time, that pattern C is "autocratic," while pattern D is a typical "business setup." Actually, of course, insofar as linkage goes, they are identical. The only difference is the arrangement of the dots on the paper. Among patterns A, B, and C, however, we may point to some real differences. For instance, in pattern A each individual can communicate with two others in the group directly—that is, without relaying a message through some other person. In patterns C and D there is only one individual in the group who can communicate directly with all the others.

To make another comparison, any individual in pattern A can communicate with any one of the others with no more than a single "relay." In pattern B two individuals must relay messages through three others in order to communicate with each other.

An experiment Do the patterns make a difference? One experiment will be described. Eight groups of college students were studied, using patterns A and B shown in Figure VII:4. Each subject was given a card upon which were printed five symbols from among these six: ○ △ ✳ □ + ◇. While each symbol appeared on four of the five cards, only one symbol appeared on all five cards. Each group's task was to find the common symbol in the shortest time possible. The subjects sat in separate cubicles. In each subject's cubicle was a box of six switches, each switch labeled with one of the six symbols. The task was considered finished when each member of the group indicated that he knew the common symbol by throwing the appropriate switch. The switches operated a board of lights visible to a laboratory assistant who recorded individual and group times and errors, an error being the throwing of an incorrect switch. The subjects communicated by writing messages which could be passed through slots in the cubicle walls. The slots were so arranged that any desired linkage pattern could be imposed by the experimenter. No restriction whatever was placed upon the content of the messages. A subject who had the "answer" was at liberty to send it along. The cards upon which the messages were written were coded so that a continuous record of the communication activities could be maintained.

Each experimental group worked on 15 successive problems. The same six symbols were used

FIG. VII:4 **Emergence of recognized leaders in different communication patterns**

The number at each position shows the total number of group members who recognized the individual in that position as the leader.

throughout, but the common symbol varied from trial to trial. Four groups worked in pattern *A,* and four other groups worked in pattern *B*. No group worked in more than one pattern.

Each of the subjects answered a questionnaire immediately after the end of the fifteenth trial. One of the questions read: "Did your group have a leader? If so, who?" The answers are shown in Figure VII:4. The findings suggest that the individual occupying the most central position in a pattern is most likely to be recognized as the leader. From direct observation of the subjects while they worked, it appears that the morale of the individuals in the most peripheral (least central) positions of pattern *B* is the poorest.

Further experiments strengthened the hypothesis that leadership is related to "centrality" of position in the communication pattern. This principle is recognized in the design of administrative organizations, where there is usually some attempt—not always successful—to give persons in high authority the readiest access to communication channels.

In another experiment using the same patterns the subjects were asked, "How did you like your job?" and "How satisfied are you with the job done?" The answers to both questions show again that those who occupy the more peripheral positions have the poorest morale. This conclusion supports the general view that participation and group morale are closely related.

Caution Conclusions from laboratory experiments using small groups are not directly applicable to large, complex organizations. However, such experiments can suggest new ways of looking at organizations and help formulate hypotheses to be tested in studies of "the real thing."

SECTION 3 INFORMAL STRUCTURE

The rules of the formal system account for much but not all of the patterned behavior in associations. Beside the formal system and interacting with it an informal structure emerges, based on the spontaneous, problem-solving interaction of persons and groups. Together the formal and informal aspects make up the *social structure* of the organization.

The informal structure is best understood as composed of patterns that develop when the participants face persistent problems that are not provided for by the formal system. The chief sources of these problems are discussed in the following paragraphs.

Impersonality The rules and prescribed roles of the formal structure are necessarily impersonal. The individual is treated as a unit in a technical, task-oriented system. In practice, however, it is often necessary to reach individuals as persons if their best efforts and their highest loyalty are to be mustered.

Some leeway must be allowed for interpersonal and group relations to supplement the formal patterns of communication and control. The importance of personal contact in organizations, not only for private advantage but to get the job done, is well known. Even in armies, where formal relations predominate, friendship and pride in one's "outfit" are important ingredients of effective organization.

Lag Like any other code of rules or laws, the formal system tends to lag behind changes in actual operations. Those who do the work must solve new problems, even problems not yet officially recognized. For example, the official rules may have been developed prior to union organizing. The elected shop stewards try to act as spokesmen for the workers on day-to-day grievances. The foreman will be under pressure to find a way to deal with the men, even though the company has not recognized the union

Informal structure: patterns that develop during spontaneous interaction of persons and groups within the organization.

values and norms	**Informal group norms** within the organization, e.g., "Don't be a rate-buster."
	Basic attitudes about work, cooperation, loyalty, etc. brought into the organization as a result of prior socialization.
	Social control devices, e.g., expressing approval or ridicule.
groups	**Friendships** exert prior claims on the individual (may be within group or from outside).
	Cliques show personal loyalty (may be friendship groups or merely alliances).
	Interest groups share a stake in existing social arrangements (may be any groups, including formal units).
status	**Informal privileges** attached to positions in the formal hierarchy.
	Power relations, e.g., balance of power between local and headquarters units, depending on source of funds, locus of membership, etc.
	Dependency patterns, e.g., dependence of "staff" on "line."

Informal structure critically affects communication and power. It is indispensable to effective functioning but may also undermine it.

FIG. VII:5   Elements of informal structure

and has developed no formal procedures for co-operating with it. Temporarily there may be an informal pattern of consultation between foremen and shop stewards. Eventually this informal procedure, usually modified and made consistent throughout the factory, may become formalized.

Generality   The rules are necessarily abstract and general. Each deals with a type of problem, but all problems cannot be anticipated. For this reason, there are limits to reliance on formal rules and authority must be delegated to the man who does the job or to his immediate supervisor, so that each decision can be made according to the circumstances.

Moreover, there are usually gaps in a system of general rules. At the operating level there may be a need to regularize behavior and make decisions routine, for example in determining coffee-time privileges or the allocation of responsibility for onerous tasks. These gaps are filled by the development of informal custom or usage. In time some patterns may become formalized, others remain outside official recognition.

Personal problems and interests   The foregoing comments assume that the participants are solely interested in attaining the organization's aims, that they are doing their best to supplement the formal rules in informal ways. It cannot be assumed, however, that individuals are solely interested in helping the organization to reach its goals. Personal needs and private concerns are also important. For example, a new supervisor may allay his anxieties by cultivating the friendship of an experienced worker. He thereby gains access to valuable information about the work and the employees. His friend may defend him when things go wrong. This relation, if stabilized, becomes part of the informal structure of the plant. It cannot be officially enforced, yet it is a significant fact that must not be overlooked by anyone who wants to understand or influence that segment of the organization.

The individual may also bring with him ingrained beliefs such as negative attitudes toward Negroes or foreigners and ties of loyalty to friends or kin. A study of a gypsum company reported that "the plant was enmeshed in a network of kinship relationships."[2] These sentiments and attachments become part of the organization's social reality.

Roles and the spillover effect   Formal relations coordinate positions and activities, not persons. The rules apply to foremen and machinists, to clerks, sergeants, and vice-presidents. However, no organization of any duration is able to restrict interaction to formally defined roles. In practice, men tend to interact as many-faceted persons, adjusting to di-

[2] Alvin W. Gouldner, *Patterns of Industrial Bureaucracy* (Glencoe: The Free Press, 1954), p. 65.

verse daily experiences in ways that spill over the boundaries set by their formal roles. The role usually calls for compartmentalization, for keeping in check personal needs, impulses, and orientations. The actor, however, is a unified personality. He has his own problems, his own priorities. This tension between person and role is characteristic of organizations.

Individuals participate in associations made up of *both* formal and informal relations. Therefore, the sociology of special-purpose associations stresses the interdependence of these aspects. The following sections, while emphasizing informal processes, show their relation to the formal devices for attaining organized, concerted effort.

SECTION 4 COHESION AND MORALE

The most effective organizations are able to win a sense of personal commitment. When the work the members do, the initiative they display, and the loyalty they give go beyond the minimum requirements of keeping a job, morale is high. The organization is then more than a technical arrangement of co-ordinated parts. It is a cohesive social group.

SOCIALIZING THE ORGANIZATION MEMBER

It is common to refer to someone as a Harvard man, a Forest Service man, or a military man. These labels suggest that the individual has been influenced by his associational experience, that is, effectively socialized. Not all organizations, however, are capable of such effective socialization.

The examples may suggest that socialization in organizations produces highly visible products, but this is not always so. Sometimes the organization's influence can be recognized only by those who are "in." Many organizations have little effect on personality. Socialization is important for the organization that requires a high degree of personal dedication and loyalty. Some organizations call for distinctive ways of thinking and responding; others must offset influences that work against their aims or policies, e.g., the civilian outlook and habits of the draftee.

When socialization is effective, the individual makes the organization's perspectives his own. This has been called the *"internalization of influence,* be-

cause it injects into the very nervous systems of the organization members the criteria of decision that the organization wishes to employ. The organization member acquires knowledge, skill, and identifications or loyalties that enable him to make decisions, by himself, as the organization would like him to decide."[3]

The effects of organizational socialization are:

1. *To strengthen group loyalty and thereby organizational security.* If the individual feels personally attacked when the organization is attacked and personal failure when it fails, he will work harder, help in crises, and require less discipline. Hence socialization motivates high levels of participation and responsibility. Socialization increases the likelihood that the members will stand united against threats from the outside. This is obviously important in voluntary action organizations such as protest groups. But it is also significant where employees have dealings with other organizations and the public, especially at the administrative level. Loyal employees are expected to defend the reputation of their organization and to pass on useful information, even if it is acquired off the job. It is probable that assessments of organizational loyalty play an important part in determining the careers of professional or executive personnel.

2. *To make official communication easier.* If the individual has absorbed the general outlook of the

[3] H. A. Simon, *Administrative Behavior* (2nd ed.; New York: Macmillan, 1958), p. 103. Italics supplied.

organization and its distinctive approach to its task and to other organizations, it will be easier to communicate instructions. They will not have to be spelled out in detail because their background and intent will be understood. The socialized organization member has internalized the decisional premises of the enterprise, that is, the bases on which decisions are made.[4] One advantage of this deeper understanding is that the member knows without being explicitly told when he may modify or even disregard instructions. Because he understands the basis of an order, he need not follow it mechanically or literally.

3. *To permit greater delegation of authority without loss of control.* When decisional premises are adequately communicated, the person who gives an order shares the same understanding of what is to be accomplished as the person who executes it. The latter may then be permitted more discretion. Thus organizational socialization substitutes informal social controls for formal administrative controls. The fact that they share values and aspirations permits the college president to delegate decision-making to a dean with confidence that the decisions will conform to the college's basic policies and interests. No such assurance would be possible if the dean were not instilled with the values and point of view of the college.

The effects of socialization in organizations parallel the effects of socialization in society itself. When aspirations and disciplines are built into the individual, personal satisfactions are linked to such social aims as hard work and patriotic sacrifice, specific rules are more thoroughly understood and more flexibly applied, and the individual can be expected to act in accordance with social values even when the official agencies of the society are not present or effective. The weaker the socialization, the more society must depend upon formal controls.

Organizations need to emphasize socialization when impersonal incentives, such as wages, are not adequate to sustain participation, when instructions are so complex that the persons who are to carry them out require extensive acquaintance with decisional premises, and when circumstances require ex-

tensive delegation of authority, for example, if subordinate offices are distant or isolated.

ORGANIZATION UNITS AS SOCIAL GROUPS

The effect of personal interaction is to create social groups within the formal organization. In many cases, the social group and the organization unit have the same membership, name, and history. When a particular division or the organization as a whole becomes the object of personal identification, develops a homogeneous personnel, and shares a common fund of tradition, it becomes more than a narrowly utilitarian organization. It takes on the character of a community.

Interest groups Group members who share a stake in existing social arrangements or unite for a common objective form an interest group. Interest groups take many forms within large organizations, from a small informal group of workers seeking protection from an arbitrary supervisor (see Adaptation 12, pp. 130 ff.) to a large department of loyal members who act as an effective social unit. Some internal interest groups are weak; others are strong. Some muster support only from within the enterprise or association; others find external allies. For example, the Army Corps of Engineers acts as an interest group within the U.S. Government, but it is also supported by private associations outside the government, such as the National Rivers and Harbors Congress. Some interest groups coincide with the formal structure and transform technical units into unities of persons. Other interest groups cut across the officially approved lines of communication and weaken the formal structure.

In many large organizations, the formation of interest groups is an expected and desired outcome of the division of labor. The personnel department upholds standards of employee selection and training; accounting is supposed to maintain standards of reporting and fiscal control; the sales department protects lines of communication to buyers; production is committed to a schedule of output. All of these units

---

[4] Simon, *op. cit.*, p. 222.

are expected to defend values as a way of executing the functions entrusted to them. They become interest groups, often vigorously promoting their special aims and methods. Within limits, and depending on the type of organization, some competition and even conflict among units may be tolerated. It is presumed that top officials are able to settle the resulting conflicts and hold the competing groups to the aims of the organization as a whole. The amount of leeway permitted internal interest groups depends on the extent to which the organization wishes to encourage initiative from below. A university, for example, must depend on the initiative of its academic departments to develop their respective fields of knowledge. The departments often act as interest groups, pressing for recognition and increased budgets and protecting standards of education and research.

Divided loyalties The social groups that develop in work situations do not necessarily follow the boundaries of formal organization units. Clerical and professional personnel, though in the same formal unit, may belong to distinct working groups with different identifications, perceptions, and interests. Differences in status and social background, combined with differences in the nature of the work, often create social groups that do not correspond with the formal division of labor.

Sometimes, when social groupings cut across formal organization lines, there are divided loyalties, especially for individuals whose daily work takes them into cooperative contact with members of other units or even of other organizations. The problem has practical implications in the relation of staff units to the operating or line organization. (See Sec. 5, p. 207.) Suppose a personnel department has the job of maintaining standards of recruitment, promotion, training, and employee morale in a large firm. A member of personnel is permanently assigned to work with the refining division (one of the operating divisions in Fig. VII:2). If he has repeated contact with members of refining, he may share its spe-

cial perspectives and be accepted by its members. To the extent that he identifies with refining, he acts as its representative, presenting its arguments and points of view to his superiors in the personnel department.

On the other hand, if he is given a variety of assignments that place him in contact with many operating units, his main identification is probably with personnel or, more accurately, with his section of personnel.[5]

If personnel department technicians are absorbed into working groups of the program or operating divisions, the policies of personnel may be weakened and in the extreme case might even endanger the continued existence of some sections of the department. The operating divisions might demand that they be allowed to work out their own personnel procedures. The personnel department could limit a staff member's contact with a particular operating division, thus forestalling his integration into a working group of the division.

PRIMARY RELATIONS

Primary relations contribute to the cohesion and effective functioning of organizations. (See PRIMARY GROUPS, pp. 134 ff.) These influences may be summarized as follows:

1. *Primary relations help morale,* that is, the maintenance of effective participation. This is accomplished by modifying the impersonality of the formal system. The individual gains direct personal satisfaction in companionship and identification with his work and with the enterprise.

2. *Primary relations aid communication.* By adapting formal rules to the individual's immediate situation, primary relations break down communication barriers. Instructions thus adapted are better understood and more readily accepted.

3. *Primary relations aid control of organization members.* When a man is a member of a primary group, he accepts its discipline. If the group is part of a larger association, it can hold its members to the aims and methods of the whole. For example,

---

[5] See H. A. Simon, D. W. Smithburg, and V. A. Thompson, *Public Administration* (New York: Knopf, 1950), p. 101.

the pressures exerted within the primary group may help reduce absenteeism. In this way, primary relations supplement the more formal controls.

Cautions (1) There is a disruptive potential in primary groups. (See "the double-edged significance of the primary group," page 134.) (2) The con-

structive contributions of primary relations are not equally available or necessary in all associations. The more the organization depends on high morale, the greater will be the significance of primary relations. Some organizations, however, are able to carry out their functions without high levels of personal commitment.

SECTION 5 COMMUNICATION AND SOCIAL STATUS

Most discussions of stratification deal with whole societies or communities, and this is the emphasis in SOCIAL STRATIFICATION. But the basic processes of stratification also occur in special-purpose associations, where they affect communication, incentive, and control.

Formal ranks and social strata The study of social stratification in organizations includes both the formal ranking systems and the informally patterned experiences of the persons who occupy the positions. The formal ranking system is readily observed. It is easy to list the official ranks between a five-star general and a buck private, between the chairman of the board of a corporation and an unskilled worker, between the president of the AFL-CIO and a rank-and-file member of a trade-union local.

Formal ranks are associated with distinctive attitudes and interests. The diverse experiences and problems of men at different levels condition (1) how individuals in similar social positions view the world and themselves and (2) the stake they have in the organization. A man's position in the hierarchy influences his manners, outlook, opportunities, and power.

Status is symbolized in many ways. The Ameri-

can office "is a veritable temple of status." [6] The carpeted office and the privilege of smoking or of first-naming one's colleagues are cues to differential status. The way names are used is important, but the significance attached to names depends on whether one is looking up or down the hierarchy. The rank order of address by executives is outlined by Potter, the student of human and other relations, in the case of Lumer Farr, a company director who liked to be called "The Guv'nor":

In the science of Christian-naming, Lumer is associated with Farr's Law of Mean Familiarity. This can be expressed by a curve, but is much clearer set down as follows:
The Guv'nor addresses:

Co-director Michael Yates as	MIKE
Assistant director Michael Yates as	MICHAEL
Sectional manager Michael Yates as	MR. YATES
Sectional assistant Michael Yates as	YATES
Apprentice Michael Yates as	MICHAEL
Night-watchman Michael Yates as	MIKE [7]

Organizations are both aided and hindered by the transformation of formal, technical rankings into social strata. Men who have feelings of deference toward their superiors more readily accept com-

---

[6] W. H. Whyte, Jr., "Status in the American Office," *Fortune* (May, 1951).

[7] Stephen Potter, *One-upmanship* (New York: Holt, Rinehart and Winston, 1952), p. 44.

mands, and the system of authority is thus sustained. On the other hand, exploitation of positions of authority for personal gratification or blind acceptance of commands because they come from a superior may subvert organizational goals.

The economy of incentives Wholehearted commitment is hard to foster because most organizations can offer only a limited range of incentives. Remuneration is no guarantee that individuals will give freely of their energy and zeal. A system of status, in addition to fixing the lines of authority and communication, also provides incentives.[8] High status conveys social prestige, inside and outside the organization, accompanied by deference and respect from others. Many persons work hard to attain even relatively small advances of status. Sometimes merely a change in job titles with no change in actual authority or salary is an effective incentive.

In addition to prestige, higher status offers special privileges, including the opportunity to execute one's own ideas. These and other social concomitants of the formal ranking system help to win fuller commitment. The design of status systems from the standpoint of the economy of incentives has not been closely studied, but its importance is widely recognized.

Line and staff as status groups Adaptation 18, pages 208–211, shows that the difference between staff officers and line supervisors is not merely one of job assignment. A broader social differentiation occurs, extending to the images each group has of the other and reflecting the insecurities they feel on the job. This differentiation is strongly influenced by the social backgrounds of the staff personnel, including both attributes that are developed within the factory and characteristics they bring with them from their earlier social experience.

Just as in the larger society, some groups within organizations are more powerful than others because of their greater ability to influence opinion or to control essential activities and resources. The struggle for power is usually less obvious in special-purpose organizations than in society at large. Partly because of this covert quality, an important phase of the sociological study of organizations is the discovery of the relative strength and weakness of the constituent groups, not as defined by formal position alone but as conditioned by their place within the social structure of the enterprise.

The Dalton study reflects this interest. One of its main themes is the relative weakness of the staff compared with the line, but this is only partly due to the formal authority of the top line officials. The staff personnel are also dependent on line officers, who are not formally their superiors. The staff men (who often seek promotion through transfer to the line organization) are dependent because of their problems of advancement and because the line supervisors can interfere with the work of the staff. Similar cases of conflict among officials in government, business, and other organizations have been reported, though few have been so carefully documented and analyzed. For example, a perennial strain is expected between the sales and production divisions in businesses, and there is often a marked difference in status, influence, and career line between the teaching and administrative groups in schools and colleges.

Communication and the chain of command Adaptation 19, pages 211–215, describes how information is filtered as it moves up and down the chain of command. The employees' efforts to protect themselves result in distortions in communication.

Although stratification may *distort* communication, the formal status system is designed to *facilitate* it. For example, when a man receives an order or request, he wants to know if it comes from someone who is in position to know the facts and who

---

[8] This point has been emphasized by Chester I. Barnard, who did much to lay the groundwork for the sociology of large-scale organizations. See *The Functions of the Executive* (Cambridge: Harvard University Press, 1938) and "Functions and Pathology of Status Systems in Formal Organizations" in William Foote Whyte (ed.), *Industry and Society* (New York: McGraw-Hill, 1946).

will back up the action taken. Usually knowledge of the sender's place in the formal status system answers his questions. As formal ranking becomes embedded in social relations, more detailed knowledge is necessary to interpret orders. One man at a given formal rank may not need to be taken seriously, but another at the same level might command prompt action. For example, communications from a "lame duck," a high official who is scheduled to leave office in the near future, are treated more casually than if his tenure in office were known to be continuing.

Adaptation 18 / Dalton STAFF-LINE CONFLICT IN INDUSTRY

This is a study of social differentiation and its consequences in two major groups of management: the line organization and the staff organization. *The line* consists of the foremen and their superiors who direct the actual work done and who are responsible for production. *The staff organization* consists of specialists who have a research and advisory function in the plant. Staff groups are relatively new in industry. They provide specialized knowledge and technical advice in such diverse fields as chemistry, statistics, public and industrial relations, personnel, accounting, and engineering.

Data on staff-line relations in this study were drawn from three industrial plants in related industries. They range in size from 4,500 to 20,000 employees and from 200 to nearly 1,000 management officials.

The problem The staff has specialized knowledge gained from training and research. In theory it advises the line officers how they can increase production and efficiency. The ideal situation involves two assumptions: (1) that the staff specialists are reasonably content to be advisors without formal authority, and (2) that their suggestions for improvements are welcomed by the line officers and carried out. This study tests these assumptions in the actual relations of the two groups as they work out their problems.

It must be emphasized that the staff-line conflict discussed here is only one of many frictions in the plants. For instance, there is competition and tension among departments, among individuals, and between union and management.

There are two major sources of friction between the staff and line in the plants considered. One is the *social background* or composition of the two groups, that is, the personal characteristics they bring to the plant. The other source of friction is the differentiation that takes place within the plant, the differences in *social position* they assume once there.

Sources of friction: social composition The two groups differ in age, formal education, and social behavior (appearance, manners, etc.).

1. *Age.* The staff members on the average are significantly younger than the line officers. This is a source of friction revealed in the ill-concealed attitude of the older line officers. They resent receiving what they regard as instructions from younger men. The staff officers often attribute their lack of success in "selling ideas" to the line to this attitude. As one assistant staff chief remarked:

SOURCE: Abridged and adapted from "Conflicts Between Staff and Line Managerial Officers," by Melville Dalton, *American Sociological Review* (June, 1950), pp. 342–351. Published in this form by permission of Melville Dalton and the *American Sociological Review*.

"We're always in hot water with these old guys on the line. You can't tell them a damn thing. They're bull-headed as hell! Most of the time we offer a suggestion it's either laughed at or not considered at all. The same idea in the mouth of some old codger on the line'd get a round of applause. They treat us like kids."

2. *Education.* The staff members necessarily have more education than the line officers. Education is part of the qualifications for staff jobs; experience is emphasized in the choice of line officers. The staff is in a position to exploit this difference in education, and it probably contributes to a feeling of superiority among them. The line, however, resents the proposals of the staff because of the educational difference involved as well as the age differential. The line often refers to the staff as "college punks," "slide-rules," "crackpots," and "chair-warmers."

3. *Social behavior.* Attention to personal appearance, cosmopolitan recreational tastes, facility in speaking and writing, poise and polish in social intercourse—these also distinguish the staff from the line. The line receives occasional snubs from the staff and feels that their emphasis on social prestige is a threat to the line man's own position and not in the best interests of the plant. To quote a line officer on the matter of social intercourse during the working day: "They don't go into the cafeteria to eat and relax while they talk over their problems. They go in there to look around and see how somebody is dressed or to talk over the hot party they had last night. Well, that kind of damn stuff don't go with me. I haven't any time to put

on airs and make out I'm something I'm not."

Sources of friction: social position within the plant The different functions the two groups perform in the plant and the different opportunities they have for advancement, salary, power, prestige, and responsibility are major sources of friction.

1. *Chances for advancement.* Line officers have better chances for advancement than staff personnel for at least three reasons: (*a*) there are approximately twice as many positions of authority in the line; (*b*) the line organization reaches higher, for it has six status levels whereas the staff has only three; (*c*) line salaries for comparable positions are usually higher.

2. *The staff is on trial.* Continuous dispute over the relative worth of the two groups is another source of friction. The line regards the staff as on trial rather than as a managerial division of equal importance. To the line officer, his authority over production is something sacred, and he resents the implication that after many years in the line he needs the guidance of an inexperienced newcomer. He is ready with charges of "crack-pot experimentation" and "costly blunders" by the staff. The lower foremen are inclined to suspect that the staff is less an engineering and technical assistance division than a weapon of top management to control the lower line officers.

The staff member is painfully aware of these feelings and of the need of his group to prove its worth. He feels bound to contribute something significant in the form of ideas helpful to management. By virtue of his greater edu-

cation and knowledge of the latest theories of production, the staff man regards himself as a management consultant, an expert. He feels that he must be, or appear to be, almost infallible once he has committed himself to top management on some point. Whereas in practice adoption of their suggestions depends upon the amount of cooperation that can be won from line officers, the staff prefer to see themselves as agents of top management, independent of the lower line, and superior to it.

3. *The line resists innovation.* The different pressures upon the staff and upon the line in day-to-day operations create additional tension. As we have seen, the staff must make contributions in the form of suggested changes in order to prove its worth. But it is the line that is called on to change its work habits. The experienced line officer fears being "shown up" before his superiors for not having thought of improvements himself. Moreover, changes in methods may bring personnel changes which threaten to break up cliques and other informal arrangements and to reduce the line officer's area of authority. Or such changes may expose forbidden practices and departmental inefficiency and waste. In some cases these fears have led line officers to strike informal bargains with the staff to postpone the initiation of new practices for a period of time in exchange for some other cooperation from the line.

The pressure on staff personnel is to develop new techniques, but they also have to consider how their plans will be received by the line. They know from experience that lower line officers can give a "black eye" to staff contributions by deliberate malpractices. Line officers may verbally accept a change, but they are in a position to sabotage it in practice. For this reason, there is a tendency for staff members to withhold improved production schemes when they know an attempt to introduce them might fail.

The study found evidence that the accommodation of staff to demands of the line included the manipulation (but not embezzlement) of company funds. Pressures from the lower line organization forced some staff groups to "kick over" some of the funds appropriated for staff use. The line was then able to hide inefficiencies and meet the constant pressure from the top to show low operating costs. In return the staff received more cooperation from the line in accepting innovations, and some staff personnel who wished transfer to the line were recommended.

Weakness of the staff It is clear in the plants studied that the line is the more powerful branch of management. The position of the staff is weak and defensive. This is due to its lack of authority over production and its dependence upon top management for approval and for advancement.

The ultimate authority in the plant rests with top *line* officials. Usually, they have risen to the top by way of the line organization. They understand and sympathize with the daily problems of the line in getting the main work done, and their functions as top officials bring them close to the day-to-day pressures and responsibilities of the line. Top officials also have influence over promotions in the higher staff positions. A staff member knows that if he aspires to one of the higher staff jobs, or wishes to transfer to the line, he must satisfy the top line officer. The staff member must show his ability to work with the line and to understand its problems. He must make contributions the line will accept, and be able to minimize the conflicts occasioned by the social differences in background and role we have described.

Conclusion The ideal conception of staff-line relations assumes that the staff is willing to function in an advisory capacity and that the line is willing to accept staff suggestions for improvement. The sources of tension inherent in this situation have been described. One result is a morale problem among new staff members, reflected in disillusionment and high turnover.

The new staff member, often selected because of his academic record, enters industry prepared to engage in logical, well-formulated relations with other members of management, and to carry out the precise, methodical functions for which he has been trained. He believes he has much to contribute and that his efforts will win early recognition and rapid advancement. He soon discovers that his freedom to function is snared in a web of informal commitments, that his academic specialty may not be relevant to his actual assignments, and that he must learn who the informally powerful line officers are and what ideas they welcome. The result is a disillusionment that contributes to a relatively high turnover of younger staff personnel.

In the plants studied, ambitious staff men, frustrated by the relatively low hierarchy through which they could move, appeared eager to increase the number of personnel under their authority. And in fact the personnel of staff groups did increase disproportionately to those of the line. There was also a trend of personnel movement from staff to line, presumably reflecting the drive, ambition, and qualifications of staff members who were striving for positions of authority, prestige, and higher income.

In general, staff-line friction reduces the distinctive contribution of staff personnel. Their relatively weak position, requiring accommodation to the line, tends to restrict their ability to engage in free, experimental innovation. On the other hand, the natural resistance of the line to staff innovations probably usefully restrains over-eager efforts to apply untested procedures on a large scale. The conflicts, however, introduce an uncontrolled element into the managerial system. Under such conditions, it is difficult to know when valuable ideas are being sacrificed.

Caution Dalton's analysis is valuable for the light it casts on the sources of group conflict within administrative organizations. While the specific conclusions are still relevant, the status of staff groups has probably risen, especially in industries that depend on "idea men" of all sorts. This is reflected in a tendency in some industries for top officials to be drawn from the staff rather than only from the line.

"In the mythology of the modern corporation, 'staff' groups are not supposed to have direct influence over line activities; but, in practice, as they gain reputation for their expertise, as they gain control over substantial amounts of company resources, and as they move from *ad hoc* advice-giving to long-range, comprehensive research and planning for the organization, they may, in fact, be setting most of the constraints within which 'line' managers operate." [9]

[9] William R. Dill, "Business Organizations," in James G. March (ed.), *Handbook of Organizations* (Chicago: Rand McNally, 1965), p. 1085.

Adaptation 19 / *Gardner* and *Moore* THE LINE OF AUTHORITY AND COMMUNICATION

The formal line of authority or chain of command in a factory provides a *channel of communication* extending from top to bottom. But it is not the simple, direct channel it is often thought to be. By its very nature as a linkage of man-boss relationships, it has a number of peculiarities which affect the quality, accuracy, and speed of communication. In fact, much of the transmission is so difficult that it is rare for a superior who is several steps removed from the work level to have comprehensive knowledge of what goes on in the shop. This adaptation reviews some of the sources of communication difficulties up and down the line.

Communication down Because each person is sensitive to his boss's moods, opinions, likes, and dislikes, there is often much confusion and misunderstanding in communication down the line. For example, we see the superintendent passing through the shop convoyed by the foreman. Being in a jovial mood, he comments that "the girls seem happy this morning, the way they are talking and laughing." The foreman thinks, "Is he hinting that I shouldn't allow them to talk? Does he think I don't keep proper discipline? Those girls ought to have sense enough to stop talking and act busy when he's around. Maybe I better move Mary off by herself because she always gets the others started talking." The boss leaves, quite unaware that his comments have been interpreted as criticism. As soon as he is gone, the foreman bawls out the girls for talking and not paying attention to their work; he moves the Marys

SOURCE: Abridged and adapted from *Human Relations in Industry* by B. B. Gardner and D. G. Moore (Rev. ed.; Chicago: Irwin, 1950), pp. 33–65. Published in this form by permission of the authors and Richard D. Irwin, Inc.

A CASE OF JITTERS

Take the case of Bob, foreman in the machine department, when he suddenly discovers that he does not have enough bronze rod on hand to complete the order of part number X37A22 for the end of the week and that it will keep two hand screw machines going steadily to make delivery on time. So he talks to Charley, the machine operator who came to him asking for the rod:

Bob: "Are you sure there isn't any of that rod over in the rack? When we started on this job, I checked the storeroom records and there was plenty on hand."

Charley: "There sure isn't now. You remember when we first started on this order somebody gave us the wrong specifications and we turned out a lot that had to be junked."

Bob: "That's right. Well, I'll call the stockroom and get some more over right away." (*Thinking*, I sure did slip up on that. I completely forgot to order more rod.)

(*He calls the stockroom.*) "I'll need two hundred pounds of that ⅜th bronze rod for part number X37A22. We're in a rush for it, got to get the order out right away and a couple of machines are waiting. Can you get it right over?"

Stockman: "Sorry, we are out of that rod. Won't be able to get it in before Friday. Why didn't you call last week?"

Bob: "Can't you get hold of any before that? If I don't deliver those parts before Monday, the gadget assembly department will be tied up."

Stockman: "We'll do the best we can, but don't expect it before Friday. Why don't you guys give us a little more notice instead of waiting until your machines shut down and then expecting us to do miracles?"

Bob: (*Thinking:* This is a terrible note! I slip up on ordering that rod the one time the stockroom is out of it. Why can't they keep some stock on hand instead of trying to work from hand to mouth. Just trying to make a good showing by keeping down inventory and they tie up production. They ought to realize that they are there to help the shop, not to give us all this trouble. Wonder what I can do now. The boss sure will give me hell when he hears this. Maybe I ought to check with Joe in gadget assembly to see how many parts they have on hand and how long before he will need more. Maybe I better let him know what's happened so he will know what to expect. Maybe he can plan his work so the people on that assembly job can do something else for a few days.

SOURCE: From *Human Relations in Industry* by B. B. Gardner and D. G. Moore (Rev. ed.; Chicago: Irwin, 1950), pp. 37–38. Reprinted by permission.

around, and it is weeks or even months before the final ripples of disturbance have died down.

Distortion up the line Because of sensitivity to the boss and dependence on him, there is much distortion in communicating up the line of authority. Along with concern for "giving the boss what he wants," there is a tendency to "cover up," to keep the boss from knowing about the things that go wrong or the things that do not get done. No one wants to pass bad news up the line, because he feels that it reflects on him and that he should handle his job so there is no bad news. Consequently, he does not tell the boss what a poor job he did or how stupid he was. That is, he does not do so unless he thinks someone else will get to the boss first. (See "A Case of Jitters," above.) When he does have to break some bad news to the boss, he will probably have things fixed

But if I tell him what's happened, he will tell his boss, and his boss will jump on my boss and my boss will jump on me for letting this happen and not letting him know. So before I tell Joe anything I better tell my boss. Maybe if I tell him, he can tell Joe's boss, and I won't have to say anything to Joe. Joe's going to be plenty sore anyway. He got kind of hot the other day when I tried to get him to let me make some changes in the base plate for that Model N job. Seemed like he was just being stubborn. Wonder if he might have enough parts on hand so he could just go along and say nothing about this affair. If I knew he had enough, I just wouldn't say anything and take a chance on getting some to him before he runs out. I'm afraid to risk it, though, without being pretty sure, because if he did have to shut down, my boss sure would raise Cain. Yeah, and Joe called the other day to know how we were coming on that lot we delivered yesterday, said he didn't want to get caught short. But Joe always does that. He starts crowding you for things long before he actually needs them. He seems to think no one will keep their promises unless he rides them. If I ask Joe how much he has on hand, he will suspect something and I will have to tell him.

Guess I better not take a chance on Joe. I will have to tell my boss first. But gee, how I hate to tell him! I know just what he will think. I know I should have remembered to order more when we spoiled that first run, but I was so busy getting caught up that I forgot. Anyway, you never would expect the stockroom to be out of a standard item like that. And if they ran this place right, they never would be. But my boss won't care about that. All he'll think is that I must be asleep on the job. He expects me to keep track of everything; and if I have to do the stockroom's job for them to keep my job going, he expects me to do that. What will I tell him, anyway, that won't make me look like a fool who doesn't know his job? Maybe I better not tell him now. It won't hurt to wait till tomorrow, and maybe then the stockroom will know when I can expect the rod. Maybe they will do better than Friday, and I might squeeze by. When I do tell the boss, I want to be able to tell him just when we will be able to start on the job again, and maybe I can plan it so we won't hold up the assembly. Guess I will wait till tomorrow and see what I can figure out.)

And Bob spends the rest of the day in a state of jitters trying to figure a way out of the predicament, or at least a partial solution which he can present to his boss when he finally is forced to tell him. He goes home that night with a terrible grouch, is cross to the children because they are so noisy, gets annoyed with his wife because she seems so cheerful, can hardly eat his supper, sleeps poorly, and hates to go to work the next morning. Such is the human element of communication up the line.

up or have developed a good excuse. People at each level develop defenses, often complicated and ingenious, to protect themselves from criticism from those above them in the chain of command.

The subordinate selects what to tell the superior, trying to anticipate what the boss wants to know or what he may want to know later, trying to present things in such a way that his boss will feel that things are not too bad, or, if they were, that they are now under control, and trying to give him good news to take the sting out of the bad. The boss goes away feeling that he knows what is going on, that he has his finger firmly on the pulse of the shop.

Filtered information   Each individual in the line acts as a filter who sorts the information coming to him and selects what he will pass on to his boss. Because the boss responds most favorably to good news, good news goes up the line quite easily and rapidly. Information about improvements in output, quality, costs, and so on are transmitted readily from level to level. On the other hand, bad news moves more slowly; everyone is reluctant to communicate his mistakes or failures. The what-will-the-boss-think-of-me feeling encourages delays, excuses, and the development of tact in presenting bad news. The filtering of information operates at all levels in the hierarchy.

The foreman's orientation   The foreman, who is usually considered the first level of management, has the most direct and detailed knowledge of the job and the workers. He plans and supervises their work; he checks and judges it; he maintains discipline and enforces the rules. To the workers he is the one who gives orders, who rewards and punishes. It is through him that the downward pressures, the demands and orders, are transmitted to the work group.

The foreman develops an orientation toward the work which is different from that of the rest of the hierarchy. In the first place, his attention is focused on the everyday details. He sees the immediate difficulties and complexities of getting the work out, and he usually knows the workers and their attitudes. As a result, he tends to be impatient with higher levels or with staff people who try to generalize on the basis of partial knowledge and make decisions which affect his job. He frequently feels that his superiors impose tasks on him and on his group without understanding the difficulties of the job.

Four characteristic orientations of foremen may be identified: (1) worker-oriented, (2) management-oriented, (3) isolated, and (4) integrated.

1. *Worker-oriented foremen.* The foreman who has strong feelings of sympathy with the work group identifies with the workers, acts as though he were one of them, and constantly defends them from his superiors and from outside organizations. Such a foreman generally maintains little social distance between himself and his work group.

There is often a much greater distinction between the foreman and his department chief. In some cases the foreman may actually avoid contacts and force the department chief to come to him. The foreman tries to keep the department chief away from his group, to be present when he is around the job, to cover up mistakes, protect individual workers from his criticism, and otherwise to build strong barriers between them. He resists demands from above for changes, finding reasons for not accepting them or for their failure if they are forced upon him.

2. *Management-oriented foremen.* The opposite type is the foreman who has a strong identification with management and his superiors, and he holds his subordinates at a distance. He tends to be critical of the workers and feels that they are not dependable or are not trying to do a good job. They correctly feel that he is aloof, and they hesitate to talk freely to him or to discuss problems with him. He is likely to seek out his superiors, both on the job and outside. He is concerned about his relationship with his department chief and tries to make a good impression.

In this situation, the workers feel forced to be on their guard against their foreman and think of him as someone who is against them rather than for them. They develop various defenses: they watch their behavior whenever he is in sight; they may restrict output without his knowledge; and they may complain about him to the union. Sometimes the tension makes contacts so uncomfortable that even he is aware of it and may withdraw to some extent from the work situation. In extreme cases, he spends most of his time at his desk, talking to his superiors, or entirely out of the department.

3. *Isolated foremen.* Sometimes a foreman is isolated from both his department chief and the work group. In these cases, there is avoidance on the part of all concerned. If the job will run with a minimum of direct supervision, the foreman may stay out of the group most of the time and stay away from his department chief, too. As long as the work goes on, the department chief also avoids the foreman and the group, and all contacts are very formal and uncomfortable. If the job does not go well, the foreman is in difficulties because his boss will be critical of him and may make arbitrary demands. At the same time, the group is defensive and does not respond to the foreman's demands. The foreman is generally critical of them, just as his boss is critical of him. Under these conditions, both the foreman and the workers are uncomfortable, and whenever there is pressure on the foreman from above, he feels isolated and defenseless and takes it out on his subordinates. In other words, such situations may be fairly stable as

long as the work is running well, but under pressure a great deal of friction between foreman and workers develops.

4. *Integrated foremen.* Sometimes, on the other hand, we find a situation in which there is strong identification and integration among all three—the workers, the foreman, and the department chief. In such cases we see very easy interaction between workers and department chief, and the department chief is usually in close touch with the details of the job and with the individuals. The foreman is comfortable under these conditions, does not worry about the presence of the department chief, and need not cover up mistakes or try to protect the group. In many instances of this kind, the whole department stands as a unit against outside pressures or against demands from above. These are the most comfortable and satisfactory work situations for the foreman and for the workers.

The foreman, communication, and morale   As we have seen, a foreman is in constant contact with the workers and has the responsibility of putting into action many of management's policies and decisions. He is the one who interprets management to the workers; he is, to a large degree, the only representative of management with whom the workers have much contact; he is the one who imposes management's controls upon them. For these reasons he influences the workers' attitudes toward the job, management, and the company generally. He is the one who can most directly affect their morale and loyalty. While his importance to employee morale has long been recognized, recent studies have shown that in many respects he is also the most important factor in the work situation.

Caution   The above description might give the impression that communication between levels in the industrial status system is completely ineffectual. Actually, of course, this is not true. People at the bottom of the structure do produce the goods, and those at the top do control production and maintain their authority over those below. But because of the nature of worker-boss relations and because status relations in the system are neither clearly recognized nor understood, communication sometimes interferes with satisfactory work relations and production.

SECTION 6 INSTITUTIONALIZATION

The social processes discussed in this chapter—group formation, stratification, communication, socialization, adaptation—have the effect of building into the organization habits, values, vested interests, and other elements of structure and policy. Each organization is a creature of its own history, the kind of people who made up its membership, the groups they formed, and the way it adapted to its environment. The outcome may be beneficial if the organization has a stable and distinctive competence, an established reputation, and a network of long-nurtured alliances. Well-established organizations often have a head start over rivals come lately on the scene.

On the other hand, the process of settling down, of becoming established and stabilized, can be costly. What began as a vigorous, purposeful group may end up institutionalized, fat, secure, and useful, but without its former energy or idealism.

Institutionalization is the development of orderly, stable, *socially integrating* forms and structures out of unstable, loosely patterned, or merely technical types of action. Stable, highly formalized technical procedures in science and industry, such as those governing the shipment of freight or the assembly of a complicated machine, do not necessarily contribute to the formation or maintenance of a social group and are, therefore, not institutional. On the other hand, some technical procedures, such as piloting a ship, may symbolize an occupation or profession for its members and take on an institutional meaning.

Four institutionalizing processes, important in the life history of associations, are: (1) formalization, (2) self-maintenance and conservatism, (3) infusion with value, and (4) development of a distinctive social composition and social base.[10]

Formalization The most obvious type of institutionalization in associations is the development of formal systems, which often emerge out of trial-and-error informal practices, as discussed on page 202. Social integration is directly and explicitly promoted by formal devices of coordination and communication. The transformation of informal groups and practices into legally recognized and formally established institutions occurs continuously, not only within associations but in the larger society as well. For example, many preexisting practices and duties regarding marriage and family life are formalized in the law of domestic relations. Similarly, zoning ordinances in a city often give formal approval to patterns of land use that have already developed in an unplanned way. Indeed zoning boards often approve variances to land use that are in violation of the ordinances. By so doing the deviations are defined as exceptions and brought under formal control.

Formalization is a way of increasing control. Practices hitherto spontaneous, governed only by tradition or the give-and-take of personal and group interaction, become subject to explicit rules and limitations. For example, labor-management legislation formalized some practices that were already worked out, but at the same time it made collective bargaining subject to greater public scrutiny and control. To take a simpler case, when the informal coffee break in an office is formalized, the practice is made legal, but it is also more readily controlled.

Self-maintenance and conservatism The quest for permanence and stability also makes for institutionalization. The demand for security usually occurs rather early in the life history of an organization because many people, and especially the leaders, have a stake in its continued existence. Therefore, priority is given to (1) maintaining the organization as a going concern, (2) minimizing risks, and (3) achieving long-run rather than short-run objectives. The leaders become willing to sacrifice quick returns for organizational security.

Adaptation 20 (pp. 218–220) summarizes Michels' study of the conservative tendencies in certain types of political organization. The conservative influence is traced to the emergence of self-perpetuating leadership, an oligarchy whose main concern is to protect its vested interests.

The institutional analysis of trade unions is concerned with the effort of union leaders to gain security for their organizations. The history of the labor movement is largely dominated by efforts to win union security through provisions for compulsory membership (the closed shop and its variants), for automatic deduction of dues payments from wages (the checkoff), and for joint consultation with management. These objectives are in the interest of long-run maintenance of the union as well as immediate gains for the members.

Large corporations are also concerned with institutional security and in recent years have been particularly sensitive to the need for a favorable climate of public opinion. Institutional advertising reflects this trend. Expensive newspaper and magazine space is bought not to promote sales, at least in the short run, but to build a favorable image of the corporation and of business in general.

Infusion with value When an individual identifies with an organization or becomes habituated to its methods or otherwise mixes his personality with it, the organization becomes for him a valued source of personal satisfaction. (See Sec. 4, p. 203.) Administrative changes are difficult when individuals are habituated to and identified with long-established procedures. For example, the shifting of personnel

[10] A classic treatment of institutionalization is Weber's analysis of "the routinization of charisma." See Max Weber, *The Theory of Social and Economic Organization* (New York: Oxford University Press, 1947), pp. 363–373.

is inhibited when individuals resist changes that threaten personalities. Infusion with value helps to institutionalize the organization, giving it a greater stability and social integration, transforming it from a mere tool into something that is valued for itself.

If an organization is merely an expendable instrument, it is altered or cast aside when a more efficient tool becomes available. If value infusion has taken place, however, there is a resistance to change. People feel a sense of personal loss; the identity of the group or community seems somehow violated; they accept economic or technical considerations only reluctantly. The Marine Corps has this institutional halo, and it resists administrative efforts to submerge its identity. In 1950 President Truman became irritated with political pressure favoring Marine Corps membership on the Joint Chiefs of Staff. He wrote a letter calling the Marines the Navy's police force and likening their "propaganda machine" to Stalin's. This raised a storm of protest that ended with a presidential apology.

From the standpoint of the national community most of the many thousands of organizations are not highly valued for themselves, although certain principles on which they are based, such as free speech or competition, may have deep cultural roots. With some very important exceptions, such as the Supreme Court, when any particular organization is threatened, no national outcry is heard. On the other hand, special groups or localities are often urged to keep an organization from dying for lack of support. For example, appeals were made to keep various major league baseball teams in their "home" cities.

Development of a distinctive social composition and social base In its day-to-day activities, an organization makes many kinds of decisions. Most are easily revised and have no permanent effect. Other decisions, however, are more binding and impart to the organization a particular character, especially when the social composition of the organization is affected. For example, selective recruiting may bring persons with distinctive backgrounds or orientations

into an organization. Sometimes this is done deliberately in private schools or colleges that attempt to preserve tradition by admitting students with appropriate family backgrounds. More often the development of a distinctive social composition is gradual and inadvertent, resulting from the unplanned selectivity that takes place because of the tendency to bring in people who share the backgrounds and perspectives of incumbent personnel. Deliberate or not, the result is a membership or personnel characterized by distinctive attitudes and habits of work.

The social base of an organization is closely related to its social composition. Many organizations, such as political pressure groups, are connected to a particular clientele or constituency upon whose support they are dependent. Because of this dependency the personnel and methods of the organization tend to reflect the social characteristics of the constituency. Even in business, adaptation to a particular market (by locality or quality of goods) may affect the habits and outlook of the sales and production departments. For example:

The first boats made by Gar Wood were high quality craft, made of the finest materials by master boat builders. Later the company decided to mass-produce a comparatively low cost speed boat for wide distribution. It developed that the entire organization found itself unable to cope with the effort to shift commitments. Workmen and shop supervisors alike continued to be preoccupied with high cost quality craftsmanship. Members of the selling staff, too, could not shift emphasis from "snob appeal" to price appeal. The quality commitment was so strong that an entirely new division—operating in a separate plant hundreds of miles away and therefore recruiting from a different labor market—had to be created to do the job successfully.[11]

Analysis of an organization's social base can reveal the pressures that play upon it and can help one understand its historical evolution and the role it plays in the community. The social base of the American Federation of Labor lay in the craft-organized skilled workers, and the split that led to the formation of the Committee for Industrial Organization (later

[11] From notes by the late Edward Boehm, formerly a Vice-President of Gar Wood Industries.

the Congress of Industrial Organizations) in 1935 reflected the effort to shift the base so as to include the semiskilled workers in the mass production industries. New social forces in the American electorate, particularly the labor and minority vote, have changed the social base of the Democratic party with significant consequences for its program and its chances of victory. The Anti-Saloon League was based on rural Protestant churches, from which it drew heavy support but whose influence in American life was waning. (See Adaptation 22, pp. 246 ff.) The structure and policies of the National Association for the Advancement of Colored People, especially at the outset, were affected by the paucity of leadership in the Negro population and an orientation toward the Negro middle class.

Adaptation 20 / Michels THE "IRON LAW" OF OLIGARCHY

"Who says organization says oligarchy." With these words the German political sociologist, Robert Michels (1876–1936), summed up his famous "iron law of oligarchy." Although his "law" is stated in unqualified form, the actual argument of Michels' book leads to more limited generalizations. His analysis does not show that organization as such necessarily leads to oligarchy, or self-perpetuating leadership. Rather, certain kinds of organization have that tendency, and then only when certain additional processes are at work. The study was based mainly on the history of socialist and trade-union organizations in Europe before the first World War.

His influential book attempts to trace a connection between the basic necessities of organization and the evolution of self-perpetuating oligarchies. Following Michels' argument, we shall first consider the general need for organization and then the special circumstances that make for the drift to oligarchy.

The need for organization The degree of organization and the importance of leadership vary with the size of the group, the permanence of its aims, and the complexity of the organization. In a small undifferentiated group, leadership may be but weakly developed; leaders arise spontaneously and serve temporarily, unofficially, and without many rewards. The leaders remain members of the group, sharing its interests and influenced by the same social conditions as the members. Since the group is small, all or most members may participate in decisions and actions. The delegated authority is limited and temporary and may be exercised by any member.

On the other hand, no organization of any size or duration can exist without leaders. Someone has to organize meetings or determine the consensus, represent the group and its decisions to other organizations or the public, and make the countless small and large decisions that are necessary to carry out its aims.

Democratic action, like any action that strives for definite ends, requires organization.

Organized, concerted action requires the delegation of special tasks, responsibilities, and powers to a few leaders.

These statements are not enough to justify the view that organization leads to oligarchy. The mere fact of organization, that is, the division of labor and delegation of tasks and powers to leaders, is not in itself undemocratic, so long as the leadership cannot perpetuate itself. Something more is needed to state the conditions that give rise to oligarchy.

Conditions making for oligarchy The delegation of tasks and

SOURCE: A summary and interpretation of *Political Parties: A Sociological Study of the the Oligarchical Tendencies of Modern Democracy* by Robert Michels (Glencoe: The Free Press, 1949). First published in German in 1911 and in English in 1915. Quoted material used by permission of The Free Press.

powers to leaders results in a concentration of skills and informal prerogatives in their hands. Not all members can perform the tasks of leadership in complex organizations. The jobs become specialized and require experience, knowledge, and individual aptitude.

Administrative *skills* are required to keep the organization functioning and to get things done. Relations with the outside world, such as diplomacy, collective bargaining, or public relations, require technical skills that the leaders alone possess. Their skills set them apart from the rank and file, and social differentiation begins. This specialization makes the members dependent on the leaders in office, because they are the ones who can keep things going and get things done that further the aims of the group. The dependence of the rank and file—a central theme in Michels' work—makes the leaders indispensable and hence gives them increased power.

Leadership carries *prerogatives.* When he chooses the organization's staff, the leader can select men whose first loyalty is to him. Thus personal machines are built. Leaders also control the channels of information within an organization, and their control gives them special access to and influence over the opinions of the members. These prerogatives and similar opportunities that characterize the social position of leadership tend to make leaders independent of the rank and file, and the power inherent in the concentration of skills is consolidated.

The position of leaders is strengthened by the members' political indifference and by their sense of obligation to those who guide them and do the main work. The ordinary member does not have the inclination or time to participate in the demanding, complex tasks of an organization, and he is glad to have the work done by someone else. Moreover, he recognizes his own incompetence compared with the skills of his leaders. The rank and file then submit willingly rather than reluctantly to the widening power of the officials.

The concentration of skills and prerogatives in the leaders' hands and the willing submission of the rank and file create opportunities for the self-perpetuation of the leaders. It is not surprising that they take advantage of the situation and try to stay in office. Michels holds that leaders try to keep their power because it is inherent in human nature to seek power and retain it. "The desire to dominate, for good or for evil, is universal." (Michels, p. 206) This is a dubious and unnecessary assumption, and perhaps Michels' weakest point.

He gives other more defensible reasons for the self-perpetuation of leaders. Certainly leaders have a desire for personal security, and the prerogatives of leadership give them social status distinct from the ordinary members. They wish to retain their status and prerogatives, including the accustomed way of living and type of employment. The union official resists returning to the shop. Leaders may also believe sincerely that they are serving the best interests of the organization and that a threat to them is a threat to the group as a whole.

Consequences of oligarchy
Self-perpetuation of leaders tends toward subversion of the aims of the organization. If leaders are independent of rank-and-file control, there is a temptation to use the organizational machinery and power to further personal aims. There is a divergence of interest between the leaders and the led, and in the absence of effective democratic control, leaders follow policies that may not serve the aims for which the group was organized.

Because he studied social reform movements, Michels was especially interested in the subversion that comes from the conservatism of an oligarchic leadership that places stability and security for the organization (and for the leaders) above all other action aims. Action is slow and cautious, risks are minimized, powerful enemies are placated, and aims are modified to assure stability. There was a strong tendency among the trade unions of Europe to move from revolutionary to more conservative aims once they had achieved extensive membership, financial security, and discipline. Organization was necessary for the achievement of the original goals, and it introduced new interests that modified group aims.

Oligarchy is inherent in democracy and cannot be eliminated. Michels holds that the social differentiation between leaders and led is universal. This does not mean that tyranny abounds everywhere but that there is a predisposition to oligarchy which requires definite social checks. "Nothing but a serene and frank examination of the oligarchical dangers of democracy will enable us to minimize these dangers, even though they can never be entirely avoided." (Michels, p. 408)

Countervailing forces   To minimize the dangers, it is necessary to capitalize on a counter-tendency of democracy to stimulate and strengthen the individual's aptitude for criticism and control. "This predisposition towards free inquiry, in which we cannot fail to recognize one of the most precious factors of civilization, will gradually increase in proportion as the economic status of the masses undergoes improvement and becomes more stable, and in proportion as they are admitted more effectively to the advantages of civilization. A wider education involves an increasing capacity for exercising control. Can we not observe every day that among the well-to-do the authority of the leaders over the led, extensive though it be, is never so unrestricted as in the case of the leaders of the poor? . . . It is, consequently, the great task of social education to raise the intellectual level of the masses, so that they may be enabled, within the limits of what is possible, to counteract the oligarchical tendencies of the working-class movement." (Michels, pp. 406 f.)

COMMENTARY

An argument similar to Michels' thesis was put forward by Berle and Means in their study of the modern corporation.[12] In the very large company there is wide dispersion of stock ownership: no individual or group owns more than a small fraction of the total shares. Even as early as 1929 no one owned more than 1 percent of the stock of the Pennsylvania Railroad, American Telephone and Telegraph, or United States Steel. Spreading ownership and risk among many shareholders permits the massing of large quantities of capital for industrial development, but the individual stockholder has only a small voice in the company's affairs and ownership is separated from control. Power is concentrated in the hands of management, which often becomes self-perpetuating.

Thus, self-perpetuating leadership is a general phenomenon, by no means restricted to the political organizations studied by Michels. The following points apply to most large-scale organizations.

1. The members of many organizations abdicate their formal right to make decisions, even important ones. They are willing for someone else to take over the task so long as their own special interests (for example, the continued flow of reasonable dividends) are not seriously affected. When members abdicate their powers in normal periods, the incumbent leaders are able to consolidate their positions, and the members find it hard to assert themselves in times of crises.

2. The weakness of members can be ameliorated if they band together in organized factions. If strong, new power centers are created in the organization, the leaders may be called to account for their actions. This is what happens in the organization of pressure groups and parties in a political democracy. (See POLITICAL MAN, pp. 523–525.) In special-purpose organizations, however, the narrowness of member interests does not sustain permanent opposition groups that can mobilize opinion and supply alternative leadership.[13]

3. The analyses of Michels and of Berle and Means indicate a basic trend toward self-perpetuating leadership in large-scale organizations. However, leaders of corporations and labor organizations are occasionally challenged or ousted, and the business pages of American newspapers report the internal contests for control of large corporations and unions. Perhaps the most notable in recent years was a financier's successful effort in 1954 to oust the incumbent management of the New York Central Railroad. Internal conflicts are exceptional, however, because the opposition must be well organized and well financed if it is to make an effective appeal to the stockholders and take over control.

[12] A. A. Berle and G. C. Means, *The Modern Corporation and Private Property* (New York: Macmillan, 1933).

[13] For a study of a deviant case, see S. M. Lipset, M. A. Trow, and J. S. Coleman, *Union Democracy: The Internal Politics of the International Typographical Union* (Glencoe: The Free Press, 1956).

CHAPTER VIII
COLLECTIVE BEHAVIOR

SECTION 1 INTRODUCTION

By common agreement the term "collective behavior" designates the study of relatively *unstructured* social situations and their products, such as crowds, riots, revivals, rumor, public opinion, fads, and social movements. These phenomena are not fully controlled by cultural norms and ordered social relations. In such situations there is often free play of emotions, a high degree of personal interaction, influence and competition, and the emergence of transitory opinions and allegiances.

Collective behavior is important, not only because dramatic events make headlines and sometimes change history, but also because spontaneous activities may give rise to new norms and values. The early phases of social change are usually marked by unstructured forms of action. The organization of workers often begins in spontaneous protests against some immediate threat to jobs or wages. Many of the respectable religious denominations of today originated in movements that excited crowd behavior. (See Adaptation 26, p. 330.) Once-popular fads, such as wearing wristwatches, collars attached

to shirts, and low-cut shoes, have become customary. The study of collective behavior illuminates the dynamics of social change and the ways new customs and institutions become established.

Through collective behavior new forms of action and new groups are created in response to felt needs, pressures, and excitements, rather than as a result of consciously coordinated activity. The development of informal structure in associations is a product of collective behavior. (See ASSOCIATIONS, p. 201.) Spontaneous actions often occur in conjunction with concerted and organized behavior, even in such dramatic episodes as mass protests and insurrections.

Collective behavior is a part of the everyday life of society and does not always take dramatic form. The study of collective behavior views the social world from the standpoint of action, of constant regrouping and continuously changing perspectives. There is always some degree of unstructuredness in human situations, because the rules cannot fully take account of all the variation in situations that may arise and the diversity of human response.

CONDITIONS OF COLLECTIVE BEHAVIOR

Three conditions characterize relatively unstructured and unstable situations:

✓ 1. *Absence or weakness of social forms.* Where existing social arrangements do not prescribe what is proper and acceptable behavior, people improvise. A crisis or disaster, such as a flood or famine, a revolution or an invasion, is something for which people are usually unprepared. Action is called for, yet routines to cope with the emergency are lacking or inadequate. The ordinary processes of orderly communication break down, and rumors, perhaps exaggerated and fear-provoking, take their place. Panic may result. In a pioneer country where law-enforcement agencies are weak or nonexistent, vigilante groups often go beyond their legitimate limits. In crowds people come into contact with each other outside the restraining influence of a social structure.

✓ 2. *Ambiguous and open decisions.* Especially in a democratic society, much government policy is deliberately left open, to be determined by expressions of public opinion. While a broad framework of orderly rules is maintained, decisions are not reached by agreement on a traditional and commonly accepted authority but are worked out in the interplay of competing interest groups. It is assumed that public opinion is not predetermined and fixed but may be influenced. As political contests progress, appeals may take on the emotional character associated with collective behavior.

3. *Changed perspectives and values.* Innovations, such as the growth of factory technology, bring about changes in goals and outlooks. Old ways are questioned, and pressure is exerted on custom and tradition. A period of fluidity ensues. When the prevailing patterns cannot be readily changed in prescribed ways, individuals often band together outside the official framework. Such conditions make for social movements, often with radical ideologies and a high degree of emotional involvement. If the movement is successful and its new perspectives are accepted, institutionalization occurs and the collective behavior aspects diminish in importance.

These conditions, widespread in modern society, lend importance to the study of spontaneous and temporary social relations and groups. Section 2 discusses crowds and collective excitement. Section 3 deals with publics, public opinion, and propaganda. Section 4 reviews social movements and social change.

Collective behavior, socialization, and the study of primary groups are the fields in sociology most closely related to psychology. Indeed, they are often studied and taught under the title "social psychology." An understanding of these topics depends in part on the development of knowledge about human motivation, emotion, perception, and communication. The sociologist is oriented to the social conditions that produce collective behavior and the effect it has on group conflict, morale, consensus, and changing patterns of social organization.

SOURCES AND READINGS

General works

Herbert Blumer, "Collective Behavior," in A. M. Lee (ed.), *New Outline of the Principles of Sociology* (New York: Barnes & Noble, 1951).

Lewis M. Killian, "Social Movements," in Robert E. L. Faris (ed.), *Handbook of Modern Sociology* (Chicago: Rand McNally, 1964), pp. 426–455.

Joseph Klapper, *Effects of Mass Communication* (New York: The Free Press of Glencoe, 1960).

Kurt Lang and Gladys E. Lang, *Collective Dynamics* (New York: Crowell, 1961).

R. T. LaPiere, *Collective Behavior* (New York: McGraw-Hill, 1938).

Wilbur Schramm, *Process and Effects of Mass Communication* (Urbana: University of Illinois, 1954).

Neil J. Smelser, *Theory of Collective Behavior* (New York: The Free Press of Glencoe, 1963).

Ralph H. Turner, "Collective Behavior," in Faris, *op. cit.,* pp. 382–425.

R. H. Turner and L. M. Killian, *Collective Behavior* (Englewood Cliffs, N.J.: Prentice-Hall, 1957).

Charles R. Wright, *Mass Communication* (New York: Random House, 1959).

On public opinion and propaganda

Gordon W. Allport and L. Postman, *The Psychology of Rumor* (New York: Holt, Rinehart and Winston, 1947).

Bernard Berelson and Morris Janowitz (eds.), *Reader in Public Opinion and Communication* (Rev. ed.; New York: The Free Press of Glencoe, 1953).

Daniel Katz (ed.), *Public Opinion and Propaganda: A Book of Readings* (New York: Dryden, 1954).

Elihu Katz and Paul F. Lazarsfeld, *Personal Influence* (New York: The Free Press of Glencoe, 1955).

Walter Lippmann, *Public Opinion* (New York: Harcourt, Brace & World, 1922).

On surveys and polling

Hadley Cantril, *Gauging Public Opinion* (Princeton: Princeton University Press, 1947).

Herbert Hyman, *Survey Design and Analysis: Principles, Cases and Procedures* (New York: The Free Press of Glencoe, 1955).

C. A. Moser, *Survey Methods in Social Investigation* (London: Heinemann, 1958).

Mildren Parten, *Surveys, Polls, and Samples: Practical Procedures* (New York: Harper & Row, 1950).

Frederick F. Stephen and Philip J. McCarthy, *Sampling Opinions* (New York: Wiley, 1958).

Public Opinion Quarterly publishes articles in this field and also reports the findings of current polls.

SECTION 2 CROWDS AND COLLECTIVE EXCITEMENT

EMOTIONAL CONTAGION

Emotional contagion occurs in a wide range of phenomena, including crowd behavior, panics, sightings of flying saucers, cheering sections, and *esprit de corps.* These phenomena, and others that are less dramatic, show a *common mood,* a state of mind affected by emotion. The mood shared in a group colors the thought and action of the participants by facilitating some acts and inhibiting others.

Elements of emotional contagion The processes that induce or sustain emotional contagion are not fully understood, but they include the following:

1. *Heightened suggestibility.* In unstructured situations people tend to look to others for cues. The readiness to take cues can be heightened by the presence of emotional tension, because *emotional tension narrows the field of consciousness.* A fearful person is alert to signs of danger and responds to cues that promise relief from anxiety. At the same time, he is apt to ignore other stimuli in his environment. An important consequence of heightened suggestibility is the *loss of critical ability.* When tension dominates consciousness, the weighing of alternative courses of action and the costs of action recede into the background.

2. *Heightened stimulation.* Different personalities show different degrees of suggestibility. However, suggestibility can be induced and the field of consciousness narrowed when there is an increase in the volume and intensity of stimuli from other persons who are excited. In large crowds where there is close physical proximity, stimulation takes the form of *circular response. A* stimulates *B* to fear. *B*'s fear not only stimulates *C* in turn but is reflected back to *A*

THE HOUSE OF COMMONS AND PARLIAMENTARY PSYCHOLOGY

On October 28 [1943], there was the rebuilding of the House of Commons to consider. One unlucky bomb had blown to fragments the Chamber in which I had passed so much of my life. I was determined to have it rebuilt at the earliest moment that our struggle would allow. I had the power at this moment to shape things in a way that would last. Supported by my colleagues, mostly old Parliamentarians, and with Mr. Attlee's cordial aid, I sought to re-establish for what may well be a long period the two great principles on which the British House of Commons stands in its physical aspect. . . . The first is that its shape should be oblong and not semicircular. Here is a very potent factor in our political life. The semicircular assembly, which appeals to political theorists, enables every individual or every group to move round the centre, adopting various shades of pink according as the weather changes. I am a convinced supporter of the party system in preference to the group system. The party system is much favoured by the oblong form of chamber. It is easy for an individual to move through these insensible gradations from Left to Right, but the act of crossing the Floor is one which requires serious consideration. I am well informed on this matter, for I have accomplished that difficult process, not only once, but twice. Logic is a poor guide compared with custom. Logic, which has created in so many countries semicircular assemblies with buildings that give to every member not only a seat to sit in, but often a desk to write at, with a lid to bang, has proved fatal to Parliamentary government as we know it here in its home and in the land of its birth.

The second characteristic of a chamber formed on the lines of the House of Commons is that it should *not* be big enough to contain all its Members at once without overcrowding, and there should be no question of every Member having a separate seat reserved for him. The reason for this has long been a puzzle to uninstructed outsiders, and has frequently excited the curiosity and even the criticism of new Members. Yet it is not so difficult to understand if

SOURCE: Abridged from *Closing the Ring,* by Winston S. Churchill (Boston: Houghton Mifflin, 1951), pp. 168–169. Reprinted by permission of Houghton Mifflin Company.

and stimulates him further. Propinquity also calls to attention such physical manifestations of emotion as heavy breathing, perspiration, and muscular tension. If emotion is present in one participant, others are likely to be aware of it.

3. *Homogeneity of experience.* To sustain emotional contagion, there must be shared dispositions and background. Crowd stimuli are not strong enough to make a guard join a prison riot. Fads and crazes are often limited to a particular age, class, or ethnic group whose members share emotional needs and attitudes. People from different ethnic, age, and educational backgrounds are less likely to develop emotional contagion.

CROWDS

In common usage any large number of people gathered in one place is called a crowd, but crowds dif-

you look at it from a practical point of view. If the House is big enough to contain all its Members, nine-tenths of its debates will be conducted in the depressing atmosphere of an almost empty or half-empty chamber. The essence of good House of Commons speaking is the conversational style, the facility for quick, informal interruptions and interchanges. Harangues from a rostrum would be a bad substitute for the conversational style in which so much of our business is done. But the conversational style requires a fairly small space, and there should be on great occasions a sense of crowd and urgency. There should be a sense of the importance of much that is said, and a sense that great matters are being decided, there and then, by the House.

Chamber of the rebuilt House of Commons, identical with the earlier House.

fer in the extent to which interaction occurs or leads to unity of feeling and behavior. The "sidewalk superintendents" gathered around a building under construction form a *casual* crowd in which interpersonal relations are at a minimum. What captures attention is of no great emotional import. Nevertheless, a crowd is a potential medium for arousing emotion and for encouraging its expression. Large gatherings provide congenial conditions for emotional contagion. Stimulation and suggestibility are heightened; the presence of others gives the individual a sense of security and approval; and crowds convey a feeling of anonymity. In times of social unrest or of racial tension, street crowds have often been transformed into *acting crowds* or *mobs*, when the event that attracts attention is exciting and stimulates existing hostilities.

By their very nature casual crowds and mobs are

not part of an organized and controlled system of social relations. They arise spontaneously without orderly preparation. There is no etiquette of crowd behavior. If feelings of hostility, anger, or resentment are aroused, the socially uncontrolled interaction of the crowd may have serious consequences. (See Adaptation 21, pp. 230–233.) In modern history the calling of general strikes has often been a prelude to revolutionary attacks upon governments. The effect of a general strike, in addition to raising the level of tension and excitement, is to draw people away from stable institutionalized activities at work and home, and to encourage the formation of street crowds. One of the first moves of a fearful government is to attempt to break up gatherings of more than two or three people, because even small knots of excited people might expand into uncontrollable street crowds.

Integrative crowd behavior Not all crowd behavior is spontaneous and unguided. Controlled emotional contagion is often encouraged and can serve a useful social function. It may offer release for emotions and tensions that ordinarily find no expression, and may stimulate feelings that enhance group solidarity. Organized gatherings of many kinds provide settings that articulate crowd behavior with the social structure.

1. *Expressive crowds.* Parties, dances, and some spectator sports are gatherings in which certain emotions and tensions can find an ordered release. In parties and dances emotional contagion makes for freer interpersonal relations. Football games permit and encourage shouting, singing, and a degree of aggressiveness. Without the unity of the crowd, people would not feel so free to engage in emotional or boisterous behavior.

2. *Audiences.* Many audiences are similar to casual crowds in their passivity and low degree of emotional unity. Nevertheless they may be susceptible to emotional contagion. In some audience situations, like lectures or concerts, the presence of others encourages expressions of enthusiasm. Performers have been known to employ claques, people hired to cheer and stimulate the spread of approval.

3. *Religious services.* Services that arouse contagious emotions of humility and piety may support deep religious feelings. In some religious sects, emotional contagion is encouraged and results in relatively uncontrolled and predominantly expressive behavior. As institutionalization develops, more restrained services appear. (See RELIGION, pp. 334–335.)

4. *Mass meetings and deliberative assemblies.* Meetings of voluntary associations usually have two functions. As deliberating bodies they hear and pass upon reports from leaders and choose new leaders. They are also designed to stimulate feelings of solidarity. Meetings in a political campaign are largely of the latter kind, and people go as they do to a football game, expecting to cheer and otherwise express their feelings. When large numbers are involved, it is common for deliberative meetings to become subject to emotional contagion. Although conventions of unions, veterans, and political parties are usually highly organized, the leaders are aware of the danger that the meeting may get out of hand. An unimportant individual may gain the attention of the meeting and develop influence he might not otherwise have.

Assemblies are called "mass meetings" when the solidarity aspect is predominant and emotional demonstrations are expected and encouraged. The emotions displayed are often stereotyped, however, and need not reflect real feelings. The "demonstrations" at national political conventions are often calculated efforts to put on a show of enthusiasm for a candidate.

In "The House of Commons and Parliamentary Psychology," page 224, Churchill takes account of the crowd potential even in the highly institutionalized British Parliament. The small rectangular chamber has two effects. At ordinary meetings, it encourages a conversational style. On the other hand, at historically significant sessions when all members are present and the chamber is packed, there is a "sense of crowd and urgency."

Integrative behavior in crisis In less than a century four American presidents met death by assassination: Lincoln in 1865, Garfield in 1881, McKinley in 1901, and Kennedy in 1963. The death of President Kennedy was the first loss of a national leader reported with the full resources of television, and the coverage, which was immediate and pervasive, reached into 90 percent of American homes. For a period of four days nearly the whole population shared a common mood. The violence attending President Kennedy's death, his youth, and the omnipresent television camera translated the assassination and its aftermath into a collective experience for the people. "Over half of all Americans apparently heard the news before the President was pronounced dead, only thirty minutes after the shooting. . . . There were times . . . when a *majority of all Americans* were apparently looking at the same events and hearing the same words." [1]

Agreement and disagreement The extent of public exposure and public involvement were without parallel, and the sense of distress and horror were almost universal. Yet reactions differed in extent, duration, and emotionalism. Some statements in a survey elicited high consensus: [2]

"It leaves the country without a leader" met strong disagreement.

". . . shows the power of the country to pull together" met strong agreement.

But other statements, such as the following, had a wide diversity of responses:

"It shows how much prejudice and hatred there is."

"It shows there's a lot of political unrest in the country."

"It's too shocking to know what to think."

Education Differences in attitudes were strongly associated with educational differences. "The college group was less suspicious of Communism, but also less likely to define the event as showing prejudice and hate; it was less likely to say there was political unrest, and less likely to say there was too much of guns and violence. In short, the college-educated were less likely to see *any* object as the cause of the event." In response to almost all propositions, the more educated in the sample were less passionate. Formal education apparently tempered and dampened the extremity of reaction. [3] The more highly educated, although fully aware and fully engaged, were less likely to seize upon some object, circumstance, or condition to blame.

Several post-assassination studies [4] suggest that the event itself and the intensive coverage on television had the following effects:

1. Allayed anxiety
2. Relieved grief
3. Reduced guilt feelings
4. Induced a sense of participation and a sense of involvement in the political system
5. Gave reassurance of institutional continuity
6. Strengthened social norms
7. In sum, the effects were reintegrative, making a single public of the American people.

MOBS

A mob is a crowd bent upon an aggressive act such as lynching, looting, or the destruction of property. The term refers to one crowd that is fairly unified and single-minded in its aggressive intent. Mob action is not usually randomly destructive but tends to be focused on some one target or identity.

The target of mob aggression is an individual or group that is resented or perceived as a source of frustration. The socially defined nature of mob action is evident in "scapegoating," in which aggression is *displaced* from the real sources of frustration,

---

[1] Wilbur Schramm, "Communication in Crisis," in Bradley S. Greenberg and Edwin B. Parker (eds.), *The Kennedy Assassination and the American Public: Social Communication in Crisis* (Stanford: Stanford University Press, 1965), p. 4.

[2] James S. Coleman and Sidney Hollander, Jr., "Studies of Changes in Responses Over Time," in Greenberg and Parker, *op. cit.*, pp. 256–258.

[3] Coleman and Hollander, *ibid.*, pp. 262–263; quotation at p. 262.

[4] See the studies collected in Greenberg and Parker, *op. cit.*

such as economic distress, to a group or individual defined as a legitimate object of hostility.

Of all the forms of action involving emotional contagion, mob activity is the most goal-oriented and the most dependent upon leadership for its direction. Mobs are composed of a nucleus of active and militant leaders and an acquiescing mass of spectators who give the leaders a sense of support and approval. The leaders in turn provide the mass with cues for aggressive behavior. Mob leaders are often those least likely to achieve leadership under ordinary circumstances. Because of the role of leadership and rumor in mob activity, situations of group conflict and social unrest are fertile soil for fanatical and irresponsible persons.

RIOTS

"Riot" connotes randomly destructive behavior, occurring in several places and possibly involving many mobs. Rioting tends to express generalized resentment and rebelliousness rather than definite purpose.

Race riots Until the recent past most American race riots were initiated by whites, although during the course of a riot Negroes sometimes attacked whites. In many cases, neither whites nor Negroes were clearly the initiators. The scenes of violence were usually Negro slums, the downtown business districts, or all-white neighborhoods where white mobs attacked individual Negroes. White marauders frequently invaded the Negro slums, and Negro mobs attacked individual whites in Negro neighborhoods.[5]

The Civil War draft riots have been referred to as "the archetype of most of the racial clashes that took place before the summer of 1964."[6] For four days in 1863, white mobs controlled much of New York city, looted stores, burned Negro dwellings, and beat or lynched Negroes. Occurring during a time of national tension and anxiety, they were a reaction by predominantly working-class whites to a requirement that they assist Negro emancipation by military service. The rioting went on throughout the city with attacks and counterattacks between whites and Negroes. In one incident, a white mob attacked, looted, and burned a Negro orphan asylum. The violence was prolonged because officials were reluctant to invoke military measures and because the troops and police sympathized with the rioters.[7]

In the 1919 Chicago race riot,[8] gangs of hoodlums and "athletic clubs" formed the nuclei of mobs. Although the initial clash between Negroes and whites occurred at a relatively isolated bathing beach, rumors and gang activity carried the conflict beyond its original locale. Soon after the spontaneous outbreaks between Negroes and whites, there was organized raiding by neighborhood gangs in search of victims. These activities went on for several days.

The release of tension and the expression of aggression in mobs signify not an individual but a group phenomenon. Even in a riot situation, where tension is high, violence is not usually committed by isolated individuals but by organized gangs or crowds transformed into mobs. Most people are not able to engage in socially destructive or violent behavior except as members of a group or an emotionally unified mob. Riot violence is, therefore, intermittent and concentrated, sparked by the transformation of crowds into mobs.

Precipitants and underlying conditions In almost every one of 76 cities in the United States where

[5] See Allen D. Grimshaw, "Lawlessness and Violence in America and Their Manifestations in Changing Negro-White Relationships," *Journal of Negro History, 44* (1959), 52–72; and "Urban Racial Violence in the United States: Changing Ecological Considerations," *American Journal of Sociology, 64* (1960), 109–119. See also Elliott M. Rudwick, *Race Riot at East St. Louis, July 2, 1917* (Cleveland: Meridian Books, 1966), and A. M. Lee and N. D. Humphrey, *Race Riot* (New York: Dryden, 1943). The last reference is a study of the Detroit riot of 1943.

[6] The President's Commission on Law Enforcement and Administration of Justice, *Task Force Report: Crime and Its Impact—An Assessment* (Washington, D.C., 1967), Chap. 9, "Riots and Crime." Quotation at p. 117.

[7] Lawrence Lader, "New York's Bloodiest Week," *American Heritage, 10* (June, 1959), 44–49.

[8] Chicago Commission on Race Relations, *The Negro in Chicago* (Chicago: University of Chicago Press, 1922). For a brief summary, see Leonard Broom and Philip Selznick, *Sociology: A Text with Adapted Readings* (3rd ed.; New York: Harper & Row, 1963), pp. 267–274.

riots occurred between 1913 and 1963, the precipitant was a confrontation between Negroes and whites in which members of one race were "wronged" in fact or in rumor by members of the other. In most cases, the alleged offense was committed by Negroes and the violence was initiated by whites.

Riot cities did not differ appreciably from other cities of similar size and location in percentage of recent increase in Negro population, white unemployment, Negro unemployment, or quality of Negro housing. On the other hand, the riot cities when compared with the non-riot cities showed a smaller Negro-white occupational difference, a smaller Negro-white income difference, a smaller number of Negro store owners per 1,000 Negro population, lower white incomes, and fewer Negro policemen per 1,000 Negro population.[9]

These findings suggest that riots of the period tended to occur where Negroes were a more definite competitive threat to whites, where whites felt more economically deprived, where few merchants in Negro neighborhoods were Negro, where few policemen were Negro, and where the means of dealing with grievances of both Negroes and whites were less adequate. Some of these apparent underlying conditions of riots may be conducive to riots initiated by one race but not by the other. For instance, a small economic advantage of whites over Negroes may predispose whites to act violently against Negroes, but a large white advantage may have the opposite effect.

In spite of these findings, the occurrence (or non-occurrence) of riots may be determined largely by chance factors. The predisposing conditions for riots are probably now present in all large American cities, and riots are likely whenever a sufficient precipitant happens to occur.

White attacks on "uppity" Negroes continue, especially in the South, but the mass violence of the mid-1960s was not directly initiated by whites. The initial incident in most cases, as in the Los Angeles riot of 1965 (see pp. 231–232), usually involved the police and individual Negroes. Such incidents were less typical of earlier riots. Beyond the precipitating event, Negroes usually have taken the initiative in recent riots, and whites have participated chiefly as law-enforcement officials, National Guardsmen, and troops. The great majority of victims as well as rioters have been Negroes, and the violence has been concentrated in the ghetto. White attacks on Negroes outside the ghetto have been rare.

Interpretations It has been suggested that in the Watts-type riot the rioters ". . . were asserting a claim to territoriality, an unorganized and rather inchoate attempt to gain control over their community, their 'turf.' "[10] This thesis is supported by (1) a low gunfire casualty rate of police despite the large volume of sniper fire and (2) apparent selectivity in the stores chosen for looting and arson. Hundreds, perhaps thousands, of rounds were fired by snipers, who shot out many street lights and auto headlights. It is thought they could have taken a far heavier toll of police. Their failure to do so supports the idea that the primary intent of the rioters may have been to intimidate and drive off the police and firemen. The second observation may be correct for Watts and some other places. Negro store owners operated on the hope that they would be given immunity and it seems their hopes were in part realized. But some riots in other places were not so discriminating, and apparently both Negro- and white-owned stores and homes were destroyed in the Detroit riot of 1967.

Another hypothesis holds that recent race riots are a "cry for help,"[11] an effort to get "Whitey" to listen. The composition of the active rioters and the interpretation of the riot by Watts residents may support this line of reasoning. (See Adaptation 21, esp. page 235.) If this hypothesis is supported, the riots

[9] Stanley Lieberson and Arnold R. Silverman, "The Precipitants and Underlying Conditions of Race Riots," *American Sociological Review, 30* (December, 1965), 887–898.

[10] Robert Blauner, "Watts and the Riots of 1966: Colonialism in Our Midst," in *Ghettos, Riots and the Negro Protest* (Houston: University of Houston, 1966), pp. 16–27; quotation at p. 16.

[11] The President's Commission, *op. cit.,* p. 121.

may be regarded as a phase of the civil rights movement.

RUMOR

A rumor is an unconfirmed, but not necessarily false, communication usually transmitted by word of mouth in a situation of anxiety or stress. Rumors spring up in unstructured situations when information is needed but reliable channels do not exist.[12]

Because they are so readily influenced by emotions, rumors tend to be rapidly disseminated and to distort or falsify the facts. A rumor may begin as an inaccurate or distorted report because of the narrowing of perception in an emotionally charged situation. It may become progressively more distorted, because all oral communication is subject to distortion. Even when emotional elements are lacking, factual reports tend to become shorter and simpler as they are passed on, with distortion of details in accordance with personal and cultural predispositions or "sets."[13]

Truth or falsity of rumor is irrelevant: a story is told and believed not because it is demonstrably true, but because it serves a need for the teller and for the listener who becomes a teller. Sometimes the need is to achieve status in the listener's opinion, and the story will be distorted in ways that will please him. The aim is not to convey information but to induce in the listener the same emotional attitude toward the alleged information that the teller has.

Rumor both contributes to and is a product of emotional contagion.

1. Rumors make for an atmosphere of tension and crisis. By means of rumors, feelings are conveyed from one person to another and from one locale to another. In the 1919 Chicago race riot rumor spread the riot beyond its originally isolated area and created a general air of tension and excitement. Anger- and fear-provoking rumors exaggerate hostile intent and tend to justify emotional and behavioral excesses.

2. Emotional contagion narrows the field of consciousness and diminishes critical ability. In times of distress, perception, which is always selective, is rendered even more so. People are apt to accept anything they hear and to revise it in accordance with their momentarily overpowering needs. Moreover they tend to misinterpret what they themselves observe.

In times of crisis and emergency, though information is of supreme importance, it is often unavailable. In a disaster like a flood or an invasion, official sources of information often disintegrate; in periods of social tension, they are often distrusted and lose their aura of authority. In such situations rumor rushes in to take the place of more secure knowledge.

[12] Tamotsu Shibutani, *Improvised News: A Sociological Study of Rumor* (Indianapolis: Bobbs-Merrill, 1966), p. 17.

[13] Gordon W. Allport, *The Psychology of Rumor* (New York: Holt, Rinehart and Winston, 1947).

Adaptation 21 / **RACE RIOT: LOS ANGELES, 1965**

The Watts riot in the late summer of 1965 lasted six days, from August 11 to 17. During the worst days from Thursday through Saturday, as many as 10,000 Negroes took to the streets. They beat up white passersby whom they pulled from their cars, overturned and

SOURCE: Based on "Violence in the City—An End or a Beginning?" (The McCone Report) by the Governor's Commission on the Los Angeles Riots, 1965; Robert Conot, *Rivers of Blood, Years of Darkness* (New York: Bantam, 1967); Jerry Cohen and William S. Murphy, *Burn, Baby, Burn!* (New York: Avon Books, 1966); The President's Commission on Law Enforcement and Administration of Justice, *Task Force Report: Crime and Its Impact—An Assessment* (Washington, D.C., 1967) Chap. 9; and press and periodical reports.

burned cars, looted stores, set buildings afire, stoned and shot at firemen, and exchanged shots with law-enforcement officers. A total of 3,927 people were arrested. The disorder spread through an area of 46.5 square miles and was ultimately controlled only with the aid of military authority and a curfew.

Thirty Negroes were killed and four whites, including a fireman and two law-enforcement officers. Of 1,032 reported injuries, 90 were Los Angeles police officers, 136 firemen, 10 National Guardsmen, 23 persons from other governmental agencies—almost all whites; and 773 civilians—the great majority of whom were Negroes.

Property loss is estimated at over $40 million. More than 700 buildings were damaged by burning and looting. Of this number, more than 200 were totally destroyed by fire. The rioters concentrated primarily on food markets, pawn shops, liquor, furniture, clothing, and department stores. Service stations and automobile dealers were for the most part unharmed. No residences were deliberately burned, and damage to schools, libraries, churches, and public buildings was minimal.

The setting The South Los Angeles area, the scene of the 1965 riot, contains the largest concentration of Negroes in the city. It includes Watts for which the riot was named. In November, 1965, three months after the riot a special 10 percent sample census survey was conducted, and the report of the survey permits comparisons with the findings of the 1960 census.[14] Interpretations should be made cautiously because part of the observed changes between 1960 and 1965, but certainly not all, may be consequences of the riot.

The South Los Angeles area roughly corresponds with the curfew zone established during the riot. The total population of 321,000 in 1965 had declined from 355,000 enumerated in the 1960 census, but the Negro population had increased from 248,000 to 260,000, or from 70 to 81 percent. At the same time whites with Spanish surnames (largely of Mexican ancestry) had declined from 43,000 to 32,000 and other whites

from 56,000 to only 24,000. In other words, South Los Angeles is a large, highly homogeneous segregated area—in current vocabulary, a ghetto. Its segregation is compounded by the lack of an efficient public transportation system so that citizens who need access to governmental offices or clinical facilities must use slow and costly buses. The area is not a ghetto in the sense of a slum made up of old tenements with a high density per acre and per room and with most dwelling units in dilapidated condition. However, about five percent of Negro-occupied dwelling units were classified as dilapidated, not suitable for habitation, and 26 percent as deteriorating. The statistics show a decline in the quality of housing compared with 1960, but despite that fact property values and median rentals had increased from $69 to $78 per month. Of the 260,000 Negro residents about 80,000, or 31 percent —the same percentage as in 1960 —were living below the poverty

line, which is defined as expenditure of a third or more of income on food. Approximately 24 percent of the total population received public assistance. The median annual income of families was $4,669, hardly changed from the 1959 figures.

Only 16 percent of male workers held white-collar jobs and 11 percent of the male labor force was unemployed. In sum, the Negro population of South Los Angeles lived in a predominantly Negro environment under poor and sometimes severely depressed conditions, highly isolated from the dominant population. Those who had the means to move elsewhere found it difficult or impossible to do so.

Initial episode (*Wednesday*) The first incident was the arrest of a Negro youth for drunk driving on the complaint of another Negro. A white motorcycle officer made the arrest under rather ordinary circumstances in a predomi-

[14] See "Characteristics of the South and East Los Angeles Areas: November 1965," *Current Population Reports* P-23, No. 18, June 28, 1966.

nantly Negro neighborhood near Watts on a hot evening, August the 11th. What began as a routine arrest with 25 to 50 curious spectators escalated as the youth's mother and brother became involved and the youth became physically resistant, eliciting forceful action by the several officers who were called for assistance. The hostility of the youth's family and the bystanders' belligerence, resistance to arrest, and use of force by the police drew a crowd of 1,000 persons within half an hour. Before the officers withdrew, five arrests were made: the driver, his brother, his mother, a young Negro woman for spitting on an officer, and a young Negro man for inciting the crowd to violence. As the last police car left, it was stoned by the now irate mob.

The crowd did not disperse but ranged in small groups within a few blocks of the arrest scene. Until midnight they stoned automobiles, pulled white motorists out of their cars and beat them, and menaced a police command post that had been set up in the area. Although the outbreak seemed to be under control by 1:00 A.M., there were sporadic reports of unruly mobs, vandalism, and rock-throwing until nearly daylight.

Atmosphere of trouble (*Thursday*) The next morning there was an uneasy calm, and a strong expectancy of further trouble kept the atmosphere tense. A meeting called by the Los Angeles County Human Relations Commission at the request of county officials failed to lower tension. The meeting was held in the early afternoon twelve blocks from the scene of the first arrests, with every available representative of neighborhood groups, Negro leaders, elected officials and members of law-enforcement agencies, as well as about 100 unexpected teen-agers, and representatives of press, radio, and television with cameras focused on the microphone.

The meeting began with discussions of how to restore law and order. Even the mother arrested the night before asked the crowd to "help me and others calm this situation down so that we will not have a riot tonight." But the tone and conduct of the meeting shifted to a discussion of grievances, especially about police conduct. A Negro high school boy grabbed the microphone and shouted: "It's like this, the way the policemens treat you round here . . . It ain't going to be lovely tonight whether you like it or not! (Shouts of disap-

San Francisco, 1964: Long-harbored resentment is openly expressed as rioters carry an injured comrade.

proval.) I was down on Avalon last night and we the Negro people have got completely fed up! They going out to Inglewood and everywhere else the white man supposed to stay. They going to do the white man in tonight!"

Catcalls and jeers from the audience drowned him out, and he was dragged away from the microphone. Other youths began to pummel him, and only the intercession of adults saved him from a beating. A youth leader returned to the microphone, declaring that the boy did not represent the consensus and that the majority of people wanted only a fair hearing. A group led by a woman Negro police sergeant pleaded with TV cameramen not to show the boy who had made the threatening speech. It was pointed out that there might be an unfortunate reaction if his isolated opinion were broadcast. The television newsmen were noncommittal. "Everybody has it. We can't say we won't use it, and then have some other station put it on the air." The inflammatory language was broadcast to television sets throughout the nation, and the boy's utterance was seldom balanced by less emotional statements made at the meeting. Some reports indicate that, during the riot, crowd behavior was deliberately manipulated for newsmaking purposes. Cameramen encouraged youths to throw stones so they could be photographed as "stars." [15]

Community proposals After the main meeting, a smaller group of leaders and representatives of youth gangs met to decide upon a

course of action. Early in the evening, they proposed to the police: (1) Withdraw uniformed officers from the troubled neighborhood and allow selected community leaders to undertake the responsibility for law and order. (2) If police found the first proposal unacceptable, substitute for white officers Negro officers in civilian clothes and unmarked cars. Both proposals were rejected, and the meeting at the 77th Street Police Station generated ill-feeling on both sides. Using only Negro officers was contrary to the LAPD policy of deploying Negro officers throughout the city and not concentrating them in the Negro area.

There were only about 200 Negroes on the force, a number far below parity, and they were scattered throughout the city, with only seven in the 77th. Police officials asserted that it would be too difficult to assemble the necessary number of Negro officers. They rejected the proposals as untested methods of handling a rapidly deteriorating situation. The police set up a perimeter to contain the trouble and to keep all others out.

About 5:00 P.M. on Thursday Police Chief Parker alerted Adjutant General Hill of the California Guard. A Guard Colonel was sent to Los Angeles as a liaison officer, and the 40th Armored Division in Southern California was alerted. In the absence of Governor Brown, Lieutenant Governor Anderson was informed of the situation.

Late in the afternoon inflammatory handbills were distributed, and around 7:00 P.M. crowds at the scene of the previous night's trouble had grown to more than

1,000. Firemen who came into the area to fight fires in three overturned automobiles were shot at and bombarded with rocks. The first fire in a commercial establishment was set only one block away, and police had to hold back rioters as firemen fought the blaze. Shortly before midnight, rock-throwing and looting crowds for the first time ranged outside the perimeter.

Lull (Friday) By 4:00 A.M. the police department felt that the situation was at least for the moment under control. At 5:00 officers were withdrawn from emergency perimeter control. Before 7:00 the intelligence officer on duty reported to the Lieutenant Governor that "the situation is rather well in hand," and the Lieutenant Governor left the city for a meeting.

Official indecision Around 8:00 A.M. crowds formed again and looting resumed. About 9:00 Mayor Yorty and Chief of Police Parker agreed by telephone to call out the Guard, but the Mayor then left the city to keep a speaking engagement in San Francisco. The Mayor told the McCone Commission: "By about 10:00 or so, I have to decide whether I am going to disappoint that audience in San Francisco and maybe make my city look rather ridiculous if the rioting doesn't start again, and the mayor has disappointed that crowd." The Mayor returned to Los Angeles at 3:35 P.M.

By late morning ambulance drivers and firemen were refusing to go into the riot area without

[15] Conot, *op. cit.,* pp. 43 and 51.

armed escort. About the same time, Chief of Police Parker thought he would need approximately 1,000 men and formally requested the Governor's executive secretary in Sacramento to send the National Guard. The Lieutenant Governor received the request at 11:00 A.M. in Berkeley but did not act on it until 5:00 P.M. in Los Angeles, although in the meantime he was in consultation with Guard officers who agreed to assemble 2,000 men at the armories by 5:00 P.M., which was said to be the earliest feasible hour.

Approximately 850 Guardsmen were available, outfitted with weapons in Long Beach (12 miles from the riot) enroute to summer camp. The McCone report criticizes the Lieutenant Governor's delay: ". . . He hesitated when he should have acted. . . . Further escalation of the riots might have been averted if these Guardsmen had been deployed on station throughout the riot area by early or mid-afternoon Friday."

Meanwhile, Governor Brown was reached by telephone in Athens and briefed on the situation. He said he felt the Guard should be called immediately, that the possibility of a curfew should be explored, and that he would return to California as fast as possible.

Early Friday afternoon, rioters drove off firemen by sniper fire and by throwing missiles. By late afternoon, gang activity had spread as far as sixty blocks to the north.

Although assembled in armories as early as 6:00 P.M., the Guard was not deployed until shortly after 10:00 P.M.

The first death occurred between 6:00 and 7:00 P.M. Friday when a Negro bystander, trapped between police and rioters, was shot and killed.

Peak of the riot On Friday night burning and looting were widespread, and the riot was out of control. At 1:00 A.M. Saturday, 100 engine companies were fighting fires—all of which were arson. Snipers shot at firemen. A fireman was killed on the fire line by a falling wall, and a deputy sheriff was killed when another sheriff's shotgun discharged in a struggle with rioters.

The law-enforcement officials tried a different tactic. Police made sweeps on foot, moving en masse along streets to control activity and enable firemen to fight fires. By midnight Friday another 1,000 National Guard troops were marching shoulder to shoulder clearing the streets. By 3:00 A.M. Saturday 3,356 Guardsmen were on the streets. Throughout the morning hours of Saturday and during the long day, the crowds of looters and arsonists spread out and increased until an 8:00 P.M. curfew was imposed on Saturday.

Beginning of control (*Saturday*) Again using sweep tactics, the Guardsmen and police were able to clear a major riot area by Saturday afternoon. Guardsmen rode "shotgun" on the fire engines and stopped the sniping and rock-throwing at firemen. Saturday evening, road blocks were set up in anticipation of the curfew.

When the curfew began at 8:00 P.M., police and Guardsmen were able to deal with the riot area as a whole. Compared with the holocaust of Friday evening, the streets were relatively quiet, with the only major exception the burning of a block of stores. Snipers again prevented firemen from entering the area, and while buildings burned there was a gun battle between law-enforcement officers, the Guard, and the snipers. By midnight Saturday 13,900 Guardsmen were committed.

During the day Sunday the curfew area was relatively quiet. Because many markets had been destroyed, food distribution was started by churches, community groups, and government agencies. Governor Brown, who had returned Saturday night, personally toured the area and talked to residents. Major fires were under control but there were new fires and some rekindling of old ones. On Tuesday Governor Brown was able to lift the curfew.

Summary 1. Watts is an isolated, predominantly Negro ghetto but not a uniformly high-density slum.

2. The Negro population includes many low-income families and has a high unemployment rate.

3. The precipitating incident was a routine encounter with the police, of a sort that occurs many times every day throughout the country.

4. Officials were slow to take decisive action in calling out the National Guard and in declaring a curfew.

5. The mass media gave preferential exposure to the more intemperate behavior and in some cases stimulated such behavior to make a "good" picture. After the riot was under way, the saturated coverage by the media may have contributed to sustaining a high level of tension.

6. The loss of life and the number of gunshot injuries were low considering the amount of gunfire and the heavy property damage. Of 1,032 reported injuries, 118 were gunshot wounds.

7. No evidence has been reported that the riot was planned, but criminal elements and extremists used the riot after it began.

Conclusions 1. *Community initiative failed.* Tentative efforts to extemporize cooperative action were rebuffed by the police. The abortive effort to establish a dialogue confirmed poor relations between police and the community. Community organization and leadership were weak, and civil rights leaders were unable to establish effective communication with the rioters.

2. *Rumor* dissemination was facilitated by hot weather, which kept people out of doors, and by ecological segregation and cultural homogeneity. Inflated and distorted rumors about the first arrests spread quickly. For example, the young woman arrested was wearing a barber's smock, and the false rumor circulated that she was pregnant and had been abused by police.

3. The police were *distant from the community* and *perceived as abrasive.* The Los Angeles Police Department is regarded as efficient and incorrupt. It is a small force for the large area and population it serves, and it depends on advanced technology for crime control and detection. It is highly motorized and mobile. The department has integrated slowly and with reluctance. In 1965 only about 200 of 5,000 officers were Negro. Little attention is given to community relations. Police officials had little interest in communicating with civilians. The Department encounters the citizenry in the line of duty, but otherwise hardly at all.

The subordinate populations, both Negroes and Mexicans, had frequently complained of the harsh and abrasive attitudes of the police. Of 586 Negroes interviewed by UCLA researchers after the riot, 90 percent thought the police were insulting and used unnecessary force in the area and about 50 percent claimed to have seen such police behavior. Nearly 30 percent said they had been insulted by police and more than 5 percent said the police had used unnecessary force on them.[16]

4. There was *wide participation.* The Watts riot was a general outbreak in which all kinds of people took part—not just agitators, adolescents, criminals, new arrivals, the unemployed, or "riffraff." Of the 3,927 people arrested, most were Negroes, but only 556 were legally juveniles (under eighteen), while 2,111 were over twenty-five; 602 were over forty. They were not predominantly people with serious criminal histories. The riot was participated in by those who had a stake in the community as well as those who did not. For example, 10 percent of those convicted of various offenses were home owners.

More than half the Negroes interviewed by the UCLA survey thought the riot had "a purpose." Expressions of "hostility, resentment and revenge" and "gaining attention" were the most commonly mentioned purposes. In the words of the Task Force report: "The implication is evident that many Negroes believe that if only the white community realized what the ghetto was like and how its residents felt, the ghetto would not be permitted to exist."[17]

[16] Reported by the President's Commission, *op. cit.,* p. 121.

[17] The President's Commission, *op. cit.,* p. 122.

SECTION 3 PUBLIC OPINION AND PROPAGANDA

In emotional contagion, individuals are united by temporary psychological bonds, and the influence of the immediate situation is strong. However, emotional contagion is not the only source of temporary and shifting unities. Some groups arise out of shared belief and common interest.

PUBLICS

A public consists of people who (1) regard themselves as affected by an event or activity, (2) can in some way register that concern, and (3) are taken into account. This is a general term that may apply to magazine subscribers, stockholders, voters, and many other groups or categories. *Political publics* develop when there is an issue, that is, a disagreement over what ought to be done, such as whether or not to support a program of medical care. Politics occurs when the public is split into factions and rival groups pursue divergent interests.

A public may be scattered. It need not have a definite membership nor a formal organization of roles. Since a public consists of those concerned with the consequences of an event, the composition of the public changes as the situation changes and the same event comes to be seen in a different light. New people become interested; others lose interest and turn elsewhere; there may be a realignment within the public. When government support of medical care is labeled "socialized medicine," some shy away from discussions; others may join a health plan at their place of work and lose interest in the general issue. Publics are temporary collectivities of varying size and composition that can be identified only by their common concern with an event or issue.

If an issue recurs, a political public may become more stable. Within each area of interest, a core of people is formed who follow developments closely and whose support can be expected. On an issue like medical care, business groups can be expected to take one side, labor unions the other side, and veterans' groups split.

The existence of relatively stable publics implies a continuity of interest in a succession of related issues. Such publics can sometimes be identified by the books, newspapers, and magazines they read. By participating in common communication channels, they tend to define situations alike. Consequently, they consistently take the same sides on a variety of issues. Such publics, however, are only partially organized, and their composition continually changes. They may provide the *social base* out of which organized groups grow and on which such groups depend. (See ASSOCIATIONS, p. 217.)

VALUES, ATTITUDES, AND OPINIONS

Personal integrity is highly prized in American culture. A man should be secure in what is most intimately his, such as his body, his ideas, and his family. This *value* affects a wide range of thought and behavior, in part by generating *attitudes.* (See CULTURE, p. 54.) For example, valuing personal integrity may dispose one to react negatively to the use of informers (who violate personal confidences), wiretapping, and the forcible pumping of a man's stomach to secure evidence against him. "An individual's attitude toward something is his predisposition to perform, perceive, think, and feel in relation to it." [18] Attitudes are in turn reflected in *opinions,* which are specific judgments on particular issues. The sequence from value to attitude to opinion moves from the general to the specific, from a broad mental set or disposition to a narrower one and finally to a specific and concrete expression of it.

Opinions are *situational,* and therefore do not reflect values directly. An opinion may run counter to a mental set because of pressures in the immediate situation. An opinion is often the complex resultant of many attitudes. For example, attitudes derived from the value of personal integrity may call for rejection of wiretapping. But a belief that the community is in danger may bring other attitudes into play. The resultant opinion may accept wiretapping, perhaps with some reservations. When opinions reflect situational pressures, they may be held weakly, as in the case of legislators who respond to group threats or to shifting climates of opinion. (See Adaptation 22, p. 247.)

GROUP BASIS OF PUBLIC OPINION

Public opinion is relatively unstable and fluctuates with changes in the immediate situation even in matters of grave consequence. As a country becomes

[18] Theodore Newcomb, *Social Psychology* (New York: Dryden, 1950), p. 118.

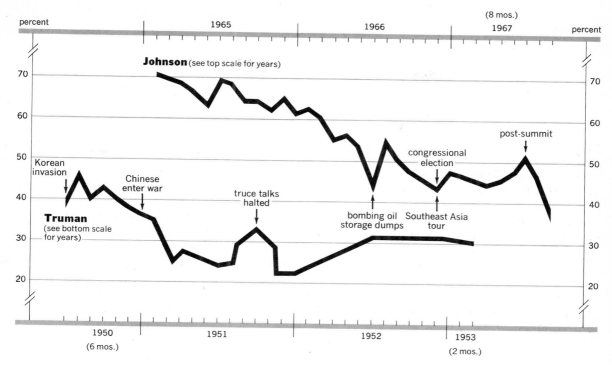

FIG. VIII:1   Popularity of President Johnson during Viet Nam War and President Truman during Korean War

Percent giving "Approve" answers to the question, "Do you approve or disapprove of the way _____ is handling his job as President?"

SOURCE: Gallup Political *Index, 18* (November–December, 1966) and Gallup Opinion *Index,* various dates.

more exposed to rapid technological change and to pressures from the rest of the world, it is increasingly difficult to make statements beginning, "The people will never stand for . . . ." Even matters on which near-consensus has been reached may become issues again in the swift movement of events. There is a large degree of unpredictability in the ebb and flow of public opinion, because the judgments are specific. The more general a judgment—for example, "The English people are our natural allies"—the more likely it is to endure. But opinions on specific policies and events—such as, "Do you approve or disapprove of the way Johnson is handling his job as President?"—tend to reflect immediate pressures.

The extent of popular approval for President Johnson and for President Truman is shown in Fig. VIII:1. Between January, 1965, and August, 1967, Johnson's "popularity" ranged from 71 percent approval to 39 percent approval, responding to transitory events as well as major trends. In a similar interval during 1950–1953, Truman's popularity was on the average far lower than Johnson's, falling below 30 percent for long periods, but it too fluctuated widely.

The level of popularity in the various sectors of the population is not a good measure of the likelihood that an officeholder would be reelected because all discontents are focused on an incumbent, dimin-

EVALUATING PERCENTAGES

How shall an analyst appraise the implication of a finding that 82 percent of a national sample believe that radio stations are doing an "excellent" or "good" job? Does this represent *overwhelming* public satisfaction? Shall the analyst note that *as many as* 18 percent were not satisfied, or shall he stress that *only* 18 percent did not show satisfaction? The extremes of zero *vs.* universal satisfaction are perhaps easy to evaluate, but here the analyst faces an intermediate figure that could be appraised in a variety of ways.

On attitudes toward advertising on the radio, about one-third of the public was found to be opposed to radio commercials. Does this represent serious criticism of the current pattern of American radio, or is this to be expected and regarded as innocuous from the point of view of change in the institution? The public was also queried on radio's degree of impartiality in handling controversial issues. Eighty-one percent regarded radio stations as being fair to both sides in general. Is this high praise of the radio industry, or should the fact be stressed that *as many as* 19 percent did not explicitly express the view that radio was fair?

In all these instances, the analyst can report the bare facts. Or he can use such neutral terms as "a majority," "a minority," and the like. But this is after all not the point of a descriptive survey. Such facts must be evaluated to be of some use, and they are bound to be capricious in the absence of norms for deciding whether such findings are large or small, frequent or rare.

Findings, apparently clear in their implications, can be misinterpreted in the absence of a standard of comparison. In a survey by the National Opinion Research Center, 37 percent of a national sample indicated that they had a favorable feeling toward the English government. Should the analyst regard this finding as indicative of serious hostility to England? While 37 percent is not a very high figure in absolute magnitude, when attitudes toward England were compared with attitudes toward other countries, 37 percent represented an unusually favorable attitude on the part of the American public. Only toward Canada did a larger proportion of the public indicate a favorable feeling.

To safeguard interpretations, the analyst usually sets norms by collecting data on parallel phenomena from the same individuals. A similar juxtaposition of parallel phenomena provided norms for the previously mentioned 82 percent of the sample who were well satisfied with radio. Parallel questions on satisfaction with the churches, newspapers, schools, and local government did not yield a figure as high as the 82 percent for radio. Radio is therefore seen to stand in *unusual* public favor.

These examples illustrate one problem in the use of norms and a method for treating it. It is obvious that there can be considerable arbitrariness in choosing the parallel phenomena to be compared. For example, one might pick only institutions toward which there is great public dissatisfaction and thereby present a misleading picture of relative satisfaction with radio. The analyst must therefore pick a series of parallel phenomena ranging over the whole probable spectrum.

SOURCE: Abridged and adapted from Herbert Hyman, *Survey Design and Analysis* (Glencoe: The Free Press, 1955), pp. 126–128. Used by permission.

ishing his general popularity. The attrition of popularity of an incumbent during his tenure in office is commonly observed. In an election, however, the public estimates the candidate against a real opponent. Consequently a fairly "unpopular" incumbent might win an election.

Despite its instability, public opinion develops within a *social setting*. The more the setting is understood, the less arbitrary and unpredictable shifts in opinion appear. Though opinion emerges from day-to-day interaction, people have social backgrounds and group affiliations: they are not separate atoms moving about randomly.[19]

1. *Social background.* An individual's social background affects the way he responds to events and consequently the opinions he forms. Although each population segment varies from one time to another in its attitudes toward an incumbent, the pattern of response shows that the following have tended consistently to be more favorable to President Johnson: men, manual workers, Democrats, Catholics, Easterners, and large-city people. Republicans, women, Protestants, Southerners, and rural people have been less favorable.

Because the categories listed are overlapping, it is necessary to break down each variable to make a precise interpretation. For instance, Catholics are heavily concentrated in urban areas. As we have seen, Catholics and big cities are favorable to Johnson. But is the preference a general large-city phenomenon or merely the consequence of a large Catholic population? To answer this question, big-city non-Catholics and big-city Catholics would have to be tabulated separately. It would then be possible to tell how much of the large-city approval is due to heavy urban representation of Catholics and how much is a large-city phenomenon without respect to religion. The statistical problem of which this is an example is called the "confounding effect."

2. *Reference groups.* Differences in social background affect perspectives and therefore opinions, because they make people sensitive to different things, provide experiences that give them feelings of weakness or strength, make them more or less verbal, more or less tradition-centered, and more or less prone to join organized groups. In addition, people tend to see themselves and the world through the framework provided by the groups in which they participate. However, a person's "reference group" (that group whose perspectives he assumes) is not always derived from his occupational role or economic position. For example, many low-income people identify with and accept the standards of middle-class life. In modern society, with wide-open communication channels, people may assume the perspectives of groups they *aspire* to be in as well as (or in place of) those to which they actually belong. Furthermore, an individual may have many reference groups, affecting his opinions on specific subjects.

Reference groups [20] should be distinguished from social categories, e.g., people in the same income level, and from membership groups like trade unions. Social categories and membership groups often *become* reference groups. In studying opinion it is important to know to what extent social categories and membership groups have been transformed into reference groups. It is also necessary to know which of the many reference groups actually influence the individual on a given issue.

3. *Strong and weak groups.* Although many groups influence public sentiment, they are not equally effective. There are wide variations in group prestige, size, resources, and in the significance they have for the individual. To the extent that people think of themselves as "middle class," regardless of income, this reference group plays a significant role in the formation of opinion. Although middle-class values and attitudes are widely held, organization among white-collar workers and consumers is relatively weak. On many specific issues, therefore, well-organized labor and business groups have greater weight. Special legislation, on tariffs and labor, for

[19] See Herbert Blumer, "Public Opinion and Public Opinion Polling," *American Sociological Review, 13* (October, 1948), 542–549.

[20] See Tamotsu Shibutani, *Society and Personality* (Englewood Cliffs, N.J.: Prentice-Hall, 1961), pp. 257–260.

example, reflects the views of these organized groups. Even strongly held opinions may not influence decisions unless they are expressed through organizations. On most subjects no popular vote is taken, and differences in organization and resources determine the final outcome.

Multiple membership accounts in part for the relatively unstable and shifting character of public opinion. The individual is constantly pulled in different directions by his various memberships and roles. Group strength is not to be judged by mere size. One interest group of 50,000 members may have little influence. Another of the same size may include a core of devoted workers who effectively mobilize the opinions of less committed members.

4. *Active and passive groups.* Those most concerned with controversial issues join or form interest groups. Others make up a large spectator-like body, interested enough to follow developments but not sufficiently concerned to participate directly. The passive elements are not necessarily without importance. As an audience whose reactions must be taken into account, they are arbiters in the struggle among interest groups. The pursuit of interests is limited not only by law and custom but also by the other members of the public whose approval is required. Interest groups try to show that their interests are tied to the general welfare, and active groups bid for the support of spectators who judge whether private and public interests are truly related. Therefore, trade unions, business associations, and professional organizations, like the American Medical Association, devote much effort to public relations.

In summary, knowledge of the group structure of society is indispensable to a proper understanding of public opinion. Opinions are affected by social experience; and the interaction of groups, varying in strength and activity, determines the weight and direction of public sentiment.

ASCERTAINING OPINION

In a free society people "vote" in many ways. They speak out at home and among their friends and associates, write letters to newspapers and legislators, join or quit organizations, and go to the polls. Because opinion is expressed in many ways, there must be a number of different research methods. One approach is to study the organizational context of opinion and to examine the rise and decline of organizations, for example, the organizational basis of prohibition sentiment. (See Adaptation 22, pp. 246–250.) Another approach is to find out what the most active people (the "opinion leaders") in a community think. Another is to assess opinion in influential business, professional, and government circles. Finally, there is the problem of determining what the public believes, how people are likely to vote, and what their votes mean.

The prediction of election returns has been justly considered an important achievement of modern social science. The polls have helped to demonstrate that the behavior of large populations can be studied through the sophisticated use of sampling techniques. In Adaptation 23, page 253, Likert shows how a small nationwide sample can accurately reflect certain characteristics of the population as a whole.

Election polls are designed to predict a single, highly complex event. This is an exacting task, for it requires not merely one prediction but a whole chain of subordinate ones. The polls must be able to analyze the "Don't know" or undecided responses and predict how they will divide on election day. The pollsters must predict how many people will vote and from what groups in society they will come, because many who state their preferences when asked do not take the trouble to vote. When the 1948 election polls were analyzed by a committee of the Social Science Research Council, it was shown that inadequate handling of the "Don't know" responses and the nonvoters probably led to the failure to predict President Truman's election.

By 1956 a number of improvements in polling techniques, referred to in Adaptation 23, were well established, and the errors in recent elections were within narrow limits. As can be seen in Table VIII:1, the surveys of 1956 and 1960 were remarkably close to the election results. The 1944 prediction was also very close, but the average error from 1936 to 1952 was over 4 percent and consistently underestimated the winner's vote.

TABLE VIII:1 GALLUP POLL ACCURACY IN EIGHT (OR NINE) PRESIDENTIAL ELECTIONS, IN PERCENTAGES

YEAR	WINNER	FINAL SURVEY [a]	ELECTION RESULT	ERROR
1936	Roosevelt	55.7	62.5	−6.8
1940	Roosevelt	52.0	55.0	−3.0
1944	Roosevelt	51.5	53.3 [b]	−1.8
1948	Truman [c]	44.5	49.9	−5.4
1952	Eisenhower	51.0	55.4	−4.4
1956	Eisenhower	59.5	57.8	1.7
1960	Kennedy	51.0	50.1	0.9
1964	Johnson	64.0	61.3	2.7
1968 [d]				

SOURCE: Based on Gallup Political *Index, 9* (February, 1966).

[a] Released to the press on the Sunday before Tuesday election.

[b] Civilian vote only.

[c] Dewey election predicted.

[d] Provision is made for inserting the 1968 results.

The election poll, however accurate, has all the limitations of the election itself as a way of ascertaining public opinion:

1. *Intensity.* A person who expresses his preference to an interviewer may or may not take his vote seriously; he may be very unhappy or quite undisturbed if his candidate loses. The strength of his opinion affects the chances that he will actually cast his ballot.

2. *Meaning.* A vote may mean quite different things to different people. Was the election merely a popularity contest? Did the voters mean to give the new administration a mandate on specific issues? Which issues were central and which peripheral? These questions remain unanswered, and there is room for interpretation after the election is over, especially when the results are very close, as they were in the Kennedy-Nixon contest of 1960.

3. *Action.* As a result of variation in intensity and meaning, it is difficult to say whether an expressed preference will lead to any action. This applies most immediately to whether a man votes at all, but beyond that it is important to know whether voting

leads to other forms of political action. The bare expression of preference does not tell.

Modern and sophisticated public opinion surveys that go beyond the simple expressions of preference attempt to overcome these limitations. Intensity can be gauged by avoiding simple yes-no answers and providing graded alternatives from which to choose. People may be asked directly whether they "strongly approve," "approve," "don't care," etc., or a more elaborate and carefully worked out series of alternatives may be presented. The problem of meaning can be handled by offering a series of increasingly specific questions on the same topic. Each succeeding question requires a more precise answer about what the words mean and what the implications of the point of view are. Superficial responses can be filtered out in this way, as shown in Table VIII:2.

TABLE VIII:2 FILTERING CONVENTIONAL RESPONSES

Do you believe in freedom of speech?	Yes	97%
	No	1
	Don't know	2
If "yes": Do you believe in it to the extent of allowing Fascists and Communists to hold meetings and express their views in this community?	Yes	23%
	No	72
	No opinion	5

SOURCE: *From Gauging Public Opinion* by Hadley Cantril (Princeton: Princeton University Press, 1944), p. 22. The questions were asked by the American Institute of Public Opinion in November, 1940.

As it becomes more sophisticated, public opinion analysis places less emphasis on specific predictions and more on understanding of underlying trends. It is more important to know whether the coalition of social groups that contributed to a party's majority is basically intact than to predict a specific election. An election may result in part from accidental circumstances, whereas a trend may be related to more enduring changes in population composition, such as the assimilation of ethnic minorities, the improvement of the economic condition of some groups, or the development of new values.

PROPAGANDA

Propaganda may be defined as the calculated dissemination of partisan ideas with the intent of influencing group attitudes and opinions. It is a form of special pleading in which truth may be, and often is, subordinated to effectiveness. Some regard propaganda as morally neutral, justified or not according to the ends it serves. Others feel it is inherently manipulative and tends to corrupt the free formation of considered judgments, whether in choosing a toothpaste or a foreign policy. This debate turns largely on a matter of degree. Most propaganda operates within limits, foregoing the bare-faced lie and the more strident emotional appeals.

In an older and more restricted usage, "propaganda" is the dissemination of a systematic doctrine, such as Catholicism. The Communists hold to this usage, distinguishing "propaganda" from "agitation." The former refers to intensive work among small groups, with emphasis on communicating fundamental ideas, e.g., Marxist economic and political theories. Agitation is the spreading of a few ideas, usually with a heavy emotional content, to a great many people. In its restricted sense "propaganda" is closer to "indoctrination" and does not have many of the characteristics associated with the use of mass communications. Here "propaganda" is used in the more general sense, without distinguishing it from agitation.

Propaganda usually refers to writings, speeches, and other symbolic behavior. In addition the term "propaganda of the deed" is used to refer to the dramatic actions of nineteenth-century anarchists who attempted to win attention to purported evils by assassinations or other acts of violence. However, in recent history there are many examples of government action taken with a view to influencing attitudes. The Russian lead in constructing the Aswan Dam in Egypt was part of a propaganda effort comparable to U.S. activities in the field of foreign aid. Both are efforts to win the "hearts and minds of the people." Any act or event can have a symbolic meaning, communicating the intentions as well as the strength or weakness of the actor.

The nature and effectiveness of propaganda depend on objectives and on the characteristics of the target population. If the aim is to sell a particular brand of cigarettes, attention-getting techniques may suffice. But if the aim is to win support for a political belief or economic doctrine, the methods must be adapted to the experiences of the listener, and this usually requires a highly selective approach to various types of audiences. This discussion considers some characteristics of propaganda aims, methods, and targets.

Aims As a mass-communications activity, propaganda tends to have short-run, situationally-defined aims with an appeal to a diverse population on the basis of immediate interests, fears, or desires. The propaganda of advertisers, interest groups, and political parties is largely of this kind. The objective is not so much to influence the individual deeply as to win his support for some immediate issue, candidate, or product. The more short-run and superficial the aims, the easier it is to use propaganda tricks and gadgets. Long-run aims, which attempt to change basic attitudes, are more difficult to achieve.

Some propaganda, though ostensibly directed outward, is really a way of bolstering group morale. Political meetings usually bring together people already committed to the organization or candidate. They are "pep rallies" designed to stimulate confidence and increase involvement, though they may also be effective propaganda as demonstrations of strength.

Methods In the study of propaganda most attention has been given to techniques and relatively little to aims or targets. See "The Tricks of the Trade," page 244. A number of characteristic propaganda methods have been identified:

1. *Gaining attention*. Many varied techniques have been used, from luminous paint to the "big lie." The effectiveness of attention-getting techniques depends on the nature of the medium used as well as the disposition of the audience. Charges against an individual often receive wide publicity in the press, whereas answers to these charges seem inherently less interesting and are given less prominent display. An

emphasis on negative attitudes, as in the early twentieth-century anti-saloon propaganda (see Adaptation, 22, p. 249), is often successful in winning attention and support because it is easier to get agreement on the existence of an evil than on some particular solution.

2. *Associating a partisan cause with existing values, attitudes, and symbols.* The propagandist, pleading for a special interest, tries to identify himself with a wider community. He tries to transfer to himself symbols that are known to elicit favorable responses. Smear tactics or guilt by association are the obverse of the same mechanism, transferring to an opponent the negative feelings attached to some despised symbol. *Glittering generalities* are emotionally loaded symbols that associate a cause directly to a general value. It is also very common to employ prestigeful figures, sometimes merely to grace a letterhead, as a way of legitimizing propaganda. (This is not necessarily to be deplored, because if the members of a public know the views of prestige figures, and prestige figures are actually involved, the device can help to identify the appeal and its source.)

In modern history the struggle for valued symbols has been a common feature of propaganda contests. Adolf Hitler took advantage of the fact that "socialist" was a high prestige word for many Europeans when he called his party the National Socialist German Labor Party.

3. *Concealing identity and aims.* The attempt to associate a cause with existing community sentiment is often jeopardized when the true aims and special interests of the sponsors are known. An evasive technique is the use of "front" organizations that have innocuous names and objectives but are controlled and manipulated by covert interests. The use of front organizations by extremists of various kinds has greatly increased the sophistication needed for effective political participation.

4. *Raising anxieties.* The critical ability of an audience may be impaired by techniques that induce anxiety and fear. This is widely practiced in advertising that makes people anxious about health, love, and status. In political propaganda *hidden* enemies are commonly emphasized.

5. *Showing strength.* Propagandists are sensitive to the reluctance of people to support a weak cause, and much effort is expended in putting on displays of strength. Sometimes this consists in propagating an ideology that history is necessarily moving in a particular direction and that the cause represents this "wave of the future." Parades, meetings, strikes, and similar demonstrations are also effective, but the turnout must in fact be impressive, lest the effort boomerang. Effective organizational work is necessary to supplement the propaganda and to sustain its effects.

Targets An understanding of the characteristics of the target and the psychological factors that influence susceptibility are essential to devising effective propaganda.

1. *Social composition and organization.* Propaganda must be adapted to the backgrounds and experiences of the audience. A knowledge of the social composition of a population can identify its *prior dispositions* to accept or reject propaganda emphases. For example, immigrant groups often retain sentiments of loyalty to their country of origin, and suburban populations are especially conscious of social status. Such interests and aspirations affect the success of propaganda themes and methods.

The way a population is *organized* determines the acceptable channels of communication. Where local leaders or special-purpose organizations are powerful, propaganda that bypasses these channels may go unheeded. Some groups are more accessible to appeals based on self-interest; others respond to ideological propaganda. This is not a matter of accident but a product of the special backgrounds and experiences of various elements in the population.

A community is made up of many different audiences, each of which responds in its own way to appeals. For example, propaganda directed at the *elites* (the most influential or self-conscious groups in a community), requires a more sophisticated and more pointed approach than propaganda aimed at a wider audience. An example of elite-oriented propaganda is the attempt to reach potentially disaffected Communists behind the "iron curtain," a project that must

THE TRICKS OF THE TRADE

Some of the devices now so subtly and effectively used by good and bad propagandists are as old as language. All have been used in one form or another by all of us in our daily dealings with each other. Propagandists have seized upon these methods we ordinarily use to convince each other, have analyzed and refined them, and have experimented with them until these homely devices of folk origin have been developed into tremendously powerful weapons for the swaying of popular opinions and actions.

The chief devices used in popular argument and by professional propagandists—together with our symbols for them—are:

Name calling—giving an idea a bad label—is used to make us reject and condemn the idea without examining the evidence.

Glittering generality—associating something with a "virtue word"—is used to make us accept and approve the thing without examining the evidence.

Transfer carries the authority, sanction, and prestige of something respected and revered over to something else in order to make the latter acceptable; or it carries authority, sanction, and disapproval to cause us to reject and disapprove something the propagandist would have us reject and disapprove.

Testimonial consists in having some respected or hated person say that a given idea or program or person is good or bad.

Plain folks is the method by which a speaker attempts to convince his audience that he and his ideas are good because they are "of the people," the "plain folks."

Card stacking involves the selection and use of facts or falsehoods, illustrations or distractions, and logical or illogical statements in order to give the best or the worst possible case for an idea, program, person, or product.

Band wagon has as its theme "Everybody—at least all of *us*—is doing it"; with it, the propagandist attempts to convince us that all members of a group to which we belong are accepting his program and that we *must therefore* follow our crowd and "jump on the band wagon."

Once we know that a speaker or writer is using one of these propaganda devices in an attempt to convince us of an idea, we can separate the device from the idea and see what the idea amounts to on its own merits.

SOURCE: Abridged from Institute for Propaganda Analysis, *The Fine Art of Propaganda* by Alfred McClung Lee and Elizabeth Briant Lee (New York: Harcourt, Brace & World, 1939). Reprinted by permission.

be based on a high degree of knowledge of the history and problems of Communism and Socialism.

2. *Susceptibility.* Some psychological mechanisms are known to affect vulnerability or resistance to propaganda. In ambiguous situations, people look for cues. They are more suggestible to ideas and rumors than they would be if the situation were clearly defined. Hence, propagandists play an important role during times of unrest. In general, whenever propaganda meets some *felt need* in the population, if only the relief of anxiety, it is likely to get a hearing. On the other hand, people *evade* propaganda by filtering out what they want to hear and rejecting the rest.

Although propaganda is significant in unstructured situations, it is not the only way opinion is influenced. In transmitting ways of looking at the world and one's self, socialization makes some ideas congenial and others alien. Furthermore, most opinions are acquired in the course of group participation rather than in response to mass communications.

Fears and prospects   When several publics exist, and each has the opportunity to weigh conflicting views according to the criterion of self-interest, the multigroup character of society is preserved. Because of heterogeneity and self-interest, the conditions that make for emotional contagion are minimized. (See above, p. 223.) However, modern mass communication tends to make many millions available to similar and simultaneous influences. The danger that emotional contagion, based upon common fears of war or subversion, will lead to excessive and irresponsible reactions has been referred to as the degeneration of publics into crowds. Lederer [21] said that the "mass-state," built upon the eradication of groups, replaces reason by propaganda, and enslaves man by delivering him to his emotions. In such a society, public opinion is not the result of the slowly working interplay of interests and ideas, but is the crowdlike response of an amorphous population.

A similar view has been expressed by Neumann:

Mob psychology, when it seizes a whole nation, destroys the web of its complex structure. Like the individual differentiation of its members, so the innumerable associations of the living community are melted into one gray mass. This process of "massification"— the dissolution of free organizations, the flattening of the social pyramid—in a way preceded the rise of modern dictators. They were the product of this disintegration of society which in turn became the basis of their established rule. [22]

Views of this kind, which emphasize the extension of crowd behavior to many aspects of social life, have been common during the past century. [23] They are usually stated in exaggerated terms, but they probably point to an authentic underlying hazard.

A graphic depiction of an imaginary society dominated by the calculated manipulation of symbols is found in George Orwell's novel *Nineteen Eighty-Four.* Orwell describes a society ruled by Big Brother and his Ministry of Truth. The Ministry systematically rewrites history and has for its slogans WAR IS PEACE, FREEDOM IS SLAVERY, IGNORANCE IS STRENGTH. The machinery of propaganda and intimidation is highly developed, including an official language, Newspeak, much of whose vocabulary is deliberately constructed for political purposes. (See "Newspeak and Expressive Symbolism," p. 53.) Orwell's account is a projection of some of the features of the totalitarian societies of Nazi Germany and Stalin's Russia.

Some of the anxiety about the future of public opinion is based on the *strong pressures toward conformity* in the mass communications industries. Since profit-making is the criterion of successful operation, the tendency is to try to please as many people as possible and to avoid antagonizing highly vocal groups. The industries are fearful of divergent views and tastes, and sensitive or controversial issues are likely to be avoided. The forums that should be available to differing opinion if the public is to be well informed

[21] Emil Lederer, *The State of the Masses* (New York: Norton, 1940).

[22] Sigmund Neumann, *Permanent Revolution* (New York: Harper & Row, 1942), p. 115.

[23] See especially Gustave Le Bon, *The Crowd* (London: Unwin, 1917); and E. A. Ross, *Social Psychology* (New York: Macmillan, 1908).

may be closed. It is also feared that a dead level of uniformity in taste, stirring no antagonisms yet rising to no new heights, may stultify the arts. No doubt these fears have some justification. On the other hand, new technological developments may change the situation drastically, making many more channels of communication available to experimental and educational activities.

Adaptation 22 / Odegard   THE ANTI-SALOON LEAGUE

In 1920 the Eighteenth Amendment to the U.S. Constitution was ratified, prohibiting "the manufacture, sale, or transportation of intoxicating liquors." Passage of the Eighteenth Amendment can largely be attributed to the national Anti-Saloon League, formed in 1895. This organization transformed the existing temperance movement from a moral appeal directed at individuals into a political power, with its strength based on Protestant churches.[24] The following account describes the nature and strategy of the Anti-Saloon League. Some implications for understanding public opinion and propaganda are noted in the concluding summary and interpretation.

The social base of prohibitionist opinion   Although in theory the Anti-Saloon League was a nonsectarian organization, in fact it was almost entirely an instrument of the Protestant churches, principally the Methodist, Baptist, Presbyterian, and Congregational denominations. Prohibitionist sentiment was strong among these groups, and the Anti-Saloon League was organized to give them effective political organization. In theory it was open to anyone; in practice it was controlled by the Protestant churches from whom it drew both its leadership and its principal membership support. The churches opened their pulpits to Anti-Saloon League speakers and provided the League with an extraordinary access to church membership. According to one account, pastors in more than two thousand churches in Illinois discussed a pending temperance measure on a single Sunday.

During the prohibitionist heyday, Protestant church members were predominantly rural and native born. Even in the cities, Protestant churches were composed largely of people born in rural areas. Where Protestants were in the majority, as in the South, prohibitionist sentiment was strong: nine of the Southern states adopted prohibition prior to 1916. Connecticut and Rhode Island never ratified the Eighteenth Amendment; Catholics made up 67 percent and 76 percent, respectively, of the total church population in these states.

The Anti-Saloon League did not have to create prohibitionist sentiment; the sentiment already existed in the rural native-born Protestant areas. Nor did it have to organize prohibitionist sentiment; it was already organized in the Protestant churches. But with singular success, the League *mobilized* the organized sentiment and directed it toward a political purpose, the passage of prohibitionist legislation.

Moral sentiment into political action   The Anti-Saloon League, formed as a national organization

SOURCE: Abridged and adapted from Peter H. Odegard, *Pressure Politics: The Story of the Anti-Saloon League* (New York: Columbia University Press, 1928). Published in this form by permission of Peter H. Odegard and Columbia University Press.

[24] See Joseph Gusfield, *Symbolic Crusade: Status Politics and the American Temperance Movement* (Urbana: University of Illinois Press, 1963).

in 1895, was, as its name suggests, a league of already established temperance organizations. Behind it lay almost a century of temperance agitation and largely unsuccessful efforts to pass prohibition legislation. One local organization, however, the Oberlin Temperance Alliance, had secured the passage of such legislation in Ohio. In 1887 the Oberlin Temperance Alliance circulated petitions demanding the passage of a state-wide Township Option Bill, by which individual municipalities might vote to outlaw the sale of liquor. The bill was put through the House and went to the Senate where, according to a preliminary poll, it had a majority of one. Two days before the vote was to be taken, Senator Crook of Dayton, one of the bill's supporters, announced that after having been visited by three committees of Dayton brewers, distillers, and saloonkeepers, he had been persuaded to vote against the measure.

Senator Crook's frankness was his own undoing. The prohibitionists reasoned that if he could be influenced by pressure from the liquor interests, he could be encouraged to return to the straight and narrow by greater pressure from the other side. That afternoon, the Rev. H. H. Russell, employed by the Alliance to push the bill, went to Dayton. Soon letters, telegrams, and petitions from citizens of that city poured in upon the recalcitrant Crook demanding that he support local option. The Senator did vote for it, and the measure was passed by a majority of one.

Senator Crook and his three committees of brewers, distillers, and saloonkeepers provided the Anti-Saloon League with a lesson in politics. Thereafter the temper-ance movement diverted its efforts from appealing to conscience to applying pressure, especially on legislators.

Single-purpose politics With the Ohio experience as a model, the national Anti-Saloon League organized itself into a legislative pressure group. It set itself up as a single-purpose organization, concentrating solely on the passage of prohibition legislation. Some prohibitionists had earlier formed themselves into a Prohibition party, arguing that the existing parties would not and could not institute prohibition. But it had never won significant electoral support, and in 1896 it split on the silver and gold issue, each side putting its own presidential candidate into the field. The Anti-Saloon League avoided all side issues upon which disagreement and factional splits could occur, and which might alienate potential supporters. Advocates of silver or of gold, of free trade or of a high tariff could all join in the Anti-Saloon League's drive for prohibition legislation without compromising their other loyalties.

Instead of entering politics as another party, the League worked through the Republican and Democratic parties, supporting whatever dry candidates were nominated. It did not care what else a candidate stood for, so long as he stood for prohibition. It frequently supported both Republicans and Democrats in the same election, provided both candidates were dry. Nor did the Anti-Saloon League insist that a candidate be a personal abstainer. The League's theory was that it is better to have a drunkard who will "vote right, than to have a saint who will vote wrong."

The League's objective was to hold the balance of power. With virtual control of a large block of voters, the League frequently forced the major parties to nominate candidates friendly to its interests, since the dry vote often spelled the difference between victory and defeat.

Having decided on a satisfactory candidate, the League did all it could to see that he was elected. Women and children were urged to gather near the polls to act as reminders of the evil of the saloon. They often paraded before polling places wearing badges: "Vote Against Whiskey and For Me," or "Vote Against the Saloon—I Can't Vote." The 19th Amendment to the Constitution, guaranteeing the right of women to vote, was not ratified until 1920. The following report in the *New York World* of May 13, 1919, describes a North Carolina election scene:

When a voter came within range he was immediately surrounded by . . . ministers . . . women and children. The clergymen employed words of advice and confined their activities to the proprieties. But the women and children were less tactful. They clutched at the coats of the voter. They importuned him to vote the dry ticket. A phrase constantly employed was "Mister, for God's sake don't vote for whiskey," repeated with parrot-like accuracy that results from thorough coaching. . . . A few of the wets ran the gauntlet of the women and children . . . but the greater majority of the voters viewed the conflict from afar and returned to their offices and homes. The drys won the day.

The League provided funds and personnel for more routine campaign activities, often employing organizers to canvass voters in their homes. In 1906 in New York it promised aid in his current campaign to any state assembly member who had voted dry and was being opposed on that account. Thirty-six dry members requested such assistance, and all were re-elected.

When prohibition legislation was pending, the Anti-Saloon League employed many kinds of direct action techniques designed to impress recalcitrant legislators with the size and strength of dry opinion. As in the campaign of the Oberlin Temperance Alliance, local League organizations saw to it that legislators received letters and telegrams from dry voters. Petitions were also effective. When national prohibition was up for debate in the House of Representatives in 1913, long slips of paper listing the names of over six million petitioners hung from the balconies filled with prohibition supporters. One Congressman suggested that the House move out of Washington to avoid pressure from the drys. That same year Congress had been petitioned to submit prohibition to the states by a parade of four thousand men and women, many of them grown gray and infirm in the long campaign, wearing the white ribbon of temperance and marching to the strains of "Onward, Christian Soldiers."

The threat of defeat for wets and the promise of victory for drys was, however, the principal political weapon of the Anti-Saloon League. In 1917, just before the House passed the resolution to submit prohibition to the states, the *Washington Times* asserted, "If the ballot on the constitutional amendment were a secret ballot, making it impossible for the Anti-Saloon League bosses to punish disobedience, the Amendment would not pass." The newspaper implied that national prohibition was about to be passed not out of conviction but out of fear of political reprisal. The League's electoral effectiveness depended on two things: (1) its control of the rural vote and (2) the dependence at that time of both the state and national legislatures on rural areas. If the rural vote had not been very nearly a solid block firmly committed on the dry issue, the League's promise to deliver votes would have been far less effective than it actually was. If the legislatures had been as dependent on the cities as they were on the rural areas, the League's hold over the rural voters would have been a less potent political weapon.

The Recruiting Sergeant for the Army of Crime: This cartoon, depicting the saloon as a natural center for vice and crime, was widely used in Anti-Saloon League publications.

Influencing the legislators
When the Anti-Saloon League turned its energies from reforming the individual to pressing for the passage of prohibition, it sought to exert its influence where the rural population had its political power. This was in the state legislatures, which tend to overrepresent rural and small town areas wherever representation is based on geographical area rather than population. In the United States Senate a sparsely settled rural state like North Dakota has as many senators as a densely populated state like New York. In addition, the movement toward the cities tends to weight legislative bodies toward rural overrepresentation, since reapportionment lags behind actual population changes. In 1917, when the League put on its strongest drive for national prohibition, one of its leaders pointed out, "We have got to win it now because when 1920 comes and reapportionment is here, forty new Congressmen will come from the great wet centers with their rapidly increasing population."

In most cases the Anti-Saloon League opposed submitting the prohibition issue to direct popular vote, trusting rather to its influence in the state legislatures. In the debate on national prohibition it was proposed that ratification be by state conventions elected by popular vote for that purpose. To this the League spokesmen objected and insisted that the more usual procedure of ratification by state legislatures be followed. They argued that since state conventions would be chosen by the same electorate that had chosen the state legislatures, the proposal to submit ratification to a more direct vote was merely a delaying tactic. Although the League had pressed for a seven-year ratification period in case ratification in some states would prove difficult, three-fourths of the states ratified within fourteen months. The speed with which the amendment was ratified surprised the wets as well as the drys. "The grip held by the Anti-Saloon League over the state legislatures was never better illustrated than in the manner in which these bodies obeyed the command to ratify. In vain were suggestions made that the lawmaking bodies were without instructions from the people on this most important question. In vain were efforts made to have the sentiment of the electorate tested by referendum voting." [25]

Propaganda strategy National prohibition was first written into the law as an aspect of food conservation during the first World War. A bill was passed under the pressure of the drys prohibiting the manufacture of foodstuffs into distilled spirits, and giving the President authority to extend the restriction to beer and wine. The war gave considerable impetus to dry propaganda, prohibition being presented as part of the war effort. Nor did the League hesitate to play upon anti-German attitudes prevalent at the time. "German brewers in this country have rendered thousands of men inefficient and are thus crippling the Republic in its war on Prussian militarism. . . ." [26]

The League directed its propaganda not so much *for* prohibition as *against* the saloon and its evils. This was an effective device because even drinkers who balked at the idea of absolute prohibition were willing to admit that the American saloon had become a noisome thing. The United States Brewers' Association itself had recognized the need for reform. Reform, however, would not satisfy the League, and it pictured the saloon as hopeless beyond redemption.

"The saloon is the storm center of crime; the devil's headquarters on earth; the schoolmaster of a broken decalogue; the defiler of youth; the enemy of the home; the foe of peace; the deceiver of nations; the beast of sensuality; the past master of intrigue; the vagabond of poverty; the social vulture; the rendezvous of demagogues; the enlisting office of sin; the serpent of Eden; a ponderous second edition of hell, revised, enlarged and illuminated." [27]

The anti-saloon propaganda of the League tried to induce a favorable attitude toward prohibition by attaching it to an already existing attitude, a negative attitude toward the saloon. It used the same strategy when it attached its fight for local option to democratic values. Local option, by which any political unit—county, city, town, or even ward—could vote to ban the saloon, was presented as an exten-

[25] *Year Book of the United States Brewers' Association,* 1919, p. 18.

[26] *American Issue,* Ohio Edition, August 3, 1917. *American Issue* was the national organ of the Anti-Saloon League, also published in state editions.

[27] *American Issue,* Kentucky Edition, April, 1912.

sion of self-government and home rule. Many people who personally disliked prohibition felt obliged to support the drive for local option as consonant with democracy. Woodrow Wilson, then Governor of New Jersey and no partisan of prohibition, wrote, "I am in favor of local option. I am a thorough believer in local self-government and believe that every self-governing community which constitutes a social unit should have the right to control the matter of the regulation or the withholding of licenses." [28]

Conclusion   1. Public opinion is usually ineffective unless it is transformed into political power. The Anti-Saloon League was distinguished from its predecessors by its use of prohibitionist opinion as an electoral weapon. It developed the political skill to defeat wets and elect drys. It concentrated its efforts on state legislatures, where prohibitionist votes were influential because of overrepresentation of the rural population.

2. Public opinion has a social base. Prohibitionist sentiment was not a matter of random individual opinion but was concentrated in native-white, rural, Protestant areas. It never gained significant following in large cities nor among immigrants and non-Protestants. The effectiveness of public opinion in determining governmental policy depends in large measure upon the social and political resources of its social base. The passage of prohibition legislation reflected the political and social importance of the rural population, especially in the state legislatures. The repeal of prohibition can be attributed in part to the growing dominance both of the political power of the city dweller and of the values and attitudes of urban life. (See URBAN MAN, pp. 438–439.)

3. Ordinarily only a minority feels strongly about any issue, and propaganda to influence others and gain allies is important in making public opinion effective. Such propaganda does not usually set out to create entirely new sentiments but to focus, strengthen, and extend old opinions. If the saloon had not become a reprehensible institution and if temperance sentiments had not already been present in large sections of the American people, the Anti-Saloon League would probably not have succeeded in its drive for legislation. But given temperance attitudes and the repugnance which many people felt toward the saloon, it was easy to transform these feelings into attitudes favorable to prohibition legislation.

4. A consensus may be temporary and unstable.

a. The social base may melt away. The conditions under which the rural population lives are quite different from what they were in the nineteenth century and early twentieth century, and the changes in these conditions have brought with them changes in attitudes and values.

b. The social base may lose its political dominance. The success of the prohibition movement came at the end of the period of rural political power. With a decline in political power, the rural population was less able to give to legislation the stamp of its own special attitudes and values.

c. Propaganda may gain allies and win a consensus on superficial or on unrealistic grounds. The adherence of many legislators to prohibitionist sentiments was not a matter of principle but of political expediency. Many people supported prohibition as a moral ideal but withdrew their support because criminals profited from prohibition and enforcement proved difficult and costly.

[28] *American Issue,* Vermont Edition, March, 1912.

Adaptation 23 / Likert PUBLIC OPINION POLLS

The following adaptation presents an assessment and critique of public opinion polls. Likert concludes that their failure to predict the 1948 Democratic presidential victory did not discredit public opinion polling but dramatized the need for improvements in techniques. As a result of the public and scientific criticism of the 1948 failure, the polling agencies were stimulated to self-criticism and to adopt more advanced methods.[29] The article on which this adaptation is based was influential in speeding the changes. [Comments in brackets have been added to indicate the situation of the 1960s.]

In 1948 Gallup forecast a 44.5 percent vote for President Truman, who actually received 50 percent of the vote and won the election. The failure of Gallup and other pollsters in predicting the outcome of the 1948 election has reinforced the skeptics of public opinion polling, who argue that the samples are too small or otherwise inadequate, that the problems are too complex to be dealt with in a few simple questions, and that the investigators are biased. How valid are these criticisms? How sound are the present polling techniques, and how reliable are their results? Is it possible to improve public opinion polling?

Polling methods The polling process divides conveniently into two major parts: (1) the population sample used; (2) the questionnaire, the method of interviewing, and the analysis of the replies. The accuracy of any poll obviously depends upon the accuracy of each of these parts.

Let us consider first the sample. In 1936 the now defunct *Literary Digest* magazine conducted a poll which forecast a Republican victory. Its conspicuous failure dramatized the fact that the design of a sample is as important as its size. Although the sample totaled more than two million persons, it erred by 20 percentage points because it was not representative of the total population. First, the poll was restricted to *Literary Digest* and telephone subscribers, that is, to those of a relatively high economic status. Second, it required that a mailed questionnaire be returned. This resulted in a further selection from an already highly-selected group; it selected out those who answer mailed questionnaires or who felt strongly enough in this case to go to the trouble to do so.

QUOTA SAMPLING

[The so-called "quota-controlled" method was the main sampling method used in public opinion polls at the time of the 1948 election. It is a relatively cheap technique and is still used for some purposes.] Quota sampling depends for its accuracy on finding those variables that have a high correlation with the behavior being studied. Thus to design a sample for predicting an election, the pollsters use their knowledge of how voting correlates with party affiliation, age, economic status, and so on. They then attempt to find out how these variables are distributed in the whole population. For example, census data will tell them how many people in the total population are Negro, how many are women, how many live in cities, and how many earn above and below certain amounts. These characteristics may be related to how people vote, and the sample must contain its proportionate quota of Negroes, women, etc. When the social composition of the sample is determined, quotas are then assigned to interviewers, that is, the interviewer must poll a certain

SOURCE: Abridged and adapted from "Public Opinion Polls" by Rensis Likert, *Scientific American, 179,* No. 6 (December, 1948). Published in this form by permission of Rensis Likert and the *Scientific American.*

[29] Social Science Research Council, *Pre-election Polls of 1948* (New York: Social Science Research Council, 1949).

number of persons in each age group, socioeconomic group, etc.

For maximum accuracy, however, a pollster would need to know all of the variables correlated with voting behavior, such as previous voting behavior, education, income, occupation, religion, party affiliation of the voter's father, mother, and close friends, and so forth. He would also need precise information on the distribution of all these variables in the population. Unfortunately for public opinion polling, these two conditions almost never exist. In the first place, many of the variables that affect voting or other behavior are unknown. In the second place, no data are available on the distribution in the population of most of the variables that are known.

In spite of these difficulties, pollsters using the quota method have usually been able to make surprisingly accurate predictions. The methods generally employed are, briefly, as follows. Quotas are set, usually on the basis of geographical region, size of community, age, sex and socioeconomic level. In some parts of the country, race also is included. In making election predictions, the results that these quota samples yield are generally tested by asking respondents how they voted in the previous presidential election and checking the percentages obtained with the actual election figures. Any discrepancy that exists is eliminated by weighting the results. For example, in a poll taken in Maine in 1944, 38 percent of the persons interviewed said they planned to vote for Franklin D. Roosevelt. An analysis of the respondents showed that the sample contained an underrepresentation of persons who had voted for Roosevelt in 1940. When a ratio correction was applied, a weighted estimate of 48 percent for Roosevelt in Maine in 1944 was obtained.

Errors in the samples A major source of bias in quota samples is the fact that interviewers, in a perfectly human fashion, endeavor to fill their quotas in the easiest manner possible. They go to places where people are readily available and seek any who will fill the age, sex, and socioeconomic specifications of their quotas. They tend, therefore, to secure a sample which is biased in that it includes more people who are easily contacted than a truly representative sample should include.

An analysis of samples obtained with the quota-controlled method shows that this method tends to obtain data with biases which at times may be serious. For example, quota samples tend to include too few respondents from high income families, too few from the lowest income groups, too many with at least high school education, and too few with only a grade school education or less.

The basic weakness of the quota-controlled method is that it does not employ a random sample. A general human failing among interviewers—or errors in the fixing of quotas—may produce a sample which is systematically biased in the same direction. In other words, when deliberate human choice enters into the final selection of respondents, the usual laws of probability governing the sampling phenomenon do not apply; the errors or deviations may not balance one another as they tend to do in a purely random sample, but at times may become cumulative and produce a bias of large and unpredictable dimensions.

PROBABILITY SAMPLING

[By the 1960s most national polling agencies had turned to probability sampling.] The fundamental requirement of probability sampling is that the final determination of just which persons are to be polled must be left to chance. Because this procedure is in conformity with statistical laws, it is possible to calculate precisely the probability that the margin of error in any sample will not exceed a given amount.

A method based on these principles is known as the "area" sample. The basic principle of this method is that each person in the population is given an equal, or known, chance to come into the sample. This is done by associating each person with one, and only one, very small geographic area and then selecting a random sample of the small geographic areas into which the country is thus divided.

The first step is to make a purely random selection of counties and metropolitan areas. Then within each of these areas a subsample of small geographic segments is selected, again by random methods. The final sample may include all the dwellings in each selected segment, or every kth dwelling, depending on the size of sample desired. The selection of persons actually interviewed in each dwelling will then depend on the purpose of the survey; if its purpose is to predict an election, the sample will consist of all the eligible voters in the designated dwellings or certain voters selected at random.

When this method is used, the interviewer has no choice whatever. He goes to the specified dwelling and interviews the specified person or persons. If a respondent is not at home he calls again and again until he gets the interview; if he finds it impossible to do so, he reports that fact to headquarters.

Results The representative character of the samples obtained by the area sampling method has been amply proved in practice. The Survey Research Center at Michigan has compared the composition of small nationwide samples (of only 500 to 3,500 persons) with the U.S. Census figures for the nation as a whole, and has found that samples obtained by the area sampling method reflect rather accurately the composition of the national population. In an analysis based upon an area sample of only 1,151 persons, the following results were obtained:

In the Survey Research Center sample, 91 percent of the persons interviewed were white; the census figure for the percentage of white persons in the whole population was 90.6.

In the sample 23 percent turned out to be in the age group 21 to 29; the census figure for the same group was 22.8 percent. In other age groups the correspondence was equally or almost equally close.

In the results on schooling, the proportion who had gone no farther than grade school was 44 percent in this survey and 46.1 percent in the census; those who had finished high school were 23 percent of the sample, 22.9 percent in the census; those who had finished college, 5 percent of the sample, 5 percent in the census.

The chief disadvantage of the area sample method is that it is more expensive. It costs more to design the sample and it costs much more for interviewers to take time to locate each respondent.

Turnout The prediction of elections involves a knotty problem which often is neglected. This is the "turnout problem"—predicting who will vote. To predict an election it is not sufficient to know what candidates are favored; it is necessary to know what candidates are favored by those persons who will actually go to the polls. This means that the pollster must know which voters are most likely to vote and which are most likely to stay home. Unfortunately, the pollsters have made few attempts to develop questions to measure the intensity of the determination to vote, and the results consequently have a large possible error.

After the 1948 election, Gallup is reported to have stated that his polls indicated a relatively small turnout, but that he did not mention this factor of uncertainty because his newspaper clients would have accused him of "hedging." As a rule, the larger the turnout the greater the Democratic vote, but this rule may not have applied. In any case, it appears likely that the "undecided" vote and the size and character of the turnout played a large part in the miscalculations of the pollsters. Had they obtained more data on these factors and analyzed them adequately, their predictions might have been less positive and less wrong.

INTERVIEWING

Questions The measurement of opinion on social, economic,

and international issues, and of public knowledge about these issues is more difficult, as a rule, than the prediction of elections. The problems in this field of polling are still so serious that opinion-poll results should be taken with even greater caution than predictions about elections.

Perhaps the greatest of these problems is that of meaning. Most of the issues of the day involve words and concepts that have different meanings for different people. On some issues large sections of the population may have no understanding of the major dimensions of the issue or the terms used. To understand the meaning of the percentages obtained in a poll, it is essential to know what respondents meant when they answered each question. Unfortunately, such data are not available. Yet polling results are often presented and discussed with the implicit assumption that each respondent understood the question and answered it from precisely the same point of view as that of the person conducting the poll.

An indication of the inadequacy of the usual polling questions can be obtained by asking a very small sample of respondents a question taken from any poll on a complex current problem and permitting these respondents to answer in their own words and to elaborate their answers. Several tests of polling questions have been made in this fashion. Quite consistently evidence has been obtained that questions on complex issues have different meanings for different people who are called upon to answer them.

Richard L. Crutchfield and Donald A. Gordon while at

Swarthmore College ran a test on the following Gallup Poll question which appeared in news releases of August 22, 1943:

"After the war, would you like to see many changes or reforms made in the United States, or would you rather have the country remain pretty much the way it was before the war?"

To test interpretations of this question, the investigators interviewed a cross-section sample of 114 New York City residents. After recording the respondent's initial reaction to the question, "the interviewer then encouraged the respondent to enlarge upon his answer in an informal conversational manner." The interviewers found that the initial response of their New York respondents gave substantially the same results as those obtained by Gallup for the country as a whole. But they also found that their respondents had seven different frames of reference in mind when answering the question. Some persons thought the question referred to "domestic changes or reforms"; others "technological changes"; others changes in the "basic political-economic structure of the U.S."; and still others thought it referred to changes in "foreign affairs of the U.S."

Respondents also had quite dif-

ferent meanings in mind when they answered "change" or "remain the same." For example, among those who answered in terms of "domestic changes and reforms" the word "change" for some persons meant shifts in a more liberal direction, such as "increases in social security," "higher pay levels," and "greater social equality for members of minority groups." Other persons meant a shift in the conservative direction, such as "change to a Republican administration," "less government control of business," and "more control of labor unions." Similarly, some of those who answered "remain the same" had in mind conservative aspects of our economy; others giving the same answer referred to liberal aspects, such as "maintaining high wages." It is obviously impossible to interpret percentages which combine into single totals answers which have such widely different meanings.

This study of what the respondents really meant by their answers substantially altered the interpretation of the poll. Thus, in their first answers, 49 percent of the New York City respondents said they wanted the country to "remain the same," and 46 percent voted for "changes or reforms." But further questioning of

those who were thinking in terms of domestic changes showed that 60 percent wanted "changes or reforms," and 40 percent favored "remain the same"—a direct reversal of the results with respect to this phase of the question. Most of those who thought the question meant technological change favored such change, while those who thought it referred to the basic political-economic structure of the U.S. did not want change.

The future of the polls The public opinion poll is only one area of application of a far more important instrument: the *sample interview survey,* one of the research tools of the social sciences. It is being used increasingly to study such widely different problems as the behavior of consumers, the distribution of income, principles of organization and management, religious behavior, the factors affecting political behavior, the production plans of farmers, and the processes of propaganda. Either alone or in combination with experimental methods, this tool enables the social sciences to deal with their problems quantitatively and on a large scale.

SECTION 4 SOCIAL MOVEMENTS AND SOCIAL CHANGE

The fluid conditions of a rapidly changing society are conducive to collective behavior. Active protests sometimes leading to violence occur when rising

aspirations are not met by speedy and visible fulfillment. Religious sects emerge when established churches fail to respond to the needs of new life situations. Swift alternations of war and peace bring widespread shifts in public opinion. Collective behavior *reflects* underlying changes, and in responding to them it *creates* new perspectives, new lines of action, and new institutions.

PERSPECTIVES AND DOCTRINES

A perspective is a complex pattern of attitudes, values, and perceptions that together make up an ordered view of the world. It includes what one sees as foreground and as background, a hierarchy of values, and specific conceptions about persons, groups, and oneself. People in similar situations tend to have *shared perspectives:* they see the world alike and have the same assessments of what is good, what is likely, and what is possible. When circumstances change, a period of uncertainty and exploratory behavior occurs until a new perspective or "definition of the situation" is adopted that seems to fit the world, as it is experienced by people in like circumstances.

In the study of social change, nothing is more fundamental than an understanding of altered perspectives. Every epoch has its distinctive evaluations of the role of the individual and the meaning of history. The nineteenth century was a period of great industrial expansion and self-confidence. Ideas that stressed the power of the individual and hailed change as progress were widely held. The twentieth century is typically an age of wars and revolutions, of pessimism and anxiety, and the idea of progress is questioned, although the development of vast resources and the expansion of productivity have raised hopes of a better life. These changes in perspective have, for better or worse, made possible and perhaps inevitable many of the movements and institutions that characterize the times, such as collectivism, bureaucratization, and increased state control.

Two types of perspectives are often associated with fundamental historical change.

1. *Perspectives affecting group identity.* Perhaps the most potent force in history is the sense of common belonging felt by many people. New perspectives may lead to the alteration of established group-ings. Citizens may think of their national interests in terms of local or linguistic factions, or color or racial identities.

2. *Perspectives that initiate change.* In the perspectives of rulers and merchants, the geographical position of England in the fifteenth and sixteenth centuries shifted from the perimeter to the center of the maritime world. The result was an epoch of trade and conquest that has only recently run its course. Religious and political ideas have also broadened perspectives and sent men out as missionaries, colonists, and warriors. Before the Pilgrims could come to New England, ordinary men had to transform their conceptions of what the world was like and what kinds of action made sense.

Perspectives of Negroes The increasing militancy of Negroes that has characterized the past decade supports the principle that protest is most likely to be expressed when there is hope and some sign of progress achieved. The absolute status of many Negroes has improved in some respects in the recent past, although it is by no means evident that their status relative to whites has improved.

Table VIII:3 shows the percentage of whites and Negroes who reported themselves satisfied on four topics in 1963–1965 and at the end of 1966. The

TABLE VIII:3 PERCENT REPORTING SATISFIED IN RESPONSE TO THE QUESTION:

"On the whole are you satisfied or dissatisfied with the work you do . . . etc.?"

	WHITES		NEGROES	
	1963–65	*1966*	*1963–65*	*1966*
Work	88	87	51	69
Children's education	73	76	43	64
Housing	76	77	36	51
Family income	68	67	34	45

SOURCE: Gallup Political *Index, 18* (November–December, 1966), 14.

percent of whites reporting satisfaction was stable, but the percent of Negroes satisfied increased for each sphere of concern. Apparently more Negroes were satisfied with their lot in late 1966 than a short time earlier.[30] Despite that fact, the percent satisfied was far smaller than for whites, and the percent dissatisfied far larger than for whites on all topics. In 1966 Negroes reported themselves dissatisfied as follows: with work 18 percent, with children's education 23 percent, with housing 44 percent, with family income 49 percent.[31] The more militant perspective of Negroes has much dissatisfaction—and realistically grounded dissatisfaction—to feed upon despite the improvement in their satisfaction index. (See SOCIAL STRATIFICATION, p. 163.)

Ideologies When self-conceptions and world views change, people grope uncertainly for some way of expressing their new understandings and hopes. The time is ripe for *ideologies,* doctrines that purport to formulate the distinctive perspectives of social groups.[32] These ideologies profess to be "true" not only in upholding certain values but in giving a correct picture of what the world is really like. Some go far in attempting to provide detailed formulations of group perspectives. In an epoch of change, ideologues are active, proposing many different systems of belief for groups to adopt. Only a few ever gain wide acceptance because to be effective the beliefs must fit the shared perspectives of many people and must make sense in terms of their historical experience.

The twentieth century has seen a waning of individualism and a development of collectivist ideologies, doctrines that stress the importance of social cohesion and planning. There are many variations and vital differences among these doctrines. Socialist and "welfare" states retain political freedom while Communism and Fascism have instituted unparalleled tyrannies. Despite these differences, collectivist ideologies are alike in calling for increased social control, a strong and active government, and more social responsibility, solidarity, and community. These ideologies have gained wide acceptance because they are in some way consistent with the understandings and aspirations of millions. It is probable that proposed alternatives to Communism and Fascism must likewise be consistent with underlying perspectives if they are not to fall on deaf ears.

SOCIAL MOVEMENTS

For the most part, social change occurs gradually and without design. However, new perspectives and aspirations often generate collective action to combat presumed evils and to institute new ways of life. Sometimes the action is sporadic and temporary, as in the case of isolated uprisings against oppressive conditions. Collective action is called a social movement when it is unified, lasting, and has the following main features:

1. *A distinctive perspective and ideology.* The women's suffrage movement arose out of redefined perspectives regarding the place of women, and these were formulated in a doctrine that was widely accepted. The ideology of a movement provides direction and self-justification; it offers weapons of attack and defense; and it holds out inspiration and hope.[33] Social movements place great emphasis on ideology, particularly when other sources of orientation and cohesion are lacking.

[30] For results from the Harris Poll, compare William Brink and Louis Harris, *Black and White* (New York: Simon and Schuster, 1967), Chap. 2, esp. p. 27.

[31] Gallup Political *Index, 18* (November–December, 1966), 14.

[32] "Ideology" is sometimes defined as a pattern of ideas that justifies and helps preserve a social system. This defensive and justifying function usually follows if a doctrine successfully formulates a group perspective. Even if an ideology includes reformist or revolutionary ideas, it is usually self-justifying from the standpoint of the group that accepts it. On the other hand, an ideology usually has other characteristics and consequences. For the more restricted view, see Karl Mannheim, *Ideology and Utopia* (New York: Harcourt, Brace & World, 1936); and on the general topic of the "sociology of knowledge," see R. K. Merton, *Social Theory and Social Structure* (Glencoe: The Free Press, 1957), Chap. XII.

[33] See Herbert Blumer, "Social Movements," in A. M. Lee (ed.), *New Outline of the Principles of Sociology* (New York: Barnes & Noble, 1951), pp. 210–211.

2. *A strong sense of solidarity and idealism.* Membership in a "movement" typically means more to the individual than other affiliations. He is a "dedicated" man and feels part of an idealistic and active enterprise. Especially in the early stages, idealism plays a role in all movements, political or religious, "progressive" or "reactionary."

3. *An orientation toward action.* The very word "movement" suggests unconventional methods of appeal, such as street meetings and the sale of propaganda tracts. Small movements can sometimes gain wide attention by dramatic actions, particularly if they involve violence. The stress on action in part reflects the problem of maintaining interest and solidarity. There is a constant need to "give the members something to do" to keep them from slipping away to other interests and involvements.

A movement is usually made up of *a variety of forms and groupings.* For example, the prohibition movement included the Anti-Saloon League, the Prohibition party, the Women's Christian Temperance Union, and many church groups. The socialist movement in England has included a number of different political parties, trade unions, newspapers, and groups of intellectuals such as the Fabian Society. This tends to give a movement a somewhat amorphous character, because there is usually no official leadership for the movement as a whole, and there is often much discussion about what constitutes the boundaries of the movement.

Civil rights movement A diversity of organizations, ideologies, and strategies is exemplified by the civil rights movement. Each organization tends to adopt a distinctive mission and role and to some extent a distinctive appeal to its constituency.[34] The National Association for the Advancement of Colored People (NAACP) has concentrated on legal change and has succeeded in winning court cases vindicating Negro rights under the U.S. Constitution. The National Urban League has defined its mission as enlarging job opportunities, and its charac-

teristic method is negotiation with businesses and business associations. The Southern Christian Leadership Conference (SCLC), headed by Reverend Martin Luther King, Jr., the Congress of Racial Equality (CORE), and the Student Nonviolent Coordinating Committee (SNCC) have organized direct action such as freedom rides, sit-ins, demonstrations, and marches. The Black Muslims, on the margin of the movement, have fostered self-improvement, Negro isolation, and the rejection of white society. As the movement has grown and passed through a series of crises, the several organizations have maintained a sometimes uneasy collaboration. To some extent the moderates depend on the radicals, whose "threats" to the white community give the moderates some leverage but also risk embarrassing the movement and alienating white support.

The goals and strategies of the civil rights movement have been strained between the polar orientations of isolation and integration. Integration with white society remains the dominant long-run goal, but many members and leaders of the movement regard "Black Power" as an essential short-run condition. As is true of many social movements, there is continuing tension between militant self-assertion and gradualism. The militants seek immediate political gain but make demands that can be fulfilled only over the long run. The gradualists strive for short-run piecemeal gains as the means to further strength and achievement. The outcome of this conflict over the "soul" of the movement depends on the experience and the changing perspectives of large numbers of Negroes who are not directly involved in civil rights organizations. Meanwhile elements in the activist wing, exemplified by the leadership of the SNCC, tend toward more radical strategies and appeals. Consequently there is an increasing possibility of a fundamental cleavage in the movement.

A social movement tends to follow a roughly discernible "career," from its origins in unrest to its end in institutionalization. (See Adaptation 26, pp. 327–333.)

---

[34] See August Meier and Elliott M. Rudwick, *From Plantation to Ghetto* (New York: Hill and Wang, 1966), Chap. 7, and William Brink and Louis Harris, *Black and White* (New York: Simon and Schuster, 1967).

CHAPTER IX
POPULATION AND ECOLOGY

SECTION 1 INTRODUCTION

The study of population is an important source of knowledge about society. "A population" is the total number of human beings in a society or community. They may be counted and classified by age, sex, occupation, or any other useful criterion. Such data are then analyzed to measure major social trends and to explore the underlying causes and significance of population facts, such as a declining birth rate, a preponderance of males, or a dearth of individuals in their productive years.

The technical study of human populations (*demography,* from the Greek *demos* meaning "*people*") largely depends on the collection of statistics either from official records like birth, death, and marriage registrations or from periodic censuses. As records and censuses become more rigorous and detailed, demographers are able to take into account a larger number of population characteristics and to examine more fully the interrelations of the various factors.

Since much knowledge about population must be interpreted by reference to sociological or economic factors, demography is closely related to sociology and economics; most courses on population in universities are given in sociology departments. The field of public health also makes use of demographic data and contributes to population analysis.

The techniques of population analysis and ecology are essential adjuncts to sociological research, especially to the study of large-scale social phenomena and major trends related to size, composition, concentration, and shifts of population. Knowledge of population composition and distribution is necessary in designing samples for social surveys and in determining how far the findings from such surveys can be generalized to the whole population.

An understanding of population phenomena offers clues to underlying forces in the society that would be difficult or impossible to perceive by compiling opinions of people or studying their life histories. For example, one of the most serious problems confronting man is the pressure of uncontrolled growth being experienced by most of the world except Western Europe and North America. The populations of

Thomas Malthus (1766–1834)

Modern work in population began with Thomas Malthus,[1] whose "Essay on the Principle of Population, etc." was first published in 1798. Malthus posed the problem of the unchecked growth of human population versus the slower growth of the means of subsistence. He held that population tends to increase up to the limit of the food supply, thus preventing any considerable rise in the standard of living.

In later editions of his work, he brought together empirical data and developed the idea of positive checks *that keep population growth from approaching a geometric ratio. The positive checks are: (1) hunger, (2) disease, (3) war, and (4) vice. He also* recognized *preventive checks which might depress the birth rate: (1) deferred marriage and (2) celibacy. He regarded the use of contraception as a "vice," which permitted men to escape the consequences of intercourse.*

developing countries are increasing with great rapidity and will continue to grow for some time. The consequent pressure on resources, on the means of production, and on land use will have profound effects on the organization of their societies and on relations among nations.

The problem of population pressure is not, however, a matter of arithmetic on one hand and of birth control technology on the other. As will be seen on pages 283–285, the future population of the world will be determined by such distinctively social considerations as the following: the willingness of people to reevaluate deeply engrained attitudes toward family size, toward preferred age at marriage, and toward interfering with biological processes.

Social or human ecology is closely related to population analysis. Population increase can be viewed as a problem in ecology in that it involves a change in the relation between mankind and natural resources and increasing competition for limited land.

The numerous blanks and question marks about the populations of many underdeveloped countries impede their progress and planning and impair the comparative analysis of international trends. No modern state can develop wise, long-term plans for the training and effective use of its human resources without the sort of knowledge compiled by sophisticated census taking. The most important single source of information on population is the census, periodically conducted in many countries. Adaptation 24 (pp. 261 ff.) briefly reviews the history and operations of the United States Census, which has become a continuing, year-round activity as well as a population count conducted each decade.

The addition of the new states of Alaska and Hawaii creates some minor reporting problems to which the reader should be alert. Many earlier statistical series are for continental United States except Alaska. Although the populations of Alaska and Hawaii combined make up less than half of one percent of the national total, they include 30 percent of all nonwhites other than Negroes. Precision dictates that a distinction be made between the 50 states taken as a whole and the continental states, excluding

---

[1] See D. V. Glass (ed.), *Introduction to Malthus* (London: Watts and Company, 1953).

Alaska. When the latter is intended, the term *conterminous* is used in Census reports and in this book. Otherwise, the designation "United States" refers to the country as it existed at the time indicated in the discussion. The same caution applies in comparing any time series during which there was change in the geographic areas being covered.

Section 2 of this chapter discusses some of the main characteristics of population and some of the elementary techniques used to present and interpret data about population composition.

Section 3 discusses the measures of fertility and mortality, trends in birth and death rates, a comparison of differences in these rates in various parts of the world, and the prospects for longevity.

Section 4 reviews in broad perspective the sweeping changes in population growth in the Western world as well as in less developed areas, and summarizes information about migration.

Section 5 introduces human or social ecology, the study of the relation of populations to their environment, both animate and inanimate, and to each other. Such relations are frequently expressed in terms of spatial distribution.

SOURCES AND READINGS

See pages 292–293 for readings in ecology.

See page 265 for the chief guides for using United States Census information and other official sources.

Texts

Paul H. Landis and Paul K. Hatt, *Population Problems* (2nd ed.; New York: American Book, 1954).

William Petersen, *Population* (New York: Macmillan, 1961).

Ralph Thomlinson, *Population Dynamics* (New York: Random House, 1965).

Warren S. Thompson and David T. Lewis, *Population Problems* (5th ed.; New York: McGraw-Hill, 1965).

Dennis H. Wrong, *Population* (Rev. ed.; New York: Random House, 1962).

Symposia and reference works

Donald J. Bogue, *The Population of the United States* (Glencoe: The Free Press, 1959).

Kingsley Davis (ed.), "A Crowding Hemisphere: Population Change in the Americas," *Annals* of the American Academy of Political and Social Science, *316* (March, 1958).

Ronald Freedman (ed.), *Population: The Vital Revolution* (Garden City, N.Y.: [Anchor] Doubleday, 1964).

D. V. Glass and D. C. Eversley, *Population in History* (London: Arnold, 1965).

Paul K. Hatt (ed.), *World Population and Future Resources* (New York: American Book, 1952).

Philip M. Hauser and Otis Dudley Duncan (eds.), *The Study of Population* (Chicago: University of Chicago Press, 1959).

Joseph J. Spengler and Otis Dudley Duncan (eds.), *Population Theory and Policy* (Glencoe: The Free Press, 1956).

Periodicals

Demography, published by the Population Association of America.

Population Index (formerly *Population Literature*), a periodical chiefly devoted to an annotated bibliography.

The Milbank Memorial Fund Quarterly

Statistical Bulletin, issued monthly by the Metropolitan Life Insurance Company.

Demographic Yearbook of the United Nations continues the *International Statistical Yearbook* published under the auspices of the League of Nations from 1927–1945. The U.N. has also assumed publication of the *Monthly Bulletin of Statistics,* formerly put out by the League.

Adaptation 24 / THE UNITED STATES CENSUS

Background The United States was the first modern nation to make a legal provision for regular census taking. A census is called for in the apportionment clause, Article I, Section 2, of the *Constitution,* which reads in part as follows:

Representatives and direct Taxes shall be apportioned among the several States . . . according to their respective Numbers, which shall be determined by adding to the whole Number of free Persons, including those bound to Service for a Term of Years, and excluding Indians not taxed, three-fifths of all other Persons. The actual Enumeration shall be made within three Years after the first Meeting of the Congress of the United States, and within every subsequent Term of ten Years. . . .

The scope of the First Census in 1790, although limited to population, was somewhat greater than that required by the *Constitution.* The name of the head of each family was recorded and the total number of persons in the family, classified as free or slave. Free persons were further classified as white or other, free whites as male or female, and free white males as over or under sixteen years of age. (See Table IX:1 Growth of the Decennial Census.) Slaves were "other Persons" in the *Constitution,* and 60 percent of their number counted in the apportionment.

The First Census was taken under the supervision of the 17 United States marshals, and the actual work of enumeration was per-

formed by about 650 marshals' assistants. The enumeration began in August, 1790, and according to law should have been completed in nine months, but double the time elapsed before the returns were all in. The returns were made by the marshals directly to the President, and he turned them over to the Secretary of State, who transmitted them to the printer. No clerical force was employed for compilation, verification, or correction, and the results were printed without the explanatory text, percentages, and detailed analyses that now accompany census statistics. The report of the First Census is contained in a pamphlet of 56 pages.

Not until the 5th Census (1830) were printed schedules used. Before that the marshals' assistants had used such paper as they happened to have, ruling it, writing in the headings, and binding the sheets together themselves. Before 1850 the family was the unit of enumeration. Because of varying family composition, it was an unwieldy unit and impeded analysis and interpretation. Beginning with the 7th Census, a number of important improvements were made. The individual became the unit of enumeration, and additional data such as age, sex, race, and occupation were reported. The change of unit greatly increased the analytic usefulness of the census by improving the accuracy of enumeration, by permitting detailed tabulations of the additional data, and by fa-

cilitating cross-tabulations. The 9th Census (1870) made the first use of machine tabulation. Another innovation was the use of maps, charts, and diagrams to present graphically the more significant facts. These were published in a separate volume called *The Statistical Atlas of the United States.*

In 1880 field operations were reorganized. Specially qualified supervisors were appointed, and they were able to give closer supervision to the work of enumeration.

The number and types of inquiries were greatly increased in the censuses of 1880 and 1890 and resulted in reports on a wide variety of subjects, but in spite of new techniques of more rapid enumeration and tabulation, publication was delayed. Two things became apparent. First, the decennial census had become burdened with fields of investigation that might better be subjects of continuous inquiry throughout the decade. Second, the process of building a completely new temporary organization for each census was no longer economical of time or money and a permanent organization was needed.

In recognition of the first problem, the 1900 decennial census was limited to four subjects: population, manufactures, agriculture, and mortality. In 1902 the Bureau of the Census was established as a permanent agency, known as the Census Office.

The 1960 Census introduced further innovations: it gathered

SCHEDULE *of the whole Number of* PERSONS *within the several Districts of the* UNITED STATES, *taken according to* "An Act providing for the Enumeration of the Inhabitants of the United States;" *passed March the 1st,* 1790.

DISTRICTS.	Free white Males of sixteen years and upwards, including heads of families.	Free white Males under sixteen years.	Free white Females including heads of families.	All other free persons.	Slaves.	Total.
* Vermont	22,135	22,328	40,505	255	16	85,539
New-Hampshire	36,086	34,851	70,160	630	158	141,885
{ Maine	24,384	24,748	46,870	538	NONE	96,540 }
{ Massachusetts	95,453	87,289	190,582	5,463	NONE	378,787 }
Rhode-Island	16,019	15,799	32,652	3,407	948	68,825
Connecticut	60,523	54,403	117,448	2,808	2,764	237,946
New-York	83,700	78,122	152,320	4,654	21,324	340,120
New-Jersey	45,251	41,416	83,287	2,762	11,423	184,139
Pennsylvania	110,788	106,948	206,363	6,537	3,787	434,373
Delaware	11,783	12,143	22,384	3,899	8,887	59,094
Maryland	55,915	51,339	101,395	8,043	103,036	319,728
{ Virginia	110,936	116,135	215,046	12,866	292,627	747,610 }
{ Kentucky	15,154	17,057	28,922	114	12,430	73,677 }
North-Carolina	69,988	77,506	140,710	4,975	100,572	393,751
South-Carolina	-	-	-	-	-	-
Georgia	13,103	14,044	25,739	398	29,264	82,548

	Free white Males of twenty-one years and upwards, including heads of families.	Free Males under twenty-one years of age.	Free white Females, including heads of families.	All other Persons.	Slaves.	Total.
S. Western Territory	6,271	10,277	15,365	361	3,417	35,691
N. Do.	-	-	-	-	-	-

Truly stated from the original Returns deposited in the Office of the Secretary of State.

TH: JEFFERSON.

October 24, 1791.

* This return was not signed by the marshal, but was enclosed and referred to in a letter written and signed by him.

In 1960, the information was entered on a schedule designed for FOSDIC (Film Optical Sensing Device for Input to Computers). FOSDIC scanned microfilm of completed schedules and from the position of marks on the schedules converted the information into magnetic impressions on tape. The tape was then processed by electronic computers. The use of FOSDIC eliminated the card-punching operation, and, thus, one important source of clerical error. The enormous capacity of the electronic computer made it possible to do much more uniform editing and coding than in earlier censuses and to ensure consistency among a large number of interrelated items.

Accuracy The management of the census must consider basic social attitudes as well as the improvement of such techniques as enumeration, computing, and tabulating. Essentially a vast reporting procedure, the census can be only as accurate as its reporters and respondents. Many countries have difficulty in conducting censuses because the people mistrust the intentions of the government and elude the enumerator or give him incomplete and faulty information. Although some people in the United States mistrust the census and regard it as an invasion of privacy, it has been remarkably free of this kind of impediment. This fact probably reflects a degree of confidence in the good intentions of the government and some awareness of the uses to which census findings can be put.

On the other hand, the American competitive spirit has occasionally affected not only the interpretation of census statistics but

more information on a sample basis than in previous years; for the first time it asked householders to fill out questionnaires instead of only responding to enumerators' questions; and it made extensive use of high-speed, electronic data-processing equipment. The census has been a leader in experimentation with statistical processing.

also their actual gathering. *The Story of the Census* reports:

Dishonest enumerators may sometimes yield to the temptation to increase their pay (which in most cases is based on the number of names turned in by them) by returning fictitious names. But the "padding" of returns from motives of personal gain has been a less serious obstacle to accurate census taking than . . . organized attempts on the part of certain cities and towns to inflate their population figures. The voice of local business interests—disguised as that of local patriotism—has sometimes called more loudly to the supervisor or the enumerator than has the voice of honor, duty, or fidelity to oath of office. After the census of 1910, 69 indictments were brought against enumerators and others believed to be responsible for the falsity of the returns in 14 cities and towns.

In 1960 some cities with aspirations to be as large as possible questioned the accuracy of census figures. The census reported in many areas that a central city had not grown very much or had even declined in population, an expected fact in view of the movement to the suburbs. This news was received with angry protests from municipal officials and local patriots and some cities incurred considerable expenses to check on the accuracy of published figures. Sociologists had predicted the census finding of slow growth or decline in many central cities as well as the civic indignation that would follow publication of the findings.

Checking census accuracy   To

check on the accuracy of the census a number of techniques are used.[2] For instance, birth and death statistics for the period between censuses are examined, and an estimate of "expected" population is made. This is done for the country as a whole and for regions and cities. Then the actual count is compared with the "expected" population. Where a significant difference exists, close analysis is made for possible error.

Toward the end of the enumeration period in 1960 many newspapers published "Were You Counted?" forms, which contained the questions asked of 100 percent of the population. The reader was urged to fill in the form and send it to the Census District Office if he

[2] This discussion is based on *U.S. Census of Population 1950,* Vol. 11, *Characteristics of the Population,* Part 1, U.S. Summary, Chapter C, 1953, pp. xxviii–xxxi.

TABLE IX:1   GROWTH OF THE DECENNIAL CENSUS: 1790–1960

CENSUS YEAR	NUMBER OF ENUMERATORS:	LENGTH OF ENUMERATION (*months*)	COST PER CAPITA	POPULATION ENUMERATED CONTERMINOUS U.S. (*in thousands*)
1790	650	18.0	$0.011	3,929
1810	1,100	10.0	0.024	7,239
1830	1,519	14.0	0.029	12,866
1850	3,231	20.5	0.061	23,191
1870	6,530	15.0	0.087	38,558
1890	46,804	1.0	0.183	62,947
1910	70,286	1.0 [a]	0.173	91,972
1930	87,756	1.0	0.321	122,775
1950	151,814	1.0	0.601	150,697
1960	159,321	3.8 [b]	0.60 (est.)	178,464

SOURCE: Based in part on *Bureau of the Census, Factfinder for the Nation, 1948; The Story of the Census, 1790–1916; U.S. Census of Population and Housing, 1960, Principal Data-Collection Forms and Procedures* (1961); and other publications of the Bureau, Washington, D.C.

[a] Not including time spent in making investigations and recounts in places where fraudulent enumeration had been detected.

[b] Enumeration was 99 percent complete in six weeks.

believed that he or members of his household had been missed in the enumeration.

In 1950 and 1960 Post-Enumeration Surveys [3] were performed by specially trained and supervised enumerators. The sample recounts found that many people had been erroneously enumerated or omitted from enumeration. The techniques of such surveys are far too costly to be used for the whole Census, but they provide a check on its methods and accuracy. Estimates of enumeration errors expressed as percents of the Census enumerated population are as follows:

Enumeration errors	1960	1950
Omissions	3.0%	2.3%
Inclusions	1.3%	0.9%
Net undercount	1.7%	1.4%

The percentages seem small, but the 1.7 percent undercount in 1960 represents about three million people, and the 1.4 percent in 1950 about two million. It might appear from the figures that the 1950 Census was more accurate than the 1960 Census, but this is probably not the case. Rather, the 1950 Post-Enumeration Survey and the methods of analysis associated with it were less precise than the survey conducted in 1960.

Probably all censuses undercount the population. The sociological usefulness of the census is somewhat impaired by this fact, but even more by the fact that different parts of the population are counted more accurately than others. The very young, old, mobile, and poor are most likely to be underenumerated.

Sampling in the Census It would be impossible for the Bureau to gather the amount of data that it does during the regular decennial census or to conduct current surveys (see p. 265) if it did not use sampling techniques. Much population information for 1950 and 1960 is based on samples—20 percent for 1950 and 25 percent for 1960—which are so identified in the census reports.

Estimates of the total number of persons with specified characteristics are obtained by multiplying by five the number of persons with these characteristics in the 20 percent sample; by four the number in the 25 percent sample. This procedure of deriving overall figures from sample figures is a matter of probability. For example, the 1950 Census shows that 17.6 percent of males twenty-five years and over *in a 20 percent sample* had completed four years of high school. On the basis of this sample, the Census reports that 7,500,000 or 17.6 percent of all males *in the total population* twenty-five years and over have completed high school, but it does not mean that the national figure is exactly 7,500,-000. On the contrary, the figure is used with the following understanding: The chances are approximately two out of three that the figure for the total population lies between 7,500,000 plus 5,440 and 7,500,000 minus 5,440. (The degree of probability and the range of accuracy claimed are derived from the mathematics of statistics.) The figure 7,500,000 falls at the midpoint of a fairly narrow range within which the actual figure probably lies.

You might argue that two out of three chances are not very good odds. One chance out of three remains that the actual figure lies outside the 7,500,000 ± 5,440 range. It is easy to increase the chances of accuracy. If you are willing to take as a reasonably accurate figure a total of 7,500,-000 ± 13,600, then the chances increase to *one hundred to one* that the actual figure for the total population lies between 7,500,000 plus 13,600 and 7,500,000 minus 13,-600.

In one sense total census figures based on sampling, like all such figures, are never precise. They are presented and must be used with the understanding that the actual figures are probably close to the computed figures. In another sense, however, they are very precise, because once the acceptable range of accuracy is specified, the degree of probability that it has been attained (e.g., odds of 2-1 or 100-1) can also be specified. Suppose a publisher is interested in estimating the potential market for a book on carpentry designed to be read by men of at least high school education. He would doubtless be pleased to know that the chances are as high as one hundred to one that his potential market lies between 7,513,600 and 7,486,400. In fact, he should be satisfied to know that the chances are two out of three that his potential market lies

---

[3] See Conrad Taeuber and Morris H. Hansen, "A Preliminary Evaluation of the 1960 Census of Population and Housing," *Demography, 1* (1964), 1–14. Tabular data at p. 4. See also U.S. Bureau of the Census Technical Paper No. 4, "The Post-Enumeration Survey: 1950," 1960.

between 7,505,440 and 7,494,560.

Although sample statistics for the U.S. as a whole may be accepted as approximating very closely the results that would have been obtained from a complete enumeration of the population, this is not true of smaller populations. In general the smaller the sample and/or the smaller the total population, the less reliable are the results of a sample.

Census sources

Guides for using the United States Census cover both decennial census publications and the results of other census surveys:

1. *Catalog and Subject Guide,* issued quarterly, cumulative since January, 1946.

2. *Catalog* of U.S. Census Publications, 1790–1945, U.S. Bureau of the Census, Washington, 1950.

The divisions of the *Catalogs* follow the organization of the Bureau of the Census:

1) *Agriculture,* first taken in 1840, quinquennial since 1920.

2) *Business,* first complete census taken in 1929, subsequently in 1933, 1935, 1939, 1948, and became quinquennial in 1954.

3) *Foreign trade.*

4) *Governments,* reports on finance and employment on state and local levels.

5) *Industrial,* prepares "Facts for Industry" series, annual surveys of manufactures since 1949; Census of Manufacturing first taken in 1810, subsequently at varying intervals, now quinquennial.

6) *Population and Housing,* the categories most frequently used by sociologists. See also U.S. Census of Population: 1960, *Availability of Published and Unpublished Data.*

Summary sources

Statistical Abstract of the United States, an annual summary of statistics on population, industry, and social, political, and economic characteristics. Convenient source book available from the U.S. Government Printing Office.

Historical Statistics of the United States (Colonial Times to 1957) should be used in conjunction with the *Statistical Abstract.* Contains a compilation of about 3,000 statistical time series. An excellent reference guide as well as a direct source of data.

Current Population Reports—In addition to the decennial census, the Bureau conducts periodically the Current Population Survey, covering a sample of about 35,000 households throughout the country.

Frequent publication of the findings from the Survey and from special censuses afford an almost continuous record of the population of the United States between decennial censuses. Current Population Survey procedures are treated in Census Bureau Technical Paper No. 7, *The Current Population Survey— A Report on Methodology,* which summarizes study design and operations up to 1963.

Other United States government sources

Monthly Labor Review, Department of Labor, Bureau of Labor Statistics, gives characteristics of the labor force. Covers some subjects formerly published by the Bureau of the Census.

Indicators (monthly), Department of Health, Education, and Welfare, summarizes vital statistics, morbidity and accident rates, and various data concerning health, education, and welfare. A good multipurpose first reference.

Trends, annual supplement to *Indicators.*

National Health Survey, Series A (Program descriptions, survey designs, concepts and definitions), Series B (Health Interview Survey results by topics), Series C (Health Interview Survey results for population groups), and Series D (Developmental and Evaluation Reports).

Monthly Vital Statistics Report, National Center for Health Statistics, reports deaths, births, and marriages.

Vital Statistics of the United States, Annual Report gives detailed breakdown of vital statistics for the year by states and smaller areas and by such characteristics as sex, age, race, etc.

Vital Statistics—Special Reports. Topic and frequency of issue vary.

In 1963 publications of Health Survey Statistics and Special Vital Statistics were revised. A new set of series, *Vital and Health Statistics,* was initiated encompassing program reports, research methods, health survey and vital statistics (supplementary to annual and monthly *Vital Statistics* reports).

Immigration and Naturalization *Reporter;* also *Annual Reports* of the Immigration and Naturalization Service.

SECTION 2 COMPOSITION

Composition refers to the characteristics of a population according to significant biological or social categories, such as race, nativity, religion, sex, age, occupation, education, and urbanization. Population figures may be presented in different ways to answer the needs of government, science, and industry. For example, the number unemployed, the numbers at specified income levels, and the number with specialized higher education provide indices of important social phenomena. The proportion of unemployed is often used as an index of the health of the economy; changes in income levels may be a sign of emergent stratification patterns; the rate of growth of the population trained in engineering may indicate whether or not educational institutions are keeping pace with the needs of an expanding technology.

A description of composition is a cross-sectional view of population at a given time, but no population is ever truly stable. To interpret composition data one must: (1) compare different populations, or (2) study a series of cross sections, that is, study the trends and changes in the same population.

A crude summary of the population composition of the United States by age, sex, and major activity is given in Table IX:2. A finer breakdown would give a more comprehensive picture but would be correspondingly more complicated. However, even this short statistical summary reveals the way the population may be differentiated into socially meaningful clusters.

Certain basic facts about composition, for instance age and sex, contribute in many ways to the understanding of society and economy.

The distribution of ages and the proportions of the sexes influence the marriage rate, the birth rate, the death rate, the ratio of producers to consumers, the percentages in the school or military ages, the numbers eligible for old-age assistance, and almost every

TABLE IX:2 POPULATION OF U.S. BY AGE AND ACTIVITY, 1965

CATEGORY AGE	POPULATION (in thousands)		FUNCTION
14 years and over	78,357		In labor force *
		2,722	In armed forces
		49,014	Civilian males
		26,621	Civilian females
	59,883		Not in labor force
		11,094	In school
		35,556	Keeping house
		11,233	Retired and other
		2,000	In institutions
5–13 years	34,455		In school
	1,433		Not in school
Less than 5 years	20,434		

SOURCE: *Statistical Abstract of the United States: 1966,* Tables 5, 43, 149, 307.

* Unemployment rate was 4.6% of civilian total.

other significant item of national bookkeeping and planning. In social and economic spheres, valid comparisons are possible only if precautions are taken to ensure that comparable age and sex groups are being used.[4]

THE SEX RATIO

The proportion of males to females within a population is called its *sex ratio* (SR) and is stated as the number of males per 100 females. A sex ratio of 100 means that the population is evenly divided between males and females; a figure greater than 100, that there are more males than females; a figure less than 100, that there are fewer males than females. For example, Alaska's sex ratio (132) is higher than that of Washington, D.C. (SR = 88); that is, the proportion of males to females is higher in Alaska than in Washington.

At birth the sex ratio for whites in the United States approximates 106, but at successively older ages the proportion of males diminishes; that is, the sex ratio declines with increasing age. The American female seems to be a more durable organism than the American male, and the life expectancy for females is higher than for males. In some other countries this is not the case, nor was it necessarily so at earlier periods in American experience.

Unbalanced ratios A sex ratio that deviates markedly in either direction is thought to be biased or "out of balance."[5] This attitude is traceable to the values of a monogamous marital system. A polygynous family system (one with plural wives) would not be concerned about an excess of females, and a polyandrous system (one with plural husbands) would welcome an excess of males.

In 1960 the sex ratio in the United States had declined to an all-time low of 97 from 106 in 1910. In the preceding century it had fluctuated between about 102 and 105, but not until the 1940s did the number of females exceed the number of males in the country as a whole. The relatively high sex ratio through much of American history was due, at least in part, to the heavier immigration of males than females, except during the light immigration of the 1930s and 1940s.

The sex ratio for Negroes in the U.S. has been consistently lower than for whites, but the reasons for this are obscure. Whatever the cause, this low ratio aggravates the adjustment problems of the Negro family. (See Adaptation 14, pp. 145–148.) The high proportion of males of marriageable age among immigrants complicates their problems of adjustment and impedes family building, especially in the early stages of an immigrant community.

Viewed regionally, New England had the lowest sex ratio (95) in 1960, and the Mountain States the highest (101). Massachusetts had the lowest sex ratio of any state (93) and Alaska the highest (132).

Rural-urban sex ratios The American city has a strong attractive power to women. In 1960 the urban sex ratio was about 94, the rural 104. The urban sex ratio was even lower between the ages of 20 and 29 (SR = 92) and consequently reduced marriage prospects for many women. The rural sex ratio in the same age group was about 106, indicating a surplus of rural males of marriageable age. These biased sex ratios reduce the rate of marriage and tend to lower the crude birth rate. Cities vary in their sex ratios, depending on the character of industry in the area. Heavy industry, such as steel, is associated with a relatively high sex ratio. On the other hand, commercial activities and light industry, such as the assembly of small equipment requiring manual dexterity, are associated with a low sex ratio. The urban concentration of women probably contributed to the development of women's political activities, which resulted in the suffrage movement and ultimately in the Nineteenth Amendment (1920) extending the franchise to women.

Despite the association between a low sex ratio and urbanization in North America and Western Europe, the relationship cannot be generalized to the whole

---

[4] T. Lynn Smith, *Population Analysis* (New York: McGraw-Hill, 1948), p. 112.
[5] Cf. Hans von Hentig, "The Sex Ratio," *Social Forces, 30,* No. 4 (May, 1952), 443.

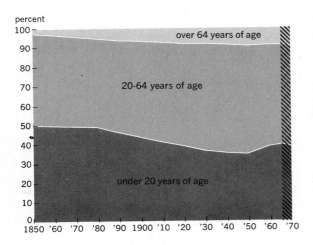

FIG. IX:1   Population of the U.S. by age categories, 1850–1965 (projected to 1970)

as does the United States, but unlike the U.S., India has a very high urban sex ratio.[6]

AGE COMPOSITION

The industrial and military potentials of a nation depend in large part on its age composition. A population with heavy concentrations in the productive years has a larger labor force and a larger potential force for mobilization in time of emergency. A population with smaller proportions in the productive years is less able to respond to threats against its security and is probably less adaptable to technological change. A population concentrated at either extreme of the age distribution has a high *dependency ratio,* that is, the number of nonproductive individuals is relatively great and burdens the productive population.

For most of its history, the United States has had a young population. Large numbers were concentrated at the early ages, the birth rate was rather high, and the death rate was fairly high. Over the decades both

world. In many countries urbanization seems to be associated with a high rather than a low sex ratio. India, for example, has a fairly high rural sex ratio

[6] Kingsley Davis, *The Population of India and Pakistan* (Princeton: Princeton University Press, 1951).

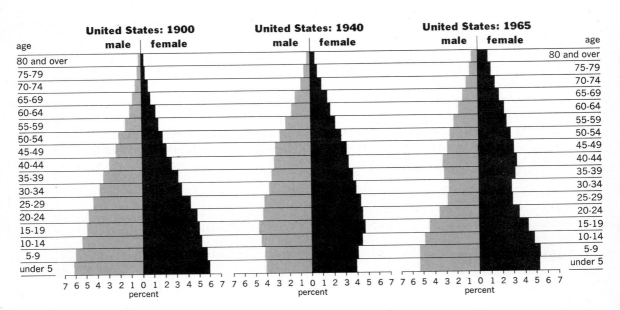

FIG. IX:2   Population pyramids, United States: 1900, 1940, and 1965

birth and death rates have declined and the proportion of the population in the lower ages has been reduced. Figure IX:1 depicts the change in the proportion of the major age groups over more than a century. Although for much of that period the population in the most productive years increased faster than the old and the young, this is not now the case. However, compared with many countries, the United States has a favorable dependency ratio.

Population pyramid The study of the population pyramids permits closer analysis of changes in the age (and sex) composition of a population. Figure IX:2 shows the age-sex distribution of the population of the United States for 1900, 1940, and 1965. Sometimes called "the tree of ages," the population pyramid summarizes age and sex characteristics at a given time. A vertical line divides the percentages of males on the left from the percentages of females on the right. The percentages indicated on the scale are calculated from population figures compiled by age categories, that is, males under 5 years of age, between 5 and 9 years old, and so on. The age groupings are shown on the pyramid steps. The figure for 1900 has the shape of a true pyramid, typical of a population increasing because of a high birth rate but also showing a high death rate. ". . . each year's crop of babies was larger than that of the year before, and the older birth classes, besides being smaller to begin with, had tended to die at a relatively early age." [7]

The 1940 figure describes a much different population. The birth and death rates had declined. The proportion of population in the most productive years (between 20 and 50) had increased. The proportion in the older dependent ages had also increased, but the proportion of children had declined. The very sharp reduction in the percentages of children under 10 years of age is undoubtedly related to the depression of the 1930s.

The pyramid for 1965 shows an increase in the population under 25 years of age—the result of the high birth rate in the 1940s and 1950s. The increase reversed the trend of the 1930s toward lower birth

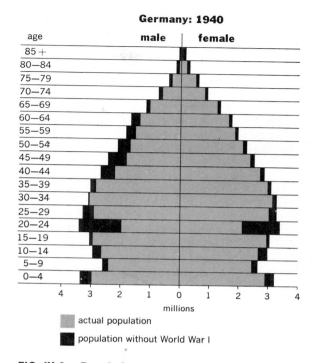

FIG. IX:3   **Population pyramid for Germany— actual and without World War I**

After Frank W. Notestein, *The Future Population of Europe and the Soviet Union* (Geneva: League of Nations, 1944), Fig. 27, p. 101.

rates. (See Sec. 3, p. 279.) The short age bars, which were at the base of the pyramid in 1940, moved up in 1965 to become a notch at ages 25–34. This pyramid graphically reveals the earlier history of a population. It does not tell the reasons for irregularities and changes; it does call attention to questions about why the irregularities occur. On page 270 "The Population Pyramid of a Minority" applies the pyramid technique to understanding some of the demographic consequences of international migration.

Depressions, wars, and epidemics leave their scars on the population pyramid, not merely for the lifetime of those directly affected but for generations. Figure IX:3 shows the effects of World War I on the

[7] Frank W. Notestein, "Population," *Scientific American, 185,* No. 3 (September, 1951), 30.

THE POPULATION PYRAMID OF A MINORITY

Figure *A* on the facing page really represents two populations, the American-born (Nisei), shown also in Figure *B*, and the foreign-born (Issei), shown separately in Figure *C*. The reading of these pyramids raises a number of questions:

1. Why are the foreign-born males (Fig. *C*) rather older than the females? The Japanese males who first came to the United States about the beginning of this century were young, single men who later brought younger women as their wives. We may conjecture that originally many of the men planned to return to Japan.

2. Why are there virtually no foreign-born Japanese under thirty years of age? Japanese immigration was controlled by the Gentleman's Agreement with Japan in 1907 and the Japanese Exclusion Act in 1924.

3. Why does Figure *A* deviate from the true pyramid of a "normal" population? This is explained by the immigration history of mature males followed by mature females and may be understood most easily by referring to *B* and *C*.

At first there were few childbearing women (arrow *1, C*), so that few persons of Japanese ancestry were born here (arrow *2, B*). A few years later more Japanese females of childbearing age (arrow *3, C*) entered as the wives of the Japanese males. These women bore the Nisei children (arrow *4, B*). But note the diminution in the number of Nisei below the age of fifteen. As the foreign-born females began to pass beyond the childbearing age, there were no foreign-born females (arrow *5, C*) to replace them, and the native-born females (arrow *6, B*) were only entering the childbearing period.

4. What can we guess about the future of this population? There should be an increase of native-born children as the native-born population reaches maturity. In turn, as they pass beyond childbearing age, the narrowing of the base should recur, although less clearly. The effect of the immigration pattern may be perceptible in this wavelike reproductive pattern for several generations.

German population of 1940: (1) the war casualties, males aged 40–64 who were of military age in 1914–1918, (2) the notch at ages 20–24, a consequence of the depletion of potential fathers, and (3) the effects of this notch reappear at the bottom of the pyramid in the reduced size of the youngest age groups.

RACIAL AND ETHNIC COMPOSITION

Homogeneous countries lack the problems of nations that have *ethnic* minorities (those set off from the main population by culture) or *racial* minorities. Presumably, homogeneous countries can achieve cohesion and consensus with relative ease because they do not experience the strain of fitting strangers into the social order. Nor do they have readily distinguishable groups whose *apparent* differences can be made the basis of discrimination.

On the other hand, countries like the United States must cope with racial and cultural diversity in building a coherent social order. This task is complicated by the fact that the diverse populations were introduced into the country rapidly, at different times, and in large numbers. Furthermore, many of the peoples are concentrated regionally or are ecologically segregated in urban areas, where they tend to develop subsocieties. Such isolation limits the access of a

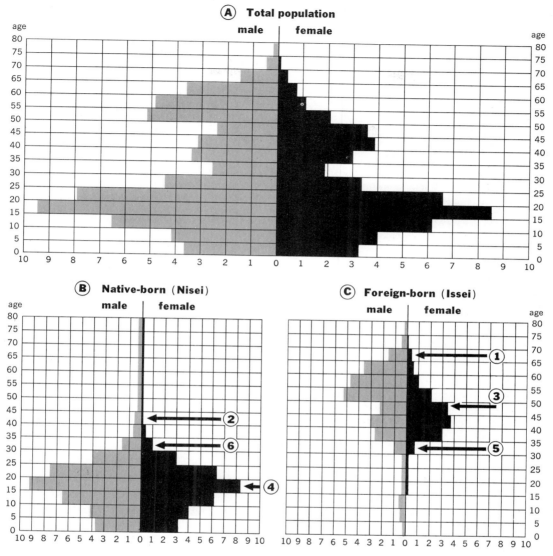

FIG. IX:4   Age and sex composition of the Pacific Coast Japanese population, 1940

SOURCE: U.S. Bureau of the Census. Figures in thousands are given for each age group.

minority to the large social order and often prolongs its subordination and deprivations imposed upon it.

Table IX:3 gives estimates of the minorities of conterminous United States. Racially defined popu-lations total about twenty-seven millions. "Negroes" include individuals ranging from persons who could easily pass as white to apparently unmixed African types. "Mexicans" include a large but unknown num-

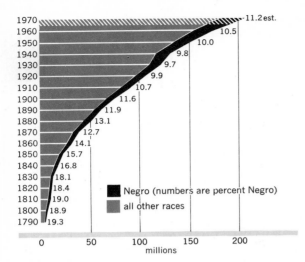

FIG. IX:5   Population of the conterminous U.S. by race, 1790–1965 (projected to 1970)

TABLE IX:3   "RACIAL" AND ETHNIC POPULATIONS, CONTERMINOUS UNITED STATES, 1965

POPULATION	NUMBER (*in thousands*)
"Racial" minorities	
Negroes	20,945
Mexicans	4,500
American Indians	650
Japanese	275
Chinese	215
Filipinos	115
Total "racial" minorities	26,700
(About 14% of total. Most physically visible.)	
Ethnic minorities	
Jews (U.S. and foreign-born)	5,250
Foreign-born French Canadians	250
Other foreign-born whites	10,500
Total ethnic minorities	16,000
(About 8% of total. Some culturally visible.)	

SOURCE: Racial estimates projected from *Census of Population, 1960,* Final Report PC(1)-1B, Table 44; foreign-born from PC(1)-1C, Table 70; Mexicans, both native and foreign-born, from reports on Spanish surname population; French Canadians from unpublished foreign-born and mother-tongue data; Jews from Current Population Reports, P-20, No. 79, February 2, 1958. The *American Jewish Yearbook, 1965,* p. 139, estimates 5,720,000 Jews for all 50 states.

ber of persons who are not different enough in their physical appearance to be distinguished from the white population, but this minority also includes many whose ancestry is largely American Indian. For this reason the United States census has had difficulty in enumerating persons of Mexican origin. In 1930 "Mexicans" were counted separately by "race," but since that time they have been included in the white population. Estimates for ethnic minorities are even less reliable than for racial groups. Many individuals in the ethnic categories are highly acculturated; others are easily identifiable as deriving from a different national or cultural background.

Because the new states of Alaska and Hawaii are so different in their composition, they are reported separately from the 48 states (see Table IX:4). Hawaii is unique in the United States in its preponderance of nonwhites and its Asian background, factors that aroused opposition to Hawaiian statehood. Now that Hawaii has achieved statehood, such antagonisms are rarely expressed.

Growth of the Negro population [8]   Figure IX:5

presents the census figures on the growth of the Negro population of the United States (conterminous) compared with the rest of the population. Through most of American history the white population increased faster than the Negro population. Between 1800 and 1965 the number of Negroes grew from about three-fourths of a million to nearly twenty-one millions. In 1800 Negroes were 19 percent of the total population, but in 1965 they were 11 percent.

Since 1930 the rate of Negro increase has exceeded that of whites. Some of the "increase" is apparent rather than real, because Negroes are now being more accurately counted. Improvements in health and living conditions are belatedly reducing death

[8] "Subject Guide to 1960 Census Data for the Negro Population," Supplementary Reports, PC(S1)-46, 1964.

TABLE IX:4 RACIAL COMPOSITION, ALASKA AND HAWAII, 1960

| | ALASKA | | HAWAII | |
	Number (*thousands*)	%	Number (*thousands*)	%
Total	226.2	100	632.8	100
Native whites	176.5	74.1	194.7	30.8
Foreign-born whites	7.1	3.1	7.6	1.2
Negroes	6.9	3.0	4.9	0.8
American Indians	14.4	6.4	0.5	0.1
Japanese	0.8	0.4	203.5	32.2
Chinese	0.1	0.1	38.2	6.0
Filipinos	0.8	0.4	69.1	10.9
Aleuts, Eskimos, etc.	28.6	12.7	—	—
Hawaiians, Part Hawaiians, etc.	—	—	114.4	18.1

SOURCE: *Census of Population, 1960. Alaska and Hawaii,* Final Reports PC(1)-3B and PC(1)-13B, Tables 15; and *Alaska and Hawaii,* Final Reports PC(1)-3D and PC(1)-13D, Tables 96.

rates for Negroes. The Negro population is younger and poorer than whites and its crude birth rate may be expected to remain higher than the white rate for some time.

The geographical distribution of the Negro population has important effects on race relations. There has been progressive dispersal of Negroes through the states and a steady reduction of the so-called "Black Belt," the area of the South with a preponderance of Negroes. Between 1900 and 1940 the number of Southern counties with 50 percent or more Negroes declined from 286 to 180, and from 1940 to 1960, the number declined to 134 (or 135, counting Washington, D.C.). The number of Negroes in such counties declined from about 4,000,000 in 1900 to about 2,600,000 in 1940, and to under 2,000,000

in the 135 counties in 1960. Negroes have been moving from the South in large numbers, and the trend of Negro migration will probably continue. The Negro population of the South, defined in the broadest terms to include seventeen states plus the District of Columbia,[°] increased 15.3 percent between 1940 and 1960, while the white population of the South increased 34.7 percent. In the same period Negroes outside the South, principally in large urban centers, increased by more than 160 percent, from 2,717,000 to 7,158,000. The percentage of Negroes in the South declined from about 79 percent in 1940 to 62 percent in 1960. Although Negroes have become more widely distributed in regional terms, their extreme concentration in central cities has maintained a high degree of ecological segregation.

[°] For the purposes of this discussion the following are counted as Southern: Alabama, Arkansas, Delaware, District of Columbia, Florida, Georgia, Kentucky, Louisiana, Maryland, Mississippi, Missouri, North Carolina, Oklahoma, South Carolina, Tennessee, Texas, Virginia, and West Virginia.

SECTION **3** FERTILITY AND MORTALITY

The future of a population is determined by rates of birth and death and by immigration and emigration. If migration is held constant, analyses of detailed birth and death rates can be used to predict the size of a population, its potential growth or decline, and its age structure.

In population literature *fertility* refers to actual reproduction, *fecundity* to potential reproduction, that is, the biologically maximum number of births. In modern urbanized and industrialized nations fertility is only a fraction of the possible number of births, and even in agrarian countries, where fertility is very high, it does not reach fecundity, the biological maximum.

THE MEASURES OF FERTILITY

A simple way to measure fertility is to calculate the percentage of new births in a population. The percentage states the number of births in a year for each 100 persons in the population. For example, in 1965 there were 3,759,000 births recorded in the U.S.[10] On the basis of a total population of 193,800,-000, new births constituted 1.94 percent of the total. Conventionally, the calculation is expressed as the number of births per 1,000 population and is called the *crude birth rate*. The formula is:

$$\frac{\text{births in a year}}{\text{midyear population}} \times 1,000 = \text{crude birth rate}$$

Substituting 1965 figures for the U.S. in the formula:

$$\frac{3,759,000}{193,800,000} \times 1,000 = 19.4$$

The U.S. crude birth rate of 19.4 is less than half the rates of Africa and parts of Latin America and

Asia. For comparisons, see Table IX:5 which reports the latest available worldwide data.

Whether a given birth rate should be interpreted as high or low depends on the number of women of childbearing age in the population. In fact the current fertility of U.S. women, compared with earlier periods in American history or with the fertility of women in Asia or Africa, is even lower than is indicated by the crude birth rate because of differing age characteristics. A relatively large proportion of the U.S. population is composed of females in the childbearing ages, whereas in less developed countries large numbers of females are children.

Measures of fertility expressed as births among women of childbearing age have analytical advan-

TABLE IX:5   ESTIMATED BIRTH AND DEATH RATES, SELECTED REGIONS, 1960–1964

REGION	RATES PER THOUSAND OF POPULATION	
	Births	*Deaths*
WORLD	34	16
Africa	47	23
North America	23	9
Latin America	41	13
Asia [ab]	38	20
Japan	17	7
Europe [b]	19	10
Australia and New Zealand	23	9
U.S.S.R.	23	7

SOURCE: United Nations, *1965 Demographic Yearbook*, 1966, p. 103.

[a] Includes Japan.

[b] Excludes U.S.S.R.

---

[10] Figures are given to the nearest thousand.

tages if the data are accurate. One such measure is the *age specific birth rate*,[11] obtained by dividing the number of births to mothers of a specific age group by the number of women of that group and multiplying by 1,000. For example, in 1959 there were 571,-000 births to mothers 15 to 19 years of age, and the age specific birth rate for that group was 90.9. In the United States births are concentrated in the age range 20–29, and relatively few births occur to women under 20 or over 34. "The Case of the G.E. Babies," pages 276–277, shows the necessity of applying appropriate measures of fertility to the correct segment of the population.

Fertility ratio Detailed vital statistics (in this case registration of births, including information on the mothers) required to calculate the age specific birth rate are lacking or imperfect in all but a few countries where human bookkeeping is most highly developed. As is so often the case, countries that might benefit most from such sophisticated information are least likely to have it. The *fertility ratio,* on the other hand, may be computed directly from census data without using birth records. To calculate the fertility ratio, it is necessary to know only the age and sex distribution of the population. The ratio is a statement of the number of small children to the number of women of childbearing age, arbitrarily defined, for example as 15–44 years of age. A typical calculation is as follows:

$$\frac{\text{children under 5 years}}{\text{women aged 15–44 inclusive}} \times 1,000 = \text{fertility ratio (FR)}$$

Substituting estimated U.S. figures for 1966:

$$\frac{19,851,000}{39,518,000} \times 1,000 = 502$$

Figure IX:6 depicts the fertility ratios of the United States since 1800. From about 1,000 in 1800 the fertility ratio declined to a low of 342 in 1942, recovered to 563 in 1960, and has since retreated to 502 in 1966. The increase in fertility following World War II was contrary to most predictions, which assumed an extension of the prolonged decline of the birth rate. The recent decline in the fertility ratio may be a reassertion of the long-term trend.

Assuming equally good enumeration of the young and the mature, within and between countries, fertility ratios are used for easy comparisons of the fertility of different countries or trends within the same country. However, if comparisons are made between interrelated areas, it is necessary to know if children live with their mothers. For example, if rural mothers migrate to the city but leave their children to be cared for in the rural areas, as is true in many developing countries, the comparison of fertility ratios for country and city would be misleading. The rural fertility ratio would be too high because of the "extra" children, and the urban fertility ratio would be too low because of the "extra" mothers.

Fertility differentials Groups within a population reproduce at different rates. Some of the fertility differentials that have been fairly well established for the U.S. are as follows:

1. Rural farm areas have higher fertility than rural nonfarm areas.

2. Rural areas have higher fertility than urban areas.

[11] Demographers use the age specific birth rate to construct a more refined measure of fertility, called the *standardized birth rate.*
Two other measures based on the age specific birth rate are the gross reproduction rate and the net reproduction rate. They are attempts to determine whether or not populations in the long run are maintaining their numbers. The *gross reproduction rate* tells us to what extent a given group of women are replacing themselves with daughters, assuming (1) that they live through their childbearing period and (2) that the age specific birth rates are maintained. To be practically useful, corrections need to be made to the gross reproduction rate. The *net reproduction rate* makes one of these corrections. It applies the age specific death rates prevalent at a given time. It assumes certain age specific birth rates, as does the gross reproduction rate. The net reproduction rate is usually expressed as follows: A net reproduction rate of 1.00 means that if the age specific birth and death rates existing in a given year continue, the population of women would just replace themselves in one generation; 1.50 means that in one generation they would increase by 50 percent; 0.50 means that in one generation they would decrease by 50 percent.

THE CASE OF THE G. E. BABIES

On January 14, 1953, General Electric announced that it would award five shares of its common stock to any employee who had a baby on October 15—the company's seventy-fifth anniversary. Originally the company said it expected about thirteen winners. It arrived at this figure by applying a daily U.S. birth rate to its own 226,000 employees. This computation actually yielded a prediction of fifteen births; but a G.E. public-relations man thought it might be nice to trim the figure to thirteen, the number of original G.E. investors. The mathematics suffered from more than public relations, however. G.E. employees, since they include no children and no one over sixty-five, are obviously a much more fertile group than the population as a whole. When this fact sank in, a company statistican made a new assault on the problem. He estimated that the size of an average G.E. family was 4.2. This meant that the total number of people in the G.E. families was close to a million. Applying the crude annual birth rate to *this* group, and dividing by 365, he came up with a new prediction of seventy-two births on the big day.

As it turned out, there were not thirteen, fifteen, or seventy-two babies born to G.E. employees on October 15. There were 189.

Subtracting the company's highest expectation of seventy-two from 189 gives 117, "extra" babies. Where did G.E. go wrong? Well, among other things, the company made no allowance for the incentive provided by its own stock. This oversight, remarkable in a company that has had a lot to say about capitalist incentives, was apparently rectified by the employees. The latter not only enjoy having children, but, it appears, they rather enjoy the idea of becoming capitalists. And they seem to have known a good thing. In a generally declining stock market, G.E. common stock rose during the pregnant months from 69⅛ to 78⅞.

SOURCE: Reprinted from the January, 1954, issue of *Fortune* by Special Permission of the Editors; Copyright, Time Inc.

WHERE DID G.E. GO WRONG?

They applied the wrong rate to the wrong group. They applied the crude birth rate to G.E. employees, assuming that only the *employees* would have babies. If the crude birth rate were to be

3. The larger the city, the lower is the fertility; that is, size of city is inversely related to fertility.

4. In general, manual workers have more children than do white-collar workers.

5. Catholic fertility tends to be higher than Protestant fertility, but its trends follow the Protestant configuration.

6. Negro fertility is higher than white fertility, but it follows white trends.

In the Western world, in recent decades lower income groups and those with relatively low education have shown higher birth rates than the middle and upper classes and the relatively well educated. However, during the "baby boom" there is evidence

used at all, it should have been applied to the whole population of G.E. *families,* not just the workers but their wives, children, and other relatives. This is what they finally did when they included families in their calculations of the crude birth rate. But the crude birth rate requires a cross section of the total population, and they did not have one. Even the whole population of G.E. families is not representative of the whole population of the U.S. For instance, G.E. families contain an abnormally large proportion of individuals in the productive (and reproductive) years and few aged persons. The G.E. statistician also failed to consider: (1) the section of the country, (2) the size of the communities where the employees lived, (3) their income, (4) their education, and (5) their race, all of which affect the birth rate.

Could G.E. have done better? They could have made a closer approximation to the true number by applying age specific birth rates to the women of childbearing ages in G.E. employee families. This number could have been further refined by correcting for seasonal fluctuations in births. Corrections for the characteristics G.E. failed to consider would be far more difficult to make and, under the conditions noted below, pointless.

Because figures for the characteristics of the G.E. population are not available, a more refined estimate cannot be calculated. Probably, but not certainly (as *Fortune* assumes), the announcement of the award was an incentive. The influence of incentive could have been estimated and the quality of the prediction further improved by interviewing a sample of G.E. wives. Of course, G.E. could have eliminated the incentive factor entirely by announcing the award eight instead of ten months before October 15. As it was, the announcement may have been timed to create maximum motivation. And a number of births may have been induced (hastened) by physicians.

There is at least one additional complication. Any estimate of a daily birth rate, even for a rather large population like the G.E. families, is subject to an additional source of error. Daily birth rates vary even more widely than seasonal or monthly birth rates. In 1950 U.S. registered crude birth rates ranged from 20.9 for the month of April to 25.5 for September. The shorter the time period, the greater the range of variation in birth rates (and the smaller the population, the greater the range of variation in birth rates). The chances of getting close to the mark on any particular day for any particular group are, therefore, not very good.

that well-educated elements shared more than proportionately in the increase. Furthermore, where large samples have permitted fine analyses of income categories, it becomes clear that the very highest income groups have greater fertility than the middle and medium high groups in such places as England, the United States, and the Scandinavian countries.

These differences in fertility have important social consequences. For example:

The burden of dependency is not evenly distributed through the population. Rural areas have a relatively greater financial burden of supporting young children.

More fertile populations may become increasingly

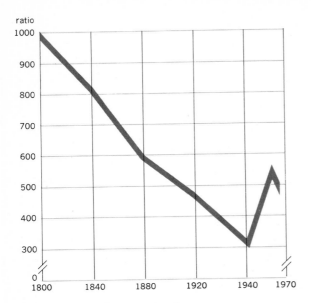

FIG. IX:6 Fertility ratio for the United States, 1800–1966

Children under 5 years of age per 1,000 women 16–44, United States.

ADAPTED from *Population Problems* by Warren S. Thompson (New York: McGraw-Hill), p. 175. Data for 1960 from U.S. Bureau of the Census, *Census of Population: 1960,* PC(1)–1B, p. xiii. 1966 estimate from sample data.

preponderant where fertility is not offset by migration or other factors. Thus, high Catholic fertility is the subject of anxious comment by some individuals from religious groups of lower fertility.

Fertility trends in the United States   In recent years the techniques of contraception have become sufficiently reliable so that people who want to limit family size can do so if they have the necessary knowledge and access to devices or materials. In the United States and other rich Western countries of high literacy, control of the timing and number of births is widely practiced.

In 1957 there were 4,334,000 births in the United States, an all-time high. Since then there has been a decline to 4,027,000 in 1964, to 3,759,000 in 1965, and to about 3,600,000 in 1966—the approximate level in 1950. This corresponds to a rate of 136 births per 1,000 married women under age 45 and is considerably below the rates after World War II but higher than the rates during the depression of the 1930s. The current decline is due to lower rates for second and subsequent children as reported in Figure IX:7. Information on birth rate by birth order is a sophisticated measure of fertility and a sensitive indicator of deliberate increase or restriction of family size.

After World War II there was a sharp increase in births, especially first births which are regarded as deferred fertility, but a *controlled* fertility may increase *or* decrease in response to historical events and economic changes.[12] The rate for first births peaked immediately after the war, the rate for second births remained high until the mid-1950s when a steady decline appeared, and the declines for third, fourth, and higher birth orders seem to have occurred in sequence. The rate for first births has been stable for several years at slightly less than 45 per 1,000 married women under age 45, but higher birth orders now show declining rates without exception. With the large cohorts of children born after World War II now reaching marriageable age, the absolute number of first births will probably increase even if the rate remains stable, and new record highs in total births may be recorded in the late 1970s. A current trend toward decreased family size is indicated by the sharp decline in the frequency with which moderate-sized families have another child, and the evidence suggests that the "baby boom" that began after World War II has ended.

MORTALITY [13]

The calculation of death rates raises the same problems discussed under fertility. The best-known death

[12] Harold F. Dorn, "Pitfalls in Population Forecasts and Projections," *Journal of the American Statistical Association, 45* (September, 1950), 332.

[13] Mortality should not be confused with morbidity, which refers to the occurrence of disease. Morbidity rates are usually expressed as the incidence of a disease or disorder per 100,000 population in one year.

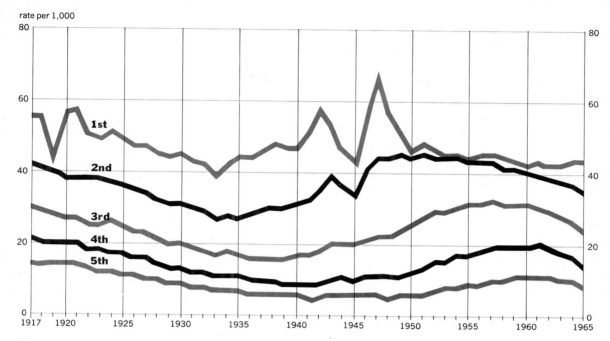

rate per 1,000

FIG. IX:7   Birth rates by order of birth, United States, 1917–1965

Births per 1,000 married women under age 45.

SOURCE: Metropolitan Life Insurance Company *Statistical Bulletin,* October, 1966, p. 2.

rate, the *crude death rate,* is calculated as follows:

$$\frac{\text{deaths in a year}}{\text{midyear population}} \times 1,000 = \text{crude death rate}$$

In 1965 the U.S. crude death rate was:

$$\frac{1,828,000}{193,800,000} \times 1,000 = 9.43 \text{ per thousand}$$

This was a bit more than half of the 17.2 recorded in 1900 in the death registration states.

Table IX:5 (p. 274) shows the spread of estimated death rates for the several world regions. As in the measure of fertility, it is necessary to relate crude death rates to age structure in order to make accurate interpretations. In fact, the low rates of North Amer-

ica and Europe as expressed by the crude death rates understate their relative superiority because the populations of these countries are older. The high African and Asian death rates occur in populations with heavy concentrations in the younger years.

Age specific death rates are expressed as the number of deaths per thousand persons of specified ages. In 1959 the U.S. age specific death rates ranged from 0.5 in ages 5–14 to 202.8 per thousand for persons 85 years and over.[14] The preoccupation of health officers with the mortality of certain groups has led to the development of special measures. Three of these follow:

1. The *infant mortality rate reports* for 1,000 live births how many infants die in the first year. The United States infant death rate was 25.7 in 1960,

[14] *Vital Statistics of the United States,* 1959, Vol. 1, Table 6-C.

compared with rates for Sweden of 17, for New Zealand of 24, and for Romania of 77.

2. *Neonatal mortality rate.* As the infant mortality rate has been brought under control, more attention has been given to the large proportion of infant deaths occurring during the first month. One-third of all infant mortality is concentrated in the first day of life; three-fifths of infant deaths occur in the first week; and more than two-thirds are in the first month.[15] A *neonatal mortality rate* is simply an age specific death rate for the age group, birth to one month. The very existence of this measure suggests how developments of medical technology and awareness of problems lead to changes in record-keeping. Viewed another way, vital statistics point out to the

medical scientist and practitioner where serious problems lie and where his efforts might be expected to produce most immediate benefits.

3. The *maternal mortality rate* states the number of mothers dying per 10,000 live births. The current American rate is under 5 maternal deaths per 10,000 live births, a decline from 58 in 1935. The risk of childbirth to the mother is greatest at the highest ages, and the most favorable period for childbearing is the early twenties. Maternal mortality statistics bear out the popular belief that the first birth is relatively the most hazardous for the mother, holding age constant.

The chances of survival   Figure IX:8 shows how

[15] *Statistical Bulletin,* Metropolitan Life Insurance Company, February, 1952, p. 1.

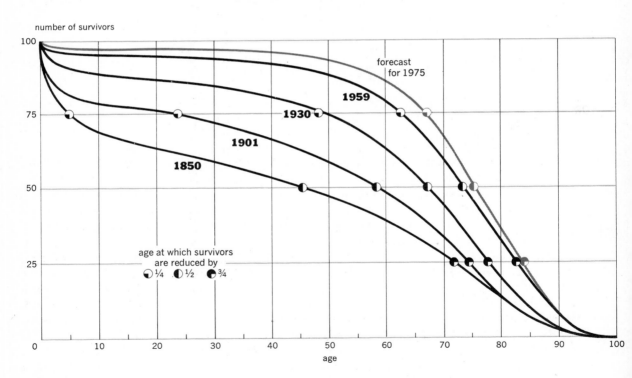

FIG. IX:8   Survivors from birth to successive ages, United States, 1850–1959

Forecast for 1975 on the basis of low mortality forecast by the Census, 1947.

SOURCE: Metropolitan Life Insurance Company *Statistical Bulletin*—March, 1952, and March, 1960.

dramatically the chances of survival have improved in a century and forecasts a slight continued improvement. In 1850 only three-fourths of the newborn in the United States reached age 5; in 1901 the same proportion reached age 24; and in 1959, the same proportion survived more than 60 years. The age to which one-half of the newborn survive increased from 45 in 1850 to more than 73 years in 1959. Great advances in medical science and technology and in public health practice, and improvement in nutrition and the standard of living are responsible for the great gains. Some important consequences of these changes are the following:

1. An increasing number of persons are living through their working years, thus contributing to the productive efficiency of the nation.

2. A larger number of persons are reaching old age, thus creating an important dependency problem.

3. The marked reduction in deaths of the young enables the population to sustain or increase its numbers with relatively fewer births.

4. "Premature" deaths have been reduced and may be reduced somewhat further, but there is no clear evidence that the upper age limits of human existence will be significantly raised. To assume so is to misinterpret improved average longevity as an extension in the limits of the human life span. Note in Figure IX:8 that the gain in survivors at the three-fourths point and above is not nearly so impressive as at one-half and one-fourth. Indeed, the 1959 curve presses closely against the 1975 forecast, suggesting relatively little anticipated improvement.[16] It would take a major breakthrough in control of the disorders of age to extend significantly the human life span.

SECTION 4 POPULATION CHANGE

WORLD POPULATION GROWTH

In three centuries the population of the world has increased nearly sixfold. Improvements in the means of production and transportation, advances in agricultural technology and medical science, and the effects of the industrial revolution have combined in a large part of the world to reduce death rates, to prolong life, and at least in the West to raise the standard of living. Carr-Saunders[17] estimates that there were half a billion inhabitants in 1650. In two centuries the population more than doubled, and in 1850 the total was about a billion and a quarter. In the last century it has again more than doubled, and the U.N. *Demographic Yearbook*[18] sets its 1965 mid-year estimate at 3,285 million. Figure IX:9 depicts the world population growth since 1800 projected to the year 2000.

In 1650 people of European ancestry made up about one-sixth of the population of the world. By 1959 they constituted almost one-third of the world's people. Asia accounts for more than half of mankind, although her share of the world's population has decreased.

The rate of increase in Western Europe and North America has been slowing. The sharp decline in death rates was followed by a decline in birth rates. By the beginning of World War II the trend had gone so far that the U.S. and countries of Western Europe appeared to be approaching stable populations. Postwar trends indicate that a stable population is uncertain or at least further away for Western Europe and North America than it seemed before the war.

Demographic transition   Students of population have tried to identify basic stages of growth and de-

---

[16] Cf. *Statistical Bulletin,* Metropolitan Life Insurance Company, August, 1965.

[17] A. M. Carr-Saunders, *World Population* (Oxford: Clarendon Press, 1936), p. 42.

[18] United Nations, *1965 Demographic Yearbook,* 1966, p. 103.

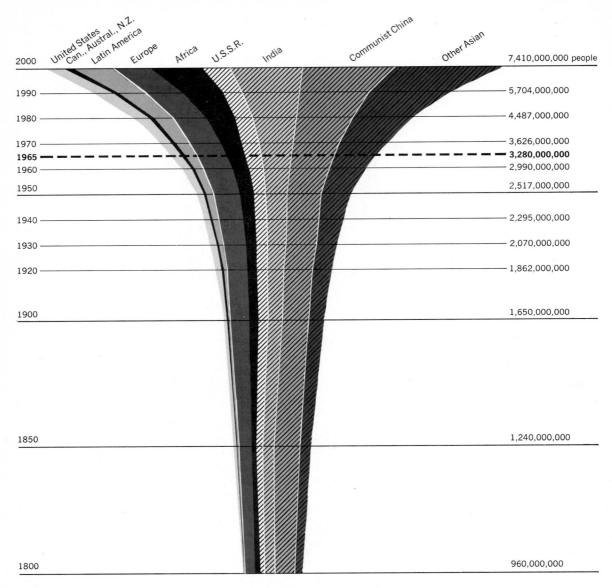

FIG. IX:9 **World population growth, 1800–1965 (projected to 2000)**

SOURCE: Chart by Alexander Semenoick for *Fortune* Magazine, June, 1966, p. 110.

cline in the populations of various parts of the world. When a population seems to be passing from one stage to another, it is called *demographic transition*. Beginning about the middle of the seventeenth cen-

tury, Europe's population passed through these stages:

1. A period of explosive growth as the death rate declined

2. A leveling off of growth as the birth rate declined

3. A change in the age structure and a trend toward population stability or decline

Western Europe before World War II had a stable or incipiently declining population and appeared to be at the natural end of a cycle. The U.S. also seemed far advanced in the cycle, and the series of stages was thought to be a *necessary* sequence. Following these assumptions, population forecasts for the U.S. predicted a stable or declining population to be reached in the relatively near future. These predictions now appear to be very conservative. The "baby boom" following World War II arrested the trend toward stability and made obsolete estimates that were only a few years old. Indeed the population of the U.S. has already exceeded some of the prewar predictions of its ultimate maximum.

Although the highly technical problem of prediction cannot be reviewed here, it seems likely that many of the estimates were incorrect in assuming that the values and beliefs responsible for the declining birth rate were permanent elements of American culture and society.[19] World War II undoubtedly had the effect of postponing some births to the immediate postwar period. The boom in births seems to be ending, but it has significantly changed the age structure of the country and the reproductive potential of coming generations. Even though some predictions have proved faulty, the main ideas of the demographic transition are instructive.

Thompson[20] groups the countries of the world in three broad categories according to the extent of their control over birth and death rates:

Group 1 countries have achieved significant control over both death rates and birth rates. Western peoples now have relatively low death and birth rates, and Thompson predicts that they will maintain relatively low rates of natural increase. This group contains the United States, Canada (except Quebec), the United Kingdom, Australia, New Zealand, and most countries of north, west, and central Europe. They include about one-fifth of the world's people.

Group 2 countries show a declining death rate, but their birth rates have only begun to decline. They lag behind Group 1 in their population trends, and their exceedingly high rates of natural increase may continue for some time. In this group are the countries of southern and eastern Europe, the Soviet Union, Japan, Quebec, and possibly north Africa, Argentina, and Uruguay. These regions also contain about one-fifth of the world's population. It is uncertain how long it will take Group 2 countries to complete the sequence of changes to a stable or declining population—or if they ever will complete the cycle.

Group 3 countries, such as most of Asia, Latin America, and Negro Africa, have high, variable death rates and high, steady birth rates. Population trends in these countries depend largely upon what Malthus called positive checks (famine, war, disease, etc.), but the checks have been altered by the introduction of modern health measures in some areas. These countries contain about three-fifths of the world's population and most of the developing areas.

Control of fertility Group 3 countries present a painful dilemma. Everyone wants to control disease and improve standards of living. But these improvements accelerate population growth, putting heavy pressure on the country's resources. Without accompanying social changes affecting fertility, the outcome may be "ever larger masses of humanity living close to the margins of existence and vulnerable to every shock in the world economic and political structure. Such 'progress' may amount to setting the stage for calamity.

[19] For a bibliography on population forecasts and a critique, see Dorn, *op. cit.* A manual for making population forecasts for sections of the U.S. is: Van Beuren Stanbery, "Better Population Forecasting for Areas and Communities" (U.S. Department of Commerce, 1952). For recent examples of population projections see Bureau of the Census, *Current Population Reports* (February 20, 1967) Series P-25, No. 359: "Projections of the Population of the United States by Age, Sex, and Color to 1990, with Extensions of the Total Population to 2015"; and (May 5, 1967) Series P-25, No. 365: "Revised Projections of School and College Enrollment in the United States to 1985."

[20] A summary may be found in Warren S. Thompson, *Population Problems* (4th ed.; New York: McGraw-Hill, 1953), pp. 267–272.

"No more striking illustration of the limitations, from the demographic point of view, of 'good government and economic development' can be given than the case of Java." [21] Between 1860 and 1930 marked advances were made in sanitation and agricultural production, and in that time the population tripled. In 1930 Java had a density of 800 per square mile. The customary way of life had changed little; there was no evidence of significant improvement in the standard of living of the masses; the limits of agricultural production were being approached; and there were few signs of a decline in fertility. If the rates of increase are maintained, by 2000 Java will have a density of 1500 per square mile.

Recent advances in techniques of birth control and the acceptance of contraceptive measures in experiments in several countries have encouraged some demographic specialists to predict that "the world population crisis is a phenomenon of the 20th century and will be largely if not entirely a matter of history when humanity moves into the 21st century." [22] Bogue bases his assertion on the following points:

1. Surveys in many countries showing widespread preference for small families

2. Political leaders in developing countries tending to favor fertility control

3. Increased professional support and the allocation of greater resources to research

4. A leveling off of progress in death control

5. Diffusion of attitudes fostering family limitation and of control techniques among the masses of the world's people

6. Improved technology of those types of contraception suitable for mass adoption by uneducated people

There is no unanimity among population specialists about how far the factors listed above are applicable to different countries. On balance, contemporary opinion is probably less confident than is Bogue about the speed of change. The end of the population explosion may be almost in sight only if present efforts are greatly expanded to improve techniques of birth control and to diffuse their use, especially in developing countries. But many of the mothers of the children of the year 2000 are already born and, barring a catastrophe, it seems inevitable that the population of the world will again double by the end of this century. (See Fig. IX:9.) A population of 7.4 (or eight) billions will place unprecedented burdens upon resources, no matter how rapidly agricultural and industrial technology may advance and no matter how rapidly their benefits are diffused throughout the world.

Increasing attention is being given to the social consequences of very large populations. Apart from questions of sheer survival for large numbers who may not have enough to eat, there is growing concern about the possible effects of very large populations and very high densities upon human behavior and the texture of social relations. The success or failure of population control will depend upon widespread preference for small families, i.e., a fundamental shift in social values and an acceptance of a family form that even in the West has become dominant only in recent decades. In other words, the answer to the demographic question of overpopulation depends upon changes in cultural values governing the preferred size of the family, relations between spouses, between parents and their children, and the accommodation of religious prescriptions to the practice of birth control. Without such changes more efficient techniques of contraception will have relatively little effect.

Adaptation 25 reports the findings of research in Ceylon, a high-fertility area. Factors considered include the nature of the family pattern, the value placed upon relations between the sexes and upon women and children, the location of authority in the family and community, and the relationship between the family and larger kin and locality groups. The

[21] Frank W. Notestein, "Summary of the Demographic Background of Problems of Undeveloped Areas," *The Milbank Memorial Fund Quarterly, 26,* No. 3 (July, 1948), 249–255. Quotation at p. 252.

[22] Donald J. Bogue, "The End of the Population Explosion," *The Public Interest,* No. 7 (Spring, 1967), pp. 11–20, quoted at p. 11.

analysis shows the necessity of taking such social and cultural factors into account and indicates the futility of using purely biological criteria in studying vital human trends.

INTERNATIONAL MIGRATION

The largest migration before 1800 was the movement of slaves from Africa, mainly to the New World. Estimates of the number of Negroes transported are unreliable, but the actual number may fall between 10 and 20 millions. Most of the slave traffic was during the eighteenth century. By comparison, the number of migrants from Europe to the New World prior to 1800 may not have exceeded 4 to 5 million. However, during the nineteenth century a massive movement from Europe took place, and perhaps as many as 75 million people have entered the Western Hemis-

phere since the beginning of the nineteenth century. This spread of European peoples is the largest intercontinental population movement in recorded history.

The opening of the New World came at an opportune time in the demographic history of Europe. Migration to the Western Hemisphere relieved population pressure during a period of explosive increase. It must not be assumed, however, that emigration is always generated by population pressure. Portugal, for example, weakened her demographic structure in attempting to man her far-flung colonies from Asia to Brazil during the period of exploration.

Although the early data are hardly more than educated guesses, estimates for the nineteenth and twentieth centuries can bear interpretation. Figure IX:10 presents the sources and destinations during the period of maximum intercontinental migration.

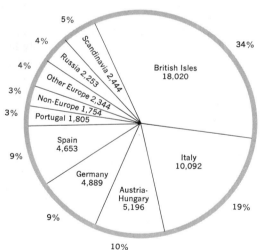

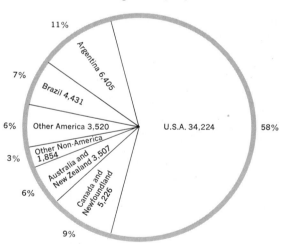

FIG. IX:10   The great intercontinental migration

For emigrants from countries specified in the left-hand figure, the period covered is 1846–1932; various dates apply for unspecified countries. For immigrants to the U.S.A., Canada, and Brazil, the period covered in the right-hand figure is 1821–1932; various dates apply for all other countries. Numbers inside the circles are emigrants or immigrants in thousands; numbers outside the circles are percentages of the total.

COMPUTED from A. M. Carr-Saunders, *World Population* (Oxford: Clarendon Press, 1936), p. 49.

All but 2 million of the 53 million people involved in intercontinental migration between 1846 and 1932 were from Europe, and more than three-quarters of the total movement was from five countries: the British Isles, Italy, Austria-Hungary, Germany, and Spain.

The figures for the countries of destination exceed the reported emigration by some 6 million. This discrepancy is due to the difference in time span—111 years compared with 86 years for the emigration data—and to the fact that there are somewhat better records on immigration than on emigration. Both statistical summaries are incomplete, but the broad outlines are clear and would not be altered significantly by addition of more recent data. The chief donor countries were European; the chief receiving countries were in the Americas, and the United States alone received three-fifths of the total immigration.

Not all of this intercontinental movement was of permanent settlers, and it is not known how many migrants were temporary residents. Carr-Saunders estimates that about 30 percent of those entering the United States (1821–1924) returned to their homes and that 47 percent of Argentine immigrants returned.[23] It is often thought that those who returned did so because they were failures in the new countries. Insofar as they adjusted poorly and did not find useful employment, this is so. However, many immigrants had intended to return to their homelands, and others who planned to be sojourners became permanent settlers. Even temporary migrants play a significant part in developing new lands. For example, between 1901 and 1930 Australia had an immigration of 2,773,000 but a net gain (immigration minus emigration) of only 536,000. Yet the transient labor supply helped to build the nation.

[23] Carr-Saunders, *op. cit.,* p. 49.

TABLE IX:6   IMMIGRATION TO THE UNITED STATES

DECADE	IMMIGRATION (*in thousands*)	CHIEF CONTRIBUTING COUNTRIES
1820–1830	152	Ireland, Great Britain, France
1831–1840	599	Ireland, Germany, Great Britain
1841–1850	1,713	Ireland, Germany, Great Britain
1851–1860	2,598	Germany, Ireland, Great Britain
1861–1870	2,315	Germany, Great Britain, Ireland
1871–1880	2,812	Germany, Great Britain, Ireland
1881–1890	5,247	Germany, Great Britain, Ireland
1891–1900	3,688	Italy, Austria-Hungary, Russia, Germany
1901–1910	8,795	Austria-Hungary, Italy, Russia
1911–1920	5,736	Italy, Russia, Austria-Hungary
1921–1930	4,107	Italy, Germany, Great Britain
1931–1940	528	Germany, Italy, Great Britain
1941–1950	1,035	Germany, Great Britain, Italy
1951–1960	2,515	Germany, Canada, Mexico, Italy
1961–1965 [b]	1,450	Mexico, Germany, Great Britain, Italy

SOURCES: *Statistical Abstract of the United States: 1966,* Tables 123 and 125. Annual Report of the Immigration and Naturalization Service, United States Department of Justice, Washington, D.C., for June 30, 1950, Table 4.

[a] Heaviest single year 1907: 1,285,000 immigrants.

[b] Five years only.

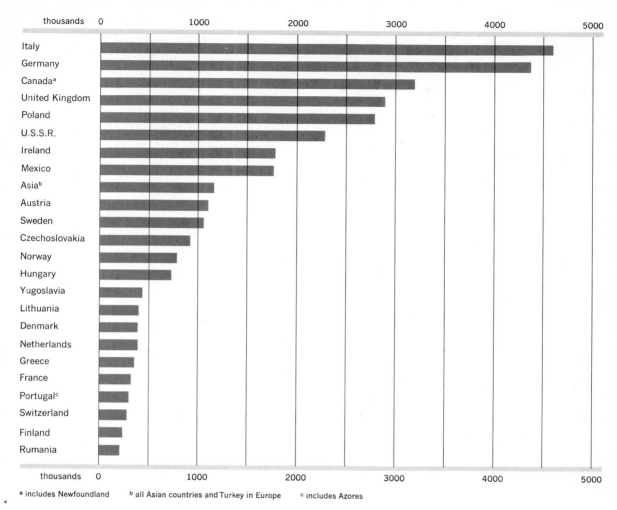

a includes Newfoundland   b all Asian countries and Turkey in Europe   c includes Azores

FIG. IX:11   Foreign stock of the United States, by country of origin, 1960

SOURCE: *U.S. Census of Population: 1960. General Social and Economic Characteristics,* Final Report PC(1)–1C (1962), Table 69. Not separately listed: Other America, 581,000; Other Europe, 492,000; Not reported, 251,000; All other, 14,000.

The United States has been a chief beneficiary from intercontinental migration. As a receiving country, it gained great human resources at relatively small cost. The expansion of the American frontier, the maintenance of an adequate labor force, the broadening of the consumer market, and the introduction of knowledge and skills were all accelerated by the uniquely sustained and diverse migration. Un-

til recently the immigration was disproportionately composed of males in their productive years, and although this fact was an economic gain, the biased sex ratio complicated the integration of the new groups into American society. Even without the high sex ratio, acculturating a large number of immigrants was bound to generate stresses in the society.

Table IX:6 summarizes immigration to the United

States. The cumulative impact of this immigration is shown in Table IX:7. The peak number of foreign born in the United States, more than 14 million, was reported for 1930. Since then, both the number and the percentage of the population foreign born have declined. The 1960 Census counted less than 10 million for the fifty states, below the number in 1900. The 10.4 million in 1900 were nearly 14 percent of the total population; the 9.7 million in 1960 were only 5.4 percent of the total. The decline in the importance of immigration is a consequence of many influences, including a restrictive immigration policy.[24] During the 1950s the reported rate of immigration recovered from the low levels of the 1930s and 1940s, but at least part of the increase was "statistical" rather than real, that is, immigration from Mexico and Canada was more accurately reported than in earlier periods. The stringent immigration policy that has prevailed in recent decades was somewhat relaxed in 1965, but it appears that in percentage terms the foreign born will continue to diminish in importance. The origins of the foreign stock of the United States are given in Figure IX:11. Compare this with Table IX:6, which reports the chief contributing countries at various periods. "Foreign stock" includes the foreign-born and the native-born population of foreign or mixed parentage. The category thus comprises all first- and second-generation Americans. The third and subsequent generations in the U.S. are called "native of native parents." In 1960 there were 34,050,000 persons of foreign stock in the U.S., or about 19 percent of the total population.

Except for Western Hemisphere countries, immigration since 1921 has been limited by annual quotas that depend on the population of foreign born or foreign stock living in the U.S. The quota laws encouraged immigration from Western and Northern Europe, but those quotas often were not filled. However, quotas for Southern and Eastern Europe were quickly oversubscribed and the laws were criticized as being discriminatory. The Immigration Act of

TABLE IX:7   FOREIGN-BORN POPULATION OF THE UNITED STATES, 1850–1960

CENSUS YEAR	FOREIGN BORN NUMBER (in thousands)	PERCENT OF TOTAL POPULATION FOREIGN BORN
1850	2,244 [a]	11.2
1860	4,136 [a]	15.0
1870	5,567	14.4
1880	6,679	13.3
1890	9,249	14.8
1900	10,445	13.7
1910	13,630	14.8
1920	14,020	13.2
1930	14,283	11.6
1940	11,657	8.8
1950	10,431	6.9
1960	9,738	5.4

SOURCES: For the period 1850–1890, *Historical Statistics of the United States, 1789–1945* (Washington, D.C., 1949), p. 30. Data for 1900 to 1960 from *Census of Population: 1960,* PC (1) 1C, *United States Summary, General Social and Economic Characteristics,* Table 66.

[a] White and free colored population only.

1965 continued the quota principle but allowed unfilled quotas to be used by "preference" immigrants whose national quotas had been exhausted. Preference immigrants are those who would be reunited with their families or who have skills and talents needed in this country. Additional special provisions are made for persons whose immediate families live in the United States.

Beginning in 1968 a yearly limit of 170,000 has been set for immigrants from countries outside the Western Hemisphere, with a 20,000 maximum from any one country. Preference is given for family reunification and needed skills. A total of 120,000 immigrants from the Western Hemisphere are to be admitted on a first-come-first-served basis with no special limit on the number from any country.[25]

It is often suggested that relief of population pres-

[24] See William S. Bernard (ed.), *American Immigration Policy* (New York: Harper, 1950); *Whom We Shall Welcome,* Report of the President's Commission on Immigration and Naturalization (Washington, D.C.: Government Printing Office, 1953); B. M. Ziegler (ed.), *Immigration* (Boston: Heath, 1953).

[25] *Statistical Abstract of the United States: 1966,* pp. 89–90.

sures in other parts of the world should enter into the formulation of immigration policy. However, emigration cannot play a significant part in relieving the problems of such countries as India and China.

These countries are so large and their reproductivity is so high that emigration of a great many people would give only fleeting relief and at the same time might transfer the problem elsewhere.

Adaptation 25 / Ryan FERTILITY AND FAMILY ORGANIZATION IN CEYLON

The population in many Asian areas is rapidly increasing, but there is no assurance that birth limitation will be practiced as it has been in Western Europe and North America. In this adaptation Bryce Ryan examines social and cultural factors that may contribute to maintaining high birth rates in Ceylon.

It should not be assumed that what happens in Ceylon must happen elsewhere in Asia. Nevertheless this study is a useful corrective to Western presuppositions that the small family system is the emergent worldwide trend.

Ceylon has recently experienced a phenomenal decline in death rates but no significant change in birth rates. Although it is possible that fertility is declining, the rate of natural increase is nearly 3 percent per year. Even if urban fertility is changing, a matter undemonstrated, it cannot be assumed that Ceylon will follow the Western pattern of persistent diffusion of the small family system. Ceylon is overwhelmingly a rural country, and the difference between city and village is much greater than in most Western nations. It is unrealistic to expect the rapid diffusion of new values and new techniques from an urban population which itself is probably largely unresponsive to them. A revolutionary development is even less likely to appear spontaneously in the countryside. Controlled fertility is typically associated with the individualistic and romantic marital union. No such social climate exists in Ceylon, nor is it likely soon to exist. If the small family pattern and birth limitation are to be introduced, they must be imposed upon a society now tied to large-family values.

The marriage pattern In Ceylon marriage is a calculated and rational extension of kinship; as a relation between two persons dominated by thoughts of each other, it is immoral and atypical. The individual is subordinated to the family. Evidence of social change may be found in the frequency of romantic suicides, which are protests against the control of the kin group, but these also show the continuous power of community and kin. The individual has a lifelong involvement with his relatives, and this is true even among urban sophisticates.

The old system is sacred, and the accepted scope of individualism simply does not provide for personal preferences in marriage. Previous acquaintance is usually of little concern to the parties involved, and there is virtually no comprehension of the concept of romance and seldom even a hint of rebellion. There is a potent and intricate *interdependence* of individual and kin. The arranged match is crucial and romantic marriage is abhorrent and socially disorganizing. Rigid criteria are applied in spouse

SOURCE: Abridged and adapted from "Institutional Factors in Sinhalese Fertility" by Bryce Ryan, *The Milbank Memorial Fund Quarterly, 30* (October, 1952), 359–381. Published in this form by permission of Bryce Ryan and The Milbank Memorial Fund.

selection: (1) membership in the same ethnic community, i.e., Sinhalese; (2) identity of caste; (3) bride younger than groom; (4) bride a virgin; (5) horoscopes of each closely matched. In addition, the dowry power of the girl's people, security and occupational prestige of the boy, and the status of family lines are considered in matchmaking.

A number of factors support familism and are inconsistent with the romantic complex. The greatest moral duty of a father is a "good" marriage for his daughter, and this duty falls on a son at the father's death. These are responsibilities to blood kin, fully as much as to the child. Desire for family prestige may press the father or brother toward almost impossible financial sacrifices.

In marriage the individual is both imprisoned and sheltered by his kinship group. The son helps with his sister's dowry and in so doing protects his own status which in turn is rewarded in dowry. A challenge to the arranged match is a challenge to the prerogatives of kin. The lineal family as a status-bearing entity in the community has its most critical time in the period of approaching marriage. Every relative has his funds or status at stake. Romantic marriage is not consistent with the rigid dictates of caste, prestige, and house honor. It threatens not merely the father's rightful authority but the honor of the generations, past and future, of which the father is the legitimate guardian. Marriage by choice has no claim upon kin for dowry, no claim for help in harvest and no claim for cooperation in marrying some ultimate daughter

of the union. Although the infrequent romantic marriages in villages do not necessarily meet with ostracism if caste propriety and other rigid matters have been observed, there is partial or complete estrangement from kinfolk. In the closely knit affairs of the village, life for such a couple may be far from pleasant.

The requirement of astrological suitability deserves special mention. Almost universally the Sinhalese, young and old, educated and uneducated, believe that suitably matched mates are perfectly revealed in the horoscopes.

Dominance of the male The Sinhalese family is usually patrilineal, descent following the male line, and patrilocal in the limited sense that the couple settles in the husband's village. A new marital unit is dominated by the husband's kin through their very proximity. The father-husband is the social authority. Except toward small children, he avoids overt expressions of affection and gives much evidence of his dignity and prerogatives. This patriarchalism is not harsh; few relations among Sinhalese are that.

From early childhood the male is schooled in his superiority. A family of many males is a "fortunate one"; one of many daughters is "burdened." To the father's position services are due and deference is paid. There is a deeply seated belief that in marriage the wife must give complete loyalty and subservience to her husband. He stands in the place of her father as well as in the role of her husband. On the other hand, it is generally agreed that the husband owes his first allegiance to his own parents rather

than to his wife. Rarely a rigid disciplinarian, the father is still *master* in a society where that concept has a living feudal history.

Marriage and fertility The village studied is in the Ceylon "Low Country," six miles from a market town. The mean age at marriage for village women (based on a one-fourth sample of existing marital units) was 21.9 years, and for men, 28.4 years.[26] There is some reason to believe that the age of women at marriage is rising, but there is no evidence of such a change among men. It is probable that the relatively high ages at marriage are influenced by the difficulties of dowry. About one-fourth of the marriages had no dowry, due to poverty, a few romantic marriages, and other reasons. The proportion of dowryless matches has not changed with passing years. Marriages by personal choice but with parental approval account for 13 percent of marriages and show no increase. Only 4 percent claim to have married in spite of their parents' wishes. More than 80 percent of all marriages and more than two-thirds of recent marriages were arranged by the parents. Most marriages conform closely to traditional patterns.

Children are viewed by all as products of destiny. When women say "all children are a blessing," they are expressing the mores of the community; but for a substantial proportion of mothers, it might be said that *many* children are *imposed* as a blessing. Many mothers accept only reluctantly a pattern of childbearing that approaches fecundity, that is, the biological limit. Women do not face continu-

---

[26] The mean age at marriage for women in the United States is about the same, and for men somewhat younger.

ous pregnancies without misgivings, although most accept them with fatalistic composure.

Attitudes toward birth control
To wish that destiny might be kind is one matter; to seek actively the prevention of birth is another. In response to this suggestion a woman said: "If a dead 'soul' wishes to be born into your family, it would be a terrible sin to prevent its birth. We will pay for such acts in our next life. Children that are to be born to you must be allowed to be born. That is how life goes on. We cannot and should not prevent this." Here speaks the voice of the community, echoed by men and women alike. A rebirth in the great cycle must not be denied to any being. (The belief in reincarnation is a basic tenet of Sinhalese culture.) A former Prime Minister of Ceylon supported this village interpretation, a position not held, however, by several other prominent Buddhist political leaders. In spite of verbal conformity by the villagers, the interviewers agree that a majority of the mothers would welcome some morally suitable relief from the imminent arrival of the next baby. They also agree that the fathers see no cause for worry and have nothing ill to say of the most fertile marriage.

The attitudes of men toward family size and birth control are not modified by the burden of childbearing and child care. Men sincerely want large families, and especially many sons: "Children are prosperity." Not once in the extensive discussions with village men was there a mention of the difficulties of child care. The personal trials and burdens of parenthood are almost wholly the mother's. Father is proud parent toward his neighbors, a caresser of infants in the home, and contributor to his kin status through well-calculated marriages. He is served by his household, and the larger his small kingdom, the greater his dignity and glory. Through children, especially sons, he gains status as a man, is assured that his responsibilities will be inherited by others and that he himself will have security in his old age. The wife has no avenue of escape from the increasing demands upon her made by the growing family. The father works no harder to provide for a large family. He merely lives less well until the youth begin earning.

The husband's sexual authority is the most important single element for an understanding of fertility. Time and again the word "property" appears, describing the wife, and frequent allusions are made to the transfer of paternal authority from the wife's father to the husband. The woman's lot is cast with an unknown male prepared for the role of patriarch. Economic dependence supports this pattern. Once a woman is given in marriage, she is expected to stick to her husband regardless of how trying married life with him may be. Her parents cannot afford to maintain grandchildren or meet the expense of a second marriage.

Only with respect to age at marriage is the Sinhalese pattern inconsistent with high reproductivity. (In the more remote districts, however, girls are frequently married soon after puberty.) For the most part family structure and mores are consistent with high reproduction, and the economic cost of children is slight. The village girl fears spinsterhood or being a childless wife; infertility is treated with contempt. However, the stigma of infertility is relieved with the birth of even a single child, and the difficulties of childbearing and child care increase in at least arithmetical ratio to numbers. With these difficulties the husband has no part and rarely much concern, for they are the natural functions of his wife and her god-given means of pleasing him. The husband is also motivated by something the wife can never fully share. Children are contributions to *his* family, not to hers; the wife is an agent for the husband's kin; he is of its very substance. To her, children may be assets of the conjugal union, but to him they are also assets in the society to which his first loyalties belong.

Doubtless a substantial minority of village women are today trying to reduce the frequency of pregnancies. Lack of technical knowledge is perhaps no greater a handicap than the unsympathetic attitudes of dominant males. It seems fair to conclude that *if* women were provided with simple contraceptive techniques which were made consistent with moral precepts, and *if* the techniques were used without their husbands' knowledge, the more youthful mothers of several children would use them. The "moral rationalization" of contraception should present no great difficulties, for the Buddhist position is not doctrinaire, and the people are skilled in adapting and compromising even rigid precepts. However, the secret use of contraceptive devices is improbable. The combined effects of male sex dominance and the distinctive male rewards for numerous progeny may retard a small-family movement more than might be expected from Western experience.

SECTION 5 ECOLOGY

INTRODUCTION

Ecology (from *oikos,* the Greek word for house, and by extension, habitat) is the study of the adaptation of living things to the environment and the mutual relations that occur in the course of that adaptation. The environment includes both other organisms and the inanimate physical setting, and the basic data for ecology are spatial distributions. Ecology as a branch of the biological sciences developed during the nineteenth and twentieth centuries and was greatly stimulated by the observations and writings of Charles Darwin (1809–1882), and by the German biologist Ernst Haeckel (1834–1919) who coined the term *ecology* in 1866.

Long before Park introduced "human ecology" in American sociology in 1921, studies of the spatial distribution of interrelated social facts such as crime rates and population characteristics were being done in Europe.[27] Such ideas became increasingly prominent through the nineteenth century, and in his *Division of Labor,* first published in 1893, Durkheim conceived of a "social morphology" to cover "(1) the study of the environmental basis of social organization and (2) the study of population phenomena, especially size, density, and spatial distribution."[28]

Cooperation and competition An important theme of ecology is cooperation-competition. Organisms and species compete for limited space and resources. Some organisms help each other to achieve a stable adjustment and to control the environment. Others compete directly and tend to displace each other, for example, man and predatory animals. In the course of this competition, certain organisms or species come to dominate a given natural area. The basic ideas of ecology (e.g., cooperation-competition) are strongly sociological, as Darwin was aware and intended. It is not surprising, therefore, that efforts were made to study the spatial distribution of human groups and their institutions in the framework of ecological ideas. The fact that the discipline cuts across biological and social sciences has encouraged some to suggest that ecology may contain the seeds of a unifying science.

Social or *human ecology* is closely related to population analysis. Many of its data are population data, and the skills required for research in this field are essentially those of the population expert. However, ecology is not concerned with all population data but primarily those which can be expressed as spatial distributions. Furthermore, it has a distinctive theoretical focus, competition for space and resources. Ecological studies have been made of areas as large as regions (and studies of regionalism [29] have some of the same basic ideas as ecological research), but thus far the American metropolis has been the chief topic for the social ecologist. Urban ecology is discussed in URBAN MAN, pages 443–453.

SOURCES AND READINGS

A. W. Hawley, *Human Ecology* (New York: Ronald Press, 1950).

[27] George A. Theodorson (ed.), *Studies in Human Ecology* (New York: Harper & Row, 1961), p. 3.

[28] Leo F. Schnore, "Social Morphology and Human Ecology," *American Journal of Sociology, 63* (May, 1958), 620, reprinted in Leo F. Schnore, *The Urban Scene* (New York: The Free Press of Glencoe, 1965).

[29] See, for example, H. W. Odum, *Southern Regions of the United States* (Chapel Hill: University of North Carolina Press, 1936); and H. W. Odum and H. E. Moore, *American Regionalism* (New York: Holt, Rinehart & Winston, 1938).

R. E. Park, *Human Communities* (Glencoe: The Free Press, 1952).

J. A. Quinn, *Human Ecology* (New York: Prentice-Hall, 1950).

George A. Theodorson (ed.), *Studies in Human Ecology* (New York: Harper & Row, 1961).

William L. Thomas, Jr. (ed.), *Man's Role in Changing the Face of the Earth* (Chicago: University of Chicago Press, 1956).

ECOLOGICAL SUCCESSION

The process of competition begins when a group or species newly enters an area. The ecologists call this entry *invasion* and if the new group displaces the original occupants, it is called *succession.*

The Hawaiian case   The principle of succession is illustrated in an analysis of changing land use and the changing occupational distribution of the various racial groups in Hawaii.[30] Prior to extensive contacts with Western civilization, Hawaiians lived under conditions of *closed* resources; that is, at their level of technological development the land and other resources were supporting the largest feasible population. It was a balanced relationship between man and the natural environment.

The advent of settlers from outside the Islands disturbed this relationship, and over the years new opportunities were created. Western technology and agricultural techniques from both East and West opened up new uses for the land and changed the condition of closed resources to one of open resources. The subsequent history of land use in the Islands has been the utilization of the land by increasingly advanced agricultural technology and progressive steps toward another state of closed resources based on new uses of the land. This took the form of a plantation economy with large production of money crops, sugar, and later pineapples, for the world market.

More manpower was needed to exploit the land because the Hawaiians could not fill the demand for workers. The plantations, therefore, imported contract labor largely from Asia. "But under the conditions of open resources [then] prevalent . . . in Hawaii, the population recruited for the plantation has been unwilling to accept plantation labor as a permanent occupational and social adjustment, and a series of movements away from the plantation and into vocations believed to be more remunerative and socially desirable has occurred."[31]

The movements away from the plantation created recurring labor shortages, which the plantations solved by successive importations.[32] Internal adjustments in the Island community were complicated by the fact that the several corps of workers came from different nations (see Table IX:8).

"Each of the major immigrant groups . . . may be conceived as invaders whose position in the new land is determined by the intensity of the existing occupation and their ability to compete. The latest arrivals occupy the places of lowest esteem in the region, and their subsequent locations measure their rise in status."[33] The earlier immigrants had advantages over those who came later, so that at any time the early migrants tended to be disproportionately located in the upper levels of the status hierarchy. The Hawaiian case is almost a model illustration of the process of invasion and succession as the immigrants entered the labor market and then followed each other up the occupational hierarchy. Table IX:9 reports the sequence in which three major immigrant populations left agricultural labor for other employment. Compare Table IX:9 with the order of immigration summarized in Table IX:8. By 1910 the process of leav-

---

[30] Andrew W. Lind, *An Island Community* (Chicago: University of Chicago Press, 1938).

[31] Lind, *op. cit.,* p. vi.

[32] Plantation systems based on slavery were devised to solve such manpower problems. They were designed to retain labor on the estates whether or not there were good work opportunities elsewhere. Nieboer holds that slavery arises as an attempt to keep labor on the land when there are ample unsettled areas, a condition of open resources. See H. Nieboer, *Slavery as an Industrial System* (The Hague: Martinus Nijoff, 1900).

[33] Lind, *op. cit.,* p. v.

ing plantation labor was already far advanced for the Chinese, the earliest immigrants, and well under way for the Japanese.

TABLE IX:8 PRINCIPAL IMMIGRATIONS TO HAWAII, 1876–1934

IMMIGRANTS	CHIEF PERIOD	TOTAL IMMIGRANTS (*estimate*) *
Chinese	1876–1900	45,000
Japanese	1890–1919	140,000
Filipinos	1909–1934	125,000

* Estimates, courtesy of Norman Meller.

TABLE IX:9 PERCENT OF MALE LABOR FORCE IN AGRICULTURAL LABOR FOR THREE RACIAL GROUPS, HAWAII, 1910–1940

RACIAL GROUP	1910	1920	1930	1940
Chinese	38.4	32.7	18.4	5.1
Japanese	55.3	47.5	26.5	19.7
Filipinos	—	82.2	83.0	69.9

SOURCE: Data from U.S. Bureau of the Census.

In addition to the sequences of occupational succession, similar changes occurred in the demographic characteristics of the immigrants, their degrees of residential segregation in the metropolitan area of Honolulu, and their patterns of intermarriage.

LIMITED ALTERNATIVES

In a pure market economy the process of ecological competition leads to the determination of land use strictly on the criteria of cost and efficiency. Land is allocated to those uses that yield the highest rents or earnings; there is complete competition between land uses as well as land users. Land which is first utilized for grazing is taken over for cultivation, then for residential development, and finally for industrial or commercial use. Each succession in such competition for occupancy leads to more intensive land use with progressively higher financial yield per acre.

Land exhaustion If there were an inexhaustible supply of all kinds of land, the objections to a free market approach would be less vehement. However, the most productive kinds of land are in short supply and the most productive soils are often those on which it is cheapest to place real estate developments or factories. Houses would cost more if they were built on slopes unsuitable to agricultural use, because of lower density and the need for expensive safeguards. But the added cost would, according to some scholars, be counterbalanced by preserving the land for agriculture.

In 1960 about 2.5 percent of all California land was in urban use, and it is estimated that by 1975 about 4 percent will be urban. Although in absolute terms 4 percent may seem a small amount, "urban expansion occurs almost entirely on the very finest agricultural land." [34] Furthermore, the increase of 1.5 percent from 2.5 percent to 4 percent is in fact an increase of 60 percent in fifteen years. The succession from agricultural to urban use is going on all over the world at a time of rapid population growth and the increasing hazard of a worldwide food shortage. The risks are complicated by the fact that the process of shifting land use changes the land. It now costs too much to return land from urban to rural use. The urbanization process is for all practical purposes irreversible, except over a long period of time. Not all ecological processes are irreversible and no strict determinacy should be assumed. However, ecological study instructs the planner to consider the cost of undoing the successively more intensive land uses.

We know that today many cities have within their present boundaries enough vacant land to take care of growth for the next twenty years. We know that if we want to we can insist that housing and industry and other developments be located on lovely rolling hills instead of on desirable agricultural land. We know that we can run our highways along the edges of the fine land instead of through it.

[34] Emil M. Mrak, "Food and Land: The Coming Shortage," *Cry California, 1* (Summer, 1966), p. 6.

Doing some of these things might cost us more money today than not doing them. But surely we will live to rue the day when we worried about the cost of housing developments and highways rather than retaining our finest agricultural areas for future production.[35]

The ecosystem and open space The foregoing quotation runs counter to the precepts of urban land use planning in that it calls for higher densities inside cities in order to preserve other lands for agricultural production. This collision of two enlightened atti-

tudes points out that the interrelation of different social uses of land needs to be studied in a broader framework than heretofore. Large regions encompassing both rural and urban land uses are coming to be viewed as systems of patterned ecological relations, in which changes in one part rebound upon the other parts of the ecosystem. However, the multitude of municipal, county, and state jurisdictions within any such region inhibit planning for the area as a whole.

The changed perspective toward open spaces was

[35] *Loc. cit.*

Encroachment of urban uses: Santa Clara and Almaden Valleys, California

ECOLOGICAL CORRELATIONS

A substantial amount of research in social ecology has attempted to relate characteristics of areas as measured by rates, averages, and the like to the characteristics of individuals within those areas. It has been shown that correlations between rates or averages for areas need not and often do not accurately represent the characteristics of the individuals within the areas.

To demonstrate the risks of inferring individual characteristics from ecological correlations, Robinson first plotted for each of the Census Bureau's nine geographic divisions (groups of states) the percentage of the population ten years old and over which was Negro in 1930 and the percentage of the population in each division which was illiterate. This is shown in the scattergram, in which the percent Negro for each division is plotted on the *x* (horizontal) axis and the percent illiterate on the *y* (vertical) axis. He then calculated the Pearsonian correlation and found it to be .946. (See p. 173.) At this point the dangers of reasoning from ecological correlations become apparent. The scattergram shows only that the divisions with relatively large proportions of Negroes are also the

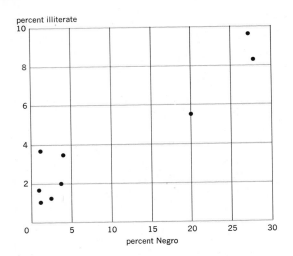

divisions with relatively large proportions of illiterates. One may erroneously assume that the Negroes contribute to illiteracy to the extent suggested by the correlation. In this case, because the correlation approaches 1.00 (unity), this faulty reasoning would lead to the conclusion that the Negroes were responsible for practically

SOURCE: Based on W. S. Robinson, "Ecological Correlations and the Behavior of Individuals," *American Sociological Review, 15* (June, 1950), 351–357.

expressed first in efforts to preserve areas in their original "natural" condition for future generations. As cities grow larger and as more people can afford to travel, they have sought respite from high density environments. But during the vacation season the efficiencies of automobiles and good roads have changed the more popular parks into rustic concentrations of urban density. The press reports smog in Yosemite National Park and the same social problems that characterize cities. The broader view of the ecosystem considers agricultural land not merely in its productive capacity but as part of the heritage of open space. It has been proposed that metropolitan regional plans provide for taxing such lands according to open-space use rather than high-density and residential use.

Caution The ideas of human ecology have been

all of the illiteracy. In fact this is not so. Table IX:10 shows how many thousands of Negroes and whites in the United States were literate and illiterate in 1930.

Negroes did include among their number a larger percentage of illiterates, but the correlation between race and illiteracy for individuals is only .203, about one-fifth of the ecological correlation. Whites as well as Negroes in the divisions of high illiteracy were illiterates. One cannot tell from an ecological correlation *which* individuals in an area are responsible for the correlations.

In political ecology the problem may present itself in the following way. Suppose that a dominantly Catholic district moves from its tradi-tional place in the Democratic column into the Republican column by a modest margin. If individual voting was not studied, three hypotheses are plausible: (1) the Catholic-Democratic bloc may be breaking down, and enough Catholics may have voted Republican to swing the district. (2) On the other hand, a minority of Protestants who had previously voted Democratic may have turned Republican, and the change in a "Catholic-Democratic" district may actually be caused by Protestants. (3) The change may be due to a difference in turnout. Individuals who did not participate in earlier elections may have decided to vote, and they may have been the decisive factor; or persons who had voted Democratic in earlier elections may not have voted at all.

TABLE IX:10 THE INDIVIDUAL CORRELATION BETWEEN COLOR AND ILLITERACY, UNITED STATES, 1930 *

	NEGRO		WHITE		TOTAL	
Illiterate	1,512	(16.1%)	2,406	(2.7%)	3,918	(4.0%)
Literate	7,780	(83.9%)	85,574	(97.3%)	93,354	(96.0)%
Total	9,292	(100%)	87,980	(100%)	97,272	(100%)

* Robinson, *op. cit.* (For population ten years old and over. Figures are in thousands.)

drawn from observations of the adaptation of the lower animals and plants to their environments. Such analogies should be used with caution. Man's behavior is not merely an immediate adaptation to an immediate environment. It is adaptive in a much broader sense. Man is capable of modifying his environment in many ways, and he may attach sentiments and values to his environment. He may then adjust according to the dictates of sentiments rather than directly to the natural environment.[36]

[36] Cf. Walter Firey, *Land Use in Central Boston* (Cambridge: Harvard University Press, 1947), *passim;* and Warner E. Gettys, "Human Ecology and Social Theory," *Social Forces, 18* (May, 1940), 469–476.

PART TWO

ANALYSIS
OF MAJOR
INSTITUTIONS

BMID TERM

CHAPTER X
RELIGION

With the collaboration of
Gertrude Jaeger Selznick

SECTION 1 INTRODUCTION

Religious beliefs and practices exist in every known society, from the most simple and isolated to the most complex and urbane. Not all individuals are religious, but some form of religious behavior is found in all human communities.

As important as the universality of religion is its remarkable diversity. Some religions believe in a single supreme being, others are polytheistic. In Buddhism the central figure is a great teacher and the idea of a deity is elusive and attenuated. In some preliterate societies religion centers around spirits, forces, and demons that are often capricious, willful, and malevolent.

Religious rituals, emotions, and prescriptions are no less varied than religious beliefs. A ritual may be a ceremony of adoration and supplication addressed to an all-wise and merciful god; it may be a way of propitiating a being who would otherwise bring evil upon the community; it may be solemn and dignified or include dancing, sexual rites, wild celebrations.

Religious emotions run the gamut from reverence to terror, joy to self-abasement, ecstasy to peace of mind.

Early efforts by social science to account for the universality of religion tended to see it as a socially-transmitted relic of man's prescientific and primitive past. Religious belief was often interpreted as a kind of error or fancy, traceable to confusion in the mind of primitive man. For example, a century ago Tylor traced the origin of the concept of a soul, and of spirits, to primitive man's attempt to account for his dreams and for death.[1]

Modern social science takes a different approach. The explanation of human religiosity is to be found in the basic functions religion performs for the individual and for society, not in error and ignorance. The universality of religion is traced not to man's propensity to make false inferences, but to traits of the human condition that persist even in an age of science.

[1] Edward B. Tylor, *Primitive Culture* (London: Murray, 1873), Chap. 11.

FOUNDATIONS OF RELIGION

The foundations of religion must be sought in the nature of human personality as well as in the requirements of social solidarity.

1. *Overcoming fear and anxiety*. To the extent that man's world is dangerous and unpredictable, he must endure and try to overcome specific fears and more general anxiety. Unease may stem from fear of natural forces and man's sense of his own weakness compared to the overwhelming power around him. Social circumstances, too, can be cruel and capricious, and there is always the uncertain certainty of death.

Man may respond to such fears and anxieties by revering the powers of nature, appeasing them, or seeking their cooperation. He may also look to a supernatural realm in which, after death, he will be safe from the frustrations of human existence.

2. *Self-justification and the quest for ultimate meaning*. In all societies there is evidence of man's search for moral meaning. He seeks an organizing principle that will validate his most important strivings, and make sense of his sufferings. Through belief in a God-given scheme of things the individual can meet frustration with greater equanimity, and can turn potential chaos and meaninglessness into an orderly scheme.

3. *The search for self-transcendence*. Most human experiences are routine and do not evoke strong emotions or strange feelings. But there are circumstances that lift man out of himself and in which he seems to transcend his everyday self. Great natural events may accomplish this by casting men into a state of extraordinary fear and awe. In addition, certain individuals are able to enter into psychological states that appear to enlarge their vision and bring them into mystic union with the world. Many religions foster this kind of experience through incantation, dance, and similar practices. A sense of self-transcendence may also be induced by drugs, as in the Peyote cult among North American Indians.[2] Recently discovered synthetics, such as LSD (d-lysergic acid diethylamid), sometimes called psychedelic or "mind-expanding" drugs, reportedly produce somewhat the same effect, giving the user a sense of transcending his everyday self.[3]

4. *Celebration of human powers and achievements*. Many religious beliefs and activities reflect pride and exultation rather than humility and despair. A victory dance, the divinity of kings, a belief in being specially chosen for a divine mission—these and many other acts and symbols celebrate man and his group and their special relation to the ultimate source of power and meaning.

5. *Making the world comprehensible*. In all societies, some effort is made to explain and interpret man's environment. This may take the form of a cosmology, explaining the origins of the earth and the heavens; various animals may be seen as mysterious beings whose special qualities of swiftness or cunning need special explanations; the fruitfulness or barrenness of the land, the cycles of birth and death, winter and summer, can all be represented in a more or less elaborate theology or mythology. This process of interpretation reflects an impulse to make the world more comprehensible, more familiar, and more meaningful.

6. *Supporting social norms and values*. Society depends on the willing cooperation of its members. For the most part, cooperation is won through ordinary processes of socialization. But socialization is to some degree imperfect. The socializers need all the help they can get, particularly when a large amount of self-discipline is required. By adding divine sanction to human values, religion buttresses the norms of society and unites its adherents into a moral community whose members feel a deep common bond because they share a belief in what is morally "true."

This classification of personal and social needs and desires does not include everything that may evoke a religious response, but it covers the major sources of

---

[2] Vittorio Lanternari, *The Religions of the Oppressed* (New York: Mentor Books, 1965), Chap. II.

[3] R. E. L. Masters and Jean Huston, *The Varieties of Psychedelic Experience* (New York: Holt, Rinehart and Winston, 1966), Chap. 9.

religious experience that have been identified and analyzed. Obviously not all men or groups have these requirements or motivations in the same degree. In some societies or historical periods, religion may be largely a way of handling fears; at another time or place the significant source of religion might be the quest for a moral identity, the celebration of human achievement, or the effort to make the world comprehensible.

An understanding of the variety of problems that tend to produce religious responses leads us away from trying to locate the origin of religion in some single factor. Religion is not a unique response to a unique problem. It is a way of meeting many different problems.

Religion is only one of the alternative ways of overcoming anxiety, integrating personality, supporting social norms, or satisfying the other conditions mentioned above. Religion is summoned and sustained by these requirements, but other social institutions, such as politics, education, science, and the arts, serve many of the same ends. Religion supplements these other social devices, sometimes competes with them, and often fills the breach when they are absent or inadequate. Supporters of religion believe that it can meet the most essential personal needs, and that without religion the moral foundations of society will wither.

The basic response Many sociologists believe that the core of religion may be found in the creation of the sacred. The basic religious response consists in man's relating himself to what he recognizes as the sacred or in the transformation of what is profane and secular into what is sacred or holy.

When something is made sacred, it is invested with a special meaning or worth, treated with reverence, awe, and respect. Anything can be made sacred: a mountain, a part of the human body, a belief, a meeting place, an animal, a cup of oil or water. But if it is sacred, it is perceived as different from the everyday world. What is sacred is not a mere means or instrument. Though it may be used in a ceremony, it is itself a thing apart toward which proper respect is due.

Sometimes the sacred is created by endowing parts of the world with a special and mysterious power. This does not necessarily involve a belief in particular gods or spirits. Thus the idea of *mana*, associated with the peoples of Polynesia and Melanesia, refers to an impersonal power that may be located in any object—a song, a man, a plant, a stone. The essential point is that mana is extraordinary power and produces extraordinary results.

If a man's pigs multiply and his gardens are productive, it is not because he is industrious and looks after his property, but because of the stones full of mana for pigs and yams that he possesses. Of course a yam naturally grows when planted, that is well known, but it will not be very large unless mana comes into play: a canoe will not be swift unless mana be brought to bear upon it, a net will not catch many fish, nor an arrow inflict a mortal wound.[4]

Mana sets things apart and gives them a unique significance. It transcends the ordinary. Therefore the principle of mana is a long step toward the creation of a sacred realm, even though all the attitudes usually associated with sacredness may not be present.

The recognition or creation of sacredness lays a foundation for faith and moral commitment. What is sacred has its own claim to respect and obedience. Because it is a special realm, the sacred may offer a new vision and a new truth unlimited by the criteria of the commonsense world.

To recognize, create, elaborate, and protect the sacred is the distinctive competence of religion. However, other institutions also participate in these tasks. The political community creates sacred documents and symbols, such as the constitution, the flag, and the founding fathers.[5] Similarly, the culture can lend an air of sacredness to basic values, such as motherhood and the preservation of human life. Whatever its source, the more sacred any act or belief, the more

[4] R. H. Codrington, "Man," in W. A. Lessa and E. Z. Vogt, *Reader in Comparative Religion* (2nd ed.; New York: Harper & Row, 1965), p. 257.

[5] W. Lloyd Warner, *American Life: Dream and Reality* (Chicago: University of Chicago Press, 1962), Chap. 1.

*Street scene in the holy
Hindu city of Benares, India:
A woman offers to a cow
cakes prepared and sold to
pilgrims for this purpose.
The cow is worshiped by
Hindus as a source of life,
and its slaughter is forbidden.*

likely it is to take on a religious quality. Thus religious institutions specialize in the sacred. And other institutions tend to become religious when they too engage in the basic religious response—the creation of the sacred.

THE ELEMENTS OF RELIGION

In the study of religion, it is necessary to distinguish the following elements or components: [6]

1. *Ritual.* All religions observe ceremonial practices or rituals. Religious rituals are prescribed acts that are sacred in themselves and also symbolize the sacred. Among Christians, the communion service is sacred and also symbolizes the sacrifice of Christ.

The ritualization of behavior is a mechanism by which sacredness is created and sustained. A way of making baskets, a family gathering, or any other socially important practice may, by being ritualized, become set apart as sacred. At the same time, whatever is sacred tends to be ritualized. In its origin the ritual practice may be simply a way of coordinating activity

and creating respect for the group and its traditions. But as the practice takes on more symbolic meaning and is connected with other religious acts and symbols, people come to think of it, and act toward it, as a religious ceremony.

2. *Feeling.* One function of ritual is to evoke appropriate feelings. The patriotic rite brings forth loyalty, pride, and a sense of closeness to one's fellow-countrymen. In this way the sacredness of the nation and of civic identity is affirmed. Religious emotions are appropriate to whatever is most sacred in the society. The religious emotion depends on the nature of the ceremony and of what is symbolized by it. Humility, reverence, and awe are common religious feelings, but ecstasy or terror may also be displayed. Whatever the feeling, it is prescribed as appropriate, it is expected, and it is stimulated and supported by the resources and techniques of the religion.

3. *Belief.* Conceivably, religious ritual and feeling may occur prior to, and independently of, specifically

[6] For a discussion of dimensions of "religiosity," see C. Y. Glock and R. Stark, *Religion and Society in Tension* (Chicago: Rand McNally, 1965), pp. 18–38.

religious ideas.[7] However, in almost all known so- cieties, there are beliefs that justify and support re- ligious rituals and feelings. Moreover, beliefs have their own powerful role to play in the creation of sacredness and in meeting the human problems to which religion responds.

In the past religious beliefs have almost always involved the supernatural. Divine beings are not of this world but outside it or above it and not subject to the ordinary limitations of man and beast. In the- ory, however, religion can exist without a belief in supernatural beings. A set of great truths or prin- ciples may be given a sacred status around which a system of auxiliary beliefs and practices is organized.

The ways of belief are variable and problematic. Some are dedicated believers; others believe in a routine way; others "believe" in an ambiguous and detached way. Some try to reinterpret religious doc- trines to make them compatible with other beliefs, such as the findings of science. They may empha- size the symbolic significance of beliefs and thus avoid taking literally views about an afterlife or the origins of the universe. Recent years have seen the development, especially among Protestant thinkers,[8] of a "God is dead" theology. This theology, accepting the radical secularization of modern society, stresses the irrelevance of traditional belief in God. At the same time, it draws on Christian symbolism and thought for a perspective that emphasizes religious action rather than doctrine.

4. *Organization.* Religious activities usually form the basis of a community of believers. (See pp. 333 ff.) Organization is needed to maintain beliefs and traditions, to conduct religious assemblies where be- lief and feeling are reinforced, to recruit and train specialists in religious ritual and doctrine, and to deal with the relations between the religious group and the rest of the society. In undifferentiated societies there may be no separate religious organization. In that case other institutions of the tribe or village do the needed organizational work, for example, se- lecting religious leaders; the religious group is co- extensive with the community.

Following Durkheim, "a religion" may be defined as a *unified system of beliefs and practices relative to sacred things, uniting into a single moral com- munity all those who adhere to those beliefs and practices.*[9] Any given religion is made up of a *com- bination* of the components mentioned above—ritual, feeling, belief, and organization. Some religions may be strong on organization but make few demands on feeling; others may emphasize ritual but not belief. In comparing religions one must specify what com- ponents, or combination of them, are being consid- ered.

The same caution applies when asking: Who is more religious? Are people becoming more or less re- ligious? Is religion declining or gaining strength? Un- less the basis of comparison is specified, incorrect con- clusions will be drawn. For example, an observed strengthening of religious organization, measured by increased membership, funds, or buildings, may or may not be associated with a strengthening of religi- ous belief or feeling.

---

[7] See Clyde Kluckhohn, "Myths and Rituals: A General Theory," *Harvard Theological Review, 35* (January, 1942), 45–79.

[8] Thomas J. J. Altizer and William Hamilton, *Radical Theology and the Death of God* (Indianapolis: Bobbs-Merrill, 1966), esp. pp. 23–50.

[9] Emile Durkheim, *The Elementary Forms of the Religious Life* (Glencoe: The Free Press, 1947), p. 47. (First published in 1912).

SOURCES AND READINGS

Michael Argyle, *Religious Behavior* (London: Rout- ledge & Kegan Paul, 1958).

Emile Durkheim, *The Elementary Forms of the Re- ligious Life* (Glencoe: The Free Press, 1947).

Joseph H. Fichter, *Social Relations in the Urban Parish* (Chicago: Univ. of Chicago Press, 1954).

Sigmund Freud, *The Future of an Illusion* (London: Hogarth, 1928).

Charles Y. Glock and Rodney Stark, *Religion and Society in Tension* (Chicago: Rand McNally, 1965).

William J. Goode, *Religion Among the Primitives* (Glencoe: The Free Press, 1951).

Thomas Ford Hoult, *The Sociology of Religion* (New York: Holt, Rinehart and Winston, 1958).

Richard D. Knudten (ed.), *The Sociology of Religion* (New York: Appleton-Century-Crofts, 1967).

William A. Lessa and Evon Z. Vogt, *Reader in Comparative Religion* (2nd ed.; New York: Harper & Row, 1965).

Thomas F. O'Dea, *The Sociology of Religion* (Englewood Cliffs, N.J.: Prentice-Hall, 1966).

Louis Schneider (ed.), *Religion, Culture, and Society* (New York: Wiley, 1964).

Glenn M. Vernon, *Sociology of Religion* (New York: McGraw-Hill, 1962).

Max Weber's studies in the sociology of religion include *The Protestant Ethic and the Spirit of Capitalism* (London: George Allen & Unwin, 1930); *The Religion of China, The Religion of India, Ancient Judaism* (published by The Free Press of Glencoe, 1951, 1958, 1958, respectively).

J. Milton Yinger, *Religion, Society and the Individual* (New York: Macmillan, 1957).

SECTION 2 SOCIAL ORGANIZATION

During most of man's history, religion has been more than "just another institution." It has been looked to as the sanctifier of human activities, the protector of group continuity, the builder of morale and solidarity, the bridge across whatever divides man from man and group from group. However, the extent to which these functions are performed, and how they are performed, depends on the place of religion in society.

FUSION OF RELIGION AND GROUP LIFE

In ancient Greece and Rome, religious practices and beliefs were an inseparable part of family and civic life. Religion was, at first, a religion of family and hearth. A sacred fire burned at an altar in every house, and care was taken that it should not be extinguished. Family ancestors were venerated and the head of the household was its priest. The gods of the family were their own. The family was a religious unit.

In his classic work, *The Ancient City,* the French historian Coulanges (1830–1889) called religion the "constituent principle" of the family in early Greece and Rome.[10] He meant that common worship was the foundation of family life and the criterion of membership. A son was no longer counted part of the family if he renounced the worship. An adopted son, on the other hand, "was counted a real son, because, though he had not the ties of blood, he had something better—a community of worship. . . . A family was a group of persons whom religion permitted to invoke the same sacred fire, and to offer the funeral repast to the same ancestors."[11] The social bond was thereby made a sacrament.

The special character of this domestic religion influenced other aspects of social life. For example, it helps explain why these communities, in contrast to others, held the idea of private property in land. The hearth was perceived as permanent, remaining forever on the same site, establishing an intimate and mysterious connection with the soil. The gods thereby "owned" the soil; but the family "owned" its gods and there was a strong identification between a particular family and its land.

---

[10] Fustel de Coulanges, *The Ancient City: A Study on the Religion, Laws, and Institutions of Greece and Rome* (Garden City N.Y.: [Anchor] Doubleday, 1956), p. 40.

[11] *Ibid.,* p. 42.

The enlargement of religious identity If each family has its own god or gods, there are many gods. When common worship is the foundation of group identity, such extreme polytheism is inconsistent with the enlargement of the group beyond the boundaries of the family. In early Greece and Rome, this problem was eased in two ways. First, the family religion began to include *gods of nature*—representations of the sea, the sun, the forest, etc.—as well as deified ancestors, and the gods of nature were universal and could be shared with other families. Secondly, the multiplicity of family gods was modified when one family and its nature god attained greater influence:

It happened, in the course of time, the divinity of a family having acquired great prestige over the imaginations of men, and appearing powerful in proportion to the prosperity of this family, that a whole city wished to adopt him, and offer him public worship, to obtain his favors. This was the case with the Demeter of the Eumolpidae, the Athene of the Butadae, and the Hercules of the Potitii. But when a family consented thus to share a god, it retained at least the priesthood. We may remark that the dignity of priest, for each god, was during a long time hereditary, and could not go out of a certain family. This is a vestige of a time when the god himself was the property of this family; when he protected it alone, and would be served only by it.[12]

As families united into tribes and tribes into a city, religion remained both symbol and bond of the new association. The union was marked by appropriate ceremonies, such as the lighting of a sacred fire, and by adoption of a common religion. Unification was strengthened when the image of the divine transcended the particularity of family and place. Ultimately, universal religions were founded on principles and symbols common to all mankind.

When religious identity and social identity are fused, we speak of *communal* religion. In a communal religion a person is considered a believer, or member of the religious community, by virtue of his membership in a family, clan, city, or state. He is born into the religion, and if he renounces it, he thereby renounces his social group. It is said that in the communal religion of ancient China, "there was no choice in religious beliefs, but neither did it occur to the common man to make any other choice. Religious values were imbedded in the traditional moral order, and religion was an integral part of communal existence, inseparable from the individual's existence."[13]

One mark of communal religion is the combination of religious and secular roles. In a family-based communal religion the father is also the priest and the home is the temple. In the broader city-based communal religion political and religious authority are combined. High priest, judge, and political chief are often one.

RELIGION DIFFERENTIATED

The differentiation of institutions is a fundamental historical trend. As societies become larger and more complex, activities become more specialized. Different functions are disentangled and become lodged in distinct institutions.

The emergence of religion as a separate institutional sphere is stimulated and supported by the following mechanisms:

1. *Voluntary religious affiliation.* When religious identity is based on voluntary choice rather than inherited status, there is a push toward differentiation. Members of the same family may adhere to different faiths. In self-defense a new faith often dissociates itself from politics. Thus early Christianity sought to distinguish what belonged to God and to Caesar; it proclaimed itself "not of this world"; it remained for many years separate from and an irritation to the political order. Thus the emergence of a new perspective—the possibility of being converted to a new faith as an individual and by free choice—helped lay the foundation for institutional differentiation.

2. *A religious officialdom.* Even when a religion is closely integrated with the political order, and mem-

[12] *Ibid.*, p. 125.

[13] C. K. Yang, *Religion in Chinese Society* (Berkeley and Los Angeles: University of California Press, 1961), p. 111.

bership is not voluntary, differentiation does occur. In a complex community the priesthood becomes a specialized activity. The community delegates to a high priest or archbishop the responsibility and authority for religious affairs and for ruling a church hierarchy. The mere existence of this religious officialdom creates a vested interest and a distinct occupational community. The churchmen are jealous of their privileges, and protective of the special values entrusted to them. The result is a greater religious self-consciousness, and lines are drawn between religion and other institutional spheres.

3. *Independence of nonreligious activities.* When religion is fused with the social order, it not only serves other institutions—it also controls them. As society becomes more differentiated, the worlds of science, art, education, law, and economics seek freedom to develop on their own. They encourage the perception of religion as a specialized sphere and set limits to the scope of religious authority.

The differentiation of religion does not necessarily keep it from influencing the secular order. Indeed, the very autonomy of religion may give it a sense of mission and make it a source of creativity. Religious leaders can develop their own ideas of what the social world should be like and try to influence that world.

The social influence of religion is not always planned or self-conscious. The Protestant Reformation had a considerable but unintended impact on the development of capitalism. (See INDUSTRIAL MAN, pp. 464 ff.)

RELIGION AND SOCIAL COHESION

From the standpoint of its role in society, one of the great potential capabilities of religion is the promotion of group cohesion. Durkheim was so impressed by this that he built his theory of religion on it. "The idea of society," he wrote, "is the soul of religion." [14]

He tried to find behind the variety of religious

rites, symbols, and beliefs the fundamental characteristic of all religions.

There is something eternal in religion which is destined to survive all the particular symbols in which religious thought has successively enveloped itself. There can be no society which does not feel the need of upholding and reaffirming at regular intervals the collective sentiments and the collective ideas which make its unity and its personality. Now this moral remaking cannot be achieved except by the means of reunions, assemblies and meetings where the individuals, being closely united to one another, reaffirm in common their common sentiments . . . . What essential difference is there between an assembly of Christians celebrating the principal dates of the life of Christ, or of Jews remembering the exodus from Egypt or the promulgation of the decalogue, and a reunion of citizens commemorating the promulgation of a new moral or legal system or some great event in the national life? [15]

In all of these activities Durkheim saw one basic function: the celebration of the social group, a clan or a larger community. By such celebrations the individual is bound into a group which he needs and which needs him. The symbols of religion, he thought, really represent society. "The god of the clan, the totemic principle, can therefore be nothing else than the clan itself, personified and represented to the imagination under the visible form of the animal or vegetable which serves as totem." [16] Religious worship is, in effect, worship of society.

Limitations of Durkheim's theory Durkheim based his analysis on anthropological reports of religion in preliterate societies, especially in Australia. However, he did not restrict his conclusions to those or similar societies. He thought he had found the fundamental significance of all religion.

As a generalization, Durkheim's view needs the following qualifications:

1. It is wrong to ignore the varied *content* of religious beliefs and symbols. Divine ancestors or

[14] Durkheim, *op. cit.,* p. 419.
[15] *Ibid.,* p. 427.
[16] *Ibid.,* p. 206.

totems may indeed be interpreted as standing for the family or clan. In such cases, it is probably correct to say that the group itself is worshiped. However, many religious ideas go beyond representation of the group. They may foster distinctive moral principles, such as the Christian idea of self-sacrificing love. The closeness of the relation between religious symbolism and the celebration of the group should be considered a *variable*. In domestic or communal religions this relation is more marked than it is in complex and differentiated religions.

2. Not all religious experience can be understood from the standpoint of its contribution to social solidarity. The quest for salvation may be an individual act and may lead to a weakening of group ties. (See SOCIAL ORGANIZATION, page 28.) Religious withdrawal from society is not uncommon. The Protestant reformers emphasized man's lonely vigil: "His life is that of a soldier in a hostile territory." [17]

3. While all religion does contribute, at least to some extent, to the cohesion of the believers, religion does not always help integrate the entire community. Again, it is necessary to distinguish between simpler and more complex societies. Religion can be a *divisive* force when a number of different religious groups compete for communicants or when religion struggles with other institutions, such as the government, for preeminence. In the latter case religion is not less divisive than the other institutions.

Religious pluralism in the United States has raised many issues, especially those affecting the relation between church and state. For example, the present public policy, as expressed by the United States Supreme Court, fosters the separation of public education and religion. It presumes that in a religiously heterogeneous society, social cohesion will be fostered if religious activity, however minor, is divorced from government sponsorship.

[17] R. H. Tawney, *Religion and the Rise of Capitalism* (New York: Penguin Books, 1947), p. 190.

SECTION 3 CULTURE

Culture includes those activities, and their products, that express the values and perspectives of a society. Some pursuits—notably philosophy, literature, and the arts—are important vehicles of cultural expression. They formulate, embody, and interpret the values and outlooks of a society. Religion is part of this expressive realm. It also gives content and direction to the arts.

RELIGION AND ART

The connection between culture and aesthetic creativity is nowhere more evident than in religious art. Although painters, sculptors, and architects have left the most visible monuments, music, dance, poetry, and drama have also served religious ends and responded to religious influences.

The intimate relation between religion and art may be accounted for, at least in part, by the importance of *symbolism* in religion. In most religions, symbols are much in evidence. They dramatize belief; they inspire reverence or fear; they form the stuff of which ceremonies are made. The true significance of a symbol lies not in its literal meaning or form but in what it connotes and suggests. A king's crown is not a mere ornament but a symbol of sovereignty and authority; that the crown is placed upon his head by a high priest may symbolize the importance and autonomy of the church—or the integration of an established church and the state. Thus acts as well as artifacts have symbolic meaning.

Although the religious symbol has a use in a larger setting, it is more than a practical instrument or tool. When a book, a cup, a picture, or a way of kneeling takes on symbolic significance, it becomes an *expressive* product. By the very way it is constructed or handled, it is meant to convey sacred meanings and

From symbolic to representational in religious art. Left, The Last Judgment *(1130–1140), sculptured relief above the west door of St. Lazare Cathedral, Autun, France. Above,* Christ the Teacher *(1205–1215), south portal, Notre-Dame Cathedral, Chartres.*

to evoke appropriate emotions. In the construction of such symbols, the artist has a special place. His craftsmanship can embellish acts and objects so as to enhance their function as symbolic carriers of sacred meanings. (See CULTURE, pp. 52–54.)

Because a religious object is symbolic rather than utilitarian, the artist is free to exploit the expressive potentialities of his medium, whether in clay, paint, or language. Though he may have to work within a definite, prescribed religious tradition, the artist is not expected to represent everyday reality or to

evoke everyday feelings. Since distortion evokes "strange" feelings, and places the object outside everyday reality, distortion is a common feature of religious art. But distortion for the sake of expressiveness is also a device of aesthetic creativity.

Religion may offer the artist a congenial framework within which to develop his talents and express his personal vision. From the standpoint of the culture, the Greek emphasis on portraying the gods was more than an affirmation of religion. It was also a kind of language, a source of known and shared meanings. For the artist this solved many problems of communication with his public. At the same time, the religious context was a rich source of ideas and starting-points for creative work. The artist served religion while he drew upon it for inspiration.

Religious orientation and art styles   Historians of art have examined the relation between specific religious beliefs and the art styles of particular cultures or epochs.[18] For example, Egyptian religion was a "funerary" religion, centered around the dead and the desire to assure them immortality. The Egyptian art that has come down to us is largely tomb art.

The static quality of Egyptian painting and the fixed remoteness and weighted ponderosity of Egyptian sculpture have been attributed to the preoccupation of Egyptian religion with death and immortality. The art style seems to strive for a sense of timelessness, transcending the present, looking to the eternity of past and future.

The religions of the ancient East emphasized the unreality of this world and preached spiritual detachment from the present. This may have been a response to the brevity and misery of most human life. Salvation was sought in a world beyond; the religious experience was preeminently a quest for mystic union with the Infinite; the seen world was but illusion. This orientation had a great influence on the art of the East, producing not only the remote, abstract, and stylized Egyptian works but also the complex, mystic patterns of Hindu art. The variations are enormous, but there is a common theme: the real world is not to be copied or glorified; it is but a starting-point for the artist's vision of a realm of spirit.

Buddhism, which conceives nature as animated by an immanent force, which force is the one order to which the whole universe conforms, must inevitably affect the whole basis of art, insofar as art is a representation of reality or of the super-reality behind natural appearances. The quality which strikes us most in Buddhism is resignation; the submission of the individual to this all-forming spirit, this destiny. The artist shares that humility, and his only desire is to enter into communion with that universal spirit. This desire has all sorts of consequences: it leads to a preference for landscape-painting above figure-painting . . . . Nature is more sublime, nearer to the universal essence, than humanity. But what the artist sees of nature he realizes is only the deceptive outward appearance of things. He will therefore not strive to imitate the exact appearance, but rather to express the spirit.[19]

In ancient Greece, on the other hand, the artist's studio "was not a lonely cave of meditation but the world of moving life."[20] In its classic form the religion of the Greeks did not demand or even encourage a flight from humanity or from what was possible in this world. The Greeks sought the divine in man and in what he could do. Perfection and excellence could make the merely human into something closer to the gods. "Through perfected mortality man was immortal."[21]

Christianity followed hard upon the civilizations of Greece and Rome, but its religious art broke with the tradition that idealized man and his works. For almost a thousand years, from the fifth century to the fifteenth, Christian art turned its back on the representation of reality and sought to glorify God in abstract, stylized, and symbolic forms.[22] The apparent primitiveness and crudeness of early Christian art cannot be attributed solely to lack of skill. A religious impulse drove the artist to disregard representation and direct his attention to the world of the spirit. In depicting that world, the presentation of symbols is more important than the reproduction of exact or even idealized men, animals, or objects.

---

[18] See Alessandro Della Seta, *Religion and Art* (New York: Scribner's, 1914); E. H. Gombrich, *The Story of Art* (Greenwich, Conn.: Phaidon, 1961); Edith Hamilton, *The Greek Way to Western Civilization* (New York: Mentor, 1948); Arnold Hauser, *The Social History of Art* (New York: Vintage, 1957); Emile Male, *Religious Art* (New York: Noonday, 1958); Andre Malraux, *The Metamorphosis of the Gods* (New York: Doubleday, 1960).

[19] Herbert Read, *Art and Society* (London: Faber and Faber, 1945), p. 53.

[20] Edith Hamilton, *op. cit.,* p. 32.

[21] *Ibid.,* p. 37.

[22] See Hauser, *op. cit.,* Vol. I, pp. 121 ff.

Tension between religion and art The alliance between religion and art has been both uneasy and intimate. Religion can inhibit the full development of the aesthetic impulse by restricting the artist to a narrow range of forms, materials, and modes of expression. Art in its turn can corrupt religious practice by encouraging idolatry and profanation of the sacred.

Art serves religion by creating visible symbols of man's faith in the invisible. But it is easy to confuse the symbol with what is symbolized, and to worship the representation rather than what is represented. This risk is important to a religion that seeks to convey the idea of a universal and invisible deity whose spirit is present everywhere.

The Old Testament condemns idolatry, the worship of objects as if they themselves were divine. So great was the horror of idol worship among the ancient Hebrews that the Second Commandment forbids the making of "any graven image or any likeness of anything that is in heaven above or that is in the earth beneath, or that is in the water under the earth." As a result of this orientation, the plastic arts did not develop among the Jews until recent times.

The early Christians shared this fear of idolatry. As Christianity grew in power, there were debates over how to decorate the churches being built throughout Europe and the Near East. Lifelike sculptures were outlawed as bordering on "graven images," but there was much disagreement concerning painting. During the sixth century Pope Gregory the Great formulated the early policy of the Roman Catholic Church. He argued that many people could not read or write and that pictures in the churches would teach them the history and substance of the Christian faith. He said: "Painting can do for the illiterate what writing does for those who can read." [23]

Disagreement over religious art was a serious problem in both the Eastern Church and Western Catholicism. The Eastern Church, centered in Byzantium (Constantinople), contained a strong faction of iconoclasts, or "image smashers," who gained power in the eighth century and forbade religious art in the Eastern churches. A century later the iconoclasts lost control and the policy of the Eastern Church was revised. The new doctrine went beyond that of Pope Gregory. The Eastern churchmen argued that religious art was holy, and that Christians could worship God through visible images without committing the sin of idolatry.[24] In time the Roman Catholic Church in the West took on somewhat the same point of view and even relaxed the ban on sculpture.

Especially during the late Middle Ages (fourteenth and fifteenth centuries) the Roman Catholic Church was plagued by the charge of idolatry. It took considerable sophistication to distinguish between worship of God, worship of Mary, and worship of a particular image of the Madonna and Child portrayed in paint or in stone. The Protestant Reformation made idolatry a major charge against the Church, and many Protestant sects took a radical stand against all religious art.

In the sixteenth century, during the Catholic Counter-Reformation, the Council of Trent reaffirmed the position of the Church favoring images and paintings as the bible of the illiterate. The Council ordained that

. . . the images of Christ, of the Virgin Mother of God, and of the other saints are to be placed and retained especially in the churches, and that due honor and veneration is to be given them; not, however, that any divinity or virtue is believed to be in them by reason of which they are to be venerated, or that something is to be asked of them, or that trust is to be placed in images, as was done of old by the Gentiles who placed their hope in idols; but because the honor which is shown them is referred to the prototypes which they represent, so that by means of the images which we kiss and before which we uncover our heads and prostrate ourselves, we adore Christ and venerate the saints whose likeness they bear.[25]

In *The Waning of the Middle Ages,* Huizinga discusses the role of the religious image in the profana-

[23] Gombrich, *op. cit.,* p. 95.

[24] *Ibid.,* p. 97.

[25] E. G. Holt (ed.), *A Documentary History of Art* (Garden City, N.Y.: [Anchor] Doubleday, 1958), Vol. II, p. 64.

tion of the sacred during the centuries immediately preceding the Renaissance and the Protestant Reformation. According to Huizinga, one consequence of the profuse use of vivid representations of Jesus, Mary, the saints, the prophets, the tortures of Hell, the Trinity, and the Crucifixion, was to make familiar and commonplace what should be mysterious, remote, revered, respected.

All life was saturated with religion to such an extent that the people were . . . in danger of losing sight of the distinction between things spiritual and things temporal. . . . In the Middle Ages the demarcation of the sphere of religious thought and that of worldly concerns was nearly obliterated. It occasionally happened that indulgences figured among the prizes of a lottery. . . . Till late in the sixteenth century profane melodies might be used indiscriminately for sacred use, and sacred for profane. It is notorious that Guillaume Dufay and others composed masses to the themes of love-songs. . . .[26]

By the late Middle Ages artists were themselves introducing a profane or secular element into religious art, foreshadowing the eventual independence of art from religion. This secular element consisted of the freer manipulation of the artist's medium for aesthetic purposes and for the expression of human emotion and temporal reality. Religious sculpture was already becoming more supple and lifelike, less stiff and stylized, more dynamic and rounded, closer to portrait than symbol. Religious art began to point less to the realm of the divine and called more attention to itself and its own virtuosity. During the Renaissance great painters continued to work for the Church and to paint religious subjects. But they introduced the classical imagery of Greece into Christian art, and technical problems of space, color, and composition began to predominate over expressions of religious piety and the evocation of religious faith. Great religious art disappeared, to be replaced by great works of art which were not inherently religious but had religious figures and episodes as their subjects.

In summary, two sources of tension between religion and art are (1) the risk of idolatry, and (2) the risk of profanation, especially the weakening of religious values and their subordination to aesthetic ends.

[26] J. Huizinga, *The Waning of the Middle Ages* (Garden City, N.Y.: [Anchor] Doubleday, 1954), pp. 156 f.

SECTION 4 SOCIALIZATION

Religion not only makes people religious but helps socialize them into the secular order. While the otherworldly ideals of religion can provide the individual with a perspective from which to criticize the secular order, religion serves more often to reconcile the individual to it. Religion helps make the secular order acceptable to the individual in several basic ways. (1) By casting an aura of sanctity over such social institutions as the state and the family, religion enhances their authority. (2) By reinforcing ethical norms with supernatural sanctions, religion aids in the acceptance and internalization of those norms.

(3) By providing religious rewards and consolations to offset secular failure and personal tragedy, religion facilitates the continuous adaptation of the individual to the circumstances of his life.

RELIGION AND PERSONAL AUTONOMY

Christianity is sometimes said to have an overly "domesticating" influence on the individual because of its strong emphasis on the virtues of obedience, humility, submission to earthly authority, and resignation to one's fate in this world.[27] Catholicism is thought to exert an especially strong influence in this

[27] See Friedrich Nietzsche, "The Genealogy of Morals," in *The Philosophy of Nietzsche* (New York: The Modern Library, 1927), pp. 616–807. On the other hand, Christian thinkers emphasize the influence of Christianity on the development of freedom and respect for the individual in the Western World. See, for example, G. K. Chesterton, *The Everlasting Man* (Garden City, N.Y.: [Image] Doubleday, 1955).

TABLE X:1 PERCENTAGE VALUING AUTONOMY ABOVE OBEDIENCE BY CLASS AND RELIGION

CLASS [a] AND RELIGION		PERCENT	NUMBER OF CASES
Upper middle:	Protestants	90	(48)
	Catholics	70	(27)
Lower middle:	Protestants	72	(65)
	Catholics	63	(59)
Upper working:	Protestants	66	(79)
	Catholics	51	(77)
Lower working:	Protestants	48	(66)
	Catholics	38	(53)

ADAPTED from Gerhard Lenski, *The Religious Factor* (Garden City, N.Y.: Doubleday, 1961), p. 201. Data for Jews and Negroes are omitted.

[a] The middle class is divided on the basis of income, with those earning $8,000 or more classified as upper-middle-class. The same is true of the working class, with $5,000 per year income for the family head providing the cutting point.

direction. (1) By emphasizing the Sacraments as the avenue to salvation, Catholicism stresses the dependence of its adherents on the Church as an institution. (2) The Catholic Church has historically allowed the layman no active direction in the affairs of his church. (3) The Catholic Church exercises authority in matters of morals—for example, divorce and birth control—that many American Protestants and Jews regard as subjects for individual decision.

A 1958 study of a sample of Detroit adults investigated whether American Catholics value "intellectual autonomy" less than do American Protestants.[28] Respondents were asked which was most important for a child to learn: to obey, to be popular, to think for himself, to work hard, or to help others. On every class level more Protestants than Catholics chose "to think for himself." However, as Table X:1 shows, class status was more important than religion. Upper-middle-class individuals tended predominantly to value intellectual autonomy over obedience *regardless of religion;* the figure was 90 percent for the

48 upper-middle-class Protestants in the sample and 70 percent for the 27 upper-class Catholics. In the lower-working-class group, regardless of religion, a majority valued obedience over intellectual autonomy. Thus, in their respect for intellectual autonomy, upper-middle-class Catholics resembled upper-middle-class Protestants more closely than they resembled their lower-working-class coreligionists. Furthermore, the proportion of Catholics valuing intellectual autonomy over obedience was higher at each higher step in socioeconomic status.

A second study, based on a sample of more than 2,000 graduate students in the arts and sciences, investigated the extent to which religious affiliation was related to the desire for personal and creative autonomy in an occupation.[29] Students were asked how important it was to them that a job provide them with an opportunity to be creative and original, to be free from supervision, and to be free from pressure to conform in their personal lives. Students who rated at least two of these job characteristics as very important were classified as "self-expressive" or autonomous in their work orientation.

As a whole, Catholic students showed least desire for autonomy on the job. However, when church attendance is taken into account, it becomes apparent that *practicing* Catholics, Protestants, and Jews resemble each other more than they resemble their less active coreligionists. The following percentages of students who frequently attended church were classified as desiring autonomy: Jewish, 33 percent; Protestant, 31 percent; Catholic, 26 percent. Therefore, it appears that *observance* of religion rather than specific religious adherence is associated with low desire for personal autonomy in an occupation.

Taken together, the two studies suggest the following tentative conclusions: (1) The desire for personal autonomy is influenced more by degree of religious involvement than by specific religious affiliation. Being religiously observant has a generally restraining influence on the desire for personal au-

[28] Gerhard Lenski, *The Religious Factor* (Garden City, N.Y.: Doubleday, 1961).

[29] Joe L. Spaeth, "Value Orientations and Academic Career Plans." (Unpublished Ph.D. dissertation, University of Chicago, 1961).

tonomy, whether the individual is Catholic, Protestant, or Jewish. (2) Though Catholics may desire personal autonomy less frequently than Protestants, and Protestants less frequently than Jews, the differences are not great, especially when religious observance and social class are taken into account.

Caution Religious affiliation is so closely related to cultural factors—for example ethnic origin—that it is extremely difficult to isolate the influence of religion *per se* upon attitudes and behavior. For example, one study found that Protestant and Jewish mothers expected their children to show "independence" at an earlier age than Catholics.[30] However, among the Catholic mothers, those of Irish ancestry looked for signs of independence a full year earlier than did those of Italian ancestry. In this case nonreligious cultural factors appear to play at least as important a role as religious affiliation.

CONVERSION AND ASSIMILATION

Most religious bodies rely upon gradual assimilation of the individual into the church through childhood indoctrination into the tenets of the faith and early participation in church activities and ritual. No special signs of faith or belief are looked for beyond ritual observance and assent to basic doctrine. Members are rarely called on to demonstrate the depth and authenticity of their faith. Regular religious observance rather than strong religious emotion is emphasized as the way to sustain a religious outlook.

While gradual assimilation into religious belief and practice is the usual process, some branches of American Protestantism stress the need for a "conversion experience," i.e., an intensely emotional episode in which the individual "takes on" or "surrenders to" his religious faith.

Conversion is often associated with overt and public confessions of faith. In certain Christian groups, revival meetings are held in which individuals are urged to come forward and "make the decision for Christ." One subject described his conversion in the following way:

I had been thinking that I should have Jesus as my personal Savior. A saintly old man, Brother Shook, preached one night. His words hammered upon me and seemed to ring in my breast. I felt I must give my life to Christ. I went to the altar where I knelt, weeping. . . . My father came and asked me if I did not love Jesus. Of course I did! And instantly my burden rolled away. I was intensely happy. All over the house I went shaking hands with everyone. My immediate aftereffect was to tell someone else about my new love. The few nights following I led three or four of my friends to the altar. I am conscious of that experience today, and it is my Bethel when I need again the joy of the Spirit.[31]

The conversion experience is encouraged by theological emphasis on man's sinfulness, a sense of the urgency of individual moral regeneration, and a belief in the capacity of religious faith to work miracles of personality transformation. Proponents of revivalism point out that church attendance does not necessarily signify a genuine religious commitment nor guarantee adherence to a Christian life. Nor do they trust the ordinary processes of religious education to provide the spiritual resources for leading an exemplary life.

Emphasis on the subjective experience of conversion is probably greatest among new religious movements that cannot rely upon gradual assimilation of the children of members but must win adult adherents. Many leaders of new religious movements report a conversion experience as a demonstration and warrant of the authenticity of the new faith, as well as a model and inspiration for its followers.

The American stress on the importance of conversion has its roots in the early nineteenth century when, it is estimated, only 10 percent of the population were church members.[32] At this time, Protestantism resembled a new religious movement. Great

[30] Fred L. Strodtbeck, "Family Interaction, Values, and Achievement," in David C. McClelland, Alfred L. Baldwin, Urie Bronfenbrenner, and Fred L. Strodtbeck, *Talent and Society* (Princeton: Van Nostrand, 1958), p. 146.

[31] Elmer T. Clark, *The Psychology of Religious Awakening* (New York: Macmillan, 1929), p. 40.

[32] Herbert W. Schneider, *Religion in 20th Century America* (Cambridge: Harvard University Press, 1952), p. 16.

revivals were carried on to awaken religious feeling among the people, establish congregations, and build the churches.

Empirical studies of religious conversion are largely limited to Protestants.[33] The conversion experience is by no means confined to Protestantism, however, nor even to religious belief. It may occur with regard to almost any belief, though it is most likely to occur when the "salvation" of the individual or of society is conceived to be at stake. Studies of religious conversion support several conclusions that are probably also applicable to political types of conversion.

1. Adolescence or near-adolescence is the age during which religious conversion is most likely to occur. Adolescence is also the age, however, when church attendance falls, religious doubts appear, and rebellious feelings are strong.[34]

2. Conversions are experienced more frequently where the group encourages them. Of 176 college students who remembered having been exposed to a theology of sin and damnation, about two-thirds reported some form of conversion experience. Of 133 who were members of nonevangelical denominations that place little importance on sudden conversion, only 8 percent reported a conversion episode.[35]

3. Conversions are rarely a sudden change from disbelief to belief; as a rule they represent an emotional "surrender" to religious faith after a period of prior socialization in the family and the church. A study of the highly successful campaigns of the American evangelist Billy Graham in England during the 1950s reported that about half of the 120,000 who came forward to make a public decision were church members at the time.[36] Most of the others were probably influenced by earlier church affiliation.

[33] See Edwin D. Starbuck, *The Psychology of Religion* (London: Walter Scott, 1899), and Clark, *op. cit.*

[34] Sidney L. Pressey and Raymond G. Kuhlen, *Psychological Development Through the Life Span* (New York: Harper & Row, 1957), pp. 481–486.

[35] Clark, *op. cit.*, p. 87.

[36] S. Herron, "What's Left of Harringway?" *British Weekly,* February 10, 1955, cited in Michael Argyle, *Religious Behavior* (London: Routledge and Kegan Paul, 1958), p. 53.

SECTION 5 PRIMARY RELATIONS

In most societies, religious practice and symbolism are a major source of support for primary groups, especially the family and the *Gemeinschaft.* (See SOCIAL ORGANIZATION, p. 48.) Moreover, some religious traditions, notably the Judaeo-Christian, celebrate love and a person-centered approach to human relations.

The writings of the Jewish religious philosopher Martin Buber (1878–1965) emphasize the distinction between "I-Thou" relations in which persons deal with one another on a basis of full communication and mutual valuing, and the "I-It" relation in which persons are more isolated and self-protective and treat one another as objects.[37]

Religious symbolism may be built upon primary relations, especially the family. In Christian theology God is the Father, Jesus is His Son. Men are the sons of God and by implication brothers to each other. In Catholicism the Holy Family plays a particularly important role. Mary, the Mother of God, and Joseph, her spouse, have been sanctified, and Mary is an intercessor for man to God. The portrayal of

[37] For a discussion of Buber's thought, including his relation to Judaism and Christianity, see Maurice S. Friedman, *Martin Buber: The Life of Dialogue* (Chicago: University of Chicago Press, 1955).

the Holy Family in Catholic art, ritual, and prayer builds a bridge between religious feeling and the more familiar emotions of everyday life, and creates a locus of intimacy and warmth within the more austere context of religious awe.

In the Judaeo-Christian tradition, the image of God reflects the double role of the patriarchal father. God is both authority and protector, the God of judgment and punishment and the God of love and forgiveness.

RELIGION AND MARRIAGE

Most religions endure over long periods because they are passed on from generation to generation. Marriage across religious lines is thus of concern to religious groups. Partly because it places in doubt the religious adherence of the children, the major religions and denominations in the United States disapprove of interfaith marriage.

The strength of disapproval of religious exogamy (marriage outside the religious group) differs from group to group. The Old Testament forbids Jews to marry non-Jews, but religious sanctions are now rarely invoked by the American Jewish community against Jews who marry outside the faith. Conversion of the Gentile partner is generally required, however, before a rabbi will perform the religious ceremony. The Catholic Church regards the marriage of a Catholic to a non-Catholic as valid only if the ceremony is performed in the Catholic Church and is preceded by an agreement that all children will be baptized and reared as Catholics. Some Protestant denominations have taken official stands against marriage to non-Protestants, especially Catholics, but the Catholic ceremony is accepted as valid.

Rates of interfaith marriage vary from religion to religion. According to a 1957 Census survey, less than 10 percent of Jewish marriages then in existence involved a non-Jewish partner. A slightly higher percentage of Protestants were exogamous, and the rate of Catholic interfaith marriage was relatively high— more than 20 percent.[38] All the rates given include both long-standing and recent marriages and do not represent present trends.

The rate of interfaith marriage appears to be increasing. Among Catholics it may now be as high as 40 to 50 percent in some areas.[39] A study of Washington, D.C., found interfaith marriage of Jewish males higher in each generation: 1.4 percent for the first generation (foreign born), 10.2 percent for the second generation (native born of foreign parentage), and 17.9 percent for the third.[40]

Interfaith marriage appears to be correlated with socioeconomic status. In a study of over 50,000 Catholic mixed marriages in an urban area, the percentage of mixed marriages was about 9 percent in lower rental areas but 18 percent in upper socioeconomic neighborhoods.[41]

Official religious opposition to interfaith marriage undoubtedly deters some individuals from engaging in close social relations with people of other faiths or from making marriages that might otherwise be congenial. However, the official doctrines of religious groups do not account for existing rates of interfaith marriage. At least three factors influence rates of interfaith marriage.

1. *The varying distribution of religious groups in the community.* In some Southern dioceses, where Catholics form no more than 2 percent of the total population, mixed marriage rates for Catholics are as high as 60 to 70 percent. In areas where Catholics are a majority, mixed marriage rates are often less than 10 percent.[42] In Iowa 42 percent of marriages contracted by Jews during 1953–1959 listed one ap-

[38] Bureau of the Census, *Current Population Reports,* P-20, No. 79, February, 1958, Table 6.

[39] John L. Thomas, S.J., *The American Catholic Family* (Englewood Cliffs, N.J.: Prentice-Hall, 1956), p. 154.

[40] Erich Rosenthal, "Studies of Jewish Intermarriage in the United States," *American Jewish Year Book,* 1963, p. 19. Based on data in Stanley K. Bigman, *The Jewish Population of Greater Washington in 1956* (Washington, D.C.: The Jewish Community Council—May, 1957).

[41] Thomas, *op. cit.,* pp. 157–158.

[42] *Ibid.,* p. 155.

plicant as non-Jewish.[43] This is a very high intermarriage rate, but there are so few Jews in Iowa that the rate of Protestant interfaith marriage is not thereby affected. The *average* incidence of Protestant interfaith marriage—about 10 percent—is as low as it is because in many areas of the United States virtually the entire population is Protestant, and there is little opportunity to marry non-Protestants.

2. *Social distance.* A particular religion may be so closely tied to ethnic background, cultural factors, residence, and socioeconomic status that individuals of different faiths do not associate with each other. For example, in some areas of southwestern United States a Catholic is likely to be of Mexican origin and low socioeconomic status, a Protestant of Anglo-Saxon origin and higher socioeconomic status. While religious difference creates social distance, social class barriers and ethnic prejudice add to the social distance that makes marriage less likely. For example, Catholics form about 30 percent of the populations of both San Antonio, Texas, and Marquette, Michigan, but the rate of Catholic interfaith marriage is only about 5 percent in San Antonio while in Marquette it is close to 40 percent.[44] In San Antonio many Catholics are of Mexican origin; in Marquette the Catholics are ethnically less differentiated from the non-Catholics.

3. *Extent of primary ties to family and ethnic community.* Resistance to interfaith marriages may reflect loyalty to family and ethnic community. Not wanting to hurt one's parents, or to be alienated from them, is apt to be more immediately important to the individual than official religious disapproval. Where the individual has close ties to an ethnic community that also shares a common religion, he may not feel at home with people of another faith—not because of religious differences but because of differences in everyday ways and attitudes.

SEX, LOVE, AND BIRTH CONTROL

Historically the Roman Catholic Church has forbidden its members to use contraceptive methods of birth control. Interference with the biological consequences of sexual intercourse has been deemed immoral, and only abstinence is a permissible way to limit births.

---

[43] Rosenthal, *op. cit.*, p. 37. For a detailed analysis see Lee G. Burchinal and Loren E. Chancellor, *Factors Related to Interreligious Marriages in Iowa, 1953–1959,* Research Bulletin 510, Agricultural and Home Economics Experiment Station (Ames: Iowa State University—November, 1962).

[44] Thomas, *op. cit.*, p. 156.

TABLE X:2 CATHOLIC USE OF BIRTH CONTROL BY AGE AND BY EDUCATION (IN PERCENTAGES), UNITED STATES, 1967

BIRTH-CONTROL PRACTICE	TOTAL	AGE			EDUCATION		
		Under 35	*35 to 49*	*50 and over*	*8th grade or less*	*High school*	*College*
Percentage using artificial device or birth-control pill	38	60	38	12	18	42	45
Percentage using rhythm method only	35	38	43	18	13	36	44
Percentage using nothing	27	2	19	70	69	22	11
Total	100	100	100	100	100	100	100

SOURCE: Louis Harris and Associates for *Newsweek,* March 20, 1967, p. 71. Based on interviews with 993 adult Roman Catholics. Copyright; Newsweek, Inc., March, 1967; used by permission.

Recently there has been a growing debate within the Church over the validity of the rule against contraception, and many Catholics do not obey it. According to a sample survey of Catholics, birth-control techniques are more commonly used by the relatively young and by the relatively better educated. (See Table X:2.) The development of doctrine on this subject is instructive for the light it sheds on Catholic interpretations of sex and love. It also illuminates the process of theological change in a highly institutionalized church.

The classic Catholic view held that the only lawful purpose of sexual intercourse was procreation. This approach dominated the thinking of Catholic theologians for many centuries, but by the seventeenth century, recognition was given to other values of sex in marriage, such as psychic health and the encouragement of fidelity. St. Paul's statement, "It is better to marry than to burn," and other Biblical sources supported enlargement of the values associated with coitus in marriage.

By the nineteenth century some Catholic theologians had come, with hesitation and qualification, to accept the fostering of love as a legitimate basis for sexual intercourse. However, the Church hierarchy continued to distinguish between primary and secondary ends, and the Church held to the position that bearing children was the primary objective of marriage.

The Vatican Council of 1965 (Vatican II, see p. 326) adopted a policy on marriage and the family that reflected the evolution of Catholic thought on the values in family life.[45] Although the Council did not deal directly with birth control, it decisively and self-consciously affirmed that sexual intercourse in marriage is to be given positive value, not only as a means of procreation, or as a grudging concession to human weakness, but as a vital ingredient of marital love. It rejected the terminology of primary and secondary ends while continuing to stress the importance of children.

The new emphasis was encouraging for those looking for change in the Church's position on contraception. If conjugal love has its own worth, and is not less important than other values in marriage, should its fulfillment be denied when the family decides to limit or space its offspring? If the values are equal in the eyes of the Church, the marital pair may assign priorities. If conjugal love is to be affirmed and procreation subordinated, then contraception may be justified. No such conclusion has been explicitly drawn from the Council document, but Catholics favorable to change have welcomed the new formulation.

[45] See *The Documents of Vatican II* (New York: The America Press, 1966), pp. 249–258, and John T. Noonan, Jr., "Contraception and the Council," *Commonweal*, March 11, 1966; also Gregory Baum, "Birth Control—What Happened?" *Commonweal*, Dec. 24, 1965. For a full historical treatment prior to Vatican II, see John T. Noonan, *Contraception: A History of Its Treatment by the Catholic Theologians and Canonists* (Cambridge: Harvard University Press, 1965).

SECTION **6** STRATIFICATION

Christianity stresses the equality of all men in the sight of God. "The Christian concept . . . is equalitarian and inclusive rather than aristocratic and exclusive." [46] Participation in the church and salvation are open to all, regardless of wealth and status.

The Christianity of the Gospels is oriented toward the poor and exalts the poor. The poor are promised a status in heaven denied to them on earth—a status unlikely to be gained by the rich and mighty.

And, behold, one came and said unto him, Good Master, what good thing shall I do that I may have eternal life? . . . Jesus said unto him, If thou wilt

[46] W. Lloyd Warner and Associates, *Democracy in Jonesville* (New York: Harper & Row, 1949), p. 153.

be perfect, go and sell that thou hast, and give to the poor, and thou shalt have treasure in heaven: and come and follow me. But when the young man heard that saying, he went away sorrowful: for he had great possessions. Then said Jesus unto his disciples, Verily I say unto you . . . It is easier for a camel to go through the eye of a needle, than for a rich man to enter into the kingdom of God.[47]

On the basis of doctrine as expressed in the Gospels, it might be expected that (1) Christianity embraces all social classes in a single religious community transcending all secular distinctions between rich and poor, the weak and the powerful; (2) church organization ignores status distinctions; and (3) the poor participate in the church more than those who have "great possessions."

SOCIAL COMPOSITION OF THE CHURCHES

It has been said that there is "more heterogeneity in class status in the average church than in any other average social grouping."[48] On the national level and for whole denominations this appears to be true. Table X:3 shows the proportions with low, middle, and high incomes in the three major religious divisions in the United States for 1963. All religions are represented at all income levels, although the income status of Jews, reflecting their urban location and high educational status, is higher than Christians.

Protestants, who are the least urbanized, have the lowest income status of the three religions.

Comparable data for 1956 are given in Table X:4. The tables differ in the cutting point between high and middle incomes and the higher income distribution in the 1963 figures. The higher 1963 figures are due to economic trends and to the fact that Negroes are not included in the sample. The larger proportion of Jews with incomes below $3,000 in 1963 is unexpected but may be due to error in the small Jewish samples.

The bottom half of Table X:4 reports five Protestant denominations separately. In 1956 almost half of Episcopalians had family incomes of $7,500 or more compared with 15 percent of Methodists and only 7 percent of Baptists. The low figures for Baptists are due in part to the large proportion of Negro Baptists as indicated in the racial breakdowns. Viewed as a whole, the Christian community includes all economic strata, but its denominational divisions reflect some of the secular realities of socioeconomic status.

Partly because of residential patterns, individual churches tend to be more homogeneous in socioeconomic status than the denominations to which they belong. In one Episcopalian congregation situated in a middle-class area in a college community, 82

[47] Matthew 19:16; 21–23; 24.

[48] Louis Bultena, "Church Membership and Church Attendance in Madison, Wisconsin," *American Sociological Review, 14* (June, 1949), 384–389.

TABLE X:3   FAMILY INCOME LEVEL BY RELIGION FOR WHITES (IN PERCENTAGES), UNITED STATES, 1963

	LOWER (BELOW $3,000)	MIDDLE ($3,000– 6,999)	UPPER ($7,000 AND OVER)	TOTAL Percent	Number of cases
TOTAL	20.7	41.5	37.8	100	12,239
Protestant	22.7	41.5	35.9	100	8,660
Catholic	15.6	43.3	41.0	100	2,884
Jewish	15.3	26.7	58.0	100	435
No religion	16.8	43.2	40.0	100	260

SOURCE: Norval D. Glenn and Ruth Hyland, "Religious Preference and Worldly Success: Some Evidence from National Surveys," *American Sociological Review, 32* (February, 1967), 78. Based on four Gallup surveys conducted between November, 1963, and March, 1965. The last survey pertains to 1964, but is combined with the earlier surveys.

TABLE X:4 FAMILY INCOME LEVEL BY RELIGION (IN PERCENTAGES), UNITED STATES, 1956

	LOWER (BELOW $3,000)	MIDDLE ($3,000– 7,499)	UPPER ($7,500 AND OVER)	TOTAL Percent	Number of cases
Protestant	28	54	18	100	4,185
Catholic	19	63	18	100	1,270
Jewish	8	50	42	100	188
Episcopalian	6	48	46	100	119
Presbyterian	20	54	26	100	272
Lutheran	26	58	16	100	328
Methodist	31	54	15	100	730
Baptist	44	49	7	100	939
White	32	57	11	100	713
Negro	64	34	2	100	226

SOURCE: Adapted from data in Bernard Lazerwitz, "Religion and Social Structure in the United States," in Louis Schneider (ed.), *Religion, Culture and Society* (New York: Wiley, 1964), p. 429. Based on national sample surveys.

percent of the adult members were college trained and more than 40 percent had attended graduate school. Though rich and poor, educated and uneducated, are members of one religious community, they tend to worship under different roofs.

The social class differentiation of American Protestantism is partly rooted in the varying economic fortunes and different ethnic backgrounds of the groups. Among Episcopalians—who are linked in origin to the Church of England—there are large numbers of people with backgrounds in the British Isles and high status who had to overcome neither a language barrier nor ethnic prejudice. The poverty of many Negro Baptists, as indicated in Table X:4, reflects the impact of racial prejudice and discrimination.

SOCIAL CLASS AND RELIGIOUS INVOLVEMENT

Social research findings indicate that the poor are less involved in the church than are those who are better off.[49] The poor are less likely to be members of a congregation, to attend church regularly, and to take part in the organized church activities. They are also less likely to be informed about religious matters. However, the poor who do go to church tend to be both more believing and more emotionally involved in their religion than better off persons.[50]

A study of 4,000 members of 12 Congregational Christian urban churches measured the religious involvement of members along four "dimensions": (1) knowledge about the Bible and religious matters in general; (2) participation in the church; (3) belief in church doctrine; and (4) religious "feeling" as indicated by faith in prayer, daily Bible reading, and belief in the necessity of a conversion experience.[51] It was found that there was a tendency for religious knowledge and participation to be associated with higher socioeconomic status, intensity of religious feeling to be associated with lower status. Differences in degree of belief were negligible for this particular denomination.

[49] See Glock and Stark, *op. cit.*, p. 187, and Erich Goode, "Social Class and Church Participation," *American Journal of Sociology*, 72 (July, 1966), 102–111.

[50] Nicholas J. Demerath III, *Social Class in American Protestantism* (Chicago: Rand McNally, 1965).

[51] Yoshio Fukuyama, "The Major Dimensions of Church Membership," *Review of Religious Research, 2* (Spring, 1961), 154–161.

To sum up: The economically well off tend to be religious in an intellectual, formal, and organizational way. They attend church regularly, they are active in the church, and they are informed about their religion. But, compared with poor churchgoers, they are apt to be less believing and less emotionally dependent on their religious faith. The poor tend to be religious in a more emotional manner. They are less regular church attenders, their knowledge is scantier, and they participate less in church activities. But, when they are religiously involved, they are apt to be more unquestioning in their faith and more reliant on it. Complete indifference to religion may, however, be commonest at lower socioeconomic levels: analysis of public opinion polls suggests that a somewhat smaller proportion of the poor go to church or show involvement in their nominal faith.[52]

Cautions   1. Findings on the relation between social class and religious involvement vary from study to study. This is partly due to the different samples used. For example, some studies deal with the relation between social class and religious involvement only among church members. Others have examined the relation in the general population, which includes both church attenders and non-attenders.

2. Measures of religious involvement are still crude and do not permit firm conclusions as to the conditions associated with "genuine" religious involvement.

RELIGION AND CLASS INTEREST

Oriented though it was to the poor, the Christianity of the Gospels did not sanction secular rebellion against class privilege and social injustice. It projected no ideal of social reform to eliminate poverty and provided no principles to guide Christians in deciding mundane questions of social, political, and economic policy.

With its success, Christianity was transformed from a religious and moral movement of the poor into the official and powerful institution of the Catholic Church. The Church assumed social, political, and economic powers. By fusing with the secular feudal order and its ruling class, the Church inevitably became a bulwark of the status inequalities of feudal society.

During the period of its European hegemony, the Catholic Church supplemented the other-worldly ethics of the New Testament with a social philosophy and an image of society based partly on the Christianity of the Gospels, partly on classical Greek and Roman thought, and partly on the realities of the feudal social system. Though modified and often abused in practice, the social philosophy of the Church contained the following elements:

1. Poverty continued to be exalted as a virtue. This was evident in monastic asceticism, in which poverty was an essential aspect of the religious life.

2. There was virtually no conception of improving the material conditions of the poor. On the other hand, the poor were not condemned as failures. Poverty was regarded as a status into which one was born, and the poor were regarded as proper objects of Christian charity and compassion.

3. Profit-making—as opposed to merely being reimbursed for one's costs and time—was condemned. The principles of the medieval Catholic Church were explicitly anticapitalist.

4. Secular society was conceived to be a divine community with the Church at its apex. All people were members of one church, and all aspects of society, including the relations between the social classes, were regarded as proper subjects of religious governance.

5. Social inequalities were not only accepted but justified. Society was compared to an organism composed of different and interdependent parts, each having its own function. The ruler and the ruled, the wealthy and the poor, were likened to the mind and the hand, one fitted only to toil, the other only to govern. Social justice was conceived as giving to each one his due. But what was due to each was defined by existing differences in wealth and power rather

---

[52] Rodney Stark, "The Economics of Piety," Publication A-66, Survey Research Center, University of California, Berkeley, 1967, processed.

than by a desire to achieve a more equitable distribution of the world's goods.

The Protestant Reformation The gradual transformation of agricultural feudal society into the commercial and industrial capitalism of the modern era was accompanied in many countries by a religious revolution against the doctrines and authority of the Catholic Church. First initiated in Germany early in the sixteenth century by the clergy and the nobility, the Protestant Reformation appealed to the rising middle classes who wanted to rid themselves of the religious, political, and economic restraints of the feudal order.

Protestantism sought and received the support of the poor. It took on, however, a distinctly middle-class coloration. Not only did the middle classes support Protestantism and gain administrative control of the churches, they also suffused it with middle-class values and attitudes. Whereas Catholic social doctrine had been formed in the context of an agricultural, feudal society, Protestantism evolved a social doctrine that reflected the realities of a commercial and industrial capitalism, organized around profit-making, employers, and wage earners.

For the middle-class Protestant, it was easy to believe that to live a Christian life was to exemplify the middle-class virtues.[53] Righteousness became identified with industry, thrift, prudence, decorum, cleanliness, self-discipline, sobriety. Sin was almost exclusively identified with the personal vices: laziness, improvidence, frivolity, dirt, swearing, gambling, drinking. Sin acquired a distinctly lower-class look, while wealth and success, once regarded as hindrances to salvation, became its very sign and reward: "No question but riches should be the portion . . . of the godly . . . ; for godliness hath the promises of this life as well as of the life to come."[54]

Poverty and salvation The exaltation of middle-class virtues and middle-class success led to a new approach to poverty and social responsibility. Though by no means universal among Protestants, the following attitudes characterized much Protestant activity and social policy for several centuries, and in some measure continue to do so.

1. Poverty was no longer seen as inevitable and necessary but became something to censure. The poor evoked not compassion but blame. Poverty, singled out by the Gospels as a blessed state because it was a guarantee against the sin of pride, was now associated with personal vices, with failure of character, and with spiritual unregeneracy.

2. A missionary rather than a charitable approach was taken toward the poor. Since secular society was no longer regarded as a divine community, into which all are born and all participate, Protestantism was faced with the task of gathering in the unchurched and of "converting" the nominal Christian. It would be inaccurate to say that the evangelical efforts of Protestantism were restricted to the poor. Nevertheless, the poor were regarded as most in need of salvation, since they were most in need of being saved from bad habits and weakness of character.

3. The concept of social justice—of giving to each his due—became identified with the distribution of rewards commensurate with merit and withholding charity from the "undeserving."

The law of God saith, "he that will not work, let him not eat." This would be a sore scourge and smart whip for idle persons if . . . none should be suffered to eat till they had wrought for it.[55]

The Marxist critique The most familiar critique of Christian attitudes toward the poor is that of Marx, who formulated the famous dictum that religion is the "opium of the masses."[56] He condemned

---

[53] See R. H. Tawney, *Religion and the Rise of Capitalism* (New York: Penguin Books, 1947) and H. Richard Niebuhr, *The Social Sources of Denominationalism* (New York: Meridian, 1957).

[54] R. Younge, *The Poores' Advocate*, 1654, quoted by Tawney, *op. cit.*, p. 221.

[55] Samuel Hartlib, *London's Charity Inlarged*, 1650, quoted by Tawney, *op. cit.*, p. 220.

[56] See Lewis S. Feuer (ed.), *Karl Marx and Friedrich Engels: Basic Writings on Politics and Philosophy* (New York: Doubleday, 1959), p. 263.

the other-worldly promises of Christianity as serving to deflect the economically oppressed from bettering their conditions in the present. Marxism saw Christianity as creating a docile laboring class, protecting the rich from threats to their wealth and power, and perpetuating secular inequalities.

In 1893, Marx's collaborator, Engels, criticized the presence in England of several famous American revivalists, implying that the industrial classes were using religion in an attempt to hold in check the rising protests and secular organization of the English working class.[57]

In some respects, the facts support the Marxist critique, but there are aspects of Christian doctrine and of church history that mitigate it. The church— both Protestant and Catholic—has attempted to develop concepts of social justice transcending mere expediency and setting ethical limits to the pursuit of material interests. Medieval Catholicism emphasized the social obligations of all classes in society. More recent Catholic thought has expanded the doctrine of social justice. Most notable is Pope Leo XIII's encyclical, *Rerum Novarum* (Of New Things), which as early as 1891 supported the formation of trade unions.[58] During the last century there grew up within Protestantism the concept of the Social Gospel that Christianity is required to work for social justice and the salvation of society, not merely for the salvation of individual souls.

The Gospels hold forth no promise of material progress, but their high valuation of the individual, rich or poor, and the assertion of man's spiritual brotherhood, laid an ethical foundation for secular reform and secular movements toward equality. While the church as an institution may be a buttress of status and privilege, its doctrines have often inspired individuals to support social idealism and economic reform.

[57] Frederick Engels, introduction to the First English translation of *Socialism, Utopian and Scientific* (New York: International Publishers, 1935), p. 24.

[58] Anne Fremantle, *The Papal Encyclicals In Their Historical Context* (New York: Mentor, 1956), pp. 166–195. More recent encyclicals emphasizing social justice and international cooperation are Pope John XXIII's *Mater et Magister* (Mother and Teacher), 1961, and Pope Paul VI's *Pacem et Terris* (Peace on Earth), 1963.

SECTION 7 ASSOCIATIONS

Although religious associations are dedicated to spiritual and transcendent ends, they are composed of human beings and face many of the same problems of organization that confront other associations. A perennial theme is the contradiction between religious purity and institutional stability. This theme appears in the discussion of two major types of religious association, the one emphasizing stability and influence, the other stressing inward purity.

THE CHURCH AND THE SECT

The church "Church" is commonly used to designate any religious group. However, sociologists use the term in a more restricted sense as a religious association characterized by (1) a relatively high degree of institutionalization (see ASSOCIATIONS, pp. 215 ff.); (2) integration with the social and economic order; (3) recruitment on the basis of residence or family membership; and (4) relatively restrained and routinized participation.

Within this broad category may be distinguished the *ecclesia* and the *denomination*. The ecclesia is a church that strives for fullest integration with the rest of society and for universal membership embracing an entire community. Unity of church and state is welcomed, and in the ideal case the ecclesia is an "established" church that counts as members all residents or citizens of a given area.

The denomination has more limited aspirations and a more restricted membership. For the most part, it is assumed that children will, in the normal course of events, be inducted into the church. Therefore family membership is the main basis of recruitment and the family is the main support of religious participation. As in the case of the ecclesia, no great demands are made upon the individual for high levels of religious commitment. Denominations are the churches of a pluralist society and are compatible with a strong belief in the separation of church and state.

The sect   The chief features of a religious sect have been summarized as follows:

It is a voluntary association; membership is by proof to sect authorities of some claim to personal merit— such as knowledge of doctrine, affirmation of a conversion experience, or recommendation of members in good standing; exclusiveness is emphasized, and expulsion exercised against those who contravene doctrinal, moral, or organizational precepts; its self-conception is of an elect, a gathered remnant, possessing special enlightenment; personal perfection is the expected standard of aspiration, in whatever terms this is judged; it accepts, at least as an ideal, the priesthood of all believers; there is a high level of lay participation; there is opportunity for the member spontaneously to express his commitment; the sect is hostile or indifferent to the secular order and to the state.[59]

Sects are concerned with purity of doctrine and with the depth and genuineness of religious feeling. As a result, demands are made upon the member to be an active participant, even a leader or missionary, as a warrant of his faith. The emphasis on purity of belief tends to create intolerance toward other groups and moves the sect toward critical assessment of the secular world in accordance with the ideals of the gospel.

Within a church, the impulse toward deeper religious commitment may be taken care of by the creation of special religious groups having selective memberships and distinctive practices. The religious

orders of the Roman Catholic Church, such as the Benedictines, Dominicans, Franciscans, and Jesuits, are good examples. The partial autonomy of these groups enables them to serve a sect-like function, but they remain within the Church and contribute to its work.

Interplay of sect and church   A number of sociologists have studied the relation between sect and church.[60] Two conclusions are important:

1. Some sects develop into denominations. If a sect is strongly interested in seeking new members, it may tend to "water down" its beliefs and take in people who are not truly committed. If in addition the sect's demands are simple, asking only that the member affirm that he feels converted, it will not be clearly insulated from the world and in time may adapt to it. Other institutionalizing processes, such as concern for a stable ministry and religious education, for respectable quarters, benefit funds, seminaries, and "good works" help this evolution along. But not all sects become denominations. One important criterion is whether the sect is *conversionist,* reaching out into the world rather than merely withdrawing from it.[61]

2. There is also a reverse movement, from church to sect. This comes about mainly by a process of schism. The watered-down belief and practice, the respectability and accommodation of the church, may become unacceptable to some of its members. Thus the poor may leave middle-class churches to form religious groups of their own, characterized by greater purity of belief, emotional fervor, a lay ministry, and an all-encompassing communal life. However, as the founders of the sect become more prosperous and respectable, they become more receptive to church-like organization and behavior. They in turn neglect the special religious needs of the poor. "This pattern recurs with remarkable regularity in the history of

---

[59] Bryan R. Wilson, "An Analysis of Sect Development," *American Sociological Review, 24* (February, 1959), 4.

[60] See especially Ernst Troeltsch, *The Social Teachings of the Christian Churches* (Glencoe: The Free Press, 1949), Vol. I, pp. 331–341; Liston Pope, *Millhands and Preachers* (New Haven: Yale University Press, 1942), pp. 118 ff.; H. Richard Niebuhr, *The Social Sources of Denominationalism* (New York: Meridian, 1957); Bryan R. Wilson, *Sects and Society* (Berkeley and Los Angeles: University of California Press, 1961).

[61] Wilson, "An Analysis of Sect Development," *op. cit.,* p. 14.

Christianity. Anabaptists, Quakers, Methodists, Salvation Army, and more recent sects of like type illustrate this rise and progress of the churches of the disinherited." [62]

Adaptation 26 illustrates some of these processes as it analyzes the relation of church and sect in Canada. Compare the discussion of institutionalization on pages 331–332 with ASSOCIATIONS, pages 216–218.

Caution Like all typologies, the church-sect distinction should be applied with the understanding that in the real world these distinctions are blurred. Many churches have some sect characteristics, and conversely a pure sect may be hard to find. The categories are starting points for analysis.

THE CATHOLIC AGGIORNAMENTO

For many years the Roman Catholic Church has been a prototype of the highly institutionalized church—the ecclesia. Catholicism gathered in whole communities and often became the established church. It has had a powerful hierarchy and a clergy largely independent of lay control; an entrenched and conservative bureaucracy, the Roman Curia, became a symbol of tradition-bound organization; an elaborate system of forms, rituals, and church laws was associated with an emphasis on authority and obedience. Although it would often accommodate to the secular world, the Church adopted a posture of lofty isolation in its dealings with other religions and ideologies.

In 1959 Pope John XXIII decided to convene a general (ecumenical) council, which would be an assembly of all the Catholic bishops throughout the world and other major church officials, such as the heads of religious orders. An ecumenical council is a rare event. Only twenty-one are recognized in the history of the Church, beginning with the First Council of Nicaea, A.D. 325. Another notable convening was the Council of Trent, 1545–1563, and nearly a century elapsed between the previous ecumenical

council and Vatican II. The proposed assembly was potentially the highest authoritative body of the Roman Catholic Church and could undertake new departures in theology, church government, and policy toward non-Catholics. After three years of preparation, the Second Vatican Council opened in the fall of 1962 and completed its final session in 1965 with more than 2,000 "council fathers" participating in the deliberations.

The keynote of the Council was set by Pope John when he used the Italian word *aggiornamento* ("renewal" or "updating") to characterize its mission. From the outset it was clear that many bishops favored change. Although many compromises were made to achieve maximum consensus, in the end a large majority voted for a new spirit within the Church. The conservative Curia, which had the main role in preparing the draft documents for consideration of the Council, lost control. The following is from an account of the first general meeting:

When a list of committee chairmen, prepared by the Curia, was presented for automatic approval [a number of cardinals] asked for a recess in order to discuss the candidates. After their first surprise, the assembled twenty-seven hundred Fathers broke into slowly thunderous applause. No vote was needed. They adjourned for *aggiornamento:* to draw up their own lists. Suddenly, dramatically, effective institutional power in Roman Catholicism had swung from the Curia to the Council of Bishops. For the first time in their episcopal lives (the last Council was in 1869), many of the bishops felt in their fingertips, so to speak, a surge of the power they were ordained to exercise. They began to be conscious of themselves as a Council. . . . In a stroke, Roman Catholicism was put on all twelves again, after having inclined for centuries in a single direction: curial Rome.[63]

In the deliberations that followed there were many revisions of the initial drafts. When its work was done the Council had taken a number of steps to change the direction of the Church: the power of the bishops relative to the Pope was increased, thus opening the way to a greater democratization; Catholic laymen were accorded a greater dignity and freedom; a more

---

[62] Niebuhr, *op. cit.,* p. 28.

[63] Michael Novak, *The Open Church* (London: Darton, Longman & Todd, 1964), p. 9.

open attitude toward Protestantism was expressed, and anti-Semitism was condemned; reform of Catholic ritual was ordained, allowing much greater variety, more use of the vernacular, and increased participation by the congregation in religious services.

The significance of the Council goes beyond the specific changes adopted. New attitudes were fostered, perhaps most important a questioning of received authority and of tradition. Although it is too soon to trace the pattern of institutional change, there are many signs of a new spirit—from new dress for nuns to a strike for academic freedom at the Catholic University of America. To some extent the process of institutionalization is being reversed.

Adaptation 26 / S.D.Clark **THE METHODIST CHURCH AND THE SALVATION ARMY**

This study is concerned with conflict between church and sect forms of religious organization in relation to the changing community structure of Canada. The view set forth is that the church requires social stability, and when such a condition is not present the church gives way to the sect form of religious organization. The church seeks the accommodation of religious organization to the community. The sect emphasizes the exclusiveness of religious organization: it thinks of the worldly society as something evil, to be withdrawn from, or to be won over by, missionary zeal. Within the church, the spirit of accommodation tends to dominate, and within the sect, the spirit of separation.

This selection from a larger study deals with the Methodist Church and the Salvation Army as they met the challenge of the Canadian city toward the end of the nineteenth century.

After about 1885, many migrants swelled the size of the Canadian city. The chief task and opportunity of religious organization became one of gaining the support of people who found themselves within a new social setting, in many cases far from their old home community and past associates. Traditional religious attachments broke down, and new ones had to be formed if religion were to maintain its hold. Established churches experienced their greatest losses to such religious movements as the Salvation Army. The Army also brought its teaching to those who had no religion. Its success came largely from its influence on the urban poor.

Methodism's social base The limitations of traditional religious denominationalism, which largely accounted for the rapid growth of new sectarian religious movements, can be most clearly seen in the case of the Methodist Church. The failure of the Methodist Church after 1885 was not a failure to grow with the city, nor was it a failure to gain influence in the social life of the urban community. The building of handsome places of worship, the employment of learned and in some cases highly paid ministers, the increasing reliance upon prominent citizens in the organization of Sunday school and missionary work, and the growing participation of the pulpit in political discussion strengthened the position of the Church in the Canadian city. The Church gained support in the better residential

SOURCE: Abridged and adapted from *Church and Sect in Canada* by S. D. Clark (Toronto: University of Toronto Press, 1948), pp. 381–429. Published in this form by permission of the University of Toronto Press and S. D. Clark.

TABLE X:5 SECT AND CHURCH

SECT	CHURCH
RELATION TO THE SOCIAL-ECONOMIC ORDER	
Membership composed chiefly of the propertyless	Membership composed chiefly of property owners
Economic poverty in church property and salaries	Economic wealth
Cultural periphery of the community	Cultural center of the community
Renunciation of or indifference to prevailing culture and social organization, including established churches	Acceptance of prevailing values and of political, economic order; cooperation with established churches
Self-centered religion based on personal experience	Culture-centered religion based on affirmation of citizenship in an existing community
A moral community excluding unworthy members	A social institution embracing all who are socially compatible
Many religious services regardless of interference with other aspects of life	Regular services at stated intervals
Adherence to strict Biblical standards, such as tithing or pacifism	Acceptance of general cultural standards as practical definition of religious obligation
PARTICIPATION AND INTERNAL CONTROL	
Unspecialized, unprofessionalized, part-time ministry	Specialized, professional full-time ministry
Voluntary, confessional bases of membership	Ritual or social prerequisites only
Principal concern with adult membership	Equal concern for children of members
Emphasis on evangelism and conversion	Emphasis on religious education
A high degree of congregational participation in services and administration	Delegation of responsibility to a small percentage of the members
Fervor and positive action in worship	Restraint and passive listening

SOURCE: Adapted from *Millhands and Preachers* by Liston Pope (New Haven: Yale University Press, 1942), pp. 122–124.

areas of the city, and its influence declined among the poorer classes.

Methodist leaders strenuously tried to avoid placing the Church in opposition to labor. Methodist religious publications expressed their sympathy for the cause of the working man and appealed to employers to improve working conditions. But such an appeal had little relation to reality as seen by the working man concerned with strengthening his bargaining position through the organization of trade unions. The Methodist appeal, which expressed the individualist philosophy of a natural harmony of interests of social classes, attacked the economic and social assumptions of working-class philosophy.

The predominantly rural background of the membership and the long rural history of the Church in Canada had much to do with the failure of Methodism to appeal effectively to labor. The conception of work as a virtue and of leisure as a temptation to sin persisted strongly in Methodist thought. The puritan outlook of persons of rural background was little different from the individualistic outlook of capitalist employers, and, whereas Methodist membership continued to be largely of rural origin, leadership passed to the capitalist elements of the urban community. The increasing influence of employers within the councils of the Church made it more difficult to develop a positive appeal to the working-class population of the cities.

Mobility of the urban workers
Only a small proportion of the working population of the city, however, was being drawn into

trade-union organization. The bulk of urban workers, unskilled and transient, lacked a working-class philosophy or a consciousness of being a part of a distinct working class. Without permanent jobs, homes, or neighborhood attachments, they had few strong loyalties and little sense of social responsibility. These elements of the population participated little in the group life of the community. They withdrew into transitory forms of association—gangs, associations of the saloon, and ephemeral groupings based upon the casual contacts of the street, rooming house, or street-corner store.

Abandonment of the practice of street preaching, as employed by the early primitive Methodist preachers , and reliance upon services held in imposing places of worship, cut the Church off from the floating population of the urban community. The problem faced by the Methodist Church in the latter decades of the nineteenth century did not only grow out of social differences between the rich and poor of the city. It resulted from a new kind of social mobility in the community for which the machinery of the Church was not adapted.

Limitations of church appeal to the lower classes Mobility imposed demands upon church organization that could be met only by new techniques. Methodism had abandoned the sectarian policy of recruiting members by religious conversion. It had come to rely upon the techniques of the church, seeking to perpetuate itself from generation to generation. The Sunday school developed as the chief means of keeping the new generation within the Church, but mobil-

ity was greatest among the younger people, and there was an increasing gap between the membership of the Sunday school and the membership of the Church. Many who had grown up in the Sunday schools were lost to the Church through the development of new interests outside the field of religion.

The house of worship was designed to meet the needs of a settled population; it did not effectively serve a floating population which had no strong local community attachments. For the masses of the urban community the street became the center of social life. Religious organization had to adapt itself to urban ecology. In failing to do so, Methodism lost the support of the more mobile elements of the population.

The churches had to do more than reach the urban population; they had to attract support through their religious appeal. A half century of effort to build itself into a denomination had led Methodism to emphasize a worldly pulpit appeal. By 1885 the Church had lost much of its evangelical drive. The polished and studied sermon took the place of the passionate exhortation calling on man to repent and seek forgiveness. The pulpit lost some of its force as a spiritually reorganizing agency among those of the city who were looking for direction and comfort and a means of securing new ties.

If churches were to be filled with people financially able to maintain them, the pulpit appeal had to be directed toward the higher social levels of the population. Evangelism and the large church edifice were incompatible. The former attracted the support of the poor, the

latter required the support of the rich. In becoming a religion of the church, Methodism increasingly depended on the settled residents of the community, upon the people who enjoyed a sense of status and security.

Church-sponsored evangelism Despite this incompatibility, an effort was made by the Church to maintain a revivalist atmosphere, in part by the use of professional evangelists who appeared in the United States about the 1870s and soon became a powerful force. Though not connected with any church, and unordained, the professional evangelist worked within rather than outside the regular churches. He gained his influence not by building up a following of his own or by developing a set of doctrinal teachings, but by making a special appeal to regular church followings. In this way, the more successful of such evangelists were able to gain a hearing among hundreds of thousands of people without interfering with the work of the Church.

The value of the professional evangelist to the regular churches was limited, however, by the fact that the churches were unable to maintain the religious interest aroused by the evangelist. The non-churchgoer who took part in revivalist services in the rink or public hall did not usually attend regular religious services. Revivalism created the urge to enter into religious fellowship, but the urge was not readily satisfied within the formal organization of the church. Revivalism was seldom successful in establishing enduring religious attachments except where it led directly to the formation of a new religious sect. Consequently, the preaching of the professional evangelists tended to strengthen new sectarian movements in the community and to weaken the regular churches. On the other hand, when the evangelists preached to people who were faithful churchgoers, they strengthened the churches, especially by getting more financial contributions.

What was needed, if the church were to reach the highly mobile elements in the city, was a body of workers prepared to go onto the city streets, into the homes of the poor, and into the public meeting places of the common man. The need of maintaining his professional dignity made it difficult for the minister to do this. Even if the evangelists had been prepared to do such work, they were too few. It required an army of workers, and such an army could only be built by drawing upon lay volunteers. In this the Salvation Army succeeded.

THE SALVATION ARMY

In 1883, the first Canadian branch of the Salvation Army was organized in London, Ontario—the beginnings of what was to become a dominant religious force in urban Canada during the next 15 years. The Army capitalized on the great evangelical revival of 1885–1900. With its sensational methods, the Salvation Army came into sharp conflict with the traditional order of Canadian society. Deeply entrenched institutions, both secular and religious, encountered a formidable challenge in its teachings. The saloon was an obvious point of attack, but the saloon was not the only institution subjected to onslaught. Nothing opposed to evangelical religion escaped. Army

workers made no nice distinction between what was considered the province of religious interest and what was not. There was no place—saloon, billiard parlor, or brothel—where the individual could take shelter from the scrutiny of Salvationists concerned about the state of his soul.

Challenge to the regular churches The established churches relied on stated places of worship, a professional ministry, and a ritual, however simple, to maintain a sense of dignity and decorum. The professional status of the minister and the social standing of the congregation in the community depended upon ridding religion of any appearance of being "queer" or irrational.

The emphasis in Salvation Army teachings on free expression of religious feelings and the willingness of Army workers to resort to any method, however spectacular, to attract attention, threatened to destroy the "good name" of religion. The Army's teachings tended to shift the prerogative of judging spiritual worth from the institution to the convert. Religion was made popular in the sense that the understanding of its mysteries was not confined to the select few. Like all religious sects, the Army attacked directly the claims and pretensions of a professional ministry. It thus attacked the whole system of ecclesiastical control and struck at the basis of authority within the church. The church could not meet the Army on its own ground. The relation was not one of competition between similar rival religious bodies; competition gave way to a fundamental conflict between types of religious organization: the church

and the sect. The loss of members by the churches to the Salvation Army represented not a shift of denominational attachments but a strengthening of a spirit of religious fellowship hostile to the whole position of denominationalism.

The Methodist Church felt most strongly the effects of Salvation Army influence. The Army originated from a schism within the Methodist Church in Great Britain, and its doctrines and teachings were very similar to those of Methodism. Therefore the Army tended to draw many recruits from the Methodist congregations, which were proportionately weakened.

Army methods and organization The methods employed by the Salvation Army won the support of footloose elements of the urban population. Street preaching was revived as a regular feature of religious work, and the combination of street preaching with parades, led by brass bands, attracted attention. Crowds gathered on street corners, in public parks and other open spaces, and when a sufficient state of religious enthusiasm had been aroused, they paraded to the barracks where a revivalist meeting took place. At no point did the Army impose any serious obstacle to the participation of the individual in religious service. He could easily join the crowds on the street and as easily depart. The Army carried on religious services in barracks and public halls, where people unaccustomed to churchgoing would feel at home. The service itself was informal and encouraged the free movement of individuals. The lack of decorum in Army meetings had a quality of homeliness and ease, in contrast to the stiff formality of the church.

The centralized organization of the Army, like that of Methodism a century earlier, was highly effective for evangelical work. Military discipline became a central feature of Army organization, and while the autocratic character of the leadership led eventually to internal dispute and schism, it was an element of strength in the early years of the Army's growth.

The movement was a religious order. The property rights of the recruit were surrendered to the organization: he lived in an Army residence, was clothed and fed by the Army, and earnings were turned over to Army headquarters. The recruits tended to be down-and-outs, the social outcasts of the community, who welcomed the economic as well as the emotional security provided by the Army. Their enthusiasm for the Cause substituted for any individual desire for gain or self-aggrandizement. The discipline of the soldier and the devoutness of the ascetic combined to build up among workers a strong feeling of group loyalty and attachment to the leaders.

The emphasis placed by the Army upon the reclamation of the individual—the drunkard, criminal, prostitute, and wastrel—led to practical results which could be demonstrated and dramatized. The sudden reformation of the individual assumed something of the character of a religious miracle, and colorful reports of such reformation provided effective advertising. The work of the Army among the down-and-outs of the city won for it the affection of those who did not feel welcome in the houses of worship of the more richly endowed denominations and the sympathy of those who had a philanthropic interest in the welfare of less fortunate elements of the population. The Army worker had no hesitation in stopping to minister to the drunkard, ex-criminal, or prostitute on the street; the Army hostel was open to those who needed food and clothing. Philanthropic activities became an important part of the Army's work. Primarily, however, the force of its appeal lay in its emphasis upon the simple message of the gospel. The Army grew with all the enthusiasm of the new religious sect. It was prepared to encourage extravagant forms of religious expression if converts to the cause were gained.

Efforts of the older churches to adopt some of the methods of the Salvation Army were an indication of their effectiveness. But the success of the Army, in the end, was not due to any particular method.

The strength of the Army lay in the fact that it was an exclusive religious sect. It expanded through its appeal to a particular class in the community. However much the older churches may have employed its methods, they were unable to make the sort of single appeal characteristic of the Army. Whatever the traditional churches did for the urban masses, the fact of social distinction was emphasized. In the Army, social differentiation disappeared in the emphasis upon spiritual worth.

Institutionalization of the Army Barracks still standing in many towns and villages provide an indication of the rapid growth of the movement. The same buildings, long since abandoned or converted to other uses, suggest an equally rapid decline. The high peak was reached about the turn of the century. Subsequent development was in the direction of limiting the field of evangelical work and strengthening the organization. Like other religious movements before it, the Army was forced away from the role of religious sect in seeking a closer accommodation with the community.

The Salvationists' evangelism had been dominated by the consciousness of souls still to be saved, and this restless search for the wicked and the damned gave their work its distinctive character. But the urge to spread ever further the message of religious salvation led inevitably to an impatience with the slow and laborious task of building up a permanent organization. Consequently many who were drawn into the Army were later lost through failure to follow up the early work of evangelization.

In the interests of the larger movement, Army Headquarters decided to withdraw from areas where sufficient support was not secured to maintain a strong local organization. The decision reflected the viewpoint of a leadership concerned with problems of administration and finance rather than the evangelist's main concern for saving souls. Necessarily, as the Army grew, greater attention had to be paid to building up a following loyal to the movement as a whole. Those served by the Army had to be taxed for its support. This meant an increasing emphasis

on organization at the cost of reducing evangelical work.

The shift in emphasis did not come about without bitter internal conflict, which on a number of occasions led to open division and the organization of rival armies. The differences were fundamental. International Headquarters was concerned with building the movement into a permanent religious organization with its own following. The dissident evangelists were concerned with saving souls wherever they might be found, with little regard to denominational lines. The one view reflected the spirit of the church, the other the spirit of the religious sect. Although the Army suffered a serious loss of support from these defections, in the end it built up a strong organization. If it were to survive, it had to rid itself of some of the very attributes which had accounted for its early success.

By 1914 the Salvation Army in Canada had ceased to be a movement of the lower class. Where the typical Salvationist had been a reformed drunkard, ex-prostitute, or ex-criminal, he was now a person of some social standing with a particular competence as a religious teacher and social welfare worker. A division developed between the Salvationists, on the one hand, and those being saved on the other. Greater attention was paid to the educational qualifications, social

position, and personality of those enlisted in officers' ranks. Establishment of a training school to equip young men and women for positions of responsibility and leadership marked the passing of the old type of Salvationist and the emergence of the professional Salvation Army worker.

The change in the character of the Army leadership was closely related to change in the general position of the Army within the community. The movement developed into a sort of social welfare organization. Rescue work among such groups as ex-convicts, drunkards, prostitutes, and unmarried mothers led to the establishment of special homes and institutions, and the management of these claimed a greater share of attention of Army leaders. Recognition of the value of its good work won for the Army a greater measure of public good will, while the increasing financial costs of the work, in turn, forced the Army to seek support from the public. The World War of 1914–1918 hastened a development already under way before 1914. Its war work secured the reputation of the Army as a patriotic organization and strengthened ties with the community. Once the support of the community had been secured, it could not easily be abandoned. Vested interests operated to check any shift back to the separatist position of the religious sect.

Conclusion   1. Rapid urbanization, accompanied by increased mobility, rootlessness, and class cleavage, affected the social basis of religious participation in late nineteenth-century Canada.

2. Institutionalization of the Methodist Church tied it to the more well-to-do elements of the community. Comfortable affluence was reflected in the leadership of the Church, its social doctrine, its methods, and the nature and location of its churches. These characteristics limited the access and appeal of Methodism to the urban lower class.

3. Church-sponsored evangelism, an effort to reach a broader population, was unsuccessful because it failed to provide a new channel for religious participation and was unable to use an aggressive corps of lay workers.

4. The Salvation Army, an offshoot of Methodism, operated as a religious sect, with unconventional methods and organization. It was thus able to gain access to the mobile city poor.

5. In time the Salvation Army itself became institutionalized, with an increasingly professional ministry, limited evangelism, and an emphasis on regularized social welfare activity.

SECTION 8 COLLECTIVE BEHAVIOR

Religious institutions are often the *locale* of collective behavior, for two reasons. (1) Collective rites and ceremonies are commonly part of religious ritual. (2) Under certain circumstances, religious gatherings arouse collective excitement and stimulate relatively uncontrolled forms of expressive behavior.

According to one theory, collective behavior is a principal *source* of religious belief and feeling. This section begins with a discussion of Durkheim's theory,[64] then considers some forms of religious expression. (See also page 308.)

THE ORIGIN OF RELIGION

Durkheim wondered how primitive man arrived at a concept of the divine—something possessing supernatural powers, upon which man is dependent and to which he owes absolute obedience, but which is able to impart to him some of its power. According to Durkheim, the answer may be that to imagine divine beings, man must experience something in his everyday life that has the characteristics men attribute to their gods. Society itself leads men to the idea of the divine. Like a god, society has absolute moral authority over the individual; it has its own ends, which often override the desires of the individual; it demands sacrifice and obedience; it seems to exist over

and above the individual and to be more powerful than he. Society gives to man greater powers than he would possess without its aid. Like a god, society is both master and helper to man.

But society works in such obscure ways that the individual does not comprehend the source of its influence on him: "Men know well that they are acted upon, but they do not know by whom."[65] Hence, man invents the concept of supernatural powers, gods, and deities to represent or symbolize his consciousness of being dependent on something greater than himself.

Durkheim saw in man's everyday social life a sufficient basis for the human concept of the divine. But he also pointed to a special relation between collective behavior and the origin of religious concepts and feelings. In collective behavior situations, the individual has the sense of being carried away by an outside force. At the same time he feels released, infused with increased energy, vitality, and intense feelings. In such situations, therefore, primitive man most easily conceives of himself as possessed by supernatural forces.

In this way the tribal gatherings of primitive peoples are transformed into religious ceremonies. Fundamental to Durkheim's view was that "the emotional and passional faculties of the primitive are only

[64] Durkheim, *op. cit.,* esp. pp. 205–239.

[65] *Ibid.,* p. 209.

imperfectly placed under the control of his reason and will. . . ." [66] Tribal gatherings lead, therefore, to crowd behavior and collective excitement; aided by rhythmic songs, dances, and sounds, the individual loses control of himself. He experiences exaltation; he feels transformed; he is transported to another world very different from the "uniform, languishing and dull" routine of his everyday life.[67] In addition, the group as a whole gains a sense of emotional unity that transcends the everyday dependence of its members on each other. Such occasions become sacred to the individual and the group, and are reinforced and elaborated by means of sacred symbols, myths, and rites.

Efforts to identify the historical origin of mankind's concept of the divine are, of course, unverifiable; there is no way of going back to a prereligious period when man had no concept of the divine and watching the transformation of secular gatherings into religious institutions. However, as a generalization about the connection between collective behavior and the creation of new faiths, Durkheim's theory has merit. New religious movements, in common with new social movements of all kinds, are apt to encourage collective excitement and emotional contagion as devices to create and spread a new faith. As new faiths become accepted and institutionalized, they rely less on extreme forms of collective behavior to generate commitment.

RELIGION AND EXPRESSIVE BEHAVIOR

In the more familiar Christian rituals, the collective nature of religious worship is controlled. The worshiping congregation is not a crowd, and the religious rites of most Christian churches set strict limits to individual expressiveness. Decorum, solemnity, reverence, humility are emphasized. Exuberance, noise, freedom of movement, and interaction among worshipers are virtually forbidden.

Historically, however, the religious gathering was one of the primary settings for extreme expressive behavior. A list of expressive practices in religious gatherings would be long indeed. One of the oldest is "speaking with tongues," that is, the shouting of meaningless words and syllables while at the height of religious ecstasy. An individual so possessed is believed to be an instrument of the voice of God. Typically, the speaker does not understand the message, which must be interpreted by another member of the congregation who is also divinely inspired.

The extreme behavior permitted within the context of some religious rites and gatherings is usually not condoned in everyday life and may even violate the regular norms of a society. For example, American and Canadian Indians who practice the Peyote religion oppose the sale and use of peyote for nonsacramental purposes.[68]

The historical connection between religious gatherings and extreme behavior has its roots in the nature of religious belief and in the intrinsically expressive and nonutilitarian character of religious rites and practices.

1. Religious beliefs validate extreme forms of behavior. The individual who believes that he is possessed by supernatural forces feels that his extreme behavior is explainable and appropriate.

2. Many religious rites, though they arouse collective excitement, provide no outlet for it. There is some evidence that when the individual has no realistic means of dealing with excessive stimulation, he experiences physiological stress expressed as uncontrollable trembling, writhing, and similar responses.[69]

3. Religious faith is difficult to experience vividly in everyday life or to demonstrate to others. Extreme manifestations of expressive behavior can demonstrate depth of faith and feeling to others and to oneself.

Revivals An important example in recent Western history of a religious gathering generating collec-

---

[66] *Ibid.*, p. 215.

[67] *Loc. cit.*

[68] J. S. Slotkin, "The Peyote Way," in Lessa and Vogt (eds.), *op. cit.,* pp. 482–486.

[69] See William Sargant, *Battle for the Mind* (Garden City: Doubleday, 1957).

tive excitement and extreme behavior is the English and American revival meeting of the eighteenth and nineteenth centuries.

Accounts of early revivals report penitent sinners writhing in agony on the floor, screaming, falling into comas, and speaking with tongues. John Wesley, the founder of Methodism, described in detail the effects of his preaching at meetings during the year 1739:

Some sunk down, and there remained no strength in them; others exceedingly trembled and quaked; some were torn with a kind of convulsive motion in every part of their bodies, and that so violently that often four or five persons could not hold one of them.[70]

Early in the nineteenth century churchmen explicitly recognized that collective religious excitement, conversions, and extreme behavior, formerly thought to be divine miracles, could be induced by the use of appropriate techniques, and lay revivalism gradually emerged as an occupation distinct from the regular ministry. As the following list reveals, revivalist techniques were based on a sound grasp of the conditions that foster emotional contagion, heighten expressiveness, and break down conventional controls.

1. Preaching was intellectually simple, dramatic, and repetitious. Often it was consciously designed to arouse intense fears of hell and damnation. Preaching was extemporaneous; revivalists were free to gesture, move about, and adapt their exhortations to the responses of the audience.

2. Revivalists were not only lay preachers but itinerants, who would come into a town, hold meetings, and leave. In this transitory situation preacher and audience could respond to each other in terms of the immediate moment and with a degree of anonymity.

3. Audience participation was actively encouraged. A hearty "Amen" from some member of the audience, besides being regarded as a visitation of the Spirit, was an encouragement to preacher and audience alike. Revivalists often explicitly exhorted audiences to be demonstrative.

Your prayers are so very cold they do not rise more than six feet high; you must strive hard and struggle —you must groan, you must agonize, why you must pray till your nose bleeds, or it will not avail.[71]

4. Revivalists developed the "protracted meeting," which consisted of "a continuous series of meetings . . . from sunrise to midnight with time out only to eat and sleep."[72] Later the protracted meeting was abandoned and for it was substituted several weeks of nightly meetings. Since revival meetings were typically led by a single revivalist, the attention of the listener was fixed for long periods of time on one subject only—conversion—and on one person only.

5. A feature of the revival was the "anxious seat" described as "some particular seat . . . [usually the front benches or pews] where the anxious may come and be addressed particularly and be made the subject of prayers and sometimes conversed with individually."[73] Besides permitting the revivalist to concentrate upon his best prospects, the "anxious seat" placed those in it under considerable social pressure to live up to expectations.

Sustained and continual stimulation of collective excitement is not possible without social organization and institutional supports. The successful revivalist was and still is dependent upon careful organization, publicity campaigns, and—most important—the cooperation of the regular churches. Of recent revivals conducted by Billy Graham in Great Britain it has been reported that half of the seats were reserved in advance by groups, usually from churches, and that many went intending to make a public decision.[74]

---

[70] Quoted in *ibid.,* p. 100.

[71] William G. McLoughlin, Jr., *Modern Revivalism* (New York: Ronald, 1959), p. 27.

[72] *Ibid.,* p. 93.

[73] Quoted in *ibid.,* p. 95.

[74] Argyle, *op. cit.,* p. 54.

SECTION 9 POPULATION AND ECOLOGY

The religious affiliations of mankind can be only roughly estimated. The approximate memberships of the five major religions are as follows:

Christian	900 million
Islam (Moslems)	450 million
Hindu	350 million
Confucian	300 million
Buddhist	150 million

All the variations of Christianity probably include less than one-third of the people of the world; Roman Catholics, with more than half a billion members, make up by far the largest subdivision. Indeed, there are more Roman Catholics than the total population of Islam. Catholics comprise between one-sixth and one-fifth of mankind; Protestants about one-twelfth.

It would be rash to estimate the varying rates of growth of the major religions. However, Christianity will probably not maintain its present share of the world's people because many of the adherents of Christianity live in developed countries with lower birth rates. The Moslem faith may grow somewhat faster than Christianity. Unless there are large and unanticipated conversions, the religions of mankind for the foreseeable future will be predominantly other than the Christian and Moslem faiths that originated in the Middle East.

RELIGIONS OF THE UNITED STATES

Data on religious affiliation for the United States are usually compilations of reports from religious bodies (churches) rather than direct enumeration of the religion of individuals. The reliability of information based on such records is, therefore, very uneven. Some small religious organizations with few churches are not reported at all. Record-keeping is costly and requires some education, and churches with lower-class membership and poorly educated officials are likely to have poor records. Some churches give only approximations of their memberships, and these can usually be recognized because they are reported in round numbers.[75] Furthermore, religious organizations have varying definitions of membership. Most Protestant churches list only those who actually join a congregation. The Roman Catholic Church and some others include as members all who have been christened. Some churches count only family heads, others include all of the members of the ethnic-religious community. Familiarity with the basis of a denomination's report of membership is essential to a meaningful interpretation of its numerical strength. Statistics reported by religious bodies, although admittedly imperfect, are published by the National Council of the Churches of Christ in the U.S.A. in the *Yearbook of American Churches,* and are summarized in the *Statistical Abstract of the United States* and other standard reference works.

Variation in record-keeping policies suggests the difficulty of defining religious adherence with precision. Similar responses to such an ostensibly simple question as "What is your religion?" have widely varying meanings. Some people who answer "Methodist" are members of the church in all meanings of membership, were reared in the church, are active and devoted practitioners, attend services regularly, send their children to Sunday school, contribute financially to the church and its missions, tithe, participate in the nonreligious activities of the church community, are visited by the minister, and are baptized, married, and buried in the church. Other respondents who answer "Methodist" merely express a preference or a sense of general identity. A full understanding of religious statistics would, therefore, depend on answers to a battery of questions on

---

[75] Paradoxically, reporting in round numbers can also suggest statistical sophistication. For instance, in large numbers totaling many thousands, the hundreds, tens, and units have little meaning. If reported, the smaller numbers suggest greater precision than probably exists.

church membership, attendance, belief, and religious practice, not merely the response to one question.

Nevertheless, even a simple question can yield valuable results when it is addressed to members of all faiths as well as nonbelievers. In 1957 for the first time the Bureau of the Census included a question on religion in one of its regular surveys. It asked a nationwide sample of persons fourteen years old and over, "What is your religion?" Of all persons in the survey 96 percent reported a religion, 3 percent stated they had none, and 1 percent made no report. Answers were voluntary.

The decision of the Census Bureau to use such a simple and general question is indicative of the fact that religion is thought to be a sensitive topic in the U.S. A more specific question, such as "What church do you belong to?" might, it was feared, seem offensive. The question was also an experiment in anticipation of the 1960 Census—an experiment to see what results could be secured and to test public reception. Apparently the results were satisfactory: the refusal rate was small. But a question on religion was not included in the 1960 Census, and even the full

findings from the 1957 sample survey have not been published. Although the available findings of the survey have been widely published and interpreted—and although social scientists have repeatedly called for a follow-up—no subsequent survey has yet been conducted.

The findings of the sample survey make it possible to construct an estimate of the religious distribution of the United States. The figures given below exclude some members of the armed forces, and some children not living with their families. It is assumed that children under fourteen years, who were not in the sample, had the same religion as the head of the family. With the foregoing qualifications, the 1957 religious composition may be described as follows:

Protestant	111,100,000	66.2%
Catholic	43,761,000	26.1
Jewish	5,020,000	3.0
Other	2,091,000	1.2
No religion	4,717,000	2.8
Not reported	1,189,000	0.7
Total	167,878,000	100.0%

TABLE X:6   RELIGION REPORTED FOR PERSONS FOURTEEN YEARS OLD AND OVER, BY COLOR AND SEX, UNITED STATES, 1957

RELIGION	NUMBER IN THOUSANDS	PERCENT TOTAL	PERCENT DISTRIBUTION			
			White		Nonwhite	
			Male	Female	Male	Female
Total, 14 years and over	(119,333)	100.0	100.0 (51,791)	100.0 (55,570)	100.0 (5,679)	100.0 (6,293)
Protestant	78,952	66.2	62.4	65.1	85.4	89.4
Baptist	23,525	19.7	15.1	15.2	59.1	62.0
Lutheran	8,417	7.1	7.9	7.7	0.3	0.2
Methodist	16,676	14.0	13.1	14.1	17.0	17.5
Presbyterian	6,656	5.6	5.8	6.4	1.0	0.8
Other Protestant	23,678	19.8	20.5	21.7	8.0	8.9
Roman Catholic	30,669	25.7	27.8	27.9	6.4	6.6
Jewish	3,868	3.2	3.6	3.6	—	0.1
Other religion	1,545	1.3	1.3	1.2	1.5	1.5
No religion	3,195	2.7	4.0	1.3	5.4	1.7
Religion not reported	1,104	0.9	0.9	0.9	1.3	0.7

NOTE: Includes about 809,000 members of the Armed Forces living off post or with their families on post.
SOURCE: Bureau of the Census, *Current Population Reports,* Series P-20, No. 79 (February, 1958).

By restricting discussion to the actual sample, a more detailed breakdown can be made, and Table X:6 gives the summary results of the survey by sex and color. The figures are based on sample data and are, therefore, *estimates* of the population aged *fourteen and older*. Protestants are the most numerous with about 79 million reported, Roman Catholics are the largest single denomination with about 30.7 million, and Jews number 3.9 million. Nonwhites are preponderantly Protestant, concentrated in two denominations, Baptist and Methodist. These two denominations are also most often reported by white Protestants, but they are not nearly so preponderant as among nonwhites. A substantially larger number of males than females say they have no religion.

By region, Roman Catholics and Jews are concentrated in the Northeast, Protestants in the South and North Central states. Jews are most urbanized and Protestants least urbanized of the three major religions. Variation in fertility by religion is related to urbanization, socioeconomic status, and other factors as well as to the influence of religious beliefs on reproduction. Baptist women have the highest fertility, Roman Catholics next, and the lowest are Jewish and Presbyterian women. The high Baptist fertility is connected to the large proportion of Negroes and the rural and Southern backgrounds of white Baptists—all factors associated with high fertility.

CHAPTER XI
EDUCATION*

* This chapter draws upon material included in the third edition of this book in Chapter XII, EDUCATION, written in collaboration with Burton R. Clark.

SECTION 1 INTRODUCTION

Most socialization is informal and occurs in the course of spontaneous interaction. However, institutionalized agencies for deliberate socialization are a universal feature of complex societies. There were schools in Egypt and China at least as early as 2000 B.C., and rudimentary agencies of formal education in charge of priests or shamans undoubtedly existed in many societies much earlier. The first schools trained priests and officials, and until recent times formal education was a device for maintaining a small "establishment," that is, a unified political, religious, military, and economic elite.

Today education is more important in size and scope than ever before in human history. In earlier times the educated man was economically unproductive; today productivity depends on wide distribution of specialized skills. Modern political systems, too, call for mass education. Effective participation in a modern society requires heavy investment in educational institutions.

Like the broader process of socialization itself, education has a dual significance. It is person-centered and society-centered. Education enhances the capabilities of the individual and contributes to his self-realization; at the same time, education does symbolic and practical work for the social system. The need to balance these functions, personal and social, poses the perennial issues of education.

FUNCTIONS OF EDUCATION

Cultural transmission The communication of received beliefs and understandings is a major function of formal education. Education is especially relied on in societies that are culturally self-conscious. Awareness of a cultural heritage is usually associated with concern that traditional values and cultural "mysteries" will be lost if no one has special knowledge of them. While cultural transmission tends to emphasize respect for tradition, values of criticism and inquiry may be passed on as well as conservative values. The function of cultural transmission encourages humanist scholarship and teaching, to preserve and perhaps examine the society's history, language, religion, and philosophy.

Social integration Formal education is a major agency for transforming a heterogeneous and potentially divided community into one bound together by a common language and a sense of common identity. The rise of national states in Europe, for example, was aided by the creation of systems of public education. The schools taught an official language, which they helped to standardize, and thereby fostered the consciousness of being French or German rather than Burgundian or Bavarian. In the United States, educational institutions have carried a major share of the task of integrating millions of immigrants; they are now expected to bring into the mainstream of American life many other millions who have been disadvantaged.

Innovation To some degree even the most tradition-bound educational institution is a source of innovation, if only because the teacher-scholar is called on to apply his wisdom or expertise to new situations. Early innovation was often accidental and unanticipated, perhaps the result of religious rather than practical intent. For instance, the calendar was first developed to order religious practices, but because it was based on systematic observation of the celestial sphere the new knowledge stimulated scientific inquiry for its own sake. In modern society innovation is increasingly institutionalized, and centers of learning are expected to contribute new ideas and new technology. As the innovative function is pressed, a strain develops between teaching and research. New forms of organization emerge, notably research institutes, to pursue innovation while maintaining only minimal educational responsibilities. Despite this trend, whose outcome cannot now be known, innovation is a dominant motif of higher education in all advanced countries.

Selection and allocation In traditional society, when only a few were educated, the school played a smaller part than family membership in determining the student's ultimate role and status. But under conditions of mass education the school system takes over the job of screening and allocating. How the individual performs in school and the course of study he chooses often determine his future occupation, income, and prestige. The school is the central mechanism for guiding and facilitating intergenerational mobility. (See SOCIAL STRATIFICATION, pp. 184–185.)

The allocating function tends to bring the educational system into close coordination with government and industry. In a period of rapidly changing technology, the school system runs the risk of turning out students who are ready for yesterday's jobs rather than today's or tomorrow's.

Personal development Formal education communicates skills and perspectives that cannot readily be gained through other socializing experiences. In addition to providing intellectual discipline and the opportunity to learn specialized subject matters, the school is often a place of transition from a highly personal to a more impersonal world; habits are learned, such as punctuality, that may be necessary in a time-conscious society. Schooling can have psychic costs as well as benefits. If the school prolongs dependency beyond maturity, instills feelings of inferiority, or exaggerates the worth of intellectuality, it may have negative effects on personal growth and well-being.

BASIC DILEMMAS

Three broad issues affecting the aims of education comprise a framework for study and debate: (1) education versus training, (2) elite versus mass education, and (3) conservatism versus change.

Education and training The question of "genuine" education as distinguished from technical training was raised by Socrates in the fifth century B.C., and the issue remains lively today. Three ideas shaped the classic Greek view of knowledge and education. First, education is the development of the power to think, not the acquisition of information.

As a Young Man   *At Eighty*

John Dewey (1859–1952) was a founder of the pragmatist school of American philosophy. A close associate of George Herbert Mead (see p. 95), Dewey rejected the oppositions of mind and self, thought and action, knowing and feeling, fact and value. He believed that ideas should be guides to action and that true learning takes place only when the individual is free to explore and test his world. Dewey's contributions to social psychology (in Human Nature and Conduct*), to philosophical naturalism (in* Experience and Nature*), to aesthetics (in* Art as Experience*), to logic (in* Essays in Experimental Logic*), and to education (in* Democracy and Education*) immensely influenced American thought for three generations.*

The educated man lives "the examined life," and education is the enlargement of understanding through the social process of questioning and being questioned. Second, education is a quest for virtue rather than technical proficiency. Third, education looks to lasting truth, based on reason, and not to mere opinion or to practical knowledge that depends on changing utilities and circumstances.

Two thousand years later, in his book *Emile*, the French-Swiss social philosopher Jean-Jacques Rousseau (1712–1778) argued for a less intellectualized, more person-centered, more experience-based concept of education. He held that education should posit the uniqueness and worth of the individual, provide a setting within which the individual's distinctive potential might develop, and allow oppor-

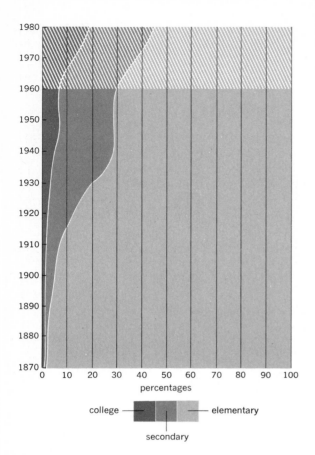

FIG. XI:1 The school population of the United States, 1870–1960 (projected to 1980)

SOURCE: *Statistical Abstract of the United States: 1966,* p. 107, and *1950,* p. 123; and *Current Population Reports,* Series P-25, No. 365, May 5, 1967. For detailed data from which this figure was constructed, see Table XI:5, page 376.

tunity for learning through experience. Rousseau thought that the practical arts could contribute to education, not as narrow training but as resources for moral development.

In this century the American philosopher John Dewey (1859–1952) carried forward with greater sophistication Rousseau's emphasis on education as the reconstruction of experience. Like most of his predecessors, Dewey also believed that virtue could be taught, but he stressed the active role of the individual and the need to cultivate personal freedom and autonomy. This ideal could be attained, he thought, only if the school provided a democratic environment.

These themes are counterposed to the view that the chief business of the schools is to train people in specific disciplines. The conflict between education and training takes place at all levels in the educational system. At lower levels it is a conflict between "child development" and the "three Rs"; at higher levels humane or general education is pitted against professional specialization. Dewey believed that the dichotomy between education and training could be overcome if, in the study of practical disciplines, the students were encouraged to explore the whole range of intellectual issues raised by the subject matter.

Elite and mass Historically, the conflict between education and training has been an aspect of the struggle of high-status groups to maintain their prestige:

Behind all the present discussions of the foundations of the educational system, the struggle of the "specialist type of man" against the older type of "cultivated man" is hidden at some decisive point. This fight is determined by the irresistibly expanding bureaucratization of all public and private relations of authority and by the ever-increasing importance of expert and specialized knowledge.[1]

The ideal of a cultivated man, as distinguished from a specialist, has been the basis of social esteem in a number of historical settings, notably the Chinese imperial government manned by "literati,"[2] and the English system of administration by "gentlemen."

Advancing technology and the spread of democracy have resulted in the extension of some form of education to virtually the entire population. In

[1] H. H. Gerth and C. Wright Mills (eds.), *From Max Weber: Essays in Sociology* (New York: Oxford University Press, 1946), p. 243.

[2] See *ibid.,* Chap. XVII, "The Chinese Literati."

the nineteenth century it became apparent that a literate labor force was needed in a modern economy; and the demand for wider participation in government added strength to the cause of universal education.

School enrollments show an extension of universal education from the primary to the secondary level and, in recent years, a rapid expansion at the college level. Figure XI:1, which summarizes the changing distribution of the school population, projects the enrollment in the three main sectors through 1980. If the trend as projected in the figure is realized, it appears that an increasingly large part of the population will have at least some college education.

The question posed by mass education, as by mass culture generally (see p. 80), is whether high standards can be maintained when large numbers participate. Attempts to deal with the problem center on the diversification of educational institutions,

that is, the creation of a variety of schools and colleges—some highly select, others oriented to mass participation. The elite schools may allow for equal opportunity based on merit, but there is a strong tendency for selective participation to be based on social origin. (See Sec. 6.)

Conservation and reform As agencies of society the schools are inevitably subject to conservative influences. Those who wish to preserve tradition insist that the schools educate the new generation in the image of the old. However, the schools are potential instruments of social change. They have unique access to the youth and resources for developing new ideas. The extent to which the schools can engage in social reconstruction and be centers of nonconformity or dissent is a subject of continuing debate. Normally the society maintains firm control over most of the educational system while allowing selected institutions to be centers of social innovation.

SOURCES AND READINGS

Orville G. Brim, Jr., *Sociology and the Field of Education* (New York: Russell Sage Foundation, 1958).

Wilbur B. Brookover, *A Sociology of Education* (New York: American Book Co., 1955).

Burton R. Clark, *Educating the Expert Society* (San Francisco: Chandler Publishing, 1962).

James S. Coleman, *The Adolescent Society* (New York: The Free Press of Glencoe, 1961).

Ronald G. Corwin, *A Sociology of Education* (New York: Appleton-Century-Crofts, 1965).

John Dewey, *Democracy and Education* (New York: Macmillan, 1916; Free Press paperback edition, 1966).

A. H. Halsey, Jean Floud, and C. Arnold Anderson, *Education, Economy, and Society* (New York: The Free Press of Glencoe, 1961).

Robert J. Havighurst and Bernice L. Neugarten, *Society and Education* (Boston: Allyn and Bacon, 1957).

A. B. Hollingshead, *Elmtown's Youth* (New York: Wiley, 1949).

Blaine E. Mercer and Edwin R. Carr, *Education and the Social Order* (New York: Holt, Rinehart and Winston, 1957).

David Riesman, *Constraint and Variety in American Education* (Lincoln, Nebr.: University of Nebraska Press, 1956).

Ralph H. Turner, *Social Context of Ambition: A Study of High-School Seniors in Los Angeles* (San Francisco: Chandler Publishing, 1964).

Thorstein Veblen, *The Higher Learning in America* (B. W. Heubsch, 1918); and (Stanford, California: Academic Reprints, 1954).

Willard Waller, *The Sociology of Teaching* (New York: Wiley, 1932).

Michael Young, *The Rise of the Meritocracy, 1870–2033* (London: Thames and Hudson, 1958).

Periodicals
Journal of Negro Education

Sociology of Education

SECTION 2 SOCIAL ORGANIZATION

As a differentiated institution, education is dependent on other institutions and reacts to their changes. It is also an independent force that influences other institutions. This section considers the extent to which education is independent of and integrated with the rest of society and the community and outlines the status of adult education.

INSTITUTIONAL AUTONOMY

The relative importance of integration and autonomy is different for every institution, but the balance between them is one of the most important problems in the study of social organization. Educators continuously strive to protect the independence of their institutions. They face encroachment from many forces in society, especially those that want to change educational policies. In resisting pressures, educational leaders feel they are protecting important public interests that have been entrusted to them. As experts and professionals, educators claim to have the training and devotion to standards that justify their autonomy.

This argument can be improperly used to avoid all criticism, but it reflects an important sociological truth. Because the values entrusted to education are general, such as "to advance learning," the work of the institution is justified on a long-run basis. Its activities cannot readily be judged by immediate results.

Most groups cannot be expected to take continuous account of the ultimate values educational institutions try to defend. This task must be left to specialists who have the necessary competence, with enough autonomy to permit them to work out and protect major policies and standards. The amount of autonomy that is needed can be determined only in the light of the specific case.

Conditions of autonomy Whether or not a particular segment of the educational institution can maintain its autonomy depends on a number of related factors:

1. *Firmness of the value.* If the values upheld by a school are well established and firmly accepted by the community, there is relatively little pressure upon the institution to justify itself by "results" or to adapt its policies to the immediate needs of specific groups. Medical education is a good example of a well-established and firmly accepted value, and medical programs are among the most secure educational activities. On the other hand, institutions that carry on activities weakly accepted as a public interest find it difficult to maintain their autonomy. They are insecure, and vulnerable to outside demands. Adult education, a good example, is discussed below.

2. *Professionalism.* Autonomy is dependent on the possibility of developing standards and training. Special skills and language ("jargon" to the outsider) are conducive to social isolation, and when they are combined with professional prestige, they make it easier to resist the efforts of laymen to intrude their judgments. Physicists and mathematicians are protected by the inability of laymen to understand their work. Elementary schoolteachers, in contrast, are vulnerable because parents live with their results and feel competent to judge their work.

3. *Source of support.* The extent of reliance on outside funds and the source from which a school or college draws its support affect its autonomy. A state college may be wholly dependent on public funds and subject to influence from the governor's office and the legislature. On the other hand, state support may free the college from the pressures of the local community, and the state constitution may protect it against gross legislative interference with educational policy. A private college may have considerable autonomy if it is well endowed and can attract students, but it is vulnerable if it is financed on a year-to-year basis or if it cannot draw enough students to guarantee a steady income from fees.

4. *Organizational scale.* Large, complex organizations are difficult to supervise from the outside. Their size obscures many activities from public view; their complexity keeps all but experienced administrators ignorant of how they actually are run—or not run. As a state college grows from 1,000 to 15,000 students, the chances of close external control decline. Authority is delegated to or assumed by the professional staff of administrators and professors. The full-time experts who are close to operations know what is going on and are able to make informed decisions.

The presence or absence of these four conditions determines the capacity of the institution to make its own policies and protect itself from outside demands and pressures.

Adult education Adult education is only weakly accepted as a public interest, and the institutions that carry on this activity are insecure and dependent.[3] The public schools are concerned primarily with the education of the young, and adult schools maintained by local school authorities compete for support and budget with the elementary and secondary schools. Supplementary funds for adult education commonly come from tuition fees or state aid, both of which are dependent on attendance. Hence, great emphasis is placed on attracting students. Classes live or die according to the enrollment of a student population that is part-time, voluntary, and casual.

The teaching staff is part-time and weakly professionalized. The program of courses must be flexible because of undependable financing and changing student interests. The career lines for teachers and principals are not well defined, and advancement often means leaving the adult school for a stable, recognized position in a high school or college.

A weakly established value, a low degree of professionalism, and heavy reliance on outside financial sources combine to place adult educators in a marginal and vulnerable position. With their low degree of independence, they often become subservient to their students.

[3] Burton R. Clark, *Adult Education in Transition* (Berkeley and Los Angeles: University of California Press, 1956).

SECTION 3 CULTURE

American culture is to a large extent a political culture. Some other societies find their identity in immemorial tradition, in ancient institutions, in ethnic homogeneity, or in a linguistic heritage, but the American way of life is more readily summed up in a set of political and social ideals. Among these is the democratic concept of equal opportunity. A country peopled by immigrants has repeatedly learned that human potentialities can be released when social and cultural barriers are lifted. The principle of equal opportunity has served both national self-interest and idealism.

Culture and mass education Equality of educational opportunity is the value-root of mass education. However, mass education raises questions whether educational standards can be maintained. This dilemma is a frequent theme in the study of education and culture: How can the ideal of equal opportunity be made consistent with the culture-sustaining activities of learning and creativity?

In a contest between opportunity and standards, it is clear from the course of American history and from the way decisions are made that opportunity would win. There is too much to be gained from education, even if that education is second-rate. However, a direct conflict between these values has been avoided by the mechanism of institutional diversification.

An outstanding feature of American education

is the patterned variety of institutions, especially at the college and university level. For example, in California a fully developed public system of higher education consists of (1) the state university, composed of several campuses, (2) the state colleges, distributed more widely throughout the state, and (3) junior colleges, in numerous communities. In an important sense, these units are interdependent. The selectivity of the university, which admits only a small fraction of high school graduates, depends

An African boy examines a passage from the Koran inscribed on a wooden tablet. Islam and the Arabic language are widespread in Africa, and their influence is growing.

on the existence of the other two types of institutions. Without the other colleges, which are less selective in admissions, the pressure from citizens to admit their children would probably make it impossible for the university to maintain a selective policy. The state colleges, too, benefit from the buffer provided by the junior colleges.

The quality of education offered at the relatively small number of highly selective colleges which aim for the highest standards of undergraduate education is in no way lowered by the extension of educational opportunities in other colleges. On the contrary, the current growth in the college-going population, far from lowering standards at these selective institutions, has markedly raised them: the number of applicants to the best (and best regarded) colleges and universities has risen steadily since World War II, and those institutions which have chosen not to expand simply skim off entering classes of higher and higher ability.[4]

While mass education may be a threat to standards, the threat is mitigated by buffer institutions able to absorb the mass of students.

The division of labor among institutions is not without its problems. In practice the elite universities are challenged by the others. The challenge is in part of their own making, for the top-level schools serve as models, and many of their graduates teach at second-level schools:

The existence of basic courses in the liberal arts and sciences at the junior colleges, and large departments in these subjects in the state colleges, force them to recruit faculty members trained in these academic disciplines at the big university graduate centers, where these men were exposed to the models towards which they strive to orient their own institutions. So the academic wings of the junior and state colleges grow, state college instructors press for more time and funds for research, and the scholarly values of liberal arts colleges and big universities are increasingly reflected throughout the system.[5]

The result is a somewhat unstable equilibrium, but in a context of mass education there is little alternative to the master strategy of diversifying institutions

[4] Martin Trow, "The Democratization of Higher Education in America," *European Journal of Sociology, 3* (1962), 244.
[5] *Ibid.,* p. 248.

within a balanced system to protect the precarious values of education and scholarship.

Student subcultures Another important cultural aspect of education is the system of norms and standards—the blueprint of behavior—found *within* the school or college. The student newly arrived on a college campus encounters a composite of guiding values and ideals. In small colleges, the cultural environment may be almost homogeneous. Usually, however, the campus culture is more diverse. Alternative orientations are held by different groups—the faculty, the alumni, and students. Adaptation 27 reviews the characteristics of the major student subcultures and relates them to trends in American education.

Adaptation 27 / B. R. Clark *and* Trow COLLEGE SUBCULTURES

This study identifies and describes four major types of student subcultures as they appeared during the 1950s and early 1960s: (1) collegiate, (2) vocational, (3) academic, and (4) nonconformist. Although the major themes vary in their emphasis at different universities, all of the forms can be recognized on most campuses. In the short time since the article was written the nonconformist subculture has had an unanticipated growth and has become much more visible.

Collegiate The *collegiate subculture* is a world of sports, dates, and fun. Its symbols are the star athlete, the homecoming queen, and the fraternity dance. Fraternities and sororities have set the pattern of the collegiate way of life. Fraternity participation in extracurricular activities extends the influence of this style, and many nonfraternal dormitories model themselves after it, from candlelight and song to float parades and panty raids. Important since the 1890s, the Joe College style is still the most visible model, the one from which have developed the stereotypes of college life found in the mass media.

The collegiate subculture usually recruits its most active supporters from the upper and upper-middle classes, for it takes money and leisure to pursue a round of social activities. It flourishes only on the residential campus.

This subsystem of values and activities is compatible with strong college loyalty. Its graduates often become devoted alumni, sentimentally tied to the college through happy memory of things past and through such events as the homecoming week and the "big" game. However, the collegiate subculture is resistant to involvement with ideas beyond what is required to pass courses and gain the diploma. This orientation is epitomized in the saw: "I have no intention of letting my studies interfere with my college education."

Vocational A second orientation is the *vocational subculture*. In this subworld, students are narrowly and directly concerned with job preparation, and see college as courses and credits leading to a diploma and a better job than they could otherwise command. They use the college to pick up credits at a rate determined by what they can afford in time, money, and energy. Symbols of this subculture are the placement office and the slide rule hanging from the engineering student's belt. Its patterns are most fully represented in the student who is poor, commutes to campus, works at an outside job between 20 and 40 hours a week, and has a wife and children. This subculture is not visible and co-

SOURCE: Abridged and adapted from Burton R. Clark and Martin A. Trow, "Determinants of College Student Subculture." Published in this form by permission of the authors. For a fuller treatment see Burton R. Clark and Martin Trow, "The Organizational Context," in Theodore M. Newcomb and Everett K. Wilson (eds.), *College Peer Groups* (Chicago: Aldine, 1966), pp. 17–70.

herent; it is simply the pragmatic, no-nonsense orientation promoted in many students by the expectations with which they enter a college and the conditions under which they attend.

The vocational subculture is not usually compatible with strong college loyalty since its members do not participate intensely in the extracurricular life of the college. Like the collegiate, the vocational subculture is resistant to intellectual demands beyond what is required to pass the courses. To many hard-driven students preparing for work directly after the bachelor's degree, ideas and schol-arship are as much a luxury and distraction as are sports and fraternities.

This subculture is likely to flourish at "streetcar" (or parking lot) colleges that recruit primarily the sons and daughters of lower-middle-class and working-class homes. It usually has little social unity. Its members interact with one another less than do those caught up in the collegiate subculture. The student role is narrow and, in the extreme, the student body is an atomized aggregation.

Academic A third blueprint for behavior is the *academic sub-culture,* the way of life of serious students who identify with the intellectual concerns of faculty members. This subculture is carried by students who work hard, get the best grades, talk about their course work outside of class, and let the world of ideas and knowledge reach them.

Their symbols are the library, laboratory, and seminar; they are liked by the professors but are "greasy grinds" in the eyes of the collegiate crowd.

The academic subculture is generally compatible with college loyalty, through identification with the faculty. It is the dominant por-

Robert Frost (1874–1963)   The poet who dropped out of Dartmouth in his first semester returns to conduct a seminar.

tion of the climate found at the academically strongest colleges. When colleges aim to upgrade themselves, they seek to recruit students already oriented in this direction. Students with serious academic orientation come from all social strata and cultural groups, but proportionately more of them are likely to come from upper-middle-class homes where parents are well educated, value books and learning, and have the financial resources to support their children through undergraduate and graduate study.

The undergraduate students most representative of this subculture look forward to graduate work or professional training. They think of graduate school as the place for pre-job training. Hence, they define their undergraduate years as a time for extending their appreciation of ideas and gaining a general education.

Nonconformist A fourth orientation is the *nonconformist subculture*. There are many types of nonconformity among college students, but a principal type is the nonconforming intellectual. His distinctive style is a rather aggressive nonconformism. Critical of the "establishment" and seeking to be independent, the nonconforming intellectuals are usually hostile to the college administration and somewhat detached from the college as a whole. These students are often deeply "concerned" with the ideas of the classroom, but even more with issues current in art, literature, and politics of the wider adult society.

Nonconforming students often strive for a personal identity, and in the process they adopt distinc-

tive styles of dress, of speech, and of attitude. In the eyes of their more conforming classmates, they are the unwashed. The nonconformist subculture, involved with ideas but not identified with the college, apparently attracts participants from all social backgrounds. It offers the rebellious student shelter and intellectual support for his rebellious idealism.

These four types of subculture emerge from the combination of two factors: (*a*) the degree to which students are involved with ideas, and (*b*) the extent to which students identify with their college:

		Involved with Ideas	
		+	−
Identify with	+	Academic	Collegiate
the College	−	Nonconformist	Vocational

Decline of the collegiate The collegiate subculture flourishes when students have money, leisure, and a light heart about their college education. But proportionately fewer students are so equipped at the present time compared to the past, and there is a trend away from dominance of campuses by the Joe College life. Career orientations are changing. More students now plan to pursue postgraduate studies, and they know that deans and graduate faculties will review their undergraduate records. More students plan to pursue careers in large organizations, and are aware that job interviewers from business corporations or public agencies will examine the transcripts that record college performance. The boy going into a small family business is less typical. The closer bearing of college performance on career has a sobering effect on campus life.

Secondly, most big city cam-

puses have a large proportion of students from working-class and lower-middle-class backgrounds, who do not have much money and feel they have no time to waste on collegiate activities. College for them is related to mobility and future security in a good job. Democratization of higher education thus tends to diminish the strength of the collegiate subculture.

Thirdly, the number of students enrolled in higher education is increasing due to the high birth rate that began after World War II and to the rising proportions of high school graduates who go on to college. The growth in numbers has created a sellers' market for colleges, and many colleges are setting higher standards of admission. In their selectivity, these colleges emphasize intelligence, good high school record, and seriousness. Selection on these grounds also weakens the collegiate subculture, and in the best colleges the collegiate is losing in competition with the academic emphasis.

These conditions of changing career patterns, democratization of college-going, and increasing selectivity in some colleges cause the collegiate subculture to decline. The fraternities and sororities on many campuses have been de-emphasizing the "rah-rah" life since the end of World War II.

The rise of vocationalism The vocational orientation is increasing rapidly, and a number of forces urge the student in this direction.

1. *Occupational change.* Professional, technical, and managerial occupations, which require advanced training, are growing rapidly. The college has more numerous and more definite training

jobs to do. The increasing undergraduate population is concentrated in applied fields, such as business administration, engineering, and education.

2. *Education as the means of mobility*. As an instrument for the achievement of higher status, college is defined as a way of getting the training and diplomas needed for the better paying jobs. People of lower social origins now entering college in larger numbers are likely to perceive college in these terms. For students of all socio-economic levels, however, college and work are increasingly interconnected and an instrumental or vocational definition of the college years is therefore encouraged.

3. *Ascendance of public colleges*. The expansion in American higher education is taking place largely in the public colleges and universities. These service-oriented institutions are usually more responsive than private colleges to state and local demands, and provide training for the growing list of occupations that require advanced skills. Public colleges are relatively inexpensive, often easy

to enter, and conveniently located to serve large numbers of students, especially job-oriented young people of lower social origins.

4. *Bureaucratization of academic organization*. The comprehensive colleges are people-processing institutions, whose administrative staffs must deal with and organize the scattered activities of large numbers of students enrolled in diverse programs. Relations between teachers and students under these conditions are fleeting and impersonal. In the university, teachers involve themselves less with students because they are busy with research, professional activity, and off-campus service.

5. *Withdrawal of student involvement*. An increasing proportion of college students enroll in nonresidential colleges. Living at home and holding part-time or full-time jobs, students visit the campus to attend class or use the library; they drop in and out of college, some finishing in six to eight years while many do not finish at all. In brief, the student role is focused on course work and

squeezed in among off-campus roles.

The trend toward vocational orientation indicates that a new cultural conflict is emerging in colleges. The older conflict was between the academic and the collegiate subcultures with the faculties upholding intellectual values and the majority of students opposing them with nonintellectual or anti-intellectual interests. With the decline of the collegiate and the growth of the vocational, the emerging conflict is between the academic and the vocational subcultures. Both of these orientations are "serious"; both are legitimate in the eyes of adults; both find proponents in the faculty as well as in the student body. The old conflict was whether students would study or play. The new conflict is whether they will study in broad fields of knowledge and concern themselves with general issues, or study in applied, narrow fields and concern themselves with acquiring the skills and certificates they need for a job.

SECTION 4 SOCIALIZATION

Since education is a form of socialization, everything in this chapter could reasonably be included under the rubric of this section. However, education is related to socialization in two more clearly defined ways: (1) the effect of education on fundamental attitudes and on personality formation, and (2) the competence of the educational system to have more than a superficial and transitory influence on the individual.

EDUCATION AND BASIC ATTITUDES

It is difficult to tell precisely what changes education induces in attitudes and values because education is highly self-selective. For example, high school students who are planning to go to college differ in some attitudes and values from those who do not plan to go. However, some effects of education are suggested by (1) national opinion polls that relate

TABLE XI:1   EDUCATION AND POLITICAL TOLERANCE

EDUCATION OF RESPONDENT	LEVEL OF TOLERANCE (IN PERCENT)			
	High	*Medium*	*Low*	*Total*
College graduate	66	29	5	100 (308)
Some college	53	38	9	100 (319)
High school graduate	42	46	12	100 (768)
Some high school	29	54	17	100 (576)
Grade school	16	62	22	100 (792)

SOURCE: Samuel A. Stouffer, *Communism, Conformity and Civil Liberties* (New York: Doubleday, 1955), p. 90. Based on persons in a national cross section who showed some interest in the news about Communists in the United States and what is being done about them. The "more interested" people totaled somewhat more than half of the sample.

attitudes to level of education and (2) studies that compare the values of college freshmen and seniors.

The national correlation   The higher their level of education, the more people tend to reject the stereotypes that constitute prejudice and express tolerance of minorities. The strong relation of political tolerance to education is shown in Table XI:1. The proportion of adults tolerant of political nonconformists in a 1955 nationwide poll varied systematically by educational level. At each higher level of education, more respondents were tolerant and a smaller proportion were intolerant. A national survey conducted in 1964 shows a similar close relation between education and tolerant attitudes toward Negroes, Jews, Catholics, and political and cultural diversity.[6] Regardless of how prejudice is measured, more people are tolerant and fewer are intolerant at each higher level of education. For example, about 1 out of 2 high school graduates scored as anti-Semitic, compared with about 1 out of 5 college graduates and 1 out of 10 postgraduates.

In brief, education is the prime correlate of many important attitudes and habits; and the correlation usually remains when the influence of occupation, religion, age, and other factors is controlled. Thus, the results of national surveys suggest that mass education significantly affects basic attitudes.

The correlation within college   Studies of changes in the attitudes of students during the college years show a widening of perspective along with increasing liberality; students tend to change toward the attitudes of academic men. The changes often, but not always, include a weakening of religious belief, indicating that college education is a secularizing influence.

A study of Bennington College in the late 1930s showed that the college exercised a marked influence on the political attitudes of many students.[7] The students came from politically conservative families, but the college was liberal in its political mood. One result was that the support for the conservative Republican candidate for president in 1936 (Alfred E. Landon) was 62 percent among the freshmen, 43 percent among sophomores, and 15 percent among juniors and seniors.

In 1952 a survey was conducted of the attitudes of 3,796 students in four Ivy League colleges (Dartmouth, Harvard, Wesleyan, Yale) and five public-supported colleges (Michigan, North Carolina, Texas, UCLA, Wayne). The students were classified in five categories, from strongly pro-civil rights to strongly anti-civil rights, and those falling in the "upper" two categories were taken as supportive of civil rights.

Table XI:2 reports, by year in college, the per-

[6] Gertrude Jaeger Selznick and Stephen Steinberg, *Antisemitism in the United States* (New York: Harper & Row, 1968).

[7] Theodore Newcomb, *Personality and Social Change* (New York: Dryden, 1943).

TABLE XI:2   YEAR IN COLLEGE AND SUPPORT OF CIVIL RIGHTS

TYPE OF COLLEGE	PERCENT SUPPORTING CIVIL RIGHTS				FRESHMAN-SENIOR CHANGE
	Freshman	*Sophomore*	*Junior*	*Senior*	
Ivy League	45	57	58	68	23
Public-supported	31	40	41	44	13

SOURCE: Norman Miller, "Academic Climate and Student Values," paper presented at the Fifty-fourth Annual Meeting of the American Sociological Association, September, 1959.

centage of students with attitudes highly supportive of civil rights (e.g., that people with dangerous social and economic viewpoints should be allowed to run for public office). The Ivy League freshmen were more supportive of civil rights than the public-supported college seniors and showed greater change over the four years, but the change in student attitude was in the same direction in both the public and the private institutions.

A study of nearly 900 students at the University of California (Berkeley) in 1957 reported a similar finding.[8] When students were classified on the basis of their attitudes on issues such as refusing a passport to a Socialist, the proportion of "highly libertarian" was 21 percent among freshmen and 40 percent among seniors.

As students progress through the educational system, they apparently become more liberal in their attitudes. The change results partly from specific knowledge and in part from being socialized to new perspectives through contact with faculties and other students and through anticipation of future careers. The higher levels of education lead to a general cultural sophistication that is characteristic of men in the professional and managerial occupations.

Cautions   1. Studies that compare seniors with freshmen are not able to take into account the effect of dropouts. The apparent change in attitude may result partly from students with one attitude dropping out while students with a second attitude re-

main, giving the senior class a different average score from the freshman class. The best method is to study the same group of students through the four years, noting who drops out and who remains. This method can compare the attitudes of the continuing students as seniors with their attitudes as freshmen. However, the longitudinal method is time-consuming and expensive.

2. Although the more educated are consistently lower in stereotyped beliefs about minorities, many of them favor such discriminatory practices as excluding Jews from social clubs.

3. Although college graduates are less prejudiced than people with less education, extent of prejudice varies according to their majors. Social sciences or humanities majors tend to be less prejudiced and more civil libertarian than, for example, majors in business administration or engineering. However, it is difficult to separate self-selection from the influence of the educational curriculum.

EDUCATION OF THE DISADVANTAGED

It is apparent that education, including mass education, contributes to public enlightenment. However, there are limitations on the competence of the schools to perform effectively as socializing agencies. The most glaring defects occur in the relations of the schools to children of disadvantaged families.

There is a relatively high rate of failure and dropout among low-income pupils. In explaining this fact, both the social background of the child and

[8] Hanan C. Selvin and Warren O. Hagstrom, "Determinants of Support for Civil Liberties," *The British Journal of Sociology, 11* (March, 1960), 51–73.

the character of the school should be considered. Low-income homes have relatively few resources for stimulating and disciplining the child in ways that are helpful in his schooling. There is less practice in reading, less use of formal language, less effective development of self-control, less effort by adults to encourage and satisfy curiosity. These deficiencies, compounded by an often turbulent and uncertain home life, contribute to school failure. Furthermore, most schools do not adequately cope with the problems of the lower-class child.

Defects of the schools A number of school characteristics have the effect of denying adequate schooling to disadvantaged children.[9] These include:

1. *Belief in limited potential.* Many administrators and teachers in low-income schools feel that most of their pupils are slow learners. Having little confidence in their achievement, the teachers do not encourage the pupils, nor do they feel it worthwhile to expend much energy in teaching. Low expectations induce low performance.

2. *Irrelevance.* Traditional children's primers are notorious for their middle-class orientation, picturing "nice" surroundings and well-behaved blonde children. There is little effort at any educational level to bring to bear the experience of slum children or realistic life situations of any kind.

Since the high school is careful to skirt and detour around real-life problems and controversial issues regarding race relations, alcoholism, materialism, religion, politics, collectivism, consumer competency, it involves the learner in a type of artificially contrived busy work and shadow boxing that either dulls the adolescent into stupor or drives him in his resentment out of school to overt aggression and resentment. In protecting youths from real-life problems, the school enters into a tragic conspiracy of irresponsible retreat from reality. The perversion of the high school curriculum to neutral and petty purposes emasculates the school program and disintegrates the ego.[10]

3. *Inappropriate teaching methods.* The perspectives and training of middle-class teachers do not prepare them for dealing with disadvantaged children. The latter have motivations and styles of conduct that must be taken into account if instruction is to be effective. Teachers are not usually prepared to deal with the slum school's cast of characters, which may include some unfamiliar figures, such as parole officers and social workers. A full appreciation of the lower-class child's social world would alter both the content and the method of teaching, as well as the teacher's role in relation to family and community.

4. *Misuse of testing.* The use of IQ tests for classification and placement of students reveals a strong middle-class bias. Such tests to a large extent measure reading skill. Lower-class children do not perform well on written IQ tests, in part because they are not encouraged to read at home. Moreover, test performance depends a great deal on the situations within which they are taken, and on practice in taking tests.

The problem is not so much in the tests themselves but rather the uses to which they are put. Despite these well-known facts of instability and class bias, most school systems and teachers still use intelligence tests as though they were stable measures of innate potential, independent of environment. One consequence is that individual teachers frequently underestimate the ability of particular youngsters and scale down their expectations and level of instruction accordingly.

5. *Discriminatory "tracking."* Public schools frequently separate students into ability groups, each with a different curriculum. The major argument for tracking is that it makes possible a better fit between the needs and capabilities of the student and the demands and opportunities of the curriculum. Slower students do not retard the progress of brighter students, and the teacher can adapt his teaching to the

---

[9] Walter E. Schafer and Kenneth Polk, "Delinquency and the Schools," in The President's Commission on Law Enforcement and Administration of Justice, *Task Force Report: Juvenile Delinquency and Youth Crime* (Washington, D.C., 1967), pp. 234–246.

[10] William Kvaraceus, cited in Schafer and Polk, *op. cit.,* p. 238.

class. The special problems of different ability groups, from "gifted" to "retarded," can be dealt with more efficiently when groups of students share the same or similar problems.

These arguments are balanced by others that take account of the social consequences of tracking. Tracking has a powerful influence on adolescent status systems, as these comments by a senior girl suggest:

If you take a college preparatory course, you're better than those who take a general course. Those who take a general course are neither here nor there. If you take a commercial course, you don't rate. . . . Those that take the college preparatory course run the place.[11]

The lower status associated with commercial and general tracks may have a debilitating effect on the student. Finding that he has been labeled as somehow less capable than other students, the commercial student may simply accept the role he has been assigned and "live down" to the expectations of his teachers and peers.

In addition, lower-income children are more likely to be placed in the low-ability tracks; the quality of instruction is poorer in the lower tracks; and the career prospects of the lower track student are sharply curtailed.

Other deficiencies of the schools include inadequate compensatory and remedial education, which would take account of the handicaps and need for greater resources of lower-class children; the inferior teachers and facilities found in low-income schools; and the distance that exists between school and community in low-income and minority group neighborhoods.[12]

The school's limitations, as noted above, are only partly due to mistakes of judgment, inadequate knowledge, and poor organization. More basic is the conclusion that the public schools have become *institutionalized in a middle-class direction*. The result is a built-in incapacity to motivate and influence the lower-class child.

Integration and academic performance The Civil Rights Act of 1964 directed the Commissioner of Education to investigate inequalities in educational opportunities for the major racial and ethnic categories of the population. Consequently a national sample survey was conducted of nearly 600,000 public school students in grades 1, 3, 6, 9, and 12, along with their teachers, principals, and superintendents. Questionnaires were submitted to the students inquiring about their home backgrounds and their educational aspirations. They were tested on ability and educational achievement. The teachers were questioned concerning their training, backgrounds, attitudes, and verbal skills. Principals and superintendents supplied information on their backgrounds and training, as well as on school facilities, curricula, supervision, and administration. Approximately 30 percent of the schools selected for the survey did not participate, but the evidence indicates that the findings were not significantly biased by that fact.[13]

Comparisons of scores on several standardized achievement tests indicate that on the average Negro students scored significantly below whites. Roughly 84 percent of the Negroes scored below the median level achieved by the whites. In other words, 34 percent more Negroes scored below a specified level than did whites. Since these differences hold for both grade school and high school students—and are actually most pronounced at the twelfth grade—it appears that, under present conditions, school experience does not enable Negroes to overcome the deficiencies with which they begin school.[14]

However, academic performance of Negro children seems more affected by the quality of their schools than does the achievement of white children. That is, the characteristics of the school are more

---

[11] A. B. Hollingshead, *Elmtown's Youth* (New York: Wiley, 1949), p. 169.

[12] Schafer and Polk, *op. cit.,* pp. 242 ff.

[13] James S. Coleman, Ernest Q. Campbell, Carol J. Hobson, James McPartland, Alexander M. Mood, Frederic D. Weinfeld, and Robert L. York, *Equality of Educational Opportunity* (Washington, D.C., 1966), pp. 550–568.

[14] *Ibid.,* pp. 20–23.

likely to make a relatively large impact for good or ill on Negro pupils.

Opponents of school integration contend that the children of neither race benefit from the experience and that white children suffer from reduced academic standards. However, the survey permits the inference that

improving the school of a minority pupil may increase his achievement more than would improving the school of a white child increase his. Similarly, the average minority pupil's achievement may suffer more in a school of low quality than might the average white pupil's. In short, whites are less affected one way or the other by the quality of their schools than are minority pupils.[15]

If, as a consequence of integration, standards are in fact temporarily lowered in previously all-white schools, this survey suggests that the white students will not be harmed nearly as much as the Negroes will be helped.

Since Negro students are more sensitive than are whites to overall school quality, their performance should improve in schools where their peers are not overwhelmingly from families of low socioeconomic status and where they have high academic aspirations and are generally optimistic about the future. A sense of hopeful expectancy is positively linked to the proportion of whites with whom Negroes attend school. Improved expectations regarding one's prospects bolster self-confidence, which in turn leads to higher academic achievement. The longer a Negro child has spent in an integrated setting, the more positive is the effect on his academic achievement.[16]

But the schools cannot rewrite the history of a child's background nor rehabilitate his environment. The difficulty of overcoming the limitations of the child's immediate social situation are additional burdens on the objectives of the school.

Schools bring little influence to bear on a child's achievement that is independent of his background and general social context; inequalities imposed on children by their home, neighborhood, and peer environment are carried along to become the inequalities with which they confront adult life at the end of school.[17]

Caution   One important limitation of this survey is that the performances of the students were examined at only one point in time rather than traced over a period of years. Since the students were not treated as a cohort and studied repeatedly, it is impossible to measure changes in their achievement resulting from their varied educational experiences, particularly those involving integration.

[15] *Ibid.,* p. 22.
[16] *Ibid.,* pp. 28–29.
[17] *Ibid.,* p. 325.

SECTION 5 PRIMARY RELATIONS

The social structure of the school determines with whom primary relations are established, the intensity of the relations, and the consequences for both the individual and the institution.

TEACHER-STUDENT RELATIONS

Pressures toward impersonality   In most settings, the teacher is expected to maintain a posture of dominance over and social distance from the students:

[In] most communities, the adults, including older teachers, expect the teacher to maintain authority over the children. . . . Failure as a disciplinarian, meaning, as a rule, failure to keep the classroom submissive, is probably the most frequently expressed reason for the dismissal of a teacher.[18]

Social distance is expected on the theory that in-

[18] Wilbur B. Brookover, *A Sociology of Education* (New York: American Book, 1955), pp. 233–234.

timacy breeds disrespect. Teachers are wary of students' "taking advantage" of them and employ numerous devices for maintaining distance, such as insisting on formal modes of address and restricting access to specific hours.

In addition to maintaining authority, social distance is helpful when potential claims on attention and emotional involvement are great. In large classes with rapid turnover, social distance protects the teacher from initiating relationships that could not be pursued. Moreover, the norm of impartiality, that is, the expectation that the same standards apply to all students, draws the teacher to an impersonal and formal pattern of behavior.

Impersonality and social distance have positive meaning for students as well as teachers:

Students in their turn have ways of fending off undue advances from teachers. The young have their reserves which they rarely cast off in the presence of their elders, and likewise the subordinate has an inner life which only his equals can penetrate. Defenses of the young against the teacher's curiosity and occasional yearning to be accepted by students consist mainly in treating the teacher as a teacher and refusing to consider him otherwise. . . . The respect of students disciplines the teacher. It is important for the teacher to know that social distance, unless it is to be quite destructive of the self-respect of the subordinated person, must always have two sides. If the teacher is to maintain his own reserves he must respect those of his students.[19]

Pressures toward personal relations Despite the rewards of impersonality, teachers are frequently ambivalent about this aspect of their role. One reason for ambivalence has to do with the nature of groups. Research has shown that groups tend to develop two leaders, one instrumental or task-oriented, the other expressive or concerned with the social and emotional aspects of the group's life. The task leader is usually more respected for his contributions, while the expressive leader is better liked. The classroom

is a setting for group dynamics, and the teacher feels some pressure to perform the expressive function as well as the task of instruction.

One study found that "dominative" (task-oriented) teachers produced resistance to themselves among their pupils; teachers whose performance tended to be "integrative" (expressive) had the opposite effect.[20] However, teachers who are overly concerned with the social-emotional aspects of the class run other risks. If they do not maintain discipline, and are unable to communicate a sense of authority, their teaching effectiveness may be impaired. A study of high school history teachers found that "authoritarian" teachers, though less well liked, were more effective than "democratic" teachers in imparting history "information." The researcher was evidently not happy with this result and added the following comment:

This does not necessarily mean that teachers must always be autocratic in order to be effective teachers of information, but rather that autocracy is more effective in groups which expect dictation. . . . If educators wish to develop democratic attitudes and techniques while maintaining the highest level of attainment in pupil learning, perhaps it will be necessary to modify the organization of our schools so that the child will expect his teacher to be friendly and democratic rather than a dictator.[21]

Another factor that influences the teacher to adopt a more personal orientation is the quest for a significant educational impact on the student. To influence the student intensively, the teacher must communicate with him on a personal level. To motivate the child to learn and to arouse his interest in topics that may not have a direct bearing on his life, the teacher must establish mutual acceptance and rapport.

The need for personal rapport is especially great in the education of underprivileged children. Lower-class children tend to be more person-oriented than

---

[19] Willard Waller, *The Sociology of Teaching* (New York: Wiley, 1932), pp. 282–283.

[20] Brookover, *op. cit.*, pp. 301–304, based on Harold H. Anderson *et al., Studies of Teachers' Classroom Personalities, I, II, III,* Three Applied Psychology Monographs of the American Psychological Association, Stanford, 1945, 1946.

[21] W. B. Brookover, "Social Roles of Teachers and Pupil Achievement," *American Sociological Review, 8* (August, 1943), 393.

*Schooling observed: A classroom in the highlands
of New Guinea engages the community's interest.*

middle-class children.[22] Impersonality is incomprehensible to one reared in a subculture that prizes personal relationships. If the teacher makes no effort to interact with the lower-class child in a personal way, the child is likely to mistake the teacher's formality for rejection, with negative effects on his self-image and motivation.

STUDENT PEER GROUPS

Childhood peer groups have both positive and negative aspects. Positively, the peer group provides the child with a series of stepping-stones to the adult world. Peer groups have a transitional function, supporting the child's personality through the period of adolescence. Negatively, peer group life may be so complete as to leave the child unprotected and overly exposed to its influence. Inadequate personality development and compulsive conformity are possible consequences.

Student groups and social status Peer relations among students are intimately involved with the status systems of adolescents, the school, and the community. They strengthen the prestige of some

[22] See Herbert J. Gans, *The Urban Villagers* (New York: The Free Press of Glencoe, 1962), pp. 89 ff.

persons and weaken that of others. The network of cliques in a high school is a status system; the student is assigned a high or low status according to his clique membership or lack of it. Some students confer prestige on a clique: a star athlete, a socially-prominent or wealthy boy, or a brilliant student may raise the status of his circle of friends. A student group may collectively move up or down due to its own actions; for example, it may lower its position in the school by engaging in criminal behavior. The lowered group status reflects on the individual members, and they, too, have lowered status.

The student gains membership in some groups because of his family status. Girls' cliques in high school are commonly related to social background. The status structure of the school is, in these respects, congruent with the status structure of the adult community. Boys' cliques are also based on social origins. However, athletic achievement plays an important role in membership in high-status groups in most schools, divorcing the boys' status system somewhat from the status structure of the parental community and perhaps conferring raised status on the athlete's parents. Many poor boys become successful athletes, and in winning for the school they become heroes of the system. They are rewarded with acceptance into the most popular crowd. This status is regarded by other students as more legitimate than that derived from family prestige. The athlete's status is achieved, while status that rests on family background is ascribed.

The attitudes and actions of teachers help to determine which activities become the basis for high status and who appears in the top-status groups. For example, teachers like to see the best scholars in the school serve as examples to the student body. But when teachers in three schools were asked: "If you could see any of three boys elected president of the senior class, which would you rather it would be? (Brilliant student, athletic star, or a leader in extracurricular activities)," the teachers preferred the activities leader to the brilliant student 73 percent to 19 percent, but only 8 percent chose the athlete.[23] The teachers avoided naming the brilliant student for this high-status position because they thought he would not have leadership ability, be close to students, or command attention.

Lament of an isolate The student peer group helps the adolescent to sustain a conception of the self in a transitional period and in the face of competition for academic and social status. Students must often weigh this support against the greater freedom they have outside the clique, for example, to study hard or to associate casually with a large number of students. Serious students frequently must choose to remain isolated, but in large schools they may band together and support one another.

Isolates are likely to have mixed feelings about their independence. Some even view their isolation as the major failure of their high school careers. One girl writes:

In school there has always been clicks [sic] and clans. I always belonged to one in grade school, one consisting of about five people, and one who wasn't the wild set. In the eighth grade, I began to separate from a single group, which I sometimes think was a mistake, and started just being friendly to all the groups. This was not too good for me because it gave me a feeling of not belonging. I really didn't notice this change till I started high school but it has been that way since. Oh, to be back in a click![24]

Adolescent freedom and student cliques In childhood and especially in adolescence the child is subject to a contest of wills between parents and peers. Traditionally, middle-class parents seem to have asserted stronger control than working-class parents, supervising closer and longer through the adolescent years. This is apparently no longer so in many communities. One study asked girls if they would join a particular club in the face of their parents' disapproval.[25] In small-town schools, the

[23] James S. Coleman, *The Adolescent Society* (New York: The Free Press of Glencoe, 1961), p. 193.

[24] C. Wayne Gordon, *The Social System of the High School* (Glencoe: The Free Press, 1957), p. 114.

[25] Coleman, *op. cit.*, pp. 287–293.

daughters of the middle-class families were *less* likely to ignore or overrule their parents' judgment than were the girls from lower social origins. But in city or suburban schools, the middle-class girls were *more* likely to say they would join despite parents' disapproval. The greatest difference lay between the daughters of traditionally middle-class parents in the small towns and the daughters of modern middle-class parents in the "elite" suburbs. Lower-class girls fell between the extremes.

This distribution of girls' reactions seems associated with the concern of middle-class parents for the child's social maturity and popularity. Both at home and in the school, they attempt to give the child self-assurance and social skills, e.g., formal instruction in social dancing in the seventh grade. Early social maturity, however, produces greater liberation in adolescence. As a result, children rely more on their own judgment or on the norms of the peer group than on adult standards. They consider themselves less subject to orders from parents and teachers.

The orientation of the middle-class children of both the small town and of the city set the tone of the high school. In both kinds of communities, particularly among girls, the leading crowd is largely composed of those with higher social origins, and the top-status cliques set the norms of the informal system of the students. In the small town, the pacesetters are the girls most subject to parental constraint; in the city or suburb, they are the girls who are most liberated.

SECTION 6 STRATIFICATION

Whether the educational system is a servant of the status quo or a vehicle of mobility and change depends mainly on who has access to what kind of education and how much of it.

DIFFERENTIAL ACCESS

Social background, especially the social station of one's family, affects educational opportunity. This influence is strongest when social status is ascribed, but even in modern industrial nations social origins are influential in determining what kind of education the young get, how clearly they (and their parents) perceive the relationship between education and advancement, and how far the young go in school. This in turn limits or opens job opportunities. The social level of the family affects opportunity, aspiration, and the ability to use the schools.

A study of two Michigan high schools found that 35 percent of working-class students were in the bottom quartile of their graduating class in academic achievement; the comparable middle-class figure was 15 percent. Middle-class students dropped out only one-fourth as often as working-class students.[26]

Compulsory attendance laws and increased interest hold almost all students in high school at least through age fifteen. Ninety-three percent of those between fourteen and seventeen years old were enrolled in school in 1965.[27] The proportion completing high school has increased considerably over recent decades. High school graduates in 1960 represented six out of ten of their fifth grade classmates, compared with less than three out of ten in 1930.[28]

Nevertheless the educational system is far from achieving a maximum utilization of the nation's

---

[26] Walter E. Schafer, "Student Careers in Two Public High Schools: A Comparative Cohort Analysis" (Unpublished doctoral dissertation, University of Michigan, 1965), pp. 88 and 179, cited in Schafer and Polk, *op. cit.,* p. 229.

[27] *Statistical Abstract of the United States, 1966,* p. 109.

[28] *A Fact Book on Higher Education* (Washington, D.C.: American Council on Education, n.d.), p. 65 and p. 253.

talent. Figure XI:2 suggests the extent to which those capable of benefiting from a college education are actually afforded the opportunity. According to the data in the figure, only one-third of those with the median intelligence level of college graduates are actually college graduates. Although this figure is based on the latest available data, they are more than a decade old. Studies currently under way are

expected to show some improvement in the ability of colleges to recruit and retain those of high intelligence. This is suggested by the increase in median school years completed for those twenty-five years old and over from 8.6 in 1940 to 11.8 in 1965.

Another measure of the influence of family background on education is shown in Table XI:3 reporting a study of 35,000 high school seniors.[29] Each

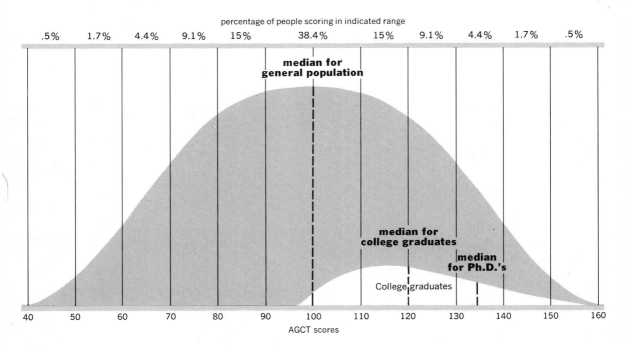

FIG. XI:2   Intelligence and college education

The large, shaded curve represents the distribution of the general population on the Army General Classification Test—roughly equivalent to IQ scores. The small, unshaded curve shows the distribution of college graduates, who fall mainly in the upper AGCT scores. It is possible to estimate the amount of wastage of talent by comparing the two curves. For example, about 16 percent of the population scores 120 (the median of college graduates) or better, but only 5 percent of the population graduate from college— a wastage of two-thirds.

Combination of figures redrawn and adapted from Dael Wolfle, "Intellectual Resources," *Scientific American,* September, 1951, p. 45.

[29] Natalie Rogoff, "Local Social Structure and Educational Selection," in A. H. Halsey, Jean Floud, and C. Arnold Anderson (eds.), *Education, Economy, and Society* (New York: The Free Press of Glencoe, 1961), pp. 241–251. See also J. A. Kahl, "Educational and Occupational Aspirations of 'Common Man' Boys," *Harvard Educational Review, 23* (1953), 186–203; W. H. Sewell, Archie O. Haller, and Murray A. Straus, "Social Status and Educational and Occupational Aspiration," *American Sociological Review, 22* (1957), 67–73; and S. M. Lipset and Reinhard Bendix, *Social Mobility in Industrial Society* (Berkeley and Los Angeles: University of California Press, 1960), pp. 91–101 and 227–233.

SECTION 6 **STRATIFICATION**

361

TABLE XI:3 PERCENTAGE OF HIGH SCHOOL SENIORS PLANNING TO ATTEND COLLEGE *

SCHOLASTIC ABILITY		FAMILY SOCIOEDUCATIONAL STATUS					ALL STUDENTS OF GIVEN ABILITY LEVEL
		(High) 5	4	3	2	(Low) 1	
(High)	4	83	66	53	44	43	61
	3	70	53	37	29	29	44
	2	65	41	31	20	21	33
(Low)	1	53	30	22	16	18	24
All students of given family status		72	47	35	26	24	40

SOURCE: Natalie Rogoff, "Local Social Structure and Educational Selection," in A. H. Halsey, Jean Floud, and C. Arnold Anderson (eds.), *Education, Economy, and Society* (New York: The Free Press of Glencoe, 1961), p. 246.

* Based on a study of over 35,000 high school seniors who constituted the entire senior class of 500 public secondary schools. The schools were a fairly representative sample of the 20,000-odd senior public high schools in the United States, 1955.

student was rated on scholastic ability (as indicated by a 20-item test) and socioeducational status of family, an index based on father's occupation, father's education, and whether older brothers and sisters had gone to college. The students were classified into four categories of ability and five status groupings that ranged from well-educated professional and managerial families to poorly educated, unskilled worker and farm families. The proportion of students planning to attend college varied by family status from 72 percent in the highest category to 24 percent in the lowest, or a difference of 48 percent; the proportion of *all* students expecting to go to college was 40 percent. Planning for college varied over the four levels of ability from 61 percent among the top ability to 24 percent among those of lowest ability, a range of 37 percent.

The columns of the table show the effect of ability with family background constant. In families of top status, 83 percent of the high-ability students and 53 percent of the lowest in ability plan to attend college, a difference of 30 percent. In the families of bottom status, just 43 percent of the high-ability students plan college and 18 percent of the low-ability stu-

dents so indicate, or a difference of 25 percent.

The rows of the table show the effect of family background on college plans, for students of similar ability. Top-ability students planning to attend college range from 83 percent to 43 percent according to family status, a difference of 40 percent because of socioeducational background, or something correlated with it. The figures reflect a loss to education of talented students from lower social origins. At the next level of ability, the loss is as great, with 29 percent in the lowest social category compared to 70 percent in the highest planning college, a 41 percent difference. These two ability categories cover the upper half of high school students.

The joint effect of social background and ability on college plans can be studied by comparing any of the figures with another. The extremes are the top-status background and top ability (83 percent) and bottom status and bottom ability (18 percent), roughly 8 out of 10 compared with 2 out of 10. The dotted line drawn through the table separates figures greater than 50 percent from those less than 50 percent; it shows the decisive role played by family background. A majority of sons and daughters in

TABLE XI:4 EDUCATION AND OCCUPATIONAL ACHIEVEMENT

PEOPLE WHO WORK IN THESE OCCUPATIONS	HAVE THIS KIND OF EDUCATION (IN PERCENT)		
	Less Than High School Graduation	*High School Graduation*	*Some College Education*
Professional and technical workers	6	19	75
Proprietors and managers	38	33	29
Clerical or sales workers	25	53	22
Skilled workers	59	33	8
Semiskilled workers	70	26	4
Service workers	69	25	6
Unskilled workers	80	17	3
Farmers and farm workers	76	19	5

SOURCE: *Manpower:* Challenge of the 1960's (U.S. Department of Labor, 1960), p. 17.

families of top status expect to go to college, even when they have little ability; at no level of ability, not even the highest, do a majority of low-family-status children plan to go to college.

EDUCATION, OCCUPATION, AND INCOME

The strong relation between amount of education and occupational achievement is shown in Table XI:4. The higher occupations are composed of the better educated; for example, three-fourths of professional and technical workers have had some college education. The broad occupational categories obscure some important groups. "Proprietors and managers" includes the small shop owner as well as the corporation executive. The small-businessman need not have advanced education, but the corporation man generally does.

Just as the relation of education to occupational attainment is strong, so is the relation of education to future income. The average annual income in 1964 of American men, ages 45–54, was directly related to the amount of education they had received: [30]

Some elementary schooling	$ 3,669
Completed elementary school	5,089
Some high school	5,798
Completed high school	6,738
Some college	8,081
Completed college	10,688
Five or more years of college	11,743

On the average, college graduates earned more than 80 percent more each year than high school graduates. In 1964 males earning $15,000 or more had on the average 16 years of schooling; those earning $3,000 or less had about half as much schooling.

The educational ladder clearly leads to higher occupations, upper social statuses, and prestigeful styles of life. Without education one has lower horizons—occupationally, socially, culturally.

What most determines life chances—social position or education, ascription or achievement? On the one hand, children from the higher social strata are likely to receive more and better education than their lower-class counterparts. Higher-level education in turn provides access to the better positions.

[30] *Statistical Abstract of the United States, 1966,* p. 115.

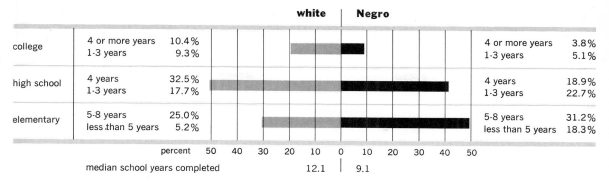

		white		Negro		
college	4 or more years	10.4%			4 or more years	3.8%
	1-3 years	9.3%			1-3 years	5.1%
high school	4 years	32.5%			4 years	18.9%
	1-3 years	17.7%			1-3 years	22.7%
elementary	5-8 years	25.0%			5-8 years	31.2%
	less than 5 years	5.2%			less than 5 years	18.3%

percent 50 40 30 20 10 0 10 20 30 40 50

median school years completed   12.1 | 9.1

FIG. XI:3   Education by race, United States, 1966,
persons twenty-five years old and over

SOURCE: U.S. Bureau of the Census, *Current Population Reports,* Series P-20, No. 158, December 19, 1966, Table 3. Sample Survey.

In this case, education stabilizes social class positions across the generations, and acts as a barrier to the social mobility of those who start from lower rungs.[31] On the other hand, some children of lower origins are upwardly mobile by virtue of the availability of schooling, persistence and success in school, and entry into some higher-status occupation to which their education admits them. Until recent decades, father's status counted more than the classroom, and mobile individuals were often mobile without education. But the effect of the school and college on social mobility grows stronger as (*a*) education becomes more widely available and (*b*) men are more often judged by the universal criteria of scholastic achievement and technical competence.

Education of minorities   The educational system may improve the status of minorities, or it may operate to maintain the status quo. Because educational deficiencies are lifelong burdens, statistics are analyzed for the population whose education is completed as well as for those actually in school. Figure XI:3 shows educational status by race for the population twenty-five years old and over in 1966. The median number of years of school for the whole

adult population of whites was 12.1, for Negroes 9.1. The discrepancy is largest at the older ages because of the poor educational opportunities for Negroes before World War II. But even the 25–29 age category shows a significant advantage for whites. In that age level there is a difference of less than two years in median years of school completed. Yet the median white male was a high school graduate, the median Negro male was not. At that age two-thirds of whites of both sexes had completed high school, but less than two-fifths of Negroes had done so.

Although retention of nonwhite students has dramatically improved since 1960, the advantage is to the whites at every age level, and at upper ages the discrepancy remains a serious impediment to the occupational future of nonwhites. For instance, in 1965 the following percentages were enrolled in schools:

Ages	Whites	Nonwhites
14–17	93.4	91.7
18–19	47.1	40.1
20–24	20.2	10.2
25–29	6.5	3.0
30–34	3.2	3.2

[31] Bernard Barber, *Social Stratification* (New York: Harcourt, Brace & World, 1957), p. 395.

Clearly whites are better able to stay in school without interruption and have a far greater likelihood of securing college and postgraduate training. The identical percentage at age 30–34 is probably due to recent remedial and vocational programs for the poor and to the fact that Negroes take longer to complete their schooling, because they often attend on a part-time basis.

The numbers show only part of the white advantage. At every level and in every region Negro education is on the average inferior to white, and this fact shows in achievement tests. Many Negroes, even those who live outside the South, attend one of approximately one hundred Negro colleges and universities. About one-third of these are unaccredited institutions that probably do not offer college-level work. Another third are accredited but not of high standard. The remainder includes such good quality institutions as Howard University in Washington, D.C., Fisk University in Nashville, the Atlanta University System, and a few others. In 1960, predominantly Negro colleges had resident enrollments of about 89,000, which included over half of all Negro college students.[32]

[32] Leonard Broom and Norval D. Glenn, *Transformation of the Negro American* (New York: Harper & Row, 1965), Chap. 5, esp. pp. 93–94. [First Harper Colophon paperback edition, 1967.]

SECTION 7 ASSOCIATIONS

The study of special-purpose organizations is a major aspect of the sociology of education. The school system itself, and specific types of institutions within it, are the most obvious examples. In addition, there are parent-teacher associations, teachers' unions, associations of scholars, and student organizations of many kinds. Sociologically speaking the educational system includes all of these units, for they all have an effect on the nature and quality of education.

BUREAUCRACY AND ALLOCATION

Like most other institutions of modern society, schools have become complex bureaucracies. There have always been administrative officials, but the rise of a corps of full-time administrators, at all levels of the educational system, is a phenomenon of recent history. The administration does not teach, but it decisively affects what is taught, by whom, and to whom. Administrators do the kind of work that is needed by any bureaucracy, but they also do some things that are peculiar to the function of education in modern society. Among these special activities are the classification and the allocation of students.

The school as people-processor The public school serves as a distribution center for society.[33] As students pass through the schools, they are sorted and classified. They are routed into one of a number of possible student careers or tracks (see p. 353), e.g., college preparatory, vocational, or even deviant careers, as a result of being classified by administrators as conduct problems. The student's educational career in large part determines his place in the social order.

The growing complexity of occupations has put pressure on the schools to identify more closely the capability of each child and help him make an appropriate choice of occupation and course of study. Schools and colleges try to do this job at minimum cost in time and effort. Toward the goal of efficiency they need to measure ability and progress and to maintain a cumulative record of performance, which leads to the development of extensive programs of testing and record-keeping. Many public school sys-

[33] See the discussion of "people-work" in Erving Goffman, *Asylums* (New York: [Anchor] Doubleday, 1961), pp. 74 ff.

tems begin a file on the pupil in the lower elementary grades, and his records accumulate and pass along through channels as the child moves up the grades.

While the student is in theory free to choose his career and field of study, in practice such decisions are frequently made on the basis of aptitude and achievement test scores. The "objective" records must be interpreted, and teachers and counselors are the custodians and interpreters of the students' files. The interpretation of any given case is the outcome of a complicated process of *social typing,* which is subject to the policies, perceptions, and stereotypes of school personnel. Consequently, the distribution of students into various educational careers is (in some unknown number of cases) less the outcome of individual student decisions than the result of administrative activity.

Role of the school counselor The "bureaucratization of the search for talent" has brought with it the professionalization of counseling in the schools, and has given the counselor a growing influence over the student's educational career.[84] Though performing an advisory function, the counselor makes many important decisions. For example, if a counselor thinks a student has low ability he may assign him to courses that do not carry college entrance credit, and the student may not realize what has happened until he tries to get into college. The counselor's influence may extend to certifying students for extracurricular activities (which may also affect admission to college), and he exercises direct influence through letters of recommendation to colleges and employers. Thus counselors occupy a strategic position in determining student opportunities.

The most important counseling activity is the interpretation of student records and test scores. In this process the counselor considers (*a*) the student's academic achievement, (*b*) his school conduct or "citizenship," and (*c*) his emotional adjustment. Within each of these categories there is social typing of the student. Academically he may be classified as an underachiever or overachiever; his demeanor and style of dress may be used to type him as a conduct problem or as part of a group that is labeled as "serious" or "rowdy"; psychologically he may be typed as well-adjusted or disturbed. These labels become part of his record and may affect responses to the student for many years.

Some dangers inherent in the process of social typing are the following: (1) Counselors may create problems where none exist. The discrepancy between the student's aptitude, as shown on tests, and his achievement, as shown by grades, may be defined by the counselor as a problem. If the student is then treated as a problem he may develop feelings of inferiority and resentment, and act out these feelings. (2) The discrepancies between test performance and class performance may simply reflect the inadequacy of the testing procedures, rather than any special difficulty or inconsistency on the part of the student. (3) Counselors may be biased against students who associate with "less desirable elements" in the school. Students with conduct problems are frequently defined as underachievers even if they perform adequately in the classroom. (4) Social typing by counselors may reduce the chances of an underachiever to improve his position. For example, some schools grade different ability groups according to different curves, on the assumption that a low performer in a high-ability group should rate a higher grade point than the best student in a lower-ability group. This is said to be necessary to avoid bias against those competing at the higher level. As a result, a student in the low-ability group who shows excellent class performance still has a poorer showing and remains defined as an underachiever, because he has received lower grade points.

Caution The above discussion is based on limited data. While there is little doubt that the high school counselor influences student careers, it is not known how much difference he makes in the lives of how many students in how many schools.

[84] Aaron V. Cicourel and John I. Kitsuse, *The Educational Decision-Makers* (Indianapolis: Bobbs-Merrill), 1963.

Cooling out The allocative function of the educational system requires the school to develop techniques for directing less competent students away from academic curricula and into vocational programs. The necessity of guiding students into less prestigeful (and less financially rewarding) careers creates a potentially explosive problem, because students must come to grips with the task of redefining their self-conceptions. The procedures developed to cope with this problem make up what has been called the "cooling-out function" of education.[35] "Cooling the mark out" is a phrase used by confidence men to refer to the ways they manage a "mark" (victim) so as to prevent him from calling the police; when the "mark" realizes he has been "taken," the confidence men try to "cool him out" gradually, that is, get him to accept his disappointment.[36] Clark argues that the idea of "cooling out" applies to schools like the California junior college, which was the subject of his study, because such colleges require large numbers of students to accept lowered expectations.

Originally the junior college was conceived as a way station on the road to a four-year college education. However, in the 1930s, the junior college became more concerned with the "terminal" student who would take a vocational program and finish his education at the end of two years. As a result of this history, there has been confusion about the purposes of a junior college education. In the eyes of the general public and many students, the junior college is simply the first two years of college. But educators and administrators, knowing that relatively few junior college students actually complete a four-year program, emphasize the terminal and vocational role of the junior college. In recognition of this change, some junior colleges have become "community colleges."

The junior college usually admits all students regardless of qualification. It has an "open door" admission policy to provide equal opportunity for higher education consistent with popular democratic ideals. However, many students fail. In the junior college studied by Clark, fewer than one-sixth of those entering completed junior college; only 24 percent of those in the transfer program later transferred to a senior college, where, as a group, they did poorly.

Most students enter junior college hoping to transfer to senior college. Caught between these expectations and knowledge of what actually happens, the junior college faces the task of redirecting the student and changing his outlook, of persuading the transfer-oriented student to accept a terminal program. First, if the student's preentrance tests are low, he is assigned to remedial classes—such as "Sub-Freshman English"—which cast doubt on his academic ability and slow his progress toward transfer. A second step is an interview with a counselor.

The assistance is initially gentle. A common case is the student who wants to be an engineer but whose test scores and school grades indicate that he is a nearly hopeless candidate. Said one counselor, "I never openly countermand his choice, but edge him toward a terminal program by gradually laying out the facts of life." Counselors can become more severe later in the sequence when they have grades as a talking point and the student is in trouble. In initial counseling, student choice still has great weight.[37]

Third, the college may require courses that are especially devised to lead the student toward a reassessment of his capabilities. For example, "Psychology 5, Orientation to College" may cover aptitude testing and evaluation of vocational choices. These courses give the teacher-counselor an opportunity to talk about the disparity between unrealistic goals and personal capacity.

By their handling of their own records, [the students] are more closely confronted with test data and the recommendations of teachers and counselors. . . . Counselors reported in interview that it was particularly in this course that they were able to talk freely to students about the disparity between per-

[35] Burton R. Clark, *The Open Door College* (New York: McGraw-Hill, 1960), pp. 71–76, 160–165.
[36] See Erving Goffman, "On Cooling the Mark Out: Some Aspects of Adaptation to Failure," *Psychiatry, 15* (November, 1952), 451–563.
[37] Clark, *op. cit.,* p. 71 f.

sonal objective and capacity. The orientation class was considered a good place "to talk tough," and to explain in an impersonal way the facts of life for the "hopeless" transfer student.[38]

A fourth step in the reorientation is assessment of the student's actual accomplishment. If he gets low grades he will be asked to see the counselor, who is then in a stronger position to redirect the student.

[38] *Ibid.,* p. 73.

Finally, the student may be placed on probation. The function of probation is not so much to push the student out of school as to direct him to the terminal program. In some junior colleges, it is possible to receive the A.A. (Associate in Arts) degree even while on probation. However, in such cases the student must agree beforehand to accept terminal status.

SECTION 8 COLLECTIVE BEHAVIOR

Each sector of the educational system has a different likelihood of being involved in collective behavior; and the forms of action congenial to each sector are also different.

Students Adolescent and young-adult students are potentially the most volatile elements in the system; they have little to lose and can often find shelter in culturally supported forgiveness of youthful misconduct. Youth is often a period of moratorium, and life at school is for many the first release from parental control: away from home, freedom is maximized.

Gathered together in age-graded groups, available to participation in mass rituals and entertainments, counterposed to an often vulnerable academic authority, set down in strange communities to which they have no commitment—all of these conditions create a potential for collective action and self-expression. The sedate rhythms of the scholarly life have ever been subject to rude interruptions.

However, student activism and expressiveness should not be dismissed as youthful aberration. The issues that agitate students may reflect legitimate and prolonged grievances; and the relatively greater freedom of students to act may cast them in the role of shock troops for social causes that go far beyond immediate student concerns. During the early 1960s college students had an important part in the civil

rights movement, especially in the initial stages of the direct-action strategy. Students were also active in less benign movements, such as the Nazi movement in Germany, which brought Hitler to power in 1933. Active student participation in a political movement probably indicates that an element of idealism is present, but it is no assurance of the rightness of the cause.

Adaptation 28 analyzes the student protest at Berkeley in 1964. The Berkeley students created some anti-University sentiment in California, but the wrath of the public was somewhat less violent than that of the public in Oxford six hundred years earlier (see p. 368). It should also be noted that at Berkeley the Governor of California responded in a way rather different from the response of King Edward III.

Faculty Traditionally teachers and administrators have a large stake in continuity and stability. They are closely bound into the educational system, which can exert social control at many points. Therefore teachers tend to respond sluggishly (or with deliberation, depending on the perspective) to events and issues. Most educational innovation is the work of professionals and does not usually involve collective excitement.

Academic self-restraint does not always prevail. Masters as well as scholars participated in the some-

ANTI-STUDENT PROTEST: OXFORD, 1354

The most spectacular features of the student life of the Middle Ages were the bloody affrays, the pitched battles, the mayhems, rapes, and homicides, which fill the records of the times with monotonous regularity. It seemed to be a maxim of University practice that the scholar or the Master, no matter what his offense, was always in the right. The lay courts had no jurisdiction over scholars, and the University or ecclesiastical courts were a farce. The immunities conferred account very largely for the unremitting hatred felt by the townsfolk for the students in their midst, and also for the tendency of the students to ride roughshod over the lesser rights and privileges of the townsmen.

The most serious riot in the annals of Oxford was the battle of St. Scholastica's Day in 1354. It originated, as did most of the University affairs, in a tavern quarrel. Certain scholars, having called for good red wine, suspected its goodness, and told mine host of their suspicions in no uncertain terms. The host retorted and the scholars emptied the lees of the disputed liquor on his head. This was an outrage not to be borne, and the innkeeper's friends ran to ring the bell of St. Martin's Church. A mob of citizens appeared as if by magic, each man with cudgel, pike, knife, or bow. Meanwhile the befuddled clerks had discreetly disappeared.

The mob was not to be balked of its prey, and proceeded to attack every scholar who happened to be in the streets. The Chancellor of the University came out in splendid array, hoping to pour oil on the troubled waters. But the irreverent mob would have none of this dignitary, and he saved his life only by a most uncanonical burst of speed. Gone were all thoughts of peace. The University roused with a will, and the scholars, armed to the teeth, poured out of the University precincts to do battle. Scholars were expressly forbidden, under the severest penalties, to carry arms of any kind, and it was the Chancellor's duty to enforce this law. But it does not seem that at this particular moment he was perturbed by the infringement of the prohibition.

All night the citizens from surrounding towns and villages poured into Oxford, thirsting to crush the hated clerics once and for all. For two days the mob rioted and pillaged and slew. The poor scholars were dragged out of their hiding-places and ruthlessly butchered; the houses were literally torn down and the schools wrecked. When the pillage was over, the University had vanished, seemingly never to return.

The fleeing Masters reassembled in distant places, and promptly the air of England was laden with their outraged cries. The King heard and gave them a terrible revenge. From that day onwards the liberties of Oxford were irretrievably broken. Henceforth, said the royal decree, the University was to have jurisdiction over the town with respect to many civic matters. No longer was Oxford a royal town; it became a hostage to the University, whose Chancellor possessed more power than its own Mayor and Council.

Nor was the Bishop of Lincoln a laggard in revenge. The town was laid under an interdict, removable only on condition that the Mayor, the Bailiffs, and three score of the chief burghers of the town appear as humble penitents each St. Scholastica's Day in St. Mary's Church, to attend mass for the souls of the slain scholars. This quaint revenge persisted down to the nineteenth century, when the University finally decided that it need not be pursued any further.

SOURCE: Abridged from Nathan Schachner, *The Medieval Universities* (London: Allen & Unwin Ltd., 1938; New York: Barnes & Noble, 1962), pp. 340, 203–206, by permission.

times turbulent academic life of the Middle Ages. In recent times, many professors have been outspoken critics of social policies, and a few have participated in collective actions, such as demonstrations against war. The next decade may see a decided increase in the willingness of teachers to engage in strikes for higher salaries and better working conditions. Teachers in big cities are less exposed to social pressures for respectability than are those in small communities. Modern teachers have more anonymity and are, in many places, better protected against arbitrary dismissal by school officials than they formerly were. With growing self-confidence, a more impersonal relation to community agencies, exposure to a social climate that validates struggle for rights, and a greater effort on the part of existing unions, teachers may well display an unaccustomed activism. To some extent, the excitement of a new trade union consciousness may blend with other forms of anti-establishment expressiveness, especially among younger teachers.

The public   Oxford University in the fourteenth century was insulated from local public opinion by its relation to King and Church. On the other hand, the public schools in the United States are decentralized and controlled by boards of laymen. Therefore the schools are highly susceptible to shifts of opinion and are a major arena of community conflict. To some extent the influence of public opinion is mitigated by the growth of an educational bureaucracy and a corps of professional educators, but the public schools are almost completely dependent on local taxation, especially taxes on homeowners. For this reason the homeowning bloc and real estate interests are vigilant about bond issues and tax rates and play an active part in school politics.

Community ideas about education may change rapidly under the impact of external events. In the recent history of American education a salient fact was the Russian achievement in putting the first satellite into orbit. After the event many neighborhoods of well-educated families changed from support of progressive education to an interest in tougher, traditional education. These families were affected by heightened national concern over the preparation of scientists and technologists, together with a personal concern that their children qualify for college. The changed mood of the educated, upper-middle class led to a revamping of the curriculum in many communities (e.g., more language and science in the elementary school) and an upgrading of the competence of teachers in the "hard" subjects (e.g., physical science and mathematics).

The militant minority. A few, active oppositionists, ideologically committed to a cause or motivated by the hope of power, sometimes exercise considerable influence on school policy. The oppositionists may be against all modern trends in education or convinced the schools are subversive.[39] They exert pressure on school authorities for changes in policy at meetings of the school board and elsewhere on public platforms. When every statement and action of school authorities is subject to the close scrutiny of a hostile group, they must give attention to the matters of concern to the minority, perhaps neglecting others. In order to relieve the pressure and get on with other school business, officials are tempted to appease the minority by making concessions on controversial policies.

[39] Cf. James S. Coleman, *Community Conflict* (Glencoe: The Free Press, 1957).

Adaptation 28 / Kornhauser **STUDENT PROTEST:**
BERKELEY, 1964

In the fall of 1964 students at the University of California, Berkeley, launched a series of mass protests. The demonstrations began as a response to new administrative restrictions on campus political activity, but they soon became a general demand for more student freedom from university authority. In classical political terms, students perceived the issue as freedom against oppressive authority, and administrators defined the issue as anarchy against order. Students and administrators confronted one another as adversaries, one side engaging in civil disobedience, the other resorting to police action. A settlement was reached only after the faculty insisted on both student political freedom and orderly procedures.[40]

Background For many years the University of California attempted to maintain a policy of political neutrality by forbidding the use of university facilities to support or advocate off-campus political or social action. Even national presidential candidates could not be invited on campus for political speeches. Students were not allowed to organize groups using campus grounds or other facilities for the support of opposing candidates or issues in local, state, or national elections.

After Clark Kerr became president in 1958, the rules were relaxed and an "open forum" policy was established. Under the new rules there was opportunity to hear all viewpoints, but "advocacy" by student groups was not allowed.

A strip of land at the main entrance of the campus had been used by students since 1961 to advocate particular causes, mostly by setting up tables to display literature and collect money. The university treated the area as if it were off-campus, thereby allowing students to acquire city permits to set up their tables. In fact the property belonged to the university.

Origin of the protest In the summer of 1964 officials of the Berkeley campus decided to take responsibility for the activity at the campus entrance. On September 16 student organizations were notified by the Dean of Students that political advocacy would no longer be permitted there, and that the tables would have to be removed. The next day representatives of 18 student organizations, including civil rights groups, Marxist clubs, Democratic and Republican clubs, organized a united front. They initiated negotiations with the Dean of Students, hoping to lift the ban.

Although the administration made some concessions, it remained adamant on the main issue. When negotiations broke down the students turned to disobedience and mass protest. They formed a Free Speech Movement (FSM) whose goal was full freedom of political speech and action. The forms of disobedience included: (1) setting up political tables and holding rallies in violation of university regulations, (2) demonstrative sit-ins in the administration building and around a police car, and (3) a student strike.

MAJOR EVENTS

The police-car incident On September 30 university rules were violated, eight students were cited for discipline, and 500 students

SOURCE: Prepared for this book by William Kornhauser.

[40] See Hal Draper, *Berkeley: The New Student Revolt* (New York: Grove Press, 1965); Clark Kerr, *The Uses of the University* (Cambridge: Harvard University Press, 1964): S. M. Lipset and Sheldon S. Wolin (eds.), *The Berkeley Student Revolt* (Garden City, N.Y.: [Anchor] Doubleday, 1965); Michael V. Miller and Susan Gilmore (eds.), *Revolution at Berkeley* (New York: Dell, 1965).

staged a nighttime sit-in. Around midnight the Chancellor announced suspension of the eight cited students. On October 1 a civil rights table was set up on the main plaza, manned by a former student. When he refused to leave, a police officer accompanying two administration representatives arrested him for trespassing. When the offender went limp in the manner of some civil rights demonstrators, a police car was brought on the plaza to remove him. The time was about noon, and over 100 early arrivals for a scheduled rally sat down around the police car. From the car top, Mario Savio, the leader of the FSM urged the gathering crowd to join the demonstrators. They did, and the demonstra-

tion immobilized the police car for 32 hours until October 2, when the president of the university agreed to last-minute negotiations with the student leaders and faculty mediators. After two hours of negotiations, while more than 7,000 students and spectators massed around the police car and 500 police stood by, an agreement was reached.

The agreement called for dropping charges against the former student (who had remained in the police car throughout the demonstration), a faculty committee to hear the cases of the eight suspended students, and a joint faculty-student-administration committee to advise on rules governing political activity.

The December sit-in and strike
Confrontations continued through October and November. During that period the Regents relaxed the rules, stating that campus facilities could be used for organizing "lawful" but not "unlawful" action in the community. This statement of rules was unacceptable to the student activists, who saw the ban on advocacy of unlawful acts as a threat to the civil disobedience tactics of the civil rights movement. On November 28 the Chancellor initiated disciplinary action against Mario Savio and three other FSM leaders for their part in the police-car demonstrations. Because of the agreement ending the demonstration, the discipline was interpreted as an act of bad faith.

Police car as podium: Mario Savio, leader of the Berkeley protest of 1964, addresses the crowd from atop a police car immobilized by demonstrating students

The response was a massive sit-in on December 2. Over 1,000 students packed four floors of the administration building. That night the Governor intervened and over 600 police arrested more than 800 students, most of whom went limp and had to be carried out of the building. Graduate students and teaching assistants led a student strike, which continued until the faculty meeting of December 8. On December 7 an abortive effort to end the strike was made by President Kerr and a council of department chairmen at an all-university meeting in the Greek Theater. Since the proposed settlement did not deal with the main issue of free speech, it was poorly received by the students. The meeting ended when Mario Savio made an unscheduled appearance at the rostrum and was unceremoniously removed by the police.

Faculty action During October and November, there was considerable activity within the faculty, and on October 13 the Academic Senate passed by a large majority a motion favoring "maximum freedom for political activity." On December 8 the largest faculty meeting ever held at Berkeley debated for three hours and passed by a vote of 824–115 a resolution calling for full freedom of speech and advocacy. The university was not to regulate the content of speech, but only "time, place, and manner." The FSM hailed the faculty resolutions, especially for rejecting the ban on "unlawful" advocacy, and ended the strike.

On December 18 the Regents said that their policies "do not contemplate that advocacy or content of speech shall be restricted beyond the purview of the First and Fourteenth Amendments to the Constitution." This statement was viewed as an acceptance of the faculty position. Two weeks later the Regents appointed a new Berkeley Chancellor who promptly announced new rules for campus political activity in line with the faculty resolutions of December 8.

NATURE OF THE CONFLICT

Conflict over rules governing campus political activity began well before the FSM. In 1961, for example, a student political party to run candidates for student government was suspended for rule violations. Four reasons may be suggested why the controversy in the fall of 1964 exploded into a conflict exceeding previous disputes at Berkeley, or perhaps at any American university: (1) the history of controversy at Berkeley had resulted in a cumulation of grievances among student activists, (2) modifications of restrictions on campus political activity encouraged students to seek greater freedom, (3) the introduction of new restrictions in September with no advance warning or consultation occurred during a presidential campaign and in an area where an increasingly militant civil rights movement had conducted two mass sit-ins the previous spring, (4) the new ban hit all political groups simultaneously, paving the way for a common effort against the administration policy.

The distinctive characteristic of the Berkeley protest was its militant direct action. For its part, the administration used police action to combat the student protest. From the beginning the conflict was a confrontation rather than a more normal political dispute. The FSM goals were not radical and the administration was not reactionary; therefore the nature of the means did not follow from the character of the ends. However, the FSM claimed that normal channels of protest were closed to students, leaving no choice except civil disobedience. The administration denied this and justified severe student discipline and even police action on the ground that usual responses were inadequate in the face of direct action.

Polarization Both sides increasingly believed that only one side could win, and that there had to be a showdown. In this the conflict resembled a classic revolutionary situation, where polarization of social forces destroys the rule and style of the moderates, who seek negotiation and accommodation of conflict within a common framework. In a highly polarized situation, each side draws on whatever resources of power it can command. To counter the administration's power, the FSM tried first to mobilize the students and then to win the support of the faculty. Hundreds and then thousands of students were persuaded to align themselves with FSM means as well as FSM aims. The power of the administration proved ineffective against the concerted action of thousands of students. Faced with this loss of consent, the administration fell back on the use of force, which further undermined its authority, and helped pave the way for a strong faculty stand in favor of the ends, although not the means, of the FSM.

NATURE OF STUDENT DISCONTENT

The FSM was successful because it gained widespread support among the students. About 3,400 students participated in one or both of the following episodes: the police-car incident in October or the administration building sit-in in December. About 4,800 actively picketed during the strike in December, and 5,600 supported the strike by refusing to attend classes. About 3,500 actively opposed the strike, and the remaining 12,000 played no active part.

Surveys of student opinion show an underlying distrust of the administration in matters affecting student rights and needs. This feeling did not extend to distrust of the faculty, nor was it an expression of dissatisfaction with the quality of their education. Surveys taken in 1964, 1965, and 1966 showed that more than four out of five students expressed satisfaction with their courses and professors; and supporters of the FSM were as satisfied in these respects as nonsupporters.[41] A third to a half of the students expressed distrust of the administration, and these students were the most likely to support the FSM. There was widespread sentiment that the administration was not interested in consulting students on university policies, and those students who felt strongly on this point were likely to support the FSM. Surveys in 1960 and 1961 showed that students held similar attitudes well before the FSM. An earlier atmosphere of distrust helped prepare the way for the FSM and was not merely the result of the free-speech controversy.

Students who distrusted the administration and supported the FSM were more likely than those who did not to (1) feel strongly about the denial of Negro civil rights in America, (2) oppose U.S. policy in Viet Nam, (3) identify themselves as liberal Democrats, (4) major in the humanities or social science, (5) have better-than-average grades, and (6) come from liberal homes.

Although the FSM activists and supporters held liberal values, they were highly critical of the liberalism of parents, politicians, university administrators, and professors. Charges of hypocrisy formed an important theme in the student criticism of university authority. Insincerity on the campus was considered of a piece with the failure of American society to live up to its ideals in the treatment of the Negro.

STUDENT LEADERSHIP AND ORGANIZATION

A classic issue in the study of revolution is spontaneity versus conspiracy. The FSM was attacked as a conspiracy by newspapers, politicians, and even by some members of the university. These attacks were partly efforts to undermine the claims of the FSM to speak for the students; but to some extent they were expressions of genuine surprise that the FSM was so effective. The administrative officials underestimated student response at almost every juncture, consistently demonstrating a failure to understand student sentiment and determination.

The main influence on FSM leadership and organization was the civil rights movement. Leaders and many activists had firsthand experience in direct action against recalcitrant authorities, for example, in Mississippi during the summer of 1964 and in the San Francisco sit-ins the previous spring. In addition, many FSM militants represented the "New Left," which was more interested in issues than ideologies, more committed to action for immediate ends than long-term strategy, and more concerned with moral appeal than with political organization.

Although the accent was on spontaneity rather than planning, initially there was organization of representatives of all political groups on campus. Subsequently a steering committee was selected by the political groups plus *ad hoc* groups of other students. The steering committee met almost continuously during crises and made many important decisions for the FSM. Many decisions were also made or ratified in mass meetings, including the noon rallies in the central plaza of the campus. But these mass decisions tended to be made by acclamation rather than after debate and discussion. Although many FSM activists feared leadership and organiza-

[41] Robert H. Somers, "The Mainsprings of the Rebellion: A Survey of Berkeley Students in November 1964," in Lipset and Wolin, *op. cit.*, pp. 530–558; Kathleen Gales, "A Campus Revolution," *British Journal of Sociology, 17* (1966), 1–19; Shirley Star, unpublished survey of Berkeley students, Spring 1966. (These surveys were conducted by professors of sociology at Berkeley, with the assistance of students taking courses in research methods.)

tion, and valued personal participation and spontaneity, they discovered that leadership and organization were indispensable.

The FSM was a reactive movement rather than a strategic organization. Almost every major action of the students was in response to the administration initiatives: notably the original ban, the suspension of eight students, and the disciplinary charges against four leaders.

The strength of the FSM was based on solidarity rather than organization, and this solidarity spread to large numbers of students because they felt that the administration was "out to get" a few FSM leaders and did not take the movement as a serious expression of student sentiment. Students were also angered by the administration's refusal to deal with the FSM. Instead it asked the opinion of the student government, which lacked legitimacy because it was widely perceived as an arm of the university administration (the 1966 survey found that only 18 percent of the students thought that the student government was effective).

When the initial aims of the FSM were substantially won, the organization disbanded. There were more student demonstrations, but without the solidarity that marked the FSM.

THE ROLE OF THE ADMINISTRATION

If the administration sometimes wondered whether the FSM was a spontaneous movement or a conspiracy, the FSM charged that the administration was part of a conspiracy with the "power structure" of the Bay Area and of the state to crush the civil rights movement. But there is as little evidence for the FSM belief as for the administration fears. The administration acted more out of weakness than of strength, more out of the anticipation of outside pressure than of demands from the "power structure," more out of concern for protecting its authority than for any political interests.

The administration, in common with other large and complex organizations, is a system of many levels of delegated authority. The University of California is especially complicated because it is a statewide system of nine campuses, of which Berkeley is only one. The statewide administration consists of the Board of Regents, the President, and his large staff. A chancellor is the chief administrative officer of each campus, and under him are vice-chancellors and deans.

What began as a matter issuing from the office of the Dean of Students on the Berkeley campus moved up the line to the Berkeley Chancellor, then to the President of the statewide university, the Regents, and finally to the Governor. In addition, newspapers, television stations, members of the state legislature, and both organized and informal community groups became deeply involved in the controversy. The controversy, then, extended beyond the university and embroiled the university in state politics. (The dismissal of President Kerr as head of the statewide university following the election of Governor Ronald Reagan in 1966 resulted in part from the FSM demonstrations.) As a result, no official of the Berkeley administration could act without worrying about its conse-

quences all the way up the line, at least as far as the Board of Regents. Therefore, the initiative was seized by the president of the statewide university, who, for example, negotiated and signed the agreement in October ending the sit-in around the police car.

The administrators were locked into a hierarchy of authority. In consequence, they tended to deal with the students at a distance. Actually, the only time Chancellor Strong spoke directly to the student demonstrators was at 3:00 A.M. on December 3 when he announced that they would be arrested if they did not vacate the administration building; and the only time President Kerr addressed the student body during the fall of 1964 was in the Greek Theater four days later.

The confrontation between a large-scale bureaucracy and a mass movement produced a glaring incongruity of style in thought and action. Each side misperceived the other as monolithic when in fact each was fragile, often chaotic. In general, the bureaucratization of the university administration resulting from the rapid growth of a statewide system decreased its communication with students and, therefore, its capacity to understand new student sentiments and styles of action.

THE ROLE OF THE FACULTY

Although the faculty comprises the core of the university, neither its organization nor its culture prepare it for institutional leadership. Hence the anomaly that the faculty was powerless in the early period of the confrontation but took a decisive role in finally resolving the crisis.

The faculty, some 1,500 teachers, merges on the one side with the student body through graduate students who are teaching assistants and instructors, and merges on the other side with the administration through professors who are deans and other kinds of officials. The faculty has an identity of its own, but this is blurred by specialization and professionalization. Especially in a leading state university like Berkeley, many professors find their major identification with their specialty wherever it is practiced, rather than with the university. The more eminent professors are likely to be least involved with the educational institution or with the students. The struggle between students and administrators developed without significant faculty participation because of this lack of faculty involvement.

Small groups of professors did play a role from the beginning, some as supporters of the FSM, some as advisors to the administration, and a few as mediators identified with neither side. However, mediation became increasingly difficult and ineffective, and the polarization of the conflict forced the faculty as a body to seek its own solution. From the beginning that solution was sought along traditional civil libertarian lines: maximum freedom for student political activity consistent with the normal functions of the university. The most difficult issue for the faculty was the use of direct action on campus. Uneasiness about civil disobedience tended to be offset by widespread dismay over the use of massive police force. In the end, the faculty, gathered together as an official body in the Academic Senate, took its stand on the side of the goals of the FSM, namely minimal regulation of student political activity on campus. But it also favored orderly procedures, and therefore supported the administration in subsequent efforts to enforce liberalized rules.

OUTCOMES OF THE STUDENT DEMONSTRATIONS

1. The concrete result of the conflict at Berkeley was liberalized rules governing political action on campus. Under the new rules there has been considerable political activity. Further confrontations, disobedience, suspensions, and police action have also occurred.

2. New ways of making rules about student political activity developed, including increased student participation in the institutional methods of rule-making.

3. New procedures for disciplining students charged with violating the rules on campus political activity were sought, with greater attention to principles of due process.

4. A faculty commission to investigate needed reforms in undergraduate education was established at Berkeley, and its report led to a number of innovations designed to improve undergraduate education.

5. Berkeley became a model for student militancy, and a rash of student protests at other universities showed the influence of the Berkeley events.

SECTION 9 POPULATION AND ECOLOGY

TRENDS IN ENROLLMENT

The school enrollment in the United States in 1966 was over 55,000,000, or over one-fourth of the total population. Table XI:5 reports enrollments at the elementary, secondary, and college levels from 1870 to 1960 with projections through 1980. The 1970 and 1980 figures are based on the low fertility/high enrollment assumptions discussed below.

An emergent trend not examined in Table XI:5 is the rapid development of the sector of graduate education. In the thirty-year span after 1930, graduate enrollment increased almost eightfold while undergraduate enrollment about tripled. The trend is apparently accelerating.

Projecting school enrollments In order to anticipate the demands that will be made on the educational system and the resources of the community, increasing use is being made of methods of popu-

TABLE XI:5 ENROLLMENTS AT THREE EDUCATIONAL LEVELS, UNITED STATES, 1870–1960, PROJECTED TO 1980 (IN THOUSANDS)

YEAR	ELEMENTARY (including kindergarten)	SECONDARY	COLLEGE AND UNIVERSITY	TOTAL
1870	7,500	80	52	7,632
1880	9,757	110	116	9,983
1890	14,181	358	157	14,696
1900	16,225	696	238	17,159
1910	18,457	1,111	355	19,923
1920	20,864	2,496	598	23,958
1930	23,739	4,812	1,101	29,652
1940	21,127	7,130	1,494	29,751
1950	22,207	6,453	2,659	31,319
1960	32,441	10,249	3,570	46,259
1970	36,471	15,005	7,424	58,899
1980	32,381	15,593	11,181	59,156

SOURCE: *Historical Statistics of the United States: Colonial Times to 1957* (Washington, D.C., 1961). *Statistical Abstract of the United States, 1950*, p. 123; *1966*, p. 107. *Current Population Reports*, Series P-25, No. 365 (May 5, 1967). Projections for 1970 and 1980 are based on low fertility/high enrollment assumptions.

lation projection. Ordinarily at least two factors are taken into account: trends in the growth of the population of school age and trends in the retention of students in the schools. As is noted in Figure XI:1 (p. 342) and Table XI:5, the school population has been growing rapidly, the upper levels of schooling accounting for an increasing proportion of students.

Table XI:6 gives four different projections of the school population based on assumptions of high and low fertility and high and low enrollment. Because the college students of 1980 were already entering or in school when the projections were prepared, only enrollment trends enter into projections at that level. Because almost all children now complete elementary school, the differences at that level are almost entirely determined by fertility trends. At the secondary level the variation in absolute numbers is small because there is a well-established tendency for students to complete high school and because many of the children who will be of high school age in 1980 were already born when the projections were done.

Present demographic thought leans to the low fertility/high enrollment assumptions. This coincides with the fertility trends discussed in POPULATION AND ECOLOGY (page 278) and is consonant with the long-term trend towards increased amounts of schooling needed by advanced nations.

Public and private schools The distribution of students between public and nonpublic (parochial and private) schools in 1960 is shown in Table XI:7. The nonpublic enrollment for the elementary and secondary levels combined has been rising in absolute numbers and as a proportion of the total school population: 1.4 million, or 8 percent in 1900; 2.7 million, or over 9 percent in 1930; 3.4 million, or

TABLE XI:6 PROJECTIONS OF SCHOOL ENROLLMENT, UNITED STATES, 1980

LEVEL OF EDUCATION	HIGH FERTILITY HIGH ENROLLMENT		HIGH FERTILITY LOW ENROLLMENT		LOW FERTILITY HIGH ENROLLMENT		LOW FERTILITY LOW ENROLLMENT	
	Number (in thousands)	Per-cent	Number (in thousands)	Per-cent	Number (in thousands)	Per-cent	Number (in thousands)	Per-cent
Elementary	40,684	(60.2)	40,451	(61.9)	32,381	(54.7)	32,233	(56.5)
Secondary	15,706	(23.2)	15,212	(23.3)	15,593	(26.4)	15,099	(26.5)
College	11,181	(16.6)	9,718	(14.9)	11,181	(19.0)	9,718	(17.0)
TOTAL	67,572	(100)	65,381	(100)	59,156	(100)	57,050	(100)

SOURCE: *Current Population Reports,* Series P-25, No. 365 (May 5, 1967).

12 percent in 1950; and 6.5 million, or 15 percent in 1960.[42] Over four-fifths of the nonpublic enrollment is in parochial schools of the Roman Catholic Church, and growth in Catholic enrollment has accounted for the increase in size of the nonpublic segment. Approximately one-half of Catholic youth attend Catholic elementary schools. Among Protestant denominations, only the Lutheran Church (the Missouri Synod in particular) has been able to maintain a sizable school system of approximately 160,000 students. Parochial schools of other churches have largely disappeared in the long-term trend toward secularization of American education.

In higher education, the private sector is now waning in relative size. The majority of college students until the early 1950s attended private institutions. Since 1952 the majority have been enrolled in public colleges, the proportion reaching 70 percent in 1963. The trend toward public higher education will almost certainly continue as a larger proportion

TABLE XI:7 ENROLLMENT IN PUBLIC AND NONPUBLIC SCHOOLS AND COLLEGES, 1960

LEVEL OF EDUCATION	PUBLIC		NONPUBLIC		TOTAL	
	Number (in thousands)	Per-cent	Number (in thousands)	Per-cent	Number (in thousands)	Per-cent
Elementary [a]	27,900	84	5,400	16	33,300	100
Secondary [a]	8,500	89	1,100	11	9,600	100
Higher [b]	2,136	59	1,474	41	3,610	100
TOTAL	38,536	79	7,974	21	46,510	100

[a] *Health, Education, and Welfare Trends* (Washington, D.C.: U.S. Department of Health, Education, and Welfare, 1961), p. 36. Figures for the school year ending 1960.

[b] *A Fact Book on Higher Education* (Washington, D.C.: American Council on Education, n.d.), p. 12. Figures for the opening enrollment, Fall, 1960.

[42] *Health, Education, and Welfare Trends* (Washington, D.C.: U.S. Department of Health, Education, and Welfare, 1960), p. 56.

of the young continue their education into the college years.

ECOLOGY OF SCHOOLS

The spatial distribution of American schools has been determined largely by the concept of the neighborhood school. Especially in elementary education, educators and parents have maintained that the school should be close to the home and serve a neighborhood, with children attending the nearest school. The neighborhood-school concept gives the elementary school a territorial base and a relatively homogeneous student body. In areas with two or more high schools, students are assigned by residence.

The educational park, a large school complex pooling several former school districts or combining the resources of several communities, has recently been urged to improve the efficiency of educational systems. Neighborhood schools are felt to be too small for economical operation and to afford the pool of specialized teachers and facilities needed for contemporary education. The educational park is also suggested as a way to solve the problems of desegregation.

Because minorities are concentrated in certain neighborhoods, the children attend segregated or largely segregated schools: the social composition of the neighborhood determines the social composition of the school. This is called *de facto* segregation in distinction from segregation by law. In a large city that has a ghetto, some schools are almost all white or all Negro, with mixed schools in the boundary neighborhoods or in areas undergoing transition.

Gerrymandering for segregation The idea that school population must be drawn from a geographic school district has been so fixed until recently that attempts to distribute students in preferred social patterns commonly take the form of gerrymandering, redrawing territorial boundaries. Thus, in a Northern industrial city, a high school district may be drawn two miles wide and ten miles long to include only

white, upper-middle-class families, because a wider zone would mix races or social classes.

Gerrymandering for integration The neighborhood-school concept is under challenge in the United States because of efforts to integrate the schools racially. Groups opposing *de facto* segregation say that proportional racial composition should be a criterion in determining the student population of schools. They claim, for example, that if a city is 20 percent Negro and 80 percent white, most of its schools should have a similar ratio rather than radically unbalanced ones. This approach, too, encourages gerrymandering of school districts or, if need be, abolishing territorial zones and transporting students to schools distant from their homes.

Extent of segregation Segregation by race among both teachers and students remains the predominant pattern.[43] Approximately 80 percent of all white children attend schools that are between 90 and 100 percent white. Nearly two-thirds of Negro students attend schools in which over 90 percent of those enrolled are Negro. While these patterns are most pronounced in the South and Southwest, they are found wherever there is a high proportion of Negroes in the population. Latin American, Asian, and American Indian children are similarly, though less thoroughly, segregated.

Segregation is somewhat less complete in teaching staffs. Over 60 percent of the teachers of Negro children are Negro, while 97 percent of the teachers of white students are white.

The racial matching of teachers is most pronounced in the South where by tradition it has been complete. On a nationwide basis, in cases where the races of pupils and teachers are not matched, the trend is all in one direction: white teachers teach Negro children but Negro teachers seldom teach white children; just as, in the schools, integration consists primarily of a minority of Negro pupils in predominantly white schools but almost never of a few whites in largely Negro schools.[44]

[43] Coleman, *et al.*, *Equality of Educational Opportunity*, p. 3.
[44] *Ibid.*

CHAPTER XII

LAW

SECTION 1 INTRODUCTION

Like religion and education, law is a major institution of social integration. Legal recognition lends coherence, regularity, and acceptance to social forms and codes of conduct. Law sustains and encourages social organization by defining what men can rely on in the conduct of others. As a sensitive indicator of cultural values, law says what men should aspire to in the ordering of their affairs.

The legal system is an arena of conflict, as well as a source of stability. Courts, lawyers, and police are preoccupied with disputes and offenses. Law is, therefore, a public, institutionalized mechanism for resolving controversies. Its contribution to social integration is active, not passive.

FOUNDATIONS OF LAW

The nature of law is best understood by considering (1) the contribution law makes to society, culture, and the individual and (2) the distinctive resources, mechanisms, and problems of law. In this perspective, law is studied as an activity or enterprise, a living institution performing social tasks. It follows

that the legal order is more than a system of norms or rules. It is also a set of agencies responding to social needs, pressures, and aspirations.

Functions of law The major social functions of a legal system are:

1. *To maintain public order.* Law offers an alternative to private warfare and vengeance. Legal machinery for the settlement of disputes supplements the more informal social processes by which men and groups adapt to each other and accommodate their interests. A legal resolution of controversy makes two contributions to public order: (*a*) it provides a basis for conclusive settlement, so that the same controversy will not be repeatedly reopened, and (*b*) if the legal process is fair to the parties concerned they may be content with the outcome.

The order-maintaining function of law is also apparent in the suppression of deviance. Although an encounter between an armed robber and his victim might be thought of as a "dispute," it is not so conceived in law or custom. In the usual case, the robber

379

is treated as someone to be suppressed, not as one who needs a legal alternative to dangerous private action.

2. *To facilitate cooperative action.* In most human interaction, people have to accept the risk that others will not do what is expected of them. Being courteous, showing up for meetings, lending a neighborly hand, and many other expectations are important to orderly social life, but for the most part they receive no legal recognition. Some expectations, however, are formally recognized and can be the basis of *claims of right.* Such a claim, if it stems from a person's status as a human being or a citizen, is usually formulated as a basic or constitutional right. Other rights are created by the parties themselves, by exchanging enforceable promises in accordance with the law of contracts. The fixing of legitimate expectations is the *reliance function* of law; without it the risks of cooperative action would be much increased. A modern industrial society is especially dependent on legal protection of rights, because there is so much cooperation between strangers who cannot rely on kinship ties or other informal social controls for the protection of their interests.

3. *To confer legitimacy.* Law moderates the struggle for power by providing criteria of legitimate succession and by saying *who* has a right to exercise *what kind* of power. The legitimating function of constitutional law is the clearest example, for it sets out the conditions for becoming a president, premier, king, or chief. But the problem of legitimacy arises in other contexts too. For example, it has long been assumed that an employer may legitimately give orders to his employees; but the nature and scope of the employer's authority have not always been clearly established in law. Similarly, the right of college administrators to govern the conduct of students has been questioned in recent years, especially where authority is presumed to be based on the principle of *in loco parentis* (in the place of a parent).

4. *To communicate moral standards.* When the law defines rights and responsibilities, and backs up its definitions with the threat of coercion, it becomes in effect a powerful agency of communication. Every act of enforcement is at the same time an act of communication. For this reason, it is important that there be close coordination of legal purpose and legal administration. Fairness at a trial may not offset the effect on public opinion of brutal or even disrespectful conduct by police at the time of arrest.

The educational significance of law accounts for the reluctance to change laws that embody moral standards. For example, many people may question the wisdom of attempting to regulate sexual conduct through law, but they want to keep the law on the books as a public expression of what is right and proper. They fear that removal of the ban on, say, homosexual relations, would be taken as public approval. By the same token, proponents of new values may be content for a while with a law that has "no teeth." They hope that having the law on the books will educate the public to the new values, in part by drawing upon the reservoir of respect for law.

Just as religion is only one way of overcoming anxiety and supporting social norms (see RELIGION, p. 303), so the functions noted above are not the exclusive province of law. Other institutions contribute in their own ways to the same ends.

Law and authority The special competence of law is to transform informal social norms into formal ones, to elevate vague obligations and privileges into recognized duties and rights, to transmute the recommendations of a mediator into decisions that bind contending parties. Thus law is the realm of formal obligation, and a key word in the study of law is *authority.*

The difference between law and no-law is the difference between a norm of conduct that will be authoritatively affirmed and one that remains informal, dependent on mutual accommodation and goodwill. People make law for themselves when they enter contracts and thereby establish explicit, binding obligations. In that case, "formal" does not necessarily mean written, for an oral agreement can create a contract. The transition from "agreement" to "contract" is an example of the emergence of law.

In a legal order, norms and decisions can always be tested for their lawfulness by putting the question: By what authority? The reply might be quite

An assertion of legal title: Mesopotamia, 1100 B.C. *Many legal records, in cuneiform script on clay tablets, have been preserved from the early civilization of Assyria and Babylon. In addition to written deeds evidencing conveyance of land, stone landmarks were used, such as the one shown here, which reads in part: "This stone is named Perpetual Fixer of Landmark. . . . If any agent or official of the said Khanbi estate shall lay claim to or take this land or shall wrongfully reclaim it or transfer it to any other party, or shall dispute this grant from the king, or shall send any fool or blind man or ignorant person to remove or destroy or hide this landmark, may the great gods curse him with incurable evil. May Shamash judge of heaven smite his countenance. May his posterity perish among the people. This stone is named Perpetual Fixer of Landmark."*

the intimate connection between legal analysis and the *critique* of authority. The demand for justification, for giving reasons, accounts for much of the flexibility and dynamism of a legal system.

Law and rules   Law has been defined as "the enterprise of subjecting human conduct to the governance of rules."[1] A *rule* is not any norm but one that is formal, explicit, and deliberately instituted. To govern according to rules is to establish standards that are general and uniform; open, not secret; usually prospective rather than retroactive; and sufficiently constant through time to be an adequate guide to action. An alternative to governing by rules is to treat each situation as unique. Most systems fall between the polar extremes of complete rulelessness, with every decision reflecting the whim, wisdom, or special interest of the decision-maker, and full adherence to rule-governed decision. Favoritism in the application of rules and vagueness in their formulation are two recurrent signs that a regime of rules (or "the rule of law") is imperfectly achieved.

Men cannot govern by rules without *being governed* by them. Rules are binding on superior and subordinate alike. In instituting rules, the superior

blunt and crude: it is the law because I the king or priest say it is. But this dialogue is the germ of legal development.

The importance of justification in law produces two major attributes of a developed legal order: (1) the right of appeal to higher authority as a way of testing the legality of a decision or rule; and (2)

[1] Lon L. Fuller, *The Morality of Law* (New Haven: Yale University Press, 1964), p. 106.

commits himself to the standards, procedures, or penalties they may establish and the reasoning that lies behind them. The authority of the rules can be invoked by the accused as well as by the accuser.

Law and the state If law is an institution for making and applying authoritative rules, then it exists outside of public government as well as within it. From a sociological point of view, law can be studied in the private associations of religious, educational, or industrial life, for these institutions also rely on formal authority and rule-making. Canon law, for example, is the law of the church, and some churches, notably the Roman Catholic and Episcopal, have elaborate legal machinery. Where church and state are separate, the decisions of church courts do not carry the sanctions of the public government. In universities a process of "legalization" may be observed when faculty rights and student rights are enunciated and demands are expressed for rule-governed, nonarbitrary decision-making by administrators. Similarly, the emergence of employee rights and systems of private adjudication in industry can be studied in the sociology of law.

In this perspective law is more general than *state law,* the legal order of an organized political community. In addition to state law there may be, as just noted, the law of special groups; and in simpler societies anthropologists have found law where there is not much political organization.[2]

This chapter deals with state law, and gives most attention to criminal law. However, non-state law should also be considered, especially in an "administered" society where great corporate entities exercise considerable power over the lives of their members and the rest of the community.

TYPES OF LAW

A sense of the legal order, and an introduction to key terms, may be gained from the following brief review of important types of law.

Common law and statute In England "common law" was developed by the King's judges, especially in the centuries after the Norman conquest of 1066.[3] The judges gradually established a uniform (common) law for the realm, replacing much local customary law. Consequently "common law" has come to refer to judge-made law, as distinct from statutory law, which is the law passed by legislatures. Judges make law by interpreting statutes (see Adaptation 29) and by adapting established legal rules or precedents to new situations. Thus in its decision on school segregation in 1954, the United States Supreme Court interpreted the Constitution, which is a kind of statute; at the same time it changed a preexisting judge-made doctrine that "separate but equal" school facilities met the constitutional requirements of "equal protection of the laws." The new judge-made doctrine said that separate public schools for Negroes and whites were inherently unequal. In the United States, judge-made rules can be changed by the legislature, which has final authority, except when the judges interpret the Constitution. In that case, the judicial rule can only be changed by a constitutional amendment.

Criminal law and civil law Much legal activity is devoted to the settlement of private disputes, such as controversies over contracts and claims resulting from automobile accidents. In such cases, the community is essentially neutral, and the objective of the law is to reestablish social equilibrium. In these civil actions damages are assessed, property is restored, rights and obligations are determined. Although "punitive damages" are sometimes granted (if the harm is done with great malice), normally the question of punishment does not arise. A crime, however, is an offense against the community. When a crime is committed, the community takes over the job of investigating and prosecuting the case, and the objective is to suppress such offenses.

Criminal and civil justice often overlap. For ex-

[2] See E. Adamson Hoebel, *The Law of Primitive Man* (Cambridge: Harvard University Press, 1954), Chap. 6.

[3] See Arthur R. Hogue, *Origins of the Common Law* (Bloomington: Indiana University Press, 1966); also Theodore F. T. Plucknett, *A Concise History of the Common Law* (Boston: Little, Brown, 1956).

ample, a "tort" is a private wrong, other than a breach of contract, such as a harm produced by negligence, slander, assault, or stealing. Some torts are also crimes, and a man may be liable to pay damages to the person he has harmed in a civil action, and also be subject to criminal prosecution.

Administrative law A major branch of law is the law of bureaucracy—the principles and rules by which official actions can be called to account in the courts. Most attention has been given to the fairness of procedures by which agencies issue licenses, regulate rates, and otherwise affect the interests of citizens. These agencies have considerable discretion, but the development of administrative law tends to limit discretion by setting standards of official conduct. For example, in 1907 a law student at the University of Minnesota was dismissed for "deficiency in his work" and the fact that he was "charged" with being insubordinate to the faculty. The case was brought to the Supreme Court of Minnesota, which held that neither of the reasons was sufficient basis for dismissal, since the student might have made up his deficiency, and the fact that he was "charged" did not mean that he was guilty.[4] In this case the court controlled administrators by insisting that they provide adequate reasons for their decisions.

The great expansion of public activities carried on through government agencies has increased the scope and importance of administrative law. The future may see further extension of administrative law to agencies hitherto relatively untouched, such as police departments, and to quasi-public agencies, such as trade unions and private universities. Administrative law is one of the main branches of "public law," which is concerned with the structure of government and its relations to the citizen. "Private law" applies to the relations among the citizens themselves. In a world of large organizations, the distinction between public and private is becoming blurred.

Positive law and "higher" law On the theory that every legal decision, no matter how high the source, should be subject to criticism and appeal, many students of jurisprudence have been reluctant to restrict the idea of law to what the courts or legislatures say. For this reason, the concept of "positive law" is used to refer specifically to what some duly constituted body has decided. Law is "positive" when a particular conclusion has been reached by an authorized agency—a conclusion expressed in a statute, a judicial decision, or an administrative regulation.

Beyond positive law, according to some theorists, is a "higher" or "natural" law, based on supernatural authority or on human reason.[5] Concepts of natural law are used to criticize positive law. For example, an asserted natural right to the privacy of one's thoughts might be used to challenge the legality of a statute requiring compulsory psychotherapy for prisoners.

Procedure and substance The legal rules that govern most human activities comprise the substantive law. They are what most law is about, e.g., real estate, inheritance, corporations, divorce, contracts. However, there is also *the law of legal decision*. Such law is called procedural or adjective law, and includes the law of arrest, how to file a suit, what evidence is admissible at trial, and everything else that bears on the legal process, including the methods of judicial reasoning and the organization of courts, public defender offices, probation departments, and parole boards.

SOCIOLOGY AND LAW

Sociology views the legal order in *context* and in *action*. The context of law is studied by exploring the social sources of legal change, especially the response of law to altered values and to new forms of social organization; by examining the relation of law to other institutions, such as medicine, or to social movements, such as the labor movement or the civil

---

[4] *Gleason* v. *Univ of Minnesota, 116* N.W. 650 (1908). [Vol. 116, *Northwestern Reporter*, p. 650]

[5] See Heinrich Rommen, *The Natural Law* (St. Louis: Herder, 1947); also Edwin W. Patterson, *Jurisprudence: Men and Ideas of the Law* (Brooklyn: Foundation Press, 1953), Chap. 13.

rights movement; and by considering the social environment within which lawyers, judges, police, and other legal officials do their jobs. For example, public apathy toward certain types of crimes is part of the context of police work, as is the enthusiasm of some groups for getting rid of deviants.

The social context sets problems for legal agencies, limits their resources, and sometimes transforms their purposes. Thus the objective of *suppressing* crime may become one of merely *regulating* it. A sensitivity to law-in-context leads to a concern for law-in-action, that is, for understanding how decisions are made.

That understanding must take account of all the social forces that play upon official agencies, those that come from outside as well as those that arise from within.

The major theme of legal sociology is the interplay of formal and informal processes. As in the study of formal organizations (see ASSOCIATIONS, pp. 196–197), sociological inquiry tends to emphasize informal structure and the informal influences on decision. This emphasis, however, does not detract from the importance of the formal or legal system.

SOURCES AND READINGS

Introductions to law

Carl A. Auerbach, Lloyd K. Garrison, Willard Hurst, and Samuel Mermin (eds.), *The Legal Process* (San Francisco: Chandler Publishing, 1961).

Harold J. Berman and William R. Greiner (eds.), *The Nature and Functions of Law* (Brooklyn: Foundation Press, 1966).

Charles G. Howard and Robert S. Summers (eds.), *Law: Its Nature, Functions and Limits* (Englewood Cliffs, N.J.: Prentice-Hall, 1965).

Frederick G. Kempin, Jr., *Legal History: Law and Social Change* (Englewood Cliffs, N.J.: Prentice-Hall, 1963).

Lewis Mayers, *The Machinery of Justice: An Introduction to Legal Structure and Process* (Englewood Cliffs, N.J.: Prentice-Hall, 1963).

Jurisprudence

H. L. A. Hart, *The Concept of Law* (Oxford: Oxford University Press, 1961).

Lon L. Fuller, *The Morality of Law* (New Haven: Yale University Press, 1964).

Roscoe Pound, *Jurisprudence* (5 vols.; St. Paul: West Publishing Co., 1959).

Julius Stone, *Social Dimensions of Law and Justice* (Stanford: Stanford University Press, 1966).

Social analysis

Jerome E. Carlin, *Lawyers On Their Own* (New Brunswick: Rutgers University Press, 1962); *Lawyers' Ethics* (New York: Russell Sage Fdn., 1966).

F. James Davis, Henry H. Foster, Jr., C. Ray Jefferey, and E. Eugene Davis, *Society and the Law* (New York: The Free Press of Glencoe, 1962).

W. Friedmann, *Law in a Changing Society* (Berkeley and Los Angeles: University of California Press, 1959).

Jerome Hall, *Theft, Law and Society* (Indianapolis: Bobbs-Merrill, 1952).

James Willard Hurst, *The Growth of American Law: The Law Makers* (Boston: Little, Brown, 1950).

Harry Kalven, Jr. and Hans Zeisel, *The American Jury* (Boston: Little, Brown, 1966).

Martin Mayer, *The Lawyers* (New York: Harper & Row, 1967).

Rita James Simon (ed.), *The Sociology of Law* (San Francisco: Chandler Publishing, 1968).

Criminology

Hermann Mannheim, *Comparative Criminology* (Boston: Houghton Mifflin, 1966).

Edwin H. Sutherland and Donald R. Cressey, *Principles of Criminology* (7th ed.; Philadelphia: Lippincott, 1966).

Paul W. Tappan, *Crime, Justice and Correction* (New York: McGraw-Hill, 1960).

Periodicals

Law and Contemporary Problems

Law and Society Review

Journal of Criminal Law, Criminology, and Police Science

SECTION 2 SOCIAL ORGANIZATION

The legal order depends for its effectiveness on an underlying social structure. Group activities and the routines of life have their own momentum and their own sources of stability. Most people meet most of their obligations most of the time, and they are sustained in doing so by the practical requirements of everyday life. Law does not so much impose social order as confirm and support it. Therefore the development of law follows closely on the evolution of social organization.

LAW AND THE DIVISION OF LABOR

The relation of law to social integration was studied by Durkheim in his *Division of Labor in Society*.[6] For Durkheim, the division of labor was more than an economic phenomenon; he saw it as a basic feature of social organization, with significance for the nature of the social bond and for the autonomy of individuals and groups. Like many other writers of his time, he thought modern society could be best understood by comparing it with an earlier stage of social evolution. To make this comparison, he developed a distinction between two types of social solidarity, *mechanical* and *organic,* the latter representing a later stage of development. Durkheim suggested that each of these stages was associated with, and indicated by a distinctive kind of law.

Mechanical solidarity is based on likeness and a sense of common identity. People are bound together by the fact that they have been brought up to act and think alike, follow similar life routines, and share a "common conscience." The main source of cohesion is symbolic experience. This solidarity is "mechanical," Durkheim thought, because it resembles "the cohesion which unites the elements of an inanimate body, as opposed to that which makes a unity out of a living body."[7] Such a society can readily break apart, as each element is a self-sufficient unit going off on its own.

Organic solidarity, on the other hand, is based on functional differentiation, analogous to a complex living body with specialized organs, each dependent on the others, and the whole dependent on the functional integration of the parts. Similarly, differentiation makes people and groups interdependent, and the outcome is organic solidarity.

In the stage of mechanical solidarity, social control through law is largely a matter of upholding the symbolic order. Group identity is reaffirmed when punishment is meted out to deviants who violate what is sacred to the group. Compared to modern law, archaic law is mainly the law of crimes. Early criminal law did not necessarily include harms to individuals, even murder, but centered on offenses

TABLE XII:1 DURKHEIM'S MODEL OF LAW AND SOCIETY

STAGE	SOLIDARITY	LAW	SANCTION	MORALITY	SOCIAL EFFECT
I	Mechanical	Crime	Repressive	Communal	Psychic cohesion
II	Organic	Contract	Restitutive	Cooperative	Functional integration

[6] George Simpson (tr.), *Emile Durkheim on the Division of Labor in Society* (New York: Macmillan, 1933). First published in French in 1893.

[7] *Ibid.,* p. 130.

against religion, custom, and authority. To enforce and reassert the common conscience, the community resorts to *punitive* law and *repressive* sanctions.

With the development of organic solidarity based on the division of labor, another type of law becomes predominant. This is *restitutive* law, which is the law of cooperation. Its purpose is to restore social equilibrium by "making a man whole," that is, to compensate him for losses incurred when someone fails to discharge his lawful obligation. The classic branch of restitutive law is the law of contracts. The contract is, wrote Durkheim, "*par excellence,* the juridical expression of cooperation."[8] One who breaches a contract is not punished but required to make up for the losses he has caused.

In organic solidarity Durkheim saw a rational basis for law and one that was compatible with personal autonomy. Each type of solidarity, and each of the two types of law, is associated with a distinctive "morality." Repressive law is a manifestation of communal morality and is suffused with the spirit of constraint. Restitutive law is the morality of cooperation; it binds together specialized groups or occupations, rather than whole communities.

Mechanical solidarity presumes that individuals are the same; organic solidarity presumes that individuals and groups are different. "The first is possible only insofar as the individual personality is absorbed into the collective personality; the second is possible only if each one has a sphere of action which is peculiar to him; that is, a personality."[9] Thus restitutive law encourages autonomy as it facilitates cooperative action.

In offering this theory of social and legal development, Durkheim understood that the stages were not "pure." No society coheres without some degree of functional interdependence; non-penal law can be found in archaic and primitive systems; and of course modern society is not without its repressive law. Durkheim was correct in his conclusion that

modern law is, relatively speaking, more concerned with restitution, and that this has much to do with the growth of commerce and industry. But the chief significance of Durkheim's analysis lies not in his historical assertions but in the theoretical connection he established between types of law and types of social solidarity. (An application of his theory in developmental psychology is discussed below in Adaptation 30, pp. 402–406.)

SELF-HELP AND THE ADVERSARY PRINCIPLE

A major preoccupation—some would say "the first problem"—of early law is to keep the peace.[10] Early law is in some respects the law of the frontier. Men are armed and they expect to take care of themselves, their families, and their property. To assert a claim or defend a right is an exercise in self-help. Law emerges to restrain self-help, to give it form and limit, but not to eliminate it.

In archaic society kinship was the basis of social organization, and when a man acted he implicated his kin group. As a result, small conflicts might escalate, with whole families or clans fighting each other. Therefore restraint on self-help went beyond protection against individual violence; it was also a way to avoid irreparable splits within the community.

For this reason early law is much concerned with "composition," that is, adjustment or settlement of a dispute by making a payment instead of returning the injury in kind. There was composition for personal injuries, including homicide, as well as for loss of property.

[I]n the laws of Ethelbert [Anglo-Saxon England, 6th century A.D.] it was provided that if one bruise another in a part covered by the clothes the *bot* or composition should be 20 *scaetts;* but if one bruise another in a part not covered by the clothes the *bot* should be 30 *scaetts.* It was not the seriousness of the bruise that was considered. The legal precept went on the extent to which the bruise would cause

---

[8] *Ibid.,* p. 123.

[9] *Ibid.,* p. 131.

[10] See Roscoe Pound, *Jurisprudence* (St. Paul: West Publication Co., 1959), vol. I, pp. 370 ff.

a desire for revenge and thus endanger peace and order.[11]

In the beginning composition was a form of retribution, not a way of compensating the injured party for damages suffered. It was a recognition in law of a right of vengeance, but carried out in accordance with rules and by means compatible with at least a minimum of social order.

The salience of kinship was often recognized by giving a man's relatives the legal right to avenge a wrong against him. Within limits the "blood-feud" was a legal action:

A striking peculiarity of criminal jurisprudence in Athens was that the most grievous offenses against the life of citizens were not considered to be directly within the range of public coercion. When an individual was killed the city left the prosecution to the relatives, and if there were no relatives or if they preferred entering into a bargain with the slayer, the latter was let off without further punishment . . . the affair was considered primarily as a private feud to be settled between the two parties by revenge or composition.[12]

There were rules to help ensure that, if a person had no close relatives, more distant ones would take responsibility for prosecuting the offender or settling with him. When a man was convicted for murder, his execution was carried out in the presence of his victim's relatives. "Thus the avengers were prevented from taking the law into their own hands . . . . They had to be content with the moral satisfaction of having destroyed their enemy at the hands of public justice." [13]

Early law had to take account of its own limited resources, and family organization was the natural substitute for what today might be done by government. Primitive legal institutions characteristically limited themselves to deciding who was right, leaving it to the parties or their kinsmen to carry out the judgment of the court.

Self-help today Modern legal process is no stranger to the idea of self-help. In substantive law, the most obvious example is the right of self-defense, and under certain conditions a man may trespass on someone else's property for the purpose of abating a nuisance or recovering something of his own. In such cases self-help is considered a necessary evil, and it is the policy of the law that citizens should seek redress through law rather than take direct action.

Although not usually thought of as such, another form of legal self-help is the formation of contracts to settle disputes and arrange new working relationships:

[Not enough has been said] about the process whereby a couple of lawyers bring two militantly hostile parties together in an office, adjudicate their disputes, draw a decree or statute called a contract to govern their conduct for the next ten years, and thereafter administer the law they have written in a way that will sensibly and faithfully carry out the legislative intent.[14]

The law of contracts is a framework within which private parties can settle their own disputes and, to some extent, make their own law. Put another way, the law of contracts is a device for encouraging voluntary social organization and thereby adding to the community's resources for social control and for social action. This sort of self-help is much approved by the legal system.

An adversary system It is in the central drama of the legal system—the process of adjudication itself—that self-help under law is most clearly institutionalized. The form it takes is a proceeding in which the parties themselves, through their legal representatives, take the initiative and carry forward the action. Where this approach is dominant,

[The] court is a passive forum for adjusting disputes, and has no power either to investigate facts or to

---

[11] *Ibid.,* pp. 377 f.

[12] Paul Vinogradoff, *Outlines of Historical Jurisprudence* (London: Oxford University Press, 1922), vol. II, p. 177.

[13] *Ibid.,* p. 180.

[14] David Cavers, "Legal Education and Lawyer-Made Law," *W. Va. Law Review, 54* (1952), 180.

initiate proceedings. Litigants themselves largely determine the scope of inquiry and the data upon which the judicial judgment is based.[15]

This statement should not be taken as a fully accurate description of all Anglo-American courts, for they sometimes do appoint experts and make inquiries; rather, the statement formulates an ideal, a concept of adjudication that maximizes the opportunity of the parties themselves to frame the issues that divide them, develop the facts as they see them, and offer arguments as to how the law applies.

Party initiative and party responsibility are manifestations of the adversary principle, which places *partisan advocacy* at the center of the legal process. The adversary principle allows and even encourages the zealous pursuit of special interest by means of self-serving interpretations of law and evidence. This pattern has been an important part of the Anglo-American tradition.

In the classic model of an adversary proceeding, the parties are presumed to have private resources. The model works best when effective social organization can be taken for granted. The wealthy and powerful come to court evenly matched. They have the resources to gather facts, hire adequate counsel, and endure lengthy litigation, including appeals to higher courts. The parties do all the spade-work required by the case. The court's task is to choose between well-prepared proofs and arguments.

Weakness of the adversary model The model breaks down (1) when the parties are grossly unequal in status or power and (2) when relatively powerless people are represented by lawyers who have their own reasons for preferring to settle rather than fight. When resources are inadequate, or bargained away, the result is impoverished advocacy, which weakens a system that presumes each individual client has effective representation.

The inequality of parties is sometimes corrected by the transformation of social organization, especially the creation of new associations to offset the power of old ones. A good illustration is the rise of trade unions. In a legal contest with his employer, for example, over injuries received on the job, the lone employee was decisively unequal. His "equality before the law" was only formal at best.

As trade unions became powerful they could intervene on behalf of their members, not only in negotiations over wages and working conditions, but also in dealing with legal agencies such as a workmen's compensation board. Supported by an organization, the individual gained social power and thereby increased his legal capability.[16]

In recent years government has given more attention to increasing the legal competence of disadvantaged persons, in both criminal and civil actions. The main problem is effective legal representation, and this has been approached in two ways: (1) enlarging the right of indigent criminal defendants to be provided with a lawyer at an early stage of the proceedings, and (2) strengthening legal resources among the poor by creating new legal-aid agencies. A legal assistance program is an important phase of the "war on poverty." One agency within that program, the San Francisco Neighborhood Legal Assistance Foundation, phrased its goals as follows:

The principal goal of the Foundation is to bring the benefits and protections of the law to those who have long been denied them. To that end the Foundation is committed to provide clients with high quality legal representation, and to increase access to these services through the establishment of neighborhood law offices in low-income areas of the city . . . to promote awareness of legal rights, and to encourage the assertion of these rights among the poor.[17]

It is understood, however, that truly effective *legal* participation depends on effective political and social participation.

---

[15] *Sale* v. *Railroad Commission,* Supreme Court of California, *15* Cal. 2d 612 (1940).

[16] For an account of this development in California, see Philippe Nonet, *Administrative Justice: A Sociological Study of the California Industrial Accident Commission* (New York: Russell Sage Foundation, 1968), Chap. IV.

[17] From an agency brochure. On the role of advocacy in the war on poverty see Edgar S. and Jean C. Cahn, "The War on Poverty: A Civilian Perspective," *Yale Law Journal, 73* (July, 1964), 1317–1352.

LAW AND ORDER

The phrase "law and order" carries a strong connotation of social peace and may even suggest that order is equivalent to or more important than law. However, in relation to social organization, and as a vehicle for the vindication of rights, law may be compatible with considerable social turbulence.

The following points should be considered:

1. Social organization creates conflict as well as order. See SOCIAL ORGANIZATION, page 14. In most social systems there is tension as well as constraint. It may be argued that the existence of tension, including that generated by new legal arrangements, shows that problems are being faced rather than avoided and that social energies are being tapped.

2. Most men prize a *kind* of order, not order in general. Passive conformity is a kind of order; so is vigorous controversy. Some people think of social order as a tight unity, or so fragile that any disturbance will destroy it. These orientations toward order affect attitudes toward social control. (See Sec. 8, p. 418.)

3. Law imposes limits on social control. Not every technique of control that might be effective is permitted under law. The police and other officials are subject to many restrictions affecting what they can do, especially in preventing crime before it occurs. There is thus a tension between law on one hand and order on the other. For a police department two aims are in conflict: The objective of "crime control" runs counter to the aim of maintaining high standards of "due process." [18]

4. The ideal of a political community based on law, with its promise of protection against the abuse of power, may spur men to close the gap between the ideal and the social reality. The result may be militant controversy, in the name of law.

[18] For a discussion of this conflict see Herbert Packer, "Two Models of the Criminal Process," *University of Pennsylvania Law Review, 113* (November, 1964), 1–68.

SECTION 3 CULTURE*

This section considers (1) cultural orientations toward law—the variety of ways justice is perceived and law is appreciated, and (2) the use of law to enforce moral standards.

CONCEPTIONS OF LAW

In any society, the various functions of law are not equally developed or valued. One society may emphasize the dispute-settling function, with a complex machinery of adjudication, frequent recourse to the courts, and high status of judges; law in another society may mainly serve to justify authority; still another society may develop technical legal instruments for manipulating property and creating associations. In one case, law may be thought of as a necessary evil and lawyers a plague on the body politic; in another it may be associated with the divine. Cultural conceptions of law determine whether the legal order will help create men that are submissive to authority or critical of it, jealous of their rights or only dimly aware of them.

Law and reason in ancient Greece A distinctive feature of Greek culture of the time of Plato (427–347 B.C.) and his pupil Aristotle (384–322 B.C.) was the celebration of law as embodying and expressing the moral aspirations of the political community. The laws of the *polis,* the city-state, defined its moral identity. They made life in the city worthwhile and distinguished civilized man from the barbarian. "The people should fight for the law as if for their city-wall," said Heraclitus.

* By Philippe Nonet in collaboration with L.B. and P.S.

Justice is symbolized in this Egyptian pictograph representing the Judgment of the Dead. The soul of Hunefer, the king's chancellor, answers for his life-conduct. Forty-two assistant judges are seated above, each responsible for a specific offense. As the accused answers, his heart is weighed in the balance on the left against the Feather of Justice on the right. The scribe (far right) announces the verdict: "Behold, I am declaring, in the home of Osiris [God of the Dead], the royal chancellor Hunefer to be true and just. His heart hath come forth in the scales, and hath not been found evil." (From the papyrus of Hunefer, about 1300 B.C.)

For the Greeks law was more than a practical machinery for settling disputes and getting the work of the community done. Law was a moral order, but not in the sense of mere customary obligation. To participate in the legal order was to act out the role of citizen. As an embodiment of virtue, law connoted a striving for excellence rather than compliance with specific rules of conduct.

In its outlook and technical concepts, Western law owes more to the Romans than to the Greeks. An-cient Greece did not evolve a distinct body of law comparable to the refined system of concepts and doctrines developed by the Romans. This is partly due to the fact that the Greeks were hostile to legal specialism. Greek laws never became the province of a special class of professional lawyers, as occurred in Rome. The Greeks insisted that the law of the *polis* belonged to and lay within the competence of every citizen. The courts were large assemblies of laymen, drawn from the eligible citizenry. Each litigant was in principle required to present and argue his own case.

Whereas the Roman heritage is a detailed, operative system of concepts and doctrines, the Greek heritage is more the *idea* of law, and especially the association of law and reason. It was believed that law and justice were founded in reason, man's most distinctively human attribute. Reason provided the principle of harmony upon which justice rested: justice, reason, and beauty were but three facets of the same overarching ideal of human excellence.[19]

Thus the Greek conception of law and justice was a morality of aspiration. Law was not a necessary evil but a positive good. And respect for law was compatible with a critical spirit, as dramatically shown in Socrates' acceptance of the judgment against him while retaining his personal autonomy.

Alternative conceptions The Greek view may be compared with some others to show how conceptions of law vary.

Law as aspiration v. law as obligation. The Hebrews had a law-oriented culture, but in contrast to the Greeks they thought of law as a set of prescriptions to be meticulously observed. The Jews formed a "community of observance." The moral obligation to obey the law was not its rationality but its sanctity. Detailed legal rules penetrated every aspect of moral life, personal as well as social. The law was perceived as a holy commandment, not as a political achievement.[20]

Law counterposed to morality. In ancient China, the followers of Confucius (530–480 B.C.) had a low regard for law, in part because they perceived it as made up of rigid and narrow rules of conduct. Law was thought incompatible with the Confucian ideal of a social order based on the harmony of status groups. The social order would rest upon *li* rather than law, that is, upon the observance by each man of the norms of propriety appropriate to his status. The realization of this ideal required virtue and wisdom more than compliance with specific or minimal standards of conduct. The means to this end were education and self-improvement rather than enforcement of law through punishment.[21] There is apparently some continuity between the Confucian dispraise of law and the modern Communist Chinese emphasis on conciliation rather than legal controversy in the settlement of disputes.[22]

Education for conformity v. education for personal growth. As we have seen, the Greeks stressed the role of law in educating citizens to virtue. An emphasis on education also appears in modern Soviet law, but with a narrower purpose. The 1961 statute on Comrades' Courts, which have jurisdiction over minor offenses, states their mission as:

contributing to the education of citizens in the spirit of a communist attitude toward work and toward socialist property, the observance of the rules of socialist community life, the development among Soviet people of a feeling of collectivism and comradely mutual assistance, and respect for the dignity and honor of citizens. The chief task of the Comrades' Courts is . . . to educate people by persuasion and social influence, and to create an attitude of intolerance toward antisocial acts.[23]

This concept of education suggests conformity and an orientation to specific rules of conduct. It is different from the Greek ideal of communicating basic principles and providing a framework for civic participation.

LAW AND MORALS

Many legal rules have little moral or symbolic significance. This variation is reflected in a traditional

[19] See Werner Jaeger, "Praise of Law," in Paul Sayre, *Interpretations of Modern Legal Philosophers* (New York: Oxford University Press, 1947), pp. 352–375; Ernest Barker, *The Political Thought of Plato and Aristotle* (New York: Dover, 1959), pp. 81–163, 321–356; and see also H. D. F. Kitto, *The Greeks* (Baltimore: Penguin Books, 1951).

[20] See W. G. DeBurgh, *The Legacy of the Ancient World* (London: Penguin Books, 1961), pp. 69–95.

[21] See T'ung-Tsu Ch'U, *Law and Society in Traditional China* (Paris: Mouton, 1961), pp. 227–281.

[22] See Jerome A. Cohen, "The Criminal Process in the People's Republic of China: An Introduction," *Harvard Law Review,* 73 (1966), 469–534.

[23] Quoted in Harold J. Berman, *Justice in the U.S.S.R.* (New York: Vintage Books, 1963), p. 289.

legal distinction between acts *mala prohibita* (wrong by prohibition) and acts *mala in se* (wrong in themselves).

Acts *mala in se* include, in addition to all felonies, all breaches of public order, injuries to person or property, outrages upon public decency or good morals, and breaches of official duty, when done willfully or corruptly. Acts *mala prohibita* include any matter forbidden or commanded by statute, but not otherwise wrong.[24]

Many violations of motor vehicle codes, such as overtime parking or driving without an operator's license, would have no moral connotation if they were not prohibited by statute. True crimes are wrong not only because the statute says they are but also because the acts are deemed wrong on the basis of general moral standards.

The modern view is that *mala prohibita* are not really crimes and should be differently classified, perhaps as "public wrongs," "regulatory offenses," or simply "prohibited acts."[25] They would thus avoid the stigma associated with criminal law, and this redefinition would help maintain the distinctiveness of the criminal law.

Between an extreme example of *malum prohibitum,* such as overtime parking, and a clear case of *malum in se,* such as murder, there are many gradations. The line between the two is blurred and moving. Littering in a public park, for example, might in an even more crowded world become *malum in se.*

Crimes without victims

A significant portion of criminal law is concerned with conduct that consists primarily in affronts to the mores (see CULTURE, p. 55) rather than in clearly identifiable harms. Laws against sexual deviation, drinking, using drugs, gambling, birth control, obscenity, and vagrancy are usually justified by reference to some harmful effect; but the alleged harm, however serious, is often hard to define, subject to debate, or only distantly connected to the offensive act. These are typically "crimes without victims."[26] Characteristically the "victim" is the person himself or someone quite willing to cooperate in the offending act, such as a prostitute.

The attempt to use law to coerce virtue raises difficult issues:

1. *Moral pluralism and liberty*. The classic argument against legislating morals is found in John Stuart Mill's essay *On Liberty:*

The only purpose for which power can be rightfully exercised over any member of a civilised community, against his will, is to prevent harm to others. His own good, either physical or moral, is not sufficient warrant. He cannot rightfully be compelled to do or forbear because it will be better for him to do so, because it will make him happier, because, in the opinion of others, to do so would be wise, or even right. These are good reasons for remonstrating with him or reasoning with him, or persuading him, or entreating him, but not for compelling him, or visiting him with any evil in case he do otherwise.[27]

This argument slights the possibility that the integrity and cohesion of the social order may depend upon the continued assertion of a common morality.[28] In effect Mill said that the use of law to uphold the "common conscience," in Durkheim's terms, might have been necessary in archaic or primitive society, but is not appropriate in a civilized community.

The reduction of liberty by the enforcement of morals may be a small problem when a single set of moral standards is widely shared in the community.

---

[24] *Commonwealth* v. *Adams, 114* Mass. 323 (1873), cited in Rollin M. Perkins, *Criminal Law* (Brooklyn: Foundation Press, 1957), pp. 57 f.

[25] See Perkins, *op. cit.,* pp. 701 f.

[26] See Edwin M. Schur, *Crimes Without Victims* (Englewood Cliffs, N. J.: Prentice-Hall, 1965).

[27] John Stuart Mill, *On Liberty* (London, 1859), reprinted in John Stuart Mill, *Utilitarianism, Liberty, and Representative Government* (London: Everyman's Library, 1910), p. 73. See also H. L. A. Hart, *Law, Liberty, and Morality* (Stanford: Stanford University Press, 1963).

[28] For a contemporary criticism of Mill, see Patrick Devlin, *The Enforcement of Morals* (London: Oxford University Press, 1959).

But under conditions of cultural pluralism, when the law enters the area of morals it may clash with the beliefs and aspirations of substantial minorities. Honest and responsible citizens may be classified and treated as criminals, and criminal law may become an expression of the social and political dominance of some over others.

Adaptation 29 shows how the United States Supreme Court dealt with a problem of moral deviance arising from group pluralism.

Sometimes laws against immoral conduct do not reflect a firm consensus based on traditional values. The history of prohibition shows the leading role of narrowly based but powerful groups. Through sustained political action, "moral entrepreneurs" [29] can push through laws that do not necessarily have majority support. Even if there is consensus on the underlying value, there may not be agreement on the wisdom of embodying such values in a penal code.

2. Costs of criminalization. The enforcement of morals has so many difficulties that there tends to be a negative effect on the integrity and reputation of the law.

Symbolic offenses tend to be vaguely defined, as in the case of vagrancy, obscenity, and outrage to public decency. This vagueness is a source of official uncertainty and leads to variable and arbitrary enforcement. The absence of a victim and the relatively private character of the proscribed activity create additional problems for the police. Without the help of complainants, the police feel they must exercise active surveillance over the community. Such practices as unlawful entrapment and illegal search and seizure are a continuing temptation to police investigators who have no other means of knowing when a crime has been committed. Where evidence cannot be lawfully secured, police may employ harassment as an alternative to prosecution. Corruption may also result from reliance on informers and from continuing contacts between the police and the underworld. The sheer difficulty of control requires enforcement to be selective and therefore discriminatory. [30]

In branding nonconformers as criminals, the law tends to cast them apart from the legitimate community. The atmosphere of secrecy, suspicion, and deviousness that comes to surround the proscribed activity may have its own degrading effect. What begins as a limited deviation may grow into a way of life, especially when the deviant comes to depend on criminal sources who supply the prohibited goods or services. In this sense, the legal sanction creates criminals. To the suppliers of contraband commodities, the legal prohibitions are a bonanza, creating opportunities for exploitation and gain they would not otherwise have. [31]

Social definition of crime The problems that arise in the area of law and morals bring home the lesson that "crime" is a social product, not a natural phenomenon. It is society that decides what shall be considered a crime and therefore subject to police surveillance and control. When law is used to uphold morals, despite the high social costs of enforcement, an underlying policy decision may be obscured. It may be unconsciously assumed that the only problem of law enforcement is to win conformity to existing legal rules. There may be a question, however, whether all acts defined as criminal should continue to be so defined. [32]

[29] See Howard S. Becker, *Outsiders* (New York: The Free Press of Glencoe, 1963), pp. 147–163; also Joseph R. Gusfield, *Symbolic Crusade* (Urbana: University of Illinois Press, 1963), on the prohibition movement; see also Adaptation 22, pp. 246–250.

[30] See Jerome H. Skolnick, *Justice Without Trial* (New York: Wiley, 1966), pp. 204–229.

[31] See Herbert L. Packer, "The Crime Tariff," *The American Scholar, 33* (1964), 551–557.

[32] See Francis A. Allen, *The Borderland of Criminal Justice* (Chicago: University of Chicago Press, 1964); The President's Commission on Law Enforcement and Administration of Justice, *Task Force Report: The Courts* (Washington, D.C., 1967), Chap. 8.

Adaptation 29 / *U.S. Supreme Court* POLYGAMY, MORALITY, AND THE MANN ACT

In 1946 the Supreme Court was faced with the problem of interpreting a statute passed by the U.S. Congress in 1910. The Mann Act made it unlawful to transport a woman across state lines "for the purpose of prostitution or debauchery, or for any other immoral purpose." In the case of *Cleveland* v. *United States,* a group of defendants appealed to the United States Supreme Court to reverse their convictions under the Mann Act. They were members of a Fundamentalist Mormon sect that still practiced polygamy, and they had traveled across state lines with their wives. The Court had to decide whether the language of the statute, especially "immoral purpose," should be applied in this case.

Through such interpretations, the Court makes law, for its decisions apply not only to a specific case but to future cases whose facts are similar. In interpreting or "construing" statutes, courts follow certain traditional rules. Among these is the rule of *ejusdem generis* (of the same kind). The rule is needed because in establishing the scope of a statute, legislatures often set out a few specific examples, followed by a general word or phrase to define a class of phenomena in order not to restrict the statute to the particular examples given. Thus a college rule might read that it applied to "intramural games, political rallies, and other activities." Clearly something more is intended than intramural games and political rallies, but would scheduled classes and dating be included? The doctrine of *ejusdem generis* authorizes the court to limit the scope of the general phrase to what it deems to be "of the same kind" as the enumerated examples. This is not always easy to do, as the Cleveland case suggests. A process of classification is involved, and it may be influenced by social knowledge, as the dissenting opinion shows.

First, the opinion of the Court, which means in this case of a majority of the justices, is presented, followed by a dissenting opinion of Justice Murphy. An interesting concurring opinion by Justice Rutledge, in which he gives his own reasons for coming to the same conclusion as the majority, is omitted.

Mr. Justice Douglas delivered the opinion of the Court.

Petitioners are members of a Mormon sect, known as Fundamentalists. They not only believe in polygamy; unlike other Mormons,[33] they practice it. Each of petitioners transported at least one plural wife across state lines, either for the purpose of cohabiting with her, or for the purpose of aiding another member of the cult in such a project. They were convicted of violating the Mann Act.

The Act makes an offense the transportation in interstate commerce of "any woman or girl for the purpose of prostitution or debauchery, or for any other immoral purpose." The decision turns on the meaning of the latter phrase, "for any other immoral purpose."

SOURCE: Abridged from *Cleveland* v. *United States,* 329 U.S. 14 (1946). [Vol. 329 of United States Reports (official Reports of the Supreme Court) at page 14.]

[33] The Church of Jesus Christ of Latter-Day Saints has forbidden plural marriages since 1890.

United States v. *Bitty* [1908] involved a prosecution under a federal statute making it a crime to import an alien woman "for the purpose of prostitution or for any other immoral purpose." The act was construed to cover a case where a man imported an alien woman so that she should live with him as his concubine. Two years later the Mann Act was passed. Because of the similarity of the language used in the two acts, the *Bitty* case became a forceful precedent for the construction [interpretation] of the Mann Act. Thus one who transported a woman in interstate commerce so that she should become his mistress or concubine was held to have transported her for an "immoral purpose" within the meaning of the Mann Act. *Caminetti* v. *United States,* 242 U.S. 470.

It is argued that the *Caminetti* decision gave too wide a sweep to the Act; that the Act was designed to cover only the white slave business and related vices; that it was not designed to cover voluntary actions bereft of sex commercialism; and that in any event it should not be construed to embrace polygamy which is a form of marriage and, unlike prostitution or debauchery or the concubinage involved in the *Caminetti* case, has as its object parenthood and the creation and maintenance of family life. In support of that interpretation an exhaustive legislative history is submitted which, it is said, gives no indication that the Act was aimed at polygamous practices.

While *Mortensen* v. *United States* rightly indicated that the Act was aimed "primarily" at the use of interstate commerce for the

conduct of the white slave business, we find no indication that a profit motive is a *sine qua non* to its application. Prostitution, to be sure, normally suggests sexual relations for hire. But debauchery has no such implied limitation. In common understanding the indulgence which that term suggests may be motivated solely by lust. And so we start with words which by their natural import embrace more than commercialized sex. What follows is "any other immoral purpose." Under the *ejusdem generis* rule of construction the general words are confined to the class and may not be used to enlarge it. But we could not give the words a faithful interpretation if we confined them more narrowly than the class of which they are a part.

That was the view taken by the Court in the *Bitty* and *Caminetti* cases. We do not stop to reexamine the *Caminetti* case to determine whether the Act was properly applied to the facts there presented. But we adhere to its holding, which has been in force for almost thirty years, that the Act, while primarily aimed at the use of interstate commerce for the purposes of commercialized sex, is not restricted to that end.

We conclude, moreover, that polygamous practices are not excluded from the Act. They have long been outlawed in our society. As stated in *Reynolds* v. *United States:*

Polygamy has always been odious among the northern and western nations of Europe, and, until the establishment of the Mormon Church, was almost exclusively a feature of the life of Asiatic and of African people. At common law, the second marriage was al-

ways void (2 Kent, Com. 79), and from the earliest history of England polygamy has been treated as an offence against society.

As subsequently stated in *Mormon Church* v. *United States,* "The organization of a community for the spread and practice of polygamy is, in a measure, a return to barbarism. It is contrary to the spirit of Christianity and of the civilization which Christianity has produced in the Western world." Polygamy is a practice with far more pervasive influences in society than the casual, isolated transgressions involved in the *Caminetti* case. The establishment or maintenance of polygamous households is a notorious example of promiscuity. The permanent advertisement of their existence is an example of the sharp repercussions which they have in the community. We could conclude that Congress excluded these practices from the Act only if it were clear that the Act is confined to commercialized sexual vice. Since we cannot say it is, we see no way by which the present transgressions can be excluded. These polygamous practices have long been branded as immoral in the law. Though they have different ramifications, they are in the same genus as the other immoral practices covered by the Act.

Petitioners' second line of defense is that the requisite purpose was lacking. It is said that those petitioners who already had plural wives did not transport them in interstate commerce for an immoral purpose. The test laid down in the *Mortensen* case was whether the transportation was in fact "the use of interstate commerce as a calculated means for effectuating sexual immorality." There was evidence that this group of petitioners in order to cohabit with their plural wives found it necessary or convenient to transport them in interstate commerce and that the unlawful purpose was the dominant motive. In one case the woman was transported for the purpose of entering into a plural marriage. After a night with this petitioner she refused to continue the plural marriage relationship. But guilt under the Mann Act turns on the purpose which motivates the transportation, not on its accomplishment.

It is also urged that the requisite criminal intent was lacking since petitioners were motivated by a religious belief. That defense claims too much. If upheld, it would place beyond the law any act done under claim of religious sanction. But it has long been held that the fact that polygamy is supported by a religious creed affords no defense in a prosecution for bigamy. *Reynolds* v. *United States, supra.* Whether an act is immoral within the meaning of the statute is not to be determined by the accused's concepts of morality. Congress has provided the standard. The offense is complete if the accused intended to perform, and did in fact perform, the act which the statute condemns, viz., the transportation of a woman for the purpose of making her his plural wife or cohabiting with her as such.

We have considered the remaining objections raised and find them without merit.

Mr. Justice Murphy, dissenting.

Today another unfortunate

chapter is added to the troubled history of the White Slave Traffic Act. It is a chapter written in terms that misapply the statutory language and that disregard the intention of the legislative framers. It results in the imprisonment of individuals whose actions have none of the earmarks of white slavery, whatever else may be said of their conduct. I am accordingly forced to dissent.

The statute in so many words refers to transportation of women and girls across state lines "for the purpose of prostitution or debauchery, or for any other immoral purpose." The issue here is whether the act of taking polygamous or plural wives across state lines, or taking girls across state borders for the purpose of entering into plural marriage, constitutes transportation "for any other immoral purpose" so as to come within the interdict of the statute.

The Court holds, and I agree, that under the *ejusdem generis* rule of statutory construction the phrase "any other immoral purpose" must be confined to the same class of unlawful sexual immoralities as that to which prostitution and debauchery belong. But I disagree with the conclusion that polygamy is "in the same genus" as prostitution and debauchery and hence within the phrase "any other immoral purpose" simply because it has sexual connotations and has "long been branded as immoral in the law" of this nation. Such reasoning ignores reality and results in an unfair application of the statutory words.

It is not my purpose to defend the practice of polygamy or to claim that it is morally the equivalent of monogamy. But it is es-

sential to understand what it is, as well as what it is not. Only in that way can we intelligently decide whether it falls within the same genus as prostitution or debauchery.

There are four fundamental forms of marriage: (1) monogamy; (2) polygyny, or one man with several wives; (3) polyandry, or one woman with several husbands; and (4) group marriage. The term "polygamy" covers both polygyny and polyandry. Thus we are dealing here with polygyny, one of the basic forms of marriage. Historically, its use has far exceeded that of any other form. It was quite common among ancient civilizations and was referred to many times by the writers of the Old Testament; even today it is to be found frequently among certain pagan and non-Christian peoples of the world. We must recognize, then, that polygyny, like other forms of marriage, is basically a cultural institution rooted deeply in the religious beliefs and social mores of those societies in which it appears. It is equally true that the beliefs and mores of the dominant culture of the contemporary world condemn the practice as immoral and substitute monogamy in its place. To those beliefs and mores I subscribe, but that does not alter the fact that polygyny is a form of marriage built upon a set of social and moral principles. It must be recognized and treated as such.

The Court states that polygamy is "a notorious example of promiscuity." The important fact, however, is that, despite the differences that may exist between polygamy and monogamy, such differences do not place polygamy in the same category as prostitution or debauchery. When we use those terms we are speaking of acts of an entirely different nature, having no relation whatever to the various forms of marriage. It takes no elaboration here to point out that marriage, even when it occurs in a form of which we disapprove, is not to be compared with prostitution or debauchery or other immoralities of that character.

The Court's failure to recognize this vital distinction and its insistence that polygyny is "in the same genus" as prostitution and debauchery do violence to the anthropological factors involved. Even etymologically, the words "polygyny" and "polygamy" are quite distinct from "prostitution," "debauchery" and words of that ilk. There is thus no basis in fact for including polygyny within the phrase "any other immoral purpose" as used in this statute.

One word should be said about the Court's citation of United States v. Bitty and the statement that the interpretation of the statute there involved is a forceful precedent for the construction of the White Slave Traffic Act. The thought apparently is that the phrase "any other immoral purpose," appearing in the White Slave Traffic Act, was derived from the identical phrase used in the statute regulating the immigration of aliens into the United States, the statute which was under consideration in the Bitty case. That case concerned itself with the portion of the immigration statute forbidding "the importation into the United States of any alien woman or girl for the purpose of prostitution, or for any other immoral purpose." Significantly,

however, the statute made separate provision for the exclusion of "polygamists, or persons who admit their belief in the practice of polygamy." Thus the phrase "any other immoral purpose," following the reference to prostitution, certainly did not comprehend polygamy. And if that statute, or the interpretation given it in the Bitty case, is to be any authority here, the conclusion to be drawn is inconsistent with the result reached by the Court today. As a matter of fact, Congress has always referred to polygamy by name when it desired to deal with that subject, as distinguished from immoralities in the nature of prostitution.

The result here reached is but another consequence of this Court's long-continued failure to recognize that the White Slave Traffic Act, as its title indicates, is aimed solely at the diabolical interstate and international trade in white slaves, "the business of securing white women and girls and of selling them outright, or of exploiting them for immoral purposes." The Act was suggested and proposed to meet conditions which had arisen in the years preceding 1910 and which had revealed themselves in their ugly details through extensive investigations. The framers of the Act specifically stated that it is not directed at immorality in general; it does not even attempt to regulate the practice of voluntary prostitution, leaving that problem to the various states. Its exclusive concern is with those girls and women who are "unwillingly forced to practice prostitution" and to engage in other similar immoralities and "whose lives are lives of involuntary servitude." A reading of the

legislative reports and debates makes this narrow purpose so clear as to remove all doubts on the matter. And it is a purpose that has absolutely no relation to the practice of polygamy, however much that practice may have been considered immoral in 1910.

Yet this Court in Caminetti v. United States closed its eyes to the obvious and interpreted the broad words of the statute without regard to the express wishes of Congress. I think the Caminetti case can be factually distinguished from the situation at hand since it did not deal with polygamy. But the principle of the Caminetti case is still with us today, the principle of interpreting and applying the White Slave Traffic Act in disregard of the specific problem with which Congress was concerned. I believe the issue should be met squarely and the Caminetti case overruled. It has been on the books for nearly 30 years and its age does not justify its continued existence. Stare decisis [the principle that precedents should be followed] certainly does not require a court to perpetuate a wrong for which it was responsible, especially when no rights have accrued in reliance on the error. Otherwise the error is accentuated; and individuals, whatever may be said of their morality, are fined and imprisoned contrary to the wishes of Congress. I shall not be a party to that process.

The consequence of prolonging the Caminetti principle is to make the federal courts the arbiters of the morality of those who cross state lines in the company of women and girls. They must decide what is meant by "any other immoral purpose" without regard to the standards plainly set forth by Congress. I do not believe that this falls within the legitimate scope of the judicial function. Nor does it accord the respect to which Congressional pronouncements are entitled. Hence I would reverse the judgments of conviction in these cases.

SECTION 4 SOCIALIZATION

This section considers three aspects of socialization and law: (1) the development of a sense of justice; (2) the problem of criminal responsibility; and (3) criminality as a product of socialization.

THE SENSE OF JUSTICE

Adaptation 30 summarizes an effort to observe justice in a natural setting. Piaget studied how concepts of fairness develop, taking account of both personality and social relations.

There is a close affinity between Piaget's theory of moral development and Durkheim's ideas as discussed in Section 2, pages 385–386. The "two stages" of each study are basically the same. Durkheim's mechanical solidarity corresponds to Piaget's morality of constraint; organic solidarity corresponds to the morality of cooperation.

In a lengthy commentary on Durkheim, Piaget argues that Durkheim lost his early insight, expressed in *The Division of Labor in Society,* that there are two moralities, one based on conformity to established norms, the other arising out of the necessities and opportunities of the division of labor. In his later writings on education, Durkheim seemed to recognize only one source of moral development—acceptance of authority.[34]

PSYCHIATRIC JUSTICE

Law is a way of holding men responsible for their acts. In Western culture, moral and legal responsibility is attributed only to conduct that is deliberate and to people who are capable of making mature choices. A *pure* accident carries no moral responsibility; an accident caused by negligence is blamed on the person who was careless. Young children are not considered responsible, and therefore the law does not recognize them as capable of forming contracts or committing crimes.

A vexing problem for the legal system is the fact that not all members of society have the capacity to conform to legal rules. This incapacity may be due to biological defects, which limit the possibilities of effective socialization, or to mental disorders that often have their roots in early childhood.

The M'Naghten rule   The modern law of criminal responsibility, as affected by mental illness or defect, begins with a case that arose in 1843 when Daniel M'Naghten attempted to assassinate Queen Victoria's prime minister. The prime minister escaped, but his secretary was killed. M'Naghten apparently suffered from delusions of persecution, and a jury found him "not guilty by reason of insanity."

At M'Naghten's trial new ideas about insanity were introduced, which cast doubt upon an eighteenth century "wild beast" test—that a man was not responsible for his acts if he did not know what he was doing, any more than a wild beast. M'Naghten's lawyers, referring to Dr. Isaac Ray's treatise on *Medical Jurisprudence of Insanity,* argued that no single aspect of personality should be considered decisive, because the mind is a unity, each part or aspect affecting the other. A man might know what he was doing, or might be able to distinguish right and wrong, and yet be so governed by mental illness as to be incapable of making sane choices.

[34] Jean Piaget, *The Moral Judgment of the Child* (New York: The Free Press of Glencoe, 1965), Chap. 4.

There was considerable uneasiness in high places about M'Naghten's acquittal, and the Queen, who had already suffered three attempts on her life, was in no mood to coddle assassins. She insisted that the law of insanity be clarified. Consequently, the Lord Chief Justice and fifteen other judges met and formulated what came to be known as the M'Naghten rule or test. Their response was a conservative one, for the Lord Chief Justice had "the Queen's breath upon him." [35]

Under the M'Naghten rule a man can be acquitted by reason of insanity only if it is proved that "at the time of the committing of the act, the party accused was laboring under such a defect of reason, from disease of the mind, as not to know the nature and quality of the act he was doing, or, if he did know it, that he did not know he was doing what was wrong." The central difficulty with the rule is that in psychological experience knowing and acting may be split. A man may be unable to control his actions yet be capable of making intellectual distinctions. He may even be able to act on those distinctions, for example, by hiding from the police, yet be unable to avoid the offending conduct.

In a number of American jurisdictions a supplement to the M'Naghten test was accepted, known as the "irresistible impulse" rule. A man might be acquitted if at the time of the offense he was overwhelmed by a compulsion he could not control, even though he knew what he was doing and that it was wrong to do it. But "irresistible impulse" has a narrow, situational focus. It presumes a momentary loss of self-control rather than a general incapacity.

The Durham rule   A major change did not occur until 1954, when the federal court of appeals for the District of Columbia heard the case of Monte Durham. The court brushed aside M'Naghten and established a new criterion of criminal responsibility. A man would not be held responsible "if his unlawful act was the product of mental disease or defect." Nothing was said about knowing or about "right and wrong." It was necessary only to show that the defendant was suffering from mental incapacity and that the illness or defect was the cause of the offending act.

The Durham rule is an example of judge-made law. As such, it applies only to the jurisdiction of the court, in this case the District of Columbia. (When the Supreme Court makes a new rule, it applies to the whole country.) However, the importance of the Durham decision derived from the considerable legal ferment it created.

Law in action   Criticism of the Durham rule has centered on three points: (1) it is very difficult to tell whether a specific act is the "product" of mental disease or defect; (2) the psychiatrist is given too much power, compared to judge and jury; (3) psychiatric decisions are often influenced by the way medical practice is organized, especially the conditions that exist in mental hospitals.

[The problem of "usurpation"] was strikingly illustrated in 1957, when a staff conference at Washington's St. Elizabeth's Hospital reversed its previous determination and reclassified "psychopathic personality" as a "mental disease." Because this single hospital provides most of the psychiatric witnesses in the District of Columbia courts, juries were abruptly informed that certain defendants who had previously been considered responsible were now to be acquitted. . . . It seems clear that a test which permits all to stand or fall upon the labels or classifications employed by testifying psychiatrists hardly affords the court opportunity to perform its function of rendering an independent legal and social judgment. [36]

A study of how the Durham rule worked during the years 1959–1963 concluded that the psychiatrists of St. Elizabeth's were predisposed to believe that only psychotic disorders were true instances of mental illness. There was thus a built-in bias against de-

---

[35] *United States* v. *Freeman,* 357 Fed. 2d 606 (2d Cir. 1966). This refers to an opinion of a United States Court of Appeals, Second Circuit; opinions of these federal appellate courts, which are below the Supreme Court, are published in a series called *Federal Reporter.* Thus the citation is read as volume 357, *Federal Reporter,* 2d Series, at page 606; the opinion is from the Second Circuit and was issued in 1966.

[36] *United States* v. *Freeman, op. cit.,* p. 622.

fendants who could not be classified as psychotics. Since the hospital was overcrowded and had inadequate facilities, the staff doctors tended to modify their purely medical judgments by taking account of economic and administrative limitations. One psychiatrist said that he chose "to accept a stricter legal standard [of what constitutes mental illness], because if I did not we would be flooded with undesirables, who are not acutely ill and who would clutter up our facilities which are already strained to the breaking point." [37]

These conclusions call attention to the fact that legal change depends for its effectiveness on the way rules are administered. To enunciate a rule is one thing; to apply it may be quite another. When the courts rely on probation departments, mental hospitals, or prisons for the implementation of policies aimed at more humane diagnosis and treatment, what they achieve in fact must depend on the competence of those institutions to do what is asked of them. [38]

CRIMINALITY AS A PRODUCT OF SOCIALIZATION *

Almost all members of modern societies commit some crimes, but most persons do not consider themselves criminals and are not so considered by the members of their groups. Even prisoners who do not identify themselves with the typical criminal insist that they are not really criminals. In everyday conversation we use such phrases as "criminal personality," "hardened criminal," "confirmed criminal," or "incorrigible delinquent" to refer to persons who conceive of themselves as criminals and persist in their criminality. Usually when we speak of a delinquent or criminal, we have in mind a person who apparently is an incorrigible outcast, but the criminality of such persons, like the criminality of persons who commit only occasional crimes, is learned.

In the efforts of families and other groups to fore-stall delinquency, children are often unintentionally driven into groups in which acquisition of a "criminal personality" is almost inevitable. The sequence of alienation may be outlined as follows: [39]

1. In the eyes of a child, behavior which is proper as play may include breaking windows, climbing over roofs, or greasing streetcar tracks. Such definitions of "play" are akin to "fun" on Halloween. But to many adults, including parents, policemen, and the victims of the play, the behavior is evil or delinquent and must be curtailed or suppressed.

2. Demands for suppression of the evil are made on the child by community members, including his parents. The demands may lead to a shift away from the definition of the specific *acts* as evil to a definition of the *actor* as evil.

3. In the face of the demands of adults, the child feels that an injustice is being done to him and, more important, that his community and, perhaps, his parents, consider him different from good children. This recognition on his part leads to closer integration with the group that shares his play activities, for the other members are encountering similar experiences.

4. The community then scrutinizes and looks with suspicion upon all his activities, his companions, his hangouts, his speech, and his personality, and becomes more certain of its definition of him as evil or bad.

5. The child discovers that he has been defined as bad and that even his efforts to be good are interpreted as evidence of his badness. He becomes more closely integrated with his play group, which has been redefined as a delinquent gang by both the community and the group members, and he begins to look upon himself and his companions as bad. He is defined as bad and becomes bad because he has been defined as bad.

6. Once the community has defined him as bad,

---

* In collaboration with Donald R. Cressey.

[37] Richard Arens, "The Durham Rule in Action: Judicial Psychiatry and Psychiatric Justice," *Law and Society Review, 1* (June, 1967), 41–80. Quotation at p. 71.

[38] See Thomas J. Scheff (ed.), *Mental Illness and Social Processes* (New York: Harper & Row, 1967).

[39] Cf. Frank Tannenbaum, *Crime and the Community* (Boston: Ginn, 1938), pp. 17–21.

it knows how to cope with him; it does not, in fact, know how to deal with him until it defines him as bad. He is threatened, punished, counseled, analyzed, supervised, and committed to an institution. He gets a "record" with the police and other agencies.

7. As the community copes with him, it crystallizes its conception of him and *his conception of himself*. He defines himself as he is defined, as an "incorrigible," a "delinquent," or a "criminal." He has adopted the community's classification system, the separation of the good and bad, the right and the wrong. He becomes loyal to groups in which the membership consists of bad persons like himself, becomes educated in crime, and learns that the community which has been defining him as bad contains many elements which support his badness.

This dramatization of evil probably plays a greater role in making the confirmed criminal or criminal personality than any other experience. One process for making a criminal is ". . . a process of tagging, defining, identifying, segregating, describing, emphasizing, making conscious and self-conscious; it becomes a way of stimulating, suggesting, emphasizing, and evoking the very traits that are complained of." [40]

Secondary deviation When society responds to deviant conduct by degrading, isolating, and stigmatizing the offender, he may become a person "whose life and identity are organized around the facts of deviance." [41] Whereas the initial or "primary" deviation might have been caused by any number of factors, such as sexual excitement or

[40] Tannenbaum, *op. cit.*, pp. 19–20.

[41] Edwin M. Lemert, *Human Deviance, Social Problems, and Social Control* (Englewood Cliffs, N.J.: Prentice-Hall, 1967), p. 41.

Ratero en accion: A pickpocket exploits a distracting crowd situation.

group pressure, secondary deviance results from the society's reaction to the original conduct. In addition to defining the individual as deviant, and thereby influencing his conception of himself, the society's punitive responses are often experienced as unfair and demeaning. Bitterness, withdrawal, and ultimate acceptance of deviance as a way of life may be the outcome. In this way, the society's reactions, especially when they involve a sense of outrage and rejection, may aggravate a problem instead of solving it.

Adaptation 30 / *Piaget* **THE CHILD'S CONCEPTION OF JUSTICE**

Jean Piaget (1896–   ) is a Swiss psychologist who has strongly influenced the study of intellectual and moral development. His work has important continuities with Durkheim and G. H. Mead and shows the interaction of philosophical, psychological, and sociological perspectives. As a student of philosophy, he directed his attention to the structure of mind and the nature of moral judgment. A sensitivity to the social setting brought him to conclusions similar to Mead's, especially the view that genuine socialization brings an appreciation of cooperative living as well as support for personal autonomy.

In his research on children, Piaget first undertook studies of language and thought judgment and reasoning. He then turned to the question of morality, especially the development of a sense of justice. In this study Piaget and seven collaborators observed and interviewed a total of 382 children who were pupils at various schools in Switzerland. Different groups of children participated in different phases of the research. A characteristic technique was to tell the child a brief "story" and elicit a response.

Morality and rules Piaget begins with the premise that "all morality consists in a system of rules, and the essence of morality is to be sought for in the respect which the individual acquires for these rules." (p. 13) He used the game of marbles to study the child's conception of rules. By observing the children and asking them to explain the game and respond to possible variations, he uncovered an intricate "jurisprudence" of marbles, a system of rules governing nearly every contingency that might arise in the course of play. However, Piaget was not primarily interested in the content of the rules but in how the child perceived his obligation. Two kinds of rules were identified:

1. Rules based on respect for authority, in which the child's feeling of obligation stems from his respect for the person who enunciates the rule—an adult or an older child. To the child the rule is a "divine law," the meaning of which is incomprehensible but which he must blindly obey. He does not understand that there is a purpose to a rule; instead, compliance is effected by punishment. Thus the first type of rule is a *coercive rule*.

2. Rules based on mutual respect among peers. In this context the child understands that rules are necessary to ensure fair and open competition in the game. Cheating

SOURCE: A summary and interpretation of Jean Piaget, *The Moral Judgment of the Child* (New York: The Free Press of Glencoe, 1965). First published in 1932. Quoted material cited to pages in the 1965 edition is published in the United States by permission of The Macmillan Company and of The Free Press, a Corporation. All other world rights granted by permission of Routledge & Kegan Paul, Ltd., London. This adaptation was prepared with the assistance of Saul Geiser.

is wrong because it is unfair to others, not simply because it invites punishment. Rules founded in this type of obligation are *rational rules*.

The morality of constraint Having formulated his basic concepts—coercive *v.* rational rules, respect for authority *v.* mutual respect, constraint *v.* cooperation—Piaget applies them in the study of developmental differences. He concludes that there are two major stages in the development of moral judgment in children, the first (ages 3 to 8) characterized by respect for authority and the morality of constraint, the second (ages 9 to 12) by the gradual ascendancy of mutual respect and the morality of cooperation.

Until he is seven or eight years old (Piaget cautions against over-emphasizing the specific ages), the child tends to perceive rules as fixed, externally imposed laws. He interprets them literally and does not understand that the spirit of the rules must at times override the letter if the purpose for which the rules were set up is to be achieved.

For the young child, good is defined in absolute terms: Any act that conforms to the literal rule is good; any act that does not so conform, regardless of extenuating circumstances, is bad. In spite of this rigid adherence to the letter of rules, there is little inward acceptance of them. Rules are exterior to the child. Like physical laws, they are perceived as external "realities" which influence behavior by force of nature, not force of principle or purpose. This orientation Piaget calls "moral realism."

Piaget asked children to compare two stories, the first about a boy who accidentally broke fifteen teacups that had been left out of sight behind a door, the second about a boy who broke a single cup while in the act of stealing jam from a cupboard. Here are two characteristic responses:

G., age 6: "Have you understood these stories?—*Yes.*—What did the first boy do?—*He broke eleven cups.*—And the second one? —*He broke a cup by moving roughly.*—Why did the first one break the cups?—*Because the door knocked them.*—And the second? —*He was clumsy. When he was getting the jam the cup fell down.* —Is one of the boys naughtier than the other?—*The first is because he knocked over twelve cups.*—If you were the daddy, which one would you punish most?—*The one who broke twelve cups.*—Why did he break them?—*The door shut too hard and knocked them. He didn't do it on purpose.*—And why did the other boy break the cup?—*He wanted to get the jam. He moved too far. The cup got broken.*—. . . Have you got a brother? *No, a little sister.*—Well, if it was you who had broken the twelve cups when you went into the room and your little sister who had broken one cup while she was trying to get the jam, which of you would be punished most severely?—*Me, because I broke more than one cup.*"

S., age 6: "Have you understood the stories? Let's hear you tell them.—*A little child was called in to dinner. There were fifteen plates on a tray. He didn't know. He opens the door and he breaks the fifteen plates.*—That's very good. And now the second story?—*There was a child. And then this child wanted to go home and get some jam. He gets on to a chair, his arm catches on to a cup, and it gets broken.*—Are these children both naughty, or is one not so naughty as the other?—*Both just as naughty.*—Would you punish them the same?—*No. The one who broke fifteen plates.*—And would you punish the other one more, or less?—*The first broke lots of things, the other one fewer.*—How would you punish them? The one who broke the fifteen cups: two slaps. The other one, one slap.*"

The striking fact about these responses is that both children ignore the *intentions* of the boys. It is the number of cups broken, not the intent, that defines the moral quality of the act. Beyond age eight the reverse is true: Older children hold the thief responsible. Piaget sees the failure of the younger children to take intent into consideration as resulting from their conception that rules have nothing to do with the "insides" of people.

The externality of rules is both a cause and consequence of adult constraint. Because the child is not yet able to comprehend that rules have a purpose, that they are means to the end of order and cooperation, it is difficult for parents to control the child's behavior without exercising constraint. The child of four or five cannot be "persuaded" that obedience to rules is good because it promotes solidarity and mutual respect. At the same time, adult constraint serves to reinforce the young child's restricted conception of rules.

The idea of justice After about age eight, the morality of cooperation gradually replaces the morality of constraint. Piaget studied this development by examining the child's conception of justice. Among the aspects of justice considered were: (1) fairness in punishment (retributive justice); (2) fairness in allocation of benefits (distributive justice); and (3) attitudes toward authority.

(1) Piaget queried his young subjects about the "justness" of various punishments for rule violations, using stories such as the following to elicit responses:

Story I. A boy has broken a toy belonging to his little brother. What should be done? Should he (1) give the little fellow one of his own toys? (2) pay for having it mended? (3) not be allowed to play with any of his toys for a whole week?

Story II. A child is looking at a picture book belonging to his father. Instead of being careful, he makes spots on several of the pages. What shall the father do? (1) The child will not go to the Cinema that evening. (2) The father will not lend him the book any more. (3) The child often lends his stamp-album to the father; the father will not take care of it as he has always done up till then.

Piaget found a clear difference between older and younger children with respect to the kinds of punishment they thought were fair. Younger children (ages 6 to 7) were more likely to choose severe punishments, whatever the rule violation, while older children (ages 8 to 12) favored milder punishments. For the younger group, "justice" was associated with severity of punishment.

In contrast to this "primitive" notion of retributive justice, the older children develop a more advanced conception of justice, based on the principle of *reciprocity*.

B., age 9, responding to Story II: *"I would dirty his album for*

him, because that would be the fairest punishment. It would be doing the same thing to him as he did. —And of the other two, which is the fairest?—*I wouldn't have lent him the book again because he would have made spots on it again.* —And how about the first punishment to stop him going to the Cinema?—*That one is the least fair. It does nothing to the album, the book. It has nothing to do with the book."*

R., age 10: "Which punishment do you think the fairest?—*Not the one of the Cinema, because that's rather too strict for having made spots.*—And which of the other two?—*The one of making spots on his album . . . it was right to do to him what he had done."*

B., age 12½, responding to Story I: The fairest statement is that he *"should give one of his toys to the little boy.*—Did you choose that one just because it came into your head, or because it seems to you more just?—*He took a toy away from the little boy, so it is right that he should give one back to him."*

Invoking the principle of reciprocity, the child conceives of "just" punishment as one that causes the offender to suffer the same consequences as he has caused others to suffer; in this way, he is made to realize the significance of his misdeeds. He is persuaded that the rule should be obeyed, not merely because he might be punished, or simply because the rule "is," but because to disobey the rule is to destroy mutual respect and reciprocity among one's peers. Piaget argues that this represents a radical shift from the idea of coercive punishment to a concept of punishment aimed at restoring the bonds of solidarity.

(2) The problem of distributive justice was approached by eliciting the children's attitudes toward favoritism.

A mother had two little girls, one obedient, the other disobedient. The mother liked the obedient one best and gave her the biggest piece of cake. What do you think of that?

In one group of 167 children, 70 percent of the young children (age 6 to 9) but only 40 percent of the older children (age 10 to 13) approved of the mother's action. Piaget concludes that "the children's reactions evolve according to a relatively constant law. With the little ones punishment outweighs equality, whereas with the older ones the opposite is the case." (p. 264) Piaget also notes a difference in the quality of the children's responses:

[The younger children] do not attempt to understand the psychological context; deeds and punishments are for them simply so much material to be brought into some sort of balance, and this kind of moral mechanics, this materialism of retributive justice, so closely akin to the moral realism studied before, makes them insensible to the human side of the problem. Whereas [the older children show] a singularly delicate moral sense— the mother's preference for the obedient child will discourage the other, will make it jealous, lead it to revolt, and so on. . . . It is in this sense, once again, that we can mark the contrast between cooperation, the source of mutual understanding, and constraint, the source of moral verbalism. . . . [C]hildren who put retributive justice above distributive are those who adopt the point of view of adult constraint, while those who put equality of treatment above punishment are those who, in their relations with other children, or more rarely, in the relations between themselves and adults, have learnt better to understand psychological situations and to judge according to norms of a new moral type. (pp. 267 f.)

Piaget recognizes that the desire for distributive justice, for fairness in allocation, may stem from adult example and tutelage. But he clearly prefers the hypothesis, without being able to prove it, that "the idea of equality develops essentially through children's reactions to each other and sometimes at the adult's expense. . . . The relation between child and adult as such does not allow for equality. And since equalitarianism is born of the contact of children with one another, its development must at least keep pace with the progress of cooperation between them." (p. 275)

(3) In his early years, the child is unable to distinguish a just rule and an authoritative rule. Until about age 7, justice and authority are one.

Once there was a camp of Boy Scouts (or Girl Guides). Each one had to do his bit to help with the work and leave things tidy. One had to do the shopping, another washed up, another brought in wood or swept the floor. One day there was no bread and the one who did the shopping had already gone. So the Scoutmaster asked one of the Scouts who had already done his job to go and fetch the bread. What should he do?

B., a girl, age 6½: *"She ought to have gone to get the bread.—Why? —Because she had been told to.— Was it fair or not fair to have told her to go?—Yes, it was fair, because she had been told to."*

Z., a boy, age 6½: *"He ought to have gone.—Why?—To obey. —Was it fair, what he had been* asked to do?—*Yes. It was his boss, his chief."*

Compare these responses, which associate justice with submission to authority, to those of children only slightly older:

L., a boy, age 7: *"He shouldn't have done it because it wasn't his job.—Was it fair or not to ask him to do it?—Not fair."*

C., a girl, age 9: *"She oughtn't to have done it. It was not her job to do it.—Was it fair to do it?— No, it was not fair."*

Now the child differentiates quite sharply between justice and authority; the question of the fairness of the rule is dissociated from the fact that the rule originated with adult authority.

Piaget contends that an essential feature of the child's idea of justice is the growing sense of equality that emerges during the seventh and eighth years. This sense of equality explains, in great part, the child's new capacity to discriminate between what is just and what is merely authoritative. The idea of equal treatment for all provides an autonomous standard against which the child may evaluate the authoritative commands of adults. To the extent that adult rules facilitate equality, the child judges them fair and just; but where adult rules are opposed to equality, the child rejects adult authority.

A developmental model Figure XII:1 shows the major variables studied by Piaget. Each stage of moral evolution is the result of three interdependent influences: (1) the level of development of the child's *personality*—egocentric or autonomous; (2) the nature of *rules*—coercive or rational; (3) the kind of *social relations* to which the child is exposed—constraining or cooperative.

Stage one relates egocentricity, coercive rules, and the morality of constraint. The young child's egocentricity has two aspects: he is basically a "loner," unable to engage in genuine cooperation: his play is characteristically mechanical and imitative; at the same time, he is dominated by respect for

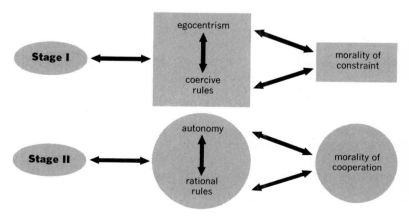

FIG. XII:1   Piaget's two stages of moral development

adult wishes. At this stage the child does not distinguish his own perspectives from the perspectives of others. "[I]n order to become conscious of one's ego, it is necessary to liberate oneself from the thought and will of others. The coercion exercised by the adult or the older child is therefore inseparable from the unconscious egocentrism of the very young child." (p. 93)

The morality of constraint is a morality of punitive rules and subordination to authority. The psychological bases for criticism of authority have not been laid.

The transition to stage two is marked by the child's increasing freedom from adult constraint. In the peer group cooperation takes hold. Cooperation entails communication by way of shared meanings. Group participation encourages a more generalized, less egocentric approach to the world, and helps the child to discover the boundaries that separate him from others. As his own autonomy grows, he gains respect for the autonomy of others. Cooperation presumes the participation of autonomous individuals. "So long as the child does not dissociate his ego from the suggestions coming from the physical and social world, he cannot cooperate, for in order to cooperate one must be conscious of one's ego and situate it in relation to thought in general." (p. 94)

Rational rules go together with autonomy and cooperation. In contrast to coercive rules, rational rules gain force from the child's understanding of them, not from fear of punishment. Rational rules therefore presuppose an autonomous individual, capable of consenting or withdrawing consent.

Later research   A recent review of studies conducted to test Piaget's hypotheses concluded that many of his findings have been confirmed, especially his theory that "the child's earliest morality is oriented to obedience, punishment, and impersonal forces, and that it progresses toward more internal and subjective values."[42] Some more specific conclusions, such as the importance he gave to the peer group in producing the morality of cooperation, have not been supported.

[42] Lawrence Kohlberg, "Development of Moral Character and Moral Ideology," in Martin L. Hoffman and Lois Wladis Hoffman, *Review of Child Development Research* (New York: Russell Sage Foundation, 1964), p. 399.

SECTION 5 PRIMARY RELATIONS

At first glance, nothing seems more remote from law than the realm of spontaneous, informal, person-centered relations. In fact, however, the legal order is closely concerned with primary relations: (1) The prototypical primary group—the family—is so important a part of social life that it inevitably becomes subject to legal rules. (2) Primary relations, and the groups based upon them, are decisive instruments of social control and therefore can determine the fate of "law and order."

MARRIAGE AND DIVORCE

In traditional legal doctrine, marriage combines both the idea of contract and the idea of status. A valid marriage is contractual at its inception. Marriages are formed voluntarily, by mutual assent, without duress. On the other hand, marriage is more than a contract; once established it takes on a new dimension. Marriage contemplates a permanent union and the conferral of status. To be a husband or wife is to be endowed with rights and obligations by operation of law and in accordance with public policy. Above all, the relation differs from contract in that the partners cannot dissolve it by mutual consent.

Freedom *to* marry is limited mainly by rules against marrying near relatives, forbidding plural marriages, and limiting marriages of young people. Until recently, in the United States, there were laws

406 - 408

174

35 - 36

against interracial marriages. In addition, some states prohibit marriages by habitual drunkards, narcotics addicts, insane people, parolees, and even paupers.

On the whole, however, the law has been less concerned with the opportunity to marry than with the problem of divorce. Here the social origins of the law, and the problem of adapting law to social reality, are plainly revealed.

The religious influence　The Anglo-American law of divorce shows the strong influence of Christian doctrine. "Wherefore they are no more twain, but one flesh. What therefore God hath joined together, let not man put asunder." (Matthew, 19: 6) At an early date marriage was proclaimed a holy sacrament. A valid marriage, consummated by sexual intercourse, was considered indissoluble.

The impossibility of divorce, somewhat mitigated by the law of annulment, has remained the doctrine of the Roman Catholic Church. The Protestant reformers of the sixteenth and seventeenth centuries rejected this absolute prohibition, and most Western countries do permit divorce. However, the Christian influence makes itself felt in the persistent legal doctrine that divorce may be granted only when one of the parties is guilty of a grievous fault, such as adultery, desertion, or extreme cruelty. There must be a guilty party and an innocent party; if both are guilty, the divorce is withheld.

Under Catholic church (canon) law, it is the duty of husbands and wives to live together, but they may appeal to church courts for permission to separate. The canon law developed rules on separation, not divorce. Adultery is the only basis for permanent separation, but temporary separations are allowed for other causes.

Under canon law, therefore, separation is relief for the innocent spouse from the duty of cohabitation because of the guilt of the other spouse. For the offending spouse it is a punitive measure, and for neither is there any possibility of remarriage. This is

the seedbed from which our civil law has sprung.[43]

Divorce law in the United States took over the canon law philosophy. Roughly speaking, what were grounds for *separation* under the canon law became grounds for divorce in the civil courts.

Secular policy　The persistence of the fault principle can be explained in part by the continuity of religious and secular perspectives. Although justified theologically, the concept of indissoluble marriage was a way of affirming the community's stake in family life. That stake remains, regardless of theology. Modern secular communities value the family for the contribution it makes to social life, especially in socialization and social control. Therefore secular policy begins with the premise that marriages should be preserved. The fault doctrine, with its deep historical roots and wide, almost automatic acceptance, was useful to the secular state as a way of placing barriers in the way of divorce.

A purely contractual view of marriage would (1) allow the parties to decide what their rights and obligations should be during the marriage, (2) permit dissolution by mutual consent, and (3) insist that the contract be for some definite term of years, after which even one of the partners could dissolve the marriage. This approach has not been accepted, although it was tried in an even more radical form by the Soviet Union, which in 1917 established the principle of free divorce, without reasons and available on request of one or both parties. However, by 1936 divorce was made somewhat more difficult and in 1944 the basic policy was changed, requiring an attempt at reconciliation and the granting of divorce only for good reasons.[44]

Assuming a social policy of preservation of marriage, the alternative to fault is the "breakdown" principle.[45] This is the view, accepted in some European countries, that a divorce should be granted if the marriage is in fact irretrievably disrupted. Even in those countries, however, the fault idea is not entirely elimi-

---

[43] Caleb Foote, Robert J. Levy, and Frank E. A. Sander, *Cases and Materials on Family Law* (Boston: Little, Brown, 1966), pp. 647 f.

[44] John N. Hazard and Isaac Shapiro, *The Soviet Legal System* (Dobbs Ferry, N.Y.: Oceana, 1962), pp. 100 f.

[45] W. Friedmann, *Law in a Changing Society* (Berkeley and Los Angeles: University of California Press, 1959), pp. 210 ff.

nated, and in Anglo-American law it is still dominant.

Institutionalized evasion The heavy moral overtones of divorce law expose it to some of the difficulties noted above in the discussion of law and morals (p. 393). There is reluctance to give up the symbolic function of traditional law in upholding moral standards; yet there is wide acceptance in fact of the futility of attempting to hold together marriages that are no longer viable. The result is a great gap between theory and practice.

The fault doctrine is attenuated in practice when judges give a very wide meaning to such terms as "cruelty," when divorce proceedings are perfunctory, and when collusion and perjury become common practice. Most divorces are uncontested. In the absence of an adversary proceeding, which would involve cross-examination and conflicting testimony, any plausible story by the plaintiff and his corroborating witnesses will be accepted, so long as everyone follows the rules and says what is expected of him. In fact, such a proceeding amounts to divorce by consent.

The gap between theory and practice in divorce law is widely recognized as *institutionalized evasion* of the legal norms. In other words, the evasions are patterned, systematic, and predictable:

The evasion of matrimonial laws throughout the country is manifested in four patterns of behavior:
(1) The laws explicitly refuse to allow divorce through the mutual consent of the spouses, but most divorces appear to be based on mutual consent; (2) collusion between parties is prohibited, yet some degree of collusion is probably present in nearly every divorce action; (3) the law assumes that matrimonial actions will be contested, but most of them are not; (4) matrimonial actions are decided on the basis of evidence presented in court, but such evidence bears little relationship to the actual causes of marital disruption. In brief, every major premise underlying most matrimonial laws is persistently denied in the majority of matrimonial cases.[46]

For many years faked evidence and fraudulent testimony were rampant in New York, where until 1966 adultery was the sole ground for divorce.

PRIMARY GROUPS AND SOCIAL CONTROL *

Social control is most effective when the individual must take account of the consequences of his conduct for his job, career, family, and friends. In the usual case, he finds himself bound into the social order through the commitments he has built up to people and groups who are themselves dependent on the community's resources and goodwill. The weaker this system of social integration, the more attenuated is social control. When informal social controls are weak, the burden on the legal order is increased.

In a normal community, most primary groups contribute to social integration. They "mediate" between the individual and the larger social structure. (See p. 134.) But this positive contribution to social control is not invariable. The primary group may also have a negative influence, from the standpoint of the larger system. Loyalty, for example, is a two-way street. A man may be respectable and exercise self-control out of loyalty to his family and fear that they may suffer; but he may also expect protection by his family if he should need it. As centers of intimacy and loyalty, primary groups always have a certain ambivalence in their relation to the social order.

The family and criminality Delinquency and criminality may be *fostered* by the family in the following ways:

1. Attitudes, values, and behavior patterns conducive to delinquency and crime may be present in the home. A child may become delinquent simply because he has learned delinquency at home.

2. The family determines the geographic and social class position of the child in the community. This, in turn, largely determines the kind of primary relations the child encounters outside the family. If the child's home is located in a high-delinquency area, the activities of play groups he encounters tend to be defined as delinquent. Similarly, belonging to a lower

---

* This section draws on material written in collaboration with Donald R. Cressey.

[46] Hubert J. O'Gorman, *Lawyers and Matrimonial Cases* (New York: The Free Press of Glencoe, 1963), pp. 20 f.

socioeconomic class may bring the child into association with neighborhood primary groups that do not fully share the dominant values of the broader society.[47]

3. The family determines the prestige of various persons and consequently affects the child's preferences for certain types of social relations. He learns to appraise persons as important or not according to their language, bearing, occupation, nationality, or other traits. These preferences greatly affect his chances of becoming delinquent. If the persons he respects and with whom he seeks primary relations outside the home are delinquent in their attitudes and values, the probability is high that he will become delinquent. Both the *type* of delinquency and the *incidence* of delinquency are determined by the types of persons who are highly esteemed in a neighborhood.

According to the theory of *differential association,* a person may be well socialized—in the sense that his training has not been neglected—and yet become a criminal if the norms of his groups are at variance with the official norms codified in criminal law. Children begin life disposed neither to crime nor to lawful behavior. However, they are both deliberately and unintentionally trained to conform to the behavior of the groups surrounding them.[48]

4. The family may fail to provide a harmonious and pleasant place for the child to live. If the primary relations in the family are obnoxious, the child may leave them, either by physically abandoning the family or by withdrawing psychologically. The family thus loses control over him. Delinquency is higher in unbroken but unhappy homes than it is in broken homes.[49] Whether a child from an unhappy or broken home becomes a delinquent, however, is determined by the kinds of outside relations he encounters when he leaves the family.

5. The family may fail to train the child to be law-abiding. It may neglect his training completely or it may overprotect him and fail to acquaint him with the rules of the outside world or with the kinds of delinquencies he will be expected to resist in the community. Whether such a "neutral" child becomes delinquent or not will, of course, depend upon the primary relations he encounters outside the home. However, the family is expected to produce not neutral children but *anti*delinquent children, whose attitudes and values will resist delinquent influences.

Most of the family conditions associated with delinquency probably become effective as indicated in paragraphs 4 and 5. Family poverty, parent alcoholism, a broken home, harsh discipline, psychological tensions or emotional disturbances in the family—all these result in failure to provide antidelinquent primary relations.

Gangs From the point of view of a gang member, the gang *is* the world. "To earn the right to belong he [the youth] will adopt whatever code of behavior the gang or group prescribes, regardless of how much it conflicts with society's standards or demands."[50]

Delinquent gangs arise chiefly from play groups that engage in delinquent or quasi-delinquent activities. The members of a play group develop a we-feeling and start referring to themselves as the "bunch" or "crowd." Group solidarity may be further promoted through rivalry with other gangs, and the delinquent character of the gang is emphasized when policy and property owners try to suppress its activities. The gang then becomes a subsociety, with values and codes in conflict with those of the larger society. The conflict with other gangs, the school, the family, and the police distinguishes a gang from a play group. Gang formation appears to be more characteristic of urban than of rural adolescent society.

---

[47] Albert K. Cohen, *Delinquent Boys: The Culture of the Gang* (Glencoe: The Free Press, 1955); Solomon Kobrin, "The Conflict of Values in Delinquency Areas," *American Sociological Review, 16* (October, 1951), 653–661.

[48] Richard A. Cloward and Lloyd E. Ohlin, *Delinquency and Opportunity* (Glencoe: The Free Press, 1960); and Edwin H. Sutherland and Donald R. Cressey, *Principles of Criminology* (7th ed.; Philadelphia: Lippincott, 1966), pp. 83–98.

[49] F. Ivan Nye, *Family Relationships and Delinquent Behavior* (New York: Wiley, 1958), p. 47.

[50] John R. Ellingston, *Protecting Our Children from Criminal Careers* (Englewood Cliffs, N.J.: Prentice-Hall, 1948), p. 35.

Visita conyugal: *In some societies the family unit is maintained even if the father is imprisoned. Mexican prisons permit intimate association between inmates and their families.*

Only 22 percent of a group of the rural boys in a correctional institution were known to be members of delinquent gangs, while 87 percent of the urban boys were members of such gangs.[51]

Groups and corrections The study of gangs and delinquent subcultures (see CULTURE, p. 71) has shown that to a large extent delinquency is a group phenomenon. The delinquent pattern is learned in social interaction and is supported by the satisfactions and pressures of peer-group relations. On the basis of these conclusions, some efforts have been made to design programs for the correction of delinquency that build upon the peer group.

One such experiment has been carried out in Provo, Utah.[52] In the Provo program a group of twenty "habitual offenders" are assigned by the juvenile court to a daytime treatment center instead of being placed on probation or sent to the reformatory. The boys are thus under the control of the court and their participation in the program is mandatory. A unique feature of the program is the deliberate creation of powerful peer groups among the boys.

Attempts to involve a boy with the peer group begin the moment he arrives. Instead of meeting with and receiving an orientation lecture from authorities, he receives no formal instructions. . . . Adults will not orient him in ways that he has grown to expect, nor will they answer any of his questions. He is forced to turn to his peers.[53]

The group is given a great deal of power. Daily group discussions are the core of the program in its first phase, supplemented by work in the community. The group is free to exercise strong pressure on the individual; it has a say in deciding when a boy should be released; it participates actively with the staff in solving problems and exercising controls. In the discussions the boys' values and attitudes are subjected to severe testing. Since the focus is on self-revelation and problem-solving, the tendency of the group is to move itself and the boy toward greater realism about the outcome of continued delinquency.

Programs of this kind are still in their infancy,

---

[51] William P. Lentz, "Rural-Urban Differences in Juvenile Delinquency," *Journal of Criminal Law, Criminology and Police Science, 47* (September–October, 1956), 331–339.

[52] See LaMar T. Empey and Jerome Rabow, "The Provo Experiment in Delinquency Rehabilitation," *American Sociological Review, 26* (October, 1961), 679–695; also LaMar T. Empey, *Alternatives to Incarceration* (Washington, D.C.: Office of Juvenile Delinquency and Youth Development, U.S. Dept. of Health, Education, and Welfare, 1967), pp. 37 ff.

[53] Empey and Rabow, *op. cit.,* p. 686.

but some success is claimed.[54] They represent a radical departure from the traditional approach of corrections, which has emphasized the need to protect authority by espousing the norm of "doing your own time" and isolating the prisoner from sustained group interaction.[55]

[54] See Empey, *op. cit.* (1967), p. 39.

[55] Richard A. Cloward, "Social Control in the Prison," in Richard A. Cloward, *et al., Theoretical Studies in Social Organization of the Prison* (New York: Social Science Research Council, 1960), pp. 24 f.

SECTION 6 SOCIAL STRATIFICATION*

In a highly stratified society, where the principle of fixed status prevails, "equality before the law" is unlikely to be recognized. The privileged classes are such in law as well as in fact. Thus Blackstone, writing of the "incidents of nobility," said:

A peer, or peeress (either in her own right or by marriage) cannot be arrested in civil cases. . . . A peer, sitting in judgment, gives not his verdict upon oath, like an ordinary juryman, but upon his honor; but, when he is examined as a witness . . . he must be sworn: . . . The honor of peers is, however, so highly tendered by the law, that it is much more penal to spread false reports of them and certain other great officers of the realm, than of other men: . . .[56]

A "peer of the realm" shared in the king's sovereignty, and a jury of his peers would be composed of other noblemen.

The movement toward legal equality began with the demand that those equal in status be treated as such before the law; the barons demanded of the king that he grant *them* the benefits of the rule of law. There followed a progressive expansion of those entitled to such benefits and in democratic societies the community of legal equals came to include all "citizens," and ultimately all "persons."[57]

THE BIAS OF THE LAW

Historically, the law has been mainly concerned with upholding constituted authority, controlling disorder and crime, and protecting property. In the settlement of private disputes, property rights have had priority, for to a large extent the law was made by "haves" to protect themselves against the "have-nots." In addition, a regard for property rights simplified the task of the courts: they could limit cases to matters fairly easy to prove, and they could offer remedies for tangible losses.

Favored parties The weak legal position of those who have little money and no property is manifest in the landlord-tenant relationship.[58] The law protects the property owner and ensures that rents will be paid. In most cases the tenant is obliged to continue paying rent even when the premises are not kept in good repair. If he refuses to pay, he may be evicted. The practice of withholding rents to enforce tenants' rights against landlords, especially in urban slums, has been initiated in some cities in recent years; and a few states have enacted repair-and-deduct laws, which allow the tenant to make repairs himself and

* This section is based in part on materials prepared by Elliott Currie and Jerrold Guben.

[56] William Blackstone, *Commentaries on the Laws of England,* edited by William Carey Jones (San Francisco: Bancroft-Whitney Co., 1915), vol. 1, pp. 557 f. First published in four volumes, 1765–1769.

[57] On the extension of citizenship see Reinhard Bendix, *Nation-Building and Citizenship* (New York: Wiley, 1964), Chap. 3; also T. H. Marshall, *Class, Citizenship, and Social Development* (Garden City, N.Y.: Doubleday, 1964), Chap. 4.

[58] See Jerome E. Carlin, Jan Howard, and Sheldon L. Messinger, "Civil Justice and the Poor: Issues for Sociological Research," *Law and Society Review, 1* (November, 1966), 13–15.

deduct the cost from the rent. However, these changes are new and limited. The law's historic preference for the landlord remains largely intact.

The law also protects creditors more than debtors. It is assumed that the man who borrowed money or otherwise went into debt did so voluntarily and with full understanding of what he was doing. The emphasis of the law is on holding people to the obligations they have contracted. Although usury statutes impose limits on the amount of interest that can be charged, these restrictions are inadequate as protections of the consumer, and the law is framed to ensure that the lender or installment seller gets his due.

Welfare law Recent studies of law and poverty have revealed many areas in which the poor face legal discrimination.[59] An example is the recipient of welfare benefits who becomes defined as a public dependent. Once that status is entered, special legal disabilities accrue. For example, in some states rules affecting "relatives' responsibility" may require children to contribute to their parents' support. While the rule applies to anyone who accepts public assistance rather than to the poor as such, in fact most welfare clients have little choice; poverty creates the dependency and therefore makes the poor subject to special legal rules.[60]

DIFFERENTIAL ADMINISTRATION

Formal discrimination, built into the legal rules themselves, is only a part of legal inequality. More important for most people is the way law is administered and experienced. The rich and the poor have very different encounters with law-enforcement agencies and legal personnel. To the poor man and his family,

the law appears in the guise of a policeman, truant officer, social worker, or bill collector. The rich man hires a lawyer to protect or increase property. The poor trade cheap time for scarce money and accept jail sentences in lieu of fines. The rich pay fines in lieu of jail terms. For one, the law is largely punitive; for the other it may be mostly opportunity and protection.

Police practice There is abundant evidence that in the United States the poor and racial minorities are more likely·than middle-class whites to be arrested and to be treated with disrespect or worse. The U.S. Commission on Civil Rights found that police are frequently distrustful of and prejudiced toward Negroes.[61] A study of police encounters with juveniles found that differences in arrest rates between Negro and white youths are in part due to the fact that Negroes more often displayed a demeanor disapproved of by the police. An uncooperative youth was more likely to be arrested—and more Negroes than whites were uncooperative.[62]

Police practices probably produce some "secondary deviance" (see p. 401), and thus inflate the rates of crime and delinquency among the minority poor compared to middle-class whites. However, it is not known how much of this occurs.

A balanced judgment would seem to be that, while there is indeed unreported delinquency and slower resort to official police and court sanctions in middle-class areas than in the central sectors of our cities, there is also an absolute difference in the amount and types of crimes committed in each area. In short, the vast differences represented in official statistics cannot be explained by differential police or court action toward children of varying backgrounds. There are, in fact, real differences leading to more frequent as-

---

[59] See "Symposium: Law of the Poor," *California Law Review, 54* (May, 1966), also published as Jacobus ten Broek and Editors of the *California Law Review* (eds.), *The Law of the Poor* (San Francisco: Chandler Publishing, 1966).

[60] On welfare and its significance for family law see Jacobus ten Broek, "California's Dual System of Family Law: Its Origins, Development, and Present Status," *Stanford Law Review, 16* (March, 1964), 257–317; *16* (July, 1964), 900–981; *17* (April, 1965), 614–682.

[61] U.S. Commission on Civil Rights, *Justice* (Washington, D.C., 1961), pp. 24–25; see also The President's Commission on Law Enforcement and Administration of Justice, *Task Force Report: The Police* (Washington, D.C., 1967), pp. 178–186.

[62] Irving Piliavin and Scott Briar, "Police Encounters with Juveniles," *American Journal of Sociology, 70* (September, 1964), 213.

saults, thefts, and breaking and entering offenses in lower socioeconomic areas of our urban centers.[63]

Bail v. jail A high proportion of defendants are unable to make bail, which is scaled to the crime rather than ability to pay. Defendants able to raise money quickly can often secure immediate release. Those who cannot pay will be detained or must depend on a bail bondsman.

The bondsman sells a service for profit. For a fee (a premium) he gives surety that the defendant will appear in court when called. A poor defendant may seem a poor risk to the bondsman, if he has no property to pledge and is unable to pay the premium in cash.

A defendant detained in jail is hindered in preparing his case and locating witnesses; he cannot take advantage of postponements, with the possibilities of attrition of the case against him. In a Philadelphia study of 946 cases, 82 percent of those who were in jail while awaiting trial were convicted, but only 52 percent of those out on bail were convicted. Of those convicted, the percentages who received prison sentences were 59 and 22 respectively.[64] Bail, therefore, appears to make a significant difference in the administration of justice. And failure to make bail, which is largely a function of poverty, removes the poor person from the labor market, confirms his poverty, and lessens the chances of accumulating the funds to aid in his defense.

As a result of such findings a movement for bail reform has developed, initiated by a private foundation, the Vera Institute of Justice. In 1964, the Attorney General of the U.S. sponsored a National Conference on Bail and Criminal Justice, which underscored the inefficiency and unfairness of the system. Bail practices have been changed in about 100 communities.[65] The new procedure is based on an assessment of the risk of flight, rather than on the nature of the alleged offense. The arrested person is interviewed and his background is investigated. If he is evaluated as a good risk, on the basis of his employment history and family relations, release without bail is recommended. While defendants who are poor risks might still receive unequal treatment, at least the criteria are more realistic and the procedures more flexible. The Federal Bail Reform Act of 1966 follows the new approach. The Act, which applies to federal, not state courts, "diminishes reliance on money bail and allows imposition of conditions commensurate with the risks presented."[66]

THE RIGHT TO COUNSEL

As was noted in Section 2 (p. 388), adequate legal representation is a virtual necessity in an adversary system of justice. It is widely recognized that "reliance upon the judge or prosecutor to protect the interests of defendants is an inadequate substitute for the advocacy of conscientious defense counsel."[67]

Familiarity with legal rules and procedures is only a part of the lawyer's contribution. He can also help the defendant organize his thoughts, bring out the facts that may help him, and stiffen his morale, especially his capacity to resist official intimidation. In that sense, the opportunity to have an attorney is probably also of value in systems of criminal justice not governed by the adversary principle.

The Sixth Amendment to the U.S. Constitution says that "in all criminal prosecutions, the accused shall enjoy the right . . . to have the Assistance of Counsel for his defense." However, the Supreme Court held in 1833 that the first ten amendments (the Bill of Rights) applied only to the federal government, not to the states. (Note that the First Amendment says *Congress* shall make no law respecting an

[63] Stanton Wheeler and Leonard S. Cottrell, *Juvenile Delinquency—Its Prevention and Control* (New York: Russell Sage Foundation, 1966), pp. 12–13.

[64] Patricia Wald and Daniel J. Freed, *Bail in the United States, 1964* (Washington, D.C.: Vera Foundation, 1964), pp. 15–19, 26–33, 46–48.

[65] The President's Commission on Law Enforcement and Administration of Justice, *Task Force Report: The Courts* (Washington, D.C., 1967), p. 38.

[66] *Ibid.,* p. 39.

[67] *Ibid.,* p. 52.

establishment of religion, etc.) The principles, though not all the specific provisions, of the Bill of Rights have been applied to the states under the authority of the Fourteenth Amendment, adopted after the Civil War, which says that no state shall "deprive any person of life, liberty, or property without due process of law; nor deny to any person within its jurisdiction the equal protection of the laws." The right to counsel has been interpreted by the Supreme Court as part of both "due process" and "equal protection." The principle of equal protection was applied in a 1956 case,[68] in which a defendant could not appeal to a higher state court because he did not have the money to pay for the necessary transcript of his trial record. It was apparent that differential treatment of the rich and the poor was a decisive issue in the case.

The abstract phrases of the Constitution do not settle how far the principle of right to counsel should be pressed. For example, narrowly interpreted, the right might mean only that the defendant must be *allowed* to have a lawyer, not that he must be provided with one if he cannot afford to hire his own. There is also a question whether the right applies only to what happens in the trial court, or also to what happens in the police station or at other stages of the case.

In 1932, in the famous Scottsboro Boys case, the Supreme Court ruled that the State of Alabama had the duty to assign counsel in the special circumstances of that case, which involved capital punishment. A "special circumstances" rule applied until 1963, when for the first time it was laid down that counsel must be provided in all criminal cases, at least where the offense is a felony.[69] The Court has also recognized a right to counsel, not only at the trial stage, but also at earlier stages, and at the time of appeal.

TABLE XII:2   TYPE OF COUNSEL BY FINAL DISPOSITION, NEGRO INMATES

FINAL DISPOSITION	COURT-APPOINTED COUNSEL		PRIVATE COUNSEL	
	N	%	N	%
Executed	93	91.2	9	69.2
Commuted	9	8.8	4	30.8
Total	102	100.0	13	100.0

SOURCE: Marvin E. Wolfgang, Arlene Kelly, and Hans C. Nolde, "Comparison of the Executed and the Commuted Among Admissions to Death Row," *Journal of Criminal Law, Criminology, and Police Science, 53* (September, 1962), 309.

The availability of counsel, and the type of counsel, may literally mean the difference between life and death. Table XII:2 reports on executions and commutations of Negro death-row inmates in Pennsylvania for the period 1914–1948. Although the numbers involved are small, the findings are suggestive. In the most serious cases the availability of adequate counsel may critically influence the fate of the defendant, overshadowing other disadvantages that may arise from poverty or race. Other studies have shown that guilty pleas are more frequent when the defendant is represented by a lawyer assigned by the court rather than by his own lawyer.[70] Private attorneys apparently are more successful in securing dismissals before trial and enter fewer guilty pleas.[71]

[68] *Griffin* v. *Illinois,* 351 U.S. 12 (1956).

[69] *Gideon* v. *Wainright,* 372 U.S. 335 (1963). For an extensive account of this case and its background, see Anthony Lewis, *Gideon's Trumpet* (New York: Random House, 1964).

[70] Lee Silverstein, *Defense of the Poor* (Chicago: American Bar Foundation, 1965), p. 22.

[71] Dallin H. Oaks and Warren Lehman, "Lawyers for the Poor," *Trans-action, 4* (July/August, 1967), 25–29; see also Edwin M. Lemert, "Juvenile Justice—Quest and Reality," *Trans-action, 4* (July/August, 1967), 40.

SECTION 7 ASSOCIATIONS*

Organizations participate in the legal order in three basic ways:

1. As *agencies* of state law. In a developed legal system, justice is administered through a complex array of organizations: police, courts, public prosecutors, public defenders, prisons, parole agencies—to mention only the most obvious examples. In addition, many specialized laws, such as those affecting commerce or labor relations, are administered by agencies that investigate complaints, enforce compliance, and often exercise quasi-judicial powers. The characteristics of the agency determine, to a large extent, what the law is in practice and what, if anything, it can accomplish.

Prisons are the legal agencies that have been most studied by sociologists.[72] These studies have emphasized the conflicting goals of prison management and the difficulty of using prisons for rehabilitation of offenders. Less attention has been given to the police and other agencies, until recently.[73]

2. As *subjects* of legal regulation. Important branches of the law, especially the law of corporations and labor law, specify the powers and duties of private associations.[74] Constitutional law is also relevant, because of the relation between free speech and freedom of association. One of the connections between law and sociology is the need of law to have a correct assessment of the social nature of corporations, trade unions, colleges, and other associations.

3. As relatively autonomous *private* legal systems. It was noted above (p. 382) that large organizations develop their own rules and decision-making procedures, affecting the rights of both members and nonmembers. This phenomenon, sometimes called "private government," is manifest in industry, education, professional associations, and churches. Rule-making by these organizations may have more significance for the life of the employee and his family, or for the student, than many of the actions of public government.[75]

This section discusses one aspect of law and associations—how important assumptions of the system of criminal justice are affected by the realities of administrative decision-making.

ADMINISTRATIVE JUSTICE

The model of a trial by judge and jury dominates the popular image of criminal justice. In fact, how-

---

* In collaboration with Jerome H. Skolnick.

[72] See Donald R. Cressey (ed.), *The Prison: Studies in Institutional Organization and Change* (New York: Holt, Rinehart and Winston, 1961); David Street, Robert D. Vinter, and Charles Perrow, *Organization for Treatment* (New York: The Free Press of Glencoe, 1966); Daniel Glaser, *The Effectiveness of a Prison and Parole System* (Indianapolis: Bobbs-Merrill, 1964); Elliot Studt, Sheldon L. Messinger, and Thomas P. Wilson, *C-Unit: Search for Community in Prison* (New York: Russell Sage Foundation, 1968).

[73] See David J. Bordua (ed.), *The Police* (New York: Wiley, 1967); Michael Banton, *The Policeman in the Community* (New York: Basic Books, 1965); Wayne R. LaFave, *Arrest: The Decision to Take a Suspect into Custody* (Boston: Little, Brown, 1965); Jerome H. Skolnick, *Justice Without Trial* (New York: Wiley, 1966).

[74] See Edward S. Mason (ed.), *The Corporation in Modern Society* (Cambridge: Harvard University Press, 1959); W. Friedmann, *Law in a Changing Society* (Berkeley and Los Angeles: University of California Press, 1959), Chaps. 9, 10.

[75] Eugen Ehrlich, one of the founders of the sociology of law, paid close attention to the "inner order" of associations. See his *Fundamental Principles of the Sociology of Law* (Cambridge: Harvard University Press, 1936), Chaps. 2, 3; also Charles E. Merriam, *Public and Private Government* (New Haven: Yale University Press, 1944); Corinne Lathrop Gilb, *Hidden Hierarchies: The Professions and Government* (New York: Harper & Row, 1966); William M. Evan, "Public and Private Legal Systems," in William M. Evan (ed.), *Law and Sociology* (New York: The Free Press of Glencoe, 1962), pp. 165–184.

ever, most cases do not come to trial. The police or the district attorney's office may decide not to press a charge, or the defendant may plead guilty.

In many communities between one-third and one-half of the cases begun by arrest are disposed of by some form of dismissal by police, prosecutor, or judge. When a decision is made to prosecute, it is estimated that in many courts as many as 90 percent of all convictions are obtained by guilty pleas.[76]

The system is operated by *informal* magistrates who weigh evidence, interpret laws, and make most of the decisions. When a policeman decides to arrest a suspect, or not to do so, he makes a complex judgment about the facts of a specific case, including what the person intended by his action and what might be the outcome of an arrest. The officer may decide that the apparent offender ought not be punished because the law was not meant to be applied to him. For example, a statute forbidding card-playing for money may be unenforced against "social" gambling if the police do not believe the legislature intended the law to apply to such cases. Often a law includes a broad definition of the offense in order to avoid loopholes; the police and prosecutors are expected to use discretion and enforce the law in the light of its "true" objectives.[77]

The exercise of discretion by law-enforcement officers, from the patrolman to the district attorney or sheriff, gives rise to an administrative system of criminal justice. The system is administrative because (1) the officers have tasks to perform and objectives to achieve—they are not passive dispensers of fairness; and (2) the officers belong to organizations that have internal problems and are subject to external pressures. Thus men who decide the fate of other men do so, not as fully independent judges, but as officials who must keep organizational needs in mind.

Presumption of innocence   When a police officer makes an arrest, he usually assumes that the man is guilty; otherwise he would not arrest him. The of-

ficer's assumption tends to be accepted by the other officials in the system. Within an administrative setting, it is natural to conclude that mistakes are unusual and that officials do not act without sufficient reason. This is called the presumption of administrative regularity and in the present situation leads to a *de facto* presumption of guilt. The advantages enjoyed by the accused from a legal presumption of innocence are reduced and administrative officials, rather than the accused, are given the benefit of the doubt. The burden of proof tends to shift to the suspect, it becomes more difficult for him to maintain a posture of innocence, and his right to remain silent may appear obstructive. The handling of traffic offenses is the clearest example of the erosion of the presumption of innocence in an administratively oriented system, but that erosion must be expected wherever the investigators and accusers also act as judges.

Plea bargaining   In the consideration of serious criminal charges, usually called felonies, an administrative orientation results in "plea bargaining." The plea of guilty is negotiated, usually by the prosecutor and defense attorney. The outcome is an agreement under which the accused will plead guilty in exchange for a reduced charge or a favorable sentence to be recommended by the prosecutor to the judge. Even when there have been no explicit negotiations, defendants relying on prevailing practices often act on the assumption that a guilty plea will be followed by a more lenient sentence.

From the standpoint of the courts, the plea of guilty is a matter of urgent economy. "There are simply not enough judges, prosecutors, or defense counsel to operate a system in which most defendants go to trial."[78] In partial justification for giving a heavier sentence to one of five defendants who refused to plead guilty, a federal judge wrote, in a 1960 opinion:

[I]f in one year, 249 judges are to deal with 35,517 defendants, the district courts must encourage pleas

[76] President's Commission, *Task Force Report: The Courts, op. cit.,* p. 4.

[77] See LaFave, *op. cit.,* pp. 89 ff.

[78] President's Commission, *Task Force Report: The Courts, op. cit.,* p. 10.

of guilty. One way to encourage pleas of guilty is to establish or announce a policy that, in the ordinary case, leniency will not be granted to a defendant who stands trial.[79]

One aspect of the negotiated plea of guilty that has received attention is its possible effect on the role of the defense attorney.[80] When most cases are subject to negotiation, and the issue is the size of the penalty rather than guilt or innocence, there is a tendency for defense lawyers to "cooperate" with the prosecutor by avoiding zealous or "obstructive" defense tactics. The prosecutor is more amenable when he is not forced to meet every possible challenge or the costs of every possible delay. A cooperative attitude on the part of the defense attorney is further encouraged when his client is not an isolated case but is part of a case load which the attorney must learn to manage efficiently.

Plea bargaining tends to win over the defense lawyer to the idea that the defendant is probably guilty of something. As a result, the defense may not take seriously the possibility of pressing for acquittal. This pattern probably prevails in the *routine* case, and may well benefit most defendants. It is not known, however, to what extent attorneys become insensitive to the nonroutine case in which the interests of justice, and of the client, would be best served by standing fast on a plea of innocence.

There is always the danger that a defendant who would be found not guilty if he insisted on his right to trial will be induced to plead guilty. The defendant has an absolute right to put the prosecution to its proof, and if too much pressure is brought to discourage the exercise of this right, the integrity of the system, which the court trial is relied on to vindicate, will not be demonstrated. When the prosecution is not put to its proof and all the evidence is not brought out in open court, the public is not assured that illegalities in law enforcement are revealed and corrected or that the seriousness of the defendant's

crimes are shown and adequate punishment imposed. Prosecutors who are overburdened or are insufficiently energetic may compromise cases that call for severe sanctions.[81]

Visibility Perhaps the major weakness of administrative justice is the relative *invisibility* of decisions. In principle, legal decisions affecting the rights of persons are formal and public, therefore subject to scrutiny, criticism, and control. When such decisions become part of administrative routines, such as patrolling an area, investigating complaints, or negotiating with defense counsel, they tend to be obscured, sometimes deliberately so. For example, a defendant may be asked specifically by the judge whether his guilty plea was made voluntarily and without inducements, yet there was inducement and even the judge may know it. Because of this hidden character, the process of plea bargaining is not subject to formal review and assessment. Invisible decision-making offers opportunity for bias, corruption, or simply random effects.

Yet administrative justice is inevitable, for no system of social control can operate without the exercise of judgment and discretion at all levels. The apparent answer is not to eliminate discretion—or the role of informal magistrate—but to make it more visible and more responsible. The presence of counsel at all stages can help increase both visibility and responsibility. In addition, such processes as plea bargaining can be made subject to greater control by formalizing the agreement to plead guilty, reducing it to writing and thus making it subject to scrutiny. This would require explicit recognition that inducements to plead guilty have a proper and controllable place within the system of criminal justice. Such a development would not be strange to legal history, which has often followed a pattern of formalizing hitherto informal procedures.

---

[79] Quoted in Skolnick, *op. cit.,* p. 13.

[80] See Jerome H. Skolnick, "Social Control in the Adversary System," *The Journal of Conflict Resolution, 11* (March, 1967), 52–70; Abraham S. Blumberg, "The Practice of Law as a Confidence Game," *Law and Society Review, 1* (June, 1967), 15–40; David Sudnow, "Normal Crimes," *Social Problems, 12* (Winter, 1965), 255–276.

[81] President's Commission, *Task Force Report: The Courts, op. cit.,* p. 10.

THE OFFICIAL PERSPECTIVE

The discussion of administrative justice suggests that in the legal order, as elsewhere, there is a persistent conflict between the needs of *systems* and the needs of *persons,* between institutional ideals and institutional realities. Legal agencies are "going concerns," and they are prone to give the system the benefit of the doubt, assigning a high priority to its stability and survival. Viewed from the official perspective (or the system perspective) the end of law is to uphold authority and order rather than to enhance rights and achieve full civic participation. In the official perspec-

tive "one assesses the factors of freedom and security from the standpoint of the official processors of government." [82] Almost invariably freedom comes off second-best.

The sociological study of legal agencies, such as the police or prisons, is largely devoted to showing how administrative needs gain priority over other values, such as the right to protest or the humane treatment of prisoners. This approach should be compared with the discussion of Michels (ASSOCIATIONS, p. 218) and of the Methodist Church (RELIGION, p. 327). Both studies explore the official or system perspective in other contexts.

[82] Edmond Cahn, "Law in the Consumer Perspective," *University of Pennsylvania Law Review, 112* (November, 1963), 5.

SECTION 8 COLLECTIVE BEHAVIOR

As the product of relatively unstructured and even chaotic events, collective behavior is bound to be a source of trouble for the legal order. Law rests on consensus and trust, yet collective action may challenge consensus and undermine trust. Collective excitement is often not compatible with respect for orderly process and constituted authority; hence it sometimes poses a serious challenge to government by law.

CIVIL DISORDER AND FREEDOM OF EXPRESSION

The dilemma of law is acute when free public expression must be weighed against the public interest in peace and safety. To balance these values the law must assess the dynamics of protest, the community structure, and the alternatives open to agencies of social control. Resolution of the dilemma hinges on the

understanding that expectations regarding public order are socially defined.[83] For example, disputes between employers and employees were at one time considered serious threats to public order, but later were accepted as normal conflicts of interest. In the nineteenth century, and the early decades of the twentieth, many courts ruled that picketing by trade union members was inherently unpeaceful:

There is and can be no such thing as peaceful picketing, any more than there can be chaste vulgarity, or peaceful mobbing, or lawful lynching. When men want to converse or persuade they do not organize a picket line.[84]

Laws banning picketing were in effect in some American jurisdictions until 1940, when the Supreme Court decided that picketing was a form of speech protected by the First Amendment.[85] In this and later decisions the Court enlarged the meaning of speech to

[83] See Allan Silver, "The Demand for Order in Civil Society: A Review of Some Themes in the History of Urban Crime, Police, and Riot," in David J. Bordua (ed.), *The Police* (New York: Wiley, 1967), pp. 1–24.

[84] From the opinion of a federal circuit court, 1905, quoted in Joseph Tanenhaus, "Picketing as a Tort: The Development of the Law of Picketing from 1880 to 1940," *University of Pittsburgh Law Review, 14* (1953), 188.

[85] *Thornhill* v. *Alabama,* 310 U.S. 88 (1940).

Caryl Chessman was executed in the gas chamber at San Quentin Prison, California, on May 2, 1960. A prolonged sequence of legal delays postponed the death penalty for almost twelve years. Because of the protracted legal maneuvering, world attention was drawn to the case, and he became a symbol of opposition to capital punishment. Ironically, the availability of due process made the legal system vulnerable to attack. Due process carried to an extreme was itself conceived as a punishment even though it was Chessman who pursued the series of court actions that delayed the execution.

include demonstrative acts of public expression. It thereby changed the standard of acceptable risks to public order.

Speech and direct action Many participants in public life draw no distinction between speech and action. To speak is to advocate and to advocate is to initiate action. Moreover, "action" is not necessarily confined to established and routine channels. "Direct action" bypasses the expected ways and seeks a stark, often personal confrontation with established authority or "the system." One form of direct action is terrorism—the use of physical intimidation and even assassination. Another form, notable especially in the Indian struggle for independence (see POLITICAL MAN, p. 505), and in the civil rights movement, has exploited the nonviolent *symbolic deed* as a tactic for the mobilization of support and for the initiation of new forms of public dialogue.[86]

From about 1955 to 1965 nonviolent direct action —sit-ins, boycotts, and marches—characterized the Negro civil rights movement. These actions followed a great legal victory—the Supreme Court's 1954 decision declaring segregation in public schools unconstitutional—but they expressed frustration with the normal political process. The Negro militants carried their struggle to the streets. Although they did so in a disciplined manner, insisting on self-restraint and nonviolence, their actions inevitably produced many tense encounters with the police.

Direct action in the civil rights movement was meant to be a particular form of public expression. Its objectives were (1) to demonstrate, through dramatic self-sacrificing, attention-getting action, the strength of the participants and the depth of their moral commitment; (2) to focus the white community's attention on continuing racial prejudice and discrimination; (3) to communicate to the mass of quiescent Negroes that the time had come to join an all-out struggle; (4) to demand of the local white community that its leaders listen to and negotiate with the black leadership.

These objectives show how public expression depends on the historical role of the action group, the nature of the constituency it seeks to mobilize, and the interests it opposes. The civil rights movement made clear that in some contexts at least, the expression of deeply felt commitments and the effort to win support must be expected to call upon the forms and resources of collective excitement. Earlier in the century, the labor movement and the movement for women's suffrage had offered the same lesson, though in less self-conscious ways.

Demonstrations and the law The communication of ideas by overt acts, even in a context of potential disorder, has been protected in Supreme Court decisions. In 1949 the Court said that speech "may indeed best serve its high purpose when it induces a condition of unrest, creates dissatisfaction with conditions as they are, or even stirs people to anger."[87] In order for the larger community to discharge its civic responsibilities, it needs to be aware of the grievances of minorities. And overt demonstrations may be the only means available to groups that do not otherwise have ready access to the means of communication and to the society at large.

The legitimacy of demonstrations is legally recognized, but only if other interests are safeguarded. The courts do not condone violence, intolerable burdens on traffic or the safety of the streets, or unjustified interference with private property. In the protection of these interests, modern legal doctrine holds that judgment be *contextual,* taking account of concrete circumstances, and the importance of free public expression. Thus what is a noisy demonstration depends on the setting; words that may be incitement to riot for one audience may be protected before another. While violence is against the law, it does not follow that any act of violence justifies forcibly dispersing

---

[86] See Mulford Q. Sibley, "Direct Action and the Struggle for Integration," *The Hastings Law Journal, 16* (February, 1965), 351–400.

[87] See "Regulation of Demonstrations," *Harvard Law Review, 80* (June, 1967), 1773–1788. Quotation at p. 1774, from *Terminiello* v. *Chicago,* 337 U.S. 1, 4 (1949).

a crowd of demonstrators. The police have the duty of crowd *control* as distinguished from crowd destruction; they are not permitted to leap to the conclusion that the crowd is uncontrollable and therefore that they are free to act repressively.

Similarly, "obstruction of traffic" cannot lawfully be used as an excuse for banning all demonstrations. Traffic regulation must be reasonable and take account of the alternatives available to the demonstrators. Demonstrators are entitled to seek access to large numbers of the public, preferably by making arrangements that do not excessively burden normal activities. The public, however, can be asked to bear some inconvenience in the interests of free speech.

The protection of private property is not absolute. The Supreme Court upheld the right of civil rights demonstrators to trespass on private property when they were demanding equal service from a business that discriminated against Negroes. The Court relied on the Civil Rights Act of 1964, which forbade discrimination by places of public accommodation. Under current principles the Court would probably protect the right to demonstrate on private property used to serve the public if there were some connection between the business and the protest, for example, consumers protesting food prices at a supermarket.[88]

Caution The above discussion of the law of demonstrations reports the trend and some of the reasoning of judicial decisions, especially of the Supreme Court. But the Court's decisions may have only a limited effect on the day-to-day conduct of the police or of other officials who regulate demonstrations.

[88] See *ibid.,* p. 1779.

SECTION 9 POPULATION AND ECOLOGY

THE AMOUNT OF CRIME

Official statistics about crime and criminals only estimate the amount of crime at any time, and they are almost useless for determining trends. A large proportion of crimes are undetected; others are detected but not reported; and others are reported to the police but not officially recorded. Since unrecorded crimes do not appear in the statistics, such official publications as the *Uniform Crime Reports* (UCR) issued by the Federal Bureau of Investigation can only approximate the true crime rate.

The course of events following a crime is summarized in Figure XII:2, which is based on a national sample survey. The process of erosion is divided into six stages in the figure:

1) Given a "real" victimization, the police were or were not notified. [Of the 2,077 instances in which individuals reported that they had been victims of a crime, only half notified the police.]

2) Once notified, the police came to the scene of the victimization or in some way acknowledged the event—or not.

3) Once they came, the police did or did not regard the incident as a crime.

4) Regarding the matter as a crime, the police made an arrest or not.

5) Once an arrest was made, there was a trial (including plea of guilty) or not.

6) The outcome of the trial was to free the suspect or punish him "too leniently" or to find him guilty and give him the proper punishment.[89]

Official records are therefore derived from the third stage in the attrition process. These crimes reported to the police and recorded by them are called "crimes known to the police." Such information as

[89] Philip H. Ennis (National Opinion Research Center), *Criminal Victimization in the United States: A Report of a National Survey* (Washington, D.C., 1967), p. 48.

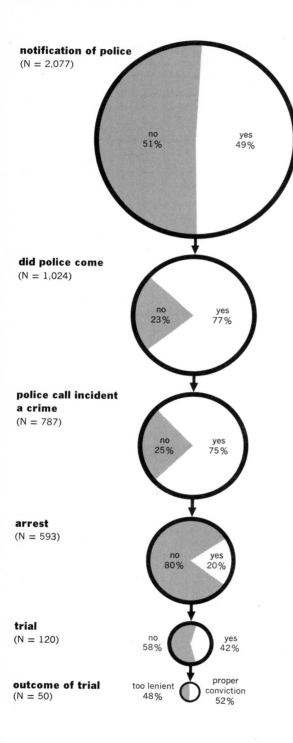

notification of police
(N = 2,077)

no
51%

yes
49%

did police come
(N = 1,024)

no
23%

yes
77%

**police call incident
a crime**
(N = 787)

no
25%

yes
75%

arrest
(N = 593)

no
80%

yes
20%

trial
(N = 120)

no
58%

yes
42%

outcome of trial
(N = 50)

too lenient
48%

proper
conviction
52%

published in the *Uniform Crime Reports* is the best *official* index of crimes committed because it is the one "closest" to the crimes. The more remote an indicator is from the crime, the greater are the number of procedures that may distort the index. Therefore crimes known to the police are better indicators than arrest statistics, which are better than court statistics, which are better than prison statistics for measuring the amount of crime.

However, not all crimes known to the police appear in the UCR because reporting to the FBI by local enforcement agencies is voluntary. Even as late as 1965, 8 percent of the population lived in areas in which police did not report to the Bureau.

A study of victims   To secure an estimate of the amount of serious crime that would not suffer from the limitations of official statistics, a survey was conducted in the summer of 1966. Interviews were done in a national sample of 10,000 households to identify those individuals who had been victims of crimes during the preceding 12 months. The survey focused on crimes of violence and property against individuals, excluding crimes against corporations and other institutions. Interviewed individuals reported for other members of the household as well as for themselves, and there is evidence of loss of data on that account. Furthermore, the survey method did not attempt to identify criminal activity in which the individual himself might be implicated. As the preliminary report put it, "People are simply not going to report their participation in illegal activities. . . . Nor is it desirable for the survey method to be used as an instrument of confession." [90] Despite limitations and qualifications that may reduce the figures, the survey found twice as much serious crime as was reported by

[90] Ennis, *op. cit.,* p. 3.

FIG. XII:2   Attrition in the legal process

SOURCE: Philip H. Ennis, *Criminal Victimization in the United States: A Report of a National Survey* (Chicago: National Opinion Research Center, 1967), reproduced by The President's Commission on Law Enforcement and Administration of Justice. See also Philip H. Ennis, "Crime, Victims, and the Police," *Trans-action, 4* (June, 1967), 36–44.

the police to the FBI. Comparison between the survey findings and the UCR figures required a correction to restrict the latter to individual or residential rates, eliminating crimes against organizations and institutions, and this is taken into account in Table XII:3, which compares the two sources on serious crimes expressed as rates per 100,000 of population. Only the rate for motor vehicle theft was lower in the survey than in the UCR. The survey homicide "rate" represented a single homicide and has no statistical merit. All other crimes showed a much higher rate in the survey than in the *Uniform Crime Reports*. Forcible rapes were more than three and one-half times the UCR rate, burglaries three times, aggravated assaults and larcenies ($50 and over) more than double, and robbery 50 percent greater.

Senseless indicators Attempts of government agencies to communicate to the public the amount and seriousness of crime often lead to the use of dramatic devices that deform rather than clarify statistics. One such device is the "crime clock," [91] widely reported in the newspapers, which purports to state how frequently serious crimes occur. For instance, it is said that a murder occurs in the United States every hour. Such information may have the effect of startling the reader but it does not inform him. A correct and interpretable measure of the incidence of crime is annually per 100,000 of population, not how many per minute or hour.

AGE AND SEX RATIOS *

Sex ratios in crime [92]   Compared with females, males have a great excess of crimes in all nations, all communities within nations, all age groups, all periods of history for which we have statistics, and all types of crime except sex-related crimes such as

TABLE XII:3   ESTIMATED RATES OF MAJOR CRIME, UNITED STATES, 1965–1966

CRIME	NORC [a] SAMPLE	UCR [b]
Homicide	3.0	5.1
Forcible rape	42.5	11.6
Robbery	94.0	61.4
Aggravated assault	218.3	106.6
Burglary	949.1	296.6
Larceny ($50+)	606.5	267.4
Vehicle theft	206.2	226.0
Total	2,119.6	974.7

SOURCE: Philip H. Ennis (National Opinion Research Center), *Criminal Victimization in the United States: A Report of a National Survey* (Washington, D.C.: Government Printing Office, 1967), p. 8.

[a] Estimated rate per 100,000 population, 1965–1966. Based on a survey of 10,000 households in continental United States.

[b] Individual or residential rates per 100,000 population, 1965. Crimes against businesses and organizations excluded to allow comparison with survey findings.

prostitution. In 1965 males in the United States were arrested for serious crimes approximately seven times as frequently as females. The male rate was 1,097 per 100,000 of population; for females it was 164. [93]

The sex ratio for apprehended criminals varies with place, time, and age. One study indicated a criminal sex ratio of 350 males per 100 females for Belgium compared with a ratio of approximately 3,000 in Algiers and Tunis. It was concluded that the criminal sex ratios are highest in countries where females are rigidly supervised, and lowest in the countries in which females have the greatest freedom and the closest approximation to equality with males. [94] The ratio is lower in American cities than in small towns,

* This discussion draws upon material written in collaboration with Donald R. Cressey and included in earlier editions of this book.

[91] *Uniform Crime Reports, 1965*, p. 15.

[92] For a discussion of sex ratios see POPULATION AND ECOLOGY, pp. 267–268.

[93] The President's Commission on Law Enforcement and Administration of Justice, *Task Force Report: Crime and Its Impact,* 1967, p. 78.

[94] E. Hacker, *Kriminalstatistische und Kriminalaetiologische Berichte* (Miskolc: Ludwig, 1949).

probably reflecting the differences in the amount of freedom permitted in the two types of communities. In large cities, the criminal sex ratio is lowest in high-delinquency and crime areas and highest in low-delinquency areas. There is evidence that the criminal sex ratio has been decreasing, especially in recent years, as women have acquired statuses more nearly equal to those of men.

The sex ratio indicates the difficulty of relying on "factors" which traditionally have been considered the causes of crime. For example, among boys and girls who live in the same homes, in equal poverty, in the same neighborhoods, which are equally lacking in recreational facilities, and with the same alcoholic or ignorant parents, the boys are much more frequently delinquent than are the girls. The significant difference is that girls are supervised more closely than boys and behavior consistent with legal codes is taught to girls with more consistency and care than to boys.[65]

Age ratios in crime Age appears to be closely related, directly or indirectly, to the frequency and type of crime committed. Since the statistics on the incidence of crime by age are ordinarily in the form of arrests or convictions, they probably tend to exaggerate the crime rates of young adults. Older criminals commit crimes which are less likely to be detected than those committed by young adults.

After this bias is taken into account, the statistics seem to justify the following conclusions:

1. The crime rate is highest during or shortly before adolescence. English statistics show that the age of maximum criminality is about age 12 or 13 for males and 16 or 17 for females.[96] FBI statistics place the age of maximum criminality somewhat higher—

between 18 and 24—but the English statistics probably report youthful criminality more completely than do the U.S. figures.

2. The age of maximum criminality varies with the type of crime.[97] Among American males, the age group 15–17 has the highest official rate for burglaries, larcenies, and automobile theft with a rate of 2,467 per 100,000 persons. For crimes of violence the peak years are from 18–24, but for fraud, embezzlement, gambling, and vagrancy, the rates are highest for offenders over 24.

3. The age for maximum general criminality and for most specific offenses is older for females than for males. For example, ages 20–24 have the highest female rate for automobile theft as well as robbery and forgery.

4. The concentration of certain crimes, such as burglary and robbery, in the young adult ages has been observed for several centuries. English statistics indicate that burglars and robbers of the fifteenth and sixteenth centuries were approximately the same age as the contemporary burglar and robber.

5. The crime rate, for both males and females, decreases from the age of maximum criminality to the end of life. In the United States the arrest rate of males decreases after the peak at about age 20, and the rate of females decreases after about age 23. This phenomenon has been observed in many nations.

6. The age of first delinquency and the type of crime typically committed at different ages varies from area to area. In cities, the age of first criminality is younger in areas of high delinquency than in areas with low-delinquency rates; boys aged 10–12 commit robberies in some areas of large cities while boys of the same age in less delinquent areas commit only petty thefts.

---

[65] See Jackson Toby, "The Differential Impact of Family Disorganization," *American Sociological Review, 22* (October, 1957), 505–512.

[96] Sutherland and Cressey, *op. cit.,* p. 134.

[97] President's Commission, *Task Force Report: Crime and Its Impact, loc. cit.*

PART THREE

MASTER TRENDS

CHAPTER XIII
URBAN MAN

SECTION 1 URBANIZATION

In man's history there have been very few changes so drastic and so pervasive in their consequences that they signal true breaks with the past. The emergence of the city is one such break marking a definitive change in man's relation to the physical world and to his fellows.

The concentration of population in villages began during the Neolithic Age, perhaps eight thousand years ago. These first stable communities were farming settlements of a few hundred people. With improvements in agriculture in a friendly environment, some grew substantially larger, but they cannot be called cities because they were composed largely of full-time farmers. Even in the modern period in Africa and Asia there are concentrations that are not true cities but rather settlements of several thousand farmers, almost all of whom regularly till their fields. Population size and food surplus are necessary but not sufficient conditions for urban life.

EARLY CITIES

The first cities were not merely large village dormitories for farm families, but were set off from the countryside and somewhat detached from the soil and the preoccupations of agricultural production. In several different places at different times a fundamentally new social form called the city emerged. The following are some of the modifications in the social order and man's relation to the environment that were involved in the development of the first cities:

1. Increase in occupational specialization
2. Release of a few individuals from immediately productive work and their elevation to a priesthood
3. Transformation of religious activities related to fertility, rainfall, and the streams into the administration of the water supply (the irrigation system) and the management of lands and herds
4. Emergence of a political leadership and organization of the work force
5. Increased differentiation of rewards for more diversified tasks
6. Assignment of some manpower to protect the food supply and the security of the city
7. A market for exchange of goods

The outcome of these changes is vague in detail

but clear in principle: an evergrowing complexity and division of labor, increasing specialization, freeing few and then many men from day-to-day subsistence tasks. The beginnings of urban life, inferred from archaeological findings in Mesopotamia, are described in Adaptation 31, pages 434–437.

The earliest cities in the fertile valleys of the Tigris-Euphrates, the Indus, and the Nile were followed by the growth of the Mediterranean city-states. By 600 or 500 B.C. a few Greek cities were colonizing throughout the Mediterranean, but most Greek cities remained dependent on the immediate countryside for food and building materials. Because the Greek terrain had a limited amount of arable land, even Athens of 400 B.C. probably did not exceed 100,000.[1]

The Mediterranean seaports of the ancient world were centers of government and religion as well as trade, and their growth and decline were tied to the fortunes of political and commercial empires. It is commonly agreed that Rome was the largest city of ancient times, but its population size, like that of other early cities, is conjectural. The Roman census reported an increase from 900,000 in 69 B.C. to more than 4,000,000 in 28 B.C., but it is unlikely that Rome increased four-and-a-half times in forty years. The statistical change may have been due to a number of causes: some increase in population, the inclusion of elements of the population not previously counted (women or children), a rapid extension of citizenship, or counting some population that did not actually reside in the city.[2] In any case the populations of early cities probably fluctuated rather widely, and estimates of their size are based on doubtful data.

As the empires of the ancient world declined, the cities also declined. By the middle of the fourth century A.D. Rome may have had a population of less than 200,000, and by the sixteenth century only

55,000.[3] The latter figure, however, is not a low point. By that time Rome, like other medieval cities, had begun to respond to the growth of the market and the renewal of trade and travel.[4]

The prevalence of cities The development of cities in modern times is an outgrowth not only of an increase in agricultural productivity (which made possible surplus to support an increasing population), but also centralization of work in machine-powered factories. The growth of cities has not been a smooth accumulation. Many cities have declined or disappeared, but urban life is now the characteristic form of human settlement in Europe, Australia, and North America. It is also the emergent form for most of the rest of the world.

Table XIII:1 shows the distribution of large cities in the major world regions. In the past decade the number of cities exceeding 100,000 has increased from less than 900 to more than 1400, and cities in the 1,000,000 and larger class have more than doubled to 121.

Outside Europe and North America, the largest cities tend to be located in coastal areas.[5] The preponderantly coastal location of the major Asian and African cities is indicative of their history and function. In large part they are the outgrowth of commercial and imperial relations with the West. They are administrative centers for government and commerce, and entrepôt (transshipment) centers for handling raw materials and redistributing finished goods. Some are preindustrial in the sense that they are at an early stage of the industrial revolution. However, even the least industrialized organize the economies of surrounding small cities and villages, and are the chief locations of more advanced industrial activity in their respective countries. Through the spread of communication and trade with coastal cities, and stimulated by growing na-

[1] Lewis Mumford, *The City in History* (New York: Harcourt, Brace & World, 1961), pp. 130–131.

[2] Cf. William Petersen, *Population* (New York: Macmillan, 1961), pp. 346–347.

[3] Petersen, *op. cit.,* p. 351.

[4] Henri Pirenne, *Medieval Cities: Their Origin and the Revival of Trade* (Princeton: Princeton University Press, 1925).

[5] Paul K. Hatt and Albert J. Reiss, Jr. (eds.), *Reader in Urban Sociology* (Glencoe: The Free Press, 1951), p. 147.

TABLE XIII:1 CITIES OVER 100,000 POPULATION IN MAJOR WORLD REGIONS, 1960

REGION	1,000,000 AND OVER	500,000 to 1,000,000	250,000 to 500,000	100,000 to 250,000	TOTAL CITIES
Africa	3	9	14	73	99
Asia [a]	42	43	103	297	485
North America	33	19	43	120	215
South America	8	11	20	52	91
Europe	25	32	65	229	351
Oceania	2	3	1	7	13
U.S.S.R.	8	21	41	118	188
TOTAL	121	138	287	896	1442

COMPILED from United Nations *Demographic Yearbook, 1965* (New York, 1966), pp. 140–162.

[a] Excludes U.S.S.R., includes Near East.

tionalism, the internal regions of Asia and Africa are being drawn into the urban world. Man is becoming urban man.

THE ASIAN CITY

The Asian cities in the forefront of change are the product of the interplay between East and West: [6] political, industrial, and commercial interests from the West and manpower, raw materials, handicrafts, and trade interests of the East. Djakarta, Saigon, Manila, Hong Kong and other Asian centers are highly cosmopolitan with a background of colonial administration, organized by Europeans in the eighteenth and nineteenth centuries to tap the resources of the countryside and extend European economic and political control. Around the busy ports, systems of river, canal, and land transport expanded, and these networks of communication created national unity where none existed before. The commercial center was also the colonial administrative center, and the colonial capital was retained as the capital of the new country when the colonial authority withdrew.

In architecture, land use, and life-style, the cities reflect their dual origins. In the commercial quarters of Djakarta, Manila, and Hong Kong are the same kinds of streets, banks, stores, hotels, and office buildings that are found in Holland, the United States, or England. The residential suburbs of the commercial and governmental administrators are also modern and Western. But among the office buildings are small retail shops, many of them run by Chinese or Indians, and scattered through the back alleys are small factories, stalls of marginal enterprise, and itinerant peddlers who have no permanent location. A few steps from the prosperous commercial streets and the European-type residential districts is the Asian slum, a warren teeming with thousands of people, many of them homeless newcomers, who live out their lives on the streets, eating and sleeping on the sidewalks and footpaths.

The administrators of Asian countries are preoccupied with agricultural efficiency, new industry, and education, and have little energy or money left over for the underprivileged urban dwellers. Some countries hope to reverse the trend of urban migration and return some of the population to the country. But this plan runs counter to the worldwide urban trend and does not take into account the magnetic power of the city even in its least attractive

[6] This discussion is indebted to "The Asian City," The University of Sydney, *Current Affairs Bulletin*, Vol. 19, No. 5 (December 24, 1956). The urban centers of Japan and Communist China are not considered here.

form. Nor does the widespread agricultural land shortage leave a choice for many displaced peasants.

Continuing urbanization seems inevitable. But the migration should not be thought of as the aimless drift of human flotsam into the cities. No doubt some migrants have weak social attachments, but many bring with them ties transferable to the new setting. Hong Kong, an extreme example of a commercial city, has elaborate networks of social organization, many of which have ties with mainland China through mechanisms that operated in traditional Chinese cities.[7] Common kinship, common village or regional origin, common occupation, religion, and membership in associations (e.g., the secret societies, now outlawed in Communist China) continue to act as bonds with the homeland. Even the most unfortunate immigrant need not be cast into a situation of total anomie, for there are anti-Communist organizations, Chinese and foreign, ready to extend a welcoming hand. The typical immigrant usually finds a niche somewhere in the web of social relationships where he is protected until he can find productive employment.

URBAN AND RURAL

Although there is agreement that some areas are rural and that others are urban, many localities fall between the obviously urban and the obviously rural. How these localities and their populations are to be classified is important when trends in urbanization are traced or international comparisons are made.

The most commonly used distinctions are population density and size. The city is a locality in which a large number of people live and work in close proximity. The rural area, by contrast, has low population density or only a small number of people in a dense cluster. Sociologists frequently add a third criterion—heterogeneity of the population in age, sex, and occupation. This criterion excludes from the term "city" such settlements as peasant villages, mining camps, prisons, and many military installations.

The ecological city Having selected population density and size as criteria, one must decide at what points to draw the line between city and noncity. The following criteria are widely used by urban sociologists: (1) The *ecological* or *natural* city has a population density great enough so that most of the land is devoted to residential, commercial, and industrial use (including transportation). (2) It is separated from other cities by space (either land or water) devoted largely to agricultural or extractive use or not used at all. (3) This separating space is broad enough to make daily commuting across it impractical for most workers.

The ecological city includes the central *legal* city (which is under a municipal government), its contiguous suburbs, and detached satellite settlements, which are socially and economically integrated with the central city. The U.S. census unit called the "urbanized area" is roughly equal to the ecological city, which is usually larger than the legal city. The larger ecological cities in the United States contain several legal cities. For instance, the ecological city of Greater Chicago includes the legal cities of Evanston, Glencoe, Skokie, Cicero, Harvey, and Park Forest, to name a few. The ecological city of New York includes Jersey City, Newark, Yonkers, and many other separately incorporated municipalities outside the limits of the legal city and even outside the state of New York. The populations of many ecological cities (the urbanized areas) now are more than double the populations of their central legal cities.

Since legal cities are often separated from one another by an invisible boundary—the middle of a street, a river, a bay, or a short span of open countryside—the ecological city is a more meaningful sociological unit. Therefore, when available, data for the ecological city are usually employed in sociological research. The use of data for the legal city rather than for the ecological city can often be misleading. For instance, newspaper and magazine articles played up the fact that most of the largest

---

[7] Based on an unpublished paper by Franz Schurmann, with permission of the author.

Skyscrapers built in A.D. *692: Some of the 500 seven-and-eight-story buildings which make up the city of Shibaam in South Arabia. This is the view from just outside the city, where women of Shibaam draw water for their goats. On this side the lowest windows are 30 feet above the ground. All entrances are from inside the city. The structures were built of sun-dried bricks and palm tree trunks.*

American cities lost population between 1950 and 1960. From this one might conclude that New York, Chicago, and Philadelphia are economically decadent and that large numbers of people are moving away, but this is not the case. All of the largest ecological cities gained population. The population decline was in *central* cities and was largely a consequence of decentralization of metropolitan areas.

The minimum population size for a city is placed at 2,500 by the U.S. Bureau of the Census, but a somewhat lower minimum would be more meaningful in the United States, since several demographic and economic variables, such as the sex ratio, change abruptly below 1,000 population.[8]

[8] Otis Dudley Duncan, "Community Size and the Rural-Urban Continuum," in Paul K. Hatt and Albert J. Reiss, Jr. (eds.), *Cities and Society* (Glencoe: The Free Press, 1957), pp. 35–45.

Comparisons In countries where farmers cluster in villages rather than living on isolated homesteads, a population of 10,000 is an appropriate breaking point between rural and urban. Such agricultural villages are rural in their social, cultural, and economic characteristics.

The fact that different criteria are used in various countries to distinguish rural and urban areas is in one sense an impediment to comparative research, but insofar as the criteria are appropriate to local conditions, varying definitions of the city do not make comparative research impossible. It has been found for a long list of countries that officially reported percentage urban, however defined, has a high correlation with the percentage of the population in ecological cities of 100,000 or more.[9]

Thailand, Pakistan, and India are among the least urbanized nations, with less than 10 percent of their population in metropolitan areas of the 100,000 class or larger. The United States, the United Kingdom, Israel, and Australia are among the most urbanized. More than 75 percent of the population of the U.K. is urban.

The high urban position of Australia may be surprising because the overall density of the country is low. In fact Australia is an extreme case of concentration, a dominant trend in the growth of urbanized societies. Argentina and Canada are other examples of high urban concentrations and low overall densities.

By any measure the United States is one of the most highly urbanized nations in the world. Figure XIII:1 shows the growth of the population of the United States since 1790 and its change from a rural country to one dominated by large metropolitan areas, with a total urban population approaching 75 percent.

The rural-urban continuum Many sociologists feel that a simple rural-urban dichotomy of communities and populations is inadequate. Obviously, the community of 5,000 people and the great metropolis of 5,000,000 are very different in many respects, yet their residents are grouped together as urban population. Communities might be classified not as urban *or* rural, but rather along a continuum from rural to urban.

It is apparent that communities form a continuum in population size, but students of the city sometimes find one community "more urban" than another of the *same* population size. In order to take into account such differences, proponents of the rural-urban continuum have added other defining criteria for urban and rural to the two basic ones of population density and size. These additional criteria —fertility and employment of women, for example —are social, cultural, economic, or demographic characteristics that are believed to be associated with high population density and size (in the case of the urban criteria) and with low population density and size (in the case of the rural criteria). With these criteria added, one can assert that community A with 20,000 people is more urban than community B with 20,000 people.[10]

Metropolitan dominance The city does not stop at its municipal boundaries but ". . . extends as far as [it] exerts a dominant influence."[11] Ecologically the central city is the organizing core that dominates the rest of the metropolitan community and integrates it with other regions. Smaller centers within the metropolitan region are incomplete and are dependent on the main center. "The metropolitan community, therefore, comprises a cluster or constellation of centers. Smaller cities and towns tend to group themselves around larger ones, somewhat as planets group themselves around a sun."[12]

The influence of a city diminishes with distance

---

[9] Jack P. Gibbs and Kingsley Davis, "Conventional Versus Metropolitan Data in the International Study of Urbanization," *American Sociological Review, 23* (October, 1958), pp. 504–514.

[10] For discussion and critique of the concept of the rural-urban continuum, see Duncan, *loc. cit.,* and Horace Miner, "The Folk-Urban Continuum," *American Sociological Review, 17* (October, 1952), 529–537.

[11] R. D. McKenzie, *The Metropolitan Community* (New York: McGraw-Hill, 1933), p. 70.

[12] *Ibid.,* p. 71.

from the center, and the extent of its influence is related to its size. Cities may be conceived of as competing with each other for influence over the hinterland. In his study of metropolitan dominance, McKenzie measured metropolitan influence in several ways, for instance in the buying practices of merchants, in banking procedures, and by newspaper circulation. Comparing the circulation of papers from one city with that of other cities and with the circulation of local papers, he showed how competition between metropolitan areas is worked out and how spheres of urban influence are defined.

Unlike Great Britain, where the *Guardian* and the London *Times,* for example, have nationwide distribution, the United States has no national daily press. Because of distances, distribution costs, and time lags, competing metropolitan papers tend to be from the same or neighboring centers, the Los Angeles *Times* and the San Francisco *Chronicle,* for instance.[13]

The countryside in the city Cities differ in the ways they are related to their countryside and the extent to which rural forms survive in the city. In climates where several crops can be produced in a year, intensive truck gardening may be carried on in the urban area. Productivity may be high enough to pay the large land rent and give the urban farmer a fair return for his work. Until recently Los Angeles was such an agricultural center.

In countries where distribution systems for foodstuffs are not highly organized, city dwellers interact closely with the countryside. Some products are sold at markets where housewives or servants bargain with farmers. Other products are sold by vendors who encompass the whole system of production and distribution from the planting of the seed to the selling of the fruit at the door of the consumer. This pattern was once common even in advanced countries, but the farmer-vendor is disappearing from the large cities, and a touch of the country has gone

[13] The technology of national publication and distribution in the U.S. was pioneered by the specialized paper, *The Wall Street Journal,* which publishes simultaneously in several metropolitan centers.

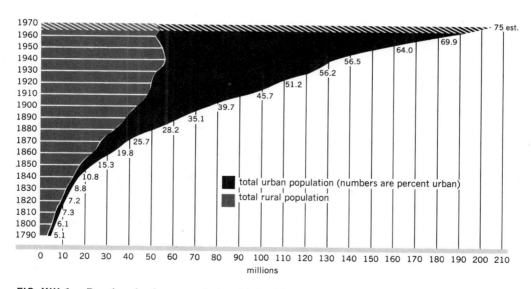

FIG. XIII:1 Rural and urban population, United States (conterminous), 1790–1965 (projected to 1970)

SOURCE: *Statistical Abstract of the United States: 1960,* p. 21, and *Census of Population: 1960,* PC(1)–1A, Table 3. Figures for 1950 and later are "new" definition of urban.

from the city streets. Rationalized distribution systems and the growth of cities have made this kind of vending spatially difficult and economically unsound. The change has been hastened by bureaucratization, an authentically urban influence. City and state bureaus hedge the distribution system with licenses and regulations. Small vendors who find licensing too costly and are not sophisticated enough to cope with the red tape of the metropolitan bureaucracy are pushed out of business.

SOURCES AND READINGS

Nels Anderson, *The Urban Community* (New York: Holt, Rinehart and Winston, 1959).

Fortune (eds.), *The Exploding Metropolis* (New York: Doubleday, 1958).

Jack P. Gibbs, *Urban Research Methods* (Princeton: Van Nostrand, 1961).

Noel P. Gist and Sylvia Fava, *Urban Society* (5th ed.; New York: Crowell, 1964).

Scott Greer, Peter Orleans, Dennis C. McElrath, and David W. Minar (eds.), *The New Urbanization* (New York: St. Martin's Press, 1967).

Jeffrey K. Hadden, Louis H. Masotti, and Calvin J. Larson, *Metropolis in Crisis: Social and Political Perspectives* (Itasca, Ill.: Peacock, 1967).

Paul K. Hatt and Albert J. Reiss, Jr. (eds.), *Cities and Society: Revised Reader in Urban Sociology* (Glencoe: The Free Press, 1957). For bibliography, see pp. 827–852.

Philip M. Hauser and Leo F. Schnore, *The Study of Urbanization* (New York: Wiley, 1965).

Lewis Mumford, *The City in History* (New York: Harcourt, Brace & World, 1961).

Lewis Mumford, *The Culture of Cities* (New York: Harcourt, Brace & World, 1938).

Robert E. Park, *Human Communities* (Glencoe: The Free Press, 1952).

Stuart A. Queen and David B. Carpenter, *The American City* (New York: McGraw-Hill, 1953).

Leo F. Schnore, *The Urban Scene: Human Ecology and Demography* (New York: The Free Press of Glencoe, 1965).

Eshref Shevky and Marilyn Williams, *The Social Areas of Los Angeles* (Berkeley and Los Angeles: University of California Press, 1949).

Scientific American, 213 (September, 1965), issue on Cities.

Adaptation 31 / Adams THE ORIGIN OF CITIES: ARCHAEOLOGICAL EVIDENCE

The rise of cities was preeminently a social process, an expression more of changes in man's interaction with his fellows than in his interaction with his environment. For this reason it marks not only a turning but also a branching point in the history of the human species.

Food surplus, technological advances, and growth in numbers were associated with occupational specialization and the allocation of land and water. Archaeological evidence reveals the emergence of the social as well as the physical conditions of urban life.

Early culture growth was directed at ways of better exploiting the natural environment. The distinguishing features were new tools and techniques and the discovery of new and more dependable resources for food and shelter. In contrast, the urban revolution was a decisive cultural and social

SOURCE: Abridged and adapted from Robert M. Adams, "The Origin of Cities," *Scientific American, 203* (September, 1960), pp. 153–168. Used in this form with permission of author and publisher.

change. To be sure, it rested ultimately on the capacity of farmers to produce more than their own requirements and to make the surpluses available to city dwellers engaged in other activities. But the essential element of the urban revolution was a whole series of new institutions and the vastly greater size and complexity of the social unit, rather than basic innovations in subsistence. In short, the differing forms of early urban societies are essentially the products of differently interacting political and economic—human—forces. And the interpretive skills required to understand them are correspondingly rooted more in the social sciences and humanities than in the natural sciences.

Precursors Knowledge about the oldest civilization and the earliest cities, those of ancient Mesopotamia, rests primarily on archaeological data. By 5500 B.C., or even earlier, it appears that the village-farming community of 200–500 individuals had fully matured in southwestern Asia. As a way of life it then stabilized internally for 1,500 years or more, although it continued to spread downward from the hills and piedmont, where it had first crystallized, into the great river valleys.

Then came a sharp increase in tempo. In the next 1,000 years some of the small agricultural communities on the alluvial plain between the Tigris and Euphrates rivers not only increased greatly in size, but changed decisively in structure. They culminated in the Sumerian city-state with tens of thousands of inhabitants, elaborate religious, political, and military establishments, social strata, advanced technology, and widely extended trading contacts.

The river-valley agriculture on which the early Mesopotamian cities were established differed considerably from that of the uplands where domestication had begun. Most important, agriculture in the alluvium depended on irrigation, which had not been necessary in the uplands. For a long time the farmers made do with small-scale systems, involving breaches in the natural embankments of the streams and uncontrolled local flooding. The beginnings of large-scale canal networks apparently followed the establishment of fully developed cities.

Where in this pattern were the inducements, perhaps even preconditions for urbanization? First, there was the productivity of irrigation agriculture. In spite of many natural handicaps, farming yielded a dependable surplus of food.

Second, the very practice of irrigation must have helped induce the growth of cities. By engendering inequalities in access to productive land, irrigation contributed to the formation of a stratified society. And by furnishing a reason for border disputes between neighboring communities, it promoted a warlike atmosphere that drew people together in offensive and defensive concentrations.

Social differentiation Finally, the complexity of food production on the flood plains may have indirectly aided the movement toward cities. Institutions were needed to mediate between herdsman and cultivator, between fisherman and sailor, between plowmaker and plowman. Whether through a system of rationing, palace largess, or a market, the city was a logical and necessary setting for storage, exchange, and redistribution.

The gathering forces for urbanization first become evident around 4000 B.C. Which of them furnished the initial impetus is impossible to say, if indeed any single factor was responsible. Growth in the size of settlements alone does not imply technological or economic advance beyond the level of the village-farming community. In our own time the Yoruba of western Nigeria maintained sizable "cities" that were in fact little more than overgrown village-farming settlements. They were largely self-sustaining because most of the productive inhabitants were full-time farmers.

Temples The evidence suggests that at the beginning the same was true of Mesopotamian urbanization: immediate economic change was not its central characteristic. The first clear-cut trend to appear in the archaeological record is the rise of temples. Conceivably new patterns of thought and social organization crystallizing within the temples served as the primary force in bringing people together and setting the process in motion.

From the archaeological record most is known about religious institutions. Religion can be traced from small shrines in early villages to more elaborate shrines with features that later permanently characterized Mesopotamian temples. The first persons released from direct subsistence labor were probably priests, whose activities are depicted in early seals and stone carvings. Quite early, the priests also became economic administrators, as attested by ration or wage lists found in temple premises, among the earliest known examples of writing. For a long time temples seem to have been the largest and most complex institutions in the communities growing up around them.

The beginnings of dynastic political regimes are much harder to trace. Probably early political authority rested in an assembly of adult males, convoked only to select a short-term war leader to meet sporadic external threat. Later, perhaps, successful war leaders were retained even in times of peace. Herein lies the apparent origin of kingship. At times springing up outside the priestly corporations, at times coming from them, new leaders emerged who were preoccupied with warfare against neighboring city-states.

Stratification As society shifted its central focus from temple to palace, it also separated into strata. Archaeologically the process can best be followed by studying grave offerings in successively later cemeteries. Earliest graves hold only pottery vessels. Later, some royal graves were richly furnished with beautifully wrought weapons, ornaments, and utensils of gold and lapis lazuli, although many graves of the same period were less elaborate, and some resembled earlier ones. Both cuneiform texts and archaeological evidence indicate that copper and bronze agricultural tools were beyond the reach of the ordinary peasant. However, graves of well-to-do persons show conspicuous consumption of copper in the form of stands for pottery vessels.

Substantial differences in the allotments to parishioners appear in temple records. Other texts describe the sale of houseplots or fields, often to form great estates held by palace officials and worked by communities of dependent clients who may originally have owned the land. Still others record the sale of slaves and the rations allotted to slaves producing textiles under the supervision of temple officials, although as a group slaves constituted only a small minority of the population.

In the temple communities on the threshhold of becoming cities, full-time craft technology was directed toward supplying seals, statuary, and ornate vessels of carved stone, cast copper or precious metals for cult purposes. Production in the later city-states was stimulated by three new kinds of demand. First, metal weapons, armor, and elaborate equipment such as chariots were made for the burgeoning military establishment of the palace. Second, a considerable volume of luxury goods was commissioned for the palace retinue. And third, a moderate private demand for these goods implies at least a small middle class.

The urban landscape By 2500 B.C. there is a fairly full picture of the general layout of a city. Radiating out from the massive public buildings toward the outer gates, were streets, unpaved and dusty, but straight and wide enough for the passage of solid-wheeled carts or chariots. Along the streets lay the residences of the more well-to-do citizenry, usually arranged around spacious courts and sometimes provided with latrines draining into sewage conduits below the streets. The houses of the city's poorer inhabitants were located behind or between the large multi-roomed dwellings. They were approached by tortuous, narrow alleys, were more haphazard in plan, less well built, and very much smaller. Mercantile activities were probably concentrated along the quays of the adjoining river or at the city gates.

Around every important urban center rose the massive fortifications that guarded the city against nomadic raids and the more formidable campaigns of neighboring rulers. Outside the walls clustered sheepfolds and irrigated tracts, interspersed with subsidiary villages, ultimately disappearing into the desert. And in the desert dwelt only the nomad, an object of mixed fear and scorn to the sophisticated court poet. By 2500 B.C. several of the important capitals of lower Mesopotamia included more than 250 acres within their fortifications. The city of Uruk extended over 1,100 acres and contained possibly 50,000 people.

These later cities provide written records from which the makeup of the population can be estimated. The overwhelming majority (possibly as high as 80 percent) of the able-bodied adults still were engaged in primary agricultural production, compared with perhaps 95 percent for the temple-towns a thousand years earlier. But many who were engaged in subsistence agriculture also had other roles: herdsmen, soldier-laborers, fishermen, sailors, pilots, oarsmen, scribes, craftsmen, etc. In addition, most were expected to serve in the army in time of crisis.

Conclusion   There is not a single origin of cities, but as many origins as there are independent cultural traditions with an urban way of life. Along the streams flowing into the Persian Gulf man made a major break with his past. Uruk of 3000 B.C. and its contemporaries were cities by any standard. Archaeological reconstruction establishes them as benchmarks in the development of human society.

Cautions   1. Many of the qualities we think of as civilized have been attained by societies that failed to organize cities. Some Egyptologists believe that civilization advanced for almost 2,000 years under the Pharaohs before true cities appeared in Egypt. The period was marked by the development of monumental public works, a formal state superstructure, written records, and the beginnings of exact science. In the New World scholars are still searching the jungles around Maya temple centers in Guatemala and Yucatán for urban agglomerations of dwellings. For all its temple architecture and high art, and the intellectual achievement represented by its hieroglyphic writing and accurate long-count calendar, classic Maya civilization apparently was not based on the city. These facts do not detract from the fundamental importance of the urban revolution but underline its complex character. Every high civilization other than possibly the Mayan did ultimately produce cities. And in most civilizations urbanization began early.

2. Some authorities consider technological advance, which they usually equate with the development of metallurgy, a major stimulant or even a precondition of urban growth. Yet, in southern Mesopotamia at least, the major expansions of metallurgy and of specialized crafts came only *after* dynastic city-states were well advanced. While the spread of technology probably contributed further to the development of militarism and social stratification, it was less a cause than a consequence of city growth. The same situation is found in New World civilizations.

SECTION 2 URBAN SOCIETY

DIFFUSION OF URBAN LIFE-STYLES

In industrial countries, the social and cultural differences between rural and urban areas are rapidly disappearing. Urban patterns of life and values now dominate much of the countryside. "The distinctive feature of the mode of living of man in the modern age is his concentration into gigantic aggregations around which cluster lesser centers and from which radiate the ideas and practices that we call civilization." [14]

The urbanization of the United States has had a profound effect on the nonurban as well as on the urban parts of the society. Urban life-styles, values, and tastes are diffused to the countryside by the mass media, the transportation network, the schools, and ties of kin and friends. The economic well-being of small-town and rural people depends to a large extent upon decisions made in Washington, D.C., in state capitals, and in the metropolises in which the giant corporations are headquartered, and the people depend more and more on the state and federal

[14] Louis Wirth, "Urbanism as a Way of Life," *American Journal of Sociology, 44* (1938), 2.

rather than local governments for public services. The rural and small-town populations can hardly escape the growing metropolitan domination of American society, but they retain an image of rural people as the source of national strength and of rural life as the good life.

Small town in mass society   The relations between a small town and the mass society are analyzed in a study of social conditions in a town of 1,000 people in upper New York state.[15] "Springdale," like many other small towns, has not shared in the population growth and economic expansion that has characterized most larger American communities during the past two decades. As the countryside has been drained of its population and as automobiles and paved roads have made it possible for the remaining rural residents to speed past the once busy hamlets to larger towns for shopping and entertainment, the loci of economic and social activity in America have shifted from hundreds of "Springdales" to fewer but larger communities. However, unlike many communities of similar size, Springdale is not declining. The postwar prosperity of farmers and the settlement of commuting industrial workers have prevented its decline, and it probably exemplifies much that is characteristic of contemporary small-town life.

Springdalers are ambivalent toward the larger society. Technological innovations and many other cultural elements of the urban society are accepted willingly, and the professional people and other carriers of urban culture enjoy enhanced status. However, the stereotype of urban life held by Springdalers is totally negative: cities are breeders of vice, corruption, atheism, un-Americanism, and other ills. By contrast, rural America, and especially Springdale, is the stronghold of morality, honesty, Godliness, and the other traditional American virtues. The villagers believe they can enjoy the material advantages of the urban society while remaining somewhat apart from it, but they overestimate their degree of independence from the mass society. There is no indigenous Springdale culture, and even the idealized image of rural life comes from mass media.[16]

The discrepancy between the villagers' illusions about small-town life and its true dependent role in the mass society creates frustration and personal conflict, particularly among merchants who find it increasingly difficult to compete with more efficient mass merchandising in nearby cities. They react by working longer hours, extending credit more liberally, and depending on personal friendship to hold their clientele. Professionals are faced with sharp limits on their economic mobility as long as they remain in Springdale. Those who stay express their mobility strivings in patterns of consumption and leisure activities that may improve their status.

Rural-urban balance of power   Writing of the United States of the 1830s, when less than 9 percent of the population was urban, Tocqueville said,

America has no great capital city, whose direct or indirect influence is felt over the whole extent of the country; this I hold to be one of the first causes of the maintenance of republican institutions in the United States. In cities men cannot be prevented from concerting together and awakening a mutual excitement that prompts sudden and passionate resolutions. Cities may be looked upon as large assemblies, of which all the inhabitants are members; their populace exercise a prodigious influence upon the magistrates, and frequently execute their own wishes without the intervention of public officers.[17]

Tocqueville distrusted the urban populations and he saw the preponderance of a rural influence as politically beneficial.

The apportionment clause of the Constitution (see Adaptation 24, p. 261) was intended to ensure that the allocation of seats in the House of Representatives would correspond to the distribution of population.

---

[15] Arthur J. Vidich and Joseph Bensman, *Small Town in Mass Society* (Princeton: Princeton University Press, 1958).

[16] *Ibid.,* pp. 102–103.

[17] Alexis de Tocqueville, *Democracy in America,* Vol. 1 (New York: Knopf, 1945), pp. 289–290.

Due to changes in geographical distribution of the population as well as urbanization, there have been many reapportionments. The results of the 1960 Census called for a reallocation of seats in the House directly affecting twenty-five states, nine gaining seats and sixteen losing them. Where changes are indicated, state legislatures are supposed to redistrict their states. If the legislatures do not redistrict, the states gaining seats elect the additional Congressmen from the whole state, that is "at large." If states lose Congressmen and do not redistrict, all candidates for the House of Representatives must run "at large."

In large part recent changes reflect the shift in population to the new centers of urban and industrial growth and a shift in political power to the more urban states. The rural-urban shift is also occurring within states. Although 43 states have constitutional provisions requiring the reapportionment of one or both of their legislative houses at least every ten years, many states have not complied with the law.

In 1955 some urban Tennessee voters instituted a suit in the state court, contending that although the Tennessee Constitution calls for reapportionment of the state's voting districts every ten years, the legislature had not acted since 1901. In the meantime the state had grown more than 50 percent and the largest gains were in the big cities. By failing to act, the legislature gave disproportionate weight to rural voters. Since there was no redistricting 2,340 voters in rural Moore County elected one representative, while 312,000 voters in Shelby County, in which Memphis is located, elected only seven. In other words, a Moore County vote was worth nearly 20 Shelby County votes.

The case was eventually appealed to the U.S. Supreme Court, and in 1962 the Court held [18] that the Tennessee Constitution had been violated and that the Tennessee legislature must redistrict the state. The decision precipitated legislative and judicial action in other states. A major alteration in political power is under way, and many legislatures, formerly controlled by rural interests, are falling into urban hands. The reapportionment process will take years to complete and of necessity will lag behind population change. The long-delayed victory for the cities will be the end of a battle, but not the end of political conflict between rural and urban interests.

Diversity Ancient Rome was made up of varied social and ethnic populations from the far-flung empire, and distinctions between victors and vanquished persisted in its social organization. Contemporary cities are heterogeneous in their segregated ethnic subcultures, extensive division of labor, and wide variations in income, power, and prestige.

Two factors contribute to heterogeneity of modern cities: selective migration and division of labor.

1. *Selective migration.* The city recruits part of its population from rural areas, from other countries, and from other cities. It offers economic and social opportunities to many kinds of people.

Since cities are composed of many persons whose early training and environment were rural or foreign, differences in child rearing, leisure time activities, and morals are to be expected. These differences may be reinforced by segregation. With the decrease in foreign immigration to the United States and the spread of urban ways of life to rural areas, a leveling of cultural differences is taking place. [19]

2. *Division of labor.* Work in the city is compartmentalized into thousands of specialized occupations. While it would be extreme to call each occupation a subculture, broad groups of occupations do develop distinctive patterns. Common interests and adaptation to similar problems tend to produce among professional groups, businessmen, or skilled workers

---

[18] See Baker *v.* Carr, 369 U.S. 186 (1962). This legal citation should be read as volume 369 *United States Reports* (Official Reports of the Supreme Court), page 186.

[19] Ronald ˙Freedman, *Recent Migration to Chicago* (Chicago: University of Chicago Press, 1950); Homer H. Hitt, "Peopling the City: Migration," in Rupert B. Vance and Nicholas J. Demerath (eds.), *The Urban South* (Chapel Hill: University of North Carolina Press, 1954), Chap. 4, pp. 54–77.

distinctive ways of viewing the world. The artisans, the warriors, and the philosophers in ancient Greek cities perceived their environment differently, as laborers, soldiers, and teachers do today.

URBAN CULTURE AND PERSONALITY

Adaptation to city life is thought to produce distinctive attitudes and personality traits.[20] The urbanite has been characterized by his sophistication and cosmopolitanism, his rationality, matter-of-factness, and reserve in social relations. Obviously, this characterization is partly a caricature, and no one urban personality is identifiable because of the wide variation among areas, occupations, and backgrounds.

However, the large numbers, the density, and the diversity of people in a city necessarily affect personality and social relations. Every day the urbanite sees many strangers with whom he has no social relations. With many others he has only brief, impersonal contacts. While he is physically close to large numbers of people, he is socially close to few. He may think of people as

"numbers," "addresses," "clients," "customers," "patients," "readers," "laborers," or "employees." The typical rural individual has fewer of these indirect communications. His face-to-face relations (with his family, minister, teacher, neighbors, etc.) compose a much larger part of his whole system of interaction than that of a typical urbanite.[21]

Sophistication, in large part an ability to conceal feelings and to manipulate situations, is fostered by anonymous and depersonalized urban social relations. The city dweller is highly *rational* in most of his relations. Servicemen, clerks, storekeepers, and conductors serve immediate ends and are judged by their ability to serve those ends. The urbanite expects the gas station attendant to serve him quickly and efficiently; the quality of the service does not vary a

great deal if the attendant likes, dislikes, or is indifferent to the personality of the customer. The city dweller is dependent upon predictable behavior; if he is to get to work on time, the bus driver must be on schedule. The personal factors in the bus driver's life that cause him to be late are of no concern to the commuter. The urbanite does not know whether someone who is in his environment today will be there tomorrow.

Time-consciousness of the urbanite is related to the complexity of city life and the necessity of integrating relations and activities in a workable way.

If all clocks and watches in Berlin would suddenly go wrong in different ways, even if only by one hour, all economic life and communication of the city would be disrupted. . . . [the] technique of metropolitan life is unimaginable without the most punctual integration of all activities and mutual relations into a stable and impersonal time schedule.[22]

A blasé attitude—a lack of reaction to new sensations—is a result of the rapidly changing stimuli presented to the city dweller.[23] He becomes indifferent to the changing panorama of faces and street scenes and to the insistent demands for his attention from newspapers, advertising, radio, and television. Simmel suggests that the blasé attitude, the cool, indifferent, outer self of the city man, serves as a psychological defense against such pressures.

Rural and urban socialization In a rural community the family is the most important source of socialization. When rural societies are isolated and have low mobility, the density of kinship ties increases, and, after a few generations, "everyone is kin to everyone else." The "clans" of the Southern Appalachian mountaineers are a case in point. This extension of the web of kin provides a way of relating oneself to a great many people. For the child, the kin are to be treated with filial respect, and they in

[20] Discussions of urban personality are found in *The Sociology of Georg Simmel,* tr. and ed. by Kurt H. Wolff (Glencoe: The Free Press, 1950), "The Metropolis and Mental Life," pp. 409–424; and Wirth, *op. cit.,* pp. 1–24.

[21] Pitirim Sorokin and Carle C. Zimmerman, *Principles of Rural-Urban Sociology* (New York: Holt, Rinehart and Winston, 1929), pp. 51–52. Reprinted by permission of Henry Holt & Co., Inc.

[22] Simmel, *op. cit.,* p. 413.

[23] *Ibid.,* pp. 413 ff.

turn support him because of their kinship. The kin relation may even be extended to non-kin: "In the peasant or rural village neighborhood, the teacher and the neighborhood itself are often described as an extension of the family." [24]

The country household socializes the child to patterns consistent with rural life: the rural child lacks alternate models to copy, and he is constrained by the work to be done. There is, therefore, less individualization of life-styles in rural environments.

In contrast to the rural family, the city family is a small, conjugal unit. (See SOCIAL ORGANIZATION, pp. 34–35.) Many of its socializing functions have been taken over by other agencies, such as the playground, the day nursery, and the peer group. The effects on personality of a wide variety of socializing agents are not well understood. Variation does, however, afford the opportunity for the city child to learn alternate patterns of behavior.

Caution Generalizations about broad differences in personality between rural and urban individuals should be viewed with care:

1. Differences in values and styles of life between urban and rural communities are rapidly diminishing.

2. Studies of rural-urban personality differences are contradictory and inconclusive. They are burdened with technical difficulties, such as the lack of comparability in personality tests. Many studies have been dominated by a bias in favor of the folk-rural way of life. Investigators have assumed that rural values are the criteria for adjustment and integration of personality. Rural personalities are said to be more integrated and unified because of homogeneous primary contacts, and a smaller range of personality differences has been assumed. The urban milieu, in contrast, is said to produce heterogeneous and unintegrated personalities. However, improved techniques of analysis and less biased investigations may

uncover more heterogeneity and less personality integration in rural settings than has been assumed. [25]

Urbanism and satisfaction Evidence on the effects of size of place on happiness is inconclusive. As shown in Table XIII:2, the smallest percentage of "very happy" people are to be found in the biggest cities, but the largest percentage are in intermediate sized places, not rural areas.

TABLE XIII:2 HAPPINESS AND COMMUNITY SIZE—PERSONS WHO SAY THEY ARE "VERY HAPPY"

SIZE OF PLACE	PERCENTAGE
Under 2,500 and rural	48.4
2,500–49,999	52.0
50,000–499,999	56.3
500,000 and larger	42.8

SOURCE: Compiled from Gallup polls conducted in 1963.

When the question of satisfaction is broken into several components, the category of largest places shows a fairly uniform low score, but the results are otherwise indecisive. Intermediate sized places are highest on work satisfaction and income but small towns and rural areas also score fairly well.

Mental illness and urbanization It is often claimed that the individuation, competitiveness, role conflict, rapid pace of activities, intense status striving, and other conditions of life in modern industrial cities result in a high incidence of mental disorders. A comparison between rates of first admissions to mental institutions in Massachusetts in the mid-nineteenth century and recent rates of admission found no increase except in the age category of fifty and older. [26] The rates for people below fifty remained about the same despite a trend toward hos-

[24] Charles P. Loomis and J. Allan Beegle, *Rural Social Systems* (New York: Prentice-Hall, 1950), p. 479.

[25] See Melvin Seeman, "An Evaluation of Current Approaches to Personality Differences in Folk and Urban Societies," *Social Forces, 25* (1946), 160–165. This article presents a summary and critique of the studies of rural and urban differences in personality and character. See also T. Lynn Smith, *The Sociology of Rural Life* (New York: Harper & Row, 1953), pp. 112–125.

[26] Herbert Goldhamer and Andrew Marshall, *Psychosis and Civilization* (Glencoe: The Free Press, 1949).

pitalization of patients with less extreme forms of mental illness.

Since Massachusetts became one of the most urbanized states in the intervening years, from 50 percent urban in 1850 to 90 percent urban in 1940, these findings suggest that city life does not produce mental disorders of the more serious types, except possibly among the elderly. It would seem that urban life is not characterized by more stress than rural life, or stress is not an important factor underlying the functional psychoses. Perhaps greater insecurity, competitiveness, and similar conditions of life in modern industrial cities produce neurotic personalities but not psychotic ones.

An increase in the number of hospitalized patients with arteriosclerotic psychoses (due to hardening of the arteries) accounts for the increase in the admission rate for older persons. The presumed greater stress or some other condition of modern urban life may have increased the incidence of arteriosclerosis, more persons with senile psychoses may now be institutionalized rather than given home care, or both of these changes may have occurred.

Although urban life as a whole may not be conducive to psychosis, extreme forms of personality deviation are not randomly distributed through the city. There is a high concentration of mental illness in the deteriorated residential areas surrounding the main business district. In their study of mental patients in private and public hospitals in Chicago, Faris and Dunham found that the rooming-house, Negro, and foreign-born slum areas had high rates of mental illness.[27] Low rates were found along the lake-front, hotel and apartment house communities, and in outlying residential areas. The main types of mental disease were more highly concentrated in some areas than in others. For example, paranoid schizophrenia had the highest rate of incidence in the rooming-house district, and manic-depressive psychoses in areas with higher rentals.

The spatial distribution of suicide follows a similar pattern of concentration in areas of transition. In Seattle and Minneapolis, Schmid found high rates of suicide in the business districts and surrounding areas.[28]

Much further study is needed before the relations between the social and cultural milieu on the one hand and mental disease and suicide on the other are clearly understood. It is not known to what extent the various urban environments *generate* these types of behavior, that is, are underlying causes of them, and the extent to which the urban environments *precipitate* mental illness and suicidal tendencies which may have been long latent in the individual. Understanding of these problems is further complicated by the fact that there is much internal mobility in the city. Deviant personalities may tend to drift toward some areas, where their breakdowns finally occur, although their difficulties may have started in other environments, either in the city or in rural areas. In the case of the Chicago study, many of the slum dwellers had been long-time residents, and this fact suggests a direct relation between social conditions in slum areas and personality disturbances. If there is in fact a causal connection between personality disorders and slum living, the determining factors may lie in the social isolation and anomie of deteriorated areas.

[27] Robert E. L. Faris and H. Warren Dunham, *Mental Disorders in Urban Areas* (Chicago: University of Chicago Press, 1939). Studies of other cities have shown similar patternings of mental disorders. See, for example, Clarence W. Schroeder, "Mental Disorders in Cities," *American Journal of Sociology, 48* (1942), 40–47.

[28] Calvin F. Schmid, *Social Saga of Two Cities* (Minneapolis: The Minneapolis Council of Social Agencies, 1937); and Calvin F. Schmid, *Social Trends in Seattle* (Seattle: University of Washington Press, 1944). Similar distributions have been found in Chicago and San Francisco. See Ruth Shonle Cavan, *Suicide* (Chicago: University of Chicago Press, 1928); Ernest R. Mowrer, *Disorganization: Personal and Social* (Philadelphia: Lippincott, 1942); and Aubrey Wendling, "Suicides in the San Francisco Bay Region" (Ph.D. dissertation, University of Washington, 1954).

SECTION 3 URBAN ECOLOGY

The ideas of social ecology are most extensively applied in the study of the city. The entry of several culturally visible immigrant populations into major urban centers is dramatic demonstration of the process of ecological invasion. The replacement of earlier settlers by later waves of immigrants epitomizes the process of succession. This section discusses two aspects of urban ecology: residential segregation and the ecological patterning of cities.

SEGREGATION

Residential separation of Negroes and whites is the most obvious and most consequential form of segregation, but the segregation of new urban settlers is a long-standing feature of the American metropolis. Each migration during the nineteenth and twentieth centuries established communal clusters—ethnic neighborhoods, which in language, diet, values, and style were transplanted from the old country. But as the immigrant generation died out and their children became acculturated to the new ways and moved out of the areas of first settlement, they were replaced by the newest immigrants. In many cases the same locality over a period of several decades would serve as the place of initial settlement for a succession of immigrants. The concentration of Negroes in central cities, therefore, is the most recent of a long series of such population movements.

Degree of segregation Residential segregation of Negroes and whites has significant consequences for the organization of cities, for the texture of urban life, for race relations, and for the culture and institutions of Negroes. Recent research provides detailed evidence on segregation in all large American cities

in 1960 and in most large cities in 1940 and 1950.[20] The degree of segregation is measured by an *index of segregation* based on the percentage of nonwhites in a city who would have to relocate in order for each city block to have nonwhites and whites distributed proportionally to their numbers in the city as a whole. For instance, if ten percent of the population of a city is nonwhite, proportional representation would be achieved if ten percent of the population of each block were nonwhite. The index score then would be zero. No intermixture of whites and nonwhites on any block would produce a score of 100, or complete segregation.

In the 207 cities that had 50,000 or more people in 1960, the index values varied from 60.4 to 98.1 —in other words, from high segregation to almost complete separation of whites and nonwhites. San Jose, Sacramento, Salt Lake City, San Francisco, and Bridgeport (Connecticut) had the lowest index values but were still highly segregated by an absolute standard. Furthermore, all of these cities except Bridgeport contain a significant number of nonwhites who are not Negroes; if the index could have been computed for whites and Negroes (instead of whites and nonwhites) the index scores would be significantly higher.

The most highly segregated cities were Fort Lauderdale, Orlando, Miami, West Palm Beach, and Jacksonville (all in Florida); Shreveport and Monroe in Louisiana; Inster, Michigan; and Winston-Salem, North Carolina. The mean segregation index was higher in the South and North Central Region (90.9 and 87.7) than in the Northeast and West (79.2 and 79.3), but there were very highly segregated cities in all regions. Degree of segregation did

[20] Karl E. Taeuber and Alma F. Taeuber, *Negroes in Cities: Residential Segregation and Neighborhood Change* (Chicago: Aldine, 1965).

not vary consistently with size of city, number of nonwhites, or percentage of nonwhites.

The greater average segregation in the South than in other regions is a reversal of the historical condition. As recently as 1940, Southern cities were less segregated on the average than cities in the rest of the country, and at the beginning of the century there was only a moderate amount of segregation in some Southern cities. However, whites and Negroes did not live together on a basis of equality. Rather, Negro servants customarily lived on the premises or behind the residences of well-to-do whites. The same condition can be observed in a few upper-income neighborhoods in the North. In recent decades the average level of segregation has increased in the South; outside the South it declined slightly between 1950 and 1960.

Segregation by economic level accounts for only part of segregation by race. As the occupational gap between whites and Negroes has become narrower, residential segregation has not declined proportionately. In cities with large numbers of other minorities, the segregation of Negroes is much more nearly complete than the segregation of any other minority.

Consequences of segregation   Contrary to popular impressions, Negroes who move into previously all-white neighborhoods are often of higher socioeconomic status than their white neighbors and are generally of higher status than other Negroes in the city. Neither new Negro migration into a neighborhood nor an increase in the percentage of Negroes in racially mixed neighborhoods typically has much effect upon the socioeconomic characteristics of the neighborhoods.

A decline in property values rarely follows increased Negro settlement.[30] However, the widely-held *belief* that property values decline causes some panic selling and temporary fluctuations in prices. The climate of anxiety invites speculation and manipulation of the market by unscrupulous operators,

who play upon the fears of householders in order to drive prices down and who then sell at inflated prices to Negroes desperate for housing.

Because residential segregation limits the amount of communication between the races and may lead to institutional by-products such as *de facto* segregation in the schools, the character of Negro residence has become a topic of increasing concern. Large, homogeneous settlements are often called ghettos, signifying the high degree of isolation and the involuntary nature of the boundaries.[31]

In 1948 the U.S. Supreme Court held that restrictive covenants (agreements between property owners not to sell or rent their property to persons of certain racial or ethnic categories) were unenforceable in the courts. The court decision enabled an owner to sell or rent his house to anyone without fear of punitive legal action but did not assure an automatic increase in the area opened to settlement by Negroes or others. It affected only the few who were willing to sell to Negroes. Customary restrictions and informal pressures remain, although not supported by the courts.

Consequently a more direct approach has been tried in a number of places. "Open housing" ordinances have been put on the ballot that would require an owner to sell or rent without taking into account the racial characteristics of his prospective tenant or purchaser.

Open housing is opposed on grounds that the seller should have absolute freedom to choose among prospective buyers or renters, that the seller should not be put in a situation where he might suffer reprisals from his neighbors, and that he should have the right to take their preferences into account. Finally it is argued that in the case of rentals the householder should be able to control his own home.

On the other hand, the drastic limitation on available housing in the ghetto results in crowding, further deterioration of already undesirable housing and, because of the severe competition for space, abnormally high rentals and property prices. Spokes-

[30] See Luigi Laurenti, *Property Values and Race: Studies in Seven Cities* (Berkeley and Los Angeles: University of California Press, 1960).

[31] For earlier usage of the term, see Louis Wirth, *The Ghetto* (Chicago: University of Chicago Press, 1928).

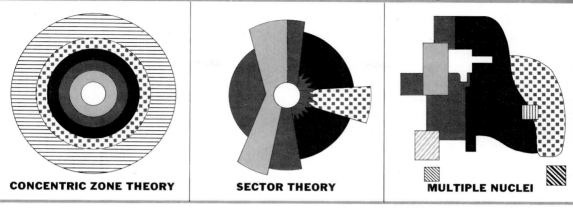

CONCENTRIC ZONE THEORY   SECTOR THEORY   MULTIPLE NUCLEI

Concentric zone terminology with Burgess-Locke family types*

1. business zone (nonfamily)
2. rooming-house zone (emancipated family)
3. immigrant zone (semipatriarchal)
4. workingmen's zone (patricentric)
5. apartment-house zone (equalitarian)
10. suburban zone (matricentric)

Detailed terminology†

1. central business district
2. wholesale light manufacturing
3. low-class residential
4. medium-class residential
5. high-class residential
6. heavy manufacturing
7. outlying business district
8. residential suburb
9. industrial suburb
10. commuters' zone

FIG. XIII:2   Three generalizations of internal structure of cities

* After Ernest W. Burgess and Harvey J. Locke, *The Family* (New York: American Book Co., 1953), p. 101.

† After Chauncy D. Harris and Edward L. Ullman, "The Nature of Cities," *Annals* of the American Academy of Political and Social Science, *242* (November, 1945), 12. By permission of the American Academy of Political and Social Science.

men for these concerns urge a free market in real estate unaffected by racial preferences.

ECOLOGICAL PATTERNING

The ideas of ecology were adapted to the study of the city by Park, Burgess, and McKenzie. (See Adaptation 32, pages 449–453.)

A number of different schemes have been devised to describe the spatial patterns of cities. Figure XIII:2 diagrams three of the schemes for describing the internal structure of cities: (1) the concentric zone theory, (2) the sector theory, and (3) the multiple nuclei theory.

1. *The concentric zone theory.* The best-known approach to the ecological analysis of cities is the Burgess concentric zone theory.[32] The elementary features may be outlined as follows (see Fig. XIII:2).

[32] Robert E. Park, Ernest W. Burgess, and Roderick D. McKenzie, *The City* (Chicago: University of Chicago Press, 1925), Chap. 2; Ernest W. Burgess, "The Determination of Gradients in the Growth of the City," *Publications of the American Sociological Society, 21* (1927), 178–184. For family types in the various zones, see Ernest W. Burgess and Harvey J. Locke, *The Family: From Institution to Companionship* (2nd ed.; New York: American Book, 1953), pp. 100–103. Figure XIII:2, which is designed for purposes of comparison, differs from the conventional numbering given the Burgess Zones.

Zone 1 is the center of the city, the area of the main business district and of the most intensive land use. In Chicago, where the Burgess scheme was developed, Zone 1 is known as The Loop. The administrative functions for the commerce, finance, and management of the city are located here. The populations in the area are transient residents in hotels and the daytime population of commuting workers in offices and stores.[33] It is the nonfamily area where unattached men predominate.

Zone 2, labeled in the figure "wholesale light manufacturing," is also called the zone in transition. It lies just outside Zone 1, and land is often held by real estate speculators in anticipation of Zone 1 expansion and consequent higher land values. In many cities land speculation in Zone 2 proved to be a good risk. A part of the zone in transition lived up to its name and became merged with the central business district. In other cities the business district did not greatly expand, and the zone in transition became a blighted area because speculators were unwilling to risk improving property. Whether it is an area of transition or blight, it tends to be associated with delinquency and crime and to provide residences for groups, which because of financial or other reasons are unable to find more desirable places to live. As a residential area it is the rooming-house zone and the location of the childless family, called emancipated.

Zone 3 is a lower-class residential district, and includes immigrants who have improved their status and have been able to move out of Zone 2. The characteristic family form is semipatriarchal.

Zones 4 and 5 comprise the residential zone where apartments and private dwellings have higher rentals than Zone 3, and there is a higher rate of home ownership. In the Burgess classification Zone 4 is the area of workingmen's homes and the patricentric family. Zone 5 with its apartment houses is the site for equalitarian families.

Zone 10, the commuters zone of residential communities, lies on the outer periphery of the city. It includes suburbs beyond the city limits and is the location of much recent population growth. The characteristic family type is matricentric.

Burgess and his associates found in Chicago that a number of social characteristics[34] which could be expressed as rates were distributed in an orderly way from the center of the city to the periphery. For example, home ownership was lowest in the center of the city and progressively higher in the outlying zones, i.e., home ownership increased with distance from the center of the city. The percentage of the population foreign born, the rate of male juvenile delinquency, and the sex ratio were all highest in the center of the city and declined toward the periphery.

Studies in St. Louis and Rochester, New York, verified the zonal theory for those cities.[35] On the other hand, the analyses of Davie and Firey show that the concentric zone theory is not directly applicable to New Haven and Boston.[36] Firey found that "sentiment and symbolism," the valuation of particular neighborhoods, such as the traditionally upper-class area of Beacon Hill in Boston, prevented "rational" forces from operating. The area retained an upper-class character long after it would have changed if the forces of zonal development had determined land use.

The concentric zone theory appears most applicable to cities of rather rapid growth that (1) were not impeded unduly in their orderly expansion by hills or other peculiarities of the topography, (2) were not greatly influenced by the automobile, and (3) developed during the period of mass Euro-

---

[33] See Gerald Breese, *The Daytime Population of the Central Business District* (Chicago: University of Chicago Press, 1949).

[34] See Ernest W. Burgess, "Urban Areas," *Chicago, An Experiment in Social Science Research,* ed. by T. V. Smith and L. D. White (Chicago: University of Chicago Press, 1929), pp. 113–138, and Burgess, *op. cit.*

[35] Stuart A. Queen and David B. Carpenter, *The American City* (New York: McGraw-Hill, 1953), p. 101; and Raymond Bowers, "Ecological Patterning of Rochester, New York," *American Sociological Review, 4* (April, 1939), 180–189.

[36] Maurice R. Davie, "The Pattern of Urban Growth," in *Studies in the Science of Society,* ed. by G. P. Murdock (New Haven: Yale University Press, 1937), pp. 133–162; and Walter Firey, *Land Use in Central Boston* (Cambridge: Harvard University Press, 1947).

pean immigration. Contemporary cities are much changed, but abundant traces of the zonal pattern may still be found in some places.

2. *Sector hypothesis.* A second theory is the Hoyt *sector hypothesis,*[37] which views the large city as a number of sectors rather than concentric zones (see Fig. XIII:2). These sectors are products of the growth patterns of cities, just as the zones are. Hoyt's analysis is largely based on a study of rental values and residential characteristics. He found that populations tended to move along well-defined axes of transportation as the city grew, with higher income groups showing a greater rapidity of movement than lower income groups.

According to this view, fashionable areas do not fill a whole concentric zone, but rather occupy segments of zones just outside the fashionable areas of earlier periods. A fashionable area located in the eastern quadrant of the city would move outward as the city grew, but would remain in the eastern quadrant. Other kinds of housing located in other sectors would also move toward the edge of the city but would tend to remain in their original *sectors.*

3. *Multiple nuclei.* (See Fig. XIII:2.) Still another approach to the problem of describing the internal structure of cities was made by Harris and Ullman.[38] They suggest that the land-use patterns of many cities are organized around several distinct nuclei rather than a single center. The nuclei are distinguished by their functions and the relation of the functions to certain kinds of terrain or communication. Four main factors are suggested in the development of nuclei:

1. Certain activities require specialized facilities. The retail district, for example, is attached to the point of greatest intracity accessibility, the port district to suitable water front, manufacturing districts to large blocks of land and water or rail connections, and so on.

2. Certain like activities group together because they profit from cohesion. . . . Retail districts benefit from grouping which increases the concentration of potential customers and makes possible comparison shopping. Financial and office-building districts depend upon facility of communication among offices within the district.

3. Certain unlike activities are detrimental to each other. The antagonism between factory development and high-class residential development is well known.

4. Certain activities are unable to afford the high rents of the most desirable sites. . . . Examples are bulk wholesaling and storage activities requiring much room, or low-class housing unable to afford the luxury of high land with a view.

The number of nuclei which result from historical development and the forces of localization varies from city to city. The larger the city, the more numerous and specialized are the nuclei.[39]

The effects of terrain The characteristics of the terrain condition the internal structure of all cities, modify the location of functions, break up areas and confuse the application of generalizing theories, such as the concentric zone theory and the sector theory. For example, Chicago's location on Lake Michigan is more nearly a segment of a circle than circular, with Zone 1 fronting on the lake. Hills, rivers, the underlying geological structure, and other features of the natural environment may divert land use, interrupting the sequences of growth and the functional relations between areas that would have occurred if the surface had been uniformly flat.[40]

Social area analysis A somewhat different approach to urban research was introduced by Shevky in a study of Los Angeles.[41] In this technique the

[37] Homer Hoyt, *The Structure and Growth of Residential Neighborhoods in American Cities* (Washington, D.C.: Federal Housing Administration, 1939), especially Chap. IV; and Homer Hoyt, "The Structure of American Cities in the Post-War Era," *American Journal of Sociology, 48* (January, 1943), 475–492.

[38] Chauncy D. Harris and Edward L. Ullman, "The Nature of Cities," *Annals* of the American Academy of Political and Social Science, 242 (November, 1945), 7–17.

[39] *Ibid.,* pp. 14–15. Reprinted by permission of the authors and the American Academy of Political and Social Science.

[40] Queen and Carpenter, *op. cit.,* pp. 95–99.

[41] Eshref Shevky and Marilyn Williams, *The Social Areas of Los Angeles* (Berkeley and Los Angeles: University of California Press, 1949). See also Eshref Shevky and Wendell Bell, *Social Area Analysis* (Stanford: Stanford University Press, 1955) on the San Francisco Bay area.

UNITS OF ECOLOGICAL ANALYSIS: CENSUS TRACTS

The cost and difficulty of making individual case studies of many urban phenomena stimulated the ecological approach to urban analysis. By studying areas instead of individuals, research on large population centers became feasible. According to the concepts of ecology, the units of analysis should be *natural areas,* that is, areas of land inhabited by a single dominant species. In the case of human ecology the areas should be dominated by one type of population or land use. This, however, was one of the problems the social ecologists were trying to solve: what and where were the natural areas of the city?

When quantitative urban studies were first made in the United States, political and administrative divisions, such as precincts and wards, were the units used for the compilation of statistical data. Although the divisions vary in size in different municipalities, most such units are too large for convenient statistical analysis. Their boundaries are not permanent, and the populations they contain are often quite heterogeneous.

THE CENSUS TRACT

In 1906 Walter Laidlaw, director of population studies for the Federation of Churches in New York, divided the city into relatively small and homogeneous tracts,* which he persuaded the Bureau of the Census to adopt for enumeration and tabulation of the 1910 Census. The seven other cities, which at that time had populations of 500,000 or more (Baltimore, Boston, Chicago, Cleveland, Philadelphia, Pittsburgh, and St. Louis), were also tracted. In 1920 census tract data were again tabulated for the list of cities. In New York a Census Committee put out the first major publication based on tract data, and soon afterward tract data were used for ecological research in Chicago.

The number of tracted cities, in some cases including their adjacent areas, has been increased, and in 1960 there were 180 tracted areas. A list of tracted areas may be found in any *Census Tract,* PHC (1) bulletin.

Census tracts usually contain from 3,000 to 6,000 persons. Where feasible, natural boundaries (rivers, etc.) are used, and each tract is drawn so as to include as nearly as possible a homogeneous population. The same tract boundaries are retained for each Census, so that studies of changes in an area are facilitated. If an area increases markedly in population, the tract may be subdivided, but it is possible to recombine the statistics of the subdivided tract for comparative analysis over time. In exceptional cases the external boundaries of tracts are changed; for instance, tracts for Providence were completely revised in 1950.

Tract bulletins report such information as the following: † race, national origin of foreign stock, family composition, marital status, education, residence in 1955, income, age by sex and race, and labor force and housing characteristics. For tracts with 400 or more nonwhites, there are details on the nonwhite population.

* Census Tract Manual. Fourth Edition, Bureau of the Census, 1958.

† Some of the data reported by census tracts are based on a 25 percent sample. In using such information, care must be taken to refer to the instructions on sampling contained in the tract bulletins.

Block Statistics Bulletins, HC (3) supply limited data on the characteristics of dwelling units for many cities that are not tracted. Reports are available for 467 places with population exceeding 50,000.

census tract is usually employed as the unit of analysis. Each tract is given a numerical score on *social rank* as measured by such factors as occupation, education, and rental value, and a score on *urbanization* as indicated by fertility, the proportion of women in the labor force, and house type. A third variable, *segregation,* is measured by the ratio of minority people in a given tract to their proportion in the city as a whole. Tracts are then grouped according to the similarity of their scores irrespective of their geographic distance from each other. Since the initial study was published in 1949, there have been a number of replications both in the United States and elsewhere and an extensive literature debating the technical merits of the method.

Because homogeneous clusters of tracts tend to be similar in other characteristics, such as life-styles, family type, and age distributions, social area analysis is of value in comparing different cities, in tracing trends in any one city, and in the general study of the spatial organization of social phenomena. By showing how geographically distant tracts with the same characteristics may be found in the same "social space," the method contributes to the comparative analysis of urban areas and generalizations about spatial phenomena.

The Chicago studies In the period between World Wars I and II the University of Chicago was the dominant force in American sociology. Under the leadership of Park, Thomas, Ellsworth Faris, Burgess, Wirth (and Mead in Philosophy), it granted a large proportion of advanced degrees, published the *American Journal of Sociology,* and contributed extensively to the advancement of the discipline.[42] A distinctive feature of this scholarly enterprise was an approach to studying the city of Chicago. The city was viewed as a "social laboratory," and it was subjected to intensive, prolonged, and systematic study. Adaptation 32 outlines some of the theoretical principles underlying the Chicago studies and some of the major lines of investigation. The monographic works listed on page 453 grew out of the research program and largely originated as doctoral dissertations. In the aggregate they represent an impressive body of knowledge about an American metropolis at a significant period in its growth. Adaptation 32 draws on these monographs as well as the collections of papers listed.

[42] See Robert E. L. Faris, *Chicago Sociology, 1920–1932* (San Francisco: Chandler Publishing, 1967).

Adaptation 32 / CHICAGO AS A SOCIAL LABORATORY

The intellectual foundation of the Chicago studies is exemplified in the background of Robert E. Park. He was intimately acquainted with European sociology, and his Heidelberg degree was earned with a theoretical treatise on collective behavior. Park's wide experience as a newspaper reporter and city editor led him to test theories by direct observation in the field.[43] His close association with W. I. Thomas supported his preference for viewing the surrounding city as a laboratory. He was familiar with urban studies in Europe and sensitive to the research merits of social surveys such as the famous *Life and Labour of the People in London* by Charles Booth (first published in 1891–1903).

The Chicago studies were influenced in part by ideas from plant and animal ecology. Suggestive analogies were drawn between plant and human communities, and the concepts of plant ecology, such as competition, dominance, accommodation, succession, and invasion, were adapted to the sociology of the city.

The development of [human ecology in the United States] was given

[43] E. C. Hughes in Buford H. Junker, *Field Work* (Chicago: University of Chicago Press, 1960), pp. ix–x.

(L) *Ernest W. Burgess (1886–1966) Park's long-time co-worker at the University of Chicago, he contributed to research in the family, social disorganization, aging and retirement, as well as urban studies.*

(R) *Robert E. Park (1864–1944) In association with E. W. Burgess and W. I. Thomas, he powerfully influenced the study of the urban community and race relations. In the ecological studies Park worked closely with R. D. McKenzie.*

an indigenous turn by the special conditions of American life. . . . It saw community life as a rapidly growing organism, with an expanding area, with increasing land values, and with an increasing number and complexity of institutions. Affected by the theories of *laissez faire* and free enterprise, ecologists saw an ever-competing and expanding business center as the dominant center of the community."

Ecological processes Park thought of the city as having ". . . a characteristic organization and a typical life history." Towns generally develop along lines of communication, at the junction of two or more land or water routes. Population and businesses concentrate about this point of maximum access, and the highest land values are found in such locations. As towns grow larger, competitively weaker facilities, such as residences, are pushed outward. *Competition,* a key ecological concept,

determines which businesses remain at the center and thus form the central business district. The growth of local transportation increases the number of people who work and transact business in the central business district, resulting in increased land values and concentration of offices, banks, and stores.

In a growing city the central business district must expand, and this expansion as well as the anticipation of it affects the surrounding area, called the zone in transition. Land values in the transition zone rise, but the buildings and the neighborhood deteriorate. Old buildings are not repaired and are put to temporary uses, but new construction awaits the growth of the central business district. When different land uses begin to encroach on the area, the process of *invasion* is under way.

Residents able to afford higher rents and the costs of commuting

from outlying areas into the central business district begin to move to the periphery. When the change in land use from residential to business is complete, *succession* has taken place. In the interstices between the business and industrial developments are slums, immigrant communities, rooming-house areas, hobohemia, and bohemia. These areas tend to be separated by such barriers as transportation arteries, wedges of business and industry, park and boulevard systems, and topographical features that modify the hypothesized concentric zonal pattern. For example, lakes modify the zonal pattern of cities like Chicago and Cleveland into concentric semicircles. The areas with a predominant land use or occupancy are termed *formations* by the plant ecologist and *natural areas* by the human ecologists—natural because the areas are products of natural forces, without design.

" Emma C. Llewellyn and Audrey Hawthorn, "Human Ecology" in Georges Gurvitch and Wilbert E. Moore (eds.), *Twentieth Century Sociology* (New York: Philosophical Library, 1945), pp. 469–470.

Park suggested that the metropolis selects out through competition those individuals best suited to live in a particular region and milieu; every individual finds the place where he can or must live. These areas exemplify *segregation,* as understood by the plant ecologist, and in their self-sufficiency and isolation tend to resist invasion of other land uses.

Social disorganization The natural areas within the zone in transition, as well as the zone itself, were a major focus of interest for the Chicago studies, because human ecologists hold that succession, accompanied by a high rate of mobility, results in social disorganization.

The constant comings and goings of its inhabitants is the most striking and significant characteristic of this world of furnished rooms. This whole population turns over every four months. . . . And at least half of the keepers of these houses had been at their present addresses six months or less.[45]

Zorbaugh characterized the Near North Side of Chicago as one of restless succession: fashionable residential streets into rooming-house districts; rooming-houses into tenements; tenements sometimes reclaimed for studios and shops. Frazier reporting on Negroes and Wirth on immigrants observed these populations tending to move out of the deteriorated areas as their economic condition improved.

Within the zone in transition are areas of social homogeneity such as the ghetto, which according to Park "made it possible for two unassimilated peoples to live together, participating in a common economy, but preserving separate cultures," and, incidentally, representing the phenomenon termed *accommodation* by the plant ecologist. Within the zone are other areas, such as the rooming-house district, where social solidarity is completely absent.

Special institutions cater to the needs of the residents of this zone where social controls have, to a great extent, broken down. Within the rooming-house district, for example, are taxi-dance halls, established to meet the demand for companionship of homeless and lonesome men.[46] In the zone in transition the hobo can find a cheap "flop" and the Skid Roader a cheap glass of wine. Many of the 1,313 boy gangs studied by Thrasher were located in this area. Here, also, where social control is weak and anonymity is high, are the centers of commercialized vice.

The slum is a bleak area of segregation of the sediment of society; an area of extreme poverty, tenements, ramshackle buildings, of evictions and evaded rents; an area of working mothers and children, of high rates of birth, infant mortality, illegitimacy, and death; an area of pawnshops and second-hand stores, of gangs, of "flops," where every bed is a vote . . . the slum . . . has reached the limit of decay and is on the verge of reorganization as missions, settlements, playparks, and business come in.[47]

For the immigrant, the slum had three attractions: rents were low; it was within walking distance of work; and absentee landlords offered little resistance to people with a low standard of living and an alien culture.

The human ecologists paid less attention to the areas beyond the zone in transition—the zone of workingmen's homes, the residential zone, and the zone of commuters—but they did compare the rates of various social problems. They found, for example, that rates of crime, delinquency, illegitimate births, family breakup, poverty, vice, mental illness, and even hotel transiency decline in relation to distance from the central business district.

When different groups move from one zone to the next, their incidence of social problems varies depending on the direction of their movement. Faris and Dunham,[48] for instance, showed that different types of mental illness are characteristic of different areas, and Frazier[49] showed that social problem rates vary by area for the Negro population as for the white population. The incidence of social problems of Negroes as for whites declines with movement toward

[45] Harvey W. Zorbaugh, *The Gold Coast and the Slum* (Chicago: University of Chicago Press, 1929), pp. 71–72.

[46] E. W. Burgess, "Introduction" to Paul G. Cressey, *The Taxi-Dance Hall* (Chicago: University of Chicago Press, 1932).

[47] Zorbaugh, *op. cit.,* p. 9.

[48] Robert E. L. Faris and H. Warren Dunham, *Mental Disorders in Urban Areas* (Chicago: University of Chicago Press, 1939).

[49] E. Franklin Frazier, *The Negro Family in Chicago* (Chicago: University of Chicago Press, 1932), pp. 249–252. See also Adaptation 14, pp. 145–148.

the periphery and into the more organized social communities.

The conceptions and interpretations of the human ecologists were influenced by the ideas of Social Darwinism and natural selection: competition distributes and segregates residences, occupations, and businesses. For the human ecologist, each area selects those individuals who can afford it or survive in it, and each area of the city "is suited for some one function better than for any other." As Park describes it:

[The city's] growth is, fundamentally and as a whole, natural, i.e., uncontrolled and undesigned. The forms it tends to assume are those which represent and correspond to the functions that it is called upon to perform.[50]

The human ecologists held that natural growth tendencies should be taken into account in the development of city plans.

Division of labor A contrast between the village and the city and between communal and impersonal social controls is also a recurrent theme in the writings of the Chicago group. Except for immigrant communities, which maintain a degree of traditional solidarity, cities tend to isolate individuals and break down local attachments. The weakened restraints are related to the incidence of vice and crime.[51] Man is thrown upon himself as custom is replaced by public opinion and law. The new social order is pragmatic and experimental: education is no longer ritual, politics is empirical, religion is a quest.[52] Law, fashion, and public opinion replace traditional controls, and primary relations in general are replaced by secondary relations.

The chief force creating this new society is the division of labor. The division of labor tends to break down or to modify the older social and economic organization of society, which was based on family ties, local association, custom, and status. Developments in urban transportation and communication, radically separating place of residence and place of work, help to create secondary relations. There is a decline of neighborhood public dance halls and neighborhood theaters in favor of large dance gardens and movie palaces.[53] New agencies take over some of the duties that home, neighborhood, and communal organizations can no longer perform adequately.[54] But men who live in the same locality do not necessarily have the same common interests; there is difficulty in maintaining the intimate contacts of the small town when people live in hotels or lodging houses, or are transient.[55]

Zorbaugh[56] contrasted certain areas of the Near North Side with its superficial and external contacts, social distance, self-absorption, and high population densities with the town or village where everyone knows everyone else "clear down to the ground." The diversity of cultural backgrounds increases social distance in the city. Economic activities in the city take men outside their local community and give them separate interests and points of view. In the village, on the other hand, economic activities are a source of the community's common body of experiences. With separation of place of work and residence, the range and the frequency of social contacts are increased. The consequent dissolution of public opinion and decay of social solidarity makes strangers out of neighbors. Recreation ceases to be spontaneous and communal. Instead it becomes commercialized and segregated in the Loop or "bright lights" area. The village fiesta is abandoned for the pool hall or the movie.

Tönnies' distinction between *Gemeinschaft* and *Gesellschaft* (see p. 48) and Durkheim's ideas about the division of labor and the interdependence of diverse social types influenced Park's thinking. These themes occur in the studies of occupations, such as *The Saleslady* and *The Professional Thief.* Like the more pointedly ecological monographs, they helped to mark

[50] Robert E. Park, Foreword in Louis Wirth, *The Ghetto* (Chicago: University of Chicago Press, 1928), p. x.

[51] Ernest W. Burgess, "The Growth of the City: An Introduction to a Research Project," in Robert Park, Ernest W. Burgess, and Roderick D. McKenzie (eds.), *The City* (Chicago: University of Chicago Press, 1925), p. 59.

[52] Park, "The City as a Social Laboratory," in *Human Communities* (Glencoe: The Free Press, 1952), pp. 74–75.

[53] Park, "Can Neighborhood Work Have a Scientific Basis?" in *The City, op. cit.,* p. 151.

[54] Park, "Community Organization and Juvenile Delinquency," in *Human Communities, op. cit.,* p. 61.

[55] Park, "Local Communities in the Metropolis," in *Human Communities, op. cit.,* p. 90.

[56] Zorbaugh, *op. cit., passim.*

off a major area of sociological research. But the occupational studies should not be thought of as entirely distinct from ecology. On the
contrary, occupational types are
seen in ecological terms as fitting
into niches in the urban zones and
in the economy. Workers find
their places by natural selective
processes into both work locations
and residential locations.

Conclusion   Among the theoretical bases of the Chicago studies, two stand out:

1. The application to human and especially urban society of ideas originally derived
from plant and animal ecology

2. The theory developed by Tönnies and Durkheim that modern society is the product
of evolution from a communal, relatively undifferentiated social order to a social system
based on specialization, the division of labor, and the functional interdependence of diverse social types

Caution   The growth of Chicago occurred rapidly and at a time when one after another different immigrant populations entered the city and worked their way up the occupational and residential ladder. The trend of Chicago's development was well established
before the automobile became the major means of urban-suburban transportation. Generalizations about the details of zonal change pertain to large, industrial, expanding cities
at a particular stage in American urban history.

A chronological listing of the Chicago studies

(Unless otherwise indicated, they are publications of
the University of Chicago Press.) Numerous periodical articles are not separately referred to, but many
of them appear in the listed collections. Monographs
about other places are excluded even though they are
part of the same intellectual tradition.

Chicago Commission on Race Relations, *The Negro
in Chicago* (1922).

Robert E. Park, E. W. Burgess, R. D. McKenzie, and
Louis Wirth, *The City* (1925).

Ernest W. Burgess (ed.), *The Urban Community*
(1927).

Frederic M. Thrasher, *The Gang* (1927).

Louis Wirth, *The Ghetto* (1928).

Clifford R. Shaw, F. M. Zorbaugh, H. D. McKay,
and L. S. Cottrell, *Delinquency Areas* (1929).

T. V. Smith and Leonard D. White (eds.), *Chicago:
An Experiment in Social Science Research* (1929).

Harvey W. Zorbaugh, *The Gold Coast and the Slum*
(1929).

Paul G. Cressey, *The Taxi-Dance Hall* (1932).

E. Franklin Frazier, *The Negro Family in Chicago*
(1932).

Walter C. Reckless, *Vice in Chicago* (1933).

Norman S. Hayner, *Hotel Life* (1936).

Robert E. L. Faris and H. Warren Dunham, *Mental
Disorders in Urban Areas* (1939).

Nels Anderson, *Men on the Move* (1940).

Robert E. Park, *Human Communities* (Glencoe:
The Free Press, 1952).

OCCUPATIONAL STUDIES

Frances R. Donovan, *The Woman Who Waits* (Boston: R. G. Badger, 1920).

Nels Anderson, *The Hobo* (1923).

Frances R. Donovan, *The Saleslady* (1930).

Clifford R. Shaw, *The Jack-Roller* (1930).

Edwin H. Sutherland and C. Conwell, *The Professional Thief* (1937).

Frances R. Donovan, *The Schoolma'am* (New York:
Frederick A. Stokes, 1938).

SECTION 4 CHANGING CITIES

CENTRAL CITY AND SUBURB

Perhaps the most dramatic change in large American cities during recent years has been the movement of people from the central zones to suburban and satellite areas. Although the suburban movement has accelerated since World War II, its beginnings were observed as early as 1899,[57] and a few commuters' settlements had grown up along railroads near large cities some fifty years earlier. This movement involved very few people, however, until the invention of the electric train and streetcar in the late nineteenth century made intermediate-range commuting both economical and convenient.[58] Metropolitan areas then expanded outward along the train and streetcar tracks and took on a starlike configuration. Most people still lived within walking distance of the public transportation routes, however, and these did not reach many of the outlying areas. The automobile provided a more flexible means of transportation and made possible an even greater dispersal of people within the metropolitan area, but the full impact of the automobile was retarded first by the Great Depression of the 1930s and then by World War II.

In every decade since 1920 the percent increase has been greater outside central cities. Since 1960 central cities have grown at an average rate of less than one percent per year, but metropolitan growth outside central cities has averaged between three and four percent per year. This nationwide trend is most rapid in the Western states.

Satellites and suburbs Although outlying places are commonly thought of as suburbs, they are not all primarily residential.[59] *Satellites* function largely as centers of employment, producing goods and services that are largely consumed elsewhere. They are centers of production, and their workers are commuters who live in other communities. They employ more workers by day than they house by night. *Suburbs,* on the other hand, send out workers and draw in goods and services for consumption by their residents. The number of residents is greater than the number employed within their boundaries. In sum, employing satellites consume labor and supply commodities while residential suburbs consume commodities and supply labor.

Not surprisingly, the resident populations of satellites grow more slowly than do those of suburbs. Satellites, which are older than suburbs, gradually convert from residential to industrial, commercial, and transportation functions. This trend drives out many residents and discourages construction of new homes. Those who remain are frequently too poor to afford higher housing costs so that the socioeconomic level of the average satellite is markedly below that of the typical suburb. The problems of satellites are frequently in miniature the problems of central cities.

Suburbanization occurs in nuclei, or small communities, around the central city as well as around the satellite cities of the metropolitan area. So extensive is growth in some areas that original suburbs of the main city have merged with suburbs of satellite cities.[60]

---

[57] Adna F. Weber, *The Growth of Cities in the Nineteenth Century* (New York: Columbia University Press, 1899).

[58] William F. Ogburn, "Inventions of Local Transportation and the Patterns of Cities," *Social Forces, 24* (May, 1946), 373–379.

[59] See Leo F. Schnore, "Satellites and Suburbs," *Social Forces, 36* (1957), pp. 121–127. Reprinted in Leo F. Schnore, *The Urban Scene* (New York: The Free Press of Glencoe, 1965), Chap. 7.

[60] Cf. Donald J. Bogue, "Metropolitan Decentralization: A Study of Differential Growth," Scripps Foundation *Studies in Population Distribution,* No. 2, (August, 1950).

Post-World War II suburbs have been the subjects of increasing research, and the accumulating findings provide the basis for some tentative generalizations about their social, cultural, economic, and demographic characteristics.[61] The movement from the central city to the outlying areas has far-reaching social consequences. Suburbs are populated mainly by young, married adults and their children, and the family tends to be child-centered. Single and unattached adults and married couples without children are rare. There is a preponderance of people below age thirteen and between the ages of thirty-five and forty-four. Although the suburban sex ratio is well below 100, the excess of females is not as great as in the urban population as a whole. Fertility rates are higher than in the central city, but not as high as in rural areas.

The socioeconomic status of suburbanites averages well above that of people in the central city. Average income is higher and a larger proportion of the workers are in professional and business occupations. Many of the families are upwardly mobile and the move to the suburbs signifies their social mobility. Furthermore, high rates of geographic mobility characterize suburbia. Although most of the families are making payments on a home, the payments are regarded like rent, and equities are readily traded and sold. For those whose careers are most successful, each move may be to a more prestigeful and expensive suburb and may symbolize a step in their upward movement.

As in the rural neighborhood, primary relations in the suburbs are often based upon proximity of residence rather than upon commonality of interests. (See SOCIAL ORGANIZATION, pp. 20–26.) There is a return to "neighboring" and a trend away from the impersonality and anonymity of the central city. Participation in community organizations, including religious ones, is high. Politically, suburbanites are more conservative than people in the central city. Morally, they are more conventional.

Each suburb tends to be homogeneous in the size and appearance of homes, in the income of residents, and in the patterns of consumption. Conspicuous consumption is avoided, getting ahead of the Joneses is apparently as strongly disapproved as failure to keep up with them. Even leisure activities are highly uniform.

Caution These generalizations do not apply to all suburbs and sometimes have been called "myths of suburbia." A study of a suburb populated by automobile workers questions the propositions that organizational participation is higher in the suburbs, that residential mobility is greater, that the suburbs are characterized by political conservatism and a renewed interest in religion, and that suburban culture is essentially middle class.[62] The working-class suburb may itself be a deviant case, and generalizations based on the suburban studies thus far completed should be regarded as tentative. The trends of decentralization and the growth of industrial satellites may result in two major types of suburban residence and life-styles: outlying neighborhoods in which middle-income commuters live and working-class suburbs.

Central city as living environment The pace of suburbanization has resulted in the deterioration of the urban core. Central cities are decaying faster than they are being rebuilt. The middle-income populations—mostly whites—continue to flee to the suburbs, to be replaced primarily by the poor—Negroes and others whose need for special services burdens shrinking civic resources. The tax base of the central city is diminished by the movement of industry to satellites, and this process has been hastened by tax-supported federal subsidies that favor highway construction over mass commuter transportation. The quality of such vital public services as education suffers from the decline in tax revenue. City streets become more congested as

---

[61] See especially William M. Dobriner (ed.), *The Suburban Community* (New York: Putnam, 1948), and William H. Whyte, Jr., *The Organization Man* (New York: Simon and Schuster, 1956).

[62] Bennett Berger, *The Working-Class Suburb* (Berkeley and Los Angeles: University of California Press, 1960).

traffic pours in from new superhighways. In attempts to salvage the central city, urban governments struggle to gain support for rapid transit systems that would afford a practical alternative to the automobile.

Urban decay and the growth of suburbs are due to the uncoordinated choices of large numbers of citizens and to public policy. While middle-income families have fled the deteriorating central cities in search of low-density housing in the suburbs, federally subsidized urban renewal has replaced slums with commercial and industrial sites and high-income housing.[63]

Low-cost housing for those displaced by slum clearance was originally a prime goal of the federal renewal subsidy program, but not more than one-fifth of the first $3 billion provided has been used to improve the housing of poor families. A major reason for this is political resistance to publicly-owned low-cost housing and rent subsidy plans.

Belatedly the federal government is pressing local communities to improve relocation procedures. However, the years of inattention to the problems of poor families dislocated by slum clearance have left a legacy of distrust now expressed as wholesale opposition to all renewal proposals that call for large-scale relocation.

City planners are caught in a dilemma. They want to purge the city of the most deteriorated buildings, which are unsightly and sometimes dangerous. They want to reduce crowding, to improve the physical environment, admit light and air, and bring trees and grass to the heart of the city. But their aspirations are more frequently than not frustrated by the scarcity and the high cost of land that dictate intensive use and dense occupancy. Housing projects, therefore, tend to increase the number of persons per acre even though the amount of space between buildings is greater than before the slums were "cleared."

Superblocks versus neighborhoods Many city designers try to develop areas of large homogeneous units. They plan in superblocks in order to gain open space, but slum clearance without reference to prior land use destroys neighborhoods and substitutes environments without past or personality. Recent opinion has become sensitive to the consequences of earlier policies that began urban renewal by knocking down everything in the neighborhood. But there is a persistent tendency to label as slums viable neighborhoods with which planners are unfamiliar.[64] Partially deteriorated neighborhoods that are adapted to their residents' needs may be heedlessly destroyed because the positive values contained in the slum environment are not recognized by middle-class planners.

The rehabilitation of established neighborhoods and the preservation of the original buildings without displacing residents is gaining increased favor with social scientists, some planners, and neighborhood groups, which have become increasingly militant and sophisticated in resisting the more ruthless of slum clearance practices. Furthermore, the technology of renewal has rapidly improved. It is now possible to restore structures economically and with such efficiency that the residents may return within a few days to a building in which the interior was entirely replaced. Selective renewal that does not displace the residents makes possible the continued existence of neighborhoods and is supported by those who object to area-wide clearance.

A parallel point of view [65] pleads for neighborhood diversity through the following means: (1) a "close-grained mix" of ground-floor stores and residences, (2) the preservation of short blocks, which tend to facilitate neighboring, (3) the preservation of old buildings to give a sense of continuity and architectural variety, and (4) high density with much of the land covered by buildings.

---

[63] William G. Grigsby, "Housing and Slum Clearance: Elusive Goals," *Annals* of the American Academy of Political and Social Science, *352* (1964), pp. 109–110.

[64] Herbert Gans, *The Urban Villagers* (New York: The Free Press of Glencoe, 1962), p. x.

[65] A vigorous (and controversial) presentation is found in Jane Jacobs, *The Life and Death of American Cities* (New York: Random House, 1961). For the other side, see, for example, Lewis Mumford, *The Culture of Cities* (New York: Harcourt, Brace & World, 1938), and Clarence S. Stein, *Toward New Towns for America* (New York: Reinhold, 1957).

In her argument for a "close-grained mix," Jacobs shows that sidewalks perform social functions beyond their manifest use: (1) The busy foot traffic of a well-used city street makes the street safe for women and children because the street is constantly under surveillance from its windows, stoops, and shops. (2) The street is a location for *un*organized play and for socialization of children by neighbors as well as peers. (3) The sidewalk and its shops are a communication network and a place where privacy is balanced against varying kinds of contact.

The uniform areas of office buildings stand in stark contrast to the round-the-clock activity of heterogeneously used blocks. In Washington, D.C., for example, massive and homogeneous offices cover acre after acre. Some of the buildings are admirable —if it is assumed that every building ought to be a monument—and the lawns lend a park-like quality to the city. But the center of a national bureaucracy, vigorously active during the working day, is deserted at night, populated by a few janitors and police. Belatedly there has been a shift in the thinking of Washington planners, and new office needs may be met by smaller buildings located in residential areas where at least some of the workers might live. The official buildings and their grounds would add variety to neighborhoods without overwhelming them. Washington then might become something less of a park to be looked at by tourists and something more of a city in which people live.

Renewal of business districts Renewal projects for revitalizing central business districts have had greater success than residential renewal. In addition to new office buildings, specialty shops, department stores, prominent restaurants, theaters, and other entertainment attractions combine to attract some of the affluent back from the suburbs to conveniently situated townhouses and high-rise apartments expanding on the fringes of the central business district.

The townhouses and high-rise apartments offer some new residential choices within the spatial limits imposed on metropolitan areas. Where metropolitan populations exceed roughly two million, the huge concentrations of people induce high land values that necessitate high proportions of row-houses and apartment construction.[66]

The suburban exodus of the last two decades has been stimulated by rising incomes, relatively full employment, liberal mortgage financing subsidized by federal and state government, and superhighways.[67] Many city planners decry this process primarily on the grounds that it weakens the urban core and creates monotonous and sterile tracts that engulf the dwindling farm and open-space land on the urban fringes. (See POPULATION AND ECOLOGY, p. 294.) To the critic, mass suburbanization has created sprawling "slurbs" and left slums in its wake. However, if the process were reversed the resulting recentralization would raise urban land values still further, making slum clearance even more expensive and imposing even greater restrictions on residential choices.

MEGALOPOLIS

On the Northeastern seaboard of the United States, in Great Britain, in the Low Countries, and in Western Germany, a new type of urban entity has grown up—the megalopolis. The megalopolis consists of two or more cities, once separated by broad bands of countryside, but now joined by strips of urban or semiurban settlement. Within the connecting strips there is an intermingling of urban, suburban, and rural land uses and a new relationship of the urban and the rural. The residents of the "super cities" are more widely dispersed than the residents of traditional compact cities, and their activities are not organized around any one central core. However, they have a higher degree of interdependence than the residents of any other area of comparable extent.

Although megalopolis has social and ecological unity, it lacks political unity. Unified planning and action are needed to handle transportation and re-

[66] Grigsby, *op. cit.,* p. 114.
[67] *Ibid.,* pp. 115–117.

source conservation, which transcend the bounds of the politically separate cities, but most planning and social action within the super cities have been piecemeal. Institutional adaptation has lagged behind the needs of these new social entities.

Administrative fragmentation　The numerous jurisdictions are jealous of their authorities and prerogatives, and as yet no "natural" agency has grown up to fill the gaps in management, to bridge authorities, or to devise overall plans. The following comment, written during World War II, depicts Metropolitan London as a bombing target, and as a problem in administration.[68]

Centered on teeming Charing Cross, the London area is the most compact and circular conurbation in the world, and by the same token it is the most deadly target for aerial bombardment that man could ever have devised. . . . There are ten official Londons overlapping one another, like concentric circles around a bull's-eye, each one representing the metropolis in its various stages of governmental growth. These are the City of London, the County of London, Police London or Greater London, Port London, Drainage London, Water London, Electricity London, Transport London, Planning London, and Traffic London. Increasing in radius and in population from the London nucleus the whole southeastern corner of England is engulfed by the Metro London that began to emerge long before the present war.

Near the center of the bull's-eye is the City of London, now badly gutted by incendiary bombing, with only one square mile of territory not much larger than Chicago's Loop, and a resident population of only nine thousand souls (1937 estimate). The City plays primarily a financial and economic role, comparable to New York's Wall Street. Governmentally, too, it is still a powerful municipal corporation in spite of the fact that its Guildhall has been bombed out. It has, for example, a police force of its own that is independent of even Scotland Yard, and it exercises important extraterritorial functions including that of acting as the Port of London's Sanitary Authority.

Though its more important docks and harbors are within the City of London, Port London goes far beyond the city boundaries, for it is an elongated district extending sixty-nine miles from Teddington on the west to the Thames's mouth on the east, and is responsible for the second largest port in the world.

The analysis also enumerates the boundaries and functions of each "London," which together make up the super city.

The Northeastern American megalopolis is an extreme example of political fragmentation.[69] This strip city extends from southern New Hampshire to the Virginia suburbs of Washington, D.C., a distance of some 425 miles. One can travel from one end to the other of this super city without leaving territory that is predominantly urban in its land use, its occupations, and the way of life of its people. Within the area, about 20 percent of the nation's people are concentrated on less than 2 percent of its land. Ten state governments, the District of Columbia, and hundreds of city, county, town, and village governments—each has jurisdiction over a portion of this megalopolitan belt. Smaller strip cities are developing along major transportation routes in the Midwest, in California, in Texas, and in other areas.

URBAN NEIGHBORHOODS

Slum clearance and urban redevelopment projects that use the formal authority of government to achieve their objectives undermine the communal structure of established neighborhoods. Small shops are destroyed and their customers displaced, churches lose their congregations and displaced families must live for months or years in places they did not choose. Even if the old residents eventually do return to the old localities, the neighborhood is gone. A new community may grow up but this will be harder to achieve because the old shops and small service facilities have been destroyed, and with them the sense of identity that is the product of spontaneous and prolonged associations. These costs, too,

---

[68] Albert Lepawsky, "The London Region: A Metropolitan Community in Crisis," *American Journal of Sociology, 46* (1941), 828–829.

[69] A detailed treatment of the economic and demographic characteristics of this area is given in Jean Gottman, *Megalopolis* (New York: The Twentieth Century Fund, 1961).

are the by-product—the unintended by-product—of change.

Urban neighborhoods seem to have a typical life cycle—a period of rapid growth, an interim of stability, and a prolonged senescence of blight and decay.

The typical life cycle of urban neighborhoods is due to the durability of buildings and the housing shortage, which has accompanied the rapid growth of American cities.[70] Because of these factors, old buildings remain profitable to their owners long after their condition falls below requirements of the upper and middle classes. Since to demolish these buildings would destroy property of considerable value, new residential construction is largely in previously uninhabited areas, and the old neighborhoods become slums.

The few upper- and upper-middle-class neighborhoods in large cities in which succession to lower-class residential usage has not occurred are rare enough to attract attention. Beacon Hill in Boston survives as a fashionable district, in spite of its great age and the encroachment of commercial activities, because it has become a symbol of upper-class standing and an object of strong sentiment among old Boston families.[71] An old residential area near the central business district in Chicago, the Gold Coast, has remained an upper- and upper-middle-class area, the old mansions having been gradually replaced by expensive high-rise apartments and residential hotels. A favorable location on the lake-front is a necessary, although probably not a sufficient, condition for this anomaly.

Among the few other examples of highly desirable residential areas that have resisted decay, one warrants special attention. Its conservation as a middle-class area shows that seemingly natural and inevitable social processes can be resisted through social planning and concerted social action. At the same time it illustrates some of the difficulties involved in social planning in a democratic and competitive society.

Planned change and group conflict Hyde Park–Kenwood is an area of some 70,000 people in Chicago's South Side.[72] The community began as a railroad suburb in the 1850s and was engulfed by the growth of Chicago before the turn of the century. Residential building occurred in several waves from the era following the Civil War to 1920–1924. By the latter date, the residential plant was all but completed. By the 1950s, therefore, the newest residential buildings of any large number were more than a quarter of a century old, and a substantial proportion were at least fifty years old. The community was middle-aged and beyond.

From their beginnings, the neighborhoods in Hyde Park–Kenwood were fashionable or above average in desirability. Kenwood emerged as a cluster of large and expensive single-family dwellings on spacious lots, and most of Hyde Park was built up with commodious and substantial (although crowded) walk-up apartments and single-family dwellings. During the last major building wave in the area, a number of luxury high-rise apartments and residential hotels were built in East Hyde Park.

In 1950 the community was still far above Chicago as a whole in a number of social and economic indices, although its relative position had declined somewhat from 1940. Even though it was almost engulfed by the expansion of the "Black Belt," only 6.1 percent of its population were nonwhite.

That Hyde Park–Kenwood survived so long as an above-average residential area without concerted action to preserve its middle-class character can be attributed largely to a cluster of institutions: the University of Chicago, which has dominated the area physically and culturally almost since its founding in 1892, the American School, George Williams College, the Chicago Osteopathic School, and the Museum of Science and Industry. The cultural attrac-

---

[70] Nelson N. Foote *et al., Housing Choices and Constraints* (New York: McGraw-Hill, 1960).

[71] Walter Firey, *Land Use in Central Boston* (Cambridge: Harvard University Press, 1947), Chap. 3.

[72] See Peter H. Rossi and Robert A. Dentler, *The Politics of Urban Renewal* (New York: The Free Press of Glencoe, 1961).

tions, the beaches, and several parks nearby have helped retain the upper-income residents of Kenwood and East Hyde Park, and the employees of the institutions comprise a large professional population.

After 1950, however, parts of the community began to deteriorate rapidly. Negroes began to settle in several localities, and the percentage of the nonwhite population increased to 36 percent by 1956. Between 1950 and 1956, an estimated 20,000 whites left Hyde Park–Kenwood and were replaced with 23,000 nonwhites. The first of the Negroes were mainly business, professional, white-collar, and skilled workers, but the later arrivals were predominantly domestic servants and unskilled and semiskilled workers. Two Negro families sometimes moved into an apartment or house vacated by one white family. The Negro areas became crowded and littered. Transition to a low-income neighborhood was well under way.

Hyde Park–Kenwood, however, was unlike most areas entering on the final stage of deterioration. (1) The large institutions in the area, particularly the University of Chicago, had heavy capital investments in the area and thus had a material interest in preserving its middle-class character. With a growing shortage of top-quality academic personnel in the nation, a slum location would be a distinct handicap to the University in its attempts to retain its position as a leading university. Furthermore, its undergraduate enrollment was dropping, in part due to a shortage of student housing in the vicinity. (2) The community in general had a liberal-intellectual orientation. Many of its residents, at least verbally, favored a biracial community, even though they wished to retain its middle-class character. Another element of the liberal-intellectual orientation was a belief in the possibility and desirability of planned social change. (3) The community was "hyperorganized" and had an above-average rate of political participation. (4) The University of Chicago, with its excellent social science departments, afforded an unusual planning resource.

Another factor which made conservation of the community possible was the passage of the Federal Housing Act of 1954, which authorized federal assistance for "urban renewal." Among other things, the bill provided that federal funds, supplemented by local funds, could be used to purchase blighted property to be sold below cost for private redevelopment or to be used for public housing. Launching of urban renewal projects depends entirely upon local initiative. Although the program adopted to conserve and rehabilitate Hyde Park–Kenwood came under "urban renewal," the groundwork for the program was laid before 1954.

Community organization The prime mover of the program to conserve and renew the community was the University of Chicago. As early as 1939 the University was active in efforts to maintain the middle-class character of its surroundings, but until 1952 its principal action had been the extension of racially restrictive covenants and the subsidizing of two community associations, which worked for enforcement of zoning and housing codes. In 1952 the University embarked upon a more positive effort. For this purpose it formed the South East Chicago Commission, which became the principal planning agency for the community. In 1954 the Commission assigned planning functions to a separate committee.

The second major participant in the efforts to conserve the community was the Hyde Park–Kenwood Community Conference, an organization with wide community support, founded in 1949 under the leadership of ministers, rabbis, and laymen from liberal religious groups. At times the Conference influenced the conservation planning process, but its chief role was to serve as a transmission belt between the Planning Unit and the citizens. The support and confidence of the citizenry was necessary for two reasons. (1) The community could not be conserved if the residents did not have enough confidence in its future to remain, and (2) popular support or at least the lack of strong popular opposition was needed if public officials were to approve the plan. The Community Conference helped provide the mass support.

Conflicting perspectives At first there was near

consensus on the desirability of taking positive action. However, as details of the plan were worked out, it became evident to many that the plan would work to their detriment. Persons who had received the plan warmly became less enthusiastic when they learned they were to be planned out of the community. Many learned that Hyde Park–Kenwood was to become so "renewed" that they could no longer afford to live there. Businessmen who at first looked with favor upon plans for a new shopping center were less favorable when they learned that the total number of business establishments would be reduced and not all of them would be able to relocate in the community. Particularly cool to the plan were the Negro residents in areas selected for clearing. For most, the movement into Hyde Park was upward mobility. Their housing was better than they had before and better than they could find elsewhere in Chicago. People who had invested money and work on their homes resented having them defined as dilapidated. Blighted areas to older residents were pleasant neighborhoods to new arrivals.

Controversy arose among the leaders in the conservation movement. Racial liberals were disturbed that the renewal would greatly reduce the Negro population in the area. Racial conservatives were disturbed by the guarantees of nondiscrimination that would come with participation in the federal urban renewal program. In the end, the liberals accepted less biracialism than they desired, and the conservatives accepted more. Many middle-class Negroes were ambivalent toward the plan. As one prominent Negro put it, "every Hyde Park Negro leader is almost driven schizophrenic trying to decide whether to act as a 'Race Man' or in terms of his social class position." [73]

[73] *Ibid.,* p. 181.

Opposition to the plan also arose from other sections of Chicago. The effects of the renewal would not be strictly local. If the population density in Hyde Park–Kenwood was to be reduced, the displaced population was likely to contribute to overcrowding in other parts of the city. People in other white areas bordering the "Black Belt" feared that stemming the Negro movement into Hyde Park–Kenwood would increase pressure for Negro entry into their neighborhoods. The Chicago Negro leaders generally opposed the plan because it would reduce the amount of housing available to Negroes. The NAACP, the Chicago Urban League, the Cardinal's Committee on Conservation and Urban Renewal, and the Packinghouse Workers Union were among the opponents.

Some of the opposition to the plan from within Hyde Park–Kenwood subsided as compromises were made and people became reconciled·to being displaced. An association of residents in South West Hyde Park opposed through litigation the use of condemnation procedures to clear an area in that neighborhood, but the efforts were unsuccessful. The city-wide opposition to the urban renewal plan delayed approval of the plan by the City Council, but the opponents did not gain wide public support.

Final approval of the plan came late in 1958, six years after the formation of the South East Chicago Commission. In its final form the plan was a compromise that satisfied no one completely. For instance, liberals were chagrined that no guarantee for public housing was included in the plan. However, the plan was generally acceptable to the interests of the University of Chicago and those Hyde Park–Kenwood residents who wished to keep the community solidly middle class.

CHAPTER XIV

INDUSTRIAL MAN*

SECTION 1 EARLY INDUSTRIALIZATION

Among the master trends of modern history is the rise of industrialism—an economic and social order based on machine technology and on large-scale highly specialized systems of production. Industrialization began in western Europe and has now become worldwide. Men everywhere seem destined to know and experience, to enjoy and endure, the distinctive features of an industrial society.

This chapter considers, first, some aspects of the early stages of industrialization, especially the problems of motivation and discipline that accompany the break from traditional society. The discussion draws on studies of early capitalism and on analyses of non-Western society. Section 2 traces the development of two major institutions of industrial society—the business firm and the labor union. Section 3 discusses the impact of technology on human relations with emphasis on the theory of alienation. Finally, Section 4 presents some highlights of the composition of the labor force.

SOCIAL RELATIONS AND INDUSTRIAL CAPITALISM

Under feudalism, social life centered on the economically self-sufficient manorial estate controlled by a lord. Economic roles were fixed by tradition and custom, and division of labor was limited to broad categories—farmers, supervisors, soldiers, and village artisans, such as blacksmiths, carpenters, and masons. An individual's occupational position and his status as freeman or serf were inherited. Unfree tenants or serfs were bound to the estate by tradition and law, and everyone, whether free or serf, was obligated to render services to the lord and pay taxes in goods or money. In return the lord resolved disputes, avenged wrongs to his people, and protected the manorial community from foreign invasion and marauding bands.

The breakdown of feudal rights and obligations freed workers to go where early capitalist enterprises

* This chapter draws upon some material included in earlier editions written in collaboration with Helen Beem Gouldner.

The Butcher and His Servant

The Coppersmith

The Hatter

During the Middle Ages there was little occupational specialization; a worker and his assistants carried the process to completion. The modern organization of production involves an extreme differentiation of skills: about 22,000 separate occupations are defined in the Dictionary of Occupational Titles, *3rd edition, United States Department of Labor, 1965.*

were located. Propertyless workers provided the labor force necessary to industrial capitalism.

With a free labor force, the entrepreneur was not responsible for his workers as was the feudal lord. He could hire and fire according to the needs of his factory.[1]

Achieved status Under feudalism a person's occupation and station in life were ascribed, fixed by tradition and inheritance. The son of a serf was also a serf, and the son of a blacksmith in a feudal village was trained to become a blacksmith. In a system of free labor, ascription gave way to individual choice and achievement.

Division of labor on an achieved rather than inherited basis is congenial to the development and expansion of industrial capitalism for the following reasons: (*a*) Achievement is better adapted to specialization, which is a characteristic feature of in-

dustrial capitalism. When occupations are inherited and training takes place within the family, the number of possible specializations is limited. (*b*) With technological advance, job requirements change and new jobs are created. It is unlikely that the technological advances that have played a major role in the expansion of industrial capitalism could have developed to such an extent without emphasis on achieved status and its accompanying ideals of initiative and acquisition. On the relation between social organization and machine technology, see Adaptation 33, pages 469–472.

RELIGION AND CAPITALISM

An economic order depends on beliefs and sentiments that make for effective participation in economic activities. The "spirit" or "ethos" of capitalism is expressed in the virtues of individualism, hard work, thrift, self-discipline, accumulation, initiative,

[1] Max Weber, *The Theory of Social and Economic Organization* (New York: Oxford University Press, 1947), pp. 276–278; Wilbert E. Moore, *Industrial Relations and the Social Order* (2nd ed.; New York: Macmillan, 1951), pp. 420–421 and 425–427.

Max Weber (1864–1920) was one of the German economic historians and sociologists who attempted to trace the distinctive features of the capitalist social and economic order. He undertook a vast comparative study of world religions in order to see the relation between religious ideas and economic development. The best-known product of this work is The Protestant Ethic and the Spirit of Capitalism. *He also wrote extensively on bureaucracy, law, and the logical foundations of social science.*

and rationality. These beliefs, not shared by the whole society, were characteristic of middle-class

entrepreneurs. The values are put forward as *duties* in Benjamin Franklin's "Advice to a Young Tradesman" (p. 467).

These personal aspirations and disciplines were especially important in the formative years of capitalism. Early capitalism depended on the enterprise and work of individuals rather than on complicated and impersonal large-scale organizations. The development of capitalism needed businessmen and manufacturers who were motivated to work hard, save, compete for markets, expand their enterprises, and accumulate capital. For both the entrepreneur and his subordinates, self-discipline and industriousness were essential to fulfilling the requirements of the business. To the extent that a similar ethic extended to the workers, regular attendance in the factory and continuous operation of the machines were furthered. "Grass may grow and sheep may graze if the peasant lies drunk under the hedge occasionally, but the wheels of mills cannot turn steadily if boiler stokers must have frequent debauches." [2]

The cultural origin of industriousness, self-discipline, initiative, and acquisitiveness has been much debated. The problem is this:

. . . how is it possible that strata of enterprisers and workers emerge that are willing to engage in methodically persistent, hard work and thereby gain a competitive advantage over less principled, more traditionalist economic agents? These men forego the traditional enjoyments of wealth—the expansion of their consumption, or the investment of wealth in ostentatious ways. How is it, then, that men arise who work hard, despite the fact that in the value terms of their economic tradition and epoch they have no understandable motives for doing so? [3]

The Protestant ethic In *Protestant Ethic and the Spirit of Capitalism,* Max Weber suggests that the main roots of capitalist ideology grew with the spread of Protestantism throughout Western societies. The main points in his study—how Protestant doctrine

[2] Charles A. Beard, "Individualism and Capitalism," in *Encyclopaedia of the Social Sciences* (London: Macmillan, Ltd.), *1.* Quotation at p. 149.

[3] Hans Gerth and C. Wright Mills, *Character and Social Structure* (New York: Harcourt, Brace & World, 1953), p. 215. Used by permission.

shaped the personalities of the rising class of entrepreneurs in which capitalism had its origins—are summarized below.[4]

1. *Self-discipline and work.* The Calvinist doctrine of predestination held that men were to be either condemned to everlasting hell or to "live in the House of the Lord forever." Because believers in this doctrine were uncertain whether they were among the elect, they were anxious and insecure. Strict self-discipline, rejection of worldly pleasures, and righteous success in this world through hard work came to be regarded as signs of grace, evidence that one was in God's favor. Relief from religious anxiety was thus sought in disciplined effort. To work was to pray, and work was a calling. Independent, honest business was interpreted as a calling particularly acceptable to God.

2. *Initiative and acquisition.* Hard work and self-discipline won economic advantage over competitors and led to the acquisition of wealth. Since the Puritans were supposed to avoid worldly pleasure, be thrifty, and abhor waste, they could not use wealth in traditional ways. They could, however, use their capital to expand their business activities. Individual initiative was rewarded, since success in work was interpreted as a sign of God's blessing. Furthermore, continual work in one's calling alleviated constant anxiety about salvation. No matter what a Puritan accomplished in this world, he had no guarantee of salvation. Therefore, he could not relax.

3. *Individualism and competition.* Puritans believed that man is alone before his Maker, that he should not trust the friendship of men, that only God should be his confidant because even those closest to him might be among the damned. Each individual could seek success as the sign of grace, and this striving was consistent with economic competition. He dealt honestly and righteously with other men, but he was ready to take advantage of his opportunities even if that meant outdoing his competitors. (See RELIGION, p. 323.)

The capitalist spirit did not flow directly from the

John Calvin (1509–1564), Swiss theologian, was a leading architect of the Protestant Reformation. At the age of twenty-six he published The Institutes of the Christian Religion, *one of the most influential religious books in history. Calvin stressed the depravity and corruption of human nature, the need for redemption through faith and repentance, and the doctrine of predestination and election. His views led to emphasis on personal traits of self-denial and self-discipline, which Weber linked to the "capitalist spirit." Sponsor and leader of a theocracy in Geneva, Calvin had no thought of contributing to economic or political individualism. While he profoundly influenced Protestantism as a whole, his impress was strongest in Puritan England, Scotland, and New England, especially in the seventeenth century.*

religious revolution of Luther and Calvin. But the revolution did go beyond religion to influence more

[4] Translated by Talcott Parsons (London: Allen and Unwin, 1930). See also R. H. Tawney, *Religion and the Rise of Capitalism* (New York: Harcourt, Brace & World, 1926). On the relation of religion and capitalism and for an exposition of Weber's thesis, see Gerth and Mills, *op. cit.*, pp. 234–236 and 360–363.

general cultural attitudes toward work, poverty, individual obligation, and the worth of trade and industry. The rising merchant and industrial classes of the seventeenth and eighteenth centuries embraced the new values, were strengthened by them, and in turn helped mold religion to the requirements of a commercial age.[5]

Religion and mature capitalism   As the new economic order became more formalized and institutionalized, and as accounting systems and other controls developed, capitalism leaned less heavily on the personal qualities of individuals. It depended less on religious motivations and disciplines. Even by the time Franklin wrote the "Advice," printed on page 467, it was possible to take for granted the values of thrift and economic prudence without explicit religious reference.

However, many of the ideas embodied in Protestantism continue to support modern industry. Self-discipline and the ability to defer gratification are highly prized, as are initiative, hard work, and success. These values eliminate the need for extensive socialization within industry, at least in the Western world. The individual comes to his job already inculcated with appropriate habits and beliefs.

INDUSTRIALIZATION IN NON-WESTERN SOCIETIES

As industrialization spreads throughout the non-Western world, social scientists have the opportunity to observe the impact of machine technology on social life, the transformation of values, and the interdependence of economic activities and social organization.[6]

Adaptation 33 outlines the social patterns accompanying the introduction of machine technology in non-Western societies. The study shows how industrialism causes the old social order to break down by separating economic activities from the total social system, by placing new individuals in positions of power, and by changing levels of aspiration among the workers. New social relations develop in the course of adjustment to machines. Impersonal relations replace personal ties, and achieved status becomes more important than family relations in the division of labor.

The dual society and labor commitment[7]   In some settings industrialization takes over completely. This is especially likely where an indigenous population is sparse and has a weakly developed technology. In Australia, for example, the small numbers of aborigines are peripheral to the industrial economy and influence it in no important way.

Another possibility is the emergence of a *dual society,* the coexistence of an industrial social system with a preindustrial one. This occurs when industrialism is introduced into densely populated agrarian societies. The imported system may be mature capitalism, socialism, communism, or a blend of systems. Dual societies now exist in much of Eastern and Southern Asia, Africa, and Latin America.

In dual societies the divergent values of the industrial and preindustrial world affect each other in complicated and not always predictable ways. In Western society many men can be found who are willing to go on accumulating wealth they may never spend. Even the ordinary worker may come to believe that he "cannot afford" to give up a well-paying job.

Preindustrial man does not want to accumulate wealth for its own sake. Employees often work hard to satisfy an immediate need but cannot be spurred to further effort once that need is satisfied. In industrial societies higher pay usually holds down the rate of labor turnover. Preindustrial workers tend to leave the job when their requirements are satisfied, and higher pay may, therefore, result in increased labor turnover.

[5] Cf. Tawney, *op. cit.*

[6] Wilbert E. Moore, *Industralization and Labor* (Ithaca: Cornell University Press, 1951). See also Bert F. Hoselitz (ed.), *The Progress of Underdeveloped Areas* (Chicago: University of Chicago Press, 1952).

[7] This discussion is indebted to J. H. Boeke, *Economics and Economic Policy of Dual Societies* (New York: Institute of Pacific Relations, 1953), and Wilbert E. Moore, *op. cit.* in ftn. 6.

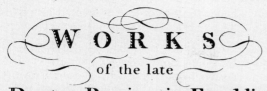

WORKS
of the late
Doctor Benjamin Franklin

Consisting of

HIS LIFE WRITTEN BY HIMSELF,

together with

Efsays, Humorous, Moral & Literary,

Chiefly in the Manner of

THE SPECTATOR.

ADVICE TO A YOUNG TRADESMAN.

WRITTEN ANNO 1748.

REMEMBER that *time* is money. He that can earn ten fhillings a day by his labour, and goes abroad, or fits idle one half of that day, though he fpends but fixpence during his diverfion or idlenefs, ought not to reckon *that* the only expence; he has really fpent, or rather thrown away, five fhillings befides.

Remember that money is of a prolific generating nature. Money can beget money, and its offspring can beget more, and fo on. Five fhillings turned is fix; turned again, it is feven and three-pence; and fo on till it becomes an hundred pounds. The more there is of it, the more it produces every turning, fo that the profits rife quicker and quicker.

Beware of thinking all your own that you poffefs, and of living accordingly. It is a miftake that many people who have credit fall into. To prevent this, keep an exact account, for fome time, both of your expences and your income. If you take the pains at firft to mention particulars, it will have this good effect; you will difcover how wonderfully fmall trifling expences mount up to large fums, and will difcern what might have been, and may for the future be faved, without occafioning any great inconvenience.

In fhort, the way to wealth, if you defire it, is as plain as the way to market. It depends chiefly on two words, *induftry* and *frugality*; that is, wafte neither *time* nor *money*, but make the beft ufe of both. Without induftry and frugality nothing will do, and with them every thing. He that gets all he can honeftly, and faves all he gets (neceffary expences excepted), will certainly become *rich*—if that Being who governs the world, to whom all fhould look for a bleffing on their honeft endeavours, doth not, in his wife providence, otherwife determine.

AN OLD TRADESMAN.

Labor commitment Much has been written about the problems of recruiting a committed, reliable, and stable labor force in societies undergoing industrialization. The limited economic wants of workers are only one obstacle to a committed labor force. For instance, in nonindustrial societies kinship systems are also economic systems, and the marked change in a man's economic role when he enters the industrial labor force disrupts his accustomed social relations. The social penalties of this disruption may keep him home even if he has economic incentives for working. Furthermore, peasants and artisans often dislike or think they would dislike the rigid time schedule and discipline of the factory. An expected loss of personal autonomy was a major obstacle to industrial employment in a Mexican village.[8] However, actually confronted by the schedule of discipline of industrial employment, workers adjusted well.

Although the problem of obtaining a committed industrial labor force in dual societies is formidable, it is not insurmountable. Industrialism is advancing throughout the world, perhaps impeded but never stopped by a lack of committed labor. Workers enter and remain in the industrial labor force despite countervailing influences.

The first industrial recruits are usually the landless, the hungry, the politically powerless, and the socially disaffected, who are pushed rather than pulled into industrial employment. The push is often provided by the beginning of industrialization itself. Cheap manufactured goods lessen the demand for handicraft goods and make it necessary for artisans to seek new means of livelihood. Basic needs can no longer be satisfied in traditional ways. The reduced mortality that accompanies industrialization spurs population growth, increases rural population density, and makes it difficult for peasants to subsist by tilling the land.

It has been thought that in India the conservatism of the traditional village society and a caste system would impede the development of an industrial labor force. However, the recruitment of commited workers has gone forward faster than expected.

The desperate poverty of the countryside made available a large labor supply that was eager to move into industry as opportunity appeared. Once employed in the factories, the workers on the whole rather readily adjusted to the disciplinary requirements of mechanized industry. Early in the history of the steel company at Jamshedpur an intensely committed labor force emerged. In Bombay, although the evidence is somewhat less conclusive, commitment to industrial employment was not difficult to achieve. Neither the multiplicity of language nor the institutions of caste seriously affected employers' ability to obtain a labor force committed to the factory system.[9]

The extent to which a labor force is incorporated into the industrial complex is measured by the degree to which the following conditions hold:

1. Acceptance of factory routines, time schedules, and discipline

2. Surmounting traditional obstacles to interaction on the job, e.g., caste barriers or race prejudice

3. Free geographic movement of labor to places of manpower shortage

4. Labor stability, i.e., little absenteeism and capricious quitting

Cautions 1. The end product of industrialization is not necessarily complete Westernization. For example, Japan has acquired an industrial technology and an efficient labor force. But the organization of the labor force is in some sectors of the economy more paternalistic and regimented than in the West. Many of the adaptations of modern Japan are evolutions of Japanese culture rather than of Western culture. The future development of Japan will be away from the traditional society but not necessarily toward Western forms.[10]

2. This discussion emphasizes worker adjustment to an industrial order. Management must also assume responsibility in creating a committed labor force. Worker adjustment is retarded when management

---

[8] Moore, *op. cit.,* Chap. 12.

[9] Morris David Morris, "The Labor Market in India," in Wilbert E. Moore and Arnold S. Feldman, *Labor Commitment and Social Change in Developing Areas* (New York: Social Science Research Council, 1960), pp. 197–198.

[10] See James C. Abegglen, *The Japanese Factory* (Glencoe: The Free Press, 1958).

tries to maintain traditional, paternalistic authority without assuming the obligations of paternalistic responsibility, or when management treats new recruits from villages as if they were experienced and committed workers.

3. In the non-Western world, a highly developed technology is being brought to societies that may lack the supports present in the West during its period of industrialization. In Europe and North America the transformation was costly in human suffering, but it came more gradually, was more closely tied to other social changes such as the rise of science, and there was more time for economic, social, and cultural adaptation. Because the histories are different, different strains and outcomes should be expected.

SOURCES AND READINGS

Reinhard Bendix, *Work and Authority in Industry* (New York: Wiley, 1956).

Peter M. Blau and Otis Dudley Duncan, *The American Occupational System* (New York: Wiley, 1967).

Theodore Caplow, *Sociology of Work* (Minneapolis: University of Minnesota Press, 1954).

Melville Dalton, *Men Who Manage* (New York: Wiley, 1959).

Robert Dubin, *The World of Work* (Englewood Cliffs, N.J.: Prentice-Hall, 1958).

B. F. Hoselitz and W. E. Moore (eds.), *Industrialization and Society* (Paris and The Hague: UNESCO and Mouton, 1963).

Arthur Kornhauser, Robert Dubin, and Arthur M. Ross (editors), *Industrial Conflict* (New York: McGraw-Hill, 1954).

Rensis Likert, *New Patterns of Management* (New York: McGraw-Hill, 1961).

Delbert C. Miller and William H. Form, *Industrial Sociology* (2nd ed.; New York: Harper & Row, 1964).

Wilbert E. Moore, *The Conduct of the Corporation* (New York: Random House, 1962).

Wilbert E. Moore, *Industrial Relations and the Social Order* (2nd ed.; New York: Macmillan, 1951).

Manning Nash, *Primitive and Peasant Economic Systems* (San Francisco: Chandler Publishing, 1966).

Sigmund Nosow and William H. Form (eds.), *Man, Work, and Society* (New York: Basic Books, 1962).

Eugene V. Schneider, *Industrial Sociology* (New York: McGraw-Hill, 1957).

Neil J. Smelser, *Social Change in the Industrial Revolution* (Chicago: University of Chicago Press, 1959).

Charles R. Walker, *Modern Technology and Civilization* (New York: McGraw-Hill, 1962).

William H. Whyte, Jr., *The Organization Man* (New York: Simon and Schuster, 1956).

Periodicals

Economic Development and Cultural Change

Human Organization

Adaptation 33 / Theodorson INDUSTRIALISM AND SOCIAL RELATIONS IN NON-WESTERN SOCIETIES

Some leaders of nonindustrial societies have said they want only machines from the Western world, but they oversimplify the meaning of industrialism. The extensive use of

SOURCE: Abridged and adapted from George A. Theodorson, "Acceptance of Industrialization and Its Attendant Consequences for the Social Patterns of Non-Western Societies," *American Sociological Review, 18* (1953), 477–484. Published in this form by permission of George A. Theodorson and the *American Sociological Review.*

machines requires semiskilled and skilled workers, factory organization, and a money economy. The introduction of these elements in non-Western societies leads to the development of new social relations, which in time tend to resemble dominant patterns of Western industrialized society.[11]

If it can be learned what changes must accompany industrialization in order to prevent confusion and the waste of time, money, and effort, planners may be able to anticipate and control some of the consequences of industrialization. It is also important to know what need not change, for this knowledge may soften somewhat the impact of industrialism.

This essay suggests how industrialization causes the old social order to break down and new social relations to emerge. The social changes emphasized here are typical of many newly industrialized societies. However, there are wide variations in the social and cultural conditions of societies prior to the impact of industrialism and in the ways industrialism is introduced. Any particular society, therefore, may only approximate the changes outlined.

Disruption of the traditional order Before the introduction of mining and railroads, Northern Rhodesia in many respects typified nonindustrialized societies. It was inhabited by small groups living in village communities limited to a very small area and isolated from the outside world. Social relations were personal relations between kin and between lifelong intimates.

Our man in Nigeria: a representative of the Singer Company.

Subsistence agriculture or cattle-keeping seldom involved a man in cooperation with any save friends and relatives who lived near by. Marriage was a local affair and seldom joined families more than thirty miles apart. Religious ritual, ceremonial, warfare, hunting and fishing were only occasionally organized on any large scale; normally they were confined to the family, the village and the local district or chiefdom; and so a high degree of autonomy in each primitive community was inevitable.

The economic life of primitive Northern Rhodesia, being part of its general social life, was parochial; it consisted, above all, of the cooperation of groups of close kinsfolk and close neighbours; most things that men wanted were produced within their bounds. Hence, there was little specialization and techniques remained simple. These groups were both the main factories and the main markets of primitive life, for the circle of exchange only occasionally passed outside them.

In primitive Northern Rhodesia, then, the bonds of kinsfolk and neighbourhood were as much a matter of business—that is of reciprocal economic advantage—as of affection, duty and respect. It was upon them that a man depended for his daily bread and his whole livelihood. For a primitive African the obligations which bound him to a wife, to parents, to parents-in-law, to children, and so on, were as much determined by the fact that he could not prosper without them as by personal affection, or by the legal, moral and conventional codes of his tribe.[12]

[11] Further illustrations on industrialization of non-Western countries from Godfrey Wilson, *Economics of Detribalization in Northern Rhodesia, Part 1* (Livingstone: The Rhodes-Livingstone Institute, 1941); Wilbert E. Moore, *Industrialization and Labor* (Ithaca: Cornell University Press, 1951); Audrey I. Richards, *Land, Labour and Diet in Northern Rhodesia* (London: Oxford University Press, 1939); and Ralph L. Beals, "The Village in an Industrial World," *Scientific Monthly, 77* (1953), 65–75.

[12] Abridged from Wilson, *op. cit.,* pp. 9–12. Used by permission.

Throughout the world, many such isolated communities have been affected by industrialism. Improved transportation facilities have brought villagers in contact with nearby cities and have made possible urban employment and trade. Modern factories or mines have been established near primitive villages, workers have been drawn from nearby communities, and the traditional social organization is disrupted. Characteristically three major changes occur:

1. *Economic relations are separated from the integrated social system.* In nonindustrialized societies, it is often difficult to separate economic activities from other areas of behavior. Trading, domestic roles, and cooperative endeavors, such as planting and harvesting, are intimately bound up with familial ties and obligations and the social life of the community. Exchange of food, for example, may involve specific kinship obligations, a religious ceremony, and a display of family status.

When villagers leave home to work in a distant city or a nearby factory or mine, their economic activities are separated from the system of rights and obligations in the community. As the worker gains money and skills, he is no longer economically dependent on his immediate and extended family, and his kinship ties thereby become weaker. The authority and unity of family and community are undermined. For example, among the Bantu of Southern and Eastern Africa:

. . . family economy is sufficiently

disrupted so that the ordinary mode of supplying enough cattle for the bride price (lobola) through the obligations of the father and gifts or loans from other kinsmen no longer operates. The young man then may seek work not only to pay taxes but to *buy* cattle in order to complete the marriage agreement. This is already a radical and disruptive step. Its logical successor is the complete commutation of the necessary cattle-price into its monetary equivalent, thereby removing the whole arrangement from its functional context in the village economy, the customs and rituals of marriage and kinship, and the symbols of familial cohesion. At this juncture the original institutions have been mortally wounded and simply collapse, leaving the individual who is money-oriented to work out new familial arrangements in the absence of precedent and tradition.[13]

2. *New individuals are placed in positions of power.* Industrialism introduces new skills, tools, and money, which bring new rewards and satisfactions, make some persons economically independent of the old order, and create new social statuses. Under industrialism there may be an emphasis on skills that were insignificant in the old system. For example, trading and mechanical abilities gain new prestige.

The creation of new economic roles, new rewards, and the increased prominence of previously unimportant resources and skills tend to place new individuals in positions of power. The new power structure challenges the old and later tends to produce a new elite. The power and influence of new

merchants and manufacturers are most pronounced, and the new factory workers may improve their status. Previously higher classes who remain in agricultural pursuits may lose status. Among the Bemba of Northern Rhodesia, for example, those aspiring to leadership may gain followers through the distribution of goods. Mine workers are able to use their wages to buy goods and win positions of importance.[14]

Even if the new elite consists only of members of the old elite, the power structure is modified. The fact that they are the same individuals makes little difference, for they must learn new attitudes, expectations, and values in order to perform their new roles.

Opposition to industrialization may be encountered from those who expect to lose most from change. While new roles are being created, old roles and skills decline in importance. The fears of the threatened members are based on sound fact and are not simply irrational reactions to change. In New Guinea, for example, workers returning to their home communities are taking over the authority of older men.

3. *Levels of aspiration are changed.* One result of industrialization, the production of large quantities of cheap goods, further disrupts the old order. It makes available to the masses material products they never expected to own. The peoples of many societies are accustomed to poverty, drought, and famine. But small improvements brought about by in-

---

[13] Moore, *Industrialization and Labor,* pp. 81–82 (used by permission of the Cornell University Press). See Monica Hunter, *Reaction to Conquest* (London: Oxford University Press, 1936).

[14] Richards, *op. cit.,* pp. 211–218.

dustrialization may suggest the possibilities of even greater betterment, and this may lead to impatience and general dissatisfaction. (See POLITICAL MAN, pp. 503 f.)

Prolonged disorganization The transition from an old social order to a new one is accompanied by a conflict of social ties and values: the factory system versus the family system, orderly patterns of work versus less disciplined work habits. Obviously, not all systems undergo equal amounts of stress in the process of change. In some cases the transition is relatively smooth; in other instances disorganization is prolonged and serious.

Industrialization introduces new economic patterns but not a total social system. When the recruit is unhappy and discontented in the factory, it is not simply because he is nostalgic for the traditional atmosphere of his youth. It may be rather that the new environment does not afford him the satisfactions and security of a well-rounded and integrated pattern of life.

One of the most common barriers to the recruitment of a new labor force is the reluctance of the worker to give up the secure traditional patterns of village life. As a result, a pattern of intermittent, casual or migratory labor is often found. This allows the laborer to enter employment at intervals while maintaining contact with his home community.[15]

New social relations Social disorganization is not likely to be permanent. New social relations develop, reflecting in part adjustment to the factory system. Because machines are expensive, they must be used economically. In the early stages of industrialization, labor is far less scarce than machinery, and there is a strong incentive to adjust labor to the machines. Teaching and enforcing of these adjustments leads to new social relations, detachment of the worker from his home community, and emphasis on achieved status in the factory. The changes are first experienced by the factory workers and through them are communicated to those who are not directly involved in industry.

1. *Impersonality.* The worker must adjust to the long hours he has to spend away from his home community. Old values, the social controls of the village, and his ties to the home community are weakened. His immediate family tends to occupy an increasing proportion of his free time and his extended family diminishes in importance.

With the introduction of mining and railroads in Northern Rhodesia, the relations of workers to kin and villagers have become more and more tenuous. In fulfillment of traditional obligations, the mine worker still occasionally visits his village with gifts of cash and clothes. He fears to neglect his obligations both for religious reasons and because he still desires the respect and approval of his relatives. However, the bonds are weakened; the worker faces new obligations in his town and factory environment and is physically separated as well as economically independent of his kinship ties.[16]

The village of Nayon—near Quito, the capital of Ecuador—recently changed from an agricultural to a market economy. Before transportation facilities made the capital city accessible, the villagers lived primarily in association with relatives. Now villagers are often away on trading trips or in the city on business, and social relations within the village are more impersonal. There is little visiting among relatives and practically none among nonrelatives. "Characteristically, people in Nayon do not know what their neighbors are doing; moreover, they have comparatively little interest in knowing." [17]

2. *Achieved status.* In nonindustrialized communities kinship is an important basis for assigning roles. But machine operators are selected largely on the basis of technical competence. The factory system emphasizes assignment to jobs on the basis of achieved criteria rather than family relations. It is not who you are but what you can do that counts.

---

[15] Moore, *op. cit.,* in ftn. 13, pp. 21–35.

[16] Wilson, *op. cit.,* p. 39.

[17] Beals, *op. cit.,* p. 69.

SECTION 2 MANAGEMENT AND LABOR IN TRANSITION

As discussed above, industrialism brought new social relations, aspirations, and disciplines. Industrial man was freed from older attachments and constraints. Especially in England and in the United States in the nineteenth century, this trend produced a "rugged individualism." At the same time a contrary trend was in the making. Industrialism was creating new social institutions, which in the twentieth century created new centers of authority, new social bonds, new opportunities for collective action and group membership. Industrial man became "organization man."

Two of the major institutions created by industrialism are the *business enterprise* and the *labor union.* This section considers the changing nature of these institutions, with emphasis on leadership and on group conflict and accommodation.

The factory system was a new way of organizing human effort. Workers, machines, capital, and management were brought together to create a "company," "firm," or "enterprise," which might or might not be legally incorporated.

The idea of an established enterprise recognizes that organizational continuity and effectiveness are vital to productivity and profit. In the early stages of capitalism when manufacturing was mainly handicraft, the businessman was more nearly a trader or middleman than an organizer of production. In later stages of industrialism, the businessman becomes a builder of organizations.

TYPES OF INDUSTRIAL MANAGEMENT

The major trend in the history of industrial organization has been from family-based management to professional management. Both types still exist, but professional or bureaucratic management is representative of modern society. Family management (sometimes called patrimonial) is characteristic of an earlier era:

Patrimonial management is a common first stage in a country's march toward economic development. In countries where the family is one of the dominating social institutions in the society, the family enterprise is a simple and logical instrument of business activity. Loyalty and trust within the hierarchy are assured. The forces of tradition and religion support the essential integrity of the family dynasty. The enterprise provides the means for safeguarding the security and the reputation of the family.[18]

As the business expands family management loses ground. Even the extended family is unable to supply enough capital, ideas, or managerial personnel to meet the crises of business growth. For a time outsiders can be hired without loss of control and without changing the character of the business. But eventually the professionals outnumber the family members and take over more and more responsibility for making business decisions. At last, the family recognizes that its own interests are served best by turning over the day-to-day operation of the enterprise, and even the most important policy decisions, to professional managers.

The Ford Motor Co. postponed this development longer than many other large family enterprises, but during the past generation it has taken on professional management. The fact that family members continue to hold executive positions does not necessarily change the basic phenomenon. Under the new conditions, the family member in the firm becomes a part of professional management. He adapts to the

---

[18] Frederick Harbison and C. A. Myers, *Management in the Industrial World* (New York: McGraw-Hill, 1959), p. 69.

organization and does not attempt to bend it to his will. In some cases, he may be given a peripheral managerial post (a "division" of his own) instead of displacing a professional executive at the top of the business hierarchy.

Nepotism Favoring family members is often seen as violation of two basic norms, advancement according to criteria of performance, and equality of opportunity. Nepotism is probably most common and least objectionable in small businesses, which are regarded as family property, but concern about nepotism increases step by step from the family enterprise to the professionally managed business and to government operations. It has been suggested that the problem of nepotism disappears as large businesses develop impersonal merit systems.[19]

Family vs. bureaucratic management The transition from family (or patrimonial) to bureaucratic organization may be more closely specified by considering (1) managerial authority, (2) rational procedure, and (3) managerial ideologies.

Managerial authority. Patrimonial management is typically one-man rule. The "boss" resists delegation of authority and is inclined to make as many decisions as possible on his own. His relations with his staff are personal and he expects unreserved loyalty and obedience.

In the bureaucratic setting authority is more impersonal, more systematic, more limited, and more effectively delegated. Respect is shown for authority based on technical competence. And all officials, including top management, accept a framework of established rules. In this sense, bureaucratic authority is "constitutional."

In many firms having professional management the principle of command is modified. Ultimate authority still rests at the top, and directives are issued down the line, but there is increased consultation. Those whose work may be affected by an impend-

ing decision are given a chance to be heard. This is not democracy in the sense of majority rule, but the base of managerial decision is broadened to take advantage of professional expertness and practical knowledge at lower levels of the organization.

Rational procedure. The pre-bureaucratic business leader was impatient with formal rules and procedures. He liked to keep his accounts in his hat and to run the organization from day to day without clear-cut policies. Much was done in accordance with tradition—"this is the way we always do it"—or by improvisation to fit the requirements of the moment. The intuitive understanding derived from one man's experience, often a rich experience, was the foundation of decision-making in the enterprise.

The bureaucratic way is directly contrary. Systematic procedure based on "principles of sound management" is the ideal. Rules and policies are developed to guide decision-making in all phases of activity. Men are hired in accordance with criteria worked out by a personnel department; they are trained, assigned, and supervised according to specified routines. Tradition is never its own justification but is subject to question and revision by specialists in organization planning and human engineering. A "web of rules" governs behavior at all levels of the enterprise.

The web of rules becomes more explicit and formally constituted in the course of industrialization. At the very early stages, the very notion of a rule may be alien, and individual incidents are confronted without regard to their more general implications. The continuing experience of the same work place, the growth in its size, the same workers, and the emergence of managerial staff tend to result in customs and traditions which begin to codify past practices. . . . Some rules may later emerge which anticipate problems rather than merely summarize past decisions. The statement of the rule then becomes more formal and elegant, particularly as specialists are developed in rule-making and administration.[20]

Detailed rules also existed in the early days of the

---

[19] Perrin Stryker, "Would You Hire Your Son?" *Fortune, 55* (March, 1957), 132 ff.

[20] Clark Kerr, J. T. Dunlop, F. H. Harbison, and C. A. Myers, *Industrialism and Industrial Man* (Cambridge: Harvard University Press, 1960), pp. 198–199.

factory system, but at that time the rules applied mostly to the discipline of the work force rather than to other policies and practices of management. The worker was subject to close supervision, and was required to abide by many regulations governing his conduct both on and off the job. At a later stage rules became protective as well as restrictive, and more of them applied to management as well as to the worker.

Managerial ideologies. The perspectives and self-justifications of management have changed with the evolution of industrial organization.[21] In eighteenth- and early nineteenth-century England, the philosophy of management was "stern and responsible tutelage," and workers were viewed as dependent, inherently irresponsible, and unreliable—in need of a firm governing hand. According to this ideology, the owner-manager stood *in loco parentis* to his work force. His exercise of command was justified because it was needed, not only by society but by the workers themselves. At the same time management had a moral responsibility to the employees as well as to the enterprise. In this scheme of things, "the dependence of the poor and the responsibility of the rich are the valid moral rules of the social order." [22]

As industrial development quickened its pace, this early point of view was discarded. In the nineteenth century and in the first decades of the twentieth, the morality of individualism, self-reliance, ambition, effort, and the "survival of the fittest" was extended from the middle-class entrepreneurs to the entire industrial community. "The militant language of an ethics of the jungle was applied to the relations between employers and workers. Riches and poverty merely reflect differences of ability and effort. The employer's success is evidence of his fitness for survival, and as such justifies his absolute authority over the enterprise." [23]

With the rise of professional management the influence of this ethic has waned. It has been replaced by a perspective better adapted to the needs of complex organizations run by specialized, expert, and interdependent staffs. In the ethic of "organization man" cooperation, group-mindedness, and security are the compelling themes.[24]

UNIONS AND SOCIETY

In 1779, in Leicestershire, England, a youth named Ludd, angered by boys of the village, entered a house where stockings were manufactured and broke some of the spinning frames. The news of the act spread and became legend. In 1811–1816, English rioters who broke machinery in various textile factories were called Luddites. They thought that the industrial revolution was producing unemployment. For a modern response to the threat of technological unemployment, see "Dead Horse and the Featherbird" (pp. 478 f.).

Desperate outbreaks against the new technology occurred sporadically, but they had no lasting effect. An important response by workers to industrialization is the creation of labor or trade unions as organizational counterparts to the business enterprise. Unions have assumed diverse forms and served different ends depending on their own development and the social context.

1. *Social protest and political radicalism.* Some labor unions have been primarily political and ideological, more interested in creating a mass base for political change than in establishing working arrangements with employers. Political unionism is characteristically found where organized labor is weak. Unable to win concessions from employers, the unions turn to political action. They form a general union, which although not strong at the factory level, plays a conspicuous role in politics. This pattern is

---

[21] See Reinhard Bendix, *Work and Authority in Industry* (New York: Wiley, 1956); W. H. Whyte, Jr., *The Organization Man* (New York: Simon and Schuster, 1956); F. W. Howton, *The Changing Self-Image of the American Businessman,* unpublished Ph.D. thesis, University of California, Berkeley, 1959.

[22] Reinhard Bendix, "Industrialization, Ideologies, and Social Structure," *American Sociological Review, 24* (October, 1959), 614.

[23] *Ibid.*

[24] W. H. Whyte, Jr., *op. cit.*

found in a number of underdeveloped countries such as Indonesia and Egypt.[25]

A similar development occurred in the United States during the latter part of the nineteenth century. The National Labor Union, organized in 1866, turned away from bargaining for better working conditions and looked to political solutions. The Knights of Labor, which had considerable influence from about 1879–1890, attempted to create a general union rather than an organization based upon the interests of particular groups of workers. "The aims of the Knights were idealistic, humanitarian, and political." [26]

A more extreme example of radical unionism in the United States was the Industrial Workers of the World—the "Wobblies"—organized in 1905. The I.W.W. program drew its ideas from a number of left-wing groups of the time, including Marxists, anarchists, syndicalists, and just militant unionists. The Wobbly program had two distinctive features. First, the organization hoped to transform society by direct economic action. The unions would take over the major industries and thus do away with capitalism. The idea was to build One Big Union that would prepare for One Big Strike. Second, the I.W.W. was more interested in agitation and strike leadership than in settlements and industrial stability:

Despite the fact that probably millions of workers came under the sway of the IWW in one conflict or another, its permanent membership never amounted to much more than 60,000. The chief reason for this was that the IWW did not concentrate on building strong permanent unions. Instead, it devoted its energies to educating the workers to its revolutionary philosophy through militant strikes. Wherever a battle was brewing, IWW leaders stepped in. Their aim was twofold: To win immediate gains for the workers involved, and to develop in them a sense of class consciousness and a feeling of class solidarity. Though the "Wobbly" organizers often achieved these results, they rarely remained on the scene to consolidate their gains and build a strong union organization after the strike had been concluded.[27]

In the United States, radicalism played an important part in the history of trade unionism, but its influence has diminished markedly.

2. *Job control, collective bargaining, and interest-group politics.* In advanced industrial nations of the non-Communist world, unionism has become non-ideological and "pragmatic." The major unions are solidly based on effective power at the factory level. They long ago rejected the Wobbly complaint:

> Why do you make agreements that
> divide you when you fight
> And let the bosses bluff you with
> the contract's "sacred right"?

On the contrary, the union contract is now perceived as a charter of industrial justice and a key to industrial stability.

Pragmatic unionism offers the member three main services in exchange for his loyalty and his dues: (1) protection of his job against potential competitors, (2) protection against unfair treatment by the company, and (3) continuous effort, through collective bargaining, to improve wages and working conditions. In addition, through the federation to which it usually belongs, the union may act as a political lobby and pressure group. It protects itself against restrictive legislation and supports more general legislation, e.g., for social insurance, that may be in the best interests of the union members. Despite its involvement in politics, the pragmatic union seeks no general reconstruction of society. It limits itself to specific objectives that may be gained within the existing political and economic framework.

3. *Labor discipline.* Where unions are free institutions, not controlled by the government, their main function is to represent the interests of the members. However, once firmly established in the plant, the union assumes responsibility for fulfilling its contract and must maintain discipline among its members to deter them from unauthorized "wildcat" strikes and slowdowns. Without such discipline, the authority of

[25] See Walter Galenson (ed.), *Labor and Economic Development* (New York: Wiley, 1959), pp. 8–15.

[26] Robert F. Hoxie, *Trade Unionism in the United States* (New York: Appleton, 1926), p. 87.

[27] Aleine Austin, *The Labor Story* (New York: Coward-McCann, 1949), p. 167.

the union leaders at the bargaining table would be undermined.

In advanced industrial countries, unions are widely accepted as integral parts of the industrial organization. Many employers, especially in large-scale manufacturing, have agreed to the checkoff (deducting union dues from the workers' pay), the "union shop" (requiring all employees to become members of the union), and other devices for strengthening union leadership. At first, these agreements were made with great reluctance, but after some experience, employers came to recognize the potential contribution of the union to maintaining labor discipline and reducing costly work stoppages.

In Communist countries trade unions are controlled by the state and the right to strike is not recognized. In the Soviet Union under Stalin (1922–1953), trade unions were agencies for promoting labor discipline and production and for administering welfare services. In 1958, as part of the post-Stalin trend toward easing totalitarian control, union powers were expanded and they were made more effective in protecting workers' rights. While wages are not subject to collective bargaining, the local unions have become more active as critics of management and as participants in redressing worker grievances. With respect to the central organization of Soviet trade unions, a recent study reports:

At the top the union central committees and the Central Council of Trade Unions, led by trusted communists, function as agents of the Communist Party and the state, more like sections in a governmental department of labor than as independent trade union centers. The national union bodies are not independent organizations expressing the will of their members. Their rights were given them by the party, not derived from the power of the working class. At any time, their work is oriented to the current instructions from the party. But they also have the duty and right to speak in the name of workers before governmental bodies. . . . Top union leaders, as communists, have strong reasons for seeking gains in living and working conditions that affect morale and confidence in the system. The CCTU functions as a watchdog over the unions, to see that they work

along approved lines; but also to a degree it acts as a watchdog for the workers, seeking better protection of their interests.[28]

In the West, too, there is often an important difference between local and national unions, with more active participation and control and more turnover of leadership at the local level.

PROSPECTS

As industrialization proceeds, the business enterprise and the union become stable institutions. Conflicts become less frequent and less intense. Labor and management no longer differ over basic principles, such as whether unions should exist at all or what the future of society should be. Most disagreements are on matters of detail and are subject to compromise. The government intervenes as mediator and stabilizer. The whole system is watched and tended to maintain production at desired levels.

The foregoing description is more nearly an image of the future than an accurate rendering of the present. It fairly depicts what is happening in the most advanced sectors of the economy in the most industrialized nations of the free world. The struggle for union recognition still goes on in some areas, such as in industrialized farming, even in the United States. But where stabilization has been achieved, the drift toward professional management of labor relations, involving representatives of management, labor, and government, is apparent.

Two important consequences of this trend may be identified:

1. Although many unions began as agencies of social reform, in the industrialized nations they are not proponents of major social change. Unionism as a "movement," either in itself or as part of a larger political effort, is in decline. As institutions with vested interests of their own, and with many commitments to other institutions, the unions are losing any special role they may have had as focal points of social criticism or reconstruction. Indeed, many unions in the United States have supported restrictive policies on immigration and have maintained

---

[28] Emily Clark Brown, *Soviet Trade Unions and Labor Relations* (Cambridge: Harvard University Press, 1966), pp. 319–320.

DEAD HORSE AND THE FEATHERBIRD

* * * * The composing room of the newspaper is comparatively quiet; no linotype machines chatter harshly, nor does the floor quiver from the running of the presses in the basement. It is the lobster shift—those off-hours when the printers set type without the pressure of a deadline. The men stand at their long composing tables adjusting metal rules, checking type against the copy for the advertisement at their elbow, and occasionally talking with each other.

The foreman walks over to a hook on the wall, a spike festooned with printed copies of advertisements that appeared in the newspaper days before. He takes one off the hook and carries it to a printer who has just finished tying up the type and metal for an ad that will run in tomorrow's paper.

"Here," the foreman tells the printer, offering him the printed ad. "We're falling behind on reset. Get this one."

The printer looks up sullenly. "What do you think I am—a lousy amateur? I don't want to set that stuff. I'm no blacksmith. Give me some live copy, not that dead horse."

The foreman does not argue. He calmly puts the advertisement down on the table and walks away, saying over his shoulder, "Get started before I call the chapel chairman over."

The printer begins to set the type for an advertisement that had already been run some months earlier. The copy announces an Easter sale in a department store, and it is now the end of summer. Mumbling to himself, the disgruntled printer starts work on the ad knowing the foreman has authority to demand that the work be done and that the chapel chairman of the shop (the union's chief steward) would back up that authority.

The compositor slaps together whatever type he can find which fits that of the ad, encloses the type in a metal form, and walks over to a table where he slams it down beside a dozen similar forms of ads that had also appeared earlier in the paper. Soon, another printer will pick up these forms from the table and take them over to a proof press where a proof copy will be made of each one. Then, the proof copy will be checked for errors and the necessary corrections made in the type. Finally, another proof of the ad will be pulled and the printer's work will be ready for its final destiny: to be destroyed without being used—melted down in the "hell box" where used type becomes hot lead once again.

This is the process by which printers do "unwork"; work that is actually performed and paid for but goes unused. It is called "reproduction," "reset," "bogus," or "dead horse."

* * * * The jet airplane seems prepared to hang in the air forever until that moment when its wheels touch the concrete runway and it is instantly transformed from a graceful creature of the air into a screaming, speeding, metal monster, ungainly and awkward out of its natural element. With a frantic roar, the jet engines are reversed and the plane protestingly slows

SOURCE: By Paul Jacobs. From a *Report* to the Center for the Study of Democratic Institutions, Santa Barbara, 1962, pp. 3–6.

down. It taxies up to the landing area and in moments a horde of attendants are swarming over it, chocking its wheels, moving up the passenger ramps, unloading baggage, and readying the ship for its next voyage.

Finally, the last passenger walks down the ramp, speeded on his way by the fixed smile of the stewardess at the door, mechanically repeating the airline farewell: "Goodbye now. Come back and fly with us again." Their work finished, the crew members walk down the ramp with the captain-pilot first, followed by copilot and flight engineer—American culture heroes in their natty uniforms, each carrying one bag of luggage and one black valise stuffed with the maps, charts, and manuals that are the paraphernalia of their craft. They walk across the oil-stained concrete ramp to the flight operations office.

Inside the office they are met by a crew from another airline who will cajole the same jet into the skies for the next leg of the journey. They talk a bit of the new traffic pattern at the Los Angeles airport, of the near-miss one of their group had with an Air Force jet, and always of the weather. But this second group of fliers has an additional man in it, for the company that flies the next segment of the trip in the very same plane does it with four crew members instead of three.

That fourth flier is a "featherbird" airman. When he arrives back at his home base, he will walk into the flight operations office there and ask the superintendent, "Any chance of getting back to flying yet? I'm a pilot, not a damned chair-warmer." The superintendent may shake his head sympathetically. "Negative, there's nothing open for you on pistons."

*   *   *   *   Thirty thousand feet of vertical space separate the newspaper compositor setting type that will never be used from the airman squeezed into a seat with no instruments in front of him. But "unwork" is a common link between them. The industries in which they perform their "unwork" are widely separated, too —by different histories, structures, economic patterns, and by contrasting relationships to government: newspaper publishing is relatively free of state regulation while commercial aviation is subject to rigid supervision by a number of governmental bodies. There is a difference also in costs. The setting of not-to-be-used type is not a heavy economic burden upon most publishers; the presence of a fourth crew member represents an airline expenditure of millions of dollars.

But despite the differences between these two industries, setting "dead horse" and flying as a "featherbird" have much in common. They derive from the same source, could not exist without management collusion, and have the same demeaning consequences for the men who are paid to perform "unwork." Even more, the common source of "unwork" that links together pilots and printers affects millions of other workers, all of them sharing a fear of unemployment and a consequent loss of identity. Thus, they can be viewed as two examples from a catalogue of meaningless work and fruitless effort carried on in America today. Current apprehension about unemployment related to our technological advance, to automation and "cybernation," make the "unwork" of these two industries symbolic of a major issue in the 1960s—how to maintain a full and free economy without a fully employed work force.

practices of racial discrimination and segregation as well as nepotism at the local level.

Unions do, however, make a significant contribution to building a system of industrial justice, thus enhancing the security and dignity of workers on the job.

2. When unions are militant and struggling for recognition, participation can bring psychological as well as material benefits to many members. To be a member of the union is to have a special and valued identity. Some have seen in this a basic justification for unionism:

The union returns to the worker his "society." It gives him a fellowship, a part in a drama that he can understand, and life takes on meaning once

again because he shares a value system common to others. Institutionally the trade-union movement is an unconscious effort to harness the drift of our time and reorganize it around the cohesive identity that men working together always achieve.[29]

However, the limited aims of the bureaucratized unions turn them into service agencies. The achievement of widespread labor recognition and labor peace makes member enthusiasm and devotion irrelevant most of the time. The significant work is done by union officials and participation of the member is not needed. The member pays his dues to support an officialdom that renders a valued service. In such an institution, psychologically meaningful participation is not easily to be achieved or sustained.

[29] Frank Tannenbaum, *A Philosophy of Labor* (New York: Knopf, 1952), p. 10.

SECTION 3 TECHNOLOGY AND HUMAN RELATIONS

Section 1 of this chapter analyzed some of the effects of machine technology on human relations in traditional society. It was shown that mechanization disturbs and reconstructs patterns of residence, employment, status, and leadership.

In later stages of industrialism the influence of technology on society continues. Every area of modern life—from making love and rearing children to politics, war, and the arts—has been in some way affected by technological change. Some of these effects are limited, others sweeping; some are highly beneficial to health and welfare, while others threaten human survival.

This section considers the significance of technology as an *environment* within which the modern industrial worker lives and which limits or expands his chances of attaining satisfaction in his work.[30]

Sociotechnical systems It is useful to think of the setting within which a man does his assigned work as a "sociotechnical system."[31] This idea emphasizes the close interdependence of technology and human relations. The sociotechnical system is a blending of the social and technical aspects of organization.

The *technical system* refers to the physical plant,

[30] The discussion of sociotechnical systems, alienation, and automation in this section is based on materials prepared by Robert. Blauner. See also Robert Blauner, *Alienation and Freedom: The Factory Worker and His Industry* (Chicago: University of Chicago Press, 1964). The relation between "technical organization" and "human organization" in the industrial plant is discussed in F. J. Roethlisberger and W. J. Dickson, *Management and the Worker* (Cambridge: Harvard University Press, 1939), Chap. 24. (See Adaptation 12, pp. 130 ff.) For a more recent discussion emphasizing the significance of technology for social organization, see Charles Perrow, "A Framework for the Comparative Analysis of Organizations," *American Sociological Review, 32* (April, 1967), 194–208.

[31] F. E. Emery and E. L. Trist, "Sociotechnical Systems," in Charles R. Walker, *Modern Technology and Civilization* (New York: McGraw-Hill, 1962), pp. 418–425.

the machinery, and the way mechanical processes are organized. The nature of the technology and the criterion of cost limit the alternative ways of getting the job done.

There is no technical system without a social system. The technical system determines important aspects of the group situation. For example, the technology may dictate how much detailed supervision is needed and what opportunities there are for informal contact among the workers. At the same time, the technical system depends upon the "human factor"—the skills, motivation, and discipline called for by the mechanical processes.

ALIENATION

In his early writings, Karl Marx advanced the theory of alienation, an influential hypothesis concerning the impact of technology on human relations in industry.[32] In Marx's view, factory technology, the increasing division of labor, and capitalist property institutions brought about the estrangement of the industrial worker from his work. Highly mechanized systems replaced craft methods of production in which the artisan had been master of his tools and materials. In the new factories, the intelligence and skill previously expressed by the craftsmen were "built into" the machines. Workers were left with routine and monotonous jobs. In the preindustrial period both skilled craftsmen and peasants had considerable control over the rhythms and movements of work. But the machine system governed the pace of work and restricted the employee's free movements. This loss of freedom, this subordination to the machine, turned the worker into a mere instrument and made him feel *powerless*.

The increasing division of labor within the factory made jobs simpler, and each employee's area of responsibility diminished. In order to rationalize production the work was broken down into minutely subdivided tasks. The highly specialized operation might be very important, but it separated the worker

from the total process. He did not need to understand how his work fit the whole. Responsibility, problem-solving, and decision-making were removed from the employees by the systematic division of labor and became the work of supervisors, engineers, and others on the technical staff. The fragmented relation of the individual to his work robbed him of a sense of purpose. This *loss of meaning* is an aspect of alienation.

Capitalism and alienation   According to Marx, the property relations of capitalist society alienated the employee. The factory belongs to the entrepreneur who has the legal and social power to hire labor, sell the products of the enterprise on the market, and take its profits for himself. The worker does not own what he produces. He has nothing to sell but his labor. Because the factory belongs to the capitalist, the workman is not likely to identify psychologically with its fortunes or its products. Because the profits do not benefit him personally, he is not motivated to work with all his energy and intelligence. Thus the property institutions of capitalism produce a third form of alienation—the employee's *sense of isolation* from the system of organized production and its goals.

Thus capitalist economic institutions and modern factory technology deprive the employee of a truly human relation to his work. Loss of control means loss of freedom, initiative, and creativity. Specialization simplifies and degrades labor; it makes the goals of the enterprise so remote that a sense of meaningful participation in a work community cannot be attained. The worker does not identify with the productive organization, but feels himself alienated from its purposes. When work does not permit responsibility, evoke a sense of purpose, or encourage larger identifications, the job is simply a way to make a living. Marx believed that unalienated productive work was essential to man's psychic well-being. Alienation reduced work to the merely instrumental,

---

[32] As a more general idea, the theme of alienation appears in the writings of a number of sociological theorists. See Robert A. Nisbet, *The Sociological Tradition* (New York: Basic Books, 1966), Chap. 7. For a discussion of the dimensions of alienation, see Melvin Seeman, "On the Meaning of Alienation," *American Sociological Review, 24* (December, 1959), 783–791.

which could only result in widespread suffering and degradation.

These ideas of the youthful Marx in the 1840s reflected a point of view widely held among intellectuals of the period. The rise of industrialism was viewed with misgivings, and intellectuals were concerned about the effects of the new order on the individual's organic relation to his community, his work, and his sense of himself as a creative and autonomous person. The concept of alienation, referring to the estrangement of man from important sources of his psychic and moral well-being, was "in the air."

As Marx sharpened his attack on capitalism, and predicted growing class conflict and political struggle, he lost interest in the more general moral issues. His emphasis shifted to the conflict of interest between workers and capitalists, and he did not pursue the theme of alienation. If he had done so, he might have come to realize that his critique was directed not toward capitalism as such. Rather, its most important elements apply to aspects of any industrial society, capitalist or socialist.[33]

The theory of alienation in industry contains important insights regarding the effects of sociotechnical systems on human satisfaction. It illuminates some basic trends in modern work organization and accurately describes the situation of many employees. However, Marx greatly exaggerated the uniformity of modern industry. While the theory is suggestive, it underestimates the diversity of sociotechnical systems, some of which encourage a sense of responsibility and purpose.

INDUSTRIAL VARIATIONS

Empirical studies of modern work organization reveal that alienation occurs unevenly in the work force. These variations become evident when three industries with different technology—craft, assembly line, and continuous process—are compared. The printing, automobile, and industrial chemical industries are contemporary examples of each of these forms of technology. Each develops characteristic sociotechnical systems.

Craft technology The printing industry is still largely based on craft technology. Its products are not standardized, and many traditional practices govern the way work is done. Historic craft specialities persist. The work force is predominantly skilled. There is variety and interest in the work of compositors, who set type, and pressmen, who run printed pages off the presses.

Craft workers are not dominated by the technical system. They control the pace at which they work, the quality of the product, and the quantity of output. They determine many of the techniques and methods involved in production and constantly meet to solve problems in the course of their work. Unlike other employees who often are under intense pressure, printers are able to resist external control and maintain personal independence. This reflects the opportunities presented by the technology as well as the strength of the powerful craft trade unions in the printing industry.

The craft worker is not limited to a small, subdivided part of the product, and therefore his work has meaning as fashioning a product with which he can identify. Craft production is usually carried on in relatively small units rather than in very large plants. The small shops characteristic of the printing industry lack the sense of isolation and anonymity common in mass-production industry. Workers in craft industry suffer little alienation because craft technology provides challenging work, a satisfying amount of control over how the work is done and opportunity for meaningful participation in a work unit.

In a survey of factory workers in many industries, printers were the most likely to report that their jobs gave them a chance to try out their own ideas. Four

---

[33] On Marx's concept of alienation, see Erich Fromm, *Marx's Concept of Man,* with a translation from Marx's economic and philosophical manuscripts by T. B. Bottomore (New York: Ungar, 1961). Students of Marx disagree on the extent to which he shifted his views about or his emphasis on alienation. See Fromm, *op. cit.,* pp. 69 ff.; Lewis Feuer, "What Is Alienation? The Career of a Concept," New Politics, *1* (Spring, 1962), 116–134; and Daniel Bell, *The End of Ideology* (New York: The Free Press of Glencoe, 1960), pp. 335–397.

out of five printers felt that they were able to express personal initiative in work, compared to one out of two in the entire sample.[34] Printers were among the least alienated from their occupation. Only 36 percent of the printers said they would choose a different trade or occupation if they could start over again at the age of fifteen, compared to 59 percent of all factory workers, and 69 percent of automobile workers.

Assembly-line technology Automobile production is based on the assembly line. As the incomplete motor vehicle moves along a conveyor belt, workers at every point on the line assemble one of the component parts. Three features of the assembly-line work organization are (1) extreme subdivision of jobs, (2) predetermination of work methods, and (3) the mechanically set speed of the conveyor belt. These features color the whole atmosphere of the assembly line.

The average assembler's job consists of only one or two operations. Little skill or training is required. The work is extremely repetitive, and little initiative is possible because engineers and time-study personnel have figured out in advance how each job is to be done. Assembly-line workers have virtually no control over their sociotechnical environment. The speed of the line brings 30 to 45 cars every hour and sets the pace of work and the quantity of output. The automobile worker cannot even leave his work station on the line without being relieved by another assembler.

Just as his job denies him control and meaning, the social atmosphere of the large assembly plant intensifies his sense of isolation. Assembly-line technology inhibits the formation of informal work groups, which contribute to internal solidarity in most factories. With little interest in the work or company, the typical job means little more than a weekly paycheck.

Caution The assembly line is an extreme form of technology that is highly mechanized yet relies on a large number of human operators. The assembly line symbolizes the engineering mentality and has influenced other less fully mechanized work settings. However, the numerical importance of assembly-line workers should not be exaggerated. Perhaps less than 5 percent of American manual workers are on the line. Even in the automobile industry, less than one-fifth of blue-collar workers were on the line in the 1950s.

Continuous-process technology In a continuous-flow system, the characteristic technology of the modern oil and chemical industries, the product flows automatically through an extensive network of pipes and reactor units. Within each unit a particular process or reaction is carried out. Manual workers do not deal with the product directly, as they do in craft and assembly-line industries, but control the reactions of the invisible oils and chemicals by monitoring control boards, watching gauges and instruments, and adjusting valves. Only the maintenance crew, which repairs breakdowns in the automatic equipment, uses traditional manual skill.

Each team of operators is responsible for a particular chemical process and for the expensive equipment in its unit. Yet instead of feeling dominated by the towering technology, which in physical size and capital cost is many times greater than assembly-line technology, the operators feel they control the apparatus. Although production is regulated automatically, they control the pace at which they read instruments and patrol the plant. There is freedom of movement because automated work environments are relaxed and free of pressure. When operations are running smoothly, routine readings take up only a fraction of work time, and there is considerable "free" time.

Yet unpredictable breakdowns do occur, and then the energies of the workers are employed in locating the cause of the problem and restoring production to normal flow. The chemical operator's attitude toward breaks in production is in sharp contrast to that of the alienated automobile worker. The chemical worker feels in control when production is

[34] Blauner, *op. cit.*

Thorstein Bunde Veblen (1857–1929), an American economist, was a caustic critic of modern business society. His best-known book, The Theory of the Leisure Class, *analyzed the functions of "conspicuous waste" and "conspicuous consumption." Veblen believed that technology—especially the way work is organized—governs institutions and habits of thought. In* The Engineers and the Price System *he stressed the conflict between "the instinct of workmanship" and the "pecuniary values" of the business world.*

running smoothly; therefore he willingly works hard to eliminate the crisis. The assembly-line worker, on the other hand, feels powerless when the line is moving normally. He *welcomes* breakdowns and is likely to give a sigh of relief when the conveyor is stopped for repairs.

The continuous-process technology seems to produce a sociotechnical system with low alienating tendencies. The loss of meaning that results from an extreme division of labor is absent, because the individual's responsibility encompasses an entire produc-

tive process. The nature of the work leads to closer integration of employees with management rather than alienation from the company. Because the operator is responsible for an expensive process, and develops firsthand familiarity with its operations, he may be consulted frequently by engineers and supervisors.

Continuous-process technology also helps reduce alienation by its effect on the occupational structure within the plant. In the oil and chemical industries there is a balanced distribution of skills. Jobs exist at all levels of skill—low, middle, and high, gradations that create opportunities for advancement. Movement from one skill and pay level to the next is a normal part of employment experience. Possibilities for advancement are reflected in the employees' optimism. Thus, in the factory survey reported in Table XIV:1, chemical and oil workers were the two categories most optimistic about promotions. In contrast, a much smaller percentage of automobile workers reported that they had jobs that would lead to a promotion. The rather uniform and low level of skill required of auto workers restricts opportunities for promotion. In printing the opportunities for promotion are also relatively low, but for a different reason. Craft technology demands a highly skilled work force, and printing craftsmen, already at the top of the skill hierarchy, have nowhere to go except into management.

Many sociotechnical systems in modern industry cannot be classified as strictly craft, assembly-line, or continuous-process. Because of great diversity in work environments, it is not possible to estimate the quality of human relations and the level of employee alienation throughout the whole industrial system.

AUTOMATION

The word automation suggests a world of automatic factories and business concerns, run by computers without workmen. In fact, highly automated processes are being used in the manufacture of oils and chemicals, in the machining of automotive engine blocks, in the production of television sets, and in the processing of insurance premiums and bank statements, but there is no inevitable progression toward

TABLE XIV:1   PERCENTAGES OF FACTORY WORKERS WHO FEEL JOBS LEAD TO PROMOTIONS, BY INDUSTRY, 1947

INDUSTRY	YES, PROMOTION	NO, PROMOTION	DON'T KNOW	NUMBER OF RESPONDENTS
Chemicals	79%	12%	9%	(78)
Oil refining	63	31	6	(52)
Furniture	59	32	8	(260)
Transportation equipment	57	33	10	(93)
Paper	55	30	15	(106)
Sawmills and planing	54	38	7	(68)
Nonferrous metals	52	46	2	(90)
Food	51	32	18	(297)
Machinery	49	44	7	(297)
Printing	48	32	20	(112)
Iron and steel	46	45	10	(409)
Apparel	43	50	7	(272)
Textiles	40	52	8	(410)
Automobiles	39	53	8	(180)
Stone, clay, glass	34	50	17	(109)
Leather	28	53	18	(130)
All factory workers	47%	42%	10%	(2,963)

SOURCE: Robert Blauner, *Alienation and Freedom,* p. 206. Data from a Roper survey for *Fortune,* 1947. Deviations from 100 percent are due to rounding.

a totally automated technology. Less advanced methods still predominate, and in many industries automatic techniques are not easily applicable.

The possibilities of automation depend on the nature of the end products, and on the extent to which a company is willing to commit itself to turning out a few standardized items. Gasoline production readily lends itself to automation because gasoline is fluid and homogeneous. Automobile production is less readily automated because motor vehicles are made up of thousands of heterogeneous parts. Automation confronts almost insuperable obstacles in the shoe industry because of the enormous variety of sizes, widths, styles and materials that make up a diversified product line.[35]

There are many stages and types of automated production. Much controversy over the impact of

automation on sociotechnical systems and employee alienation is due to this diversity. Worker reaction to automation depends on the nature of the work setting *before* automation. For example, in some offices traditional clerical jobs have been displaced by the introduction of electronic data processing systems. When this takes place, the employee's job is simplified, but his control over the work and his freedom of physical movement are reduced.[36] Another study of office automation found that when a high-speed computer system was introduced into an insurance firm where clerical procedures had already been mechanized (using a keypunch card process), the result was a widening of the employee's responsibility.[37]

It is difficult to distinguish the effects of automation as such from the effects of changeover to a

[35] James R. Bright, *Automation and Management* (Boston: Harvard Business School, 1958).

[36] Ida Russakoff Hoos, "When the Computer Takes Over the Office," in Sigmund Nosow and William H. Form (eds.), *Man, Work and Society* (New York: Basic Books, 1962), pp. 72–82.

[37] Bureau of Labor Statistics, "The Introduction of an Electronic Computer in a Large Insurance Company," (mimeographed) Number 2 of *Studies of Automatic Technology* (October, 1955).

new system. A common finding is that installation of automation replaces physical fatigue with mental tension. However, the "jumpiness" that workers in newly automated plants report may be due to difficulties in adjusting to a radically changed way of work. In the oil and chemical industries, which have been automated for many years, operators are habituated to the job, and rarely complain of mental tension. But automatic technology never stands still, and the introduction of new techniques means that employees must become accustomed to frequent changes in operations. Automated processes require workers who are more adaptable and flexible than the average mass-production worker or low-skilled clerical employee. That is why automated firms seek better-educated employees.

Despite the difficulty in generalizing about automation, a number of consequences seem firmly established. Work in the factory becomes lighter and cleaner. Manual skills decline in importance. Employee responsibility is heightened. Advanced automation in both factory and office tends to enlarge jobs rather than further subdivide the work. Most important for its impact on sociotechnical systems, automation enhances the interdependence of all employees and contributes to the integration of the organization. Since events in one segment of the process have immediate repercussions on the total system, communication increases both horizontally and vertically. There is more consultation between employees and supervisors, between engineers and foremen, between the office and the factory.

Dramatic long-range consequences of automation have provoked much comment, but it is too early to estimate their importance. Automation may reduce the distinction between factory and office, between hand and brain work, which has been a central element in the stratification system of industrial society. Blue-collar operators in the new clean, office-like factories will be responsible employees, much like the white-collar employees in the new, more mechanized, factory-like offices.

GROUP PERFORMANCE

Although most studies of work groups concentrate on "problem" behavior, such as turnover, absenteeism, morale, and low productivity, they offer insights into the basic processes underlying behavior in organizations. The findings show that the social variables of the immediate work situation, such as the attitudes of workers toward each other and toward their supervisor, the character of supervision, and group cohesiveness, are related to performance.

Social factors that affect the performance of work groups include group cohesiveness and supervisory behavior:

1. *Group cohesiveness.* A cohesive group is characterized by teamwork or group unity and has the following features: (*a*) friendly interaction of members, (*b*) common interests and shared goals, (*c*) identification of the members with the group, and (*d*) norms that establish "proper" behavior of members. Several indicators of these characteristics—pride in the work group, positive sociometric choices, cooperation, lack of persistent antagonisms, and acceptance of group goals—are positively associated with group performance.[38]

The members of a long-established cohesive group with standards of high production are likely to maintain high levels of individual and group performance. If, however, the norms of a cohesive group are oriented toward restriction of production, the performance is accordingly lower. An extreme case of the effect of group norms and pressures is illustrated in Figure XIV:1.

2. *The behavior of the supervisor.* At least two aspects of supervisory behavior are related to high productivity of work groups:

a. An active leadership role. A supervisor who performs an active leadership role differentiates between the functions of supervisor and worker, spends more time in actual supervision than in doing the same sort of work as his subordinates, plans and oversees the work of the group, and helps his sub-

---

[38] Rensis Likert, *New Patterns of Management* (New York: McGraw-Hill, 1961), esp. Chap. 3; and Peter M. Blau and W. Richard Scott, *Formal Organizations* (San Francisco: Chandler Publishing, 1962), esp. Chap. 4.

ordinates. Supervisors of high-producing groups tend to define themselves as group leaders to a greater extent than supervisors of low-producing groups.[39]

b. A "human relations" approach to supervision. A supervisor who has the "human relations" approach is not overly critical of his subordinates, shows an interest in their personal and job problems, encourages them to make suggestions for improvement of work methods and the work situation, keeps them informed about the work situation and their performance, and allows a maximum amount of freedom on the job. His supervision concentrates on people rather than on work production, and may be described as group- or person-oriented. Supervisors of high-producing groups tend to be more group-

and person-oriented than supervisors of low-producing groups.[40]

Participation in decision-making The apparent success of the "human relations" approach to supervision has led its advocates to urge full participation of subordinates in making decisions that directly affect them. Some feel that participation will increase production and employee morale and reduce turnover, absenteeism, and resistance to change. One study that supports this viewpoint is outlined in Adaptation 34. This experiment found that participation of workers lowered resistance to change in the production routine and increased production. Adaptation 34 also illustrates research procedures, specifically experiments using control groups.

[39] Daniel Katz, Nathan Maccoby, and Nancy C. Morse, *Productivity, Supervision and Morale in an Office Situation* (Ann Arbor: University of Michigan, 1950); and Daniel Katz, Nathan Maccoby, Gerald Gurin, and Lucretia G. Floor, *Productivity, Supervision and Morale Among Railroad Workers* (Ann Arbor: University of Michigan, 1951).

[40] Katz *et al.,* as in ftn. 39.

Adaptation 34 / Coch and French AN EXPERIMENTAL STUDY OF RESISTANCE TO CHANGE

This adaptation reports the findings of a study that attempted to isolate the causes of, and develop techniques to reduce, resistance to change in work groups. It also illustrates the use of experimental and control groups in research.

STEP 1. THE PROBLEM

The first step in any research is to delineate the problem to be studied. Unless the area of investigation is carefully defined and limited, research is apt to be unsystematic and findings inconclusive.

This experimental study was designed to discover why people re-

sist change and what can be done to overcome the resistance. The locale was a pajama factory where frequent and necessary changes of work procedures and shifts in personnel were met by strong resistance. Special monetary allowance for transfers to different jobs did not lower the resistance, which was expressed in grievances, high

turnover, low efficiency, restriction of output, and marked aggression toward management.

STEP 2. COLLECTING BACKGROUND INFORMATION

The investigator needs to (1) review pertinent literature and (2) become acquainted with the characteristics of the organization or

SOURCE: Abridged and adapted from Lester Coch and John R. P. French, Jr., "Overcoming Resistance to Change," *Human Relations, 1* (1948), 512–532. Published in this form by permission of the authors and Tavistock Publications, Ltd.

groups to be studied. Background information helps him locate the factors operating in the situation and formulate a theory and hypotheses.

Employees in the pajama factory worked on an individual incentive system. Piece rates were set by time study and were expressed in units. One unit was equal to one minute of "standard" work, and 60 units per hour equaled the standard efficiency rating. It required a great deal of skill to achieve 60 units per hour. The rate of each pieceworker was computed every day.

The investigators thought that learning a new job after transfer might be a factor in resistance to change. They compared the speed with which operators learned their jobs on first entering the factory with the relearning speed of several hundred experienced operators who had been transferred to new jobs. They found that relearning after transfer to a new job was often slower than learning on first entering the factory. Only 38 percent of the transferred operators recovered to the standard rating of 60 units per hour, and the other 62 percent either became chronically substandard operators or quit during the relearning period.

What accounts for differences between initial learning and learning after transfer? Why should so many operators fail to recover their former ratings and even quit? Investigation indicated that the interference of previous work habits in the learning of new skills apparently did *not* play a crucial part.

The investigators interviewed a number of workers, analyzed production records and turnover, and from their findings developed the tentative theory that resistance to change was a result of two factors:

1. The frustrations of transfer, including the learning of the new job, the contrast of new status with former status, and the difficulties of reaching the standard piece rate.

2. Negative attitudes induced in the individual from his work group. The preliminary interviews suggested that groups with high "we-feeling" and positive cooperative attitudes about the change were the best relearners. On the other hand, groups with high "we-feeling" and negative attitudes toward management expressed strong resistance to change. Aggregations of individuals with little or no "we-feeling" showed less resistance to change.

These tentative conclusions suggested that the problem of resistance to change could be attacked by (1) reducing the frustration of transfer and (2) developing positive attitudes toward the change within the groups to be transferred. Would the group's participation in the plans for the change positively affect both of these factors? If group members were permitted to help plan the way their new jobs should be done and were consulted about the new standard piece rates, would the frustration of transfer (including the perceived difficulty of reaching a new arbitrarily set standard piece rate) be reduced? Through participation was it possible that the group, as a group, would agree that the

change was necessary and develop positive attitudes toward the change? If so, the individual within his work group would be receptive to the change.

STEP 3. STATING THE HYPOTHESIS

The hypothesis should be stated in such a way that it can be supported or refuted by the findings of the study. The hypothesis guides the collection of pertinent data, provides a standard by which to evaluate the findings, and allows other investigators to repeat the study.

The following hypothesis was suggested from the theory of resistance to change: *The greater the group participation in the plans for change, the less the resistance to the change and the faster the speed of relearning a new job.*

STEP 4. THE EXPERIMENTAL DESIGN

In an experimental design, a group called *the experimental group* is subjected to influences introduced by the investigator. *The control group* is not subjected to the experimental conditions. The groups are matched on certain variables to give the experiment more precision.

Four groups were roughly matched for (1) efficiency ratings (each group had reached a stable level slightly above the standard production of 60 units per hour); (2) degree of change that would be involved in the transfer; and (3) the amount of "we-feeling" observed in the group.

After [41] the experimental con-

---

[41] There are many variations of this basic "before and after" design. See, for example, Samuel A. Stouffer, "Some Observations on Study Design," *American Journal of Sociology, 55* (1949–1950), 355–361.

FIG. XIV:1   Pressure on the presser

A presser in a pajama factory worked 20 days in a group and 20 days alone. After the presser reached the standard production rate of about 50 units per hour, he exceeded the established group level. "Scapegoating" began, and his production declined. When the group was dispersed, the presser's production increased markedly and remained high.

Data from Lester Coch and John R. P. French, Jr., "Overcoming Resistance to Change," *Human Relations, 1* (1948), 519–520.

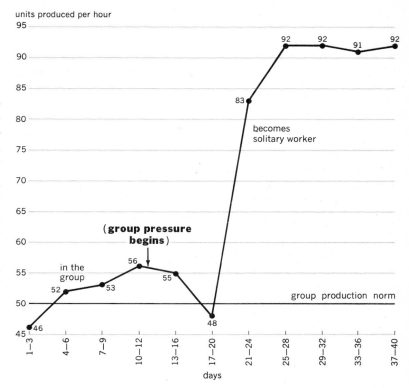

ditions have been imposed, the groups are observed to see what changes occur. If the experimental group manifests change after the experimental conditions have been imposed and the control group does not, the investigator may state with some assurance that the change is related to the experimental conditions and not to some extraneous factors.

The four groups in the present study differed in their degrees of participation in the planning for the changeover.

Experimental group I had a meeting to discuss the need for the change and agreed that the change could be made without affecting their chances of earning high efficiency ratings. Management then presented a plan for changing over to the new job. The group approved the plan, which included choosing several operators for special training and setting new piece rates by time studies. The special operators met, management asked for their suggestions about job procedures, and they worked out the details of the new job in consultation with the engineer. The new job and piece rates were presented at a second group meeting to all the operators, and the special operators trained the rest of the group on the new job.

Experimental groups II and III held meetings similar to those of experimental group I, but since the groups were smaller, all operators participated directly in the designing of the new jobs.

The control group (group IV) did not participate in the plans for change. The production department modified the job and set a new piece rate. At a meeting the group was told that the change was necessary because of competitive conditions in the market.

STEP 5. THE EXPERIMENTAL RESULTS

The experimental findings are stated as supporting or rejecting the hypothesis. Negative findings are as "good" and scientific as positive results.

The results of the present study support the original hypothesis. The rate of recovery to the standard efficiency rating was directly proportional to the amount of participation. Furthermore, turnover and aggression were inversely proportional to the amount of participation. The study is summarized in Figure XIV:2.

The specific findings were as follows:

1. Experimental group I, at the end of 14 days, averaged 61 units per hour (the quota was 60 units per hour). No one quit in the first 40 days, and only one act of aggression against the supervisor was recorded. Observations indicated that the attitude of the group was cooperative.

2. Experimental groups II and III recovered faster than group I. After a slight drop on the first day of change, the efficiency ratings returned to a prechange level and showed sustained progress thereafter to a level about 14 percent higher. They worked well with their supervisors, and no indications of hostility were observed. There were no quits in the first 40 days.

3. The control group did not reach its former production standard. There was no progress after transfer for a period of 32 days, and marked expressions of aggression against management occurred. Three of the 18 workers quit in the first 40 days, and there was deliberate restriction of production.

To make sure that the results depended on group participation rather than on other factors, such as the personalities of members of the control group, the investigators brought the remaining members of the control group together again two and a half months after the change. They were again transferred to a new job. This time they had the opportunity to participate in planning the new job procedures. The group then exceeded its previous level of efficiency, and

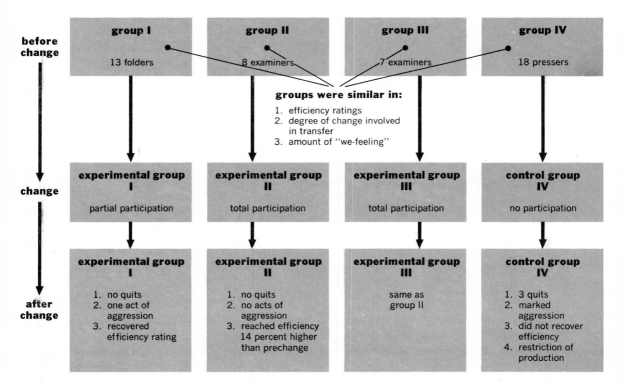

FIG. XIV:2   The "before and after" experiment

there was no aggression or turn-over for 19 days. This retesting of the control group strengthens the assumption that the important factor reducing resistance to change was the participation technique. However, at the time of the second change the group had lost three of its members, and they may have been dissident and obstructive ones.

STEP 6. INTERPRETATION OF THE FINDINGS

The basic conclusion of this study is that participating groups exhibit less resistance to change than non-participating groups. The findings suggest two further generalizations: (1) pressures generated within a group for change are more compelling than pressures from outside, and (2) pressures for change will occur within the group if there is shared realization of the need for change.

SECTION 4 THE LABOR FORCE

THE WORLD LABOR FORCE [42]

Of the three billion people in the world, about 1,300 million or 43 percent are in the labor force. The largest national working populations are China (roughly 300 million), India (190 million), U.S.S.R. (110 million), but size is only one significant aspect of the labor force. Other important considerations are the ages at which people start and stop working, the economic participation of women, and the allocation of workers to the three major industrial divisions or "sectors": agriculture, industry, and services.

The three sectors are sometimes identified as the primary, secondary, and tertiary forms of production.[43] Primary refers both to a stage of industrial development and to the fact that workers deal directly with raw materials. The *primary* industries include agriculture, fishing, and forestry. *Secondary* industries, which include manufacturing, construction, and mining,[44] are involved in the conversion of raw materials into goods. *Tertiary* industries include services—both professional and personal—trade, transportation, and communication.

As societies become industrialized, the distribution of workers among various economic activities tends to change in a predictable way. In the early stages of industrial development, the population is preponderantly engaged in the cultivation and collection of raw materials for food, clothing, and shelter. With the advance of technology and industrialization, the productivity of agriculture rises, and workers are drawn into manufacturing and construction where their efforts yield higher earnings. The proportion in agricultural employment decreases, the proportion in manufacturing increases, and a third trend appears. Growing numbers of workers enter service industries, such as the distribution of raw and finished products, the maintenance of communication, trade, and transport, and the training and care of the population. The shift of workers into industry and the services raises the efficiency of farmers with machinery, research, and improved management techniques.

Despite the phenomenon of increasingly rapid industrialization, more than half the world's workers are in agriculture. Perhaps three-fourths of the work-

[42] The statistics in this discussion are the latest available data, usually for 1960. SOURCE: U.N. *Demographic* and *Statistical Yearbooks,* various dates; and International Labor Office, *U.S. Monthly Report on the Labor Force* and *Monthly Labor Review.*

[43] See Colin Clark, *The Conditions of Economic Progress* (3rd ed.; London: Macmillan, 1957), esp. Chap. 9.

[44] Because modern mining usually involves some form of processing and leaves few materials in a raw state, it may be classified as a secondary rather than a primary industry.

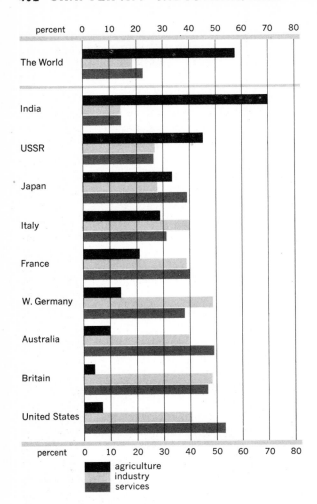

FIG. XIV:3 Industrial distribution of the labor force, world and selected countries, in percentages, 1960

ADAPTED and redrawn from *The Economist, 223* (April 1, 1967), 55. Based on International Labor Office data.

agriculture. Japan, the most industrialized Asian nation, employs one-third of its workers in primary production, but the United States less than 6 percent and Britain only 4 percent. (See Fig. XIV:3.) There is a worldwide trend toward a decline in the proportion of workers in agriculture but the trend is fastest in advanced countries. Advanced nations have about a third of the world labor force but 62 percent of the industrial labor force.[45] The industrial or secondary sector is predominant in such countries as Italy, Czechoslovakia, and West Germany, highly advanced but not the most highly advanced nations. Only in Canada and the U.S. does the service or tertiary sector account for a majority of workers. Australia is on the borderline with 50 percent, and several other countries have crossed the 40 percent line.

THE UNITED STATES LABOR FORCE

In the early nineteenth century the United States was an agricultural nation with three-fourths of its workers in primary production, but now less than 6 percent of its workers are in agriculture. (See Fig. XIV:4.) Agricultural efficiency has nearly tripled in the period since 1940 when the average farmer raised enough to feed 10 persons. In fact the agricultural output per man-hour has increased much more rapidly than output in nonagricultural industries.[46] A third of the working force were employed in manufacturing and construction early in this century, and the percentage has remained about the same. Employment in the services paralleled the growth of industry until the beginning of the century, when it rapidly outstripped manufacturing. Service activities now employ about 60 percent of the working force.

The size of the labor force is affected by the age composition of the population, the education required to operate the technological system, and the efficiency of the system of production, which determines the ability of the economy to support nonworkers. In 1820 approximately 30 percent of the

ers in Africa and nearly that proportion in Asia are in primary production. Surprisingly, for a country of high technological achievement, more than 40 percent of the labor force of the U.S.S.R. work in

[45] *The Economist, 223* (April 1, 1967), 55.

[46] *Statistical Abstract of the United States: 1966,* Table 330.

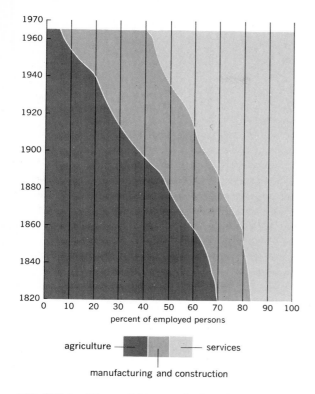

agriculture ———— ———— services

manufacturing and construction

FIG. XIV:4 The working population of the United States, 1820–1965

AFTER Eshref Shevky and Marilyn Williams, *The Social Areas of Los Angeles* (Berkeley and Los Angeles: University of California Press, 1949), p. 4. Data for 1950, and 1960 from *Census of Population;* for 1965 from *Statistical Abstract of the United States: 1966*, Tables 307 and 314.

population were gainful workers, and in 1900, 37 percent. At present a large part of the population of the United States is in the productive years, and in 1965 the labor force comprised about 40 percent of the national total. (See POPULATION AND ECOLOGY, pp. 268 ff.)

As the U.S. has become a mature industrial society with increasing education requirements, the age of entering the labor force has been postponed. In 1900 more than three out of five boys between fourteen and nineteen years of age were in the working force; in 1965 about 44 percent, which is the projected rate through 1980.[47]

Women in the labor force [48] In 1900 only 18 percent of workers were female, in 1965 the figure was 34 percent, and there is every likelihood that a larger proportion of women will be employed. Changes in family structure and changed participation of women in the labor force have gone hand in hand. Traditionally women's major economic contribution to the family was not earnings but such activities as making cloth, clothing, and household goods, and producing and preparing food. As women have lost their economic productivity in the family, and as rising consumption standards demand more money income, women have gone outside the home for employment. The result has been an increase in the number of married women of all ages in the labor force. (See Fig. XIV:5.) Since 1890 the greatest increase has taken place between the ages of

Togetherness in the textile industry: child labor was often family labor.

[47] Bureau of Labor Statistics, "Projections of the Labor Force, 1970–1980," *Special Labor Force Report,* No. 49.

[48] This discussion draws on material written in collaboration with Ralph H. Turner and included in earlier editions of this book. For a recent analysis see Glen C. Cain, *Married Women in the Labor Force* (Chicago: University of Chicago Press, 1966).

thirty-five and sixty-five. The children of women in this age group are usually in school or have left home so that the mothers are free to seek work.

Occupational classification The preceding discussion has emphasized the industrial composition of the labor force. An alternative breakdown is the grouping of workers into occupational categories according to the kind of work they do, irrespective of their industrial classification. Table XIV:2 shows the relative occupational distribution of whites and nonwhites for 1940–1965. Operatives (e.g., bus drivers, meatcutters) and kindred workers were the

largest category of employed persons in 1965, whereas half a century earlier farmers and farm managers were most numerous. The professional and clerical categories promise continued growth.

Both industrial and occupational classifications of workers are important in determining policies and in making long-term plans for training and using manpower. Not only education, but welfare, retirement, and other programs must be based on an understanding of labor force trends. For example, there is often a large gap between the supply and demand for certain types of labor. The present shortage of engineers is one example, but workers are sometimes

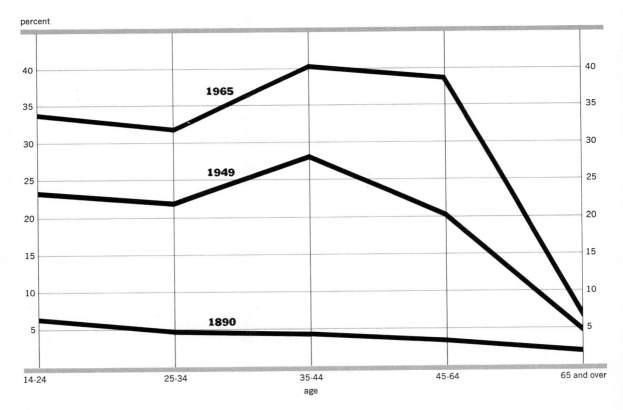

FIG. XIV:5   Percentage of married women in the working force by age, United States

AFTER A. J. Jaffe and Charles D. Stewart, *Manpower Resources and Utilization* (New York: Wiley, 1951), p. 172. Data for 1965 from *Statistical Abstract of the United States: 1966*, Table 320.

trained for jobs in little demand. This results in a surplus of manpower in some industries and occupations and a shortage of manpower in others. As the economy becomes more complex and as educational requirements are raised, full knowledge of the characteristics of the labor force is necessary to avoid serious misallocation of manpower and needless unemployment.

The nonwhite labor force   The nonwhite labor force, more than 90 percent of whom are Negro, dif-

fers markedly from the white labor force in employment, union, occupational, age, sex, and educational characteristics. Unemployment has been consistently higher among nonwhites. At the time of the 1960 census, 9 percent of the nonwhite labor force was unemployed compared with 5 percent of the white labor force. Although nonwhite unemployment diminished somewhat after the United States involvement in the Viet Nam war, in 1967 it was still over 7 percent, twice as great as white unemployment. Nonwhites are concentrated in industries and occu-

TABLE XIV:2   RATIO OF ACTUAL TO EXPECTED * PROPORTION OF NONWHITE WORKERS IN EACH OCCUPATIONAL CATEGORY, 1940–1965

	1940	1950	1960 [a]	1965 [a]
White collar				
Professional, technical and kindred workers	.36	.40	.49	.55
Managers, officials, and proprietors, except farm	.17	.22	.23	.25
Clerical and kindred workers	.12	.29	.46	.53
Sales workers		.18	.23	.29
Blue collar				
Craftsmen, foremen, and kindred workers	.27	.38	.49	.52
Operatives and kindred workers	.57	.94	1.08	1.15
Laborers, except farm and mine	2.06	2.56	2.59	2.40
Service workers				
Service workers, except private household	1.53	2.00	2.02	1.94
Private household workers	4.66	5.92	5.46	4.10
Farm				
Farmers and farm managers	1.31	1.22	.78	.58
Farm laborers and foremen	2.57	2.28	2.46	2.25

SOURCE: Norval D. Glenn, "Some Changes in the Relative Status of American Nonwhites, 1940 to 1960," *Phylon*, 24 (Summer, 1963), Table 1. Ratios for 1965 are computed from basic data in Department of Labor, Bureau of Labor Statistics, *Monthly Labor Review* and *Employment and Earnings Report on the Labor Force.*

* The "expected" proportion of nonwhites in each occupational group is the proportion of *all* workers in that category. For instance, in 1965, 12.3 percent of all employed workers in the United States were professional, technical, and kindred workers, and therefore one would "expect" 12.3 percent of the employed nonwhites to be in that occupational category. However, only 6.8 percent of employed nonwhites were actually so employed. Thus the ratio of actual to expected is .55, that is, $\frac{6.8}{12.3} = 0.55$. If nonwhites were proportionately represented, the ratio would be 1.00, a ratio of more than 1.00 indicates overrepresentation, and a ratio less than 1.00 indicates underrepresentation.

[a] Inclusion of nonwhites in Hawaii in 1960 and 1965 accounts for a small part of the change between 1950 and later dates.

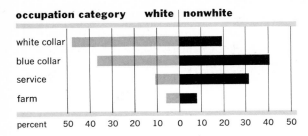

occupation category   white | nonwhite

white collar
blue collar
service
farm

percent   50   40   30   20   10   0   10   20   30   40   50

FIG. XIV:6   Major occupation categories by color, United States, 1965

SOURCE: *Statistical Abstract of the United States: 1966*, p. 229. Data refer to employed persons.

pations in which unemployment occurs most often, and they tend to be the last hired during periods of economic expansion and the first fired during recessions.

Nonwhites are overrepresented in most of the poorly rewarded occupations and are underrepresented in all the more highly rewarded ones. The proportion of employed whites and nonwhites in each broad occupational level is shown in Figure XIV:6. Only a fifth of the nonwhites, compared with nearly half of the whites, have white-collar jobs. A more detailed breakdown shows that whites in each of these broad levels generally rank above the nonwhites in the same level. (See Table XIV:2.) Even within each of the eleven occupational groups listed in the table, nonwhites are concentrated in the lower-paid occupations. For instance, most of the nonwhites in the professional and technical category are clergymen and teachers rather than doctors, lawyers, engineers, or other highly paid professionals.

Unfavorable though it is, the present occupational status of nonwhites is an improvement over the past. Changes in nonwhite representation in the occupational groups from 1940 to 1965 are shown in Table XIV:2.

Although nonwhite representation is increasing in both the upper and intermediate levels, the greatest gains are at the middle levels, in skilled manual and lower white-collar work. There has been a modest gain in the professional and technical category but nonwhite representation as managers, officials, and proprietors has hardly changed since 1950. The decline in farm work, in other labor, and in private household service is significant because it indicates a shift of nonwhites into jobs where advancement can be achieved more readily.

CHAPTER XV
POLITICAL MAN

With the collaboration of
William Kornhauser

SECTION 1 INTRODUCTION

A feature of modern industrial and urban society is the ever-increasing penetration of politics and government into the direction and control of urbanization and industrialization. In the twentieth century a large measure of government responsibility for industrialization is taken almost for granted. The shape of the city and the allocation of land and other resources are increasingly determined by governmental decisions or by the failure of government to assume responsibility. Politics is inextricably mixed with the major social changes discussed in the preceding two chapters.

Of equal sociological interest is the effect of social change on the political order. Industrialization with its accompanying changes in social relations has produced political crises and upheavals, some of which have had the gravest consequences for the security and freedom of millions. Even when not accompanied by wars and revolutions, these master trends have transformed the role of government. Compared to an earlier age, many more people participate in political affairs; many more are directly affected by

the government's decision to tax, conscript, or educate. Modern man is political man no less than he is urban and industrial man.

The standpoint of political sociology   As in the study of industry, education, and other spheres of life, there is need to place political activities and institutions in a broader social context, to see the influence of social groups and forces upon the workings of the political machinery. The sociologist contributes to this fuller understanding in part by inquiring into the political consequences of phenomena with which he is already familiar, such as stratification, primary groups, collective behavior, and population movements.

Political sociology is interested in the *underlying social conditions* that affect government and politics. An understanding of changes in the group structure of society, such as the assimilation of ethnic minorities, may throw light on the pattern behind the shifting results of national elections. The outcome of elections, the stability of governments, the rise of new movements and parties—these and many other political events depend on what is happening in other areas of social life.

The social factors that influence the way men are governed and the way they make political decisions have been recurrent themes in the history of thought for many centuries. In *The Republic* Plato traced the connection between the integrity of statesmen and their social circumstances, holding that a degree of social isolation is necessary to protect the philosopher-guardians of an ideal state from the temptations and involvements of ordinary men. Aristotle studied the degeneration of government and stressed the need for a middle class as a stabilizing force in the political order. Madison, in the famous tenth Federalist paper, called attention to the impact of group pressures on government and noted that "the most common and durable source of factions has been the various and unequal distribution of property."[1] Today these problems are still being explored, with somewhat less emphasis on speculative inquiry and more attention to the empirical testing of hypotheses.

Within political sociology, three broad areas may be distinguished:

1. Social foundations of political *order,* especially the way political arrangements depend upon social organization and cultural values. The main problem of political order is the regulation of the struggle for power, and political sociology considers basic constitutional questions. However, sociologists are less concerned with the formal aspects of government and law than with the underlying supports of these institutions.

2. The social bases of political *behavior.* Among contemporary social scientists political behavior refers mainly to the participation of individuals in politics—why and how they vote, hold political opinions, belong to political associations, and support political movements.

3. Social aspects of political *process,* including the types of organized groups in politics and their patterns of interaction. A major topic is the study of how interest groups, parties, and movements change or stabilize the political order.

The above topics are considered in the course of analyzing some of the political phenomena of the modern world. Section 2 deals with nationhood and political modernization. In Section 3 the nature of social revolutions is examined, followed in Section 4 by an outline of the chief characteristics of totalitarian society. Finally, Section 5 discusses the social foundations of freedom and problems of participation in a democratic political order.

[1] Alexander Hamilton, John Jay, and James Madison, *The Federalist* (Everyman's Library edition; London: J. M. Dent, 1942), p. 43. First published in 1787/88.

SOURCES AND READINGS

G. A. Almond and J. S. Coleman, *The Politics of the Developing Areas* (Princeton: Princeton University Press, 1960).

Gabriel A. Almond and Sidney Verba, *The Civic Culture: Political Attitudes and Democracy in Five Nations* (Princeton: Princeton University Press, 1963).

Reinhard Bendix, *Nation-Building and Citizenship* (New York: Wiley, 1964).

B. R. Berelson, P. F. Lazarsfeld, and W. N. McPhee, *Voting: A Study of Opinion Formation in a Presidential Campaign* (Chicago: University of Chicago, 1954).

Eugene Burdick and A. J. Brodbeck, *American Voting Behavior* (Glencoe: The Free Press, 1959).

Angus Campbell, P. E. Converse, W. E. Miller, and D. E. Stokes, *The American Voter* (New York: Wiley, 1960).

Robert A. Dahl, *Who Governs?* (New Haven: Yale University Press, 1961).

Vladimir Orlando Key, Jr., *The Responsible Electorate* (New York: Knopf, 1961).

William Kornhauser, *The Politics of Mass Society* (Glencoe: The Free Press, 1959).

S. M. Lipset, *Political Man* (New York: Doubleday, 1960).

R. M. MacIver, *The Web of Government* (New York: Macmillan, 1947).

Lester W. Milbrath, *Political Participation* (Chicago: Rand McNally, 1965).

SECTION 2 THE CREATION OF NATIONS

Of all the social forces in the modern world, none is more important than nationalism. The nation is in many ways the decisive unit of social organization. It can summon profound loyalties; it can organize great economic and military efforts; it can give to millions of people a consciousness of kind, a sense of common fate, a collective identity.

For many centuries kinship, social class, and local community were the abiding centers of loyalty. In Europe nationhood emerged only gradually as new institutions (1) defined and defended national boundaries, (2) broke down local barriers to trade and communication, (3) became politically integrated under an effective central government, and (4) created a system of education transmitting an official language and a sense of common heritage.

Many conditions had to exist before these changes could be accomplished. Germany and Italy did not become fully organized nations until the nineteenth century, although centuries earlier the Florentine, Machiavelli (see p. 193), wrote an eloquent plea for the unification of Italy. In France and England vigorous monarchies contributed to the formation of nations, even though the royal houses had to change their own perspectives and self-images. The ruler had to "make up his mind whether he was the first of the nobles or the first of the magistrates and administrators."[2] As kings and queens came to think of themselves as chief administrators, they built up a corps of tax collectors, judges, police, and other officials throughout the country, completely dependent on the central government. This helped lay the basis of the modern integrated nation-state.

The emergence of nations is a phenomenon of *widening loyalty and consciousness.* If national identity is to be achieved, loyalty must extend beyond the immediate bonds of locality and kinship. The individual embraces a more general and abstract idea—the concept of being French, Indian, Congolese, or Swiss. Extending or generalizing the sense of civic identity is one of the most profound aspects of nation-building.

National consciousness broadens loyalties and gives them focus and depth. New aspirations are created, especially the demand for national autonomy. The nationalist patriot wants his own government to symbolize and protect the identity of his country. In this sense nationality also *limits* perspectives.

The combination of these broadening and limiting effects of nationalism generates a potent political energy. Nationalism creates power by making more men available for participation in its larger community. At the same time, this potential energy is given impetus and direction by the tendency of nationalism to enhance patriotic pride and fervor.

Today the nation-state plays an ambiguous role. On one hand it is a threat to world stability. On the other hand its capacity to mobilize people and change old ways of life makes the nation the major agency of modernization. All over the world economic development and nationalism are closely associated.

[2] Albert Guerard, *France: A Modern History* (Ann Arbor: University of Michigan Press, 1959), p. xi.

COLONIALISM AS NATION-BUILDING

For four centuries (1500–1900) European powers penetrated the preindustrial areas of Asia, Africa, and the Americas. Spain, Portugal, Holland, France, Belgium, England, Italy, and Germany—all took part in the great commercial and political adventure called colonialism. They sought resources, markets, settlements, pride, power, and religious conversions. As they exploited, traded, settled, aggrandized, subjugated, educated, and converted, they brought with them the culture of the Western world, which they transmitted with obscure intent and uneven success to at least the top layers of the societies with which they dealt.

For the most part the European powers entered lands that were prenational as well as preindustrial. Some areas, such as North America, were relatively sparsely populated or had governments incapable of coping with the European conquerors. Almost everywhere the conquerors took advantage of existing conflicts within the indigenous population.

Where the Europeans came to stay, and were not merely casual visitors, traders, or pirates, they faced the problem of establishing order. In doing so they themselves laid the foundations for the emergence of new nations. They did this in three ways:

1. *By defining national boundaries.* In many areas the colonial governments simply drew lines on a map and gave a name to the new "country." Indonesia and the Philippines are good examples:

The scattered lands inhabited by the peoples of Malay stock, including therein the Philippines, the entire Indonesian archipelago, and such parts of the Malay Peninsula as were primarily Malay were not laid out by nature or originally so settled by man as to make any one political partition of them more self-evident than another. The existing frontiers are, as far as both geography and ethnology are concerned, essentially arbitrary and reflect the limits of the colonial spheres carved out in the conflict of imperialisms.[3]

The new "national" boundaries were set partly for

administrative reasons, so that the responsibilities of the colonial governor for a given territory could be fixed. Boundaries were also needed to establish claims and work out accommodations with rival European powers.

2. *By creating a more integrated social organization.* The colonial administrator typically established centralized control over his domain. He had to pacify the territory, collect taxes, and protect his fellow-countrymen as they exploited and developed the resources of the colony. To achieve these ends, transportation and communication were improved, a national currency was established, and at least a rudimentary educational system was created. The result was easier and safer movement within the colonial boundaries, both for government agents and for the native peoples. Patterns of mutual dependency sprang up. It was easier to do business with people inside the colonial boundaries and this tended to establish new and enduring social bonds.

3. *By stimulating national consciousness.* The colonial government, it is said, created the conditions of its own destruction. By its very existence as a central administration for a defined region, the colonial government brought a new focus of loyalty and pride to people who would demand freedom in the name of patriotism and national honor.

Perhaps most important, the colonial government itself became the target of opposition and rebellion. Anti-colonial sentiment stimulated national consciousness, even among settlers from the home country. Among non-Europeans, those who struggled for independence did not seek a return to the situation as it was before the Europeans came. Rather, they sought independence for that nation which was the creature of the colonial power. For example, after the Indonesians gained their freedom following World War II they laid claim to the entire territory of the old Netherlands East Indies, which includes Irian (Western New Guinea), although the people of New Guinea are unlike the Indonesians both in race and culture.

---

[3] Rupert Emerson, *From Empire to Nation* (Cambridge: Harvard University Press, 1960), p. 124.

Colonial nationalism has been strongest where the colonial government was most constructive. Where it invested in economic development, educated the people, brought them into government administration, and created or allowed free institutions, such as political parties and trade unions, nationalism grew rapidly. The British were relatively benign colonial rulers. By the same token, they did much to make rebellion a practical possibility.

Direct and indirect rule   The policies and practices of the colonial powers in dealing with a diversity of problems followed no single pattern. However, the two main types of colonial rule had different effects on national development.

Under *direct rule* the colonial power set up its own administration and tried to regulate in detail the economic and social life of the colony. For example, the British in Burma replaced the old monarchy with a governor-general,

whose staff gradually increased until the Secretariat came to house all types of departments and ministries expected of a modern government. Burma proper was divided into eight divisions, each consisting of three or four districts. In a ruthlessly logical fashion two or three subdivisions were created in each district, two to four townships in each subdivision. The townships were each divided into nearly fifty village tracts that became the prime units of local government.[4]

This is an extreme example of the effort to bypass existing social organization and superimpose a centrally controlled administrative hierarchy upon the country.

In exercising direct rule, the colonialists used the principles and methods they knew. They introduced Western concepts of law and administration, as the British did in creating a Civil Service and a Western-style judiciary in India. Direct rule limited and sometimes destroyed indigenous institutions, but it allowed the recruitment of educated natives to serve in the government bureaus.

Under *indirect rule* colonial authority was exercised through native leaders—kings, tribal chiefs, and village elders. This was the policy of the Dutch in Indonesia and of the British in some African territories. This system tended to minimize the Western impact and support local institutions and customs.

The choice of direct or indirect rules was usually pragmatic, depending on the traditions and strength of the colonial power. If it had only a weak outpost in the colony, intermittently reinforced or supplied from a home base thousands of miles away, it was obviously prudent to come to an agreement with the native leaders who would, for a price, control their own populations. Indirect rule required fewer paid officials and was cheaper.

Economic policy influenced the choice of direct or indirect rule. Where the colonialists sought only a kind of tribute of cocoa, rubber or some other product, this could be done through the use of local chieftains. On the other hand, if the native population was seen as a market for goods manufactured abroad, or if local manufacturing was developed, direct rule was more appropriate.

What are the effects of direct and indirect rule on nation-building? Paradoxically direct rule, though apparently more oppressive, lent itself more readily to the evolution of a united nation. Direct rule tends to create a cohesive political community *before* independence. When independence is achieved, the new rulers have something to work with. At least part of the job of centralization and training has already been done.

Indirect rule often helped make social change more acceptable to a tradition-bound people. Working through existing institutions has the effect of moderating the pace of change and associating it with a familiar and accepted local authority. On the whole, however, indirect rule kept the society weak, fragmented, and unprepared to enter the modern world. Usually indirect rule did not foster the development of an educated class. The central government, dependent on the cooperation of village leaders, remained weak.

[4] Lucian W. Pye, *Politics, Personality and Nation Building: Burma's Search for Identity* (New Haven: Yale University Press, 1962), p. 82.

The strength of traditional authorities sustained by indirect rule creates difficulties after independence. When the colonial power leaves, the local leaders are reluctant to give up their power and they lack a strong commitment to the new state. Hence they represent a force for separatism along regional or ethnic lines.

Tribalism The architects of the new nations of Asia and Africa must take account of preexisting social organization. In their quest for modernization they lead populations still largely tradition-bound. Many millions of their people are untouched by the Western world. To them the immemorial ties of personal relatedness, ritual, and traditional authority are the true sources of security and satisfaction. For thousands of villages, isolation is still a paramount fact of life.

In the Congo, the village of Lupupa has its own way of describing the world:

The earth is conceptualized as a round, flat platter; if one approaches the edge (although the distance is too great to conceive of this as a real possibility) and is not careful, he will tumble off and into a limitless sea beyond which is only the unknown. In the exact center of this platter is Lupupa and, by extension, the Congo, while somewhere around the rim are placed America, Belgium, and Portugal. These three countries, it is evident, figure in the world scene because they are the only ones known—America, because there had been American visitors there, Portugal because of the presence in Tshofa [a nearby village] of a Portuguese trader, and Belgium for obvious reasons. . . .

The most sophisticated person in the village knew that this picture of the world was untrue, and told us so. He had learned the truth in school, he said, and the world, far from being a flat platter, was in reality a flat triangle, with Lupupa in the center, and Belgium, Portugal, and America at the various angles of the figure.[5]

Among these people, nationhood has little meaning. Moreover, for the villager the idea of a nation is very new, whereas local legends may trace the tribe back to the beginning of the world. It is reasonable to expect some reluctance to trade his old identity for a new one.

The tribe is a kinship-based, tradition-centered unit of social organization, composed of people who share a sense of personal relatedness rooted in a real or imagined common descent. Tribal society of the African Gold Coast "was an amalgamation of family units into larger and larger kinship groupings in which totemic genealogy provided a major social guide."[6] Tribes may occupy a particular territory, but territory is less important for tribal organization than for the modern nation-state. It has been estimated that there are as many as six thousand tribes in Africa.[7]

Traditionally, the tribal bond has been an extension of family loyalties. One belonged to the tribe through family membership, and the authority of the tribe over the individual was channeled through his kinship group. This was effective in rural areas where the family was an economic unit and organized virtually the total life of the individual. As the tribesman moves to the city, however, family authority and identity weaken. The tribe comes to have a more direct influence on the person. In a subtle way, this may serve as a transition to a sense of national citizenship, because loyalty is shifted to a larger unit, but the immediate effects are to obstruct national unity.

NATIONHOOD AND MODERNIZATION

The emerging independent nations in Asia and Africa encounter many problems not faced by earlier new nations. Today's new nations enter a world scene charged with political and ideological conflict. The great industrialized protagonists feel the need to win cooperation and allegiance from the less developed countries. This has created unprecedented opportunities for international aid to promote development.

[5] Alan P. Merriam, *Congo: Background of Conflict* (Evanston: Northwestern University Press, 1961), p. 176.

[6] David E. Apter, *The Gold Coast in Transition* (Princeton: Princeton University Press, 1955), p. 80.

[7] These are listed in George P. Murdock, *Africa* (New York: McGraw-Hill, 1959), pp. 425–456.

Below: A Pakistani campaigning for office displays his party symbol.

Above: A first voter in Colombia, with daughter, happily shows her registration form.

At the same time, the new nations welcome industrialization and seek full participation in the world community.

The revolution of rising expectations For many centuries the lives of millions of people in tradition-centered societies remained unchanged. A poor existence and short life were fatalistically accepted. But one of the sources of change in the modern world is the breakdown of these traditional perspectives, the increasing demand for better health, more comfort, and all else that technology can provide. The change has been so drastic that a new term has been coined —"the revolution of rising expectations." [8]

These new expectations are partly due to lessening isolation. As communication increases, bringing news of high living standards to remote places, people become aware of alternatives to poverty. The newly awakening peoples feel that they, too, are entitled to the benefits of advanced technology.

Aspirations are also raised by the dynamics of nationalism. The governments of the new nations attempt to bind together their heterogeneous peoples by building up internal trade, improving transportation and communication, expanding educational facilities, establishing government-sponsored health clinics, damming rivers for electric power, and creating military establishments. Indirectly, these activities introduce new values and perspectives.

The struggle for independence from the colonial power brought with it hopes for a better life. In the course of the struggle, nationalist progaganda

[8] On the significance of changing perspectives, see COLLECTIVE BEHAVIOR, pp. 255 f.

offered visions of a rosy future once the foreigners were ejected. The very fact of a changed status helped produce the sense of an expanding world.

The revolution of rising expectations should be viewed in the light of an important generalization: *Poverty or hardship as such does not produce rebellion or other collective action; rather action is stimulated by a new awareness of alternative possibilities.* As a leader of the Russian Revolution of 1917 said, "In reality the mere existence of privations is not enough to cause an insurrection; if it were, the masses would always be in revolt." [9]

The charismatic leader   The combination of continuing traditionalism, tribalism, and rising aspirations affects the nature of political life in the new nations. Among the characteristic phenomena resulting from these circumstances is the "charismatic" leader.

In Greek, charisma means "endowed with grace," and its ancient usage had primarily a religious connotation. Weber used the term in his analysis of authority and leadership to mean "a certain quality of an individual personality by virtue of which he is set apart from ordinary men and treated as endowed with supernatural, superhuman, or at least exceptional powers or qualities." [10] The charismatic leader is perceived as a heroic, saintly, or otherwise peculiarly gifted man whose authority is based on his personal qualities. It is not just that he occupies high office but that he is perceived as especially deserving of respect and even adoration.

Leadership tends to be based upon personal charisma *when institutions are weak or under stress.* Thus charismatic leaders become prominent in wartime and in periods of social upheaval. Winston Churchill and Adolf Hitler were charismatic leaders of the past generation—examples which show that charisma may attach to either good or evil leaders.

The charismatic leader serves as a unifying symbol for new countries whose national institutions are weak. He can summon loyalty to the nation through devotion to his own person. Such a figure was Kwame Nkrumah, first president and prime minister of Ghana, the former British colony known as the Gold Coast.

Before independence in 1957, Nkrumah's Convention People's Party recited nationalist prayers at mass meetings. A nationalist creed identified Nkrumah with Christ and the British Governor with Pontius Pilate. Nkrumah's imprisonment by the British in 1950 only added to his stature. "The word spread that the jail could not hold him and that he slipped out every night in the guise of a white cat." [11]

Nkrumah did much to cultivate his charisma. The Constitution of Ghana named him Osagyefo—Redeemer and Leader. He was Life Leader of the Convention People's Party. His likeness was reproduced on stamps and coins and on the masthead of the party newspaper. In Accra, the capital, a large statue placed before the new Parliament building was inscribed, "Kwame Nkrumah, Founder of the Nation."

In 1966 a military *coup* overthrew Nkrumah, who was unable to cope with the country's economic crisis and had become an increasingly arbitrary ruler. In a sense, charisma was his undoing:

Nkrumah openly cut himself off from his original source of power, the masses, and retired behind the walls of Flagstaff House, where his feelings of loneliness and unreality grew day by day. A less megalomaniac leader, one less remote from reality, might have successfully asked the people to tighten their belts for the greater glory of Ghana. But Nkrumah seemed hardly to care about their plight and let the party newspapers listlessly make the admonitions. Nor did the party sycophants around him try to wake him—how would you explain to a "messianic majesty" and "national fount of honor" that the

---

[9] A comment attributed to Leon Trotsky. See Crane Brinton, *The Anatomy of Revolution* (New York: Vintage, 1957), p. 34.

[10] See the picture and commentary, p. 464. For a discussion of charisma, see Max Weber, *The Theory of Social and Economic Organization* (New York: Oxford University Press, 1947), pp. 358–392, and Reinhard Bendix, *Max Weber: An Intellectual Portrait* (New York: Doubleday, 1960), Chap. X.

[11] John Gunther, *Inside Africa* (New York: Harper & Row, 1955), p. 804.

Jawaharlal Nehru (1889–1964) was the political heir of Mohandas Gandhi (1869–1948), who led the movement for Indian independence and developed the tactic of Satyagraha. This was a form of collective action, often involving civil disobedience, based on militant, self-sacrificing nonviolence. In his time Gandhi was the greatest charismatic figure of the non-Western world. A religious as well as a political leader, he became known as Mahatma, "great soul."

Nehru was born into a prosperous, upper-caste family. He was educated in England and joined Gandhi's movement about 1919. He spent ten years in jail, off and on, and was released for the last time in 1945, shortly before he became Prime Minister of India.

economy was collapsing and that grumbling, not only of stomach but of mouth, was mounting? [12]

Similar problems and a similar fate overtook President Sukarno of Indonesia who was displaced by a military revolt in 1966. Sukarno's personal following was recognized by the leaders of the revolt, who

[12] J. Kirk Sale, "And Now Nkrumah: The Generals and the Future of Africa," *The Nation, 202* (March 21, 1966), 290–291, in Wilson C. McWilliams (ed.), *Garrisons and Governments: Politics and the Military in New States* (San Francisco: Chandler Publishing, 1967). See also Henry L. Bretton, *The Rise and Fall of Kwame Nkrumah: A Study of Personal Rule in Africa* (New York: Praeger, 1966).

EGYPT'S POPULIST REGIME

The Egypt of King Farouk and the Egypt of Colonel Nasser are in a sense opposite models of the political evolution of countries that seek to change from a traditional agricultural to a modern industrial society. Though Farouk's regime was not liberal, it allowed a certain amount of freedom and political dissent. Partly, this was the result of a balance of forces among the palace, the British, and the various Egyptian groups who opposed both; the hesitation or fear of each one to assume all power enabled the others to survive and express themselves. But it stemmed also from the nature of the monarchy as a pre-populist regime. Such a regime and social system does not rest on public opinion. It retains considerable latitude by ignoring the masses, by not drawing them into political life, but leaving them undisturbed in their private misery and political apathy. It can therefore allow greater freedom at the top to the articulate groups—the press, political parties, professionals, students. By leaving the masses dormant, it affords some freedom for the elites.

Nasser's populist Egypt is something else. Having destroyed the organizations (especially the political parties and the economic bases of the groups that supported them) which enjoyed a modicum of freedom under its predecessor, the populist regime cannot allow these erstwhile elites or their remnants the same degree of freedom in politics. Instead, it seeks mass support by drawing new classes into the political process. These are the peasants and urban workers, who are wooed to add the strength of numbers to the regime's support in the army and the upper levels of the civilian bureaucracy. The political process no longer embraces competing parties and relatively free parliaments. Rather it includes (1) a single mass organization to arouse and channel political consciousness, (2) professional associations, peasant cooperatives, trade unions, and religious groups harnessed to the regime's goals, and (3) plebiscites, and parliaments without parties.

Because the populist regime depends on the systematic cultivation of formerly isolated and ignored groups, it must rely on exhortation and propaganda to a greater extent than does the pre-populist regime. It communicates with the masses more directly and more often, creates opinions in them, arouses their passions, stimulates their desires and tries to make them work harder for the elite's goal of modernization. In such a society, where mass opinion is stirred, the expression of any opinion becomes all the more significant because it is no longer confined to the homogeneous and articulate thin layer at the top. The populist regime suppresses freedom at the top because freedom may now penetrate the lower levels and have serious consequences. And precisely because opinion and communication may now move the masses being brought into the political spectrum, the populist regime seeks to control expression everywhere. Increased communication does not itself constitute democracy though it enhances the role of classes formerly ignored.

SOURCE: Abridged from *The Arab World Today* by Morroe Berger (New York: Doubleday, 1962), pp. 419–423. Published in the British Empire by Weidenfeld & Nicolson, Ltd., London. Used by permission of the publishers.

1. Social Processes

	PRE-POPULIST	POPULIST
Communication	limited to elites and periphery	extended to whole society
Voluntary organizations	permits existence, makes some effort to control; few formal organizations, based either on religion or kinship	destroys or co-opts; creates mass organizations, substituting politics for kinship and religion; nationalizes loyalties
Education	emphasis on higher education and liberal professions; foreign schools permitted	greater emphasis on primary education and on science and technology; foreign schools nationalized
Social structure	loose, many differences; individual closely bound to family and other groups and to locale	greater individual freedom from family and all nonpolitical associations but deliberate effort to produce national uniformity

2. Economic Processes and Policies

Organization	loose controls, private enterprise dominant	extensive controls, claims of socialism
Industry	small but growing	great emphasis on industrialization
Agriculture	large holdings	land reform, state-controlled cooperatives
Ownership	private, with considerable foreign interests	nationalization in two senses: transfer of foreign property to native control; state acquisition of private property
Taxation	burden on middle and upper classes; chiefly indirect	extension of direct taxation to lower-income groups; appeals for "voluntary" contribution of labor and wages
Prices	few controls	increasing control, mainly of food staples

3. Political Processes and Programs

Nationalism of dominant elite	strong but mixed with older loyalties	intensified, less influenced by other loyalties
Participation	masses left largely quiescent	goads, exhorts, draws in masses
Freedom: meaning	Western sense: individual liberty	synonymous with national independence
Freedom: incidence	some freedom resulting from competition for power among foreign interests, native elite in office, new native elite seeking power	no challenge to native ruling elite permitted
Class distinctions	form basis of regime's policies	emphasis on social equality, economic democracy and appeal beyond classes
Parties	several	one, or a mass political organization not called a party
Legislation	by parliament, with strong executive	rule by decree of leader or cabinet: parliament, if existing, based on plebiscite
Public administration	civil service a personal appendage to ruler; little effort at reform	efforts to introduce modern bureaucracy

retained him as nominal President but took away his powers.

The charismatic leader combines qualities of the traditional authority figure with those of the modern statesman-politician. As chief he is a personal and continuing source of power. This is important in nations unaccustomed to the periodic orderly change-overs of leadership that accompany elections in stable democracies. Personal loyalty is familiar and meaningful to people not far removed from traditional ways of life. They can feel an attachment to the national hero which they cannot so readily feel for the abstract notion of nation-state. "In short, the hero helps to bridge the gap to a modern state." [13]

The quest for bureaucracy The modern state requires a dependable officialdom—a bureaucracy. In the new nations government is responsible for stimulating and directing the economy, and administrative rationality is an urgent necessity.

Achieving rationality in a new nation is no simple task. It requires a reconstruction of traditional approaches to the recruitment and supervision of government employees. This is the same basic process discussed in connection with the growth of rationality in economic behavior: from personal to impersonal relations, from ascribed status to achieved status, from an emphasis on traditional loyalties and routines to a willingness to do what is needed to accomplish the task at hand. (See INDUSTRIAL MAN, pp. 473–475.)

To the people in the developing areas, attitudes of impersonality and strict adherence to norms of rationality are strange and may even be considered immoral. For example, in the Philippines:

First, and most important, is loyalty to the family. Kinship ties more than any other factor determine political loyalties. Public office is often viewed more as an opportunity for fulfilling family responsibilities than as one for meeting responsibilities to the nation.

For an appointing officer to fill a vacancy with a well-qualified stranger when a relative is looking for a job would subject him to a severe family criticism. [14]

Nepotism is only one obstacle to the development of a modern civil service. Political loyalties also play a large part. When government jobs are rewards for political support, it is difficult to maintain professional standards of administration, especially when patronage extends to the lower levels of government administration. In the United States federal government and in many states, politics affects the appointment of high officials, but the lower levels tend to be recruited on the basis of the impersonal standards of the Civil Service. At an earlier period, however, the United States faced much the same problem, with respect to politics and administration, that now confronts the new nations.

From the standpoint of the modernizing country, impersonality and formality can be overdone. Development should be seen as *the creation of effective organizations.*[15] And organizational effectiveness depends on a blending of formal and informal relations. Creation of new opportunities for personal satisfaction and group loyalty is as important as the breakdown of nepotism and other traditional ways. In the attempt to create a modern bureaucracy, legalism and formality are sometimes overemphasized, with the result that government is less able to deal flexibly and rationally with complex problems.

Democracy and the modernizing elite In the new nations there is a continuing tension between democracy and authoritarianism. The dominant trend is toward increased popular participation in political life—voting, membership in mass parties, attendance at political rallies and demonstrations. Political awareness is part of the larger process by which national consciousness and loyalty are created. Voting for nation-centered parties and for national officers helps build a national civic identity. In addition the

[13] Immanuel Wallerstein, *Africa: The Politics of Independence* (New York: Vintage Books, 1961), p. 99.

[14] David Wurfel, "The Philippines," in George M. Kahin (ed.), *Governments and Politics of Southeast Asia* (Ithaca: Cornell University Press, 1959), p. 467.

[15] Pye, *op. cit.,* p. 38.

new leaders seek popular support to strengthen themselves against the more traditionalist or separatist chiefs, or against other political opponents.

However, the modernizing leaders are not equally committed to mass participation. The table on page 507 summarizes a useful distinction between pre-populist and populist regimes, but it should be remembered that there are many mixed situations.

The emphasis on mass opinion by populist regimes does not necessarily mean that a great deal of political freedom is allowed. In Egypt under Nasser, for example, a mass organization, rather than competing political parties, is used to arouse and channel political consciousness. Voting is a plebiscite rather than a real choice among alternative candidates. Other organizations, such as trade unions and professional associations, are controlled by the government. See "Egypt's Populist Regime," pages 506–507.

The modernizing elite is mainly committed to economic development and increased national strength. It is little concerned with political forms. Democracy may be a slogan and a call to action rather than a specific way of making decisions. New labels, such as "tutelary democracy" or "guided democracy," describe regimes that encourage some forms of mass participation, but maintain effective control at the top.

In analyzing the weakness of democracy in the new nations, the following should be considered:

1. Modernization under unfavorable social conditions may require considerable government initiative and control. And the political turmoil following independence may leave little alternative to a temporary authoritarian solution. It does not follow, however, that all cases in which freedom is abrogated can be justified on these grounds.

2. In some new or less industrialized nations, a relative lack of political freedom may be a transitional phenomenon. As economic and political development proceeds, democratic institutions may become stronger. However, where political freedom has been extinguished or not allowed to emerge, such optimism is misplaced.

SECTION 3 THE AGE OF SOCIAL REVOLUTION

In the modern world the common man becomes an actor on the stage of history. He learns to hold opinions and to make his aspirations known. His acceptance of things as they are is not taken for granted. He is wooed and placated, flattered and consulted. He is summoned to participate in great events. This "awakening of the masses" is a fundamental social fact of our era.

Two key words of modern times are *democracy* and *equality*. The loosening of older social bonds has been accompanied by (1) a steady pressure to give more and more people a voice in political decision-making; and (2) a demand that traditional forms of inequality, especially those based upon inherited status, be modified. To a large extent, the expansion of democracy and equality has been a gradual process, the old order giving way in piecemeal fashion to limited demands. On the other hand, the attack upon the old order sometimes has been accompanied by great social upheavals.

THE MEANING OF SOCIAL REVOLUTION

In its broad sense, a social revolution is any profound transformation of society or of some aspect of society. Thus "industrial revolution" designates extensive changes in values and in social organization. A "managerial revolution" alters the social composition of the industrial and governmental elites in modern society.[16] When used in this way, nothing is indicated as to the *method* of change. It is assumed that many forces, acting in a variety of ways, have a profound and cumulative effect upon the social order.

The more restricted meaning of social revolution focuses upon a definite set of events. In this sense social revolution is *a form of collective action* that has the following features:

1. It is directed at the overthrow of a government and the ousting of the social groups that support it from positions of power.

2. Popular support is mobilized through direct action such as mass demonstrations, rioting, refusal of soldiers to obey their commanders, and seizure of factories or of large agricultural holdings. These acts challenge existing authority and set passive elements of the population into motion.

3. Demands are general rather than limited, extending to basic changes in the political and social order.

There is a high probability that violence will be used in a revolution of this sort, either in the course of mass action or by soldiers recruited to the revolutionary cause. However, force is not essential to a social revolution. Little or no violence may occur, if the government is weak and chooses to capitulate in the face of a well-organized and widely supported revolutionary group. Revolutionaries may use force *after* they come into power, in suppressing opposition to the new regime, even though they used little force in actually taking over the government.

The social revolution as a form of collective action is distinguished from the *coup d'état,* in which a group outside the government takes over power, though with limited goals and without stirring a general social upheaval. Thus in 1962 the military leaders in Peru formed a "junta," and ousted the existing government in order to nullify the results of the presidential election. This *coup* had none of the features of a social revolution. On the other hand, a *coup d'état* can be *part* of a social revolution. A case in point is the Bolshevik *coup* in November,[17] 1917, which ousted the Provisional Government formed when the Czar was overthrown the preceding March. In this case the *coup* was a phase of the broader drama called the Russian Revolution.

Although they may involve mass action, social revolutions do not necessarily favor the extension of political democracy. The German Nazi regime of 1933–1945 was created by a social revolution, but it was contemptuous of democracy and extinguished democratic institutions. Nor were the Bolsheviks (later called Communists) favorable to democracy. In each case, a self-appointed "vanguard" asserted the right to speak for the people and rule in their name, without, however, submitting itself to the test of free elections. The Nazi and Communist revolutions are examples of a great historical paradox: the use of mass action and the summoning of popular support for dictatorial movements and governments.

THE REVOLUTIONARY SITUATION

The conditions that make a society "ripe" for revolution are complex and varied, and no simple formula can be stated. Nevertheless, several conclusions can be drawn from the evidence of history.

1. *Aspiration is as important as deprivation in stimulating revolution.* The significance of rising expectations has already been indicated (p. 503), but the lowest, most oppressed strata of the population do not take the lead. Social revolutions are likely to be organized and led by groups that are fairly well-off economically. For example, the Jacobin clubs of the French Revolution, which were important centers of agitation and organization, were of distinctly middle-class composition. (See Table XV:1.) The members "represent the abler, more ambitious, and successful of the inhabitants of a given town. It

[16] James Burnham, *The Managerial Revolution* (New York: John Day, 1941).

[17] This is the New Style date, according to the Gregorian calendar. Before the Revolution, Russia used the Old Style (Julian) calendar. Under that system, the Czar was overthrown in February, 1917, and the Bolsheviks seized power in October. These dates become March and November under the New Style, which conforms to Western usage. The terms "February Revolution" and "October Revolution" are sometimes used in referring to the Russian events of 1917.

TABLE XV:1 SOCIAL COMPOSITION OF THE
JACOBIN CLUBS DURING THE
FRENCH REVOLUTION

	MODERATE PERIOD 1789–1792 (*Percent*)	VIOLENT PERIOD 1793–1795 (*Percent*)
Middle class	66	57
Working class	26	32
Peasant	8	11
Total	100	100
Members	4,037 in 12 clubs	8,062 in 42 clubs

SOURCE: Crane Brinton, *The Anatomy of Revolution* (New York: Vintage Books, 1960), p. 101.

is as if our present-day Rotarians were revolutionists."[18]

The respectable and relatively well-situated revolutionists revolt because they feel that the existing order does not give them the social status and the freedom of action to which they are entitled. For many, this represents a quest for full recognition and complete economic opportunity rather than a desperate effort to escape intolerable conditions.

Deprivation, however, does play a part because the revolutionary situation is often marked by severe hardships brought on by food shortages, a sharp decline in the value of money, new and burdensome taxes, or a demand for unpopular military service. Desperation at the lower levels of society may produce sporadic outbreaks that highlight the weakness and incompetence of the government, encouraging the better-off elements to take action. At the same time, those most deprived become available for mass action in support of the revolutionary leaders. For all groups, it is *relative* deprivation that sharpens resentment and stirs revolt.[19]

2. *Social revolutions occur when the ruling elite is weak and divided.* In the revolutionary situation a state of disorganization spreads throughout the whole

Vilfredo Pareto (1848–1923), an Italian economist, studied the nonrational bases of human conduct. No devotee of verbal economy, he produced a million-word treatise, The Mind and Society. *His theory of elites considers decay within the governing class as a prelude to revolution. According to Pareto, divisions within the governing class and conflict among elites lead to social change. Social stability, on the other hand, presumes the "circulation of elites," that is, free access to the governing class by men of talent and determination and elimination of weaker members of the elite. While Pareto stressed the importance of elites, he did not defend aristocracy, which tends to interfere with the circulation of elites.*

[18] Brinton, *op. cit.*, p. 102.

[19] See James C. Davies, "Toward a Theory of Revolution," *American Sociological Review, 27* (February, 1962), 5–19.

society. The revolution is a crisis of confidence, and the wealthy and the powerful lose *self*-confidence. Members of the ruling elite are affected by new ideas and by criticism of the existing order. Just before the French and Russian revolutions, many of the nobility were highly critical of the regimes and doubtful that the old way of life could continue for long. Beset by internal criticism and self-doubt, the government hesitates to take strong countermeasures. Yet it is incapable or slow to institute the reforms that might stave off the revolution. Or such action may be too late.

Consequently, there is a breakdown of solidarity within the governing class. Some of its members openly espouse revolution and even undertake to lead it. These upper-class rebels may be conservative in their backgrounds and social views, but they feel that the crisis can be met only by overthrowing the government.

3. *The crisis puts at issue the type of government represented by the existing regime.* Limited rebellions may demand only that particular men in power be turned out. Thus kings sometimes were forced to abdicate, to be replaced by another member of the royal family who might be thought more competent, less corrupt, or simply more willing to follow the policies proposed by the rebels.

In a social revolution, however, the attack goes beyond particular officeholders. A change in the form of government is demanded. The interests of those who derive their privileges from the existing form of government and its institutions are threatened.

Thus the revolution reveals weakness and incompetence at the top, widespread loss of confidence in the existing political order, and the availability of alternative groups in the society whose aspirations and self-confidence are high. Clearly, revolutionary change is not a simple thrust from below. It is preceded by a corrosion that affects the entire social system.

THE NATURAL HISTORY OF REVOLUTIONS

The overthrow of the old regime is not an end but a beginning. What is most significant in social revolu-

tions occurs *after* the initial event. How far social change will be pushed, and upon what principles the society will be organized, depends on the character of the revolutionary leadership.

In the classic cases of France and Russia, power was at first transferred from the monarchy to a group of *moderates* who represented the official parliamentary bodies and who sought a limited change in the nature of the government and society. But these men had inherited an ineffective government organization and a host of political and social problems. Moreover, they were unprepared to assume the leadership of an aroused and excited public, because their moderate views inclined them toward compromise and gradual change rather than toward direct action and drastic measures. At the same time, they were committed to a new atmosphere of political freedom and this made them hesitate to curb those who held more radical views. The radicals believed that the political changes in overthrowing the old government were not enough. They insisted that the political revolution should become a social revolution.

Dual power The weakness of the moderates was acutely revealed in the existence of "dual power." In the early stages of the revolution, rival governments appeared. One was the official government, controlled by the moderates; the other was an unofficial government.

Lenin, the leader of the Russian Bolsheviks, described the situation in this way:

The highly remarkable feature of our revolution is that it has established a *dual power;* . . . side by side with the Provisional Government . . . there has developed *another government* . . . — the Soviets of Workers' and Soldiers' Deputies. . . . *This* power is of exactly *the same type* as the Paris Commune of 1871. The fundamental characteristics of this type are: (1) The source of power is not a law previously discussed and passed by parliament, but the direct initiative of the masses from below . . .; (2) the direct arming of the whole people in place of the police and the army, which are institutions separated from the people and opposed by the people; order in the state under such a power is maintained by the armed workers and peasants *themselves,* by the armed peo-

V. I. Lenin (1870–1924), organizer of the Bolshevik Revolution, addresses a crowd. To the right of the stand is Leon Trotsky, another intellectual who became a revolutionary.

ple *itself;* (3) officials and bureaucrats are either displaced by the direct rule of the people itself or at least placed under special control.[20]

Lenin wrote this statement in April, 1917, about a month after the overthrow of the Czar and six months before he himself was to assume power. When he speaks of "the people" he means that groups not hitherto in power are capable of becoming powerful centers of loyalty. Dual power exists when these groups take over some of the functions of government, such as the maintenance of order, while acting independently of the official government.

Russia of 1917 is the clearest case of dual power. On one side was the Provisional Government; on the other were the Soviets (Councils) within which the Bolsheviks and other radical groups were active. The same phenomenon, though not always so plainly evident, has occurred in other revolutions. In the English revolution of the 1640s, the radicals controlled the New Model Army, which represented a dual

power rivaling the moderate-controlled Parliament. In the French Revolution of 1789–1795, a network of radical Jacobin societies provided the organizational basis of dual power.

The essential sociological feature of dual power is *the withdrawal of loyalty* by groups capable of establishing an alternative government. Such groups take varied forms. Sometimes they have a geographical basis, as in the American South just prior to the Civil War; at other times, a sector of the official government—often the army—may become a "government within a government"; or new organizational forms may appear based upon preexisting political parties, churches, trade unions, or other associations. In the 1930s a dual-power situation was created by the German Nazis, who built a network of organizations, including their own military units, that challenged the existing civil authority.

A pattern of dual power also existed in Palestine during the period of rising Zionist influence prior to

[20] "A Dual Power," in V. I. Lenin and J. Stalin, *The Russian Revolution* (New York: International Publishers, 1938), pp. 20 f.

the establishment of the State of Israel in 1948. Although the British governed Palestine under a League of Nations mandate, a number of Jewish organizations, notably the labor federation (Histadrut) and a military organization (Haganah), constituted a separate system of community institutions.

The phenomenon of dual power suggests two conclusions regarding the dynamics of social revolution:

1. The dramatic days of insurrection, when the old government is deposed, may only confirm and complete, with a minimum of violence, a transfer of power that has already occurred. If the unofficial rival government has established its own machinery, and won over the loyalty of units of the army or police, the revolution will already have taken place. In such cases, the final showdown will bring no surprises.

2. Social revolutionists do not so much "seize" power as destroy and re-create it.[21] The old institutions, already weakened, are helped to die. New ones, typically more vigorous and ruthless, are established. These new groups do not simply replace the old. They are more dynamic and bring additional resources into political life. Therefore, the total quantity of effective political power is increased in the course of the revolution.

Victory of the extremists The great social revolutions witnessed a deepening conflict between the moderates and the radicals. In part, these conflicts took place *within* the rival or shadow governments. The extremists pressed their views inside the Soviets, the Jacobin societies, military staffs, or other bases of dual power. When they became dominant there, they were ready for a final test of strength with the legal government of moderates who had replaced the old regime.

Although characteristically the extremists are only a small part of the total population, they come to power in two basic ways. First, by intimidating opponents, both physically and psychologically, they *neutralize* large parts of the population. As the crisis deepens, more and more people withdraw from political participation. Political life tends to be polarized, with high activity at the extremes but passivity among large numbers. Fear and confusion put many on the sidelines. The political arena is abandoned to those who are most ruthless and determined.

Second, because of their discipline and political passion, the extremist minorities are able to take advantage of popular manifestations of resentment or desperation. They place themselves at the head of the "masses," that is, of the most active and excited elements. This greatly increases their power, at least temporarily.

Once in power the radicals establish a "revolutionary dictatorship." Firmness and terror are the order of the day. Step by step, all opposition is suppressed. New and drastic measures are introduced. The social revolution is pressed from above. The government itself is now the main source of social change and the chief mobilizer of the people. Especially in the revolutionary dictatorships of communism and fascism, there is an emphasis on demonstrations of mass support, with huge parades and meetings addressed by the revolutionary leaders. Instead of holding elections, the leaders offer these "direct" activities as evidence of popular approval.

Thermidor The leaders of the French Revolution underlined their break with the past by instituting a new calendar. For the warmest season of the year they chose the name Thermidor ("gift of heat"). On 9th Thermidor of the year II (July 27, 1794), the revolutionary leader Robespierre was deposed. He was executed the next day. There followed a period of reaction against the militancy of the revolution and the way was paved for Napoleon Bonaparte. This transition, to some extent duplicated in other social revolutions, has since been called the "Thermidorean Reaction."

As a phase in the natural history of revolution, Thermidor has the following significance:

1. The centralized power created by the revolu-

---

[21] See George S. Pettee, *The Process of Revolution* (New York: Harper, 1938), pp. 4–5.

tion is taken over and stabilized by a "strong man" —Cromwell in England, Bonaparte in France, Stalin in Russia.

2. Revolutionary fervor is abated and accommodations are made with more moderate groups and older traditions. The revolutionary extremists are suppressed; peace is made with older institutions, such as the church; historic nationalist aspirations are reasserted.

3. The reaction is not complete. There is no return to the prerevolutionary situation. Although many of the ideals of the revolutionaries are shucked off, the period of Thermidor maintains and consolidates the chief social changes wrought by the revolution. Thus under Stalin socialism became identified with state ownership of industry and state initiative in economic development, but the revolutionary ideals of "workers' control" and the "classless society" were abandoned.

The outcome   A great social revolution is not the work of a handful of conspirators or fanatics. Disciplined minorities play a decisive role, but the upheavals occur because there are real problems that the old order seems incapable of solving. Some of these problems are immediate and relatively short-run, such as might be brought on by defeat in war or an economic crisis. These are not likely to lead to a social revolution unless important sectors of the society are ready to accept fundamental changes in the position of great institutions or social classes.

The Russian Revolution was begun by idealists that included in their number both moderates and extremists. "They dreamed of power with the object of abolishing power; of ruling over people to wean them from the habit of being ruled." [22] But the regime they created soon humiliated and destroyed the generation of militant idealists. Within a few years, a dictatorship had suppressed all opposition and set itself to build up its own and the country's power. Indeed, the chief accomplishment of the revolution was the modernization of Russia. [23]

Caution   The above discussion identifies patterns that are discernible in at least some revolutions. However, it is not possible to generalize for all revolutions. There is no single pattern of natural history, no inevitable set of stages.

NATIONALISM AND SOCIAL REVOLUTION

Adaptation 35 is a case study showing how national aspirations can be combined with revolutionary action. In a number of cases, including the Nazi revolution in Germany, national feeling provided much of the political energy for staging the revolution and supporting its victorious leadership. [24] The French Revolution, too, had its nationalist aspects, especially in the defense of the Revolution against foreign armies representing governments hostile to the overthrow of the aristocracy.

[22] Arthur Koestler, *Darkness at Noon* (New York: Modern Library, 1946), p. 59.

[23] John Strachey, "The Strangled Cry," *Encounter* (London), November, 1960, pp. 7–8.

[24] On nationalism and revolution in non-Western countries, see John H. Kautsky (ed.), *Political Change in Underdeveloped Countries: Nationalism and Communism* (New York: Wiley, 1962).

Adaptation 35 / Johnson **PEASANT NATIONALISM AND COMMUNIST POWER**

Following the outbreak of the Sino-Japanese War in 1937, the Chinese Communist Party (CCP) enlarged the territory under its control by establishing "guerrilla bases" in rural areas behind the Japanese lines. By the time of Japan's surrender in 1945, one-fifth of the population of China lived in the guerrilla bases and followed the CCP, but the Communist government of China was not formally proclaimed until October, 1949.

The Communists' success during the war was in marked contrast to the decade preceding the war, when they first tried to organize the peasantry. Although the CCP was in effective control of various small enclaves in the Chinese countryside from 1927 on, its efforts during that period to set up rural "soviets" were far less successful than during the blackest period of the Sino-Japanese war.

Many interpretations of the Communist rise to power in China have been advanced since the revolution of 1949. Some analysts emphasize the economic distress of the Chinese peasantry and the attraction of Communist proposals, such as land reform. Others contend that the appeals of Communism are irrelevant because Communist parties are self-serving conspiracies indifferent to the attitudes of the populations under their control. Still others argue that the Chinese Communist success was due to military superiority alone, and they discount the social and political environment of wartime China as of secondary importance in producing a Communist victory.

The view advanced here is that the Communist rise to power should be understood as a species of nationalist movement originating in resistance to the Japanese occupation of China during World War II. The Chinese masses—the peasants—were unified and brought to political consciousness in the course of the drastic restructuring of Chinese life that accompanied the Japanese conquest of north and east China. This wartime awakening became the basis for a new order in China following Japan's collapse: after the war the resistance leaders were confirmed by their followers in positions of legitimate national authority.

The following account is based in part on a study of documents in the archives of the Japanese Army and other Japanese agencies, made available after World War II.

PREWAR CHINA

Before World War II, Nationalist China, controlled by the Kuomintang party and its leader Chiang Kai-shek, was violently anti-Japanese. This early nationalism was an expression of Westernized, or cosmopolitan, educated Chinese. But for all the political activity and ferment among the prewar elites, their movement was a head without a body. Nationalism was a powerful sentiment among leadership groups, but the social milieu in which they acted was not nationalistic. The Chinese peasantry had no stake in the Chi-

SOURCE: Abridged and adapted from Chalmers A. Johnson, *Peasant Nationalism and Communist Power,* with the permission of the publishers, Stanford University Press. © 1962 by the Board of Trustees of the Leland Stanford Junior University.

nese literary culture. (China's total population in 1949, estimated at 557,000,000, was about 90 percent villagers.) The earlier humiliations of China at the hands of the European powers were largely meaningless to the agricultural masses. The prewar peasant was absorbed in local matters, had only the dimmest sense of "China," and was politically quiescent.

Until 1927, the CCP had shared with the Kuomintang (KMT) the leadership of the early anti-imperialist, anti-Japanese movement among the intellectual and urban classes. However, with the establishment of Chiang Kai-shek's regime in 1927, the KMT purged the CCP and the Communists withdrew to Kiangsi province in south China. From 1929 to 1934 the Communists consolidated and enlarged their position in Kiangsi, south China, but in 1934 KMT armies drove out the Communists, forcing the Long March to Yenan in north central China, where the Communists gained effective control of a number of guerrilla bases.

EFFECTS OF THE JAPANESE INVASION

The most important consequence of Japan's invasion in 1937 and subsequent occupation of China was its impact upon the peasant masses. The invasion heightened the peasant's interest in and awareness of national defense, citizenship, treason, legitimacy of government, and the long-range betterment of the Chinese state. In short, the war mobilized the peasantry, creating the conditions under which mass nationalism could emerge.

Because of the isolation of the peasantry from Chinese nationalist elites, Japanese intelligence had expected little or no resistance on the part of the peasants. However, the devastation and exploitation that accompanied the Japanese invasion produced a radical change in the political attitudes of the northern Chinese; north China became the center of guerrilla resistance during the war.

A number of factors contributed to the awakening and mobilization of the peasantry:

A visible, ruthless enemy The hostile activity of easily identifiable foreign soldiers against Chinese soldiers and civilians had a decisive political effect. Although the peasantry, on the eve of the war, was no more opposed to the Japanese than to other authorities, it became anti-Japanese because of the conduct of Japanese troops. Anti-Japanese feelings, stimulated by the invasion itself, were exacerbated by the "mop-ups" which were aimed directly at the peasantry.

Because the Japanese could not distinguish a guerrilla from a villager, they took ruthless action against the entire rural population. In Hopei, the Japanese implemented a "three-all" policy—"kill all, burn all, destroy all." The essence of "three-all" was to surround a given area, kill everyone in it, and make the area uninhabitable. For example, in May, 1942, Japanese forces surrounded the village of Peihuan in central Hopei, pumped poison gas into the tunnels that were used as shelters by the peasants, and 800 Chinese were killed. The effect of such actions was to arouse even the most parochial of village dwellers. The peasants became receptive to a new political appeal—the defense of the fatherland.

Flight of local officials As the armies of the Chinese Central Government retreated most local officials went with them, and a political vacuum was created. The villagers responded by establishing self-defense forces and, in some cases, guerrilla units. Hundreds of local anti-Japanese governments were set up behind Japanese lines. The feeling of belonging and of having a stake in government was entirely novel to the Chinese masses; it brought an exhilarating sense of self-determination.

The Japanese puppet government In 1940, the Japanese established a puppet government, whose purpose was to create popular support for the invaders. Because of inept administration, continuing Japanese exploitation, and heavy-handed military activities, the facade of Chinese sovereignty surrounding the Japanese-sponsored government never won the support of the Chinese peasantry.

These developments broke the hold of parochialism on the Chinese peasant. The war destroyed the rural social order and sensitized the Chinese peasant to new associations, identities, and purposes. The new environment was the most favorable the Communists had encountered since the Party's founding in 1921.

ROLE OF THE COMMUNIST PARTY

The source of the Communist Party's authority in China today dates from the wartime period when it led the mobilized masses of previously non-Communist areas in their struggles with the Japanese army. Propaganda, organization, and military action were the means by which the Communists took advantage of the opportunity created by the Japanese invasion, the crumbling of existing authority, and the response of the peasantry.

Propaganda The propaganda effort launched by the CCP was remarkably free of Communist ideology. The Communists did not repeat their political failure of the prewar period; they eschewed old slogans of class warfare and radical redistribution of property and concentrated solely on national salvation. An example of the wartime propaganda is a CCP leaflet found by the Japanese Army:

Exterminate the Traitor, Peace Preservation Committees! Japan has invaded our Shansi, killed large numbers of our people, burned thousands of our houses, raped our women in countless numbers, robbed us of our food and wealth, trampled on the graves of our ancestors, forced our wives and children to flee, destroyed our famous places, . . . and made the joy of peace impossible. . . . Everybody! Rise up and join a guerrilla self-defense unit! Exterminate the Peace Maintenance Committee which sells out the nation! Defend our anti-Japanese patriotic people's government! Assist the all-out resistance of Commander Yen! Act in unison with Army and people to overthrow Japanese imperialism!

Organization A second source of Communist strength was the organizational expertise of the Communist Army. Communist-controlled troops included regulars, guerrillas, and militia. The regulars were uniformed, mobile divisions,

"field forces," which were the best-equipped and best-officered. They were transferred from one area to another in response to military developments. The guerrillas were full-time military units, but remained in the area where they were mobilized and were not usually in uniform. Often guerrilla units were set up prior to the arrival of regular Communist forces and were subsequently incorporated into the Communist Army. The militia was made up of farmers, both men and women, who engaged in local military activities as needed. They also collected intelligence, controlled movements between villages (by means of an elaborate passport system), and mined roads.

As guerrillas and militia the peasants encountered the enemy and identified with the resistance. The regular forces, however, provided the organizing leadership. Training and propaganda activities were the special duties of "political departments" attached to all regular Communist military units.

Political specialists or "cadres" used regional dialects to communicate with the majority of the people. A Communist Army guide, entitled "Problems of Working with Youth in Peasant Villages," emphasized the necessity of obtaining information on the political, economic, and cultural life of the village, as well as on pro-Japanese sentiment. The manual also instructed political workers to dress and talk like peasants, and to respect local superstitions.

The manual also said, "the broad peasant class is the chief object of mass movement work, but the peasantry has two distinctive characteristics: (*a*) a conserv-

ative or nativistic viewpoint, and (*b*) limited organization with no clear perception of the future." To meet this difficulty, the manual advised that initial efforts be directed at handicraft workers, middle-school students, small-businessmen, and "self-respecting" bureaucrats and landlords who sense the existence of a "national crisis." The support of such people would facilitate work with the peasants.

Mass-movement associations The end product of a successful campaign was the creation of mass organizations. The most common were "National Salvation Associations," separately organized for peasants, women, young people, workers, teachers, merchants, and cultural workers. These large, hierarchically structured organizations had little internal democracy; their chief function was to educate their members politically and train them in reading and other skills. From these associations, auxiliary resistance units such as self-defense corps, stretcher units, and transportation corps were recruited.

Although they were not intended to exercise political power, the mass associations contributed to the guerrilla government by electing representatives. The aim was to afford the population a sense of direct participation in the resistance movement and thereby to ensure continued popular support for the Communist Army. The mass associations' true contribution to Chinese political life was not democracy but, as the Communists themselves stated, mass mobilization.

Guerrilla warfare A third factor accounting for the success of the CCP was the effective military action of the Communist Army against the Japanese. When the Communist armies engaged the enemy, they inflicted serious damage. The usual Japanese report, however, was "no enemy force encountered"—a consequence of the Communist armies' strict adherence to the principle of guerrilla warfare: fight only at times of your own choosing. The success of such tactics depended on support from the rural population, for guerrilla warfare is not so much a military technique as a political condition. In guerrilla warfare the conflict is between a professional army, possessing the advantages of superior training and equipment, and an irregular force, less well trained, less well equipped, but actively supported by the population. The people free the guerrillas from dependence on supply lines, provide them with nearly perfect intelligence concerning enemy movements, and hide fugitives.

Conclusion   Between 1937 and 1945 north China witnessed a confrontation between two expanding political domains: the Chinese Communists and the Japanese. Having squeezed out the Kuomintang as a third participant early in the war, they fought between themselves—winner take all. When the Japanese were defeated, the Chinese Communists took all of north China (except for some major cities that the KMT managed to reoccupy for a few years). North China thus became the chief stronghold from which the Communists waged their successful civil war against the KMT during 1947–1949.

In China Communist power rests basically upon indigenous national aspirations. The reality underlying that power is a quickened national awareness and an unprecedented mobilization of the people. The transformation took place under the banner of Communism, but its roots lie deeper than attachment to Communist political ideas and leadership. The nationalist foundation of Communist rule must inevitably lend a distinctive character to the evolution of Communism in China.

SECTION 4 TOTALITARIAN SOCIETY

In the nineteenth century, social change was social progress, and the future of society seemed clear and hopeful. Industrialism and democracy would advance together. Traditional society based on status, privilege, and ignorance would be swept aside. A new and permanent era of rationality and enlightenment would gradually extend its sway. This optimistic view of a progressive society assumed that the darkest pages of human history, measured by brutality, tyranny, and political hatred, belonged to the past.

In the twentieth century, there is a more pessimistic note. Industrial society, and the technology on which it is based, have conferred many benefits. But they have also presented problems and produced some unexpected and drastic responses. One of the most important of these responses is the emergence of twentieth-century totalitarianism.

Totalitarianism represents a fusion of state and society, an entire social system in which politics profoundly affects the whole range of human activities and associations. The totalitarian social system differs markedly from older authoritarian dictatorships. In the latter, power is concentrated in the hands of a ruling few, but many spheres of life, such as religion and the family, are more or less free from state control. Autocratic rulers of the past were often cruel, despotic, and ready to sacrifice others to their own power and glory, but they lived in societies poorly adapted to the exercise of centralized power. It is one thing to have the trappings and the doctrine of autocracy; it is another to have the means to put it into practice. Modern technology and social organization provide the most advanced tools of political dictatorship.

Total power In totalitarianism the government accepts no limitation on the *amount or kind* of coercion it may use to achieve its ends. It can exe-

Henry VIII (1491–1547) consolidated the power of the monarchy and split the English Church from Rome. Nevertheless, his power was limited by the social structure of his time. As king, Henry had no large standing army, no effective police, no extensive bureaucracy to carry out his will. He depended on the landed gentry and the merchant classes, without whose cooperation he could not govern. His regime was autocratic and authoritarian, but not totalitarian.

cute people, exile them, place them in prison or in labor camps—all without effective restraint. Totalitarian power is also unlimited in *scope*. It is all-embracing. The government asserts the right to control and regiment every phase of life.

Total power is not easily achieved or maintained. Every totalitarian regime supplements conventional powers of government by new devices and strategies for subjecting people to detailed surveillance and control. The most important controls are the following:

1. *The official political party.* Although there are no significant contests in the totalitarian state, much effort is devoted to maintaining a party organization. The regimes are sometimes called "party states" because of the important role played by the single political party in strengthening the top leaders. The totalitarian party consists of a relatively small percentage of the population, but includes the most dedicated supporters of the system.

The party is a training ground for future leaders and administrators; it is an army of volunteers who stimulate and reinforce support for the government; its members greatly enhance the capacity of the government to observe the population and report subversive activities. Within the party, there are sometimes conflicts and debate among top leaders, but the membership itself does not participate in the determination of policy or the selection of leaders. The party is a dependable instrument of total power controlled from the top.

2. *Official ideology.* The totalitarian government is a propagandist and agitator that demands total conformity to an orthodox set of political beliefs. The government gains prestige as the spokesman for a new set of moral beliefs. The ideology provides material for the political indoctrination of the people, who thus learn whom to hate, what to cheer, and why they must sacrifice; loyalty is tested and "dangerous thoughts" detected and combated. Under totalitarianism the official ideology stands unchallenged. No competing doctrines may be openly promulgated. Furthermore, the official ideology is not restricted to politics, religion, or economics, but

it is a total ideology, guiding all phases of conduct and belief. The common thread is subordination of the individual to the will of the state.

3. *Monopoly of public communication.* The government takes over the entire system of public communication: newspapers, radio, television, cinema, and publication of books, magazines, and even academic journals. This monopoly has several uses for totalitarian rule. Most important, the prohibition of independent media of communication stifles the organization of opposition groups, since they cannot maintain themselves without some means of communication. In addition, the government can filter out any news that might create unfavorable attitudes or undertake campaigns of "public education" to create a favorable climate of opinion.

4. *Control of organized group life.* When the totalitarian regime comes to power, it either breaks up or takes over most independent social groups, including trade unions, business associations, youth groups, churches, schools, and political parties. It even places loyalty to the state above loyalty to family and friends. It attempts to curtail the autonomy of primary groups, especially in the early stages of totalitarian rule when the values transmitted by the family do not conform with those of the state.

But totalitarianism is not the absence of social organization. On the contrary, associations of all kinds are created and supported by the totalitarian state. Government-controlled youth leagues, hiking clubs, trade unions, and other "people's" organizations have been important under both fascism and communism. Social groups under totalitarianism, however, are not autonomous. They are instituted and controlled from above to mobilize people for courses of action desired by the ruling elite and to prevent the development of independent groups and opinion.

5. *A managed economy.* The totalitarian state assumes control over the main sectors of the economy, especially the big corporations and banks. Under communism all major enterprises are owned and run by the government. Under Hitler, private owner-

ship remained, but the government established control over business management. Total power is not possible when the government must defer to the independent decisions of businessmen or when the free play of the competitive market is allowed to decide who produces what and how much at what price.

6. *The police state.* Because the totalitarian regimes depend on the extensive use of arbitrary police power, they are often referred to as "police states." The police become weapons in the struggle for total power, and special police agencies, partly secret, act as arms of the government in maintaining political surveillance of the population and in ferreting out potential opponents. Moreover, the police are not restrained by legal requirements of speedy trial or fair treatment.

In its quest for total power, the totalitarian state combines the threat of violence with organization and mass persuasion. The ultimate achievement of total power would rest on complete and willing acceptance of the system and its existing leaders by the population. However, no totalitarian government is willing to test its hold on public opinion by removing the threat of imprisonment or worse and permitting the open debate of public issues.

Since the death of Stalin in 1953, there has been some relaxation of totalitarian control in the Soviet Union:

Purges of the elite within the Communist Party and political terror directed against the population at large were for a long time defined by many observers as distinctive and irremovable features of Soviet totalitarianism. Political controls of essentially nonpolitical activities and restrictions on freedom of movement and expression continue to characterize Soviet society. But the formerly ubiquitous forced labor camps have apparently largely been closed down, the purging of the ranks of the Party greatly reduced, and even the treatment of defeated "enemies" at the highest levels of the Party transformed from inevitable shooting to probable demotion and "internal exile."[25]

---

[25] Alex Inkeles and Kent Geiger, *Soviet Society: A Book of Readings* (Boston: Houghton Mifflin, 1961), p. 249.

This relaxation is accompanied by an increased concern for consumer needs, some restraints on police power, and possibly a greater degree of professional and academic freedom. However, the government maintains the decisive instruments of total power. The government's continued stability and self-confidence may reduce the harshness with which these powers are used, and if this goes on for a long time the totalitarian character of the system may change.

Totalitarianism and industrial society Although as a political system the totalitarian state is alien to constitutional democracy, the similarities of the two industrial systems should not be overlooked.

1. The modern totalitarian state is a vehicle of rapid industrialization. Its power rests on advanced technology. Its values include a prizing of scientific and engineering progress. Indeed, in accordance with Marxist doctrine, the communists accept material progress as the main criterion of social worth. Insofar as advanced industrial organization defines the character of a society, communism has points in common with other industrialized systems.

2. Totalitarian society, like the rest of the modern world, is a *participant* society. The totalitarian rulers ask more of their people than simple obedience. Through a large variety of government-controlled organizations and programs, the people are called upon to participate actively in public life—to volunteer for special duties, to show enthusiasm for their leaders, to read the government newspapers, to join in public criticism of lesser officials, to vote for the official slate of candidates. The more totalitarian the society, the greater is the emphasis on *mobilization,* on driving the population toward greater effort to serve the state.

The emphasis on participation, plus the glorification of "the people" in totalitarian ideology, lends a pseudodemocratic cast to life in the totalitarian world. The very term "democracy" becomes identified with participation and popular consent, even if it does not involve the free choice of leaders, freedom of speech, or freedom of association. In the democratic age, the symbols of democracy, and some of its forms, are associated with even the harshest dictatorial regimes. Mass dictatorship is a parody of the democratic ideal.

SECTION 5 SOCIAL FOUNDATIONS OF FREEDOM AND DEMOCRACY

The revolutionary changes discussed above—especially the rise of totalitarianism—direct renewed attention to the study of freedom and democracy:

1. The problem of *freedom,* that is, the restraint on the power of government and the protection of the individual from actual or potential oppression.

2. The problem of *democracy,* and the *quality of self-government,* that is, the degree to which civic participation is widespread, rational, and effective.

This section deals with these problems by considering (*a*) the legitimacy of authority, (*b*) pluralism as a foundation of freedom, and (*c*) political participation.

POWER AND LEGITIMACY

Legitimacy is power justified by reference to accepted values. When power is made legitimate, it is called *authority*. By means of legitimation, consent to the exercise of power is gained, and governing is freed from primary reliance on naked force. The quest for legitimacy is universal, but the *principles* of legitimacy vary: each culture justifies authority in accordance with its major values. Some of the different principles which have made power acceptable in specific groups are mentioned in the following quotation:

. . . ruling classes do not justify their power exclusively by *de facto* possession of it, but try to find a moral and legal basis for it, representing it as the logical and necessary consequence of doctrines and beliefs that are generally recognized and accepted. So if a society is deeply imbued with the Christian spirit the political class will govern by the will of the sovereign, who, in turn, will reign because he is God's anointed. So too in Mohammedan societies political authority is exercised directly in the name of the caliph, or vicar, of the Prophet; or in the name of someone who has received investiture, tacit or explicit, from the caliph. The Chinese mandarins ruled the state because they were supposed to be interpreters of the will of the Son of Heaven, who had received from heaven the mandate to govern paternally, and in accordance with the rules of the Confucian ethic, "the people of the hundred families." . . . The powers of all lawmakers, magistrates, and government officials in the United States emanate directly or indirectly from the vote of the voters, which is held to be the expression of the sovereign will of the whole American people.[26]

Some rule, and others obey, in part on the basis of shared beliefs in the desirability of the arrangement. However, merely because legitimacy justifies a system of power, it does not follow that principles of legitimacy are "mere quackeries designed to trick the masses into obedience." [27] Rather, such principles answer real needs felt by rulers and ruled alike.

Legitimate power tends to be *restrained* power. Principles of legitimacy state what power-holders cannot do as well as what they are justified in doing. For example, if the principle of legitimacy is popular election, then the governing group cannot appoint its own successors but must hold elections to justify its continued power. In the case of monarchy, established principles of legitimacy governing accession to the throne, such as the right of birth or election by a council of barons, have checked the power struggles of feudal lords. The principle of legitimacy supports the broader notion of a restraining law that stands above the rulers, to which they are responsible and by virtue of which they govern.

"Even the tyrant must sleep," wrote Hobbes, and dictators as well as democrats strive for legitimacy. However, power made legitimate is the first indispensable step toward a system that permits the questions: By what right do you govern? How do you justify your decisions?

The contribution legitimacy makes to freedom depends on the specific principles invoked. When Hitler justified his regime by claiming to represent the historic spirit of the German *Volk,* or when appeal is made to tradition as the basis of authority, it is difficult to make the principle an effective basis for criticizing and restraining the exercise of power. When legitimacy rests on specifically delegated power, or on a particular competence, the possibilities of critical assessment are enhanced.

PLURALISM

Political freedom can be realized only in group membership. A single individual facing the power of government is too weak to resist encroachments on his freedom. But if he joins with others, he can find protection. The collective power of organized groups helps the individual to resist arbitrary interference with his liberty in other spheres of life as well as in his relations to government. A worker's freedom is enhanced because his union is able to prevent management from treating him arbitrarily, and this has been a chief reason for the widespread growth of trade unions in modern times.

Many different social groups contribute to political freedom. Professional associations, trade unions, business organizations, churches, fraternal orders, veterans groups, for instance, generate social power that can protect the individual, standing between him and hostile forces.

Three patterns of social organization affecting political freedom are:

1. *Concentrated power.* When power is in a few

[26] Gaetano Mosca, *The Ruling Class* (New York: McGraw-Hill, 1939), p. 70. Used by permission of McGraw-Hill Book Company, Inc.

[27] *Ibid.,* p. 71.

hands the freedom of individuals and of other groups is endangered. There is so much strength on one side that opposition can be isolated and quickly destroyed. This situation is encountered where one group dominates a community or internationally when a single country dominates a continent.

When a single group or combination of groups achieves a virtual monopoly of power, it no longer has to take account of the interests of other groups. There are no effective checks on its power. Even though motivated by high ideals, any group with a monopoly on power endangers the freedom of others.

2. *Fragmented power.* Freedom is also endangered when power is so widely dispersed among competing groups that no group or combination is strong enough to organize the community and establish effective social control. A frontier society, in which each man is his own police force, is a case in point. Moreover, where power is fragmented, the community is vulnerable to any strong group that may arise. The conquest of England in 1066 by a small force from Normandy was made easier because of the fragmented character of social organization. Power was dispersed among many local lords, bishops, and sheriffs, and no adequate stabilizing force existed.

3. *Countervailing power.* Freedom is best protected when there are a number of groups powerful enough to check each other and strong enough to maintain social order and organize the main activities of the society. Such a pattern of social organization is usually called "pluralism."

[The pluralist society is] characterized by the presence of large, well integrated groups representing significant divisions of interests and values. The various groups are limited in their power by the fact that the interests of other groups must be taken into account. The power of the state is limited by the power of organized public opinion and large special interest groups; the pressure exercised by business interests is counterbalanced by the forces of organized labor; both management and labor must take into account the interests of an integrated consumers' movement and other public agencies; no one religious group possesses a monopoly of spiritual values, and the various religious groups learn to accommodate themselves to one another; religious thought is denied absolute sovereignty over ideas by the presence of independent secular thought maintained by a free press, free universities, free literary movements, learned societies and organized scientific research. In the sphere of production, a pluralist society might allow for the operation of more than one form of economic organization: not only corporations and single entrepreneurships, but worker owned cooperatives and state organized collectives as well. Probably no community has ever achieved the optimum degree of pluralist organization, but the United States of America, Great Britain and Sweden may be considered as illustrative of societies tending to approximate the conditions of a pluralist society.[28]

Functions of pluralism Social pluralism limits the power of groups by providing a system of social checks and balances:[29]

1. It encourages competition among groups and rivalry among leaders and therefore inhibits monopolies of power.

2. It limits leadership control by increasing the chances that members belong to several organizations. Each group tempers its attack on others to keep from losing the cooperation of those members who belong to the other organizations.

3. Participation in a pluralist society encourages such skills of democratic politics as the use of bargaining and negotiation.

4. Pluralism increases the availability of sources of information independent of government, church, or any single organization. This permits people to consider criticisms of and alternatives to existing policies and leaders.

If pluralism is to be a workable pattern of social organization, there must be a shared belief in its validity. This consensus need not run deep; it may

---

[28] Gerard De Gré, "Freedom and Social Structure," *American Sociological Review, 11* (October, 1946), 535. See also Mosca, *op. cit.,* pp. 134 ff.

[29] See Robert A. Dahl and Charles E. Lindblom, *Politics, Economics, and Welfare* (New York: Harper & Row, 1953), pp. 303–306.

depend on the shared beliefs of "influentials" rather than on solid support and full understanding by the entire public.[30]

Agreement on fundamentals is more difficult to attain in pluralist than in communal social organization. A simple rural community is held together by strong ties of kinship, locality, and traditional belief. Pluralist social organization, however, has a greater diversity of values and interests, more impersonal relations, and, therefore, more conflicting loyalties. When few important life experiences are shared, consensus is difficult to achieve. But without agreement on fundamentals, pluralist social organization is precarious, though it may "muddle through" so long as social conflict is not intense.

The significance of pluralism for political freedom is discussed further in Adaptation 36, pages 531–532.

PARTICIPATION

The democratic ideal suggests that everyone should be interested in politics and act effectively. Many, however, do not take the trouble to vote, even in presidential elections. National elections in the United States bring less than two-thirds of the eligible population to the polls. Other forms of participation, such as attending meetings, wearing buttons, or contributing money involve far fewer people. Opinion surveys have shown that on many political issues one-third or more of the respondents indicate that they have no opinion or information.[31] The broad picture is one of many active minorities bidding for the support of a fluctuating mass of relatively uninvolved individuals.

Who votes[32]   About two weeks after the 1964 presidential election the Current Population Survey (CPS) of the Census Bureau conducted interviews in 33,000 households, which included 65,000 people of voting age.

The CPS found differences in voter participation rates on almost every characteristic: age, sex, race, region of residence, urbanization, educational level, employment status, occupation, income level, and family status. As indicated in Table XV:2, which reports the extremes, education, income, region, and age are important determinants of voting participation. The original report gives more refined data showing some interrelations that are only suggested in the table. For instance, voting participation was 93.4 percent for females with four or more years of college and with family incomes of $10,000 or more, but was 39.4 percent for females with less than eight years of education and with family incomes under $3,000.

All voting surveys have their limitations and almost all report higher voting participation than the actual vote.[33] The present survey, although based on a large and excellent sample, capably executed and interpreted, overestimates by 6 million the number of votes cast. The survey estimates 76.6 million voters out of 110.6 million persons of voting age in the civilian noninstitutional population. Official counts show 70.6 million votes cast for the presidential candidates.

The principal sources of the discrepancy are the reluctance of a respondent to admit he did not vote or actual mistakes in reporting the voting participation of another household member. Such overstatements might run between 5 and 10 percent. Despite admitted limitations, the differences are not explained away, and the findings probably correctly reflect relative tendencies to vote in various parts of the population.

---

[30] See Herbert McClosky, "Consensus and Ideology in American Politics," *American Political Science Review, 63* (June, 1964), 373.

[31] Angus Campbell, P. E. Converse, W. E. Miller, and D. E. Stokes, *The American Voter* (New York: Wiley, 1960), p. 174.

[32] *Current Population Reports,* Series P-20, No. 143, "Voter Participation in the National Election: November, 1964," Washington, D.C., October 25, 1965. (Prepared by Mary G. Powers and Richard W. Dodge.)

[33] *Ibid.,* pp. 4–5.

TABLE XV:2   EXTREMES IN VOTING PARTICIPATION (IN PERCENTAGES)
UNITED STATES, 1964

VARIABLE	HIGHEST PARTICIPATION		LOWEST PARTICIPATION	
Age	45–54 years	76.1	21–24 years [a]	51.3
Sex	Men	71.9	Women	67.0
Race	White	70.7	Negro	58.5
Region	North Central	76.2	South	56.7
Residence	Metropolitan	70.8	Nonmetropolitan	66.5
Education	College (4 years or more)	87.5	Elementary (0–7 years)	51.2
Family income	$10,000 and over	84.9	Under $2,000	49.6
Occupation	White collar	82.7	Farm workers	65.2
Employment status	Employed	73.0	Unemployed	58.0

SOURCE: *Current Population Reports,* Series P-20, No. 143, October 25, 1965. Percentages are based on "all persons," which includes a small number whose voting participation was not reported.

[a] In Alaska, Georgia, Hawaii, and Kentucky the voting age is less than 21 years. Only 39.2 percent of eligibles under 21 years of age actually voted.

Apathy and political competence   Differences in skill and feeling affect both the extent and quality of political participation.[34] The complexities of modern politics make great demands on the understanding of the electorate. Candidates must be judged not only by the party they represent, but also by the particular wing within the party. A multitude of complex issues, from foreign policy to tax programs, need to be assessed for their long-run as well as short-run effects.

Voters are very different in their political skill. The educational and job experiences that produce such skills are not uniform throughout the population. Social position has much to do with the ability to write letters, use the telephone easily, read the newspapers, and speak at meetings. Both poise and knowledge affect political competence. The conditions of lower-class life probably do not train people in techniques of cooperation and leadership that are taken for granted among middle- and upper-class people.

Whether or not people have the skills, many do not *feel* competent to deal with political affairs. A sense of impotence keeps them out of politics because they wish to avoid areas of life that are frustrating. One study showed that the higher the income, the greater the feeling that individual political action does (or can) have an impact on politics. (See Table XV:3.) Another found that "among the poorly educated, lower-income manual workers the sense of involvement in public, and particularly international, affairs tends to be extremely limited and passive." [35] Among the lower classes the belief prevails that politics is not comprehensible or manageable. Even among higher-status groups, there are individuals who feel at the mercy of forces beyond their control.

A five-nation study of political participation found significant differences in the "sense of civic competence." [36] This state of mind was measured by asking a sample of respondents in each country whether they

[34] This discussion is based on: David Riesman and Nathan Glazer, "Criteria for Political Apathy," in Alvin W. Gouldner (ed.), *Studies in Leadership* (New York: Harper & Row, 1950); and David Riesman in collaboration with Reuel Denney and Nathan Glazer, *The Lonely Crowd* (New Haven: Yale University Press, 1950).

[35] Gabriel Almond, *The American People and Foreign Policy* (New York: Harcourt, Brace & World, 1950), p. 130. See also Campbell *et al., op. cit.,* especially pp. 103–105, 479–481, 490–491.

[36] Gabriel A. Almond and Sidney Verba, *The Civic Culture* (Princeton: Princeton University Press, 1963), Chap. 7.

TABLE XV:3 INCOME AND THE SENSE OF POLITICAL EFFICACY

INCOME	SENSE OF POLITICAL EFFICACY		
	High	Medium	Low
Under $2,000	11%	49%	38%
$2,000–2,999	19	54	25
$3,000–3,999	25	57	17
$4,000–4,999	33	51	16
$5,000 and over	43	46	10

SOURCE: A. Campbell, G. Gurin, and W. E. Miller, *The Voter Decides* (Evanston: Row, Peterson, 1954), p. 191. A national sample of 1,582 persons replied to questions designed to gauge their "feeling that individual political action does have, or can have, an impact upon the political process, i.e., that it is worth while to perform one's civic duties. It is the feeling that political and social change is possible, and that the individual citizen can play a part in bringing about this change." The sample was asked to agree or disagree with such questions as: "Sometimes politics and government seem so complicated that a person like me can't really understand what's going on." (*Ibid.,* pp. 187–188.)

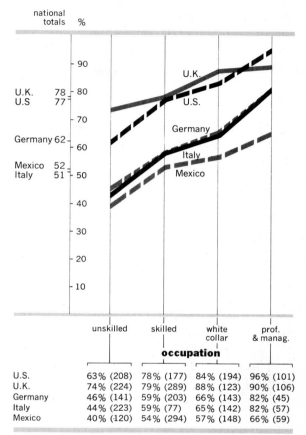

(Numbers in parentheses refer to the base upon which percentage is calculated.)

FIG. XV:1 Percentage in five countries who say they can do something about an unjust law, by occupation of family breadwinner

ADAPTED from Gabriel A. Almond and Sidney Verba, *The Civic Culture* (Princeton: Princeton University Press, 1963), p. 210.

thought they could succeed in changing an unjust law. Figure XV:1 shows variation by country and the direct relationship between sense of efficacy and occupational status in all five countries.

Apathy and political affect The great differences in feeling or emotion that people bring to politics are due in part to the wide variety of motives behind political interest. Traditionally, Americans have been exhorted to participate in politics in order to defend their private interests and to fulfill their duties as citizens. Self-interest is indeed a potent political incentive. The farmer, for example, must attend to politics in an era of government-supported prices, crop quotas, and subsidies. But for many citizens, private interests are only obscurely related to politics; the links to government action may seem remote or invisible, and even when clear, feelings of impotence may make political concern for private interests seem pointless. In mass democracy, self-interest is no sure motive for political involvement.

A sense of public duty is often a strong incentive. When social values are deeply implanted in the individual, he may feel the obligation to protect those values in politics, as in other spheres of life. Such a sense of duty has been historically most closely associated with upper-class tradition, for example in England and in New England. On the other hand, some people turn to politics for amusement, conformity, a sense of belonging, psychic escape, and other forms of gratification. They often turn away from politics for similar reasons.

Combinations of competence and affect Different proportions of emotional involvement and skill are associated with what Riesman has called "political styles." These ways of responding to politics cut across party affiliation or political ideology. They are rooted in socialization and character.

1. People of very low political competence and affect are *indifferent* to politics. They neither understand it nor feel personally involved in it. Politics to them is something alien, the province of others unlike themselves. Indifference was widespread at one time among women who viewed politics as the prerogative of men and among lower-class people who thought of politics as an upper-class responsibility. These "traditional indifferents" still form a large but indefinite proportion of the electorate in the United States. In less politically mature countries, they remain the great majority.

2. People with more emotions than competence in politics often express themselves in an *indignant* manner. They respond to political disappointments with strong feelings of self-righteousness. Extreme "political indignants" are vulnerable to the appeal of ideologies and movements that promise to destroy all those groups not in agreement with their beliefs and to usher in a utopian order of "perfect morality."

3. People with a high level of political competence but little emotional involvement often express themselves in a *manipulative* manner. They see politics as an opportunity to manipulate people and things rather than as a way of supporting valued ideas and groups. They avoid being on the losing side. The manipulative person is careful not to become so emotionally involved in anything that he cannot change his position. His lack of firm values does not provide a stable psychological base for democratic institutions.

4. An additional category is made up of people of high competence and high commitment. Such individuals are almost inevitably drawn to leadership roles. The most conspicuous cases are from families that have a long history of public service and regard politics as a worthy and challenging career.

The independent voter Among the more important conclusions of modern research on voting is a new assessment of the independent voter.

The ideal of the Independent citizen, attentive to politics, concerned with the course of government, who weighs the rival appeals of a campaign and reaches a judgment that is unswayed by partisan prejudice, has had such a vigorous history in the tradition of political reform—and has such a hold on civic education today—that one could easily suppose that the habitual partisan has the more limited interest and concern with politics. [However], far from being attentive, interested, and informed, Independents tend as a group to be somewhat less involved in politics. They have somewhat poorer knowledge of the issues, their image of the candidates is fainter, their interest in the campaign is less, their concern over the outcome is relatively slight, and their choice between competing candidates, although it is indeed made later in the campaign, seems much less to spring from discoverable evaluations of the elements of national politics.[37]

These conclusions, like many others in social science research, are based on the comparison of percentages. For example, Table XV:4 shows that in one study 82 percent of people who strongly identified with a political party cared "very much or pretty much" about the outcome of an election. The corresponding percentage for independents was 51 percent. Many independents are interested, although not so large a proportion as affiliated persons.

The view of the independent voter in the quotation above has been challenged. A study of "switchers" in recent presidential elections showed that many independents choose candidates in the light of the positions they hold on important issues.[38] It is apparent that each point of view emphasizes different aspects of the voting and opinion data. In fact there are many independent voters who act self-consciously and rationally, many others whose

---

[37] Campbell *et al., The American Voter, op. cit.,* p. 143.

[38] See V. O. Key, Jr., *The Responsible Electorate* (Cambridge: Harvard University Press, 1966).

TABLE XV:4 STRENGTH OF PARTY IDENTIFICATION AND CONCERN OVER OUTCOME

	STRONG PARTY IDENTIFICATION	WEAK PARTY IDENTIFICATION	INDEPENDENTS
Care very much or care pretty much	82%	62%	51%
Don't care very much or don't care at all	18	38	49
Total	100%	100%	100%
Number of cases	609	621	395

SOURCE: Angus Campbell, P. E. Converse, W. E. Miller, and D. E. Stokes, *The American Voter* (New York: Wiley, 1960), p. 144.

reasons for voting as they do are obscure and perhaps irrational. How many there are of each type is not known.

In a democracy, group membership is vital to the political process, partly to support a pluralist political order, as discussed above. In addition, the voting studies suggest that the affiliated citizen is more likely to be politically competent and involved than his "free-floating" compatriot.

A democratic order needs large numbers of people who are socialized in the skills of political participation and who believe that democratic values are worth having and protecting. However, it is not necessary that all members of the electorate must be politically involved all the time. A sizable group of less involved citizens is desirable to "cushion" the intense action of highly-motivated partisans. If everyone were highly and continuously interested in all issues, compromise and gradual solution might be reduced.

Adaptation 36 / Tocqueville **THE DEMOCRATIC AGE**

Alexis de Tocqueville was born in Verneuil west of Paris in 1805 and died at Cannes in 1859. He studied law and, as a young man, began a career in the judiciary. In succeeding years, he developed a broad interest in the structure of French society, especially in the problems created by the interplay of a continuing aristocratic tradition and the rising tide of democracy.

In 1831, together with his lifelong friend, Gustave de Beaumont, Tocqueville obtained a commission from the French government to study the prison system and prison reform in the United States. This project was faithfully carried out, but the real interest of the two men lay in the entire political system of the new country. The result was a two-part study, *Democracy in America*. Part I appeared in 1835, Part II in 1840. This book has been called "perhaps the greatest work ever written on one country by the citizen of another."

SOURCE: Abridged and adapted from *Democracy in America* by Alexis de Tocqueville. Translated by Henry Reeve and edited by Francis Bowen (Cambridge: Sever and Francis, 1862). For easy reference to other editions, general locations of quoted passages are shown.

Tocqueville saw the United States as a social laboratory. Here was a new country in which democratic institutions were being rapidly developed and given free rein. Here, if anywhere, the full significance of democracy might be studied. His aim was to draw some lessons from this experience for the guidance of his own countrymen. In pursuing this task, Tocqueville adopted a distinctly sociological perspective. He asked: What social conditions *sustain* the democratic political order? What are the consequences of democracy for manners and customs, for nonpolitical institutions, for the quality of life?

The following passages from Tocqueville show some of his major concerns. The passages have not been edited for this adaptation but are taken directly from the translation.

It is not, then, merely to satisfy a legitimate curiosity that I have examined America; my wish has been to find there instruction by which we may ourselves profit. Whoever should imagine that I have intended to write a panegyric would be strangely mistaken, and on reading this book, he will perceive that such was not my design: nor has it been my object to advocate any form of government in particular, for I am of opinion that absolute excellence is rarely to be found in any system of laws. I have not even pretended to judge whether the social revolution, which I believe to be irresistible, is advantageous or prejudicial to mankind. I have acknowledged this revolution as a fact already accomplished, or on the eve of its accomplishment; and I have selected the nation, from amongst those which have undergone it, in which its development has been the most peaceful and the most complete, in order to discern its natural consequences, and to find out, if possible, the means of rendering it profitable to mankind. I confess that, in America, I saw more than America; I sought there the image of democracy itself, with its inclinations, its character, its prejudices, and its passions, to learn what we have to fear or to hope from its progress. [I. Introduction]

Despotism and democracy No sovereign ever lived in former ages so absolute or so powerful as to undertake to administer by his own agency, and without the assistance of intermediate powers, all the parts of a great empire: none ever attempted to subject all his subjects indiscriminately to strict uniformity of regulation, and personally to tutor and direct every member of the community.

When the Roman Emperors were at the height of their power, the different nations of the empire still preserved manners and customs of great diversity; although they were subject to the same monarch, most of the provinces were separately administered; they abounded in powerful and active municipalities; and although the whole government of the empire was centred in the hands of the Emperor alone, and he always remained, in case of need, the supreme arbiter in all matters, yet the details of social life and private occupations lay for the most part beyond his control. The Emperors possessed, it is true, an immense and unchecked power, which allowed them to gratify all their whimsical tastes, and to employ for that purpose the whole strength of the state. They frequently abused that power arbitrarily to deprive their subjects of property

or of life: their tyranny was extremely onerous to the few, but it did not reach the many; it was fixed to some few main objects, and neglected the rest; it was violent, but its range was limited. [II. Bk. 4, Chap. 6]

The notion of secondary powers, placed between the sovereign and his subjects, occurred naturally to the imagination of aristocratic nations, because those communities contained individuals or families raised above the common level, and apparently destined to command by their birth, their education, and their wealth. This same notion is naturally wanting in the minds of men in democratic ages, for converse reasons; it can only be introduced artificially, it can only be kept there with difficulty; whereas they conceive, as it were without thinking upon the subject, the notion of a single and central power, which governs the whole community by its direct influence. Moreover, in politics as well as in philosophy and in religion, the intellect of democratic nations is peculiarly open to simple and general notions. Complicated systems are repugnant to it, and its favorite conception is that of a great nation composed of citizens all formed upon one pattern, and all governed by a single power. [II. Bk. 4, Chap. 2]

I believe that it is easier to establish an absolute and despotic government amongst a people in which the conditions of society are equal, than amongst any other; and I think that, if such a government were once established amongst such a people, it would not only oppress men, but would eventually strip each of them of several of the highest qualities of humanity. Despotism, therefore, appears to me peculiarly to be dreaded in democratic times.

On the other hand, I am persuaded that all who shall attempt, in the ages upon which we are entering, to base freedom upon aristocratic privilege, will fail; that all who shall attempt to draw and to retain authority within a single class, will fail. At the present day, no ruler is skilful or strong enough to found a despotism by reestablishing permanent distinctions of rank amongst his subjects: no legislator is wise or powerful enough to preserve free institutions, if he does not take equality for his first principle and his watchword. All of our contemporaries who would establish or secure the independence and the dignity of their fellow-men, must show themselves the friends of equality; and the only worthy means of showing themselves as such is to be so: upon this depends the success of their holy enterprise. Thus, the question is not how to reconstruct aristocratic society, but how to make liberty proceed out of that democratic state of society in which God has placed us. [II. Bk. 4, Chap. 7]

Freedom and association Aristocratic countries abound in wealthy and influential persons who are competent to provide for themselves, and who cannot be easily or secretly oppressed: such persons restrain a government within general habits of moderation and reserve. I am well aware that democratic countries contain no such persons naturally; but something analogous to them may be created by artificial means. I firmly believe that an aristocracy cannot again be founded in the world; but I think that private citizens, by combining together, may constitute bodies of great wealth, influence, and strength, corresponding to the persons of an aristocracy. By this means, many of the greatest political advantages of aristocracy would be obtained, without its injustice or its dangers. An association for political, commercial, or manufacturing purposes, or even for those of science and literature, is a powerful and enlightened member of the community, which cannot be disposed of at pleasure, or oppressed without remonstrance; and which, by defending its own rights against the encroachments of the government, saves the common liberties of the country. [II. Bk. 4, Chap. 7]

There are no countries in which associations are more needed, to prevent the despotism of faction or the arbitrary power of a prince, than those which are democratically constituted. In aristocratic nations, the body of the nobles and the wealthy are in themselves natural associations, which check the abuses of power. In countries where such associations do not exist, if private individuals cannot create an artificial and temporary substitute for them, I can see no permanent protection against the most galling tyranny; and a great people may be op-

Alexis Charles Henri Maurice Clerel de Tocqueville

pressed with impunity by a small faction, or by a single individual.

The most natural privilege of man, next to the right of acting for himself, is that of combining his exertions with those of his fellow-creatures, and of acting in common with them. The right of association therefore appears to me almost as inalienable in its nature as the right of personal liberty. [I. Chap. 12]

Amongst the laws which rule human societies, there is one which seems to be more precise and clear than all others. If men are to remain civilized, or to become so, the art of associating together must grow and improve in the same ratio in which the equality of conditions is increased. [II. Bk. 2, Chap. 5]

Tyranny of the majority In my opinion, the main evil of the present democratic institutions of the

United States does not arise, as is often asserted in Europe, from their weakness, but from their irresistible strength. I am not so much alarmed at the excessive liberty which reigns in that country, as at the inadequate securities which one finds there against tyranny.

I do not say that there is a frequent use of tyranny in America at the present day; but I maintain that there is no sure barrier against it, and that the causes which mitigate the government there are to be found in the circumstances and the manners of the country, more than in its laws.

It is in the examination of the exercise of thought in the United States, that we clearly perceive how far the power of the majority surpasses all the powers with which we are acquainted in Europe. The authority of a king is physical, and controls the actions of men without subduing their will. But the majority possesses a power which is physical and moral at the same time, which acts upon the will as much as upon the actions, and represses not only all contest, but all controversy. [I. Chap. 15]

When the ranks of society are unequal, and men unlike each other in condition, there are some individuals wielding the power of superior intelligence, learning, and enlightenment, whilst the multitude are sunk in ignorance and prejudice. Men living at these aristocratic periods are therefore naturally induced to shape their opinions by the standard of a superior person, or superior class of persons, whilst they are averse to recognize the infallibility of the mass of the people.

The contrary takes place in ages of equality. The nearer the people are drawn to the common level of an equal and similar condition, the less prone does each man become to place implicit faith in a certain man or a certain class of men. But his readiness to believe the multitude increases, and opinion is more than ever mistress of the world. Not only is common opinion the only guide which private judgment retains amongst a democratic people, but amongst such a people it possesses a power infinitely beyond what it has elsewhere. At periods of equality, men have no faith in one another, by reason of their common resemblance; but this very resemblance gives them almost unbounded confidence in the judgment of the public; for it would not seem probable, as they are all endowed with equal means of judging, but that the greater truth should go with the greater number.

The fact that the political laws of the Americans are such that the majority rules the community with sovereign sway, materially increases the power which that majority naturally exercises over the mind. For nothing is more customary in man than to recognize superior wisdom in the person of his oppressor. The intellectual dominion of the greater number would probably be less absolute amongst a democratic people governed by a king, than in the sphere of a pure democracy, but it will always be extremely absolute; and by whatever political laws men are governed in the ages of equality, it may be foreseen that faith in public opinion will become a species of religion there, and the majority its ministering prophet.

If the absolute power of a majority were to be substituted, by democratic nations, for all the different powers which checked or retarded overmuch the energy of individual minds, the evil would only have changed character. Men would not have found the means of independent life; they would simply have discovered (no easy task) a new physiognomy of servitude. There is,—and I cannot repeat it too often,—there is here matter for profound reflection to those who look on freedom of thought as a holy thing, and who hate not only the despot, but despotism. For myself, when I feel the hand of power lie heavy on my brow, I care but little to know who oppresses me; and I am not the more disposed to pass beneath the yoke because it is held out to me by the arms of a million of men. [II. Bk. 1, Chap. 2]

Democracy and anomie In certain remote corners of the Old World, you may still sometimes tumble upon a small district which seems to have been forgotten amidst the general tumult, and to have remained stationary whilst everything around it was in motion. The inhabitants are, for the most part, extremely ignorant and poor; they take no part in the business of the country, and are frequently oppressed by the government; yet their countenances are generally placid, and their spirits light.

In America, I saw the freest and most enlightened men placed in the happiest circumstances which the world affords: it seemed to me as if a cloud habitually hung upon their brow, and I thought them serious, and almost sad, even in their pleasures.

The chief reason of this contrast

is, that the former do not think of the ills they endure, while the latter are forever brooding over advantages they do not possess. It is strange to see with what feverish ardor the Americans pursue their own welfare; and to watch the vague dread that constantly torments them, lest they should not have chosen the shortest path which may lead to it.

Their taste for physical gratifications must be regarded as the original source of that secret inquietude which the actions of the Americans betray, and of that inconstancy of which they daily afford fresh examples.

If, in addition to the taste for physical well-being, a social condition be super-added, in which neither laws nor customs retain any person in his place, there is a great additional stimulant to this restlessness of temper. Men will then be seen continually to change their track, for fear of missing the shortest cut to happiness.

Amongst democratic nations, men easily attain a certain equality of condition; but they can never attain as much as they desire. It perpetually retires from before them, yet without hiding itself from their sight, and in retiring draws them on. At every moment they think they are about to grasp it; it escapes at every moment from their hold. They are near enough to see its charms, but too far off to enjoy them; and before they have fully tasted its delights, they die.

In democratic times, enjoyments are more intense than in the ages of aristocracy, and the number of those who partake in them is vastly larger: but, on the other hand, it must be admitted that man's hopes and desires are oftener blasted, the soul is more stricken and perturbed, and care itself more keen. [II. Bk. 2, Chap. 13]

When every one is constantly striving to change his position; when an immense field for competition is thrown open to all; when wealth is amassed or dissipated in the shortest possible space of time amidst the turmoil of democracy, —visions of sudden and easy fortunes, of great possession easily won and lost, of chance under all its forms, haunt the mind. The instability of society itself fosters the natural instability of man's desires. [II. Bk. 2, Chap. 17]

The worth of democracy In the present age, when the destinies of Christendom seem to be in suspense, some hasten to assail democracy as a hostile power, whilst it is yet growing; and others already adore this new deity which is springing forth from chaos. But both parties are imperfectly acquainted with the object of their hatred or their worship; they strike in the dark, and distribute their blows at random.

We must first understand what is wanted of society and its government. Do you wish to give a certain elevation to the human mind, and teach it to regard the things of this world with generous feelings, to inspire men with a scorn of mere temporal advantages, to form and nourish strong convictions, and keep alive the spirit of honorable devotedness? Is it your object to refine the habits, embellish the manners, and cultivate the arts, to promote the love of poetry, beauty, and glory? Would you constitute a people fitted to act powerfully upon all other nations, and prepared for those high enterprises which, whatever be their results, will leave a name forever famous in history? If you believe such to be the principal object of society, avoid the government of the democracy, for it would not lead you with certainty to the goal.

But if you hold it expedient to divert the moral and intellectual activity of man to the production of comfort, and the promotion of general well-being; if a clear understanding be more profitable to man than genius; if your object be not to stimulate the virtues of heroism, but the habits of peace; if you had rather witness vices than crimes, and are content to meet with fewer noble deeds, provided offences be diminished in the same proportion; if, instead of living in the midst of a brilliant society, you are contented to have prosperity around you; if, in short, you are of opinion that the principal object of a government is not to confer the greatest possible power and glory upon the body of the nation, but to ensure the greatest enjoyment, and to avoid the most misery, to each of the individuals who compose it,—if such be your desire, then equalize the conditions of men, and establish democratic institutions.

But if the time be past at which such a choice was possible, and if some power superior to that of man already hurries us, without consulting our wishes, towards one or the other of these two governments, let us endeavor to make the best of that which is allotted to us, and, by finding out both its good and its evil tendencies, be able to foster the former and repress the latter to the utmost. [I. Chap. 14]

Conclusion   Tocqueville's argument may be summarized as follows:

1. In the democratic age, equality becomes a paramount value. This equalizing tendency breaks down the power and self-confidence of traditional elites. Whatever their defects, these elites did exercise some restraint on kings and other sovereigns. Democracy tends to create a strong centralized government before which all citizens are equal. Tocqueville thought this equality might become an equality of weakness. As a result, he saw a latent despotism in democratic society.

2. To make the citizens stronger, Tocqueville emphasized the importance of the autonomous association in the democratic community. He would have seconded the slogan of his contemporary, the French anarchist Proudhon, who said, "Multiply your associations and be free."

3. Tyranny can be cultural and psychological as well as political. Democracy, which gives all opinions equal worth, and honors the views of the majority, may usher in an age of conformity. This danger he referred to as the "tyranny of the majority."

4. Democracy and equality tend to stimulate ambition, loosen social bonds, and lessen respect for established forms of conduct. Thus democracy tends to be "anomic" (Tocqueville himself did not use that term) and runs the risk that dissatisfaction will produce irrational political responses.

Comment   Tocqueville's analysis should be understood as a diagnosis of some of the inherent weaknesses of democracy. In this sense, it is similar to the study by Michels (Adaptation 20, pp. 218 ff.). Tocqueville wrote mainly as a friend of democracy. Although he drew on his aristocratic background and inclinations, at a number of points he expressed his faith in self-government.

CREDITS

Below are listed the pages on which illustrations appear by special permission, which we gratefully acknowledge. (Figures are suitably acknowledged at the place of their appearance.) We appreciate the right to reproduce the following illustrations:

4—Frontispiece from *The Positive Philosophy of Auguste Comte,* tr. and ed. by Harriet Martineau (New York: Blanchard, 1858)

27—Courtesy of The Macmillan Company

28—United Press International Photo

46—Frontispiece from *An Autobiography,* Vol. I, by Herbert Spencer (London: Williams and Norgate, 1904)

55—Courtesy of Maurice R. Davie

60—Courtesy of Professor R. M. Glasse

61—The Bettmann Archive

80—From the Collection of the Philadelphia Museum of Art (By A. J. Wyatt, Staff Photographer)

81—John Launois, Black Star

85—Courtesy of Professor Harry F. Harlow, Primate Laboratory, University of Wisconsin

91—(Top left) Courtesy of Philip Selznick; (Top right) Courtesy of Leonard Broom; (Bottom) Courtesy of Douglas Davidson, Honolulu

95—Frontispiece from *The Philosophy of the Act* by George Herbert Mead (University of Chicago Press, 1938)

112—*The Toronto Telegram*

116—Wide World Photos

121—Courtesy of Rentscheler Studios

122—(Top and Bottom right) Courtesy of Standard Oil Co. (N.J.); (Bottom left) John Zimmerman for *Sports Illustrated*

123—Courtesy of Standard Oil Co. (N.J.)

127—Courtesy of the U.S. Army

131—From *Management and the Worker* by F. J. Roethlisberger and William J. Dickson (Harvard University Press, 1942). Used by permission.

139—Courtesy of the U.S. Army

146—Courtesy of the American Sociological Association

175—Culver Pictures

193—The Bettmann Archive

225—British Crown Copyright. Reproduced by permission of the Controller of Her Britannic Majesty's Stationery Office.

232—Jerry Telfer, *San Francisco Chronicle*

259—Frontispiece from *Essai sur le principie de population* (Paris: Guillaumin et Ce, 1852)

295—Air-Photo Co., courtesy of Santa Clara Planning Department, California

304—Richard Lannoy, Paris

341—(Left) The Bettmann Archive; (Right) Frontispiece from Paul Schilpp, ed., *The Philosophy of John Dewey,* published 1939, 1951 by Library of Living Philosophers, Inc. (New York: Tudor Publishing Co.)

346—Courtesy of Professor Georges Balandier

348—Courtesy of Standard Oil Co. (N.J.)

357—Department of Territories, Commonwealth of Australia

371—UPI Photo

381—From *A Panorama of the World's Legal Systems* by John Henry Wigmore (St. Paul: West Publishing Co., 1928), Vol. 1, p. 68.

390—*Ibid.,* p. 47.

401—Courtesy of Jenaro Olivares G.

410—Courtesy of LIFE Magazine. © Time Inc.

419—Wayne Miller, Magnum

431—Wide World Photos

450—Courtesy of The University of Chicago Library

463—Facsimile of engravings on wood, designed and engraved by J. Amman, sixteenth century.

From Paul Lacroix, *Manners, Customs, and Dress during the Renaissance Period* (London: Chapman and Hall, 1876). Reproduced by permission of the publishers.

464—From *Max Weber: ein Lebensbild* by Marianne Weber (Tübingen, 1926)

465—Frontispiece from *Histoire de la Vie . . . de Jean Calvin* by Hierosme Hermes Bolsec (Lyon: N. Scheuring, 1875). From a portrait in the Geneva Library

470—Courtesy of The Singer Manufacturing Co.

484—Moffett Studio, Chicago

493—Courtesy of International Ladies' Garment Workers' Union, New York

503—(Left) Pierre Streit, Black Star; (Right) Courtesy LIFE Magazine, F. Scherschel. © Time Inc., 1960

505—Wide World Photos

511—Frontispiece from *The Mind and Society,* Vilfredo Pareto, tr. by A. Livingston and A. Bongiorno. By permission of The Pareto Fund.

520—Frontispiece from *Henry VIII* by Edward Hall (London: T. C. & E. Jack, 1904)

531—The Bettmann Archive

NAME INDEX

Abegglen, J. C., 181, 468
Adams, J. B., 34
Adams, R. M., 434–437
Allen, F. A., 393
Allport, G. W., 223, 230
Almond, G. A., 498, 526, 527
Alston, J. P., 157, 166, 174
Altizer, T. J. J., 305
Anderson, C., 233
Anderson, C. A., 343, 360, 361
Anderson, H. H., 356
Anderson, N., 434, 453
Anshen, R. N., 33
Apter, D. E., 502
Arens, R., 400
Argyle, M., 305, 316, 335
Aristotle, 389, 498
Arnold, M., 51
Aronson, E., 88
Auerbach, C. A., 384
Austin, A., 476

Baldwin, A. L., 315
Bales, R. F., 18, 125
Baltzell, E. D., 174
Banton, M., 17, 415
Barber, B., 157, 363
Barker, C. H., 108
Barker, E., 391
Barnard, C. I., 207
Bates, F. L., 168
Baum, G., 319
Bavelas, A., 199–201
Beals, R. L., 51, 56, 470, 472
Beard, C. A., 464
Beaulieu, M. R., 143
Beaumont, G. de, 529
Becker, H. S., 105, 393
Beegle, J. A., 441
Bell, D., 482
Bell, N. W., 33, 143
Bell, W., 447
Bendix, R., 157, 166, 168, 179,
    180, 181, 187, 198, 360, 411,
    469, 475, 498, 504
Benedict, R., 57, 102, 114

Bensman, J., 438
Bentham, J., 61
Berelson, B. R., 223, 498
Berger, B., 455
Berger, M., 506
Berger, P. L., 107
Berle, A. A., 220
Berman, H. J., 384, 391
Bernard, W. S., 288
Bernstein, B., 101
Biddle, B. J., 17
Bidney, D., 70
Bigman, S. K., 317
Blackstone, W., 411
Blalock, H. M., 177
Blau, P. M., 17, 18, 157, 195, 469,
    486
Blauner, R., 229, 480, 483, 485
Blumberg, A. S., 417
Blumer, H., 222, 239, 256
Boas, F., 51
Boehm, E., 217
Boeke, J. H., 466
Bogue, D. J., 260, 284, 454
Boll, E. S., 88
Bonaparte, L. (Napoleon III),
    188, 189
Bonaparte, N. (Napoleon I), 514,
    515
Bonjean, C. M., 168
Booth, C., 449
Bordua, D. J., 72, 415, 418
Borgatta, E. F., 125
Bossard, J. H. S., 88, 103
Bott, E., 143
Bottomore, T. B., 78, 157, 187,
    482
Bowen, F., 529
Bowers, R., 446
Bradburn, N. M., 172, 177
Breese, G., 446
Bretton, H. L., 505
Briar, S., 412
Bright, J. R., 485
Brim, O. G., Jr., 88, 343
Brink, W., 256, 257

Brinton, C., 504, 511
Brodbeck, A. J., 498
Bronfenbrenner, U., 100, 101,
    102, 176, 315
Brookover, W. B., 343, 355, 356
Brown, E., 233, 234
Brown, E. C., 477
Brown, R., 88
Bryson, L., 51
Buber, M., 316
Bultena, L., 320
Burchinal, L. G., 318
Burdick, E., 498
Burgess, E. W., 17, 35, 110, 445,
    446, 449, 450, 451, 452, 453
Burke, P. J., 177
Burnham, J., 510
Burnight, R. G., 171

Cahn, E., 63, 418
Cahn, E. S., 388
Cahn, J. C., 388
Cain, G. C., 493
Calvin, J., 465
Campbell, A., 498, 525, 526, 527,
    528, 529
Campbell, E. Q., 354
Campbell, Z., 161
Cantril, H., 223, 241
Caplovitz, D., 172, 177
Caplow, T., 155, 195, 469
Carlin, J. E., 384, 411
Carpenter, D. B., 434, 446, 447
Carr, E. R., 343
Carr-Saunders, A. M., 281, 285,
    286
Cartwright, D., 125, 199
Cavan, R. S., 35, 442
Cavers, D., 387
Centers, R., 156
Chancellor, L. E., 318
Chessman, C., 419
Chesterton, G. K., 313
Chiang Kai-shek, 516
Childe, V. G., 77
Chinoy, E., 191

Christ, 304, 312, 315, 316, 504
Churchill, W. S., 224–225, 226, 504
Cicourel, A. V., 365
Clark, B. R., 339, 343, 345, 347–350, 366
Clark, C., 491
Clark, E. T., 315, 316
Clark, S. D., 327–333
Clinard, M. B., 29
Cloward, R. A., 409, 411
Coch, L., 487–491
Codrington, R. H., 303
Cohen, A. K., 72, 409
Cohen, J., 230
Cohen, J. A., 391
Coleman, J. S., 220, 227, 343, 354, 358, 369, 378, 498
Comte, A., 4
Conot, R., 230, 233
Converse, P. E., 498, 525, 529
Conwell, C., 453
Cooley, C. H., 92, 120, 121, 124, 125, 126
Corwin, R. G., 343
Coser, L. A., 17, 48
Coser, R. L., 85
Cottrell, L. S., 413, 453
Coulanges, F. de, 306
Cressey, D. R., 384, 400–402, 408–411, 415, 423–424
Cressey, P. G., 451, 453
Crockett, H. J., Jr., 186
Cromwell, O., 515
Crutchfield, R. L., 253
Currie, E., 411

Dahl, R. A., 498, 524
Dahrendorf, R., 157, 187, 189, 192
Dale, E., 197
Dalton, M., 207, 208–211, 469
D'Antonio, W., 169
Darwin, C., 75, 292
Davie, M. R., 446
Davies, J. C., 511
Davis, A., 165
Davis, E. E., 384
Davis, F. J., 384
Davis, K., 104, 192, 260, 268, 432
De Burgh, W. G., 391
De Gré, G., 524
Demerath, N. J., 439
Demerath, N. J., III, 321
Denney, R., 103, 104, 526
Dentler, R. A., 459

Devlin, P., 392
Dewey, J., 121, 341, 342, 343
Dickson, W. J., 130–133, 149, 480
Dill, W. R., 211
Dobriner, W. M., 455
Dodge, R. W., 525
Donovan, F. R., 453
Dorn, H. F., 278, 283
Dornbusch, S. M., 110–113
Douglas, W. O., 394–396
Draper, H., 370
Dubin, R., 469
Duncan, O. D., 157, 186, 260, 431, 432, 469
Dunham, H. W., 442, 451, 453
Dunlop, J. T., 474
Durkheim, E., 26–30, 292, 305, 308, 333–334, 385, 386, 398, 402, 452

Edward III, 367
Eels, K., 99, 165
Ehrlich, E., 415
Eisenhower, D. D., 138, 241
Elkin, F., 88
Ellingston, J. R., 409
Elliott, D. L., 102
Embrey, N. G., 143
Emerson, R., 500
Emerson, R. M., 20
Emery, F. E., 480
Empey, L. T., 410, 411
Engels, F., 77, 187, 323, 324
Ennis, P. H., 421, 422, 433
Erickson, E. C., 169
Etzioni, A., 195
Evan, W. M., 415
Eversley, D. C., 260

Fadiman, C., 174
Fallers, L. A., 33, 191
Farber, B., 143
Faris, E., 124, 449
Faris, R. E. L., 12, 222, 442, 449, 451, 453
Farouk, 506
Fava, S., 434
Feldman, A. S., 468
Feuer, L. S., 187, 189, 323, 482
Fichter, J. H., 305
Firey, W., 297, 446, 459
Fiske, M., 80
Floor, L. G., 487
Floud, J., 343, 360, 361
Folger, J. K., 185

Foote, C., 407
Foote, N. N., 459
Forde, C. D., 56
Form, W. H., 469, 485
Foster, H. H., Jr., 384
Franklin, B., 464, 466
Frazier, E. F., 144, 145–148, 451, 453
Freed, D. J., 413
Freedman, R., 260, 439
Fremantle, A., 324
French, J. R. P., Jr., 487–491
Freud, S., 50, 90, 117, 305
Friedman, M. S., 316
Friedmann, W., 45, 384, 407, 415
Fromm, E., 93, 116, 117, 482
Frost, R., 348
Frost, S. L. 88
Fukuyama, Y., 321
Fuller, L. L., 381, 384

Galenson, W., 476
Gales, K., 373
Gallup, G., 241
Gandhi, M., 183, 505
Gans, H. J., 35, 357, 456
Garbin, A. P., 168
Gardner, B. B., 165, 211–215
Gardner, M. R., 165
Garfield, J. A., 227
Garrison, L. K., 384
Geer, B., 105
Geiger, K., 521
Geiser, S., 402
Gerth, H. H., 17, 154, 342, 464, 465
Gettys, W. E., 297
Gibbs, J. P., 30, 432, 434
Gibbs, M., 43
Giedion, S., 80
Gilb, C. L., 415
Gilbert, C. W., 169
Gilmore, S., 370
Gist, N. P., 434
Glaser, D., 415
Glass, D. V., 259, 260
Glazer, N., 103, 104, 526
Glenn, N. D., 153–193, 320, 364, 495
Glock, C. Y., 304, 306, 321
Gobineau, J. A., 51
Goffman, E., 18, 19, 106, 107, 195, 364, 366
Goldenweiser, A., 69
Goldhamer, H., 441
Golembiewski, R. M., 125

Gomberg, W., 176, 192
Gombrich, E. H., 311, 312
Goode, E., 321
Goode, W. J., 19, 176, 306
Gordon, C. W., 368
Gordon, D. A., 253
Gottman, J., 458
Gough, E. K., 33
Gould, J., 12
Gouldner, A. W., 202, 526
Gouldner, H. B., 462
Graham, B., 316, 335
Greenberg, B. S., 227
Greer, S. A., 17, 434
Gregory I (The Great), 312
Greiner, W. R., 384
Grigsby, W. G., 456, 457
Grimshaw, A. D., 228
Guben, J., 411
Guerard, A., 499
Gunther, J., 504
Guralnick, L., 171
Gurin, G., 487, 527
Gurvitch, G., 450
Gusfield, J. R., 246, 393

Hacker, E., 423
Hadden, J. K., 434
Hagstrom, W. O., 352
Hall, E. T., 64–68
Hall, J., 384
Haller, A. O., 360
Halsey, A. H., 343, 360, 361
Hamilton, A., 498
Hamilton, E., 311
Hamilton, W., 305
Handel, G., 176
Handlin, O., 82
Hansen, M. H., 264
Harbison, F. H., 473, 474
Hare, A. P., 125
Harlow, H. F., 85
Harlow, M. K., 85
Harris, C. D., 445, 447
Harris, L., 256, 257, 318
Hart, H. L. A., 384, 392
Hartley, E. L., 88, 100, 176
Hartlib, S., 323
Hatt, P. K., 260, 428, 431, 434
Hauser, A., 311
Hauser, P. M., 260, 434
Havighurst, R. J., 165, 343
Hawkes, G. R., 88
Hawley, A. W., 292
Hawthorn, A., 450

Hayner, N. S., 453
Hazard, J. N., 407
Henry VIII, 520
Henry, A. F., 29, 30
Henry, W. E., 106
Heraclitus, 389
Herrick, V. E., 99
Herron, S., 316
Hertzler, J. O., 185
Hitler, A., 49, 138, 243, 367, 504, 521
Hitt, H. H., 439
Hobson, C. J., 354
Hodge, R. W., 167, 168
Hoebel, E. A., 56, 382
Hoffman, L. W., 406
Hoffman, M. L., 406
Hogue, A. R., 382
Hoijer, H., 51, 56
Hollander, S., Jr., 227
Hollingshead, A. B., 165, 343, 354
Holt, E. G., 312
Homans, G. C., 17, 125
Hoos, I. R., 485
Hoselitz, B. F., 466, 469
Hoult, T. F., 306
Howard, C. G., 384
Howard, J., 411
Howton, F. W., 179, 475
Hoxie, R. F., 476
Hoyt, H., 447
Hughes, E. C., 105, 449
Huizinga, J., 312, 313
Humphrey, N. D., 228
Hunter, F., 168
Hunter, M., 471
Huntington, M. J., 105
Hurst, J. W., 384
Hurst, W., 384
Huston, J., 302
Hyland, R., 320
Hyman, H., 223, 238
Hyman, M. D., 177
Hymes, D., 56

Inkeles, A., 521

Jackson, E. F., 177, 186
Jacobs, J., 456, 457
Jacobs, P., 478–479
Jaeger, G., *see* Selznick, G. J.
Jaeger, W., 391
Jaffe, A. J., 494
Janowitz, M., 135–140, 223
Jay, J., 498

Jefferey, C. R., 384
Jensen, A. R., 102
Jespersen, O., 81
John XXIII, 324, 326
Johnson, C. A., 516–519
Johnson, L. B., 144, 237, 239, 241
Jones, E., 119
Jones, W. C., 411
Junker, B. H., 449

Kahin, G. M., 508
Kahl, J. A., 157, 172, 360
Kahn, R. L., 195
Kalven, H., Jr., 384
Kardiner, A., 113
Katz, D., 195, 223, 487
Katz, E., 223
Kaufman, H. F., 166
Kautsky, J. H., 515
Keller, A. G., 55
Kelley, H. H., 125
Kelly, A., 414
Kempin, F. G., Jr., 384
Kendall, P. L., 105
Kennedy family, 43
Kennedy, J. F., 227, 241
Kerr, C., 370, 372, 374, 474
Key, V. O., Jr., 498, 528
Killian, L. M., 222, 223
King, M. L., Jr., 257
Kinsey, A. C., 174, 182
Kitsuse, J. I., 365
Kitto, H. D. F., 391
Klapper, J., 222
Klein, J., 125
Kluckhohn, C., 50, 54, 56, 60, 69, 70, 71, 75, 305
Knudten, R. D., 306
Kobrin, S., 409
Koestler, A., 515
Kohlberg, L., 406
Kohn, M. L., 100
Kolb, W. L., 12
Komarovsky, M., 80, 101, 176
Kornhauser, A., 469
Kornhauser, W., 48, 370–375, 497–534
Kroeber, A. L., 50
Kuhlen, R. G., 316
Kuznets, S., 162
Kvaraceus, W., 353

Lader, L., 228
La Fave, W. R., 415, 416
Laidlaw, W., 448
Landis, P. H., 260

Landon, A. E., 351
Landsberger, H. A., 130
Lang, G. E., 222
Lang, K., 222
Lanternari, V., 302
La Piere, R. T., 222
Larson, C. J., 434
Lasswell, H. D., 50, 119
Lasswell, T. E., 157
Laurenti, L., 444
Lazarsfeld, P. F., 223, 498
Lazerwitz, B., 321
Leach, E. R., 60, 183
Le Bon, G., 245
Lederer, E., 245
Lee, A. M., 222, 228, 244, 256
Lee, D., 57, 59, 73–75
Lee, E. B., 244
Leggett, J. C., 192
Lehman, W., 414
Leighton, A. H., 114
Lemert, E. M., 88, 401, 414
Lenin, V. I., 512, 513
Lennard, H., 143
Lenski, G., 157, 166, 177, 180,
    185, 192, 314
Lentz, W. P., 410
Leo XIII, 324
Lepawsky, A., 458
Lerner, D., 48, 50
Lerner, M., 80
Lessa, W. A., 303, 306, 334
Levin, H., 88
Levy, M. J., 33
Levy, R. J., 407
Lewis, A., 414
Lewis, D. T., 260
Lieberson, S., 229
Lifton, R. J., 108
Likert, R., 141, 195, 240, 251–254,
    469, 486
Lincoln, A., 227
Lind, A. W., 293
Lindblom, C. E., 524
Lindesmith, A. R., 88
Lindzey, G., 88
Linton, R., 33, 56, 57, 68
Lippitt, R., 141
Lippmann, W., 223
Lipset, S. M., 157, 166, 168, 179,
    180, 181, 187, 192, 220, 360,
    370, 373, 499
Little, R. W., 135
Llewellyn, E. C., 450
Locke, H. J., 35, 445
Loeb, M. B., 165

Loomis, C. P., 48, 441
Lord, W., 175
Low, J. O., 165, 185
Lowenthal, L., 80
Lowie, R. H., 32
Ludd, 475
Lunt, P. S., 165
Luther, M., 465
Lynes, R., 160

McCarthy, P. J., 223
McClelland, D. C., 315
McClosky, H., 525
Maccoby, E. E., 88, 100, 176
Maccoby, N., 487
McCone, J. A., 230, 233, 234
McElrath, D. C., 434
McGee, R. J., 155
Machiavelli, N., 193, 499
MacIver, R. M., 499
McKay, H. D., 453
McKenzie, R. D., 432, 433, 445,
    450, 452, 453
McKinley, W., 227
McLoughlin, W. G., Jr., 335
MacNeish, R. S., 78–79
McPartland, J., 354
McPhee, W. N., 498
McWilliams, W. C., 505
Madison, J., 498
Male, E., 311
Malinowski, B., 116, 117–119
Malraux, A., 311
Malthus, T., 259
Mandelbaum, D. G., 58
Mannheim, H., 384
Mannheim, K., 48, 256
Maraini, F., 45
March, J. G., 195, 211
Marden, P. G., 171
Marshall, A., 441
Marshall, T. H., 157, 190, 411
Martin, C. E., 174, 182
Martin, W. T., 30
Marx, K., 15, 77, 78, 154, 187–
    190, 191, 323, 324, 481, 482
Mason, E. S., 415
Masotti, L. H., 434
Masters, R. E. L., 302
Matthew, 320
Matza, D., 72
Mayer, K. B., 157
Mayer, M., 384
Mayers, L., 384
Mayo, E., 30
Mazlish, B., 50

Mead, G. H., 9, 90, 94–98, 99,
    102, 121, 341, 402, 449
Mead, M., 114, 116
Means, G. C., 220
Meeker, M., 165
Meier, A., 257
Meller, N., 294
Mencher, J. P., 33
Mercer, B. E., 343
Mermin, S., 384
Merriam, A. P., 502
Merriam, C. E., 415
Merton, R. K., 17, 105, 106, 256
Messinger, S. L., 411, 415
Michels, R., 9, 216, 218–220, 534
Middleton, R., 34
Milbrath, L. W., 499
Mill, J. S., 392
Miller, D. C., 469
Miller, D. R., 88
Miller, H. P., 157, 162, 163, 171,
    179, 184, 185
Miller, M. V., 370
Miller, N., 352
Miller, S. M., 157, 176, 187
Miller, W. B., 72
Miller, W. E., 498, 525, 527, 529
Mills, C. W., 17, 154, 169, 173,
    174, 342, 464, 465
Minar, D. W., 434
Miner, H., 432
Mood, A. M., 354
Moore, B., Jr., 190
Moore, D. G., 211–215
Moore, H. E., 292
Moore, W. E., 192, 450, 463, 466,
    468, 469, 470, 471, 472
Morgan, L. H., 76
Morris, M. D., 468
Morris, R. T., 153, 157–161
Morse, N. C., 487
Mosca, G., 523, 524
Moser, C. A., 223
Mosse, G. L., 50
Mowrer, E. R., 442
Moynihan, P. J., 144
Mrak, E. M., 294
Mumford, L., 79, 428, 434, 456
Murdock, G. P., 32, 33, 57, 68,
    446, 502
Murphy, F., 394, 396–398
Murphy, W. S., 230
Myers, C. A., 473, 474

Nagel, E., 51
Nam, C. B., 185

Napoleon, *see* Bonaparte
Nash, M., 469
Nasser, G. A., 506, 509
Nehru, J., 505
Neugarten, B. L., 343
Neumann, S., 245
Newcomb, T. M., 88, 100, 176, 236, 347, 351
Nieboer, H., 293
Niebuhr, H. R., 323, 325, 326
Nietzsche, F., 313
Nimkoff, M. F., 32, 33, 34
Nisbet, R. A., 49, 481
Nixon, R. M., 241
Nkrumah, K., 504, 505
Nolde, H. C., 414
Nonet, P., 388, 389–393
Noonan, J. T., Jr., 319
Nosow, S., 469, 485
Notestein, F. W., 269, 284
Novak, M., 326
Nye, F. I., 409

Oaks, D. H., 414
O'Dea, T. F., 306
Odegard, P. H., 246–250
Odum, H. W., 292
Ogburn, W. F., 454
O'Gorman, H. J., 408
Ohlin, L. E., 409
Olson, D. M., 168
Orleans, P., 434
Ortega y Gasset, J., 48
Orwell, G., 52, 53, 245

Packer, H. L., 389, 393
Palmer, G. L., 179
Pareto, V., 511
Park, R. E., 17, 110, 292, 293, 434, 445, 449, 450, 451, 452, 453
Parker, E. B., 227
Parker, W., 233, 234
Parsons, T., 465
Parten, M., 223
Patterson, E. W., 383
Paul VI, 324
Pellegrin, R. J., 157
Perkins, R. M., 392
Perrow, C., 415, 480
Petersen, W., 260, 428
Pettee, G. S., 514
Pettigrew, T. F., 184
Piaget, J., 88, 103, 398, 402–406
Picasso, P., 80
Pilate, P., 504
Piliavin, I., 412

Pirenne, H., 428
Plato, 389, 498
Plucknett, T. F. T., 382
Polk, K., 353, 354, 359
Pomeroy, W. B., 174, 182
Pope, L., 325, 328
Porter, J., 157
Postman, L., 223
Potter, S., 206
Pound, R., 384, 386
Powers, M. G., 525
Pressey, S. L., 316
Presthus, R., 195
Proudhon, P. J., 534
Pye, L. W., 501, 508

Queen, S. A., 34, 434, 446, 447
Quinn, J. A., 293

Rabow, J., 410
Radcliffe-Brown, A. R., 113
Rainwater, L., 144, 176
Ray, I., 398
Read, H., 311
Reader, G. G., 105
Reagan, R., 374
Reckless, W. C., 453
Redl, F., 90, 93
Reeve, H., 529
Reiss, A. J., Jr., 157, 428, 431, 434
Reissman, L., 157
Rice, S. A., 119
Richards, A. I., 470, 471
Riesman, D., 103, 104, 114, 169, 343, 526
Riessman, F., 176
Roberts, H. V., 10–12
Robertson, W., 76
Robespierre, M. de, 514
Robinson, W. S., 296–297
Roethlisberger, F. J., 130–133, 149, 480
Rogoff, N., 179, 186, 360, 361
Rommen, H., 383
Roosevelt, F. D., 241, 252
Rosenberg, B., 80
Rosenthal, E., 317, 318
Ross, A. M., 469
Ross, E. A., 245
Rossi, P. H., 167, 168, 459
Rousseau, J.-J., 341, 342
Rubel, M., 78, 187
Rudwick, E. M., 228, 257
Rutledge, W. B., 394
Ryan, B., 289–291

Sale, J. K., 505
Sander, F. E. A., 407
Sapir, E., 52, 58
Sargant, W., 334
Savio, M., 371, 372
Sayre, P., 391
Schachner, N., 368
Schafer, W. E., 353, 354, 359
Scheff, T. J., 400
Schein, E. H., 108
Schmid, C. F., 442
Schneider, E. V., 469
Schneider, H. W., 315
Schneider, L., 306, 321
Schneier, I., 108
Schnore, L. F., 292, 434, 454
Schramm, W., 222, 227
Schroeder, C. W., 442
Schur, E. M., 392
Schurmann, F., 430
Scott, W., 81
Scott, W. R., 195, 486
Sears, R. R., 88
Seeman, M., 441, 481
Seigel, P. M., 167
Selvin, H. C., 352
Selznick, G. J., 54, 84–119, 301–339, 351
Semenoick, A., 282
Sequoyah, 83
Seta, A. D., 311
Sewell, W. H., 360
Shapiro, I., 407
Shaw, C. R., 453
Shevky, E., 434, 447, 493
Shibutani, T., 88, 230, 239
Shils, E. A., 135–140
Shodara, H., 59
Short, J. F., Jr., 29, 30
Shostak, A. B., 176, 192
Sibley, M. Q., 420
Silver, A., 418
Silverman, A. R., 229
Silverstein, L., 414
Simmel, G., 47, 48, 440
Simon, H. A., 195, 203, 204, 205
Simon, R. J., 384
Simpson, G., 26, 385
Skolnick, J. H., 393, 415, 417
Slotkin, J. S., 334
Small, A. W., 47
Smelser, N. M., 88, 222, 469
Smelser, W. T., 88
Smith, S., 199
Smith, T. L., 267, 441
Smith, T. V., 446, 453

Smithburg, D. W., 205
Socrates, 340
Somers, R. H., 373
Sorokin, P. A., 157, 180, 440
Spaeth, J. L., 314
Spencer, H., 46
Spengler, J. J., 260
Spitz, R. A., 85
Spock, B., 101
Spykman, N. J., 48
Srinivas, M. N., 183
Srole, L., 165
Stalin, J., 513, 515, 521
Stanbery, V. B., 283
Star, S., 373
Starbuck, E. D., 316
Stark, R., 304, 306, 321, 322
Stein, C. S., 456
Steinberg, S., 351
Stendler, C. B., 101
Stephen, F. F., 223
Stevenson, H. N. C., 183
Stewart, C. D., 494
Stocking, G. W., Jr., 51
Stokes, D. E., 498, 525, 529
Stone, J., 384
Stouffer, S. A., 351, 488
Strachey, J., 515
Straus, M. A., 360
Strauss, A. L., 88, 105
Street, D., 415
Strodtbeck, F. L., 315
Strong, E. W., 374
Stryker, P., 474
Studt, E., 415
Sudnow, D., 417
Sukarno, 505
Summers, R. S., 384
Sumner, W. G., 55, 57, 70
Sutherland, E. H., 384, 409, 424, 453
Svalastoga, K., 157, 181
Swanson, G. E., 88

Taba, H., 165
Taeuber, A. F., 443
Taeuber, C., 264
Taeuber, K. E., 443
Talmon-Garber, Y., 38–42
Tanenhaus, J., 418
Tannenbaum, F., 400, 401, 480
Tappan, P. W., 384
Tawney, R. H., 309, 323, 465, 466
Tax, S., 57, 69, 70
Ten Broek, J., 412

Theodorson, G. A., 292, 293, 469–472
Thibaut, J. W., 125
Thomas, E. J., 17
Thomas, J. L., 317, 318
Thomas, W. I., 449, 450
Thomas, W. L., Jr., 293
Thomlinson, R., 260
Thompson, V. A., 205
Thompson, W. S., 260, 278, 283
Thomsen, M., 62
Thrasher, F. M., 453
Tien, H. Y., 182
Toby, J., 424
Tocqueville, A. de, 80, 438, 529–534
Tönnies, F., 48, 452
Treiman, D. J., 168
Trist, E. L., 480
Troeltsch, E., 325
Trotsky, L., 504, 513
Trow, M. A., 6–8, 184, 220, 346, 347–350
Truman, D. B., 30
Truman, H. S., 217, 237, 240, 241, 251
Tumin, M. M., 192
T'ung-Tsu Ch'U, 391
Turner, R. H., 31, 223, 343, 493
Tylor, E. B., 51, 76, 301

Udry, J. R., 171
Ullman, E. L., 445, 447

Vance, R. B., 439
Veblen, T., 157, 171, 343, 484
Verba, S., 498, 526, 527
Vernon, G. M., 306
Vico, G. B., 50
Vidich, A. J., 438
Vinogradoff, P., 387
Vinter, R. D., 415
Vogel, E. F., 33, 143
Vogt, E. Z., 303, 306, 334
Von Hentig, H., 267

Wald, P., 413
Walker, C. R., 469, 480
Waller, W., 343, 356
Wallerstein, I., 508
Wallis, J., 81
Wallis, W. A., 10–12
Walton, J., 169
Warner, W. L., 160, 165, 166, 181, 185, 303, 319
Warren, R., 169

Weber, A. F., 454
Weber, M., 47, 154, 166, 216, 306, 342, 463, 464, 465, 504
Weiner, D., 157
Weinfeld, F. D., 354
Wendling, A., 442
Wesley, J., 335
Westoff, C. F., 182
Wheeler, S., 88, 413
White, D. M., 80
White, L. D., 446, 453
Whorf, B. L., 58, 59
Whyte, W. F., 128–130, 149, 174, 207
Whyte, W. H., Jr., 20–26, 31, 206, 455, 469, 475
Wilensky, H. L., 195
Williams, M., 434, 447, 493
Williams, R., 50
Williams, R. M., Jr., 17, 54, 57
Willmott, P., 35
Wilson, A. B., 102
Wilson, B. R., 325
Wilson, E. K., 347
Wilson, G., 470, 472
Wilson, T. P., 415
Wilson, W., 250
Wineman, D., 90, 93
Wirth, L., 437, 440, 444, 449, 451, 452, 453
Wolfenstein, M., 101
Wolff, K. H., 48, 440
Wolfgang, M. E., 414
Wolfle, D., 360
Wolin, S. S., 370, 373
Wright, C. R., 223
Wrong, D. H., 260
Wurfel, D., 508

Yancey, W. L., 144
Yang, C. K., 307
Yates, M., 206
Yinger, J. M., 306
York, R. L., 354
Yorty, S., 233
Young, M., 35, 343
Younge, R., 323

Zander, A., 125, 199
Zeisel, H., 384
Ziegler, B. M., 288
Zimmerman, C. C., 440
Zimmerman, R. R., 85
Zorbaugh, F. M., 453
Zorbaugh, H. W., 451, 452, 453

SUBJECT INDEX

Accommodation, 37
Acculturation, 81–82
  defined, 81
  of ethnic groups, 82–83
  of migrants, 82
  selectivity in, 81–82
Achieved status, 182, 463, 472
  and industrialization, 463
Activism, 367, 370–375
Adaptation
  dynamic, 92–93
  static, 92–93
Administrative justice, 415–418
Administrative law, 383
Adolescents
  class differences in parental control, 358–359
  parent conflict, 104–105
  student peer groups, 357–359
Adversary principle, 386–388
Adversary system and right to counsel, 413–414
Age
  composition of population, 268–271
  composition of U.S. population, 268
  and crime, 424
  and illiteracy rates, 11–12
Aged
  social category, 30
  and weakened primary group ties, 126
Aggiornamento, 326–327
Agricultural labor force, 491–493
Alaska, racial composition, 273
Alienation
  and the assembly line, 483
  and capitalism, 481–482
  and continuous-process technology, 483–484
  and craft technology, 482–483
  among industrial workers, 481–484
  in industry, 481–484
Allocative function in schools, 364–367
Altruistic suicide, 26–27
American culture characteristics, 54

Anomie
  and democracy, 532–533
  and suicide, 28–29
  see also Social disorganization
Anthropology
  and sociology, 5
  and the study of culture, 50–51
Anti-Saloon League, 246–250
Anti-student protest, 368–369
Anxiety
  in children, 89–90
  and the human condition, 117
  and interpersonal relations, 128–130
  and religion, 302
Apathy, political, 526–529
Arapesh culture, 114–115
Armies. *See* Military organizations
Art and religion, 309–313
Ascribed status, 182, 463
Aspiration
  in emerging nations, 503–504
  levels and industrialization, 471–472
  and social revolution, 510–511
Assassination
  and integrative behavior, 226–227
  and mass media, 227
  of President Kennedy, 226–227
Assimilation, 37
  and socialization, 110
Associations, 194–220
  and bureaucracy, 199
  church and sect, 324–326, 327–333
  cohesion and morale in, 203–206
  and communication, 194–195, 207–208, 211–215
  and control, 194–195
  democratic and authoritarian forms, 198–199
  and discipline, 197
  and education, 364–367
  formal ranks and strata, 206–207
  formal structure, 134, 201, 203
  and incentives, 194–195, 207
  informal structure, 134, 201–203

Associations—*continued*
and institutional autonomy, 344, 345
institutionalization, 215–218
interest groups, 204–205, 207–211
and the law, 415–418
line and staff, 207–211
and oligarchy, 218–220
opposing groups, 205
and primary relations, 134, 205–206
and rationality, 197
religious, 324–333
and security, 194–195
self-perpetuating leadership, 218–220
social base, 217–218
social composition, 217–218
and social status, 206–211
socialization in, 203–204
staff-line conflict, 208–211
Attitudes
change and education, 350–352
distinguished from values and opinions, 236
education as affecting, 350–352
Attrition in legal process, 421–423
Authoritarian forms of organization, 198–199
Authority, 380–381
avuncular, in socialization, 117–119
and communication, 211–215
delegation in associations, 196
and law, 380–381
as legitimate power, 522–523
and Oedipus complex, 117–119
parental, in socialization, 117–119
patriarchal, 119
and socialization, 117–119
Automation, 484–486
and unemployment, 479
Autonomy, 73–75
institutional, 344–345
and religion, 313–314
and sociability, 20, 24–25
and social structure, 73–75

Bail, 413
Belief, religious, 304–305
Berkeley student protest, 370–375
Bias and the law, 411–414
Bilineal descent, 32
Biological basis of socialization, 84–85

Birth control
by Catholics, 318–319
see also Fertility control
Birth rate
age specific, 275
crude, 274
standardized, 275
U.S., by order of birth, 278–279
world, 274
see also Fertility
Bourgeoisie, 188–190
Buddhist
art style, 311
world membership, 336
Bureaucracy, 46, 199
as basis of social organization, 46
defined, 199
distinguished from family management, 473–474
in education, 350, 364–367
in emerging nations, 508
see also Associations
Bureaucratic management in industry, 473–475

Canon law, 382
Capitalism
and alienation in industry, 481–482
and Protestant ethic, 463–466
Capitalistic ethos, 463–466
Career mobility, 181–182
Caste
Indian, 183
and open-class systems, 182–183
Catholicism
attitudes toward the poor, 322–324
and personal autonomy, 314–315
symbolism in, 316–317
Catholics
and birth control, 318–319
interfaith marriage, 317–318
in parochial schools, 377
and Prohibition movement, 246
U.S. population, 337
Census, U.S., 261–265
accuracy, 263–265
electronic processing, 262
history, 261–263
and religion, 336–338
required by constitution, 261

Census, U.S.—*continued*
  sampling, 261–262, 264–265
  tracts, 448
Centralization in modern society, 48–49
Ceylon
  birth control, 291
  dowry, 290
  fertility, 284, 289–291
  fertility and family, 289–291
  male dominance, 290
  marriage pattern, 289–290
  valuation of children, 290–291
Change. *See* Collective behavior, Culture change, Demographic transition, Migration, Population change, Social change, Social mobility, *and* Technology
Charismatic leadership, 504–508
Cherokee, written language, 83
Chicago studies, 445–447, 449–453, 459–461
Child rearing
  fads, 101–102
  social class differences, 101, 176
  see also Socialization
Chinese law, 391
Chinese revolution, 516–519
  communist party, 517–519
  guerrilla warfare, 518–519
  Japanese invasion, 517
  mass-movement associations, 518
Christianity
  world membership, 336
  see also Catholicism, Protestantism, *and* Religion
Church and sect, 324–326, 327–333
Churches
  church services and revivals, 334–335
  social composition in U.S., 320–321
  see also Religion
Cities, 427–461
  ancient, 427–428
  Asian, 429–430
  central, 454–457
  Chicago studies, 445–447, 449–453, 459–461
  and cultural diversity, 439–440
  ecological distinguished from legal, 430–431
  ecology of, 443–453
  ecology of family types, 445
  happiness and size, 441
  megalopolis, 457–458

Cities—*continued*
  and mental illness, 441–442
  metropolitan areas, 454, 457–458
  neighborhoods, 456–457, 458–461
  origin of, 427–428, 434–437
  prevalence of, 428–429
  satellites, 454
  social areas, 447–449
  and suburbanization, 454–455
  world distribution, 428–429
  see also Ecology, Suburbs, Urbanism, *and* Urbanization
Civic participation. *See* Social participation
Civil disobedience of Gandhi, 505
Civil law, 382–383
Civil rights movement, 257
Class
  consciousness in U.S., 191–192
  differences and socialization, 101–102
  homogeneity of religious congregations, 320–321
  interest and religion, 322–324
  privileged and the law, 411–414
  see also Social class *and* Social stratification
Cliques
  formation, 358–359
  and residential patterns, 20–23
Coast Guard Academy, 110–113
Cohesion. *See* Social cohesion
Collective behavior, 221–257
  community moods, 369
  conditions of, 222
  and education, 367–375
  emotional contagion, 223–235
  forms, 224–230
  and the law, 418–421
  and mass society, 245
  and public opinion, 235–241, 251–254
  and religion, 333–335
  social change, 254–257
  social movements, 254–257
Collective settlements in Israel, 38
College subcultures, 347–350
  academic, 348–349
  collegiate, 347, 349
  nonconformist, 349
  vocational, 347–348, 349–350
Colonialism and nation-building, 500–502

Color
  and illiteracy rates, 11–12
  and income, 163
Common law, 382
Communication
  in associations, 194–195, 196, 199–201, 203–204, 206–207
  and authority, 211–215
  channeled, 196
  filtered, 213–215
  and group conflict, 36–37
  and informal structure, 133–134
  Mead's theory, 95–97
  nonverbal, 64–68, 95
  in primary groups, 141–142
  and status, 207–208, 211–215
  in task groups, 199–201
Communism, 108–110
  and Chinese brainwashing, 108–110
  see also U.S.S.R.
Community
  defined, 31
  and family in Israel, 38–42
  organization, 460
  quest for, 48–49
  religious, 31
  and the self, 98
  in suburbs, 20–26
Competition, 36. *See also* Ecological processes
Conflict, 36–37
  and communication, 36–37
  cultural, 61–64
  group, 36–37
  parent-youth, 104–105
  and urban planning, 455–457, 459–461
Conformity
  and deviation, 61–64
  and norms, 61–64
  and sociability, 102–103
  and socialization, 87–88, 100–101, 103
  in suburbs, 24–26
Confucian, world membership, 336
Conjugal family, 33. *See also* Nuclear family
Consanguine family, 33. *See also* Extended family
Consciousness of kind, 30–31
Consensus in public opinion, 250
Consistency, status, 177
Conterminous U.S., defined, 260

Contract, 94, 386, 387
  and social organization, 45
Control in associations, 194–195
Conversion
  religious, 315–316, 334–335
  see also Resocialization
Cooling out in colleges, 366–367
Cooperation, 37–38. *See also* Ecological processes
Cooperative settlements in Israel, 40–41
Coordination, 196
Correlations, interpretation of, 173
Craft technology, 482–483
Crime
  and family, 408–409
  indexes of, 421–423
  and police, 412
  rates, 421, 423
Criminal
  law, 382–383
  responsibility, 398–400
Criminality
  and the family, 408–409
  and socialization, 400–402
Criminalization, 393
Crisis and integrative behavior, 226–227
  functions of, 227
Crowds, 224–226
  integrative behavior, 226
  and publics, 236
  in race riots, 228, 232, 235
  types of, 224–226
Cultural
  conformity, 61–64
  deviation, 61–64
  diversity, 68–75
  ideals, 61
  relativism, 70–71
  selective adjustment, 69
  universals, 68–69
  values, 54
Cultural evolution. *See* Culture change
Culture, 50–83
  acculturation, 81–83
  and civilization, 50–51, 75
  defined, 50–51
  and education, 339, 345–350
  folk, 48
  and language, 58–61, 64–66

Culture—*continued*
  and law, 389–398
  mass, 80–81
  norms, 54–55
  and personality, 114–115
  pervasive influence, 57
  and religious art, 309–313
  shock, 61–62
  and social organization, 55–56
  and space perceptions, 66–67
  strain to consistency, 57
  and symbolism, 51–54
  and technology, 77–80
  themes, 54
  themes in America, 54
  and time perceptions, 64–65
  variation, 68–71
Culture change, 75–83
Custom, 55. *See also* Culture *and* Norms

Death rate, 278–280
  age specific, 279
  crude, 279
  world regions, 274
  see also Mortality
Definition of the situation, 255
Delinquency
  gangs, 409–410
  measurement of, 6–7
  and self-conceptions, 400–402
  see also Crime
Delinquent subcultures, 71–72
Democracy, 522–534
  and anomie, 532–533
  in associations, 198–199, 218–220
  and despotism, 530–531
  in emerging nations, 508–509
  social foundations, 522–534
  and social revolution, 509–510, 514–515
  symbol under totalitarianism, 522
  Tocqueville's interpretation, 529–534
  "tyranny of the majority," 531–532
Democratic forms of organization, 198–199
Demographic transition, 281–283
Demography. *See* Population
Demonstrative behavior and the law, 418–421
Denomination, 324–325
Dependency and social control, 20. *See also* Aged

Description. *See* Method
Deviance
  and conformity, 61–64
  secondary, 412
Deviation
  secondary, 401–402
  socially defined, 400–401
Differential association and criminality, 409
Differentiation
  of industrial institutions, 470–471
  of institutions, 47
  of religion, 307–308
  see also Social differentiation
Direct rule, 501–502
Disadvantaged
  education of, 352–355
  and legal assistance, 388
Disaster at sea and social rank, 175
Discrimination in law enforcement, 412–413
Division of labor, 47
  in associations, 196
  and formal structure, 196
  and law, 385–386
  urban, 435–436, 439–440
  and urban ecology, 452
Divorce
  law, 406–408
  rate in U.S., 34–35
  and suicide, 29
Drives, distinguished from instincts, 84–85
Dropouts
  and color, 363–364
  and social class, 359–363
Dual power in social revolutions, 512–514
Dual society, 466–469

Ecclesia, 324
Ecological patterns
  concentric zone, 445–446
  and family types, 445–446
  multiple nuclei, 445, 447
  sector, 445, 447
  urban, 445–449
Ecological processes, 292, 293
  in cities, 450–451
  competition, 292
  cooperation, 292
  invasion, 293

Ecological processes—*continued*
  segregation, 443–445
  succession, 293
Ecology, 292–297
  ecological correlations, 296–297
  ecological succession, 293
  invasion, 293
  limited alternatives, 294
  of schools, 378
  and sociability, 22–23
  urban, 443–453
Economic conditions and suicide, 29
Economic inequality, 161–164
  between countries, 161
  within countries, 161–162
  United States, 161–163
Economics and sociology, 5
Ecosystem, 295–296
Education, 339–378
  adult, 345
  allocative function, 184–185, 340
  and associations, 364–367
  and attitude change, 350–352
  college attendance and social class, 360–362
  and community moods, 369
  control, 344–345
  cultural functions, 345–347
  differential access by social class, 352–355, 359–363
  diversity of institutions, 346
  elite vs. mass, 342–343, 345–346
  enrollment in parochial schools, 377
  enrollment in private colleges, 376–377
  and income, 362–363
  indicators of commitment, 8
  and innovation, 340
  institutional autonomy, 344–345
  institutional diversification, 345–346
  of minorities, 354–355
  and occupational achievement, 362–363
  and primary relations, 355–359
  professionalism, 344
  and public opinion, 367–375
  and race, 363–364
  school population, 375–378
  schools as agents of social stratification, 359–364
  slum schools, 453–455
  and social mobility, 352–354, 359–364

Education—*continued*
  and social stratification, 359–364
  socializing role, 350–355
  vocationalism, 347–348, 349–350
Ego
  adequate and inadequate, 93
  created in socialization, 92
  functions of, 92, 93
  see also Self
Egoistic suicide, 27–28
Egypt, 506–507
  populist regime in modern, 506–507
  religion and art style in ancient, 311
Election polls, 237, 239–241, 251–254
Elite education, 342–343
Elites
  divided in revolutions, 511–512
  and industrialization, 471
  Machiavelli's theory, 193
  modernization and democracy, 508–509
  Pareto's theory, 511
  and propaganda, 285–286
Emerging nations
  bureaucracy, 508
  charismatic leadership, 504–505
  colonial direct and indirect rule, 501
  colonialism as nation-building, 500–501
  democracy, 506–507, 508–509
  and mass opinion, 509
  revolution of rising expectations, 503–504
  and tribalism, 502
Emigration. *See* Migration *and* Immigration
Emotional contagion, 223–224
Endogamy, 32
Environment, physical. *See* Ecology
Equalitarian family, 32
Equality, 161–164
  and democracy, 532–534
  see also Democracy *and* Social stratification
Eskimo language, 59
Ethnic groups. *See* Minorities *and* Race
Ethnocentrism, 70–71
  defined, 70
  and subcultures, 72
Evolution. *See* Culture *and* Culture change
Exogamy, 32
Experimental research. *See* Method
Extended family, 33–34

Fads in child rearing, 101–102
Family
    American matricentric, 35
    American nuclear, 34–35
    authority in, 35
    basis of religion, 306–307
    and birth control, 289–291
    and community in Israel, 38–42
    conjugal, 33
    consanguine, 33
    and criminality, 408–409
    extended, 33–35
    Hopi, 34
    law, 406–408
    management in industry, 473–474
    married women in labor force, 493–494
    Negro, 145–148
    nuclear, 33–35
    and Oedipus complex, 117–119
    organization and fertility, 289–291
    patriarchal authority, 117–119
    persistence in Israel, 39–42
    and primary relations, 142–148
    Sinhalese, 290–291
    and social change, 34–35, 38–42
    and social organization, 31–35, 38–42
    in socialization, 99–102
    systems, 142–143
    types, 32–35
    working wives, 493–494
    see also Divorce, Marriage, and Sex
Fealty, 43–44
    basis of social organization, 43–44
    and feudalism, 43–44
    functions, 43–44
Fecundity, 274
Fertility
    in Ceylon, 284, 289–291
    and cultural values, 284
    differentials, 274–279
    distinguished from fecundity, 274
    measures, 274–275
    trends in U.S., 278
    ratio, 274, 278
    and urbanization, 275
    and valuation of children in Ceylon family,
        290–291
    see also Birth rate

Fertility control
    factors favoring, 284
    and family in Ceylon, 289–291
Feudalism
    and Catholicism, 322
    economic roles, 462–463
Folk culture, 48
Folk society. See Gemeinschaft
Folkways, 55
Foreman, role, 19, 211–215
Formal organization. See Associations
Formal structure and channeled communication, 196
    and coordination, 196
    defined, 197
    and delegation of authority, 196
    and division of labor, 196
Formalization in institutions, 216
Free Speech Movement, 370–375
Freedom
    and human nature, 116–117
    and pluralism, 524–525
    social foundations of, 522–534
French Revolution, 510–515
Friendship
    by social strata, 172
    see also Primary groups and Primary relations
Functional view of stratification, 192–193

Gangs
    delinquent, 409–410
    in race riots, 228
Gemeinschaft, 48, 452
    elements, 124
    and urban ecology, 452
    see also Community
Generalized other, 97
Generational mobility. See Intergenerational mo-
        bility and Social mobility
German
    army, 135–150
    population pyramid, 269
Gerrymandering of school districts, 378
Gesellschaft, 48, 452
Gestures as preverbal communication, 95–96
Ghana, charismatic leadership, 504
Greek law, 389–391
Group
    loyalty and autonomy, 25–26

Group—*continued*
  relations, 16, 30–38
Groups, 30–42
  and social categories, 30–31
  types, 30–31
  see also Associations *and* Primary groups

Happiness and city size, 441
Hawaii
  ecological succession, 293–294
  immigration, 294
  racial composition, 273
Hebrew law, 391
Hindus, world membership, 336
Historical materialism, 77–80
Hopi, language, 58
Housing and social organization, 20–26
Human nature, 116–117
  and anxiety, 89–90, 117
  biological basis, 84–86
  concept, 116–117, 132
  and freedom, 116–117
  and socialization, 116–117
Human relations
  and industrial decision-making, 487–491
  and technology, 480–491
  see also Interaction, Interpersonal relations, Primary groups, Primary relations, *and* Social relations

Id, 90. *See also* Self
Identification in associations, 203, 205
Ideology, 256
  managerial, 475
  and social movements, 256–257
Idolatry, 312
Illiteracy, U.S., 10–12, 296–297
Immigration
  to Australia, 286–287
  effects of, 286–289
  and family in Israel, 38–42
  to Hawaii, 293–294
  policy, U.S., 288–289
  to U.S., 286–288
  see also Migration
Impersonality
  in associations, 201
  in industry, 472, 474

Impersonality—*continued*
  and primary relations, 140
Incentives
  in associations, 194–195, 203–204, 206–207
  in industry, 130–133
Income
  and religion, 320–321
  see also Social stratification
Indicators, 7
  empirical, 7–8
  of work performance, 486
Individual autonomy, 73–75
Individual mobility, 181–182
  factors affecting, 181–182
Individualism
  and contract, 45
  in Spencer's theory, 46
Industrial
  classification of work force, 491
  organizations and primary groups, 130–133
  sectors, 491–493
Industrial Workers of the World, 476
Industrialization
  and disorganization, 472
  early stages, 462–472
  in non-Western societies, 466–472
  and Protestantism, 463–466
  and technology, 480–486
  and totalitarianism, 522
  and traditionalism, 470–471
Industry
  primary, secondary, and tertiary, 491–493
  staff-line conflict, 208–211
  variation and alienation of workers, 482–484
  see also Industrialization *and* Technology
Inequality
  economic, 161–164
  and the law, 411–414
Informal structure, 201–205
  elements of, 202
  sources, 201–203
  see also Associations *and* Primary relations
Inner-directed, 103–104
Innocence, presumption of, 416
Instincts, 84–85
  and socialization, 84–85
Institutional differentiation, 47
Institutionalization, 216–218

Institutionalization—*continued*
   of associations, 215–220
   formalization, 216
   infusion with value, 216–217
   religious, 331–332
   self-maintenance, 216, 218–220
   social base, 217–218
Institutions
   autonomy, 344–345
   defined, 31
   differentiation, 47
Integration, racial. *See* School integration *and* Segregation
Integrative behavior in crisis, 226–227
Intelligence and college education, 359–362
Interaction
   and civic participation, 20–23
   and group loyalty, 22–24
   interpersonal, 15–26
   interpersonal patterns, 20–26
   and privacy, 24
   and socialization, 95–98
   sociometry, 148–152
Interest groups, 204–205
Intergenerational mobility, 178–181
   factors affecting, 179–181
Interpersonal relations, 15–16. *See also* Interaction *and* Primary relations
Invention and culture change. *See* Technology
Islam, world membership, 336
Isolate, 358
   in sociogram, 149
Isolated family in Israel, 41
Isolation, 20

Japan
   national character, 114
   traditional, 44
Japanese
   invasion of China, 517
   language, 58–59
Jews
   interfaith marriage, 317–318
   and personal autonomy, 314–315
   U.S. population, 337
Justice among children, 402–406

Kachin language, 60

Kibbutz, 38–40
Kinship
   basis of social organization, 31–35, 43
   and early law, 386–387
   in London, 35–36
   persistence of, 35
   social organization, 31–42, 43
   terms, 32
   see also Family
Knights of Labor, 476

Labor
   commitment, 467–469
   division of, 47, 196, 385–386, 435–436, 439–440, 452
Labor force
   in agriculture, 491–493
   industrial trends, 491–493
   in manufacturing, 491–493
   married women in, 493–494
   nonwhite, 495–496
   occupational classification, 494–495
   in service industries, 491–493
   in U.S., 492–496
   world, 491–492
Labor unions, 475–480
   airline pilots, 479
   and collective bargaining, 476
   in communist countries, 477
   institutionalized, 479–480
   and labor discipline, 476–477
   and political radicalism, 475–476
   printers, 478
   and social protest, 475–476
   and technological unemployment, 475, 478
   see also Trade unions
Land
   exhaustion, 294
   use, 294–297
Landlord-tenant law, 411–412
Language
   as cultural barrier, 64–68
   and culture, 58–60
   Eskimo, 59
   French influence on English, 81
   Hopi, 58
   invention of Cherokee writing, 83
   Japanese, 58–59

Language—*continued*
Kachin, 60
selectivity of, 58–59
the "silent" language, 64–68
and socialization, 96
and thought, 59–60
and totalitarianism, 53
Trobriand, 59–60
Latin America, cultural attitudes, 66, 68, 70
Law, 379–423
administrative, 383
adversary principle, 386–388
adversary system and right to counsel, 413–414
associations, 415–418
attrition in legal process, 421–423
and authority, 380–381
civil, 382–383
and collective behavior, 418–421
common, 382
criminal, 63–64, 382–383
criminal responsibility, 398–400
and culture, 389–398
differential administration, 412–413
discriminatory enforcement, 412–413
and the division of labor, 385–386
and the family, 406–408
and inequality, 411–414
and kinship, 386–387
landlord-tenant, 411–412
legal counsel and capital punishment, 414
M'Naghten rule, 398–399
Mann Act and Mormonism, 394–398
and morals, 391–398
and mores, 55
natural, 383
and primary relations, 406–411
self-preservation, 63–64
and social class, 411–414
social foundations, 379–382
social functions, 379–380
and the state, 382
statute, 382
types of, 382–383
welfare, 412
Leadership
charismatic, 504–508
and communication nets, 200–201
self-perpetuating, 208–211, 216, 218–220

Leadership—*continued*
sociometric choice, 148–152
Legal counsel and capital punishment, 414
Legitimacy
and constitutional law, 380
political, 522–523
and restrained power, 522–523
Liberalism and education, 351–352
Life expectancy, 280–281
Life span, 281
Limited alternatives, 294
Line and staff, 207–211
Love
and socialization, 90
see also Primary relations
LSD, 302

M'Naghten rule, 398–399
Mana, 303
Management, industrial
changes, 473–475
ideologies, 475
professional, 474–475
types, 473–475
see also Associations
Managerial ideologies, 475
Mann Act and Mormonism, 394–398
Manpower
and ecological change, 293–294
see also Labor force
Manufacturing labor force, 491–493
Marital statistics, U.S., 36
Marital status and suicide, 28
Marriage
in Ceylon, 289–290
interfaith, 317–318
law, 406–408
mate selection and social status, 174
percent married, U.S., 35–36
see also Divorce *and* Family
Marxism and religion, 323–324
Marxist model, 187–189
case of England, 190–191
critique of, 189–190
Mass culture, 80–81
Mass education, 342–343, 345–346
Mass media, 245
in Watts riot, 232–234

Mass meetings, 226
Mass society, 48, 438, 503–534
    and crowds, 245
    and *Gesellschaft,* 48
    and totalitarian society, 522
    trend toward in emerging nations, 507–509
Materialism. *See* Historical materialism
Matriarchal family, 32
    Negro family, 146–147
Matricentric family, 35
Matrilineal descent, 32
Matrilocal residence, 32
Measurement. *See* Method *and* Sociological inquiry
Medicine and the social system, 16–17
Megalopolis, 457–458
Mental health and urbanism, 441–442
Method
    before-after experiment, 487–491
    census data, 262–264
    census tract as unit of analysis, 448
    correlations, 173, 296–297
    description, 6–7
    ecological correlations, 296–297
    estimating accuracy of census, 263–265
    evaluating percentages, 238, 528
    experimental design, 487–491
    experimental study of task groups, 199–201
    hypothesis, 488
    indicators, 7
    interviewing, 253–254
    longitudinal analysis, 352
    measurement, 6–8
    measures of fertility and mortality, 274–280
    measures of population composition, 266–273
    measures of work performance, 486
    official crime reporting, 421–423
    percentages, 238, 528
    polling questions, 253–254
    prediction of birth rate, 281–283
    prediction of elections, 240–241, 251–254
    probability sampling, 252–253
    projection of school enrollments, 375–377
    public opinion polls, 240–241, 251–254
    quota sampling, 251–252
    reliability of crime statistics, 421–423
    sample survey of crime, 421–423
    sampling, 7
    sampling in census, 261–262, 264–265

Method—*continued*
    sampling in surveys, 251–253
    social area analysis, 447–448
    social stratification research, 155–156, 157–161
    sociogram, 148–152
    sociometric technique, 148–152
    survey research, 251–254
    tabular presentation, 10–12
    urban concentric zone theory, 445–447
    urban multiple nuclei theory, 447
    urban sector theory, 447
    validity, 7–8, 149
Methodism, 327–333
Methodology. *See* Method *and* Sociological inquiry
Metropolitan dominance, 432–433
Middle East culture, time perceptions, 65
Migration
    and culture contacts, 82
    intercontinental, 285–289
    to U.S., 285–288
    see also Immigration
Militancy, 368–375
Military organizations
    and primary relations, 135–140
    suicide rates, 26–27
Military status and suicide, 27
Mind, as social product, 94–98
Minorities
    distribution in U.S., 272–273
    and education, 354–355, 363–364
    and social stratification, 163–164
    see also Race *and* Segregation
Mobility. *See* Immigration, Migration, *and* Social mobility
Mobility, intragenerational. *See* Career mobility
Mobs, 227
Monogamy, 32
Moods, 223–225
Moral pluralism, 392–393
Morale
    in associations, 203–205, 215
    empirical indicators, 7–8
    war and propaganda, 137–138
Morals and law, 391–398
Morbidity, 274
Mores, 55, 70
Mortality, 278–280
    infant, 279–280

Mortality—*continued*
  maternal, 280
  measures, 278–280
  neonatal, 280
  see also Death rate
Moshav, 40–41
Moslem, world membership, 336
Mundugumor culture, 114–116
Myth and Oedipus complex, 117–119

National character, 114
Nationhood and modernization, 502
Nations, creation of, 499–509
Natural law, 383
Negro
  colleges, 364
  education, 354–355
  families, 143–148
  shared perspectives, 255–256
  see also Minorities *and* Nonwhite
Negro population of U.S., 267, 271–273
  concentration of, 270, 273
  growth of, 272–273
Neolocal residence, 32
Nepotism, 474, 508
Nonwhite
  Alaska population, 272, 273
  conterminous U.S. population, 271–273
  education, 354–355, 363–364
  Hawaii population, 272, 273
  illiteracy rates, 11–12
  income, 163
  occupational distribution, 495–496
  see also Minorities *and* Negro
Norms, 54–55
  and anomic suicide, 28–29
  conflicting, 63–64
  and deviance, 61–64
  and political legitimacy, 522–523
  and primary relations, 127, 133
  religious support for, 302–303
  salient, 55
  see also Conformity, Deviation, *and* Law
Nuclear family, 33–34

Obligations, diffuse, 45
Occupational achievement and education, 362–363
Occupational mobility, 178–181

Occupational stratification, 160, 164
Occupations
  classification, 494–495
  distribution of nonwhites, 495–496
  distribution of workers, 491–496
  prestige ranking, 166–168
  and social mobility, 178
Oedipus complex, 117–119
Oligarchy, "Iron Law," 218–220
  consequences, 219
  countervailing forces, 219–220, 523–525
Open-class and caste societies, 182–183
Opinions
  distinguished from values and attitudes, 236
  effects of education, 350–352
  see also Public opinion
Opportunity structure, U.S., 183–185
Organization
  chart, 197
  effective, 195
  special purpose, 31
  see also Associations
Other-directed, 103–104, 114
Oxford riot, 368–369

Parent-child relations, 104–105
Parliament and collective behavior, 226
Participant society, 508–509, 522
Participation
  differential, in religion, 321–322
  mass, in emerging nations, 507–509
  in mass society, 48
  political, 525–529
  see also Social participation
Particularistic ethic and American culture, 54
Patriarchal, 32, 35
Patriarchal authority and Oedipus complex, 117–119
Patrilineal descent, 32
Patrilocal residence, 32
Peer groups
  and corrections, 410–411
  in schools, 357–359
  and social control, 102–103
  and social status, 357–359
  in socialization, 102–103
Percentages, interpretation of, 238

Performance
  and group cohesiveness, 486
  and supervisory behavior, 486–487
  in work groups, 486–491
Personal autonomy and religion, 313–315
Personality
  basic, 113–114
  and culture, 114–115
  and national character, 114
  representative, 114
  see also Self *and* Socialization
Perspectives, shared, 255–256
  and ideologies, 256
  of Negroes, 255–256
Peyote, 302
Plantation, 293
Plea bargaining, 416–417
Pluralism
  functions of, 524–525
  political, 523–525
  and political freedom, 524–525, 531
Police
  and crime, 412
  in Watts riot, 233–235
Political participation, 525–529
  and apathy, 526–527
  and competence, 526–528
  and independent voter, 528–529
  voting, 525–526
Political power. *See* Power
Political science and sociology, 5
Political sociology, 497–498
Political tolerance and education, 351–352
Politics
  and fealty, 44
  participation in, 525–529
  rural-urban balance of power, 438–439
  and socialization, 525–529
Polling, in elections, 237, 239–241, 251–254
Polyandry, 32
Polygamy, 32, 34
  and the Mann Act, 394–398
Polygyny, 32, 34
Population, 258–297
  change, 280–289
  composition, 266–274
  composition of U.S., 266
  demographic transition, 281–283

Population—*continued*
  forecasting, 283
  foreign born in U.S., 288
  foreign stock in U.S., 287
  labor force, 491–496
  labor force in U.S., 492–496
  life expectancy, 279, 280
  Malthusian theory, 259
  Negro in U.S., 267, 272–273
  religious composition of U.S., 336–338
  rural and urban, U.S., 433
  in school, 342, 375–376
  sex ratio, 267–268
  see also Birth rate, Death rate, Fertility, Migration, *and* Mortality
Population change, 280–289
Population composition, racial and ethnic, 270–271, 272–273
Population explosion. *See* Demographic transition, Fertility control, *and* Population growth
Population growth
  in developing areas, 283
  European, 281
  world, 280–284
Population pyramid, 268–271
  effects of wars, 269–270
  of Germany, 269
  interpreting, 269–270
  of Japanese Americans, 270–271
  of a minority, 270–271
  of United States, 268
Populism in Egypt, 506–507
Positive law, 383
Positivism and Comte, 4
Poverty, 163–165, 174–176
  and Christianity, 323
  and the law, 411–412
  and rebellion, 504, 510–511
  slum schools, 453–455
Power
  in communities, 168–169
  concentrated, 523–524
  fragmented, 524
  and legitimacy, 522–523
  national, 169–170
  and pluralism, 523–525
  and social organization, 522–525
Prejudice. *See* Minorities, Race, *and* Segregation

Presidential popularity, 236–237
Prestige
  in communities, 166
  of occupations, 166–168
Primary groups, 120–148
  cohesion of military, 138–139
  communication in, 141–142
  defined, 120
  delinquent gangs, 409–410
  and the individual, 126–133
  and industrial organization, 130–133
  in large-scale organizations, 133–140
  mediating function, 134–135
  and rehabilitation, 410–411
  and social control, 408–411
  in society, 135
  structural variations in, 140–142
  subversive and supportive, 134
  see also Primary relations
Primary relations, 120–124
  in associations, 205–206
  characteristics, 120–124
  and criminality, 408–411
  in education, 355–359
  and impersonality, 125
  and interfaith marriage, 317–318
  and law, 406–411
  in military organizations, 135–140
  organizational functions, 134, 205–206
  and personal security, 128–130, 134
  see also Family and Primary groups
Profanation, 313
Professions and institutional autonomy, 344
Prohibition movement, 246–250
  and Protestantism, 246
  and rural vote, 248–249
Projections, school enrollments, 375–377
Proletariat, 188–190
Propaganda, 242–246
  and the German army, 137–138
  and Prohibition movement, 249–250
  targets, 243
  techniques, 242–244
  tricks, 244
Protestant ethic and capitalism, 463–466
Protestant reformation, 323
Protestantism
  attitudes toward the poor, 323–324

Protestantism—continued
  and Prohibition movement, 246
Protestants
  interfaith marriage, 317–318
  in parochial schools, 377
  and personal autonomy, 314–315
  population in U.S., 337
Psychiatry and justice, 398–400
Psychological warfare, 135–140
Public opinion
  affecting education, 367–369
  group basis, 236–240
  measuring, 237–241, 251–254
Public opinion polls, 240–241, 251–254
  accuracy in elections, 240–241
Publics
  characteristics, 236
  and crowds, 236
Puritanism and capitalist spirit, 464–466
Pyramid. See Population pyramid

Rabble hypothesis, 30
Race
  and illiteracy, 296–297
  see also Color and Nonwhite
Race riots
  Chicago, 228
  Detroit, 229
  Los Angeles, 229, 230–235
  Watts, 229, 230–235
  see also Rumor and Mobs
Racial composition
  Alaska, 273
  conterminous U.S., 270, 272
  Hawaii, 273
Rationality
  and American culture, 54
  in associations, 197
  in bureaucracy, 46, 474–475
  and impersonality, 48
  and secularism, 47–48
Reference groups, 239
  and opinion formation, 236–240
Reformation, Protestant, 323
Religion, 301–338
  and art, 309–313
  and associations, 307–308, 324–333
  church and sect, 324–326, 327–333

Religion—*continued*
  and class interest, 322–324
  and collective behavior, 333–335
  communal, 306
  conversion, 315–316
  and culture, 309–313
  defined, 305
  differentiation of, 307–308
  domestic, 306–307
  Durkheim's theory, 308–309, 333–334
  elements, 304–305
  family as a basis, 316–317
  foundations, 302–303
  Greek and Roman, 306–307
  idolatry, 312
  and income, 320–321
  and institutional differentiation, 307–308
  and intermarriage, 317–318
  involvement and socioeconomic status, 321–322
  and primary relations, 316–319
  profanation, 313
  religious communities, 31
  revivals, 334–335
  and the sacred, 303–304
  and social cohesion, 308
  and social organization, 306–309
  and socialization, 313–316
  and stratification, 319–324
  and suicide rates, 27–28
  symbolism, 309–313
  U.S. membership, 336–338
  world membership, 336
  see also Catholicism *and* Protestantism
Research. *See* Method *and* Sociological inquiry
Resocialization, 107–113
  and brainwashing, 108–110
  and religious conversion, 315–316
  in service academies, 110–113
Responsibility, criminal, 398–400
Revivals, 334–335
Revolution
  age of, 509–519
  Chinese, 516–519
  and dual power, 512–514
  French, 510–515
  and nationalism, 515–519
  natural history, 512–515
  of rising expectations, 503–504

Revolution—*continued*
  Russian, 510–515
  social, 509–510
  social conditions, 510–512
Reward and punishment, 100
Riots, 228–235
  interpretations of, 229, 235
  and mobs, 228
  race, 228–235
Ritual, as religious element, 304
Rivalry, 36–37
Role, 18–20
  actual, 18–19
  ideal, 18
  of the other, 97
  and personality, 105–107
  and role conflict, 19
  and role strain, 18–19
  and social position, 19
Roman law, 390–391
Rule, direct and indirect, 501–502
Rule of law, 381–382
Rumor, 230
  in race riots, 230, 235
Rural community
  and Prohibition movement, 249, 250
  rural-urban continuum, 432
Rural-urban
  balance of power, 438–439
  continuum, 432
  reapportionment, 439
Rural vote and Prohibition movement, 248–249
Russia. *See* U.S.S.R.
Russian Revolution, 510, 512–513, 515

Salvation Army, 327–333
Sampling
  in census, 261–262, 264–265
  see also Method *and* Sociological inquiry
Sanctions, repressive and restitutive, 385–386
Scapegoating, 227–228
School achievement and socialization, 102
School integration and academic performance, 354–355
Schools. *See* Education
Science, selectivity of, 3
Scientific method. *See* Method *and* Sociological inquiry

Secondary deviation, 401–402, 412
Sect, distinguished from church, 324–325, 328
Sectors, industrial, 491–493
Secularism, 47
  and rationality, 46–48
Security and associations, 194–195
Sects. *See* Religion
Segregation
  consequences, 444
  de facto, 378
  in schools, 378
  residential, 443–445
  see also Minorities *and* Race
Self
  Freud's theory, 90
  "looking-glass" self, 92
  Mead's theory, 90–92, 94–98
  social, 93, 96–97
Self-preservation as a legal defense, 63–64
Service industries in labor force, 491–493
Sex
  and illiteracy rates, 11–12
  norms among poor, 174, 176
  and Oedipus complex, 117–119
  and temperament, 114–116
Sex ratio, 267–268
  in crime, 423–424
  defined, 267
  of Negroes, 267
  rural-urban, 267
  in U.S., 267–268
Significant other, 97
Sioux culture, time perceptions, 64–65
Situs, 178
Sociability
  and ecology, 22–23
  and peer groups, 103
  and personal autonomy, 23–26
Social base of associations, 217–218
  Anti-Saloon League, 246, 256
  Methodism, 327–329
  and publics, 236
Social change
  in cities, 454–461
  and collective behavior, 254–257
  and the family, 34–35, 38–42
  master trends, 46–49
  and social class in England, 190–191

Social change—*continued*
  see also Culture change, Emerging nations, Industrialization, Population, Social organization, Social stratification, Technology, *and* Urbanization
Social class
  and adolescent freedom, 358–359
  and caste, 182–183
  defined, 154–155
  and French Revolution, 510–511
  Marxist model, 187–189
  and Methodism, 327–330
  objective, 188–189
  subjective, 188–189
  see also Social stratification
Social cohesion
  and associations, 134, 203–205
  and religion, 308
Social control
  and interdependence, 20
  and isolation, 20
  in primary groups, 131–133
  and primary relations, 408–411
  see also Law
Social differentiation
  in associations, 204–205, 208–211
  see also Differentiation *and* Social stratification
Social disorganization
  and industrialization, 472
  urban, 451–452
  see also Anomie
Social distance and interfaith marriage, 318
Social inequality, necessity of, 192–193
Social integration
  and suicide, 26–30
  see also Social cohesion *and* Social organization
Social interaction, 17–18. *See also* Interaction *and* Social organization
Social isolation. *See* Isolation
Social justice, 323
Social mobility
  and changes in the occupational structure, 183–185
  paths in U.S., 186–187
  pathways, 185–187
  relative rates of, 185–187
  and religion, 329
  in service academy, 112

Social mobility—*continued*
   trends in, 185–187
   types of, 178
   vertical and horizontal, 153, 178
   see also Social stratification
Social morphology. *See* Ecology
Social movements, 254–257
   civil rights, 257
Social order
   Catholic view, 322–323
   see also Social control *and* Social organization
Social organization, 14–49
   basic patterns, 42–49
   bureaucracy, 46
   contract, 45, 385–386
   and culture, 55–56
   defined, 14
   and education, 14–15
   fealty, 43–44
   field of study, 15–17
   and friendship, 20–26
   and group relations, 16, 30–38
   group structure of society, 30–42
   and the individual, 17–30
   and industrialization, 462–463, 469–472
   and interpersonal relations, 15–20
   and kinship, 31–42
   levels of, 15–17
   rational coordination, 46
   and religion, 306–309
   and social control, 20
   and social order, 16–17
   and social roles, 18–20
   as stable interaction, 18
   status, 44–45
   and suicide, 26–30
Social participation
   and civic leadership, 25–26
   see also Participation
Social problems and sociology, 4
Social psychology and sociology, 5
Social rank and disaster at sea, 175
Social relations
   and interaction patterns, 17–18
   and social roles, 18–20
   weak and strong, 18
Social research. *See* Method *and* Sociological inquiry

Social roles, 18–20
   defined, 18
   of foreman, 19, 211–215
   and personality, 105–107
   strains, 18–20
   see also Role
Social strata, 154
Social stratification, 153–193
   attitudinal correlates, 172
   characteristics of American system, 170–176, 185–187
   in cities, 445–448
   correlates of, 170–177
   dimensions of, 153
   and early city, 435–436
   and education, 164, 359–365
   and family characteristics, 170–176
   functional view, 192–193
   by income, 162
   life-style correlates, 171
   methods of research, 185–189
   and minorities, 163–164
   and Negro family, 146–148
   objective studies, 156, 160–161
   by occupation, 164–165
   of occupations by color, 495–496
   orders, 154
   and political competence, 526–527
   and poverty, 163–164
   religion and class interest, 322–324
   and religious involvement, 321–322
   reputational studies, 155, 158–160
   subjective studies, 155–156, 158
   in U.S. churches, 320–321
   Warner's studies, 165–166
   see also Elites, Social class, Social mobility, *and* Status
Social system, 15–17. *See also* Social organization
Socialization
   and access to the individual, 99
   adult, 113
   agencies of, 98–99
   aims of, 86–87
   anticipatory, 105
   in associations, 110–113, 203–204
   and authority, 117–119
   biological basis, 84–86
   and childhood dependence, 86

Socialization—*continued*
  and class differences, 101–102
  competition among agencies of, 98
  and conformity, 87–88, 103–104
  and criminality, 400–402
  defined, 84
  deliberate and unconscious, 87
  and emotional responses, 89–90
  in the family, 99–102
  and human nature, 116–117
  and instincts, 84–85
  and interactional needs, 85
  and language, 86
  and learning capacity, 86
  participatory, 100–102
  and peer groups, 102–103
  and personality, 113–119
  political, 525–529
  and religion, 313–316
  repressive, 100–102
  resocialization, 107–113
  and reward, 100
  rural and urban, 440–441
  in the school, 350–355
  and the self, 90–98
Socioeconomic status and religious involvement, 321–322
Sociogram, 148–152
Sociological analysis. *See* Method *and* Sociological inquiry
Sociological inquiry, 4–5, 6–8
  data collection, 6–7
  for descriptive purposes, 6–7
  empirical indicators, 7–8
  and ethics, 10
  and explanation, 7
  and privacy, 10
  purposes of, 3, 6–7
  and sampling, 7
  and scientific method, 4–5
  selectivity, 3
  and social problems, 4
  statistics in, 6–7
  and validity, 7
  see also Method
Sociological research. *See* Method *and* Sociological inquiry

Sociology
  and the social sciences, 4–5
  see also Sociological inquiry
Sociometric choice, 148–152
Solidarity, mechanical and organic, 385–386
Space, culturally defined, 66–67
Specialization
  as master trend, 46–47
  in Western society, 46–47
Staff-line, 207–211
Statistical method. *See* Method *and* Sociological inquiry
Statistical tables, 10–12
Status, 18, 44–45
  achieved, 182–183
  achieved and industrialization, 463, 472
  ascribed, 182–183
  in associations, 206–208
  basis of social organization, 44–45
  consistency, 177
  and contract, 45
  defined, 44
  under feudalism, 45
  groups, 154
  in Japan, 44–45
  of students, 357–359
  suppression in resocialization, 23–24, 107–110, 110–113
  system, 44
  see also Social stratification
Status and life-styles, 170–177
  the poor, 174–177
  the rich, 170–174
Statute law, 382
Stratification. *See* Social stratification
Stratification method
  objective, 156, 160–161
  reputational, 155, 158–160
  subjective, 155–156, 158
Student
  activism, 367, 370–375
  peer groups, 357–359
  protest, 370–375
  teacher relations, 355–357
Subcultures, 71–72
  delinquent, 71–72
  student, 347–350

Suburbs
    friendship patterns, 20–26
    growth, 454–455
    Park Forest, Illinois, 20–26
    working class, 455
Suggestibility and emotional contagion, 223
Suicide and Durkheim's theory, 26–30
    altruistic, 26–27
    anomic, 28–29
    and aspirations, 28–29
    and divorce rate, 29
    and economic conditions, 29
    egoistic, 27–28
    among intellectuals, 29
    and marital status, 28
    and religion, 27–28
    and social integration, 26–30
    of soldiers, 27
Superego, 90
Supervision in industry, 132–133
Survey research. See Method
Survival, chances of, 280–281
Symbolism, 51–54
    in art, 52–54, 309–310
    expressive, 52–54
    referential, 52
    in religion, 304, 309–311, 316–317

Tanala, 56
Task groups, 141
Tchambuli culture, 114–116
Teacher-student relations, 355–357
Technology
    and alienation, 481–484
    assembly-line, 483
    automation, 484–486
    continuous-process, 483–484
    craft, 482–483
    and culture, 56, 77–80
    featherbedding, 478–479
    and group performance, 487–491
    and Marx's view of social change, 481–482
    sociotechnical systems, 480–481
    and Tanala culture, 56
    and unemployment, 475, 578–579
Temperament and sex, 114–116
Tenant-landlord law, 411–412
Thermidor, 514–515

Thought and language, 59–60
Time, culturally defined, 64–65
Titanic, sinking and social status, 175
Total institutions, 107, 110–113
Totalitarianism, 519–522
    and industrial society, 522
    mechanisms of total power, 520–522
    modification of in U.S.S.R., 521–522
Tracking in schools, 353–354
Trade unions
    under communism, 477
    and featherbedding, 478–479
    functions of, 475–480
    and institutionalization, 216, 217–218
    and social reform, 477, 480
    see also Labor unions
Tradition-directed, 103–104
Tribalism and emerging nations, 502
Trobriand
    family, 117–119
    language, 59–60

Underdeveloped areas. See Emerging nations
Unemployment
    and featherbedding, 478–479
    and Luddites, 475
    see also Automation, Industrialization, and Technology
Unions. See Labor unions and Trade unions
Universalistic ethic
    and American culture, 54
    defined, 54
Urban ecology, 443–453
Urban diversity, 439–440
Urban division of labor, 452
Urban life-styles, 437–438
Urban neighborhoods, 456–457, 458–461
Urban and rural classification, 430–434
Urban and rural population, U.S., 433
Urbanism, 437–438, 440–441
    and personality, 440
    and Prohibition movement, 249, 250
    and religious organization, 328–329
    spread of, 437–438
    see also Cities and Urbanization
Urbanization, 427–437
    comparative study, 430–431
    conditions for, 427–428

Urbanization—*continued*
  index of, 432
  rural-urban continuum, 432
  and U.S. Congress, 438–439
  see also Cities *and* Urbanism
U.S.S.R.
  law in, 391
  national character, 114
  totalitarianism, 521–522

Validity. *See* Sociological inquiry
Validity of responses, 149
Validity of sociological measures, 7–8
Values, 54, 237
  cultural, 54

Values—*continued*
  distinguished from attitudes and opinions, 54, 237
  and institutional autonomy, 344
Vatican Council, 326–327
Voting, 525–526, 528–529
Voting behavior
  independent voter, 528–529
  see also Public opinion

Welfare law, 412
Work force
  industrial distribution, 491–493
  see also Labor force

Yankee City, 165–166

68 69 70   7 6 5 4 3 2